MW01625273

THE BOOK OF II KINGS

Me'am Lo'ez

בצאת ישראל ממצרים בית יעקב
מעם לועז

The Book of II Kings

Me'am Lo'ez

by
Rabbi Shmuel Yerushalmi

Translated and adapted by
Rabbi Nathan Bushwick

MOZNAIM PUBLISHING CORPORATION
NEW YORK / JERUSALEM

For information write:
Moznaim Publishing Corporation
4304 12th Avenue
Brooklyn, New York 11219
Tel. (718) 438-7680, 853-0525

ISBN 1-885220-17-0

Printed and bound in Jerusalem, Israel
by Vagshal Ltd.
Typesetting by Vagshal Ltd.
Jerusalem
Plates by Frank, Jerusalem

Printed in Israel

THE BOOK OF II KINGS

Me'am Lo'ez

II KINGS 1

1:1 וַיִּפְשַׁע מוֹאָב בְּיִשְׂרָאֵל אַחֲרֵי מוֹת אַחְאָב׃

Moab rebelled against Israel after the death of Ahab.

Ahab is remembered as a wicked king, for he was guilty of many sins, but he had a righteous side too. His good deeds revealed an inner faith and desire to serve G-d. G-d did not overlook his righteousness, and rewarded him for it by granting him a long reign, during which his kingdom enjoyed a position of power among its neighbors. Even Moab, one of Israel's traditional enemies, deferred to him and accepted him as their master.

But his son and successor, Ahaziah, shared none of his good qualities, so he was not worthy of any such rewards. His reign began with the rebellion of Moab. As soon as they heard that Ahab had been killed, they took the opportunity to test the new king to see whether he would be able to force them to submit.[1]

This was a divine warning to Ahaziah. Just as he had rebelled against G-d, so the nations would rebel against him.[2] But he stubbornly ignored it, as he did the clear signs of divine providence that he had witnessed during his father's reign. Having no merit to protect him, his doom came without delay.

As for Moab, they too were punished. Ahaziah's brother and successor, Jehoram, crushed them and laid waste their land, as we will see in Chapter Three. Thus again, we see that the wicked are punished by the wicked, who are ultimately punished themselves.

1:2 וַיִּפֹּל אֲחַזְיָה בְּעַד הַשְּׂבָכָה בַּעֲלִיָּתוֹ אֲשֶׁר בְּשֹׁמְרוֹן וַיָּחַל וַיִּשְׁלַח
מַלְאָכִים וַיֹּאמֶר אֲלֵהֶם לְכוּ דִרְשׁוּ בְּבַעַל זְבוּב אֱלֹהֵי עֶקְרוֹן אִם־אֶחְיֶה מֵחֳלִי
זֶה׃

Ahaziah fell through the lattice in his roof-house that was in

Samaria, and he became ill. He sent messengers and said to them, "Go inquire of Baal-zebub, the god of Ekron, whether I will recover from this illness."

There was a wooden lattice covering the skylight in the uppermost floor of the palace. While Ahaziah was walking on the roof he fell through and was injured.[3]

Some say the word "שבכה," means not "lattice" but "spiral staircase." It was on the stairs that led to the upper story of his palace that Ahaziah fell.[4]

1:3-4 וּמַלְאַךְ ה׳ דִּבֶּר אֶל־אֵלִיָּה הַתִּשְׁבִּי קוּם עֲלֵה לִקְרַאת מַלְאֲכֵי מֶלֶךְ־
שֹׁמְרוֹן וְדַבֵּר אֲלֵהֶם הֲמִבְּלִי אֵין־אֱלֹהִים בְּיִשְׂרָאֵל אַתֶּם הֹלְכִים לִדְרֹשׁ בְּבַעַל
זְבוּב אֱלֹהֵי עֶקְרוֹן: וְלָכֵן כֹּה־אָמַר ה׳ הַמִּטָּה אֲשֶׁר־עָלִיתָ שָּׁם לֹא־תֵרֵד מִמֶּנָּה
כִּי מוֹת תָּמוּת וַיֵּלֶךְ אֵלִיָּה:

An angel of G-d said to Elijah, the Tishbite, "Arise and go up to meet the messengers of the King of Samaria. Say to them, 'Is there no G-d in Israel, that you are going to inquire of Baal-zebub, the god of Ekron? Therefore, thus says G-d, "The bed that you have gone up onto, you will not go down from, for you will surely die!"' " So Elijah went.

Had Ahaziah not committed the additional sin of turning to the idols for advice instead of to G-d, he might have recovered. The suffering of his injury might have been sufficient punishment. But this sin sealed his fate. He wanted to know whether he would recover, and G-d relieved him of all doubt.

1:5-8 וַיָּשׁוּבוּ הַמַּלְאָכִים אֵלָיו וַיֹּאמֶר אֲלֵיהֶם מַה־זֶּה שַׁבְתֶּם: וַיֹּאמְרוּ
אֵלָיו אִישׁ עָלָה לִקְרָאתֵנוּ וַיֹּאמֶר אֵלֵינוּ לְכוּ שׁוּבוּ אֶל־הַמֶּלֶךְ אֲשֶׁר־שָׁלַח אֶתְכֶם
וְדִבַּרְתֶּם אֵלָיו כֹּה אָמַר ה׳ הֲמִבְּלִי אֵין־אֱלֹהִים בְּיִשְׂרָאֵל אַתָּה שֹׁלֵחַ לִדְרֹשׁ
בְּבַעַל זְבוּב אֱלֹהֵי עֶקְרוֹן לָכֵן הַמִּטָּה אֲשֶׁר־עָלִיתָ שָּׁם לֹא־תֵרֵד מִמֶּנָּה כִּי־מוֹת
תָּמוּת: וַיְדַבֵּר אֲלֵהֶם מֶה מִשְׁפַּט הָאִישׁ אֲשֶׁר עָלָה לִקְרַאתְכֶם וַיְדַבֵּר אֲלֵיכֶם

אֶת־הַדְּבָרִים הָאֵלֶּה׃ וַיֹּאמְרוּ אֵלָיו אִישׁ בַּעַל שֵׂעָר וְאֵזוֹר עוֹר אָזוּר בְּמָתְנָיו
וַיֹּאמַר אֵלִיָּה הַתִּשְׁבִּי הוּא׃

The messengers returned to him and he said to them, "What is this, that you have returned?" They said to him, "A man came up to meet us and said to us, 'Go, return to the king who sent you, and say to him, "Thus says G-d, 'Is there no G-d in Israel, that you sent to inquire of Baal-zebub, the god of Ekron? Therefore the bed that you have gone up onto you will not go down from, for you will surely die!'"' " He said to them, "What was the man like, who came up to meet you, and spoke these words to you?" They said to him, "A man with much hair, and girded with a leather belt on his loins." He said, "It is Elijah the Tishbite!"

The messengers were young men who did not remember Elijah. It had been many years since he had appeared publicly in Samaria, for Jezebel had sworn to kill him. Those who had been present when he built the altar on Mount Carmel would certainly have recognized him, but these messengers seem not to have been among them. Elijah had returned briefly to rebuke Ahab for the murder of Naboth, but that time he spoke to Ahab alone. He delivered his message and left.

Ahaziah, however, remembered him, and immediately suspected it was he that had intercepted the messengers. A few words were all that was needed to confirm his suspicion.[5]

1:9 וַיִּשְׁלַח אֵלָיו שַׂר־חֲמִשִּׁים וַחֲמִשָּׁיו וַיַּעַל אֵלָיו וְהִנֵּה יֹשֵׁב עַל־רֹאשׁ
הָהָר וַיְדַבֵּר אֵלָיו אִישׁ הָאֱלֹהִים הַמֶּלֶךְ דִּבֶּר רֵדָה׃

He sent him an officer of fifty with his fifty. He went up to him, and there he was sitting at the top of the mountain. He said to him, "Man of G-d, the king said, 'Come down!' "

The officer spoke to Elijah arrogantly, for he did not believe in G-d's power. He said, "I command you in the name of the king to come! If you do not come willingly, my men will arrest you and bring you by force!"[6]

1:10 וַיַּעֲנֶה אֵלִיָּהוּ וַיְדַבֵּר אֶל־שַׂר הַחֲמִשִּׁים וְאִם־אִישׁ אֱלֹהִים אָנִי תֵּרֶד
אֵשׁ מִן־הַשָּׁמַיִם וְתֹאכַל אֹתְךָ וְאֶת־חֲמִשֶּׁיךָ וַתֵּרֶד אֵשׁ מִן־הַשָּׁמַיִם וַתֹּאכַל אֹתוֹ
וְאֶת־חֲמִשָּׁיו:

Elijah answered and said to the officer of fifty, "If I am indeed a man of G-d, let fire come down from the sky and consume you and your fifty!" So fire came down from the sky and consumed him and his fifty.

Elijah saw that the officer and his men had come to defy G-d, so they deserved no mercy. He said, "Since you have defied G-d publicly, G-d will make an example of you and display His power in the eyes of all!"[7]

Having ignored the divine fire they witnessed at Mount Carmel, the Jewish People had become particularly vulnerable to fire. Elijah therefore chose fire to destroy them.[8] If anyone were to arise in their defense and object that this punishment was unduly harsh, the fire itself would call to mind that earlier miracle. They had experienced a clear proof that G-d pays close attention to their actions and rewards or punishes them accordingly. Any generation that has had such an experience should be careful about questioning G-d's power.

Elijah also wanted to intimidate Ahaziah, because he realized that Ahaziah wanted to kill him. Ahaziah, like his mother, the wicked Jezebel, had no concern for G-d and Torah. Now that Ahab was gone, they were in complete control. Even so great a prophet as Elijah did not dare endanger his life by entering Samaria now, except by G-d's explicit command.

For no prophet has control over nature, to call up miracles whenever he pleases. He can only ask G-d to perform miracles as an act of mercy. Like anyone else, Elijah was required to look out for his own life and not place himself in unnecessary danger. If he acted irresponsibly, for instance, by going to Samaria where Jezebel might catch him, he could not then ask G-d to rescue him. But as long as he made the appropriate efforts to protect himself by staying in the mountains, he did not have to fear the soldiers who came to get him.

1:11,12 וַיָּשָׁב וַיִּשְׁלַח אֵלָיו שַׂר־חֲמִשִּׁים אַחֵר וַחֲמִשָּׁיו וַיַּעַן וַיְדַבֵּר אֵלָיו
אִישׁ הָאֱלֹהִים כֹּה־אָמַר הַמֶּלֶךְ מְהֵרָה רֵדָה: וַיַּעַן אֵלִיָּה וַיְדַבֵּר אֲלֵיהֶם אִם־אִישׁ

הָאֱלֹהִים אָנִי תֵּרֶד אֵשׁ מִן־הַשָּׁמַיִם וְתֹאכַל אֹתְךָ וְאֶת־חֲמִשֶּׁיךָ וַתֵּרֶד
אֵשׁ־אֱלֹהִים מִן־הַשָּׁמַיִם וַתֹּאכַל אֹתוֹ וְאֶת־חֲמִשָּׁיו:

He again sent him another officer of fifty with his fifty, and he spoke up and said to him, "Man of G-d, thus said the king, 'Hurry up and come down!' " Elijah answered and said to them, "If I am indeed the man of G-d, let fire come down from the sky and consume you and your fifty!" So fire of G-d came down from the sky and consumed him and his fifty.

Ahaziah was stubborn and refused to give up, nor was he concerned about the lives of his servants. As for the second officer, he failed to learn a lesson from his predecessor. He too tried to take Elijah by force and suffered the same fate.

1:13,14 וַיָּשָׁב וַיִּשְׁלַח שַׂר־חֲמִשִּׁים שְׁלִשִׁים וַחֲמִשָּׁיו וַיַּעַל וַיָּבֹא
שַׂר־הַחֲמִשִּׁים הַשְּׁלִישִׁי וַיִּכְרַע עַל־בִּרְכָּיו לְנֶגֶד אֵלִיָּהוּ וַיִּתְחַנֵּן אֵלָיו וַיְדַבֵּר אֵלָיו
אִישׁ הָאֱלֹהִים תִּיקַר־נָא נַפְשִׁי וְנֶפֶשׁ עֲבָדֶיךָ אֵלֶּה חֲמִשִּׁים בְּעֵינֶיךָ: הִנֵּה יָרְדָה
אֵשׁ מִן־הַשָּׁמַיִם וַתֹּאכַל אֶת־שְׁנֵי שָׂרֵי הַחֲמִשִּׁים הָרִאשֹׁנִים וְאֶת־חֲמִשֵּׁיהֶם
וְעַתָּה תִּיקַר נַפְשִׁי בְּעֵינֶיךָ:

He again sent an officer of a third fifty with his fifty. The third officer of fifty went up and came and bowed on his knees before Elijah and begged him and said to him, "Man of G-d, let my life and the lives of these fifty of your servants be precious in your eyes! Behold, fire has come down from the sky and consumed the two first officers of fifty and their fifties! But now, let my life be precious in your eyes!"

The third officer, however, feared G-d and humbled himself before Elijah. He recognized that the deaths of the other two officers and their troops had been a divine punishment, not an accident. He made two requests. The first was for both himself and his men, that Elijah spare their lives, and not cause them to be killed as the others were. The second was for himself alone. He begged Elijah to accompany him of his own free will, for if the officer were to return without him, he feared that Ahaziah would have him killed. Therefore the first time he said, "let my life and the lives of these fifty of your servants be precious in your eyes!" but the second time he said only, "let my life be precious in your eyes!" If he returned empty handed, he alone would be blamed and punished.[9]

He also referred to himself as "your servant," meaning that even though he served Ahaziah, he considered Elijah his real master.[10]

1:15 וַיְדַבֵּר מַלְאַךְ ה׳ אֶל־אֵלִיָּהוּ רֵד אוֹתוֹ אַל־תִּירָא מִפָּנָיו וַיָּקָם וַיֵּרֶד
אוֹתוֹ אֶל־הַמֶּלֶךְ׃

The angel of G-d said to Elijah, "Go down with him! Don't be afraid of him!" So he got up and went down with him to the king.

Nonetheless, Elijah would not go until he had received explicit divine instruction. Only then could he be sure of G-d's protection.

1:16 וַיְדַבֵּר אֵלָיו כֹּה־אָמַר ה׳ יַעַן אֲשֶׁר־שָׁלַחְתָּ מַלְאָכִים לִדְרֹשׁ בְּבַעַל
זְבוּב אֱלֹהֵי עֶקְרוֹן הֲמִבְּלִי אֵין־אֱלֹהִים בְּיִשְׂרָאֵל לִדְרֹשׁ בִּדְבָרוֹ לָכֵן הַמִּטָּה
אֲשֶׁר־עָלִיתָ שָּׁם לֹא־תֵרֵד מִמֶּנָּה כִּי־מוֹת תָּמוּת׃

He said to him, "Thus says G-d, 'Since you sent messengers to inquire of Baal-zebub, the god of Ekron, is there no G-d in Israel to inquire of His word? Therefore the bed that you have gone up onto you won't go down from, for you will surely die!' "

Elijah said, "The loss of Moab and the accident that you have suffered were divine warnings, but you chose to ignore them. Worse yet, by seeking the advice of foreign idols rather than G-d's word, you made it seem as if the idols were greater than G-d and knew more. Had you not done that, your pain might have been considered sufficient punishment and you might have recovered. But for this additional lack of faith you will suffer accordingly. You were not satisfied to wait and see what the outcome of your illness would be. You belittled G-d to try to find out what your fate would be. Now He will relieve your doubts. You will indeed die!"[11]

1:17,18 וַיָּמָת כִּדְבַר־ה׳ אֲשֶׁר־דִּבֶּר אֵלִיָּהוּ וַיִּמְלֹךְ יְהוֹרָם תַּחְתָּיו בִּשְׁנַת
שְׁתַּיִם לִיהוֹרָם בֶּן־יְהוֹשָׁפָט מֶלֶךְ יְהוּדָה כִּי לֹא־הָיָה לוֹ בֵּן׃ וְיֶתֶר דִּבְרֵי אֲחַזְיָהוּ
אֲשֶׁר עָשָׂה הֲלוֹא־הֵמָּה כְתוּבִים עַל־סֵפֶר דִּבְרֵי הַיָּמִים לְמַלְכֵי יִשְׂרָאֵל׃

He died, like the word of G-d that Elijah had spoken, and Jehoram became king in his place, in the second year of Jehoram, the son of Jehoshaphat, King of Judah, for he didn't have a son. The rest of the things about Ahaziah that he did are indeed written in the Book of the Chronicles of the Kings of Israel.

By appearing personally before Ahaziah and delivering his prophecy, Elijah assured that it would become public knowledge. News of his visit spread quickly, and when Ahaziah died everyone knew that it was indeed a divine punishment, not an accident. It was according to "the word of G-d that Elijah had spoken."

Thus ended the short reign of the wicked king, Ahaziah. It lasted less than two years. He became king in the seventeenth year of Jehoshaphat, as we have already learned,[12] "Ahaziah the son of Ahab became king over Israel in Samaria in the seventeenth year of Jehoshaphat, King of Judah, and he reigned over Israel two years." The two years referred to could not have been full years, though, for later we read,[13] "Jehoram, the son of Ahab, became king over Israel in Samaria in the eighteenth year of Jehoshaphat, King of Judah." Even if he became king in the beginning of Jehoshaphat's seventeenth year and his brother, Jehoram, succeeded him in the end of Jehoshaphat's eighteenth year, his entire reign would still not have totalled two full years.

By referring to this in one verse as the second year of Jehoram, son of Jehoshaphat, and in another as the eighteenth year of Jehoshaphat, the Bible implies that there was an overlap between the reigns of these two kings. Even though a son generally did not take the throne until after his father's death, there were certain exceptions. King David had Solomon crowned before he died, to make sure that he, and not his brother Adonijah, would be the next king. Like David, Jehoshaphat wanted to establish Jehoram as his successor. But there was another reason for appointing him at that time.

As we have already learned, in the seventeenth year of his reign, Jehoshaphat agreed to accompany his brother-in-law, Ahab, King of Israel, in battle against Aram. The prophet Micaiah warned Ahab that he would not survive that battle, but he refused to heed his advice and was killed as the prophet had foretold. Jehoshaphat should have withdrawn his support when he heard that the battle was against the will of G-d, but he kept his word and went along. He reasoned that he would be safe, since the prophecy had not been directed toward him.

G-d punished him, for a great man like Jehoshaphat should not make such an error. He caused the soldiers of Aram to mistake him for Ahab, and they pursued him and almost killed him. But at the last minute he called out for mercy, and G-d had pity and saved him.

When Jehoshaphat returned home, however, he realized that he deserved to have died. He did not consider himself fit to reign any longer, so he had his son, Jehoram, crowned in his place. Seeing his sincere remorse, G-d forgave him and granted him favor in the eyes of the people. He continued to reign together with his son for seven more years, and was also respected by his nephews, Ahaziah and Jehoram, who consulted him concerning the governing of their kingdom.[14]

As has already been explained,[15] the seventeenth and eighteenth years of Jehoshaphat mentioned in reference to the beginnings of the reigns of Ahaziah and Jehoram are not calendar years, but years of the actual duration of Jehoshaphat's reign. When Ahaziah became king, Jehoshaphat had reigned sixteen full years, and was in the midst of his seventeenth. Ahaziah died and Jehoram became king in the midst of Jehoshaphat's eighteenth year. But in reckoning the total lengths of the reigns of these kings, a different system is used. They are given in calendar years, which begin in Nisan. Thus, when we are told that Ahaziah reigned two years, it only means that there were two calendar years during which he reigned. The actual duration of his reign might have been less than one year, covering only the last few months of one calendar year and the first few of the next.[16]

II KINGS 2

2:1,2 וַיְהִי בְּהַעֲלוֹת ה׳ אֶת־אֵלִיָּהוּ בַּסְעָרָה הַשָּׁמָיִם וַיֵּלֶךְ אֵלִיָּהוּ וֶאֱלִישָׁע
מִן־הַגִּלְגָּל: וַיֹּאמֶר אֵלִיָּהוּ אֶל־אֱלִישָׁע שֵׁב־נָא פֹה כִּי ה׳ שְׁלָחַנִי עַד־בֵּית־אֵל
וַיֹּאמֶר אֱלִישָׁע חַי־ה׳ וְחֵי־נַפְשְׁךָ אִם־אֶעֶזְבֶךָּ וַיֵּרְדוּ בֵּית־אֵל:

This is what happened when G-d took Elijah up to the heaven in a mighty wind. Elijah and Elisha went from Gilgal. Elijah said to Elisha, “Please stay here, for G-d has sent me to Beth-el.” Elisha said, “As G-d lives, and as your soul lives, I will not abandon you!” So they went down to Beth-el.

Gilgal was the first place where Joshua and the Jewish People camped after crossing the Jordan into the Holy Land. It was holy and greatly revered. There stood the twelve stones that they had taken from the bed of the Jordan. G-d had made the Jordan dry up for the people to cross. As a memorial of this, the first of many great miracles, each tribe took a mighty stone from the river bed and carried it to Gilgal. There Joshua erected them as a monument for future generations to see.

Then Joshua circumcised the people. Those that had been born during the forty years of wandering in the desert had not been circumcised, so he circumcised them all at Gilgal. After that they celebrated Passover.

Gilgal was also the first site of the Tabernacle in the Holy Land. All these things made Gilgal a very special place. In particular, it symbolized the observance of Torah and G-d’s commandments.

Elijah said to Elisha, “Let me take leave of you here, and here you will take over the leadership of the other prophets and of the whole Jewish People. By transferring the leadership to you at Gilgal, you will be fortified in Torah and the sanctity of the commandments, as is epitomized by this place. You will also gain the strength to unify the nation, just as it was unified here in the time of Joshua.”

But Elisha would not part with him. He said, “That is not enough. It is indeed a great thing to faithfully observe G-d's commandments and guide the people in Torah, but I want to strive for even greater heights. I will go on with you to Beth-el!"[1]

2:3,4 וַיֵּצְאוּ בְנֵי־הַנְּבִיאִים אֲשֶׁר־בֵּית־אֵל אֶל־אֱלִישָׁע וַיֹּאמְרוּ אֵלָיו
הֲיָדַעְתָּ כִּי הַיּוֹם ה׳ לֹקֵחַ אֶת־אֲדֹנֶיךָ מֵעַל רֹאשֶׁךָ וַיֹּאמֶר גַּם־אֲנִי יָדַעְתִּי הֶחֱשׁוּ׃
וַיֹּאמֶר לוֹ אֵלִיָּהוּ אֱלִישָׁע שֵׁב־נָא פֹה כִּי ה׳ שְׁלָחַנִי יְרִיחוֹ וַיֹּאמֶר חַי־ה׳
וְחֵי־נַפְשְׁךָ אִם־אֶעֶזְבֶךָּ וַיָּבֹאוּ יְרִיחוֹ׃

The sons of the prophets who were in Beth-el came out to Elisha and said to him, "Do you know that today G-d is taking your master from upon your head?" He said, "I too know! Be quiet!" Elijah said to him, "Elisha, please stay here, for G-d has sent me to Jericho." He said, "As G-d lives and as your soul lives, I will not abandon you!" So they came to Jericho.

Beth-el stood for prophecy and divine influence. There, Jacob had gone to sleep and seen the ladder to heaven. He declared that it was indeed the "House of G-d and the gate of heaven."[2] He returned there by G-d's command when he came back from Aram with his family, and built an altar there to express his gratitude.

At Beth-el Elijah, too, thanked G-d for answering him the many times that he had called out, and for saving him from the wrath of his enemies. He thanked G-d as well for the great level of prophecy that he had reached during his life.

He said to Elisha, "Let me leave you here, for now you have earned not only the leadership of the nation, but also continued prophecy. By virtue of the holiness of this place, the spirit of prophecy will never leave you."

Elisha said, "Even prophecy is not enough. I have been your loyal disciple and served you faithfully. I want to be like you, to perform miracles as you have. I will not remain here either!"[3]

The "sons of the prophets" were the students who learned Torah from Elijah and the other prophets.[4] Besides learning Torah, they shared some of the divine influence that their teacher received. For when a person, through his piety, raises himself to the level of prophecy, those around him experience some of the spirit of prophecy as well.[5]

At that time, Elijah had followers in many cities of Israel. They learned Torah from him whenever he visited them, and they taught and guided the people of their own areas. In that way, the Torah was spread throughout Israel. Only Elisha stayed with Elijah all the time, travelling with him wherever he went.[6]

When the sons of the prophets spoke to Elisha, they referred to Elijah as "Your master." Some say they considered him Elisha's master, but not their own. They thought of themselves as prophets in their own right, while they saw Elisha only as Elijah's disciple.[7] They said, "We are prophets, so it has been revealed to us that Elijah will be taken to heaven today. But you, Elisha, do you know it? You have never proclaimed a prophecy. Perhaps you are not a prophet at all, but know only what Elijah tells you."[8]

Elisha answered, "I know it too, but it is not to be mentioned. Otherwise I would have said it myself!" For indeed, it had been revealed to Elisha too. Elijah had not told him, yet he knew.[9]

2:5,6 וַיִּגְּשׁוּ בְנֵי־הַנְּבִיאִים אֲשֶׁר־בִּירִיחוֹ אֶל־אֱלִישָׁע וַיֹּאמְרוּ אֵלָיו הֲיָדַעְתָּ
כִּי הַיּוֹם ה׳ לֹקֵחַ אֶת־אֲדֹנֶיךָ מֵעַל רֹאשֶׁךָ וַיֹּאמֶר גַּם־אֲנִי יָדַעְתִּי הֶחֱשׁוּ׃ וַיֹּאמֶר
לוֹ אֵלִיָּהוּ שֵׁב־נָא פֹה כִּי ה׳ שְׁלָחַנִי הַיַּרְדֵּנָה וַיֹּאמֶר חַי־ה׳ וְחֵי־נַפְשְׁךָ
אִם־אֶעֶזְבֶךָּ וַיֵּלְכוּ שְׁנֵיהֶם׃

The sons of the prophets who were in Jericho approached Elisha and said to him, "Do you know that today G-d is taking your master from upon your head?" He said, "I too know! Be quiet!" Elijah said to him, "Please stay here, for G-d has sent me to the Jordan." He said, "As G-d lives and as your soul lives, I will not abandon you!" So the two of them went.

Jericho was the site of many miracles. There the angel appeared to Joshua and promised him divine protection in all his campaigns against the Canaanites. He was then instructed to conquer the city of Jericho in a manner that would clearly display divine intervention. For seven days the people marched around it, and on the seventh day the walls fell and sunk into the ground.

There, too, the curses that Joshua proclaimed were fulfilled. He forbade the people to take anything from the spoils of the city. Only one person, Achan, violated the ban, but for this alone the people were punished with defeat in their next campaign. Joshua also proclaimed a curse upon anyone who would rebuild the city. He would lose his children one by one, and the last would die when the city was completed. That ban was respected until Elijah's own time, when it was violated by the wicked Hiel. He suffered the curse exactly as Joshua had proclaimed it.

Jericho was also opposite the mountain of Pisga, from which Moses viewed the land before he died.

Elijah said, "Now you have earned not only leadership in Torah and prophecy, but the ability to perform miracles as well. Surely you will be satisfied with that. Remain here, then, and let me proceed alone."

But even this was not acceptable to Elisha, so great was his dedication to his teacher. He was committed to remaining with him to the very end. Furthermore, he knew that even the level of miracle worker was not equal to Elijah, and he would settle for nothing less himself. So he insisted upon accompanying him across the Jordan.[10]

Some say Elijah himself did not know where he was destined to ascend to heaven. He knew only that it would be at one of the holy places which had been the site of other great events. First he went to Gilgal, but when he arrived he realized that it would not be there. So too at Beth-el and Jericho. But as they crossed the Jordan, Elijah knew that he was nearing the place.[11]

2:7 וַחֲמִשִּׁים אִישׁ מִבְּנֵי הַנְּבִיאִים הָלְכוּ וַיַּעַמְדוּ מִנֶּגֶד מֵרָחוֹק וּשְׁנֵיהֶם עָמְדוּ עַל־הַיַּרְדֵּן׃

Fifty men of the sons of the prophets went and stood at a distance, and the two of them stood at the Jordan.

None of the fifty prophets were close to Elijah's level, so they were unable to come along. They could only stand at a distance and watch. But Elisha had risen above them all. He alone could accompany his master.[12]

2:8 וַיִּקַּח אֵלִיָּהוּ אֶת־אַדַּרְתּוֹ וַיִּגְלֹם וַיַּכֶּה אֶת־הַמַּיִם וַיֵּחָצוּ הֵנָּה וָהֵנָּה וַיַּעַבְרוּ שְׁנֵיהֶם בֶּחָרָבָה׃

Elijah took his cloak, rolled it up, and hit the water. It was divided in half here and there, and the two of them crossed on the dry land.

Having come this far, there was nowhere left from which to send Elisha back. They proceeded on together for the time being. When the time would come for Elijah to be taken away, Elisha would have no choice but to remain behind.

The word "ויגלם," "rolled it up," does not mean to fold neatly on creases, as one does with laundered clothes, but to roll or bunch up together.[13]

2:9,10 וַיְהִי כְעָבְרָם וְאֵלִיָּהוּ אָמַר אֶל־אֱלִישָׁע שְׁאַל מָה אֶעֱשֶׂה־לָּךְ בְּטֶרֶם אֶלָּקַח מֵעִמָּךְ וַיֹּאמֶר אֱלִישָׁע וִיהִי־נָא פִּי־שְׁנַיִם בְּרוּחֲךָ אֵלָי: וַיֹּאמֶר הִקְשִׁיתָ לִשְׁאוֹל אִם־תִּרְאֶה אֹתִי לֻקָּח מֵאִתָּךְ יְהִי־לְךָ כֵן וְאִם־אַיִן לֹא יִהְיֶה:

As they were crossing, Elijah said to Elisha, "Ask what I shall do for you before I am taken from you." Elisha said, "Let there be, please, double your spirit upon me!" He said, "You have asked for something very hard! If you see me being taken from you it will be so for you, and if not, it will not be."

Elijah had never before offered to grant Elisha's request, neither at Gilgal, Beth-el, nor Jericho. Perhaps he would have had Elisha agreed to remain behind at one of those places. Perhaps he had intended all along to make this his parting gift to his faithful follower.

Or perhaps, had Elisha remained at any of those places, he would not have been worthy of such an offer. Only now that he had shown his faithfulness and determination had he attained this highest of levels. He was now worthy of anything that was within Elijah's power.[14]

Some say that Elijah had not made this offer until now because he didn't realize how attached his student was to him. But now, seeing that he had in no way been able to convince Elisha to part with him, he became aware of what a bitter loss it would be. He wanted to give him something to console him. Though Elijah himself was ready to leave this world and felt no regret, he was distressed by the sight of his faithful disciple suffering so. He would do anything he could to alleviate it.[15]

What was the meaning of Elisha's request? What would it mean for him to have double Elijah's spirit? Some say that he wanted to perform twice as many miracles as Elijah had. Elijah had experienced eight miracles, five private and three public. The first private miracle occurred when he was in the desert, hiding from Ahab. For a year G-d sent ravens to bring him bread and meat to eat twice each day.

The second was the miracle that he performed for the woman of Zarephath. He blessed the small amounts of flour and oil that she had when he arrived, which were not even enough for a single day. They lasted as long as he stayed with her, never being diminished no matter how much she used.

After that, the woman's son died and Elijah revived him. That was the third miracle.

The fourth was the bread and water that were brought to him in the desert when he was running away from Jezebel.

And the fifth was the special strength given him by that food, which enabled him to live for forty days without eating anything else. All these were private miracles, witnessed only by a small number of people. The second and third were witnessed by Elijah, the woman, and her son. The rest by Elijah alone.

The first of the three public miracles was the drought that was brought on the Jewish People by Elijah's word. Part of this miracle was the divine protection that he received during that time. Ahab was unable to find him no matter how hard he searched. Another part was the immediate cessation of the drought when Elijah declared it over.

The second was the fire that came down on Mount Carmel at his request.

The third was the destruction by fire of the soldiers of Ahaziah who were sent to arrest him. These miracles were witnessed by many people, and everyone knew about them.

Elisha asked to perform sixteen miracles, twice as many as Elijah had. Indeed, eventually he did.[16]

But if this was Elisha's request, why did Elijah consider it so difficult to grant? If he could make Elisha capable of performing a single miracle, could he not make him capable of performing two, three, or any number of the same sort?

Others therefore say that the spirit that Elisha requested refers to divine influence. He wanted to achieve twice the level of prophecy of Elijah. In that case, we can well understand why Elijah answered that it would be difficult. How can one person give another more than he has himself?[17]

But Elijah did not answer that it was impossible. He only said it was difficult. For, as Elijah would ascend to heaven, he would achieve a much greater degree of divine influence than he had had while he was on earth. Elisha asked whether, during the short time that he was rising upward and his own power of prophecy was increasing, he might be able to impart to him some of that newly gained greatness before he was taken completely away. Elijah answered that only if Elisha would be present and continue to see him during that time would it be possible.[18]

According to this interpretation, it was by the act of watching Elijah ascend that Elisha himself would be elevated to this new and higher level. Even Elijah had never had such an experience, to watch someone ascend to heaven. Perhaps that is why it would impart to Elisha a kind of greatness that Elijah himself had never before attained.

Others say that it was only a sign of the strength that Elisha already possessed. Elijah said, "If you are able to withstand this experience, then indeed twice my spirit is already upon you!"[19]

An entirely different interpretation is that Elisha was asking that Elijah's spirit remain with him even after he ascended to heaven. He said, "During the time that I have been your disciple, I have risen to your level, and the two of us have been unique among all the people of the world. We have spent our time discussing Torah in a way that neither of us could have done with anyone else.

"But once you are gone, what will I do? With whom will I study? For a person must study Torah by sharing his thoughts with someone else, and there will be no one left who will be able to appreciate my insights. I therefore request that your spirit remain with me even after your body is taken away. Then we can continue to discuss Torah together, even though you will not be with me physically any more."

This was a truly exceptional request. There was no precedent for it among the earlier prophets. So it is understandable that Elijah considered it very difficult.[20] Nonetheless, according to this interpretation as well, it was not impossible. Indeed, had it been beyond the realm of possibility, Elisha himself would never have asked for it. He knew which sort of requests were reasonable and which not, and would not have asked for something that could not be fulfilled.

According to this interpretation, Elijah's response should not be translated "If you see me being taken from you" but "If you will see me when I have been taken from you." That is, if Elisha would be able to see Elijah by means of prophecy even after Elijah was no longer in this world, then they would indeed be able to continue to converse and exchange thoughts of Torah. That would depend upon Elisha's own state. If he remained pure and holy, then it would be possible. He would be fit to receive Elijah's spirit. But if, after Elijah was gone, he sunk into the ways of the physical world, he would not. Therefore Elijah referred to sight whereas Elisha had requested only spirit, which is understood to mean speech, not vision. He said, "My speaking to you is dependent upon your seeing me. As long as you can see me, I will be able to speak to you!"

Thus, throughout the ages, there have been saintly men who have purified themselves through Torah and become worthy of seeing Elijah. Once they have attained that vision, he has spoken to them.[21]

2:11 וַיְהִי הֵמָּה הֹלְכִים הָלוֹךְ וְדַבֵּר וְהִנֵּה רֶכֶב־אֵשׁ וְסוּסֵי אֵשׁ וַיַּפְרִדוּ בֵּין שְׁנֵיהֶם וַיַּעַל אֵלִיָּהוּ בַּסְּעָרָה הַשָּׁמָיִם׃

So it was that they were walking and talking, and behold, there was a chariot of fire and horses of fire, and they separated between the two of them. Then Elijah went up in the mighty wind to heaven.

While they walked they discussed the Torah as they always had. They didn't let Elijah's imminent departure distract them. Some say they were discussing the recitation of Shema, some the creation of the world, some the final redemption and rebuilding of the Temple, and some the divine chariot.[22]

G-d sent an angel to bring Elijah to heaven, but as long as they were speaking words of Torah, he was powerless. Finally he came between them and interrupted them. The moment they stopped he lifted Elijah up to heaven. Then he returned to G-d and said, "I have fulfilled the mission on which You sent me, but look what a disgrace I was forced to commit to accomplish it!"[23]

What happened to Elijah when he went up to heaven? Some say his body was burnt by the heavenly fire and only his soul remained.[24] Though his body did not remain alive, this was not like the death of ordinary people, whose souls leave their bodies. Elijah ascended bodily and was purified by this unique experience until only his soul remained, as metal is purified in the fire.

Others say that Elijah's body, too, remained whole and unharmed. He was carried through the air to the Garden of Eden where he remained hidden from the rest of mankind, except for those times that he is sent to appear to the righteous or perform other missions.[25]

Both Moses and Elijah remained strong and healthy throughout their old age. Their bodies did not become sick and deteriorate like the bodies of most old people. Moses could have continued to live indefinitely, but when the time approached for the Jews to enter the Holy Land G-d decreed that he die. He prepared a special cave for him with a bed to lie on. There he lay down, closed his eyes, and his soul left his body, passing from physical existence to a purely spiritual one. It was without pain or sorrow, for he remained awake and in contact with the divine presence throughout. This was called "death by a kiss."

Why didn't Elijah die as Moses did? Was that not the most desirable way for a person to end his earthly existence? One reason is that, unlike Moses, Elijah's task on earth was not yet completed. Moses had taken the Jews out of Egypt, given them the Torah, and led them through the desert. That was his great mission, and, having completed it, he was ready to leave this world. But Elijah had yet to herald the coming of the Messiah and prepare the Jewish People for the final redemption, as the prophet Malachi said,[26] "Behold, I am sending you Elijah the prophet, before the coming of the great and awesome day of G-d." So G-d arranged that he remain alive in the Garden of Eden until that time arrives. All his needs would be provided for there, and he would be endowed with a body that would never weaken or deteriorate.

This was the opposite of what happened to Adam. Adam was created with a perfect body, meant to remain alive forever. He was placed in the most ideal location, the Garden of Eden, where he would never experience trouble or want. But he sinned by following his physical desires, and lost both comfort and eternal life.

Elijah, on the other hand, was born an ordinary human being, destined to suffer, deteriorate, and die. But through his piety he overcame physical desire until his entire existence was dedicated to G-d. He thereby earned for himself the eternal life that Adam had lost. The rough leather cloak and leather clothes that he wore instead of softer, more comfortable material, were reminiscent of the "clothes of skin" that G-d made for Adam and Eve after they sinned. For Elijah, they represented his rejection of the pleasures of the physical world.[27] For it was only physically that these clothes were coarse and inferior. Spiritually they were among the holiest and most elevated. They were made from the skin of the ram that Abraham sacrificed in place of his son, Isaac.[28]

Another reason that Elijah was granted eternal physical life while Moses died was that Elijah's spiritual greatness came through his involvement with the physical world, while Moses' came by transcending it. Moses walked among the angels even when he was alive. So the height of Moses' greatness was reached through the separation of his soul from his body, while Elijah's was reached by their continued union.

Elijah's zeal and devotion to G-d and Torah were expressed by his burning intolerence of human imperfection. Moses, on the other hand, begged G-d to have mercy on the Jews even when they committed the gravest sins.

A third reason was that in death, Moses' body was united with the earth of the Holy Land, in which he yearned to live. But Elijah raged against the Jewish People and brought curses of fire and drought upon their land. It would not have been right that his body rest within it.[29]

2:12 וֶאֱלִישָׁע רֹאֶה וְהוּא מְצַעֵק אָבִי אָבִי רֶכֶב יִשְׂרָאֵל וּפָרָשָׁיו וְלֹא רָאָהוּ עוֹד וַיַּחֲזֵק בִּבְגָדָיו וַיִּקְרָעֵם לִשְׁנַיִם קְרָעִים׃

Elisha was watching and crying out, "My Father, my Father! Chariot of Israel and its horsemen!" Then he didn't see him any more. He took hold of his clothes and tore them into two pieces.

There are various interpretations of Elisha's exclamation. One is that the words, "Chariot of Israel and its horsemen!" referred to Elijah himself. Elisha called him that because his prayers protected the People of Israel like an army of chariots and horsemen.[30] According to this, the chariot of fire that appeared was a divine symbol of Elijah leaving the Jewish People. Therefore on that day the kingdom of Rome was established, for now that Israel's protector was no longer among them, their enemies were able to gain strength.[31]

Another interpretation is that the words referred to the chariot and horses of fire. Elisha said, "This is indeed the very fire that descended on Mount Carmel, and the same one that destroyed the soldiers of Ahaziah! It is the protecting fire of Israel, appearing in this way because it protects Israel like horses and chariots."

A third explanation is that the name "Israel" refers here not to the Jewish People, but to the patriarch Jacob himself. Elisha said, "Look, Oh my Father! This is the camp of G-d that Jacob saw and that protected him from Laban and Esau."[32]

Elisha addressed Elijah as "my Father" because any teacher of Torah, and especially the one from whom a person has received the majority of his knowledge, is considered like a father. In ways a teacher is even greater than a parent, because a parent brings a child into this world, while a teacher who guides him enables his soul to develop and reach ever greater spiritual heights, so that he may enter the world to come and enjoy greatness there. All the more so in Elisha's case, for he had left his own parents to follow Elijah.[33]

It was not by accident that Elijah's cloak fell as he rose to heaven.

The cloak was the symbol of prophecy and leadership. When Elijah first invited Elisha to become his disciple, it was by passing his cloak over him. Elisha understood this gesture and abandoned everything he had to follow him. Now, that cloak and the position of leadership it symbolized would become Elisha's. Elijah's last act as he was taken to heaven was to throw off the cloak for him.[34]

Elisha tore his clothes in mourning, as he would have had his own father or mother died, for Elijah was like a father to him. Even a student whose relationship with his teacher is not as close as Elisha's was must mourn in this way, for a teacher of Torah has the status of a parent with respect to the laws of mourning.[35]

The cloak also represented the separation between Elijah and G-d. It was with that cloak that he had covered his face when G-d passed before him in the cave on Mount Sinai. Now he let it go. He had risen to a level where such a division would no longer be necessary.[36]

Some say that Elisha not only made a tear in his clothes to demonstrate his mourning, but tore them completely to pieces. His clothes were symbolic of his status. With Elijah's departure, that had completely changed. He was no longer a disciple, but the leader of the prophets. He destroyed his old clothes to show that he would not be wearing them any more. From now on, he would wear the cloak of Elijah.[37]

2:13,14 וַיָּרֶם אֶת־אַדֶּרֶת אֵלִיָּהוּ אֲשֶׁר נָפְלָה מֵעָלָיו וַיָּשָׁב וַיַּעֲמֹד עַל־שְׂפַת
הַיַּרְדֵּן׃ וַיִּקַּח אֶת־אַדֶּרֶת אֵלִיָּהוּ אֲשֶׁר־נָפְלָה מֵעָלָיו וַיַּכֶּה אֶת־הַמַּיִם וַיֹּאמַר אַיֵּה
ה׳ אֱלֹהֵי אֵלִיָּהוּ אַף־הוּא וַיַּכֶּה אֶת־הַמַּיִם וַיֵּחָצוּ הֵנָּה וָהֵנָּה וַיַּעֲבֹר אֱלִישָׁע׃

He picked up the cloak of Elijah that had fallen from upon him, and went back and stood on the bank of the Jordan. He took the cloak of Elijah that had fallen from upon him and hit the water and said, "Where is the L-rd, the G-d of Elijah?" Even he, he hit the water and it was divided in half, here and there, and Elisha went across.

Elisha immediately went to see whether his request had been granted. Would he be able to split the Jordan as his master had? Until that time, Elisha had never performed a miracle. Some say he had never even been granted prophecy.[38] He had served Elijah faithfully, but never tried to take his place. That is the way a student of Torah should behave. He should not crave his teacher's greatness or try to take over his position. For serving a great teacher is one of the most exalted things a person can do.[39] Thus Joshua remained Moses' servant as long as Moses was alive, never trying to lead in his stead. But as soon as Moses died he became the leader of the Jewish People, and demonstrated greatness which had never been evident before.

Thus we are taught that a student may not declare a decision in the presence of his teacher unless he receives his permission first.

Some say that it was indeed twice as great a miracle for Elisha to split the Jordan than it had been for Elijah. When Elijah struck the waters, they parted for two holy men to pass, Elijah and Elisha. But when Elisha struck them they parted for him alone. Thus, in one way, Elisha's request for twice Elijah's spirit had already been fulfilled.[40]

By the words, "Where is the L-rd, the G-d of Elijah?" Elisha did not mean to doubt G-d's presence. It was a way of calling on G-d to demonstrate that even though Elijah was gone, He was still watching over His people. He had not left them without a leader and guide.[41]

After these words he hit the waters again and they split.[42]

2:15,16 וַיִּרְאֻהוּ בְנֵי־הַנְּבִיאִים אֲשֶׁר־בִּירִחוֹ מִנֶּגֶד וַיֹּאמְרוּ נָחָה רוּחַ אֵלִיָּהוּ
עַל־אֱלִישָׁע וַיָּבֹאוּ לִקְרָאתוֹ וַיִּשְׁתַּחֲווּ־לוֹ אָרְצָה׃ וַיֹּאמְרוּ אֵלָיו הִנֵּה־נָא
יֵשׁ־אֶת־עֲבָדֶיךָ חֲמִשִּׁים אֲנָשִׁים בְּנֵי־חַיִל יֵלְכוּ נָא וִיבַקְשׁוּ אֶת־אֲדֹנֶיךָ פֶּן־נְשָׂאוֹ
רוּחַ ה׳ וַיַּשְׁלִכֵהוּ בְּאַחַד הֶהָרִים אוֹ בְּאַחַת הַגֵּיאָוֹת (הַגֵּאָיוֹת קרי) וַיֹּאמֶר לֹא תִשְׁלָחוּ׃

The sons of the prophets who were in Jericho saw him from afar and said, "The spirit of Elijah has rested on Elisha!" They came to meet him and bowed to him to the ground. They said to him, "Behold, please. There are with your servants fifty brave men. Let them, please, go and seek your master, lest the wind of G-d carried him up and threw him on one of the mountains or in one of the valleys." He said, "Don't send!"

Unlike Elisha, the other students, though they had prophesied while Elijah was still alive, now lost their power of prophecy.[43] Only a short while ago they had all known clearly that Elijah was to be taken away and they hadn't hesitated to tell Elisha so. Now they seemed to doubt it.[44] Had they forgotten even the prophecy that they themselves had proclaimed? Or, now that it was only a memory and no longer an active revelation, had it ceased to seem real to them?

2:17,18 וַיִּפְצְרוּ־בוֹ עַד־בֹּשׁ וַיֹּאמֶר שְׁלָחוּ וַיִּשְׁלְחוּ חֲמִשִּׁים אִישׁ וַיְבַקְשׁוּ שְׁלֹשָׁה־יָמִים וְלֹא מְצָאֻהוּ׃ וַיָּשֻׁבוּ אֵלָיו וְהוּא יֹשֵׁב בִּירִיחוֹ וַיֹּאמֶר אֲלֵהֶם הֲלֹא־אָמַרְתִּי אֲלֵיכֶם אַל־תֵּלֵכוּ׃

They pressed him until it was too much, and he said, "Send!" So they sent fifty men. They sought three days and did not find him. They returned to him, and he was sitting in Jericho. He said to them, "Didn't I say to you, 'Don't go?' "

Elisha knew with certainty that Elijah was gone. It was useless to search for him. But, though the others accepted him as their new leader, they would not listen to him yet. Perhaps the grief of losing Elijah was too much for them to bear. Though they knew it was true, they could not accept it. Finally, seeing that he would not be able to convince them, he let them go and find out for themselves.[45]

Some say the words "עד בש," "too much," mean "until it was very late."[46] Others say they mean "until it was embarrassing." Elisha was ashamed to refuse any longer, lest they say that he didn't want to find his teacher as they did. He was afraid they would think that he wanted Elijah to stay away so that he could keep his newly acquired position of leadership.[47]

2:19 וַיֹּאמְרוּ אַנְשֵׁי הָעִיר אֶל־אֱלִישָׁע הִנֵּה־נָא מוֹשַׁב הָעִיר טוֹב כַּאֲשֶׁר אֲדֹנִי רֹאֶה וְהַמַּיִם רָעִים וְהָאָרֶץ מְשַׁכָּלֶת׃

The people of the city said to Elisha, "Behold, the dwelling-place of the city is good, as my master sees, but the water is bad and the land loses its inhabitants."

"The dwelling-place of the city is good" refers to the opinion of people who lived there.[48] They considered it a good place even though others would have rejected it because of the water. They said, "The climate here is good, the land is good, and the people are righteous and worthy of being blessed. It is only the water that makes it bad."

Some say it was Joshua's curse on the rebuilding of Jericho that had caused the water to become unwholesome. There was nothing naturally wrong with it, but G-d cursed it because the people had violated Joshua's ban. Although Joshua had only declared a curse on the builder of Jericho, G-d cursed all those who lived there as well. The curse even extended to those who settled there afterwards and had in no way assisted in the building. They had committed no sin, for there was no prohibition against settling there. Had there been, Elijah's students, who were all righteous men, would not have violated it. Nonetheless, G-d's wrath remained on the place.[49]

Some say it had just become bad that day, for otherwise Elijah himself would have cured it. Furthermore, had the water always been bad the place would not have been considered desirable in the past.[50]

The word used here to describe the death of the inhabitants of Jericho is "משכלת," which is generally used to mean losing one's children. This is reminiscent of Joshua's curse on the builder of Jericho, whose children died one by one until the city was completed. The inhabitants of a land are like its children. If they perish it becomes like a mother whose children have died.

2:20-22 וַיֹּאמֶר קְחוּ־לִי צְלֹחִית חֲדָשָׁה וְשִׂימוּ שָׁם מֶלַח וַיִּקְחוּ אֵלָיו: וַיֵּצֵא
אֶל־מוֹצָא הַמַּיִם וַיַּשְׁלֶךְ־שָׁם מֶלַח וַיֹּאמֶר כֹּה־אָמַר ה׳ רִפִּאתִי לַמַּיִם הָאֵלֶּה
לֹא־יִהְיֶה מִשָּׁם עוֹד מָוֶת וּמְשַׁכָּלֶת: וַיֵּרָפוּ הַמַּיִם עַד הַיּוֹם הַזֶּה כִּדְבַר אֱלִישָׁע
אֲשֶׁר דִּבֵּר:

He said, "Bring me a new jar and put salt in it," and they brought it to him. He went out to the source of the water and threw salt there, and said, "Thus says G-d, 'I have cured these waters! There will not be any more death and loss of life from there!'" The waters were cured until this day, like the word of Elisha that he had spoken.

Elisha asked for a new jar that had never contained anything before. He wanted it to be clear that there was nothing but salt in it. There could not have been even the trace of any earlier contents that might have been responsible for curing the water.[51]

The curing of the water was a double miracle. Salt makes even sweet water undrinkable, yet this time it made the contaminated water pure and wholesome again. A similar miracle was performed by Moses shortly after the Jews left Egypt. Having traveled through the desert for three days without water, they finally came to a spring, only to find the water undrinkably bitter. G-d directed him to cut down a tree and throw it into the water.[52] Though the tree itself was bitter, it made the water sweet.[53]

Elisha's act differed significantly from that of Moses, however, in that it was not done at G-d's command. Elisha followed the example of his master, Elijah, who proclaimed miracles and called on G-d to fulfill them. Therefore the curing of the water is described as being "like the word of Elisha that he had spoken." It was according to Elisha's word, not G-d's.

Elisha had already seen that G-d would fulfill his word when the Jordan split for him. He knew then that he had been granted the spirit of Elijah as he had requested, and was confident that the other miracles he proclaimed would be fulfilled as well. Now he demonstrated it to his followers in Jericho too. Once they saw that, they knew that though they had lost their great master, Elijah, he had left a disciple to take his place.[54]

2:23,24 וַיַּעַל מִשָּׁם בֵּית־אֵל וְהוּא עֹלֶה בַדֶּרֶךְ וּנְעָרִים קְטַנִּים יָצְאוּ
מִן־הָעִיר וַיִּתְקַלְּסוּ־בוֹ וַיֹּאמְרוּ לוֹ עֲלֵה קֵרֵחַ עֲלֵה קֵרֵחַ: וַיִּפֶן אַחֲרָיו וַיִּרְאֵם
וַיְקַלְלֵם בְּשֵׁם ה׳ וַתֵּצֶאנָה שְׁתַּיִם דֻּבִּים מִן־הַיַּעַר וַתְּבַקַּעְנָה מֵהֶם אַרְבָּעִים וּשְׁנֵי יְלָדִים:

He went up from there to Beth-el. He was going up on the way, and little boys came out from the city and made fun of him. They said to him, "Go up, baldy, go up, baldy!" He turned around and saw them, and cursed them in the name of G-d. Then two bears came out of the forest, and tore apart forty-two boys from among them.

Elisha continued to retrace his steps, going back along the way that he had come with Elijah. At each place he performed a miracle. When Elisha looked at the children who came out to tease him, he saw by the spirit of prophecy that they were devoid of any good deeds and weak of faith. The word "נערים," "boys," can also be interpreted as "מנוערים," "shaken out" and therefore empty. They were empty of the only thing of worth, good deeds. The word "קטנים," "little," alludes to how small their faith was.[55]

Some say that Elisha saw that all of them had been conceived on Yom Kippur. Their parents had violated the holiness of that day, when it is forbidden for man and wife to have intimate relations. As their beginning had been in sin, so, Elisha saw, their end would be. He cursed them not in anger or vengence, but because he saw that no good would ever come of them. It was their evil nature that had brought them to behave so nastily, and it would continue to produce wickness as long as they lived.

Others say that he saw that their hair was cut in the style of the heathens. He understood that they had already strayed so far from the ways of Torah that they would never return.[56]

Though G-d fulfilled Elisha's decree, He did not entirely approve, and Elisha was eventually to suffer for it. Three times in his life he was to be afflicted with illness. Once was for causing the death of these children. Another was for rejecting his follower, Gehazi, who had shown himself unworthy. From both these illnesses he recovered, for they were divine punishments. The third time he became ill was when his time came to die. This was not a punishment, but the vehicle of his death.[57]

Some say these boys were the children of the priests of Baal, who had been sent by their parents to annoy him. They said, "Your master was hairy and you are bald. He went up to heaven, now you go up too and leave us alone!" Elisha saw that it was not himself alone that they were mocking, but Elijah too. He was filled with indignation, and arose in defense of the honor of his master and of all the prophets. He saw, too, that these children were not only wicked themselves, but the sons of wicked fathers, raised in wickedness. There was no one to admonish them and turn them back to the path of righteousness. They would never accept the rebuke of a stranger as long as their parents remained committed to their wicked ways.[58]

Others say that these boys used to earn money bringing water to Jericho when the water there was bad. They hated Elisha for taking this source of income away from them.[59]

The two bears that killed them stood for the honor of the two great prophets whom they had mocked, Elijah and Elisha. The forty-two boys that were killed were an allusion to the Torah they had rejected. Forty-two is the numerical value of the letters "מב," and stands for Torah and holiness. G-d commanded us to teach the Torah to our children by the words,[60] "You will teach them to your children and speak of them." The numerical value of the word "of them," "בם," is forty-two. These children had not been taught Torah, so they went astray and brought on their own destruction.[61]

This was especially miraculous because no bears were known to live in that forest. Some say there wasn't even a forest there.[62]

The people of Jericho were also held responsible for the deaths of these children. Had they escorted Elisha on his way, this incident never would have happened. A host should therefore escort his guest until he reaches a place of safety.[63]

2:25 וַיֵּלֶךְ מִשָּׁם אֶל־הַר הַכַּרְמֶל וּמִשָּׁם שָׁב שֹׁמְרוֹן׃

He went from there to Mount Carmel, and from there he returned to Samaria.

Then Elisha went to the other places at which miracles had been performed for Elijah. At all of them he received renewed divine influence. He also drew from the holiness of the places themselves, that had seen miracles and prophecy in earlier times.[64]

II KINGS 3

3:1 וִיהוֹרָם בֶּן־אַחְאָב מָלַךְ עַל־יִשְׂרָאֵל בְּשֹׁמְרוֹן בִּשְׁנַת שְׁמֹנֶה עֶשְׂרֵה
לִיהוֹשָׁפָט מֶלֶךְ יְהוּדָה וַיִּמְלֹךְ שְׁתֵּים־עֶשְׂרֵה שָׁנָה׃

Jehoram, the son of Ahab, became king over Israel in Samaria in the eighteenth year of Jehoshaphat, King of Judah, and he reigned twelve years.

Earlier, the beginning of Jehoram's reign was given as the second year of Jehoram, King of Judah, but here it is referred to as the eighteenth year of his father, Jehoshaphat. As was explained there, Jehoshaphat deserved to die in the battle of Ramoth-gilead, but he was spared by divine mercy. Realizing this, he no longer considered himself worthy of being king, and had his son, Jehoram, crowned in his place. He ceased to refer to himself as King of Judah, but simply as Jehoshaphat.

But, seeing his sincere remorse, G-d forgave him and began to refer to him as king again. So in this chapter he is again called King of Judah and dates are again reckoned by the years of his own reign, not his son's. Only Jehoshaphat himself continued to refrain from using that title. So his own quotes in this chapter are introduced by the words, "Jehoshaphat said," but otherwise he is referred to as "the King of Judah."

3:2,3 וַיַּעֲשֶׂה הָרַע בְּעֵינֵי ה׳ רַק לֹא כְאָבִיו וּכְאִמּוֹ וַיָּסַר אֶת־מַצְּבַת הַבַּעַל
אֲשֶׁר עָשָׂה אָבִיו׃ רַק בְּחַטֹּאות יָרָבְעָם בֶּן־נְבָט אֲשֶׁר־הֶחֱטִיא אֶת־יִשְׂרָאֵל דָּבֵק
לֹא־סָר מִמֶּנָּה׃

He did what was evil in G-d's eyes, but not like his father and his mother. He removed the monument of Baal that his father had made. Only to the sins of Jeroboam ben Nebat who made Israel sin did he cling. He did not go away from them.

Israel sinned in two different ways. One was to worship idols, thanking them for the blessings that had really been given by G-d, and asking them for help, which only G-d can give. This is the gravest of all sins. But even serving G-d can be done in the wrong way. Some forms of service are desirable to Him and others are not. G-d doesn't want us to serve Him in the abominable ways that the pagans serve their gods. He doesn't want us to inflict injuries on ourselves or indulge in orgies. Therefore, in the Torah, He laid out a pure and noble service for us. It is uplifting to those who perform it and pleasing to Him.

Before the Kingdom of Israel began to worship idols, they had long practiced the lesser sin of deviating from the service that G-d had commanded, attempting to serve Him in other, novel, ways. That was the sin of Jeroboam ben Nebat. He made two golden calves and directed the people to worship them. These were not intended as idols of pagan deities, like the idols of the Canaanites. They were dedicated to G-d Himself. The divine presence was supposed to dwell between the horns of the calf, as it did between the cherubs in the Temple in Jerusalem. In this way, Jeroboam hoped to draw the people away from Jerusalem and the kings of the House of David, to follow him and his successors, the Kings of Israel.

But, unlike the cherubs in the Temple, these golden calves had not been ordained by G-d. The service that Jeroboam performed on the altars that he erected before them and in the sanctuaries that he built was an abomination. At first the Jewish People recognized that, but over the generations, as it became established, it no longer seemed to be a serious sin. For when people persist in a sin and become accustomed to it, it ceases to shock and repel them as it originally did. The worship of foreign gods, on the other hand, continued to be recognized as a terrible sin, and absolutely rejected until the time of Ahab. It was only under the influence of Ahab's pagan wife, the wicked Jezebel, that the worship of Baal and Asherah was introduced. Even then, it faced strong opposition.

Jehoram was therefore praised for discontinuing the worship of Baal and returning to the service of G-d, even though it was in the unacceptable form instituted by Jeroboam.[1] In that way he was considered better than his father. But, while Ahab had indeed supported Baal, he also worshiped G-d with great dedication. Jehoram lacked that redeeming quality.

As for the worship of Asherah, even Jehoram could not abolish it. Asherah was a female deity, and was supported by Jezebel alone. The priests of Asherah did not depend upon Jehoram, so he had no control over them.[2]

3:4,5 וּמֵישַׁע מֶלֶךְ־מוֹאָב הָיָה נֹקֵד וְהֵשִׁיב לְמֶלֶךְ־יִשְׂרָאֵל מֵאָה־אֶלֶף
כָּרִים וּמֵאָה אֶלֶף אֵילִים צָמֶר׃ וַיְהִי כְּמוֹת אַחְאָב וַיִּפְשַׁע מֶלֶךְ־מוֹאָב בְּמֶלֶךְ יִשְׂרָאֵל׃

Mesha, King of Moab, kept flocks, and he would send the King of Israel one hundred thousand fattened sheep and one hundred thousand rams with wool. But when Ahab died the King of Moab rebelled against the King of Israel.

Ahab was punished for his sins, but also rewarded for his righteousness. Under his rule, the Kingdom of Israel gained great power and wealth. The neighboring nations feared him and sent him tribute. Among them was Moab, from which he received one hundred thousand fattened sheep and one hundred thousand rams every year.[3]

Some say this was not really tribute. During the period of the judges, Moab had raided Israel many times and stolen their flocks, but they had been unable to resist. Sometimes they dominated the Jews and extracted tribute from them. Now that Israel had gained the upper hand, they forced Moab to gradually return what they had taken. Therefore the word used for "send" is "והשיב," which literally means "return."[4]

We already learned in Chapter One that when Ahab died Moab rebelled against his son, Ahaziah. Ahaziah had not been able to reconquer them, but Jehoram felt that he could. Perhaps he thought that since he was more righteous than his brother he would have enough merit to be worthy of divine assistance.

3:6,7 וַיֵּצֵא הַמֶּלֶךְ יְהוֹרָם בַּיּוֹם הַהוּא מִשֹּׁמְרוֹן וַיִּפְקֹד אֶת־כָּל־יִשְׂרָאֵל׃
וַיֵּלֶךְ וַיִּשְׁלַח אֶל־יְהוֹשָׁפָט מֶלֶךְ־יְהוּדָה לֵאמֹר מֶלֶךְ מוֹאָב פָּשַׁע בִּי הֲתֵלֵךְ אִתִּי
אֶל־מוֹאָב לַמִּלְחָמָה וַיֹּאמֶר אֶעֱלֶה כָּמוֹנִי כָמוֹךָ כְּעַמִּי כְעַמֶּךָ כְּסוּסַי כְּסוּסֶיךָ׃

On that day King Jehoram went out of Samaria and mustered all Israel. He went and sent to Jehoshaphat, King of Judah, saying, "The King of Moab has rebelled against me. Will you go to war against Moab with me?" He said, "I will go up! I am just like you! My people is just like your people and my horses are just like your horses!"

Jehoshaphat responded with whole-hearted support, as he had to Jehoram's father, Ahab. Although the Jewish People was divided into two kingdoms, they would stand united against any foreign enemy. He said, "You know that we disapprove of some of your practices. We condemn the cult of the golden calves that was established by Jeroboam, and all the more so the idolatry that has more recently been introduced. But we are still one nation. We are brothers, and we must always stand side by side."

Jehoshaphat also realized that if Moab succeeded in their rebellion, other vassel states might follow their example. He said, "This is not a danger to you alone. It is a danger to me too!"[5]

Jehoshaphat remembered the tragic mistake of his father, Asa. Asa had enlisted the help of Aram to fight against Baasa, King of Israel.[6] Only afterwards did he learn that had he faced Baasa himself, he would have overcome him and reunited the nation under his own rule. By enlisting the aid of a foreign nation against his fellow Jews, he lost that privilege forever. Jehoshaphat resolved not to repeat his father's mistake.

The expression "כמוני כמוך," "I am just like you! My people is just like your people and my horses are just like your horses!" literally means, "Like me, like you, like my people, like your people, like my horses like your horses." This form, using the prefix "כ," "like" twice, indicates complete equality.

3:8 וַיֹּאמֶר אֵי־זֶה הַדֶּרֶךְ נַעֲלֶה וַיֹּאמֶר דֶּרֶךְ מִדְבַּר אֱדוֹם׃

He said, "By which road shall we go up?" He said, "By the road of the desert of Edom."

Jehoram asked Jehoshaphat's advice, since Jehoshaphat was older and more experienced.[7] Jehoshaphat said, "Let us not attack directly across the border of Israel and Moab. If we do, the Moabites will see us coming and prepare to defend themselves. Instead, let us take a round-about route and catch them by surprise. Bring your army through my territory. Together we will go through the territory of Edom and attack Moab from the South. Edom is under my control, so they will help us. I will send messengers ahead to them and command them to ready their army to join us. Together we will have a massive force and will easily vanquish Moab!"[8]

3:9,10 וַיֵּלֶךְ מֶלֶךְ יִשְׂרָאֵל וּמֶלֶךְ יְהוּדָה וּמֶלֶךְ אֱדוֹם וַיָּסֹבּוּ דֶּרֶךְ שִׁבְעַת
יָמִים וְלֹא־הָיָה מַיִם לַמַּחֲנֶה וְלַבְּהֵמָה אֲשֶׁר בְּרַגְלֵיהֶם׃ וַיֹּאמֶר מֶלֶךְ יִשְׂרָאֵל
אֲהָהּ כִּי־קָרָא ה׳ לִשְׁלֹשֶׁת הַמְּלָכִים הָאֵלֶּה לָתֵת אוֹתָם בְּיַד־מוֹאָב׃

The King of Israel, the King of Judah, and the King of Edom went, and they went around on the road seven days. Then there was no water for the camp and for the animals that were with them. The King of Israel said, “Alas! G-d has called these three kings to give them over into the hand of Moab!”

The plan sounded good, but it didn’t work. They had not counted on how long it would take them to cross the desert between Edom and Moab. Now they found themselves close to the border of Moab, but without water and already weak from thirst. They could not retreat. It had taken them seven days to get there, and would take another seven to get back. They couldn’t survive that long without water. But if they attacked now, in their weakened condition, they would almost certainly be defeated. What could they do? Soon the soldiers would be forced to leave the camp in search of water. Scattered across the countryside, weak and disorganized, they would be an easy prey for Moab.[9]

Jehoram realized that it was all his fault. He was the one who had gotten the other kings and their armies into this predicament. But he could not bear accepting the responsibility, so he blamed G-d instead. He said, “G-d has led us into a trap to destroy us!”

3:11 וַיֹּאמֶר יְהוֹשָׁפָט הַאֵין פֹּה נָבִיא לַה׳ וְנִדְרְשָׁה אֶת־ה׳ מֵאוֹתוֹ וַיַּעַן
אֶחָד מֵעַבְדֵי מֶלֶךְ־יִשְׂרָאֵל וַיֹּאמֶר פֹּה אֱלִישָׁע בֶּן־שָׁפָט אֲשֶׁר־יָצַק מַיִם עַל־יְדֵי
אֵלִיָּהוּ׃

Jehoshaphat said, “Is there no prophet of G-d here, that we may inquire of G-d from him?” One of the servants of the King of Israel answered and said, “Elisha ben Shaphat is here, who poured water on the hands of Elijah.”

Jehoshaphat said to Jehoram, “Are you a prophet, that you know what G-d has in store for us? Before giving up hope and mourning for ourselves, let us find a true prophet and see what he has to say.”

Some say Jehoshaphat feared he had again made a mistake by agreeing to go along with Jehoram without consulting a prophet first. But perhaps it was not too late. If they could find a prophet now, he would obey whatever that prophet said.[10]

The people referred to Elisha not as the student of Elijah, but as the one who poured water on Elijah's hands, for those who serve the scholars of Torah are greater than those who only learn from them.[11] Those who serve are constantly with their masters and learn from their every action. They imitate their pious ways until they become ingrained in their own personalities. If the master is a prophet, the student who serves him can hope to become a prophet too. A scholar who prevents his students from serving him therefore deprives them of a valuable opportunity.[12]

Some say they were referring to the miracle that had occurred on Mount Carmel. Elijah commanded that four pitchers each be filled with water three times and poured on the altar. It was Elisha who fulfilled his instructions. As Elijah held out his hands above the altar, Elisha poured the water over them. Miraculously, as the small stream from the pitchers touched his fingers, it became a gushing torrent and the water covered the altar and filled the trench around it.[13]

Elisha's involvement with water was also of primary significance now, since it was water that they needed. They said, "Elisha has the merit to give us water. He earned the merit to perform miracles with water by serving Elijah by means of water."

3:12 וַיֹּאמֶר יְהוֹשָׁפָט יֵשׁ אוֹתוֹ דְּבַר־ה׳ וַיֵּרְדוּ אֵלָיו מֶלֶךְ יִשְׂרָאֵל
וִיהוֹשָׁפָט וּמֶלֶךְ אֱדוֹם:

Jehoshaphat said, "There is a word of G-d with him." So the King of Israel, Jehoshaphat, and the King of Edom went down to him.

Jehoshaphat said, "Surely Elisha has not come along to fight, for he is not a soldier. It could only be that G-d has sent him to be our guide or to perform miracles for us if we are in need!" Indeed, G-d had sent him with them for just that purpose, to perform miracles that might sway Jehoram to return to Torah.[14]

In this verse Jehoshaphat is not called by his title, "King of Judah" like the other two kings. They approached Elisha as kings, but he approached him humbly, as a common person.[15] He exerted some influence on the other kings as well. Though they did not remove their royal clothes, they went down to Elisha to consult him, rather than ordering him to appear before them, as kings usually do.

3:13 וַיֹּאמֶר אֱלִישָׁע אֶל־מֶלֶךְ יִשְׂרָאֵל מַה־לִּי וָלָךְ לֵךְ אֶל־נְבִיאֵי אָבִיךָ
וְאֶל־נְבִיאֵי אִמֶּךָ וַיֹּאמֶר לוֹ מֶלֶךְ יִשְׂרָאֵל אַל כִּי־קָרָא ה׳ לִשְׁלֹשֶׁת הַמְּלָכִים
הָאֵלֶּה לָתֵת אוֹתָם בְּיַד־מוֹאָב׃

Elisha said to the King of Israel, "What do you and I have to do with each other? Go to the prophets of your father and to the prophets of your mother!" The King of Israel said to him, "Don't! For G-d has called these three kings to give them over into the hand of Moab!"

But Elisha saw that Jehoram was not ready to submit to G-d, because he came as a king wearing his crown, so he refused to answer him, rebuking him instead. He said, "Your father also asked a prophet for divine guidance, but when it was not to his liking he ignored it. Are you better than him? Why should I waste my time prophesying for you, if I cannot expect you to listen to me anyway?"

"Please don't refuse me in my time of need!" begged Jehoram. "Even if I do not live up to your high standards, I am, nonetheless, a true believer in G-d. Did I not immediately admit that our present predicament was not an accident, but divinely ordained? If I thought it were a natural occurrence I would have gone to the prophets of Baal and Asherah, for they represent the forces of nature. The very fact that I have come to you shows that I believe it comes from G-d.

"Never did my father or I deny that G-d is the ultimate ruler of the universe. We only differ with you in that we believe that He has given the ordinary day-to-day events of the world into the hands of His messengers, the forces of nature. That is why we worship them. It is only in extraordinary situations that He interferes Himself. I recognize that this is one, and that is why I have come to you."[16]

"You would be better off not appealing to your faith and righteousness," said Elisha. "Those who sincerely believe in G-d know that nothing happens except by His word. There is no one else to whom it is fit to pray, and G-d has therefore forbidden it. If you were truly faithful to Him, you would have eliminated the worship of Baal entirely!

"Besides, G-d does not answer prayers and perform miracles for those who turn to Him only when they are in trouble and defy Him the rest of the time."[17]

Jehoram begged him, "Please don't call to mind our guilt for that wickedness! Have mercy on us in our time of trouble!"[18]

3:14-19 וַיֹּאמֶר אֱלִישָׁע חַי־ה׳ צְבָאוֹת אֲשֶׁר עָמַדְתִּי לְפָנָיו כִּי לוּלֵי פְּנֵי־
יְהוֹשָׁפָט מֶלֶךְ־יְהוּדָה אֲנִי נֹשֵׂא אִם־אַבִּיט אֵלֶיךָ וְאִם־אֶרְאֶךָּ: וְעַתָּה קְחוּ־לִי
מְנַגֵּן וְהָיָה כְּנַגֵּן הַמְנַגֵּן וַתְּהִי עָלָיו יַד־ה׳: וַיֹּאמֶר כֹּה אָמַר ה׳ עָשֹׂה הַנַּחַל הַזֶּה
גֵּבִים גֵּבִים: כִּי־כֹה אָמַר ה׳ לֹא־תִרְאוּ רוּחַ וְלֹא־תִרְאוּ גֶשֶׁם וְהַנַּחַל הַהוּא
יִמָּלֵא מָיִם וּשְׁתִיתֶם אַתֶּם וּמִקְנֵיכֶם וּבְהֶמְתְּכֶם: וְנָקַל זֹאת בְּעֵינֵי ה׳ וְנָתַן
אֶת־מוֹאָב בְּיֶדְכֶם: וְהִכִּיתֶם כָּל־עִיר מִבְצָר וְכָל־עִיר מִבְחוֹר וְכָל־עֵץ טוֹב
תַּפִּילוּ וְכָל־מַעְיְנֵי־מַיִם תִּסְתֹּמוּ וְכָל הַחֶלְקָה הַטּוֹבָה תַּכְאִבוּ בָּאֲבָנִים:

Elisha said, "As G-d of H-sts, before whom I have stood, lives, were it not that I respect Jehoshaphat, King of Judah, I would not look at you or see you! So now bring me a musician!" So it was, that when the musician played, the hand of G-d was upon him. He said, "Thus says G-d, 'Make this river-bed many wells!' For thus says G-d, 'You will not see wind and you will not see rain, and this river-bed will become full of water! You will drink, and your flocks and your animals.' This is easy in G-d's eyes. He will give Moab over into your hand! You will smite every fortified city, and every choice city. Every good tree will you fell, all the wells of water will you seal up, and every good field will you afflict with stones."

Some say that Elisha had not experienced divine revelation since Elijah went up to heaven. The divine presence does not reside with one who is sad, and Elisha was still mourning the loss of his teacher. Even though he could perform miracles while he was sad, he could not prophesy. He therefore asked for musicians to play and cheer him up.[19]

Others say it was his anger that prevented him from receiving G-d's word, for anger drives away both wisdom and prophecy.[20]

Elisha said, "Were it not for Jehoshaphat, I would not even look you in the face, for it is forbidden to look at the face of the wicked. A person's wickedness is apparent on his face, and influences anyone who looks at it."[21]

In the desert there are river-beds that are dry most of the year, but are briefly filled with water during the heavy rains in the winter. It was near such a river-bed that the three armies were camped. Elisha proclaimed that this river-bed would soon be filled with water. But it would not be in the natural way, by wind and rain. The skies would remain clear, yet suddenly they would see water coming. They were therefore commanded to dig wells all over the river-bed to catch the water when it came.[22]

This was Elisha's fourth miracle. It was comparable to the miracle that Elijah had performed on Mount Carmel. But it was small compared to the one that would follow it, an almost effortless victory. By these miracles, however, the Jewish People incurred the special obligation of completely destroying Moab. Even the fruit trees, which the Torah protects under normal circumstances, were to be destroyed this time.[23]

When Elisha made this proclamation the kings all said, "But doesn't the Torah say,[24] 'When you besiege a city ... don't destroy its trees!' How can you tell us to violate the Torah?"

"Indeed," answered Elisha, "that is the law for all other nations. But this nation is so lowly in G-d's eyes that even its trees are not worth preserving!"[25]

This was part of the special treatment to which Moab was condemned for their unwarranted animosity toward the Jewish People when they were wandering through the desert. The Torah says,[26] "Don't inquire after their peace and their good." The word "their good" refers to, among other things, the "good trees."[27]

3:20 וַיְהִי בַבֹּקֶר כַּעֲלוֹת הַמִּנְחָה וְהִנֵּה־מַיִם בָּאִים מִדֶּרֶךְ אֱדוֹם וַתִּמָּלֵא
הָאָרֶץ אֶת־הַמָּיִם׃

In the morning, as the offering was being brought, behold, there was water coming from the way of Edom, and the land was filled with the water.

Early the next morning, Elisha's prophecy was fulfilled. By the time of the morning sacrifice in the Temple in Jerusalem, the water had arrived.

Some say the water came from rain, far away in the mountains of Edom. It began to fall in the morning, filling the river-beds and rushing down in torrents, until, by the time of the afternoon sacrifice, it reached the camp. That explains the apparent contradiction between the words "morning" and "as the offering (מנחה) was being brought." The word "מנחה," "offering" generally refers to the afternoon sacrifice, not the morning one. If the water came when that sacrifice was being brought, it was no longer morning. According to this explanation, the two words refer to the beginning and end of the miracle.[28]

3:21 וְכָל־מוֹאָב שָׁמְעוּ כִּי־עָלוּ הַמְּלָכִים לְהִלָּחֶם בָּם וַיִּצָּעֲקוּ מִכֹּל חֹגֵר
חֲגֹרָה וָמָעְלָה וַיַּעַמְדוּ עַל־הַגְּבוּל׃

All Moab heard that the kings had come up to fight with them. They called for all who could gird on a belt and upward, and they stood on the border.

But by now Moab had found out about the impending attack and prepared to defend themselves. They were terrified, and mustered every last man. The expression "חגר חגרה," "gird on a belt" refers, of course, to the belt that holds a sword. It means anyone who was able to use a sword to fight.[29]

3:22,23 וַיַּשְׁכִּימוּ בַבֹּקֶר וְהַשֶּׁמֶשׁ זָרְחָה עַל־הַמָּיִם וַיִּרְאוּ מוֹאָב מִנֶּגֶד אֶת־
הַמַּיִם אֲדֻמִּים כַּדָּם׃ וַיֹּאמְרוּ דָּם זֶה הָחֳרֵב נֶחֶרְבוּ הַמְּלָכִים וַיַּכּוּ אִישׁ אֶת־רֵעֵהוּ
וְעַתָּה לַשָּׁלָל מוֹאָב׃

They got up early in the morning, and the sun was shining on the water. Moab saw the water from afar red like blood. They said, "This is blood! The kings have indeed been destroyed! They have smitten each other! So now to the spoils, Oh Moab!"

Though the combined army of the three kings could have conquered Moab without divine help, G-d wanted them to know that their victory was not a natural occurrence. It had been granted as a divine favor, not won by their own might. He made the sunrise particularly red that day, so that when the soldiers of Moab saw the reflection of the red sky in the water, their hopes and imagination led them to construe it as blood. It did not even occur to them that it might just be water, since that river bed was generally dry.[30] They concluded that the three allies had quarreled and fallen upon one another.

3:24 וַיָּבֹאוּ אֶל־מַחֲנֵה יִשְׂרָאֵל וַיָּקֻמוּ יִשְׂרָאֵל וַיַּכּוּ אֶת־מוֹאָב וַיָּנֻסוּ
מִפְּנֵיהֶם וַיַּבּוּ־בָהּ (וַיַּכּוּ־בָהּ קרי) וְהַכּוֹת אֶת־מוֹאָב׃

They came to the camp of Israel. Israel got up and smote

Moab, and they fled from before them. They smote it, and smote Moab.

Jehoshaphat had hoped to overcome Moab by taking them by surprise in their land, but G-d did much better. They were indeed taken by surprise, but in the most vulnerable way. They left their camp disorganized and unprepared for battle. They were not even fully armed, because they expected to find very few Jews and Edomites still alive. They left most of their weapons behind so that they would be able to carry back more spoil. But instead of a camp full of dead and wounded, they found an army of warriors, strong, confident, and eager to fight.[31]

3:25 וְהֶעָרִים יַהֲרֹסוּ וְכָל־חֶלְקָה טוֹבָה יַשְׁלִיכוּ אִישׁ־אַבְנוֹ וּמִלְאוּהָ וְכָל־
מַעְיַן־מַיִם יִסְתֹּמוּ וְכָל־עֵץ־טוֹב יַפִּילוּ עַד־הִשְׁאִיר אֲבָנֶיהָ בַּקִּיר חֲרָשֶׂת וַיָּסֹבּוּ
הַקַּלָּעִים וַיַּכּוּהָ׃

The cities did they destroy, and every good field, each man threw his stone and filled it up. Every source of water they sealed up and every good tree they felled, till there remained only the stones of the wall of Haresheth. The catapulters surrounded it and smote it.

After easily defeating the army of Moab, they laid waste the country as G-d had commanded. Only the mighty capital, Haresheth, withstood their attack. In all the other cities they were able to break through the city wall and demolish it along with the houses. But the wall of Haresheth was built of stones too large for them to move, so they bombarded it with their catapults instead.[32]

Some say "חרשת," "Haresheth," is not the name of a place, but the common noun "חרש," which means "clay." They broke the walls of the cities so diligently that no two stones remained held together by the clay that had been put between them when the wall was built.[33]

3:26 וַיַּרְא מֶלֶךְ מוֹאָב כִּי־חָזַק מִמֶּנּוּ הַמִּלְחָמָה וַיִּקַּח אוֹתוֹ שְׁבַע־מֵאוֹת
אִישׁ שֹׁלֵף חֶרֶב לְהַבְקִיעַ אֶל־מֶלֶךְ אֱדוֹם וְלֹא יָכֹלוּ׃

The King of Moab saw that the war was too strong for him.

He took seven hundred men with drawn swords with him to break through to the King of Edom, but they weren't able to.

Some say that the King of Moab was trying to kill the King of Edom and throw his followers into confusion. Perhaps he chose Edom because they were the weakest of the three armies, or perhaps they were the closest and easiest to reach. He may also have had a particular hatred for him.[34]

Others say that he hoped to convince the King of Edom to rebel against the two Jewish kings and join him instead. Whatever his goal, he was repulsed and forced back into the city.

3:27 וַיִּקַּח אֶת־בְּנוֹ הַבְּכוֹר אֲשֶׁר־יִמְלֹךְ תַּחְתָּיו וַיַּעֲלֵהוּ עֹלָה עַל־הַחֹמָה
וַיְהִי קֶצֶף־גָּדוֹל עַל־יִשְׂרָאֵל וַיִּסְעוּ מֵעָלָיו וַיָּשֻׁבוּ לָאָרֶץ׃

He took his firstborn son, who was to rule in his place, and offered him as a sacrifice on the wall. Then there was great anger against Israel. They went from upon him, and returned to the land.

Some say that Mesha sacrificed his own son to G-d, because he recognized that only G-d, and no idol, could save him. He asked his advisers, "Why does G-d do such miracles for this people?" They answered, "Their ancestor, Abraham, was ready to sacrifice his only son to G-d. G-d has never forgotten Abraham's complete dedication, and continues to protect his descendants."

Mesha thought, "If that is the case, the only way I can overcome them is to show equal dedication." So he took his own son and sacrificed him.

But that was certainly not G-d's will. Many years later the prophet Jeremiah complained about the cruel acts that had been performed in G-d's name. Though those who performed them sincerely thought they were fulfilling G-d's will, they were really abominations. G-d described these acts by the words,[35] "to burn their sons and their daughters in fire, that I did not command and that did not come up upon My heart." The words "that I did not command" refer to Jephtah, who vowed that if G-d would grant him victory he would sacrifice the first thing that came out of his house to greet him when he returned from battle. When his daughter came out first, he sadly sacrificed her to fulfill his vow. G-d said, "I never commanded him to keep such a vow!" The words, "that did not come up upon My heart" refer to Mesha, the King of Moab. Of him G-d said, "Never did I intend Abraham to actually sacrifice his son. I only wanted to test him to show that he was willing to do it."

Nonetheless, G-d did not ignore Mesha's sincerity and dedication. He became very angry with the Jews, and turned the battle against them. He said, "The King of Moab overcame even his love for his own son to please Me, but you perform abominations and idolatry to anger Me every day! Why then should I help you and not him?"[36]

Others say that he offered his son to the pagan gods.[37] Though he did not thereby please G-d, he called to mind the idolatry that they too were practicing. G-d became angry with them and abandoned them.[38]

Another interpretation is that it was not his own son that he sacrificed, but the son of the King of Edom. He captured him during his attempt to break through the lines, and now, in anger, he killed him and burnt his body. Thus the prophet Amos said,[39] "For three sins of Moab and for four I will not forgive them, for burning the bones of the King of Edom into lime." The King of Edom became angry with Jehoram, whose fault it ultimately was, and refused to fight any more. Some say Mesha had taken the son hostage some time before, and his father had come along in the hope of rescuing him. Now, he had brought about his death instead. The army fell into disorder and withdrew.[40]

II KINGS 4

4:1 וְאִשָּׁה אַחַת מִנְּשֵׁי בְנֵי־הַנְּבִיאִים צָעֲקָה אֶל־אֱלִישָׁע לֵאמֹר עַבְדְּךָ
אִישִׁי מֵת וְאַתָּה יָדַעְתָּ כִּי עַבְדְּךָ הָיָה יָרֵא אֶת־ה׳ וְהַנֹּשֶׁה בָּא לָקַחַת אֶת־שְׁנֵי
יְלָדַי לוֹ לַעֲבָדִים:

One woman from among the wives of the sons of the prophets cried out to Elisha saying, "Your servant, my husband, died, and you know that your servant was G-dfearing. Now the creditor has come to take my two sons for himself as slaves."

Elisha's fifth miracle involved helping a poor woman and saving her children from slavery. This woman's faith was the saving virtue of her generation. Had it not been for her, the entire Jewish People would have been destroyed.

As we learned at the end of the preceding chapter, G-d was angry at the Jewish People, because the King of Edom had reminded Him of their guilt. But in His mercy, He searched for some merit that might save them, and found this poor woman.[1] Therefore she is referred to as "one woman." She alone saved them all.

The woman was the widow of Obadiah the prophet. Obadiah had been Ahab's servant and chief adviser, and used his position to help other G-dfearing people. He protected them during the period of persecution initiated by Jezebel, as we learned earlier,[2] hiding one hundred prophets and providing them with food and water. There he is described as "fearing G-d very much," as his wife described him here.[3]

But Obadiah didn't always have enough money to buy food for them, so he was forced to borrow. It was to Ahab's son, Jehoram, now King of Israel, that he turned. Jehoram was not above taking interest for these loans, in direct violation of the Torah. And when Obadiah's heirs could not pay his debts, Jehoram was ready to violate the Torah further by taking them as slaves. For, though a person's property may be designated as collateral for his debts, his body may not, and certainly not his children. He cannot be forced to sell them or become a slave himself.[4]

See how easily a person who violates one commandment is drawn into violating others![5] Jehoram began by taking interest, which is a violation of property rights, and ended up attempting to kidnap, a violation of personal rights. Eventually he was punished for these, along with his other sins.

Obadiah's wife cried out two hundred and sixty-five times, but she received no answer. She didn't know what to do, so she went to the cemetery and called, "Oh G-dfearing one! Oh G-dfearing one!"

She heard a voice answer, "Which G-dfearing one do you mean? There are four here who are called G-dfearing, Abraham, Joseph, Job and Obadiah."

She answered, "I want the one of whom it says, 'He feared G-d very much!'" Then they showed her Obadiah's grave.

She knelt down on his grave and said, "Oh my master, where is the promise that you made me when you lay on your death bed? When I said, 'In whose care do you leave me and my two sons?' you replied, 'The L-rd of the world promised me,[6] "Leave your orphans, I will support them, and your widows can rely upon Me."' But now no one has come to save us!"

The orphans cried out, "Take us, Oh father, take us!"

He answered, "Go to Elisha with the little oil that you have left and he will bless you with it. For when I hid the hundred prophets in the caves, I never failed to supply them with oil for their lamps day and night. Let the prophets remind G-d of that and He will take care of you."[7]

4:2 וַיֹּאמֶר אֵלֶיהָ אֱלִישָׁע מָה אֶעֱשֶׂה־לָּךְ הַגִּידִי לִי מַה־יֶּשׁ־לָכִי (לָךְ
קרי) בַּבָּיִת וַתֹּאמֶר אֵין לְשִׁפְחָתְךָ כֹל בַּבַּיִת כִּי אִם־אָסוּךְ שָׁמֶן׃

Elisha said to her, "What should I do for you? Tell me, what do you have in the house?" She said, "Your maidservant has nothing in the house but a flask of oil."

Elisha said, "If you have nothing at all I cannot give you a blessing. I will have to try to help you in another way. For to receive a blessing you must have something to be blessed."[8]

This woman was really destitute. The oil, which was all she had, was not even enough to use for eating, but only for rubbing on the skin.[9]

She wondered whether that was enough for a blessing. But as soon as she told Elisha about it, he reassured her. "Don't worry," he said, "oil is a holy substance. It is used to anoint priests and kings. Even a small amount of oil is sufficient to receive a blessing!"[10]

The miracle that Elisha was about to perform for her was similar to the one that Elijah had done for the woman with whom he stayed in Zarephath. It involved blessing something that she already had, making it increase without limit. When Elijah came to Zarephath, the woman had only a small amount of flour and a small amount of oil. She was going to make them into bread for herself and her son. Once they had eaten it, they would be left without any more food and soon would die. But Elijah blessed the flour and the oil so that it was never used up as long as he stayed with them. Obadiah's wife was even worse off. She had no flour and very little oil. Furthermore, she was in debt and had two children to feed.

4:3,4 וַיֹּאמֶר לְכִי שַׁאֲלִי־לָךְ כֵּלִים מִן־הַחוּץ מֵאֵת כָּל־שְׁכֵנָכִי (שְׁכֵנָיִךְ קרי) כֵּלִים רֵקִים אַל־תַּמְעִיטִי: וּבָאת וְסָגַרְתְּ הַדֶּלֶת בַּעֲדֵךְ וּבְעַד־בָּנַיִךְ וְיָצַקְתְּ עַל כָּל־הַכֵּלִים הָאֵלֶּה וְהַמָּלֵא תַּסִּיעִי:

He said, "Go, borrow containers for yourself from outside, from all of your neighbors, empty containers, not just a few. Then go and close the door upon yourself and upon your sons. Pour upon all these containers, and the full ones take away."

Elisha said, "The woman of Zarephath was worthy of a great miracle. She had earned that merit by her self-sacrifice and extraordinary hospitality. Though the food she had was not even enough for herself, she was ready to share it with Elijah, who was a total stranger. You, however, do not have such merit, so the miracle that will be performed for you will be more restricted.

"You will be able to pour as much as you want from the bottle, but only one time.[11] Once you stop pouring, the miracle will stop and it will become a regular bottle of oil again. So prepare as many containers as you can to hold the oil. They need not belong to you, so borrow from your neighbors. As long as you keep pouring, the oil will continue to flow, regardless of what it goes into.

"But you must not move while you are pouring. The bottle will become like a well from which oil will flow like water from its source.

Just as a well does not move, so this bottle must not be moved for the duration of the miracle.[12]

"Most important, no one but you and your children may see it happen. This is one of the greatest kinds of miracles, because it violates a fundamental law of nature. Within nature, things move around and change from one form to another, but the total amount of material always remains the same. For the amount of oil to increase will require an act comparable to the creation of the world from nothingness. That is a much greater miracle than bringing down fire from the sky or purifying bad water by thowing in salt.

"G-d ordained the laws of nature for man to live by. Without natural regularity, man would not be able to accomplish good deeds and avoid evil ones. G-d does not want man to witness those laws being violated, for then the world would appear chaotic to him. Therefore this miracle must be performed quietly, hidden from view.

"Even you and your children will not actually see the amount of oil increase. You will only be able to deduce that it has, since it will continue to flow no matter how much has already been poured out. As for others, they may not witness even that.

"Once you have collected as many containers as you can, close the door so that no one else can enter or look in. Only then can you begin to pour, and the miracle will start."

Some say the instruction to borrow containers meant that she could use only borrowed ones, not her own. Elisha said, "Your husband committed a sin by agreeing to pay interest on his loan, because the prohibition of interest applies to the borrower as well as the lender. Even though he did it for a worthy cause, it left a curse on all of his property. Neither this house nor anything else that belonged to him can ever be blessed. Your own containers will therefore not be able to receive the extra oil. Even into the borrowed containers it will not flow while they are resting on the floor or table of your house. So you must hold the flask in your hands while you pour, and your children must hold the containers in which the oil is being collected. As soon as one is full, the child holding it must take it away and the other child can put another in its place. But once a container is full it may be placed back on the ground, for then it is no longer subject to the miracle."[13]

4:5-7 וַתֵּלֶךְ מֵאִתּוֹ וַתִּסְגֹּר הַדֶּלֶת בַּעֲדָהּ וּבְעַד בָּנֶיהָ הֵם מַגִּישִׁים אֵלֶיהָ
וְהִיא מֹיצָקֶת (מוֹצָקֶת קרי) : וַיְהִי כִּמְלֹאת הַכֵּלִים וַתֹּאמֶר אֶל־בְּנָהּ הַגִּישָׁה
אֵלַי עוֹד כֶּלִי וַיֹּאמֶר אֵלֶיהָ אֵין עוֹד כֶּלִי וַיַּעֲמֹד הַשָּׁמֶן: וַתָּבֹא וַתַּגֵּד לְאִישׁ

הָאֱלֹהִים וַיֹּאמֶר לְכִי מִכְרִי אֶת־הַשֶּׁמֶן וְשַׁלְּמִי אֶת־נִשְׁיֵכִי (נִשְׁיֵךְ קרי) וְאַתְּ
בָּנַיִכִי (וּבָנַיִךְ קרי) תִּחְיִי בַּנּוֹתָר׃

She went from him and closed the door upon herself and upon her sons. They were bringing to her, and she was pouring. When the containers were full she said to her son, "Bring me another container!" He said to her, "There isn't another container!" Then the oil stopped. She went and told the man of G-d. He said, "Go sell the oil and pay your creditors. You and your sons will live on the remainder."

When all the containers were full she said, "There are still some pieces of broken containers. Bring those now, because just as G-d can fill what is empty, so can He mend what is broken." They brought the broken pieces, and the pieces joined together to become whole as the oil flowed into them.[14]

As soon as there were no empty containers left, the oil stopped flowing. But the miracle was not finished. She still had to sell the oil so that she could pay her debt. With so much oil suddenly on the market, the price of oil would normally have gone down, and she would have gotten only a fraction of its real value. But she could not afford to keep the oil and sell it little by little. She needed the money right away. Nor would Jehoram, being a shrewd businessman, have accepted the oil itself as payment. So, though she had plenty of oil, her problems were far from over.

She went back to Elisha and asked him what to do next. Should she sell it all and risk having to accept a deflated price? He said, "Sell it and don't worry!"

Miraculously, the price remained stable. No matter how much she sold, no one offered less. She made so much money that not only were her debts paid in full, but she and her sons lived for the rest of their lives on what was left.[15]

4:8 וַיְהִי הַיּוֹם וַיַּעֲבֹר אֱלִישָׁע אֶל־שׁוּנֵם וְשָׁם אִשָּׁה גְדוֹלָה וַתַּחֲזֶק־בּוֹ
לֶאֱכָל־לָחֶם וַיְהִי מִדֵּי עָבְרוֹ יָסֻר שָׁמָּה לֶאֱכָל־לָחֶם׃

One day, Elisha passed through Shunem. There there was a great woman. She took hold of him, that he eat bread. Thereafter, whenever he passed through he went aside there to eat bread.

Shunem was a city in the Jezreel Valley, in the portion of Issachar. It was there that King Saul fought his last battle against the Philistines.

This woman was famous for her piety and good deeds. It was in that way that she was "a great woman." She was respected by all the people of her community.[16] Some say she was the sister of Abishag the Shunamite, who was King David's companion in his last years, and the mother of the prophet Iddo. Others say she was Iddo's wife.[17] She recognized Elisha's greatness, and implored him to be their guest. Some say she didn't take hold of him physically, but by her words.[18]

4:9,10 וַתֹּאמֶר אֶל־אִישָׁהּ הִנֵּה־נָא יָדַעְתִּי כִּי אִישׁ אֱלֹהִים קָדוֹשׁ הוּא עֹבֵר עָלֵינוּ תָּמִיד: נַעֲשֶׂה־נָּא עֲלִיַּת־קִיר קְטַנָּה וְנָשִׂים לוֹ שָׁם מִטָּה וְשֻׁלְחָן וְכִסֵּא וּמְנוֹרָה וְהָיָה בְּבֹאוֹ אֵלֵינוּ יָסוּר שָׁמָּה:

She said to her husband, "Behold, please, that I know that it is a holy man of G-d who passes by us all the time. Let us make a little extra room, and put a bed, a table, a chair and a lamp there for him. Then, whenever he comes to us he will go aside there."

How did she know that Elisha was a holy man? Some say she knew his reputation.[19] She had heard about the miracles he had performed and knew that only a truly holy man could have done such things.

Others say she could tell by his conduct. Some say she saw that the flies never came to the table when he ate. Others say that it was because his bed was always clean in the morning.[20] It had the fragrance of the Garden of Eden. Her husband didn't notice these things, because a woman notices more about guests than a man does.[21]

She could also tell that Elisha's student, Gehazi, was not holy like him. She therefore spoke in the singular and said, "A holy man of G-d." By this she implied that he was holy, but his disciple who accompanied him was not.[22]

She said, "This holy man passes through our community frequently, and we are honored that it pleases him to stay at our house. Such a holy man ought to have a private room when he comes. He should not have to use the same utensils as everyone else and sit where everyone can see him, for great men and scholars should not eat or attend to their affairs in public.[23] Moreover, this man is a prophet and may want to be alone to receive divine inspiration."[24]

The word "עלית קיר," "extra room," literally means an elevation of the wall. Some say it was a partition within the house, a wall raised to form a separate room. Others say it was an extension of the outer wall of the house upwards, to create a room on the roof. Some say there were already walls above the roof, and they had only to add another roof above them.[25]

4:11-13 וַיְהִי הַיּוֹם וַיָּבֹא שָׁמָּה וַיָּסַר אֶל־הָעֲלִיָּה וַיִּשְׁכַּב־שָׁמָּה׃ וַיֹּאמֶר אֶל־
גֵּיחֲזִי נַעֲרוֹ קְרָא לַשּׁוּנַמִּית הַזֹּאת וַיִּקְרָא־לָהּ וַתַּעֲמֹד לְפָנָיו׃ וַיֹּאמֶר לוֹ אֱמָר־נָא
אֵלֶיהָ הִנֵּה חָרַדְתְּ אֵלֵינוּ אֶת־כָּל־הַחֲרָדָה הַזֹּאת מֶה לַעֲשׂוֹת לָךְ הֲיֵשׁ לְדַבֶּר־לָךְ
אֶל־הַמֶּלֶךְ אוֹ אֶל־שַׂר הַצָּבָא וַתֹּאמֶר בְּתוֹךְ עַמִּי אָנֹכִי יֹשָׁבֶת׃

One day he came there, and went aside to the extra room and lay down there. He said to Gehazi, his servant, "Call this Shunamite!" He called her, and she stood before him. He said to him, "Please say to her, 'Behold, you have shown all this great respect for us. What is there to do for you? To speak on your behalf to the king or to the general of the army?' " She said, "Within my people do I live."

The righteous are generally unwilling to accept gifts, as it says,[26] "He who hates gifts will live." In this case, however, Elisha accepted the woman's help.[27] He saw that she gave it with a pure heart and sincere generosity, not because she hoped to receive a reward. That is why she was worthy of the merit of helping him, thereby taking part in his great work.[28] He accepted her help as the priests accept the gifts that G-d decreed be given to them.[29] Even so, he would only accept a small gift, equal to his needs and no more. Later, when Naaman the general of Aram gratefully offered him riches for curing him, he refused to accept anything.

Although the woman had not expected any reward, Elisha wanted to show his appreciation. He remembered that before Elijah went up to heaven, he had given him the choice of whatever parting gift he would like. Now he offered the woman a similar choice.

He said, "By the great effort that this woman has gone to on our behalf, she has shown herself to be one who sincerely respects the Torah and those who study it. Her reward is that we, in turn, show our respect for her by listening to her and accepting her words. For he who loves Torah scholars will be granted a son who is a Torah scholar, and he who honors Torah scholars will have a son-in-law who is a Torah scholar, but he who respects Torah scholars is even greater, and he will become a Torah scholar himself.

"Those three divine promises were given to all Jews. But what of a person who cannot become a scholar? What is his reward for respecting the students of Torah? It is that his words will be accepted even as the words of a true Torah scholar are. Since this woman cannot become a Torah scholar, we will make her this offer and grant whatever she requests![30]

Elisha showed his humility by saying "us" instead of "me," as if it were Gehazi, too, that she had honored.

Why did Elisha have Gehazi speak to her rather than speaking to her himself? Some say he was so holy that no woman could bear to look upon his face, so even when she stood before him, he did not address her directly, but spoke to her through his servant.[31]

Others say that he had originally only planned to express his appreciation, not to offer her anything. He called her in, thanked her, and then she left. Only after that did it occur to him that there might be something he could do for her, so he sent Gehazi to ask her what she might need.[32]

The kind of help that Elisha had in mind was natural, physical help, the sort of help that even one who was not a prophet could have given. He preferred that to performing a miracle for her.[33] Since the victory over Moab, he had gained the respect of the king and his officers. Perhaps his influence could be of use to her.

But the woman replied that she had no need of such help. She said, "Here, among my own family and community, I am known and respected. No one would hurt me, and if I were in need there would be enough people ready to come to my aid. I have no business elsewhere, and if I did, they would help me there too.[34]

This seems a strange offer in light of the last miracle Elisha had performed. If he had such influence in the court, why hadn't he simply asked Jehoram to release the wife of Obadiah from her debts? Perhaps it was only as a result of that miracle that he gained this respect. Jehoram saw that he would be better off cooperating with the prophet, since if he did not he was liable to be defeated by a miracle anyway.

Some say it was Rosh Hashanah, the day on which the deeds of each person are weighed and his future decided. On that day G-d judges the childless and decides whether they will be granted children.[35]

By the word "king," Elisha was referring not to Jehoram, but to G-d, the King of the World. Since Rosh Hashanah is the day on which G-d's kingdom is proclaimed, Elisha chose to refer to Him this way. But the woman answered, "I offer my prayers together with my community, so I need no intermediary. The prayers of a community go directly to G-d, and those who make themselves part of the community will not be judged harshly.[36]

4:14-16 וַיֹּאמֶר וּמֶה לַעֲשׂוֹת לָהּ וַיֹּאמֶר גֵּיחֲזִי אֲבָל בֵּן אֵין־לָהּ וְאִישָׁהּ זָקֵן׃
וַיֹּאמֶר קְרָא־לָהּ וַיִּקְרָא־לָהּ וַתַּעֲמֹד בַּפָּתַח׃ וַיֹּאמֶר לַמּוֹעֵד הַזֶּה כָּעֵת חַיָּה אַתְּי
(אַתְּ קרי) חֹבֶקֶת בֵּן וַתֹּאמֶר אַל־אֲדֹנִי אִישׁ הָאֱלֹהִים אַל־תְּכַזֵּב בְּשִׁפְחָתֶךָ׃

He said, "Then what is there to do for her?" Gehazi said, "But she has no son, and her husband is old." He said, "Call her!" He called her, and she stood in the doorway. He said, "At this season, in the time of life, you will be holding a son in your arms." She said, "Don't, my lord, man of G-d! Don't deceive your maidservant!"

Gehazi said, "Even though she has all her needs, she is childless. Couldn't you bless her with a son? There is no natural way for her to have a child, because she is too old. When she was young she had no children, so she certainly won't now."[37]

Some say that she was not too old, but her husband was. Gehazi said, "She cannot afford to wait for a child, because her husband is old and may die soon. But you can perform a miracle for her!"[38]

Gehazi did not seem to understand that Elisha could not control nature. He could not do whatever he wanted. In certain situations he was able to declare a miracle and it would be fulfilled, but he could not make anything happen at any time. At that moment, however, Elisha experienced divine revelation. G-d told him that that was indeed the blessing he was to give her, so he had Gehazi call her back.

This time when she came, she stood in the doorway, because she realized it had been rude to stand inside with such a holy man. Some say that is the reason Elisha spoke to her directly this time, whereas before he had spoken only through his servant. Her greater respect earned her the right of being addressed by the prophet.[39]

Some say he had not been commanded to bless her, but gave this blessing from his own heart. He trusted G-d to fulfill it, as it says,[40] "The desire of those who fear Him He will do."[41]

The expression "כעת חיה," "in the time of life," is the same one that the angels used when they told Abraham that Sarah would bear him a son. Some say it means, "at the time of birth." Elisha said, "The child will be born at its own proper time, after fully developing in the womb. Rest assured, therefore, that it will be healthy and thrive." According to this, the word "life" refers to the child. Or it may refer to the season itself. It would be a time that is conducive to birth, a time when those who are born will live.[42]

Others say the word "life" refers to the woman. A woman who gives birth is called a "חיה," "a live one." The child would be born at the time when her own body was most fit to give birth, which would therefore be the best for the child's health as well.[43] Or perhaps Elisha was guaranteeing her future health by comparing it to her present state. He told her, "Just as you are alive now, so will you be alive next year at this time and be holding a child in your arms."[44]

Some say she thought Elisha was only trying to make her feel good, but was really not planning to perform a miracle. She said, "When the angels told Sarah that she would have a child, they promised to return after their words had been fulfilled. But you did not say, 'I will return to you' as the angels did. If you were serious, why didn't you make such a commitment too?"

"Angels are eternal," answered Elisha. "They could make such a statement with confidence because they knew they would be able to fulfill it. But a human being doesn't know when he will die, so I can't make such a promise. Nonetheless, whether I am alive or not, you will have a son."[45]

Others say she did not doubt that his words would be fulfilled, but worried what would happen afterwards. She said, "Don't give me a blessing that will bring temporary pleasure, but sorrow in the end. I see that you did not mention that the son would survive and grow to adulthood. You said only that I would hold him in my arms. Is that because you foresee that he will die young? If so, let me not have this blessing. What is the use of feeding and caring for a child if he is only to die anyway? Better not to have a child at all than have one and suffer the grief of losing it! Better an empty bottle than one that was full and has spilled out.[46]

"It was surely not without reason that G-d has withheld children from me. Perhaps it is because, had I given birth to children, they would all have died young. G-d, in his mercy, spared me that grief. So do not you bless me with a son now unless it be one that will live."[47]

The word "תכזב," "deceive," refers to something that fails to proceed as it should. Thus the prophet Isaiah said,[48] "like a source of water whose water never fails (יכזבו)."[49]

4:17-19 וַתַּהַר הָאִשָּׁה וַתֵּלֶד בֵּן לַמּוֹעֵד הַזֶּה כָּעֵת חַיָּה אֲשֶׁר־דִּבֶּר אֵלֶיהָ אֱלִישָׁע: וַיִּגְדַּל הַיָּלֶד וַיְהִי הַיּוֹם וַיֵּצֵא אֶל־אָבִיו אֶל־הַקֹּצְרִים: וַיֹּאמֶר אֶל־אָבִיו רֹאשִׁי רֹאשִׁי וַיֹּאמֶר אֶל־הַנַּעַר שָׂאֵהוּ אֶל־אִמּוֹ:

The woman conceived and bore a son, at that season, in the time of life, as Elisha had told her. The boy grew up. One day he went out to his father, to the reapers. He said to his father, "My head! My head!" He said to the servant, "Carry him to his mother."

The harvest season is a dangerous time, because the sun is strong and beats down upon a person's head. People spend long hours working hard in the field reaping the grain, and if they are not careful, they are liable to suffer sunstroke.[50] So it happened to the boy that day. But his father did not realize there was anything seriously wrong. He thought the boy was just tired and wanted to go home.[51]

4:20,21 וַיִּשָּׂאֵהוּ וַיְבִיאֵהוּ אֶל־אִמּוֹ וַיֵּשֶׁב עַל־בִּרְכֶּיהָ עַד־הַצָּהֳרַיִם וַיָּמֹת: וַתַּעַל וַתַּשְׁכִּבֵהוּ עַל־מִטַּת אִישׁ הָאֱלֹהִים וַתִּסְגֹּר בַּעֲדוֹ וַתֵּצֵא:

He carried him and brought him to his mother. He sat on her knees until noon, and then he died. She went up and laid him down on the bed of the man of G-d. She closed up upon him and went out.

Now, the woman thought, her worst fears had been realized. But had not Elisha promised her it would not happen? So she went to seek his aid. She knew that he alone could save the child. First, she put him in the special room that symbolized her dedication to Elisha and the rest of the holy prophets. She said, "May the merit of this room and all the hospitality we have shown protect this child and bring him back to life. For how can a deed performed with such sincerity be repaid with sorrow?"

4:22,23 וַתִּקְרָא אֶל־אִישָׁהּ וַתֹּאמֶר שִׁלְחָה נָא לִי אֶחָד מִן־הַנְּעָרִים וְאַחַת
הָאֲתֹנוֹת וְאָרוּצָה עַד־אִישׁ הָאֱלֹהִים וְאָשׁוּבָה׃ וַיֹּאמֶר מַדּוּעַ אַתְּי הֹלֶכְתִי (אַתְּ
הֹלֶכֶת קרי) אֵלָיו הַיּוֹם לֹא־חֹדֶשׁ וְלֹא שַׁבָּת וַתֹּאמֶר שָׁלוֹם׃

She called to her husband and said, "Please send me one of the servants and one of the donkeys, and I will run to the man of G-d and come back." He said, "Why are you going to him today? It is not the New Moon and it is not Sabbath!" She said, "All is well!"

She did not tell her husband what had happened. So confident was she that Elisha would revive the boy that she felt she could sincerely reassure him that everything would be alright. She also wanted to conceal the forthcoming miracle as much as possible. She didn't even want her husband to know about it.[52]

From his question, we see that the woman followed the practice of visiting her teacher every Sabbath and holiday. This is very praiseworthy, and anyone who lives within a short distance of his teacher should observe it, at least on the major festivals. However, if it is too far to walk there and back on the same day, there is no obligation.[53]

4:24-26 וַתַּחֲבֹשׁ הָאָתוֹן וַתֹּאמֶר אֶל־נַעֲרָהּ נְהַג וָלֵךְ אַל־תַּעֲצָר־לִי לִרְכֹּב כִּי
אִם־אָמַרְתִּי לָךְ׃ וַתֵּלֶךְ וַתָּבֹא אֶל־אִישׁ הָאֱלֹהִים אֶל־הַר הַכַּרְמֶל וַיְהִי כִּרְאוֹת
אִישׁ־הָאֱלֹהִים אֹתָהּ מִנֶּגֶד וַיֹּאמֶר אֶל־גֵּיחֲזִי נַעֲרוֹ הִנֵּה הַשּׁוּנַמִּית הַלָּז׃ עַתָּה
רוּץ־נָא לִקְרָאתָהּ וֶאֱמָר־לָהּ הֲשָׁלוֹם לָךְ הֲשָׁלוֹם לְאִישֵׁךְ הֲשָׁלוֹם לַיָּלֶד וַתֹּאמֶר
שָׁלוֹם׃

She saddled the donkey and said to her servant, "Drive and go! Don't stop me from riding unless I tell you to." She went and came to the man of G-d, to Mount Carmel. When the man of G-d saw her from afar he said to Gehazi his servant, "Here is that Shunamite! Now, please run to meet her, and say to her, 'Is all well with you? Is all well with your husband? Is all well with the boy?'" She said, "All is well!"

Some say she rode on the donkey. Others say she brought it along in case she got tired, but she preferred to walk to Elisha herself, because she was bitter and upset.[54]

As she had not told her husband the reason for her visit, neither did she tell Gehazi. The only one who could help her was Elisha, so there was no point in telling anyone else.

4:27,28 וַתָּבֹא אֶל־אִישׁ הָאֱלֹהִים אֶל־הָהָר וַתַּחֲזֵק בְּרַגְלָיו וַיִּגַּשׁ גֵּיחֲזִי
לְהָדְפָהּ וַיֹּאמֶר אִישׁ הָאֱלֹהִים הַרְפֵּה־לָהּ כִּי־נַפְשָׁהּ מָרָה־לָהּ וַה׳ הֶעְלִים מִמֶּנִּי
וְלֹא הִגִּיד לִי׃ וַתֹּאמֶר הֲשָׁאַלְתִּי בֵן מֵאֵת אֲדֹנִי הֲלֹא אָמַרְתִּי לֹא תַשְׁלֶה אֹתִי׃

She came to the man of G-d, to the mountain, and took hold of his feet. Gehazi approached to push her away, but the man of G-d said, "Let her go, for her soul is bitter, and G-d has concealed from me and did not tell me." She said, "Did I ask for a son from my master? Did I not say, 'Do not mislead me?' "

The woman grabbed Elisha's feet and held fast as a sign that she would not let him go until he came with her.[55]

Some say that before she began to speak, G-d revealed to Elisha what the trouble was. Therefore Elisha said, "G-d has concealed from me and did not tell me" in the past tense. He said, "He concealed it from me until this moment, but now He has revealed it."[56]

Others say that it was not until she said "Didn't I say, 'Don't mislead me?' " that he knew what had happened. He remembered what her fear had been when he gave her his blessing. Now he prepared to fulfill his promise and revive her son.

4:29-31 וַיֹּאמֶר לְגֵיחֲזִי חֲגֹר מָתְנֶיךָ וְקַח מִשְׁעַנְתִּי בְיָדְךָ וָלֵךְ כִּי־תִמְצָא אִישׁ
לֹא תְבָרְכֶנּוּ וְכִי־יְבָרֶכְךָ אִישׁ לֹא תַעֲנֶנּוּ וְשַׂמְתָּ מִשְׁעַנְתִּי עַל־פְּנֵי הַנָּעַר׃ וַתֹּאמֶר
אֵם הַנַּעַר חַי־ה׳ וְחֵי־נַפְשְׁךָ אִם־אֶעֶזְבֶךָּ וַיָּקָם וַיֵּלֶךְ אַחֲרֶיהָ׃ וְגֵחֲזִי עָבַר לִפְנֵיהֶם
וַיָּשֶׂם אֶת־הַמִּשְׁעֶנֶת עַל־פְּנֵי הַנַּעַר וְאֵין קוֹל וְאֵין קָשֶׁב וַיָּשָׁב לִקְרָאתוֹ וַיַּגֶּד־לוֹ
לֵאמֹר לֹא הֵקִיץ הַנָּעַר׃

He said to Gehazi, "Gird your loins and take my staff in your hand and go. If you meet anyone, don't greet him, and if anyone greets you, don't answer him, and put my staff on the boy's face." The mother of the boy said, "As G-d lives and as your soul lives, I will not abandon you!" He got up and went after her. Gehazi went on ahead of them and put the staff on the boy's face, but he neither spoke nor heard. He went back to meet him and told him saying, "The boy didn't wake up."

Elisha hoped that Gehazi would become a worthy disciple, so he gave him the privilege of taking part in this miracle. That merit might one day help him become a prophet in his own right. Elisha himself had once served Elijah by pouring water over his hands, and later had been worthy of miraculously supplying water for the armies of Judah and Israel. Now he sent Gehazi ahead with his staff, by which he would be able to restore the boy's life.

However, Gehazi would not be able to participate in this miracle without some merit of his own. Elisha decided that to earn that merit, Gehazi would have to develop the quality of humility. He would have to perform the miracle without anyone else knowing, so that it would be motivated only by the desire to do G-d's will, not to impress others and win their admiration. Elisha therefore commanded him not to greet anyone on his way, or even return a greeting. In that way he would not become involved in conversation by which he might reveal his special mission.

But Gehazi's heart was not pure, and he craved exactly the fame and honor that Elisha demanded that he relinquish. So he figured out a way to circumvent Elisha's instructions. As he walked, he waved the staff in the air for everyone to see. Instead of greeting him, people said, "Hey, Gehazi, where are you going with that staff?"

Elisha had not forbidden him to answer questions, only greetings, so he eagerly replied, "This is Elisha's staff! He gave it to me to do a miracle! I'm going to revive a dead child!"

Gehazi observed the letter of Elisha's instructions, but not the spirit. He failed to demonstrate humility and earn the merit of performing a miracle. When he got there and put the staff on the boy, nothing happened.[57]

Some say that the staff was never intended to revive the child. It was only meant to preserve his body so that it would not deteriorate further before Elisha got there. To revive him would require more than a staff. Elisha would have to be alone with the child, to pray and implore G-d, and even to place his own body on the child's. None of this could Gehazi do. But Elisha gave him a small part of the miracle so that he might thereby earn some merit too. With the staff he could keep the boy closer to life, so that it would be easier to revive him and require less of a miracle.

But Gehazi did not understand that. When the boy showed no signs of life, he thought it had failed and Elisha had been mistaken in sending him.[58]

Others say that the staff was indeed supposed to revive the boy, but that Gehazi himself did not believe it, so it didn't work for him. Instead of obeying Elisha faithfully, he laughed at him as he went. When people asked him what he was doing with the staff, he said, "Elisha sent me to put this staff on a dead boy and revive him. Isn't that ridiculous?"[59]

Some say he found a dead dog on the way and decided to try out the staff. He put it on the dog and it came to life and bit him! But having misused the staff, it would not work for him anymore. When he put it on the boy, nothing happened.

The words, "אין קול ואין קשב," "he neither spoke nor heard" mean literally, "there was no voice and no listening." Gehazi thought, "Even if the boy can't speak, if he could hear me he would make some sign. Since he didn't, he must not be alive."[60]

4:32-34 וַיָּבֹא אֱלִישָׁע הַבָּיְתָה וְהִנֵּה הַנַּעַר מֵת מֻשְׁכָּב עַל־מִטָּתוֹ׃ וַיָּבֹא
וַיִּסְגֹּר הַדֶּלֶת בְּעַד שְׁנֵיהֶם וַיִּתְפַּלֵּל אֶל־ה׳׃ וַיַּעַל וַיִּשְׁכַּב עַל־הַיֶּלֶד וַיָּשֶׂם פִּיו
עַל־פִּיו וְעֵינָיו עַל־עֵינָיו וְכַפָּיו עַל־כַּפָּו וַיִּגְהַר עָלָיו וַיָּחָם בְּשַׂר הַיָּלֶד׃

Elisha came into the house, and behold, the boy was dead, laid down on his bed. He came in, closed the door on the two of them, and prayed to G-d. He got up and lay down on the boy, and put his mouth upon his mouth, his eyes upon his eyes, his hands upon his hands, and spread himself out on him. The boy's flesh became warm.

Elisha prayed, "As you did miracles and revived the dead for my master Elijah, so now revive this boy for me!"[61] He had to pray to perform this miracle even though he had not for the others, because the revival of the dead is in G-d's hands alone.[62] There are three keys that G-d keeps Himself, the key to rain, the key to birth, and the key to the revival of the dead. They are not given over to any angel or representative.[63] Elijah had briefly received the key to the revival of the dead. Now Elisha prayed to be given it too.

By placing his own body on the body of the boy, he imparted some of his life to him. One interpretation is that it was his warmth that warmed the child's flesh and enabled him to live again.[64] Another is that the contact of the two bodies symbolized the qualities that Elisha wanted the boy to receive. Such a symbol is a kind of nonverbal prayer. Sometimes it is more effective than a prayer that is uttered only by the lips. Thus we learn, "A symbol is a meaningful thing." On Rosh Hashanah we therefore eat foods whose names sound like the things for which we pray.[65] The act of eating thereby becomes a nonverbal prayer.

4:35,36 וַיָּשָׁב וַיֵּלֶךְ בַּבַּיִת אַחַת הֵנָּה וְאַחַת הֵנָּה וַיַּעַל וַיִּגְהַר עָלָיו וַיְזוֹרֵר
הַנַּעַר עַד־שֶׁבַע פְּעָמִים וַיִּפְקַח הַנַּעַר אֶת־עֵינָיו׃ וַיִּקְרָא אֶל־גֵּיחֲזִי וַיֹּאמֶר קְרָא
אֶל־הַשֻּׁנַמִּית הַזֹּאת וַיִּקְרָאֶהָ וַתָּבֹא אֵלָיו וַיֹּאמֶר שְׂאִי בְנֵךְ׃

He went back and walked around in the house, once this way and once this way, and got up and spread himself out on him. The boy sneezed seven times, and the boy opened his eyes. He called Gehazi and said, "Call this Shunamite!" He called her and she came to him. He said, "Lift up your child!"

Again, Elisha gave Gehazi an opportunity to take part in the miracle. But he didn't tell him how he had performed it, because he was not worthy of hearing that.[66]

4:37 וַתָּבֹא וַתִּפֹּל עַל־רַגְלָיו וַתִּשְׁתַּחוּ אָרְצָה וַתִּשָּׂא אֶת־בְּנָהּ וַתֵּצֵא׃

She came and fell on his feet and bowed to the ground. Then she lifted up her child and went out.

This was Elisha's seventh miracle. It corresponded to Elijah's revival of the son of the woman of Zarephath. Both had excelled in the giving of charity, and both were rewarded with the revival of a child. So too, the promised revival of the dead in the future will come about by virtue of charity.[67]

4:38 וֶאֱלִישָׁע שָׁב הַגִּלְגָּלָה וְהָרָעָב בָּאָרֶץ וּבְנֵי הַנְּבִיאִים יֹשְׁבִים לְפָנָיו
וַיֹּאמֶר לְנַעֲרוֹ שְׁפֹת הַסִּיר הַגְּדוֹלָה וּבַשֵּׁל נָזִיד לִבְנֵי הַנְּבִיאִים׃

Elisha returned to Gilgal. There was a famine in the land, and the sons of the prophets were sitting before him. He said to his servant, "Put up the large pot and cook a porridge for the sons of the prophets."

Though this is the first we hear of Elisha's teaching at Gilgal, it is called a return. Perhaps he had taught there before, but the Bible did not record it. Or perhaps it refers to his visit there on the day that Elijah ascended to heaven.[68]

A terrible famine had come upon the whole land. We will hear much more about it in the coming chapters. Elisha himself had proclaimed it because the people had refused to return to Torah. So, although the righteous suffered too, among them his own students, he did not pray that it be relieved. Perhaps he would not have been answered even had he prayed, for it was a time of divine anger.[69]

4:39 וַיֵּצֵא אֶחָד אֶל־הַשָּׂדֶה לְלַקֵּט אֹרֹת וַיִּמְצָא גֶּפֶן שָׂדֶה וַיְלַקֵּט מִמֶּנּוּ
פַּקֻּעֹת שָׂדֶה מְלֹא בִגְדוֹ וַיָּבֹא וַיְפַלַּח אֶל־סִיר הַנָּזִיד כִּי־לֹא יָדָעוּ׃

One went out to the field to gather greens. He found a wild vine and gathered wild gourds from it, enough to fill his clothes. He came and split them into the pot of porridge, for they didn't know.

The man went out to gather edible grasses, but he found a vine with gourds on it that looked like it would be much more filling. He didn't realize that they were poisonous, so he gathered them and brought them back. He broke them into pieces and threw them into the pot.[70]

Some say "ארת" means greens, such as wild chives and leeks.[71] Others say it is a kind of berry called a field-rocket, that enlightens the eyes, which is why it is called "ארת," coming from the word "אור," "light."[72]

4:40,41 וַיִּצְקוּ לַאֲנָשִׁים לֶאֱכוֹל וַיְהִי כְּאָכְלָם מֵהַנָּזִיד וְהֵמָּה צָעָקוּ וַיֹּאמְרוּ
מָוֶת בַּסִּיר אִישׁ הָאֱלֹהִים וְלֹא יָכְלוּ לֶאֱכֹל׃ וַיֹּאמֶר וּקְחוּ־קֶמַח וַיַּשְׁלֵךְ אֶל־הַסִּיר
וַיֹּאמֶר צַק לָעָם וְיֹאכֵלוּ וְלֹא הָיָה דָּבָר רָע בַּסִּיר׃

They poured out for the men to eat. But when they ate from the porridge they screamed "There is death in the pot, Oh man of G-d!" They couldn't eat. He said, "Get some flour!" and he threw it into the pot. He said, "Pour out for the people and they will eat!" There was nothing bad in the pot!

The poisonous plants had a strong bitter taste that affected the whole porridge. Everyone who tasted it immediately knew something was wrong. Had it not been a time of famine they might just have thrown it all out, but now it was all they had to eat. What could they do?

Elisha told them to pour what was left in their bowls back into the pot. Then he told them to put in some flour and dish it out again. This time the porridge tasted good and no one got sick from it.[73]

This miracle was superficially similar to the one that Elisha had performed earlier at Jericho, where he cured the water by throwing in salt. But there was a fundamental difference between them. Treating the water with salt had been a double miracle. Salt makes sweet water undrinkable, but Elisha caused it to make the bad water pure. Flour, however, would not ruin good porridge. It would make it even better. The effect of the flour was therefore in accordance with its nature, not against it as that of the salt had been.

In that way, this miracle was similar to reviving the son of the Shunamite, where Elisha had aligned certain of his limbs and organs with the boy's. The wholesomeness of the flour influenced the porridge as the life of Elisha's body influenced the body of the boy.

The miracle of the salt proved that G-d's power is above all nature, and that by G-d's word the natural order can be reversed. This miracle, on the other hand, showed that a person should strive in accordance with nature and pray to G-d to do the rest. Some say that it was not Elisha himself who threw in the flour.[74] He gave it to one of the students, to show that you don't have to be a prophet for your prayers to be answered. Anyone can pray, because G-d listens to all who call on Him sincerely.

Another interpretation is that it was to show that simple flour can sometimes accomplish more than the most advanced medicines, for ultimately it is by G-d's will that everything is accomplished.[75]

4:42-44 וְאִישׁ בָּא מִבַּעַל שָׁלִשָׁה וַיָּבֵא לְאִישׁ הָאֱלֹהִים לֶחֶם בִּכּוּרִים עֶשְׂרִים־לֶחֶם שְׂעֹרִים וְכַרְמֶל בְּצִקְלֹנוֹ וַיֹּאמֶר תֵּן לָעָם וְיֹאכֵלוּ: וַיֹּאמֶר מְשָׁרְתוֹ מָה אֶתֵּן זֶה לִפְנֵי מֵאָה אִישׁ וַיֹּאמֶר תֵּן לָעָם וְיֹאכֵלוּ כִּי כֹה אָמַר ה׳ אָכוֹל וְהוֹתֵר: וַיִּתֵּן לִפְנֵיהֶם וַיֹּאכְלוּ וַיּוֹתִרוּ כִּדְבַר ה׳:

A man came from Baal-shalishah and brought the man of G-d bread of the new crop, twenty loaves of barley bread, and fresh barley in the ear. He said, "Give to the people and they will eat!" His servant said, "How shall I put this before one hundred men?" He said, "Give it to the people and they will eat, for thus said G-d, 'Eat and have left over!' " He put before them and they ate and had left over, like the word of G-d.

Barley is the first grain to ripen, and of all the areas of the Land of Israel, the first place for any grain to ripen is Baal-shalishah. In that year of famine, however, the crops all ripened late. Although it was already after Passover, even in Baal-shalishah the barley harvest had just begun.[76]

This was similar to Elisha's earlier miracle of the oil, and Elijah's miracle of the oil and the flour. In those, a small amount become greater. In this case, rather than becoming greater, it remained small but satisfied a great number of people. It was similar to the food that Elijah ate in the desert when he was running away from Jezebel. One meal lasted him for forty days.

The expression "בכורים," which generally refers to the new crop offering that was brought in the Temple, here simply means "bread of the new crop." Elisha and his followers were not priests, so they would not have been permitted to eat of the Temple offering.[77] The fresh ears of barley were not normally eaten raw, but in time of famine people sometimes ate them that way because they could not wait for them to be dried and prepared.[78]

Some say "בצקלנו" means "in his clothes"[79] or "in his bag,"[80] describing how he brought the grain. Others say it means that the grains were still in their husks.[81]

Some say there were twenty-two loaves. The words "לחם," "bread" and "וכרמל," "and fresh barley" each add one to the number twenty mentioned in the verse. Others say there were twenty-two hundred students, so there was one loaf for every hundred of them. The words "before one hundred men" refer not to all the loaves together, but to each one. For had there been only one hundred students in all, each would have gotten about one-fifth of a loaf, a significant amount in time of famine.[82]

II KINGS 5

5:1 וְנַעֲמָן שַׂר־צְבָא מֶלֶךְ־אֲרָם הָיָה אִישׁ גָּדוֹל לִפְנֵי אֲדֹנָיו וּנְשֻׂא פָנִים
כִּי־בוֹ נָתַן־ה׳ תְּשׁוּעָה לַאֲרָם וְהָאִישׁ הָיָה גִּבּוֹר חַיִל מְצֹרָע׃

Naaman, the general of the army of the King of Aram, was a great man before his master and held in high esteem, for through him had G-d given victory to Aram. This man was a mighty warrior, but a leper.

Elisha's tenth miracle was to cure Naaman, the Aramean, of his leprosy. Naaman was blessed in many ways. He was strong, courageous, and well liked. He achieved a high position and won the respect of his people. Part of his fame was due to the key role he played in the battles against Israel. It was he who shot the arrow that killed Ahab in the battle of Ramoth-gilead.[1] G-d said, "Ahab saw my miracles, yet he refused to abandon his wicked ways. Not so Naaman. He is sincere and upright even though he was raised in idolatry. Furthermore, I know that when he sees My greatness, he will completely abandon idolatry and serve Me alone. He is worthy of being My messenger. By his hand will I punish Ahab!"[2]

The only flaw in Naaman's enviable life was his leprosy. He was never free of pain from his affliction and embarrassment from its disfiguring effects. But this made his accomplishments all the greater, for he continued to serve his king and fight for his people in spite of his suffering.[3]

Some say G-d gave him leprosy to lead him to Torah. Naaman was a sincere and pious man, but only through Torah could he attain his true potential. G-d saw his piety and rewarded him by showing him the greatness of His holy prophets. He knew that Naaman would not ignore it. But since Naaman would never see it in Aram, G-d afflicted him with leprosy so that he would go to the Land of Israel to seek Elisha's help.[4]

5:2,3 וַאֲרָם יָצְאוּ גְדוּדִים וַיִּשְׁבּוּ מֵאֶרֶץ יִשְׂרָאֵל נַעֲרָה קְטַנָּה וַתְּהִי לִפְנֵי
אֵשֶׁת נַעֲמָן׃ וַתֹּאמֶר אֶל־גְּבִרְתָּהּ אַחֲלֵי אֲדֹנִי לִפְנֵי הַנָּבִיא אֲשֶׁר בְּשֹׁמְרוֹן אָז
יֶאֱסֹף אֹתוֹ מִצָּרַעְתּוֹ׃

Aram went out in bands and captured a little girl from the Land of Israel. She served the wife of Naaman. She said to her mistress, "Let my master present his petitions before the prophet that is in Samaria. Then he will cure him of his leprosy."

During that time, Aram did not declare war against Israel, but the Arameans conducted organized raids across the border. The raiding parties consisted of bands of as many as one or two hundred men, each of whom took whatever he was able to capture for himself.[5]

Some say Naaman was afflicted with leprosy only after the girl was captured. It was a divine punishment, because he was responsible for kidnapping her.[6]

Others say it was a punishment for arrogance. Naaman was proud of his strength and success. He failed to recognize that all these were blessings given by G-d, so G-d afflicted him with leprosy to humble him. Just as leprosy comes from G-d and man is powerless to prevent it, so too, the blessings that he is granted are beyond his control, and he had no right to take credit for them.[7]

This girl is described by two apparently contradictory words, "נערה" and "קטנה." "נערה" generally means a girl of around twelve years old and "קטנה" means a young child. Some say they are used here to indicate that though she was still young, she was wise beyond her years.[8] Others say that "נערה" can mean a girl of any age, and, when modified by the word "קטנה," simply means a small girl.[9]

Another interpretation is that in this verse the word "נערה" does not mean "girl," as it usually does, but one who comes from the place called "נערון," "Naaron," a "Naaronite." The words "נערה קטנה" therefore mean "a small Naaronite girl."[10]

The girl understood that a prophet is not a magician who can do anything. He can only give a person what that person himself deserves. She therefore specifically advised Naaman to approach Elisha humbly and beg for his help. That is the meaning of "present his petition." She said, "Your recovery is dependent upon your own deeds. If you pray and conduct yourself humbly before the prophet, you will be worthy of being cured. But if you act arrogantly, there is nothing he will be able to do for you."[11]

The word used for curing leprosy is "יאסף," which literally means "to be gathered in." The Torah forbids a leper to dwell within the camp of Israel. When he is cured of his leprosy, he can reenter the camp. Being cured of leprosy is therefore called "being gathered in."[12] Even among the other nations, lepers are excluded from the general community, so this expression is not restricted to Jews.[13]

5:4,5 וַיָּבֹא וַיַּגֵּד לַאדֹנָיו לֵאמֹר כָּזֹאת וְכָזֹאת דִּבְּרָה הַנַּעֲרָה אֲשֶׁר מֵאֶרֶץ יִשְׂרָאֵל׃ וַיֹּאמֶר מֶלֶךְ־אֲרָם לֶךְ־בֹּא וְאֶשְׁלְחָה סֵפֶר אֶל־מֶלֶךְ יִשְׂרָאֵל וַיֵּלֶךְ וַיִּקַּח בְּיָדוֹ עֶשֶׂר כִּכְּרֵי־כֶסֶף וְשֵׁשֶׁת אֲלָפִים זָהָב וְעֶשֶׂר חֲלִיפוֹת בְּגָדִים׃

He came and told his master, saying, "Such and such said the girl that is from the Land of Israel." The King of Aram said, "Go and get there! I will send a letter to the King of Israel." He went and took ten talents of silver in his hand, and six thousand pieces of gold and ten changes of clothes.

Naaman wanted to convince the king to let him take the girl's advice, so when he told him what the girl had said he described her as a "נערה," an older girl, not as a "קטנה," a little girl.[14]

Some say that at first Naaman did not take the girl's suggestion seriously, but his master, the king, told him, "Don't write it off without trying it. You have nothing to lose and so much to gain!"[15]

The King of Aram naturally assumed that if there was such a great miracle worker among the Jews, he must be highly respected by the people, and above all by the king, Jehoram. He said, "The best way to approach this holy man is through the king. If their king sends you to him, he will do his utmost to cure you. So go to the king first."

5:6,7 וַיָּבֵא הַסֵּפֶר אֶל־מֶלֶךְ יִשְׂרָאֵל לֵאמֹר וְעַתָּה כְּבוֹא הַסֵּפֶר הַזֶּה אֵלֶיךָ הִנֵּה שָׁלַחְתִּי אֵלֶיךָ אֶת־נַעֲמָן עַבְדִּי וַאֲסַפְתּוֹ מִצָּרַעְתּוֹ׃ וַיְהִי כִּקְרֹא מֶלֶךְ־יִשְׂרָאֵל אֶת־הַסֵּפֶר וַיִּקְרַע בְּגָדָיו וַיֹּאמֶר הַאֱלֹהִים אָנִי לְהָמִית וּלְהַחֲיוֹת כִּי־זֶה שֹׁלֵחַ אֵלַי לֶאֱסֹף אִישׁ מִצָּרַעְתּוֹ כִּי אַךְ־דְּעוּ־נָא וּרְאוּ כִּי־מִתְאַנֶּה הוּא לִי׃

He brought the letter to the King of Israel saying, "Now, when this letter comes to you, behold, I have sent you Naaman, my servant, that you cure him of his leprosy." When the King of

Israel read the letter he tore his clothes and said, "Am I G-d, to cause to die and to cause to live, that this one sends to me to cure a man of his leprosy? For just please know and see that he is looking for an excuse to start a fight with me."

But Jehoram hated Elisha because Elisha had rebuked him. His hatred led him to deny Elisha's prophecy and wonderous deeds, even though he had seen some of them with his own eyes. So completely did he put Elisha out of his mind that when Naaman came to him it did not even occur to him to that there might be someone within his kingdom who could fulfill the King of Aram's request.[16]

See what a terrible sin it is to reject criticism! It leads a person to hate those who criticize him, and prevents him from recognizing their good qualities. Even if they bear no grudge and remain willing to help him, he cannot bring himself to approach them any more. He treats them as if they no longer exist, so he cannot avail himself of their help when he is in need.[17]

5:8 וַיְהִי כִּשְׁמֹעַ אֱלִישָׁע אִישׁ־הָאֱלֹהִים כִּי־קָרַע מֶלֶךְ־יִשְׂרָאֵל אֶת־בְּגָדָיו וַיִּשְׁלַח אֶל־הַמֶּלֶךְ לֵאמֹר לָמָּה קָרַעְתָּ בְּגָדֶיךָ יָבֹא־נָא אֵלַי וְיֵדַע כִּי יֵשׁ נָבִיא בְּיִשְׂרָאֵל׃

When Elisha, the man of G-d, heard that the King of Israel had torn his clothes, he sent to the King of Israel saying, "Why did you tear your clothes? Let him please come to me, and he will know that there is a prophet in Israel!"

Some say Elisha heard about Naaman's visit through prophecy.[18] Others say the news of the arrival of such an important Aramean official and the king's fear that it was a pretext for declaring war on Israel spread quickly through the country, and soon reached Elisha as well.

Elisha said, "Indeed, Jehoram, you are a wicked king and not worthy of being saved. Were it for your sake alone, I would not cure this man. Nor would I do it for the honor of the King of Aram. I do not respect him or fear his soldiers. But I will do it for the glory of G-d, to show Aram as well as Israel that He is above all nature, and that the prophets and teachers of the Jewish People are indeed His messengers."[19]

5:9 וַיָּבֹא נַעֲמָן בְּסוּסָו וּבְרִכְבּוֹ וַיַּעֲמֹד פֶּתַח־הַבַּיִת לֶאֱלִישָׁע׃

Naaman came with his horses and his chariot and stood at the door of Elisha's house.

Naaman wanted to impress the miracle worker with his power and status. He thought that it would take great effort to cure him, and that the man would not be prepared to go to that trouble for an ordinary person. So he appeared before Elisha together with his whole entourage.[20]

5:10 וַיִּשְׁלַח אֵלָיו אֱלִישָׁע מַלְאָךְ לֵאמֹר הָלוֹךְ וְרָחַצְתָּ שֶׁבַע־פְּעָמִים
בַּיַּרְדֵּן וְיָשֹׁב בְּשָׂרְךָ לְךָ וּטְהָר׃

Elisha sent a messenger to him saying, "Go wash seven times in the Jordan, and your skin will return to you and you will be pure."

Elisha purposely did not go out to meet him. Since his purpose was to show Naaman G-d's true greatness, he performed this miracle as undramatically as possible. He wanted to show that, far from being difficult, it required no effort at all. Nature and miracle are all the same to G-d in that way. He can do one as easily as the other. It is not that the forces of nature are independent of G-d, but less powerful, as the pagans believed. No! G-d is the source of all power. All the forces of nature are derived from Him alone, so He doesn't need to exert any effort to overcome them.

Elisha also wanted to humble Naaman. Naaman had conducted himself as a powerful and honored nobleman, not even getting off his chariot when he came to the prophet. He expected Elisha to come out and stand meekly in his presence. Elisha did just the opposite. Eventually Naaman would come to realize that it was his own arrogance that had brought this affliction upon him.[21]

The word "הלוך," "go," in the phrase "Go wash seven times" is in a noun form, similar to the English, "going." It can be understood either as a command, "go wash," or a statement, "going, you will wash." Elisha said, "I know that you will indeed do as I say. When you go, you will wash and be purified! Though at first you will reject my words, in the end you will follow them anyway."[22]

5:11,12 וַיִּקְצֹף נַעֲמָן וַיֵּלַךְ וַיֹּאמֶר הִנֵּה אָמַרְתִּי אֵלַי יֵצֵא יָצוֹא וְעָמַד וְקָרָא
בְּשֵׁם־ה׳ אֱלֹהָיו וְהֵנִיף יָדוֹ אֶל־הַמָּקוֹם וְאָסַף הַמְּצֹרָע: הֲלֹא טוֹב אֲבָנָה (אֲמָנָה
קרי) וּפַרְפַּר נַהֲרוֹת דַּמֶּשֶׂק מִכֹּל מֵימֵי יִשְׂרָאֵל הֲלֹא־אֶרְחַץ בָּהֶם וְטָהָרְתִּי וַיִּפֶן
וַיֵּלֶךְ בְּחֵמָה:

Naaman was enraged and left. He said, "Behold, I thought he would surely come out to me, and stand and call out in the name of the L-rd, his G-d, and raise his hand to the place, and the leprosy would be cured. Aren't Amanah and Parpar, the rivers of Damascus, better than all the waters of Israel? Couldn't I wash in them and become pure?" He turned and he went away in anger.

Naaman was disappointed. He had expected to be treated with honor. He thought that Elisha would come out to greet him and stand before him in awe as his own people did. Even the King of Israel trembled when he read the message. Why had this man, who was nothing but a prophet, treated him so lightly?[23] He did not yet understand that the true prophets of G-d are not like the heathen priests, for G-d is not like the idols. Kings may have pomp and glory, but the real power belongs to G-d. He gives it to His true faithful servants, so they need fear no man.

Naaman also misunderstood Elisha's answer. He thought that washing in the Jordan was intended not to invoke a miracle, but a natural remedy. He said, "I thought this man was a prophet, not a doctor. I didn't come for medical advice!"[24]

Some say "the place" refers to the place on Naaman's body that was afflicted with leprosy.[25] Others say it means the Jordan, the place where he was directed to wash.[26] Such an act might impart supernatural powers to the water. Another interpretation is that it refers to the Holy Temple. Naaman imagined that Elisha would invoke the power of the Temple.[27]

Some say that Naaman was accustomed to wash in the rivers of Damascus every day. He said, "Why should washing in the Jordan help, when washing in Amanah and Parpar never did?"[28]

The Jordan River had double significance. It was a holy river, but its name also indicated the key to Naaman's recovery. The name "ירדן," "Jordan," comes from the root "ירד," which means to go down. Naaman suffered leprosy because he was arrogant. Not until he humbled himself would he be relieved.[29]

5:13 וַיִּגְּשׁוּ עֲבָדָיו וַיְדַבְּרוּ אֵלָיו וַיֹּאמְרוּ אָבִי דָּבָר גָּדוֹל הַנָּבִיא דִּבֶּר
אֵלֶיךָ הֲלוֹא תַעֲשֶׂה וְאַף כִּי־אָמַר אֵלֶיךָ רְחַץ וּטְהָר׃

His servants approached him and spoke to him and said, "My father, had it been a great thing that the prophet said to you, wouldn't you do it? All the more so since he said to you, 'Wash and become pure.'"

His servants advised him not to act rashly. They said, "Had he told you to do something very difficult, wouldn't you have done it? Now that he has told you something so easy, what can be the harm of trying it? At worst, it will have no effect."[30] In this way they followed the example of their king, who had encouraged Naaman to go in the first place.

Another way of reading this verse is, "It is indeed a great thing that the prophet said to you! Won't you do it?" They said, "Though this seems small in your eyes, if Elisha says it, it must be great! Do it even though you don't understand it!"[31]

Some say that Naaman understood that Elisha was telling him to become more humble, but he refused to accept his advice. His servants said, "Is your honor worth such suffering? What do you gain? Humble yourself as the prophet says and you will be cured!"[32]

5:14 וַיֵּרֶד וַיִּטְבֹּל בַּיַּרְדֵּן שֶׁבַע פְּעָמִים כִּדְבַר אִישׁ הָאֱלֹהִים וַיָּשָׁב בְּשָׂרוֹ
כִּבְשַׂר נַעַר קָטֹן וַיִּטְהָר׃

He went down and dipped in the Jordan seven times, in accordance with the word of the man of G-d. His skin became like the skin of a small boy again and he became pure.

Being cured of leprosy is described as "the skin returning" because leprosy makes the skin deteriorate, and when Naaman was cured it miraculously grew back.

His skin became like the skin of a small boy, not like the skin of an adult. A little child has no pride. Like his skin, Naaman was now meek and humble.[33]

5:15 וַיָּשָׁב אֶל־אִישׁ הָאֱלֹהִים הוּא וְכָל־מַחֲנֵהוּ וַיָּבֹא וַיַּעֲמֹד לְפָנָיו
וַיֹּאמֶר הִנֵּה־נָא יָדַעְתִּי כִּי אֵין אֱלֹהִים בְּכָל־הָאָרֶץ כִּי אִם־בְּיִשְׂרָאֵל וְעַתָּה קַח־נָא
בְרָכָה מֵאֵת עַבְדֶּךָ׃

He went back to the man of G-d, he and all his camp. He came and stood before him and said, "Behold, now I know that there is no god in all the earth except in Israel! So now, please accept a blessing from your servant."

Naaman knew that in one respect, his initial reaction had been correct. There was really no difference between the water of the Jordan and that of any other river. It was the act of obeying the prophet's words that had cured him. It was therefore clear that the true prophets of G-d are not like the heathen priests. Now he understood why Elisha had not shown him reverence. No longer did he expect the prophet to stand before him. On the contrary, it was he who stood before Elisha! Elisha saw how his attitude had changed, so this time he came out to greet him.[34]

Elisha had succeeded in showing him that the G-d of Israel was really different than the idols. When Naaman came, he had thought that Elisha might be greater than the priests of the idols, but not essentially different. Now, however, the manner in which Elisha had cured him made it clear that his G-d controlled all of nature, and could do with it as He willed.

Some say that Naaman still didn't recognize that G-d controlled the entire universe. That is why he said, "in all the earth." The heavens, he thought, might be outside of G-d's domain, but as far as the earth is concerned, there is no god but Him. In this way, Naaman was greater than Jethro, who had said,[35] "Now I know that the L-rd is greater than all the gods." He believed that the other gods had power, but that G-d was stronger and could overcome them. There was a third righteous gentile who came even closer to the truth. That was Rahab, the prostitute, who helped the Jews when they conquered the Holy Land and later became a righteous convert. She said,[36] "For the L-rd, your G-d, is the G-d in the heavens above and the earth below." She recognized that there is no place outside of His control. But only Moses expressed the true extent of G-d's greatness. He said,[37] "For the L-rd is the G-d in the heavens above and on the earth below. There is none other." G-d's greatness is beyond human comprehension. Only by complete negation, "There is absolutely none other," can we express it.[38]

Naaman would never worship idols again. He was wholeheartedly dedicated to the service of G-d. But he did not convert and become a Jew. He would not abandon his position and the great responsibility he had toward his people. So he lived as a righteous gentile, keeping the seven commandments that G-d gave to Noah and his descendants, but not the Torah that was only given to the Jewish People and those who choose to join them.[39]

5:16 וַיֹּאמֶר חַי־ה׳ אֲשֶׁר־עָמַדְתִּי לְפָנָיו אִם־אֶקָּח וַיִּפְצַר־בּוֹ לָקַחַת וַיְמָאֵן׃

He said, "As G-d, before Whom I have stood, lives, I will not accept!" He pressed him to accept but he refused.

By the word "blessing," Naaman meant a gift.[40] But Elisha did not want any reward. He had performed this miracle to demonstrate G-d's power, and had succeeded.[41] What material reward could compare to that?

The prophets of the idols are always eager for reward, but the prophets of G-d refuse gifts even when they are offered. Accepting a gift would have contradicted exactly the point Elisha had just made, that G-d controls everything. It would have implied that there were some things that G-d could not give him, for otherwise, what need would he have had of human assistance? So he stubbornly refused.[42]

Thus, too, we find that Abraham refused to accept anything from the King of Sodom. He said, "Everything I have is through G-d's blessing. I have not received anything from anyone else!"

Another reason for refusing is that he had really done nothing. For what way did he deserve a reward? The miracle was performed by G-d, not Elisha. He had not even been present when it happened![43]

Some say he did not want to take Naaman's gift because it contained money derived from idolatry.[44]

But even Elisha, great as he was, found it necessary to take an oath to strengthen his conviction. The riches that Naaman offered were such a great temptation that, in order to control his evil inclination, he felt he needed to swear to accept nothing.[45]

5:17,18 וַיֹּאמֶר נַעֲמָן וָלֹא יֻתַּן־נָא לְעַבְדְּךָ מַשָּׂא צֶמֶד־פְּרָדִים אֲדָמָה כִּי
לוֹא־יַעֲשֶׂה עוֹד עַבְדְּךָ עֹלָה וָזֶבַח לֵאלֹהִים אֲחֵרִים כִּי אִם־לַה׳׃ לַדָּבָר הַזֶּה
יִסְלַח ה׳ לְעַבְדֶּךָ בְּבוֹא אֲדֹנִי בֵית־רִמּוֹן לְהִשְׁתַּחֲוֹת שָׁמָּה וְהוּא נִשְׁעָן עַל־יָדִי
וְהִשְׁתַּחֲוֵיתִי בֵּית רִמֹּן בְּהִשְׁתַּחֲוָיָתִי בֵּית רִמֹּן יִסְלַח־נָא־ה׳ לְעַבְדְּךָ בַּדָּבָר הַזֶּה׃

Naaman said, "If not, let there please be given to your servant two mules' burden of earth. For your servant will not make burnt offerings and sacrifices to other gods any more, except to the L-rd. Only for this thing may G-d forgive your servant: When my master comes to the house of Rimon to bow down there and rests on my hand, I will bow down at the house of Rimon. For my bowing down at the house of Rimon may G-d forgive your servant for this thing."

Naaman said, "I now believe in G-d and want to worship Him. But I cannot abandon my family or leave my master, the king. So let me take home some earth of the holy land to make an altar to G-d. It may seem a strange request, since earth is not valued, and people do not generally ask permission to take such a small amount of it. Nonetheless, I will not take anything without asking your permission and the permission of your king.[46]

"Don't think I merely want to add G-d to the list of idols that I have been accustomed to serve. As of now I reject them all, because I know that the ultimate power rests with G-d alone.

"I would not even enter the temples of the idols any more, were it not for my obligation to the king, my master. But I hereby declare that when I bow down together with him it will be only because I am required to assist him, not of my own free will!"[47]

How great is the respect the Jewish People receives from the nations of the world when they do G-d's will! Naaman wouldn't even take a small amount of earth from them without asking permission. He certainly would never again have raided them to take captives or property.[48]

5:19 וַיֹּאמֶר לוֹ לֵךְ לְשָׁלוֹם וַיֵּלֶךְ מֵאִתּוֹ כִּבְרַת אָרֶץ׃

He said to him, "Go to peace!" and he went from him about a mile.

Elisha assured Naaman that he would not be held guilty for accompanying his master in his idolatrous practices. Some say he also reassured him that his leprosy would not return.[49]

Some take this as proof that a righteous gentile is not required to give his life rather than bow before an idol. Others say that if there are ten Jews present, even a gentile is required to give his life, but as there would be no Jews in the temple of Rimon, Elisha told Naaman that he would be forgiven.[50]

5:20 וַיֹּאמֶר גֵּיחֲזִי נַעַר אֱלִישָׁע אִישׁ־הָאֱלֹהִים הִנֵּה חָשַׂךְ אֲדֹנִי אֶת נַעֲמָן הָאֲרַמִּי הַזֶּה מִקַּחַת מִיָּדוֹ אֵת אֲשֶׁר־הֵבִיא חַי־ה׳ כִּי־אִם־רַצְתִּי אַחֲרָיו וְלָקַחְתִּי מֵאִתּוֹ מְאוּמָה׃

Then Gehazi, the servant of Elisha, the man of G-d, said, "Behold, my master has held Naaman, this Aramean, back, by not taking from his hand what he brought. As G-d lives I will run after him and take something from him."

Here Gehazi is called "נער אלישע" "the servant of Elisha." The word "נער" is used here because it is like the word "נער," "poured out." It indicates that Gehazi was devoid of good deeds like a pot whose contents have been poured out.[51]

The word "מאומה," "something," is written "מומה," without the letter "א." "מום" means a flaw. Without realizing it, Gehazi foretold that he was to receive Naaman's flaw, his leprosy.[52] By swearing falsely he had profaned G-d's name. G-d said, "You swore by My name that you would take 'something,' 'מאומה.' By your life I swear that you will take 'מום,' Naaman's flaw."[53]

5:21 וַיִּרְדֹּף גֵּיחֲזִי אַחֲרֵי נַעֲמָן וַיִּרְאֶה נַעֲמָן רָץ אַחֲרָיו וַיִּפֹּל מֵעַל הַמֶּרְכָּבָה לִקְרָאתוֹ וַיֹּאמֶר הֲשָׁלוֹם׃

Gehazi ran after Naaman. Naaman saw someone running after him and he fell from upon his chariot to meet him. He said, "Is all well?"

The word "ויפל," "he fell," means not that he fell by accident, but that he jumped down.[54]

5:22,23 וַיֹּאמֶר שָׁלוֹם אֲדֹנִי שְׁלָחַנִי לֵאמֹר הִנֵּה עַתָּה זֶה בָּאוּ אֵלַי שְׁנֵי־נְעָרִים מֵהַר אֶפְרַיִם מִבְּנֵי הַנְּבִיאִים תְּנָה־נָּא לָהֶם כִּכַּר־כֶּסֶף וּשְׁתֵּי חֲלִפוֹת

בְּגָדִים׃ וַיֹּאמֶר נַעֲמָן הוֹאֵל קַח כִּכָּרָיִם וַיִּפְרָץ־בּוֹ וַיָּצַר כִּכְּרַיִם כֶּסֶף בִּשְׁנֵי
חֲרִטִים וּשְׁתֵּי חֲלִפוֹת בְּגָדִים וַיִּתֵּן אֶל־שְׁנֵי נְעָרָיו וַיִּשְׂאוּ לְפָנָיו׃

He said, "All is well! My master sent me saying, 'Behold, just now there came to me two boys from the mountains of Ephraim, from the sons of the prophets. Give them, please, a talent of silver, and two changes of clothes.'" Naaman said, "Agree to take two talents!" He pressed him, and he wrapped up the two talents of silver in two bags, and two changes of clothing. He gave them to his two servants and they carried before him.

King Solomon enumerated certain sins that are particularly obnoxious to G-d. The punishment for such sins is leprosy. Among them is[55] "feet that hurry to run to evil." Gehazi exemplified this bad quality.[56]

Some say the word "הואל" means "agree."[57] Others say it means "swear."[58] Naaman said, "Swear to me that you were sent by Elisha!"[59] Naaman could not believe that Elisha had changed his mind, having been so adamant before. When he heard Gehazi swear, however, he was satisfied, and sent two of his servants with him to carry the presents.

5:24 וַיָּבֹא אֶל־הָעֹפֶל וַיִּקַּח מִיָּדָם וַיִּפְקֹד בַּבָּיִת וַיְשַׁלַּח אֶת־הָאֲנָשִׁים
וַיֵּלֵכוּ׃

He came to the stronghold, took them from their hands and put them safely in the house. Then he sent the men and they left.

Some say the word "עפל," "stronghold," means a strong and secure building located on a high place where it can be easily protected.[60] Others say it means a secret hiding place.[61]

5:25 וְהוּא־בָא וַיַּעֲמֹד אֶל־אֲדֹנָיו וַיֹּאמֶר אֵלָיו אֱלִישָׁע מֵאַן (מֵאַיִן קרי)
גֵּחֲזִי וַיֹּאמֶר לֹא־הָלַךְ עַבְדְּךָ אָנֶה וָאָנָה׃

As for him, he came to his master and stood. Elisha said to

him, “From where have you come, Gehazi?” He said, “Your servant did not go anywhere.”

Elisha gave Gehazi an opportunity to repent. He hoped that when he asked Gehazi where he had gone he would admit what he had done. Then he might have been forgiven. But instead he made his sin worse by denying it.[62]

The word “מאין,” “from where” is an allusion to the dire consequences of Gehazi’s sin. It is written “מאן” without the letter “י,” which means “refuse.” Elisha said, “From where have you gone and where are you going? You have refused the reward of the righteous!”[63]

5:26,27 וַיֹּאמֶר אֵלָיו לֹא־לִבִּי הָלַךְ כַּאֲשֶׁר הָפַךְ־אִישׁ מֵעַל מֶרְכַּבְתּוֹ לִקְרָאתֶךָ
הַעֵת לָקַחַת אֶת־הַכֶּסֶף וְלָקַחַת בְּגָדִים וְזֵיתִים וּכְרָמִים וְצֹאן וּבָקָר וַעֲבָדִים
וּשְׁפָחוֹת: וְצָרַעַת נַעֲמָן תִּדְבַּק־בְּךָ וּבְזַרְעֲךָ לְעוֹלָם וַיֵּצֵא מִלְּפָנָיו מְצֹרָע כַּשָּׁלֶג:

He said to him, “No! My heart went along, when a man turned from upon his chariot to greet you. Was it time to take the silver and to take clothes, olives and vineyards, sheep and cattle, slaves and maidservants? The leprosy of Naaman will cling to you and to your descendants forever!” And he went out from before him leprous as snow.

Elisha said, “How do you imagine that you can fool me? Do you think that my power of prophecy has left me, that I do not know what you’ve done? My heart went along with you and I saw everything you did. I saw you accept the gifts from Naaman as if I had been standing right there!”[64]

Some say the words “לא לבי הלך” mean “No! What you say is not true! My heart went along with you and saw.”[65] Others say it means, “Has my heart, that is, my power of prophecy, left me, that I don’t know what you did?”[66]

Naaman should not have had to pay for his recovery. He earned it by his repentance. But once Gehazi accepted a gift from him, that gift became a ransom for his soul. By accepting it, Gehazi accepted Naaman’s affliction too!

Gehazi also deserved this punishment for trying to deceive his teacher. Later, we will see that he committed other sins as well. He was disrespectful to his teacher by referring to him by his name, and also interfered with the Torah studies of the other students.[67]

Another reason is that he swore falsely to Naaman. Thus we learn that there are seven sins for which a person may be punished with leprosy, one being swearing falsely.[68]

Gehazi had also committed other sins, for which he had not been punished. He was envious, promiscuous, and lacked faith. In particular, he denied the revival of the dead.[69]

Elisha was enraged that Gehazi not only committed a sin, but lied about it as well. He had tried to overlook Gehazi's misdeeds until now, in the hope that he would improve, but he could tolerate them no longer. He absolutely rejected him.

At that time, Gehazi had been studying the laws of the eight impure creeping animals. Elisha said, "The reward for studying Torah, like other good deeds, is to be given in the next world, for rewards in the next world are eternal. But the wicked are given all their rewards in this world and sent to the next world empty-handed, their merit totally depleted. By choosing to take Naaman's present, you have made this the time to receive the reward for your studies. For the eight impure animals you will receive eight things, silver, clothes, olives, vineyards, sheep, cattle, slaves, and maidservants, the things that you took from Naaman or that you can buy with the money he gave you. Enjoy them now, for in the next world you will have nothing!"[70]

Some say the curse of leprosy only affected those children that would be born in the future. Those that were already born would not suffer for their father's sin. But, since it affected his body, it would be inherited by any children born later on.

Others say that it affected those that were already born as well, because they knew about their father's sin and condoned it.[71]

The word "לעולם," "forever," may mean "for their whole lives" or it may mean "until the Jubilee year."[72] Thus we find in the Torah that the expression "he will be his slave forever"[73] means only until the Jubilee year.

II KINGS 6

6:1,2 וַיֹּאמְרוּ בְנֵי־הַנְּבִיאִים אֶל־אֱלִישָׁע הִנֵּה־נָא הַמָּקוֹם אֲשֶׁר אֲנַחְנוּ
יֹשְׁבִים שָׁם לְפָנֶיךָ צַר מִמֶּנּוּ: נֵלְכָה־נָּא עַד־הַיַּרְדֵּן וְנִקְחָה מִשָּׁם אִישׁ קוֹרָה
אֶחָת וְנַעֲשֶׂה־לָּנוּ שָׁם מָקוֹם לָשֶׁבֶת שָׁם וַיֹּאמֶר לֵכוּ:

The sons of the prophets said to Elisha, "Behold, please, the place that we are living there before you is too crowded for us. Please, let us go to the Jordan. Each one of us will take one beam from there, and will make ourselves there a place to live there." He said, "Go!"

As soon as Gehazi left, Elisha's following began to grow. Gehazi used to get into arguments with the other students, and many didn't want to stay while he was around. They found his behavior and bad character repulsive.[1]

Some say that although he was wicked, the other students respected him for his scholarship. But even that respect he abused, using it to mislead them. He sat outside when Elisha was lecturing rather than going in to listen. When the others came and saw him there, they stayed outside too. So the attendance at Elisha's lectures was poor and only a small building was needed.[2]

Now that Gehazi was gone, there were so many students that there was not enough room for them all. Elisha's fame was also spreading as he performed more miracles.[3] So they decided to move to a new location where they could expand.[4]

They chose the bank of the Jordan. It was from there that Elijah had departed when he went up to heaven. It was the waters of the Jordan, too, that had cured Naaman. They hoped to gain additional divine inspiration there.[5]

The "place" referred to in this verse may mean the entire area in which Elisha's students lived, or the building in which he delivered his lectures. According to the second interpretation, the phrase "המקום אשר

אנחנו ישבים" means "the place where we are sitting there before you," referring literally to their sitting in front of him when he taught.

6:3 וַיֹּאמֶר הָאֶחָד הוֹאֶל נָא וְלֵךְ אֶת־עֲבָדֶיךָ וַיֹּאמֶר אֲנִי אֵלֵךְ׃

One said, "Please agree to go with your servants!" He said, "I will go."

Elisha accompanied them to guide them and protect them in case anything went wrong.[6]

6:4,5 וַיֵּלֶךְ אִתָּם וַיָּבֹאוּ הַיַּרְדֵּנָה וַיִּגְזְרוּ הָעֵצִים׃ וַיְהִי הָאֶחָד מַפִּיל הַקּוֹרָה
וְאֶת־הַבַּרְזֶל נָפַל אֶל־הַמָּיִם וַיִּצְעַק וַיֹּאמֶר אֲהָהּ אֲדֹנִי וְהוּא שָׁאוּל׃

He went with them. They came to the Jordan and cut down trees. One was felling a beam and the iron fell into the water. He cried out and said, "Alas, my master! It was borrowed!"

As the man was striking the wood with his axe, the iron axe-blade came loose and fell off.[7] Iron tools were hard to come by in those days, so they were very expensive. Losing one was bad enough, but as it was not his own he would have to pay for it, and he had no money.[8]

6:6,7 וַיֹּאמֶר אִישׁ־הָאֱלֹהִים אָנָה נָפָל וַיַּרְאֵהוּ אֶת־הַמָּקוֹם וַיִּקְצָב־עֵץ
וַיַּשְׁלֶךְ־שָׁמָּה וַיָּצֶף הַבַּרְזֶל׃ וַיֹּאמֶר הָרֶם לָךְ וַיִּשְׁלַח יָדוֹ וַיִּקָּחֵהוּ׃

The man of G-d said, "Where did it fall?" and he showed him the place. He cut a piece of wood and threw it there, and the iron floated up. He said, "Take it up for yourself!" He reached out his hand and took it.

Some say Elisha cut a new handle just the right size to fit into the iron axe-head. Like the miracle of the salt in the water, which was done with a new bottle, this was done with a new handle. He could not have used the old one for the miracle. When the new handle was thrown into the water, it found the hole in the blade, went in, and floated back up with the blade attached.[9]

Others say he just cut a piece of wood from a tree and threw it in. The wood, which by nature should have floated, sank down, and the heavy axe-head floated to the top in its place. It was as if the wood had gone in and called the iron up.[10]

There were many easier ways by which Elisha could have retrieved the axe-head, but he took this opportunity to demonstrate that G-d is indeed above all nature. Natural order exists only by His word, so He can change it whenever He wants. This was Elisha's twelfth miracle.[11]

6:8 וּמֶלֶךְ אֲרָם הָיָה נִלְחָם בְּיִשְׂרָאֵל וַיִּוָּעַץ אֶל־עֲבָדָיו לֵאמֹר אֶל־מְקוֹם פְּלֹנִי אַלְמֹנִי תַּחֲנֹתִי׃

The King of Aram was fighting with Israel. He consulted with his servants saying, "At a covered and hidden place make my camp."

Naaman's recovery didn't make a lasting impression on Aram.[12] Soon they were back attacking Israel. Some say they pretended to be at peace, while secretly sending bands to maraud them.[13] The king decided that this time he would try to capture Jehoram, so he lay in ambush for him at a place where he was expected to pass.[14] Some say they dug pits there to trap Jehoram and his men.[15]

The word "פלני" means something concealed and covered. "אלמני" means "nameless."[16] Together they are used in place of a name that the speaker does not want to reveal, the way the expressions "such-and-such" or "so-and-so" are used in English. Thus this expression is used in the Book of Ruth to refer to the relative who refused to marry Ruth, permitting Boaz to marry her instead.

In this case, the king might have used it to keep the name of the location secret, lest someone whom he did not trust was listening. He just said "at such-and-such a place," and those who knew what he meant understood. Or it might be a description of the place itself, "a secret place that is hidden from view." According to this, the king had no particular place in mind, and was just giving general instructions.[17]

6:9,10 וַיִּשְׁלַח אִישׁ הָאֱלֹהִים אֶל־מֶלֶךְ יִשְׂרָאֵל לֵאמֹר הִשָּׁמֶר מֵעֲבֹר הַמָּקוֹם
הַזֶּה כִּי־שָׁם אֲרָם נְחִתִּים׃ וַיִּשְׁלַח מֶלֶךְ יִשְׂרָאֵל אֶל־הַמָּקוֹם אֲשֶׁר אָמַר־לוֹ
אִישׁ־הָאֱלֹהִים וְהִזְהִירֹה וְנִשְׁמַר שָׁם לֹא אַחַת וְלֹא שְׁתָּיִם׃

The man of G-d sent to the King of Israel saying, "Be careful not to pass this place, for there Aram are lying in wait." The King of Israel sent to the place that the man of G-d had told him and warned him, and watched out there, not once and not twice.

When the King of Aram failed to catch Jehoram at the first place, he tried another one. Again Elisha warned him, and that failed too. This happened "not once and not twice" but many times.[18]

6:11 וַיִּסָּעֵר לֵב מֶלֶךְ־אֲרָם עַל־הַדָּבָר הַזֶּה וַיִּקְרָא אֶל־עֲבָדָיו וַיֹּאמֶר
אֲלֵיהֶם הֲלוֹא תַּגִּידוּ לִי מִי מִשֶּׁלָּנוּ אֶל־מֶלֶךְ יִשְׂרָאֵל׃

The King of Aram's heart was very troubled about this thing. He called his servants and said to them, "Won't you tell me which of you is for the King of Israel?"

Finally, the king concluded that there must be a traitor among his servants.

6:12-14 וַיֹּאמֶר אַחַד מֵעֲבָדָיו לוֹא אֲדֹנִי הַמֶּלֶךְ כִּי־אֱלִישָׁע הַנָּבִיא אֲשֶׁר
בְּיִשְׂרָאֵל יַגִּיד לְמֶלֶךְ יִשְׂרָאֵל אֶת־הַדְּבָרִים אֲשֶׁר תְּדַבֵּר בַּחֲדַר מִשְׁכָּבֶךָ׃ וַיֹּאמֶר
לְכוּ וּרְאוּ אֵיכֹה הוּא וְאֶשְׁלַח וְאֶקָּחֵהוּ וַיֻּגַּד־לוֹ לֵאמֹר הִנֵּה בְדֹתָן׃ וַיִּשְׁלַח־שָׁמָּה
סוּסִים וְרֶכֶב וְחַיִל כָּבֵד וַיָּבֹאוּ לַיְלָה וַיַּקִּפוּ עַל־הָעִיר׃

One of his servants said, "No, my master, the king. For Elisha, the prophet who is in Israel, can tell the King of Israel the things that you say in your bedroom." He said, "Go and see where he is, and I will send and take him!" It was told to him saying, "Behold, in Dothan!" He sent horses and chariots and a mighty army there. They came at night and surrounded the city.

How foolish are those who serve idols! Even when the truth stares them in the face, they refuse to see it. If Elisha could tell where the king had laid his ambushes, wouldn't he also know that he had sent the army to capture him? He could flee before the army had even left Aram, and be far away by the time they reached his house. Or he might choose not to leave, and defeat them by a miracle instead. The king knew of Elisha's powers. He himself had sent Naaman to him to be cured. But his desire to succeed blinded him, and he stubbornly refused to admit the truth.

He sent the army by night, hoping in that way to surround the city without being noticed and capture Elisha by surprise in the morning.[19]

6:15 וַיַּשְׁכֵּם מְשָׁרֵת אִישׁ הָאֱלֹהִים לָקוּם וַיֵּצֵא וְהִנֵּה־חַיִל סוֹבֵב אֶת־הָעִיר וְסוּס וָרָכֶב וַיֹּאמֶר נַעֲרוֹ אֵלָיו אֲהָהּ אֲדֹנִי אֵיכָה נַעֲשֶׂה׃

The servant of the man of G-d awoke early to get up. He went out, and behold, an army was surrounding the city, and horses and chariots! His servant said to him, "Alas, my master, what will we do?"

It is difficult even for those who have complete faith in G-d to be calm in time of danger. The servant knew that G-d, Who controls the whole universe, was with them and could protect them from all harm. Nonetheless, he was afraid. He did not feel the nearness of G-d's presence as he did the things that he could hear and see, so he was overcome by fear.

6:16,17 וַיֹּאמֶר אַל־תִּירָא כִּי רַבִּים אֲשֶׁר אִתָּנוּ מֵאֲשֶׁר אוֹתָם׃ וַיִּתְפַּלֵּל אֱלִישָׁע וַיֹּאמַר ה׳ פְּקַח־נָא אֶת־עֵינָיו וְיִרְאֶה וַיִּפְקַח ה׳ אֶת־עֵינֵי הַנַּעַר וַיַּרְא וְהִנֵּה הָהָר מָלֵא סוּסִים וְרֶכֶב אֵשׁ סְבִיבֹת אֱלִישָׁע׃

He said, "Don't be afraid, for those that are with us are more than are with them!" Elisha prayed and said, "Oh G-d, please open his eyes that he may see!" G-d opened the eyes of the servant and he saw, and behold, the mountain was full of horses and chariots of fire all around Elisha!

Elisha wanted his servant to have a more vivid awareness of G-d's presence, even if just for a moment. He prayed that he experience it as if he were seeing it with his eyes.

Some say there weren't really any horses and chariots of fire. They were just a vision that the servant saw, symbolizing G-d's strength and indicating that He was with them.[20] Others say that they were actually surrounded by angels, who appeared to humans as fiery horses and chariots.[21] But this awesome spectacle was only to reassure the servant, for it was not by fighting against the army of Aram that they would be saved.[22]

6:18 וַיֵּרְדוּ אֵלָיו וַיִּתְפַּלֵּל אֱלִישָׁע אֶל־ה׳ וַיֹּאמַר הַךְ־נָא אֶת־הַגּוֹי־הַזֶּה
בַּסַּנְוֵרִים וַיַּכֵּם בַּסַּנְוֵרִים כִּדְבַר אֱלִישָׁע׃

They came down to him and Elisha prayed to G-d and said, "Please smite this people with blindness!" He smote them with blindness, in accordance with the word of Elisha.

This is the same sort of blindness, "סנורים," with which the angels smote the people of Sodom who tried to attack Lot. Some say it was a blinding light. Others say that they could see, but could not understand what they saw. It was an affliction of the mind, not of the eyes. They could no longer recognize even familiar things. More miraculous yet, they did not realize anything was wrong! They felt as if all their faculties were intact, but that they had simply lost their way.[23]

6:19,20 וַיֹּאמֶר אֲלֵהֶם אֱלִישָׁע לֹא־זֶה הַדֶּרֶךְ וְלֹא־זֹה הָעִיר לְכוּ אַחֲרַי
וְאוֹלִיכָה אֶתְכֶם אֶל־הָאִישׁ אֲשֶׁר תְּבַקֵּשׁוּן וַיֹּלֶךְ אוֹתָם שֹׁמְרוֹנָה׃ וַיְהִי כְּבֹאָם
שֹׁמְרוֹן וַיֹּאמֶר אֱלִישָׁע ה׳ פְּקַח אֶת־עֵינֵי־אֵלֶּה וַיִּרְאוּ וַיִּפְקַח ה׳ אֶת־עֵינֵיהֶם
וַיִּרְאוּ וְהִנֵּה בְּתוֹךְ שֹׁמְרוֹן׃

Elisha said to them, "This is not the road and this is not the city. Follow me and I will take you to the person that you are looking for." He took them to Samaria. When they came to Samaria, Elisha said, "Oh, G-d, open up the eyes of these and they will see!" G-d opened up their eyes and they saw, and behold, they were in the middle of Samaria!

The soldiers couldn't recognize Elisha even when he was standing in front of them! He told them that the man they were looking for was not in Dothan, which indeed he was not, having come out of the city to talk to them.[24] Unsuspecting, they followed him right into a trap. As they had attempted to trick Jehoram and capture him, now he had captured them! Thus they were punished according to their own wickedness.

When Elisha called upon G-d to blind the soldiers, he did not mention G-d's name, but when he prayed that they be cured he did. It is not proper that G-d's name be associated with evil and curses.[25]

6:21-23 וַיֹּאמֶר מֶלֶךְ־יִשְׂרָאֵל אֶל־אֱלִישָׁע כִּרְאֹתוֹ אוֹתָם הַאַכֶּה אַכֶּה אָבִי׃
וַיֹּאמֶר לֹא תַכֶּה הַאֲשֶׁר שָׁבִיתָ בְּחַרְבְּךָ וּבְקַשְׁתְּךָ אַתָּה מַכֶּה שִׂים לֶחֶם וָמַיִם
לִפְנֵיהֶם וְיֹאכְלוּ וְיִשְׁתּוּ וְיֵלְכוּ אֶל־אֲדֹנֵיהֶם׃ וַיִּכְרֶה לָהֶם כֵּרָה גְדוֹלָה וַיֹּאכְלוּ
וַיִּשְׁתּוּ וַיְשַׁלְּחֵם וַיֵּלְכוּ אֶל־אֲדֹנֵיהֶם וְלֹא־יָסְפוּ עוֹד גְּדוּדֵי אֲרָם לָבוֹא בְּאֶרֶץ
יִשְׂרָאֵל׃

The King of Israel said to Elisha when he saw them, "Shall I indeed smite them, Oh my father?" He said, "Don't smite! Are they captives that you took with your sword and your bow, that you would smite them? Put bread and water before them. They will eat and drink and go to their master." He prepared a great feast for them. They ate and drank and he sent them, and they went to their master. The bands of Aram didn't continue to come to the Land of Israel any more.

At that moment, Jehoram had great respect for Elisha. He called him "father" and would not make a move without his approval. Like Ahab, Jehoram vacillated between piety and wickedness. His attitude depended upon the situation.

Elisha did not want to destroy the soldiers of Aram, even though they were his enemies and the enemies of Israel. It would be far better to impress them with G-d's greatness, and also with His mercy. Perhaps, like Naaman, some of them would reject idolatry and serve G-d alone.

Nor was he afraid that by letting them free they might come and attack Israel again in the future. Indeed, they might, but as G-d had saved Israel this time, so He would again. Only a great prophet like Elisha could make such a decision, for he was guided by divine revelation, not his own judgment. He knew that G-d had not condemned the soldiers of Aram to death, so he would not let Jehoram kill them.

He said, "Had G-d given them over into your hand in war, it would have been a sign that they were to be killed, as is customary for those taken in battle. But these were captured by means of a miracle, and it is G-d's will that they be treated mercifully and freed."

The word "כרה," "feast," is an expression of peace.[26] Jehoram didn't just give them a little food so that they would not go home hungry. He made a feast to celebrate the new peace that was to be established between the two peoples.[27]

King Solomon said,[28] "Wisdom is better than weapons of war." The wisdom of Elisha helped Israel more than all the wars of Jehoram.[29]

Revealing the hiding places of Aram was Elisha's thirteenth miracle, and capturing the army his fourteenth. These miracles involved sight and knowledge. They demonstrated that G-d sees and knows all, and that it is through Him alone that man is able to perceive and understand.

6:24 וַיְהִי אַחֲרֵי־כֵן וַיִּקְבֹּץ בֶּן־הֲדַד מֶלֶךְ־אֲרָם אֶת־כָּל־מַחֲנֵהוּ וַיַּעַל וַיָּצַר עַל־שֹׁמְרוֹן׃

Afterwards, Ben-hadad, the King of Aram, gathered his whole camp and went up and besieged Samaria.

But Aram still didn't understand that even a full scale campaign would fail if it were against G-d's will. They thought it was only ambushes and raids that were doomed to failure.[30] Nor were they impressed by Elisha's mercy. Though he had fed them and let them free, they were not ashamed to besiege Samaria and starve the people to death.

6:25 וַיְהִי רָעָב גָּדוֹל בְּשֹׁמְרוֹן וְהִנֵּה צָרִים עָלֶיהָ עַד הֱיוֹת רֹאשׁ־חֲמוֹר בִּשְׁמֹנִים כֶּסֶף וְרֹבַע הַקַּב חרי יונים (דִּבְיוֹנִים קרי) בַּחֲמִשָּׁה כָסֶף׃

There was a great famine in Samaria, and now they were besieging it! It reached the point that the head of a donkey cost eighty pieces of silver, and a fourth of a kab of pigeon droppings cost fifty pieces of silver.

This was the terrible seven year famine described by the prophet Joel.[31] The first year they ate the food they had stored in their houses, the second what was in the fields, the third they ate the kosher animals, the fourth the unclean animals, the fifth the insects and crawling things, the sixth the flesh of their children, and the seventh their own flesh. Thus the prophet Isaiah said,[32] "Each person eats the flesh of his own arm."[33] Nor did they have wood to cook with. They used dung instead, and when that was used up, even bird droppings became scarce.

6:26,27 וַיְהִי מֶלֶךְ יִשְׂרָאֵל עֹבֵר עַל־הַחֹמָה וְאִשָּׁה צָעֲקָה אֵלָיו לֵאמֹר הוֹשִׁיעָה אֲדֹנִי הַמֶּלֶךְ׃ וַיֹּאמֶר אַל־יוֹשִׁעֵךְ ה׳ מֵאַיִן אוֹשִׁיעֵךְ הֲמִן־הַגֹּרֶן אוֹ מִן־הַיָּקֶב׃

The King of Israel was passing by on the wall and a woman cried out to him saying, "Help, my master, the king!" He said, "If G-d will not help you, from where can I help you? From the threshing-floor or from the winepress?"

Throughout the siege, Jehoram used to walk along the top of the wall to inspect the troops defending the city.[34] It was on one such tour that the woman approached him. At first he thought she was begging him for food. He was forced to admit his helplessness. He said, "My own storerooms are empty. What can I do for my people?"[35]

6:28,29 וַיֹּאמֶר־לָהּ הַמֶּלֶךְ מַה־לָּךְ וַתֹּאמֶר הָאִשָּׁה הַזֹּאת אָמְרָה אֵלַי תְּנִי אֶת־בְּנֵךְ וְנֹאכְלֶנּוּ הַיּוֹם וְאֶת־בְּנִי נֹאכַל מָחָר׃ וַנְּבַשֵּׁל אֶת־בְּנִי וַנֹּאכְלֵהוּ וָאֹמַר אֵלֶיהָ בַּיּוֹם הָאַחֵר תְּנִי אֶת־בְּנֵךְ וְנֹאכְלֶנּוּ וַתַּחְבִּא אֶת־בְּנָהּ׃

The king said to her, "What's the matter?" The woman said, "This one said to me, 'Give your son and we will eat him today, and my son will we eat tomorrow.' So we cooked my son and ate him. I said to her the next day, 'Give your son and we will eat him!' but she has hidden her son."

Although he had failed as protector of his people and provider, Jehoram still functioned as lawgiver and judge. So, after his initial response of hopelessness, he asked the woman what her problem was. Perhaps he would be able to help her anyway. When he heard her terrible dilemma he was shocked. The warning of the Torah had been fulfilled, as it says,[36] "You will eat the fruit of your womb, the flesh of your sons and your daughters, that the L-rd, your G-d, has given you, in the siege and in the dire straits into which your enemies will put you."

Some say the other woman's child was still alive, and she was hiding him to save his life.[37] What could Jehoram do? Ordinarily, the case would have been clear. The other woman had made an agreement and now she had to abide by it. But this was murder. The Torah permits the eating of forbidden foods to save one's life, as well as the violation of most other laws, but not murder.[38] The other woman had the right, even the obligation, to protect her son.

Others say the child had already been slaughtered and prepared, but she still refused to share it.[39]

6:30 וַיְהִי כִשְׁמֹעַ הַמֶּלֶךְ אֶת־דִּבְרֵי הָאִשָּׁה וַיִּקְרַע אֶת־בְּגָדָיו וְהוּא עֹבֵר עַל־הַחֹמָה וַיַּרְא הָעָם וְהִנֵּה הַשַּׂק עַל־בְּשָׂרוֹ מִבָּיִת:

When the king heard the woman's words he tore his clothes. Then, when he was passing by on the wall the people saw, and behold, there was sackcloth on his skin on the inside!

Only when Jehoram tore his clothes did the people see that he had already been mourning and praying for forgiveness. He recognized all along that it was his sins and the sins of the people that had brought this tragedy upon them. He repented and put on sackcloth, accepting this suffering upon himself as an atonement. But he was afraid that the people would despair if they found out, so he put on his royal garments on top. Now that they were torn, everyone saw the sackcloth underneath.[40]

Even though Jehoram had put on sackcloth, G-d had ignored his prayers until now. But publicly tearing his clothes was different. It was an act of total resignation to G-d's will. What good was it to pretend to be strong? Only G-d could save them. As soon as he did that, G-d saw and answered him, as we will soon see.

Jehoram's dress reflected his personality. Outwardly he was wicked, but in his heart he was righteous. He feared G-d and recognized that everything was in G-d's hands. He would have liked to keep G-d's commandments, but was unwilling to commit himself to a righteous life, lest he be forced to sacrifice honor and physical pleasure. So he hid his righteousness beneath a show of strength and self-confidence.

An important person like a king, or even a great scholar or communal leader, may not conduct himself like an ordinary person. He must maintain the dignity of his position. He is forbidden to wear sackcloth unless he is sure that he will be answered as Jehoram was, for if he puts on sackcloth and is not answered, he will be disgraced. People will take his failure as a sign that he is not worthy of his position. They may even suspect him of having committed some unknown sin.[41]

6:31 וַיֹּאמֶר כֹּה־יַעֲשֶׂה־לִּי אֱלֹהִים וְכֹה יֹסִף אִם־יַעֲמֹד רֹאשׁ אֱלִישָׁע
בֶּן־שָׁפָט עָלָיו הַיּוֹם׃

He said, "Thus may G-d do to me and more, if the head of Elisha ben Shaphat will stand on him today!"

But even as he repented and prayed for mercy, Jehoram tried to cast off the blame and put it on G-d and his prophets. He said, "It is Elisha's fault that we are suffering this way! He was the one who reprimanded us. He called upon G-d and proclaimed this famine. Had he left us alone G-d would have forgiven us. But he made an issue of our sins, and now we are being punished!" Thus again we see how the wicked refuse to take responsibility for their own actions. They turn their heads and will not see that they have brought the suffering upon themselves. Instead, they blame the very ones who try to save them.

Elijah, too, had proclaimed a drought, but after three years he prayed that the people be forgiven. Then it rained again. Elisha was not so easy with them. The famine he had proclaimed was now in its seventh year, yet he had not relented, even when the people were forced to eat their own children![42]

Jehoram also remembered the mercy Elisha had had him show the army of Aram when they were in his hands. He said, "Had I killed them then rather than letting them go, none of this would have happened. It's all Elisha's fault!"[43]

Some say the words "Thus may G-d do to me and more" refer to the woman and her child. Jehoram swore, "May I too kill my own child, and do even worse to myself, if I fail to take vengeance on Elisha!"[44]

6:32 וֶאֱלִישָׁע יֹשֵׁב בְּבֵיתוֹ וְהַזְּקֵנִים יֹשְׁבִים אִתּוֹ וַיִּשְׁלַח אִישׁ מִלְּפָנָיו
בְּטֶרֶם יָבֹא הַמַּלְאָךְ אֵלָיו וְהוּא אָמַר אֶל־הַזְּקֵנִים הַרְאִיתֶם כִּי־שָׁלַח בֶּן־הַמְרַצֵּחַ

הַזֶּה לְהָסִיר אֶת־רֹאשִׁי רְאוּ כְּבֹא הַמַּלְאָךְ סִגְרוּ הַדֶּלֶת וּלְחַצְתֶּם אֹתוֹ בַּדֶּלֶת
הֲלוֹא קוֹל רַגְלֵי אֲדֹנָיו אַחֲרָיו׃

Elisha was sitting in his house and the elders were sitting with him. He sent a man before him. Before the messenger came to him, he said to the elders, "Do you see that this son of a murderer has sent to take off my head? Look when the messenger comes. Close the door and push him out with the door. Indeed, the sound of his master's feet is after him!"

The words, "He sent a man before him" refer to Jehoram sending his messenger. Some say Jehoram didn't really want to kill Elisha, so he sent the messenger ahead to warn the prophet and ask him to relent. If he did and the people were saved, no harm would come to him. But if he was stubborn and refused, he would suffer the king's wrath. Jehoram himself followed close behind him, planning to hide so that he could overhear Elisha's answer.[45]

All this was revealed to Elisha even before the messenger arrived. He said, "Lock the door and don't let him in. I will speak to the king himself, for I know that soon he will be here too. I want to publicize G-d's word in his presence. It doesn't matter whether the messenger gets angry, because once he hears the good news I have to report he will be appeased."[46]

Others say the messenger was sent to kill him.[47] Elisha said to him, "That's not the way to save yourselves. You won't make things any better by killing me. The only thing to do is repent and pray for forgiveness."[48]

Elisha referred to Jehoram as the son of a murderer, alluding to Ahab's murder of Naboth.[49] He said, "The evil traits of the father have been inherited by the son. When he cannot have his way, he vents his anger on the innocent."[50]

6:33 עוֹדֶנּוּ מְדַבֵּר עִמָּם וְהִנֵּה הַמַּלְאָךְ יֹרֵד אֵלָיו וַיֹּאמֶר הִנֵּה־זֹאת הָרָעָה
מֵאֵת ה׳ מָה־אוֹחִיל לַה׳ עוֹד׃

He was still speaking with them and there was the messenger coming down to him. He said, "Behold, this evil is from G-d. Why should I pray to G-d any more?"

Some say that these are the words of the messenger. He said, "If this were a natural occurrence, it might help to ask G-d to intervene and save us. But as it is the will of G-d himself, what use is it to pray? He has decided to punish us, and there is no point in asking Him to change His mind. He is not like a human being, who can be persuaded."[51]

Others say they are the words of the king. Elisha didn't open the door until he arrived. Then he let him in together with his messenger.[52]

Or they may be the words of the prophet himself. He said, "Why have you come to ask me to pray for you? You know that this is a divine punishment for your sins. If you don't repent, what good will my prayers do?"

II KINGS 7

7:1 וַיֹּאמֶר אֱלִישָׁע שִׁמְעוּ דְּבַר־ה׳ כֹּה אָמַר ה׳ כָּעֵת מָחָר סְאָה־
סֹלֶת בְּשֶׁקֶל וְסָאתַיִם שְׂעֹרִים בְּשֶׁקֶל בְּשַׁעַר שֹׁמְרוֹן:

Elisha said, "Listen to the word of G-d. Thus says G-d, 'At this time tomorrow a measure of fine flour will cost one shekel and two measures of barley will cost one shekel at the gate of Samaria.'"

Elisha said, "G-d never turns a deaf ear to our prayers. When we are not answered, it is because we ourselves are not worthy of an answer. It is not that G-d did not hear us, or has made up His mind and cannot be influenced. On the contrary, it is He Who has our best interests in mind. We are the ones who are to blame for our troubles, as it says,[1] 'A man's own foolishness perverts his way. Then against G-d does his heart rant.'

"Had the people sincerely repented, their prayers would have been answered. But G-d, Who sees what is in the heart of every man, knows that despite your suffering you have not given up your evil ways. Once you are relieved, you will quickly return to them. You therefore do not deserve to be saved.

"However, G-d will have mercy on you despite your sins. You have questioned His kindness, so now He will prove it to you. Tomorrow the siege and the famine will both be over in a most dramatic way."

The relief is described in terms similar to those used earlier to describe the famine itself. Above it says that "the head of a donkey cost eighty pieces of silver, and a fourth of a kab of pigeon droppings cost fifty pieces of silver." In contrast, it says here, "a measure of fine flour will cost one shekel and two measures of barley will cost one shekel."

7:2 וַיַּעַן הַשָּׁלִישׁ אֲשֶׁר־לַמֶּלֶךְ נִשְׁעָן עַל־יָדוֹ אֶת־אִישׁ הָאֱלֹהִים וַיֹּאמַר
הִנֵּה ה׳ עֹשֶׂה אֲרֻבּוֹת בַּשָּׁמַיִם הֲיִהְיֶה הַדָּבָר הַזֶּה וַיֹּאמֶר הִנְּכָה רֹאֶה בְּעֵינֶיךָ
וּמִשָּׁם לֹא תֹאכֵל:

The officer upon whose hand the king was leaning answered the man of G-d and said, "Even if G-d makes windows in the sky, would this thing happen?" He said, "Behold, you will see with your eyes, but from there will you not eat."

To think that it is hopeless to pray is a mistake, but to question G-d's ability is a sin. The officer would be punished accordingly, by being denied a part in G-d's blessing. His sin was all the worse because Elisha's prophecy had not been directed to him at all, but to the king. He showed his lack of respect for the prophet by interrupting him.[2]

7:3,4 וְאַרְבָּעָה אֲנָשִׁים הָיוּ מְצֹרָעִים פֶּתַח הַשָּׁעַר וַיֹּאמְרוּ אִישׁ אֶל־רֵעֵהוּ מָה אֲנַחְנוּ יֹשְׁבִים פֹּה עַד־מָתְנוּ׃ אִם־אָמַרְנוּ נָבוֹא הָעִיר וְהָרָעָב בָּעִיר וָמַתְנוּ שָׁם וְאִם־יָשַׁבְנוּ פֹה וָמָתְנוּ וְעַתָּה לְכוּ וְנִפְּלָה אֶל־מַחֲנֵה אֲרָם אִם־יְחַיֻּנוּ נִחְיֶה וְאִם־יְמִיתֻנוּ וָמָתְנוּ׃

There were four men who were lepers at the door of the gate. They said to one another, "Why are we sitting here until we are dead? If we decide to go into the city, there is famine in the city and we are dead there. If we sit here we're dead. Now go, and we'll fall upon the camp of Aram. If they let us live we'll live, and if they kill us we're dead."

The four men were Gehazi and his three sons.[3] It was in the last year of the famine that Naaman had come to Elisha and Gehazi had been cursed.[4] Being lepers, they were not permitted to live within the city, as it says in the Torah,[5] "Outside of the camp will be his dwelling-place." This law only applies to those cities that were already surrounded by walls at the time of Joshua. Samaria was not one of them. It was built by King Omri, Ahab's father. However, the kings of Israel wanted to enhance the status of their capital and make it appear ancient and important, so they excluded lepers, enforcing this law even in time of severe famine. Some praise them for this, because it showed their dedication to those laws of Torah that they had not rejected.[6]

Nonetheless, when their situation became desparate, the lepers discussed the possibility of being permitted in anyway. Perhaps the people would be so busy with the siege and the famine that they wouldn't notice them. Or perhaps they would let them in to save them from being captured, because saving a life takes precedence over the other commandments.[7]

But, seeing that they would be no better off inside, they decided to put themselves at the mercy of the enemy. From this we see that if a person is sure that he will die otherwise, he may place himself in the hands of heathens, for instance, by entrusting himself to the care of a heathen doctor. But if he thinks he might live without their help, it is forbidden.[8]

To these lepers, the situation seemed so hopeless that they felt as if they were dead already. When discussing death, they used the past tense, "ומתנו," "we're dead," or "we have died." To actually die wouldn't make much difference. But when discussing the possibility of saving their lives, they used the future, "נחיה," "we will live." To be saved would almost be like being revived from the dead.[9]

7:5 וַיָּקֻמוּ בַנֶּשֶׁף לָבוֹא אֶל־מַחֲנֵה אֲרָם וַיָּבֹאוּ עַד־קְצֵה מַחֲנֵה אֲרָם
וְהִנֵּה אֵין־שָׁם אִישׁ׃

They got up at twilight to come to the camp of Aram. They came to the edge of the camp of Aram, and behold, there was no one there!

Why did they wait till night to go? Some say they were afraid that the other Jews would kill them if they saw them going. They would say, "If the Arameans find out how bad the famine is, they will attack right away. No one may go to their camp!"[10] Others say it was to prevent the Arameans from shooting at them as they approached. Or perhaps so that the Arameans would not see that they were lepers, for if they did, they might refuse to let them in.[11]

7:6,7 וַאדֹנָי הִשְׁמִיעַ אֶת־מַחֲנֵה אֲרָם קוֹל רֶכֶב קוֹל סוּס קוֹל חַיִל גָּדוֹל
וַיֹּאמְרוּ אִישׁ אֶל־אָחִיו הִנֵּה שָׂכַר־עָלֵינוּ מֶלֶךְ יִשְׂרָאֵל אֶת־מַלְכֵי הַחִתִּים
וְאֶת־מַלְכֵי מִצְרַיִם לָבוֹא עָלֵינוּ׃ וַיָּקוּמוּ וַיָּנוּסוּ בַנֶּשֶׁף וַיַּעַזְבוּ אֶת־אָהֳלֵיהֶם
וְאֶת־סוּסֵיהֶם וְאֶת־חֲמֹרֵיהֶם הַמַּחֲנֶה כַּאֲשֶׁר הִיא וַיָּנֻסוּ אֶל־נַפְשָׁם׃

For G-d had made the camp of Aram hear the sound of chariots, the sound of horses, and the sound of a great army. They had said to one another, "Behold, the King of Israel has hired the kings of the Hittites and the kings of the Egyptians to come against us!" They got up and ran away at twilight. They abandoned their tents, their horses and their donkeys, the camp as it was, and ran for their lives.

Where did this terrible noise come from? It was the sound of the plague of hail with which G-d had smitten the Egyptians in the time of Moses. When, at Pharaoh's request, Moses prayed that the plague stop, the hailstones and noise were suspended in mid-air. The stones remained there until the time of Joshua, when they came down and smote the Emorites.[12] The terrible noise remained until now, at the time of Jehoram, when it was released to frighten Aram.[13]

The Arameans were so confused that they didn't even take the time to saddle their horses. They could have gone much faster on horseback, but in their panic they left them and fled on foot.[14]

7:8,9 וַיָּבֹאוּ הַמְצֹרָעִים הָאֵלֶּה עַד־קְצֵה הַמַּחֲנֶה וַיָּבֹאוּ אֶל־אֹהֶל אֶחָד
וַיֹּאכְלוּ וַיִּשְׁתּוּ וַיִּשְׂאוּ מִשָּׁם כֶּסֶף וְזָהָב וּבְגָדִים וַיֵּלְכוּ וַיַּטְמִנוּ וַיָּשֻׁבוּ וַיָּבֹאוּ
אֶל־אֹהֶל אַחֵר וַיִּשְׂאוּ מִשָּׁם וַיֵּלְכוּ וַיַּטְמִנוּ׃ וַיֹּאמְרוּ אִישׁ אֶל־רֵעֵהוּ לֹא־כֵן
אֲנַחְנוּ עֹשִׂים הַיּוֹם הַזֶּה יוֹם־בְּשֹׂרָה הוּא וַאֲנַחְנוּ מַחְשִׁים וְחִכִּינוּ עַד־אוֹר הַבֹּקֶר
וּמְצָאָנוּ עָווֹן וְעַתָּה לְכוּ וְנָבֹאָה וְנַגִּידָה בֵּית הַמֶּלֶךְ׃

These lepers came to the edge of the camp. They came into one tent and ate and drank. They carried away silver and gold and clothes and went and hid them. Then they went back and came into another tent, carried away and went and hid. They said to one another, "It's not right, what we are doing. Today is a day of good news, and we are keeping quiet. If we wait until daylight, sin will overtake us. So now, let us go and arrive and tell the house of the king."

Gehazi and his sons had not abandoned their greedy ways, even after suffering the terrible punishment of leprosy. They could not resist the temptation of enriching themselves with the loot they found.[15] But when they had relieved their hunger and overcome the initial exhilaration, they remembered the other people still starving in the city.

Some say it was not just their sense of obligation and concern for the others. They knew that if they did not bring the news now, it would be discovered sooner or later anyway. Then they would be condemned for having kept it a secret. They would certainly be punished for such shameful selfishness, so they hurried to tell the news before it was too late.[16]

7:10-12 וַיָּבֹאוּ וַיִּקְרְאוּ אֶל־שֹׁעֵר הָעִיר וַיַּגִּידוּ לָהֶם לֵאמֹר בָּאנוּ אֶל־מַחֲנֵה
אֲרָם וְהִנֵּה אֵין־שָׁם אִישׁ וְקוֹל אָדָם כִּי אִם־הַסּוּס אָסוּר וְהַחֲמוֹר אָסוּר וְאֹהָלִים
כַּאֲשֶׁר־הֵמָּה׃ וַיִּקְרָא הַשֹּׁעֲרִים וַיַּגִּידוּ בֵּית הַמֶּלֶךְ פְּנִימָה׃ וַיָּקָם הַמֶּלֶךְ לַיְלָה
וַיֹּאמֶר אֶל־עֲבָדָיו אַגִּידָה־נָּא לָכֶם אֵת אֲשֶׁר־עָשׂוּ לָנוּ אֲרָם יָדְעוּ כִּי־רְעֵבִים
אֲנַחְנוּ וַיֵּצְאוּ מִן־הַמַּחֲנֶה לְהֵחָבֵה בהשדה (בַשָּׂדֶה קרי) לֵאמֹר כִּי־יֵצְאוּ
מִן־הָעִיר וְנִתְפְּשֵׂם חַיִּים וְאֶל־הָעִיר נָבֹא׃

They came and called out to the gatekeepers of the city and told them saying, "We came to the camp of Aram, and behold, there is no one there, nor human voice! Just the horses tied up and the donkeys tied up, and the tents as they were!" The gatekeepers called and told the house of the king inside. The king got up at night and said to his servants, "Let me tell you, please, what Aram has done to us. They know that we are hungry, and went out of the camp to hide in the field, saying, 'When they go out of the city we will capture them alive, and come into the city!' "

Though Jehoram had heard Elisha's prophecy, he did not believe they had really been saved. He was sure it was a trick.[17]

7:13 וַיַּעַן אֶחָד מֵעֲבָדָיו וַיֹּאמֶר וְיִקְחוּ־נָא חֲמִשָּׁה מִן־הַסּוּסִים הַנִּשְׁאָרִים
אֲשֶׁר נִשְׁאֲרוּ־בָהּ הִנָּם כְּכָל־ההמון (הֲמוֹן קרי) יִשְׂרָאֵל אֲשֶׁר נִשְׁאֲרוּ־בָהּ הִנָּם
כְּכָל־הֲמוֹן יִשְׂרָאֵל אֲשֶׁר־תָּמּוּ וְנִשְׁלְחָה וְנִרְאֶה׃

One of his servants answered and said, "Please, let them take five of the remaining horses that are left in it. Behold, they are like all of the masses of Israel that are left in it! Behold, they are like all of masses of Israel that are finished off! Let us send and see!"

The king's servant reasoned as the lepers had, that there was no point in worrying about their lives, since they were dying anyway. Nor did it matter whether they lost a few horses, since they too were weak and near death.

He repeated the words, "they are like all the masses of Israel" to indicate that, one way or another, horses and men would share the same fate. They said, "If they go and are killed by the Arameans, they will be no worse than the rest of us who remain behind and die of starvation. And if they do not go, they will starve along with the rest of us, so they will be no better off for our caution."[18]

7:14 וַיִּקְחוּ שְׁנֵי רֶכֶב סוּסִים וַיִּשְׁלַח הַמֶּלֶךְ אַחֲרֵי מַחֲנֵה־אֲרָם לֵאמֹר לְכוּ
וּרְאוּ׃

They took two chariots of horses, and the king sent after the camp of Aram saying, "Go and see."

The king agreed to let them go, but only allowed them two horses, not five. He said, "Two is all you need to go and investigate."[19]

7:15 וַיֵּלְכוּ אַחֲרֵיהֶם עַד־הַיַּרְדֵּן וְהִנֵּה כָל־הַדֶּרֶךְ מְלֵאָה בְגָדִים וְכֵלִים
אֲשֶׁר־הִשְׁלִיכוּ אֲרָם בהחפזם (בְּחָפְזָם קרי) וַיָּשֻׁבוּ הַמַּלְאָכִים וַיַּגִּדוּ לַמֶּלֶךְ׃

They went after them until the Jordan, and behold, the whole way was full of clothes and utensils that Aram had thrown away in their haste. The messengers returned and told the king.

When they saw the road strewn with clothes and other valuable things all the way to the Jordan, they knew it was not a trick. Even Aram would not have gone to such lengths to fool them.

7:16 וַיֵּצֵא הָעָם וַיָּבֹזּוּ אֵת מַחֲנֵה אֲרָם וַיְהִי סְאָה־סֹלֶת בְּשֶׁקֶל וְסָאתַיִם
שְׂעֹרִים בְּשֶׁקֶל כִּדְבַר ה׳׃

The people went out and looted the camp of Aram. Then it

was that a measure of fine flour was one shekel and two measures of barley one shekel, like the word of G-d.

When the people heard the news they rushed out in complete disorder.[20] Each one took for himself and his family. You can imagine their excitement, having been without food for so long!

7:17 וְהַמֶּלֶךְ הִפְקִיד אֶת־הַשָּׁלִישׁ אֲשֶׁר־נִשְׁעָן עַל־יָדוֹ עַל־הַשַּׁעַר וַיִּרְמְסֻהוּ
הָעָם בַּשַּׁעַר וַיָּמֹת כַּאֲשֶׁר דִּבֶּר אִישׁ הָאֱלֹהִים אֲשֶׁר דִּבֶּר בְּרֶדֶת הַמֶּלֶךְ אֵלָיו׃

The king appointed the officer upon whose hand he had leaned to be in charge of the gate. The people trampled him at the gate and he died, as the man of G-d had said, who spoke when the king came down to him.

The officer tried to establish some order in the mob that was rushing out through the gate, but no one paid any attention to him. When he tried to stand in the way of the starving masses they pushed him down and he was trampled.[21]

Some say Jehoram claimed that all the spoils belonged to him. The officer tried to force the people to bring it to the royal treasury instead of taking it for themselves, but they ignored him.[22]

Even then, it was his own fault. Had he gone along with the people instead of staying stubbornly at his post, he too would have enjoyed G-d's blessing and been saved. But he was still unwilling to accept the prophet's words and the divine kindness that he had foretold.

The thing the wicked find hardest to accept is that G-d is the ultimate and absolute ruler of everything in the world. They desperately want to feel that they themselves are in control, at least in a small way. So they oppose not only divine punishment, but divine blessing as well, for the one implies the other. Both are beyond man's control, coming to him whether he agrees or not. So the wicked sometimes prefer to suffer hunger and deprivation a little longer to prove that they themselves have control over when they obtain their desires, and it is not just up to G-d. In that way they imagine they can establish that they are able to prevent suffering as well.

7:18-20 וַיְהִי כְּדַבֵּר אִישׁ הָאֱלֹהִים אֶל־הַמֶּלֶךְ לֵאמֹר סָאתַיִם שְׂעֹרִים בְּשֶׁקֶל
וּסְאָה־סֹלֶת בְּשֶׁקֶל יִהְיֶה כָּעֵת מָחָר בְּשַׁעַר שֹׁמְרוֹן׃ וַיַּעַן הַשָּׁלִישׁ אֶת־אִישׁ
הָאֱלֹהִים וַיֹּאמַר וְהִנֵּה ה׳ עֹשֶׂה אֲרֻבּוֹת בַּשָּׁמַיִם הֲיִהְיֶה כַּדָּבָר הַזֶּה וַיֹּאמֶר הִנְּךָ
רֹאֶה בְּעֵינֶיךָ וּמִשָּׁם לֹא תֹאכֵל׃ וַיְהִי־לוֹ כֵּן וַיִּרְמְסוּ אֹתוֹ הָעָם בַּשַּׁעַר וַיָּמֹת׃

For it had been, that when the man of G-d had said to the king saying, "Two measures of barley for a shekel and one measure of fine flour for a shekel will it be at this time tomorrow, at the gate of Samaria," the officer answered the man of G-d and said, "Even if G-d makes windows in the sky, would such a thing happen?" He said, "Behold, you will see with your eyes, but you won't eat from it." So did it happen to him. The people trampled him at the gate and he died.

The Bible retells the sin of the officer to emphasize that his death was a divine punishment. It also specifically mentions that it was "when the king came down" to Elisha. The king himself had gone down humbly, ready to accept Elisha's words, but the officer remained firm and stubborn. By mocking the prophet he influenced Jehoram to return to his wickedness. His punishment was therefore particularly harsh.[23]

Saving Israel by frightening the Arameans with the terrible noise was Elisha's fifteenth miracle. It is compared to the rain that Elijah brought at Mount Carmel. His sixteenth miracle was the death of the officer, comparable to the death of the troops that had come to arrest Elijah. Bringing the famine is considered Elisha's seventeenth miracle, even though it was performed before these, because it is not attributed to him until the beginning of the next chapter.

II KINGS 8

8:1,2 וֶאֱלִישָׁע דִּבֶּר אֶל־הָאִשָּׁה אֲשֶׁר־הֶחֱיָה אֶת־בְּנָהּ לֵאמֹר קוּמִי וּלְכִי
אתי (אַתְּ קרי) וּבֵיתֵךְ וְגוּרִי בַּאֲשֶׁר תָּגוּרִי כִּי־קָרָא ה׳ לָרָעָב וְגַם־בָּא אֶל־הָאָרֶץ
שֶׁבַע שָׁנִים׃ וַתָּקָם הָאִשָּׁה וַתַּעַשׂ כִּדְבַר אִישׁ הָאֱלֹהִים וַתֵּלֶךְ הִיא וּבֵיתָהּ וַתָּגָר
בְּאֶרֶץ־פְּלִשְׁתִּים שֶׁבַע שָׁנִים׃

Elisha spoke to the woman whose son he had revived saying, "Get up and go, you and your household, and live wherever you want to live, for G-d has declared a famine, and it has also come to the land for seven years." The woman got up and did according to the word of the man of G-d. She went, she and her household, and lived in the land of the Philistines for seven years.

It was G-d Himself who declared the famine, and Elisha only informed the people of the divine declaration. For there are three things that are declared by G-d Himself: famine, plenty, and a worthy leader who provides for the needs of the community.[1]

As was mentioned above, this was the terrible seven-year famine described by the prophet Joel.[2] The righteous woman who had helped Elisha was spared the suffering of the years of famine and siege. Before the famine began, Elisha warned her to take her family out of the territory of Jehoram, for the rest of the land would not be affected. This was not mentioned above, even though it happened before the siege, because it was not significant there. Only upon her return does the Bible discuss it.

Incidentally, this verse indicates that it was indeed by Elisha's word that the famine had been declared, as Jehoram said.[3]

8:3,4 וַיְהִי מִקְצֵה שֶׁבַע שָׁנִים וַתָּשָׁב הָאִשָּׁה מֵאֶרֶץ פְּלִשְׁתִּים וַתֵּצֵא לִצְעֹק

אֶל־הַמֶּלֶךְ אֶל־בֵּיתָהּ וְאֶל־שָׂדָהּ׃ וְהַמֶּלֶךְ מְדַבֵּר אֶל־גֵּחֲזִי נַעַר אִישׁ־הָאֱלֹהִים
לֵאמֹר סַפְּרָה־נָּא לִי אֵת כָּל־הַגְּדֹלוֹת אֲשֶׁר־עָשָׂה אֱלִישָׁע׃

At the end of seven years the woman returned from the land of the Philistines, and went out to cry out to the king about her house and about her field. The king was talking with Gehazi, the servant of the man of G-d, saying, "Please tell me all the great things that Elisha did."

Jehoram feared Elisha because he was so holy and righteous. He felt Elisha's very presence as a rebuke, until he came to hate and scorn him. But he felt comfortable with Gehazi, because, like Jehoram himself, he exhibited both good and bad qualities. So, having been rejected by his teacher, Gehazi came to win the favor of the king.

8:5 וַיְהִי הוּא מְסַפֵּר לַמֶּלֶךְ אֵת אֲשֶׁר־הֶחֱיָה אֶת־הַמֵּת וְהִנֵּה הָאִשָּׁה
אֲשֶׁר־הֶחֱיָה אֶת־בְּנָהּ צֹעֶקֶת אֶל־הַמֶּלֶךְ עַל־בֵּיתָהּ וְעַל־שָׂדָהּ וַיֹּאמֶר גֵּחֲזִי אֲדֹנִי
הַמֶּלֶךְ זֹאת הָאִשָּׁה וְזֶה־בְּנָהּ אֲשֶׁר־הֶחֱיָה אֱלִישָׁע׃

Just as he was telling the king how he had revived the dead, behold, there was the woman whose son he had revived crying out to the king about her house and about her field. Gehazi said, "My lord, the king, this is the woman and this is her son whom Elisha revived!"

As soon as Gehazi started to tell the king about the miracle, G-d brought the woman herself to tell him. G-d said, "The wicked Gehazi is not worthy of telling the world about My greatness!" Thus King David said,[4] "To the wicked, G-d said, 'What business have you recounting My laws, and carrying My covenant upon your mouth?'" So it was not a coincidence that she happened to be standing right outside and entered at that moment. Even had she been at the other end of the earth, G-d would have brought her there.[5]

When Elisha had offered to help the woman years earlier, she had responded, "I don't need anything. I live within my own people." For so pious a person, such self-confidence was improper. There is no security but in G-d, because He alone controls everything. When a person refuses an offer of help, he implies that he is self-sufficient, having need of neither man nor G-d. The truly G-dfearing should never speak that way. They should act humbly, admitting their complete dependence upon G-d. They should be ready to consider any offer of help, for perhaps it was sent especially for them.

It was therefore decreed that this woman eventually suffer for her words, and need the help of king and prophet that she had rejected. Now, upon her return home, she learned that she could not always rely upon the good will of her community. Her own family and friends, no doubt somewhat jealous that she had been spared suffering the years of famine, refused to defend her rights. She was forced to bring her case before the king.

Jehoram might not have been sympathetic to her cause either, had it not been for the divinely arranged introduction she received. But having just heard about the two impressive miracles that had been done for her, he responded with enthusiasm.

8:6 וַיִּשְׁאַל הַמֶּלֶךְ לָאִשָּׁה וַתְּסַפֶּר־לוֹ וַיִּתֶּן־לָהּ הַמֶּלֶךְ סָרִיס אֶחָד לֵאמֹר הָשֵׁיב אֶת־כָּל־אֲשֶׁר־לָהּ וְאֵת כָּל־תְּבוּאֹת הַשָּׂדֶה מִיּוֹם עָזְבָה אֶת־הָאָרֶץ וְעַד־עָתָּה׃

The king asked the woman and she told him. The king gave her one officer saying, "Return all that is hers, and all the crops of the field, from the day that she left the land until now."

The woman had only asked for her property back, but the king had them return even the produce of the years of her absence.

8:7 וַיָּבֹא אֱלִישָׁע דַּמֶּשֶׂק וּבֶן־הֲדַד מֶלֶךְ־אֲרָם חֹלֶה וַיֻּגַּד־לוֹ לֵאמֹר בָּא אִישׁ הָאֱלֹהִים עַד־הֵנָּה׃

Elisha came to Damascus, and Ben-hadad, the King of Aram, was sick. He was told saying, "The man of G-d has come here!"

Having been rejected by Elisha, Gehazi went from bad to worse. Finally he left the land of Israel to live in Aram. Elisha began to regret having treated him so harshly, and went to try to persuade him to return. He said, "Indeed you have sinned and been punished, but if you repent, G-d will forgive you. Please come back and be my student again. I will help you!"

"No," replied Gehazi, "even if I repent I will never be forgiven, for I have misled the people. One who misleads the people and brings them to sin can never repair the evil he has caused. Even if he stops sinning himself, those whom he has influenced continue. As he is partially responsible for their sins, he keeps accumulating guilt."

Gehazi's sin was to give credence to the golden calves made by Jeroboam, which had become the national cult of the Kingdom of Israel. Some say he secretly put a magnet into the body of the calf, causing it to float in the air. People saw and thought that it must really have divine power.

Others say he wrote the special name of G-d and put it in the calf's mouth. The calf began to speak and pronounced the first two commandments, "I am the L-rd, your G-d, who took you out of the land of Egypt. You will have no other gods before Me." When they heard that, everyone was convinced that G-d's presence really rested in the calves, as it did in the holy of holies in the Temple.[6]

8:8 וַיֹּאמֶר הַמֶּלֶךְ אֶל־חֲזָהאֵל קַח בְּיָדְךָ מִנְחָה וְלֵךְ לִקְרַאת אִישׁ .
הָאֱלֹהִים וְדָרַשְׁתָּ אֶת־ה׳ מֵאוֹתוֹ לֵאמֹר הַאֶחְיֶה מֵחֳלִי זֶה:

The king said to Hazael, "Take a present in your hand and go to meet the man of G-d. Ask of G-d from him saying, 'Will I recover from this illness?' "

When the King of Aram heard that Elisha was visiting his country, he immediately sent to inquire of him. Elisha was feared and respected by the people of Aram, for they had witnessed his miracles. And, though there was continual conflict between Aram and Israel, they did not see him as a personal enemy. He had performed miracles both for and against Aram, as he had for his own people, and had shown Aram mercy even when they tried to capture him.

8:9 וַיֵּלֶךְ חֲזָאֵל לִקְרָאתוֹ וַיִּקַּח מִנְחָה בְיָדוֹ וְכָל־טוּב דַּמֶּשֶׂק מַשָּׂא
אַרְבָּעִים גָּמָל וַיָּבֹא וַיַּעֲמֹד לְפָנָיו וַיֹּאמֶר בִּנְךָ בֶן־הֲדַד מֶלֶךְ־אֲרָם שְׁלָחַנִי אֵלֶיךָ
לֵאמֹר הַאֶחְיֶה מֵחֳלִי זֶה:

Hazael went to meet him. He took a present in his hand, and all the goodness of Damascus, a burden of forty camels. He came and stood before him and said, "Your son, Ben-hadad, King of Aram, has sent me to you saying, 'Will I recover from this illness?' "

Some say the present Hazael brought was a precious stone, equal in worth to the whole city. That is why it is referred to as, "all the goodness of Damascus."[7]

Others say it was a gift of food. The king remembered how Elisha had rejected Naaman's gifts, and knew that he would not accept money or valuable property. But food was different. Elisha had many needy students, and he was known to accept contributions for them.[8]

That explains why the gift was so bulky. Had it consisted of gold and silver, the burden of forty camels would have been an inordinately large gift, even for such a great prophet as Elisha. The king was, after all, only asking him to foretell the future. He did not expect the prophet to cure him, if, indeed, he was destined to die.

The expression "טוב," "goodness," is used to refer to food in other places as well, as in,[9] "I will give you the goodness of the land of Egypt, and they will eat the fat of the land," and[10] "the goodness of the land will you eat."[11]

8:10 וַיֹּאמֶר אֵלָיו אֱלִישָׁע לֵךְ אֱמָר־לא (לוֹ קרי) חָיֹה תִחְיֶה וְהִרְאַנִי ה׳
כִּי־מוֹת יָמוּת׃

Elisha said to him, "Go say to him, 'You will surely recover!' but G-d has shown me that he will surely die."

This verse is written, "לך אמר לא חיה תחיה," "Go say, 'You will surely not live!' " but it is read, "לך אמר לו חיה תחיה," "Go, say to him, 'You will surely live!' " The difference is the spelling of the word "לו." It is written "לא," "not," making it part of the message, "You will surely not recover," but it is read "לו," "to him," which makes it part of the instruction, "Say to him." This reveals the double meaning of Elisha's answer. He said, "If you wish, you may tell him the truth. In that case say, 'You will surely not live, for G-d has shown me that you will surely die!' But if you prefer, you may lie instead and tell him that he will live. Of what value will it be to cause him suffering? He will die in any case, so let his last days be happy ones! Knowing that he is destined to die might even make him die sooner! In that case, consider the words 'G-d has shown me that he will surely die' to be addressed to you alone."[12]

8:11 וַיַּעֲמֵד אֶת־פָּנָיו וַיָּשֶׂם עַד־בֹּשׁ וַיֵּבְךְּ אִישׁ הָאֱלֹהִים׃

He turned his face away for a long time, and the man of G-d cried.

But there was more to Elisha's vision than he had revealed, for he saw that Ben-hadad's death would be followed by terrible suffering for the Jewish People. He did not want to tell Hazael about that part, so he turned away and hid his face. But, as it became more and more vivid in his mind, he could control no longer himself and began to cry. Then Hazael knew something was the matter.[13]

8:12 וַיֹּאמֶר חֲזָאֵל מַדּוּעַ אֲדֹנִי בֹכֶה וַיֹּאמֶר כִּי יָדַעְתִּי אֵת אֲשֶׁר־תַּעֲשֶׂה
לִבְנֵי יִשְׂרָאֵל רָעָה מִבְצְרֵיהֶם תְּשַׁלַּח בָּאֵשׁ וּבַחֻרֵיהֶם בַּחֶרֶב תַּהֲרֹג וְעֹלְלֵיהֶם
תְּרַטֵּשׁ וְהָרֹתֵיהֶם תְּבַקֵּעַ׃

Hazael said, "Why is my master crying?" He said, "For I know that you will do evil to the Children of Israel. Their strongholds will you set afire, their young men by the sword will you kill, their babies will you dash to pieces and their pregnant women rip open."

At first, Hazael thought Elisha was crying over the king's impending death. He said, "Why are you, of all people, so upset about it? Ben-hadad has been the enemy of your people and caused them so much suffering!"[14]

Having been asked, Elisha had to tell the truth. He said, "It is not that at all, but another vision that I see. For you yourself will one day cause greater suffering to the Jewish People than your master ever did."

8:13 וַיֹּאמֶר חֲזָהאֵל כִּי מָה עַבְדְּךָ הַכֶּלֶב כִּי יַעֲשֶׂה הַדָּבָר הַגָּדוֹל הַזֶּה
וַיֹּאמֶר אֱלִישָׁע הִרְאַנִי ה׳ אֹתְךָ מֶלֶךְ עַל־אֲרָם׃

Hazael said, "What is your servant but a dog, that I do this great thing?" Elisha said, "G-d has shown you to me as King of Aram!"

Hazael could not understand how such a thing was even possible. He said, "I am in no position to do that! I am but a servant, like a dog who can only do his master's bidding."

Having been asked this obvious question, Elisha revealed yet another part of his prophecy. He said, "Though you are but a servant now, you will one day become king yourself!"[15]

8:14 וַיֵּלֶךְ מֵאֵת אֱלִישָׁע וַיָּבֹא אֶל־אֲדֹנָיו וַיֹּאמֶר לוֹ מָה־אָמַר לְךָ אֱלִישָׁע
וַיֹּאמֶר אָמַר לִי חָיֹה תִחְיֶה׃

He departed from Elisha and came to his master. He said to him, "What did Elisha say to you?" He said, "He said to me, 'You will surely live!' "

Hazael took Elisha's advice and concealed the truth from his master. Perhaps he also wanted to avoid being questioned about the rest of the prophecy. He could certainly not reveal that he himself had been designated as his successor, since that would lead the king to suspect him of conspiring against him.

8:15 וַיְהִי מִמָּחֳרָת וַיִּקַּח הַמַּכְבֵּר וַיִּטְבֹּל בַּמַּיִם וַיִּפְרֹשׂ עַל־פָּנָיו וַיָּמֹת
וַיִּמְלֹךְ חֲזָהאֵל תַּחְתָּיו׃

The next day he took the blanket and dipped it in water. He spread it on his face and he died. Then Hazael became king in his place.

Some say the king's death was an accident. Hazael was trying to relieve the king's fever, but the shock of the cold cloth was too much for him and he died.[16]

Others say he intentionally murdered him. Knowing that he was destined to become king, he felt no compunctions about hastening his master's death.[17]

Some say the word "מכבר" means a cloth, others a blanket or a pillow.[18]

8:16-19 וּבִשְׁנַת חָמֵשׁ לְיוֹרָם בֶּן־אַחְאָב מֶלֶךְ יִשְׂרָאֵל וִיהוֹשָׁפָט מֶלֶךְ יְהוּדָה מָלַךְ יְהוֹרָם בֶּן־יְהוֹשָׁפָט מֶלֶךְ יְהוּדָה: בֶּן־שְׁלֹשִׁים וּשְׁתַּיִם שָׁנָה הָיָה בְמָלְכוֹ וּשְׁמֹנֶה שנה (שָׁנִים קרי) מָלַךְ בִּירוּשָׁלָם: וַיֵּלֶךְ בְּדֶרֶךְ מַלְכֵי יִשְׂרָאֵל כַּאֲשֶׁר עָשׂוּ בֵּית אַחְאָב כִּי בַּת־אַחְאָב הָיְתָה־לּוֹ לְאִשָּׁה וַיַּעַשׂ הָרַע בְּעֵינֵי ה׳: וְלֹא־אָבָה ה׳ לְהַשְׁחִית אֶת־יְהוּדָה לְמַעַן דָּוִד עַבְדּוֹ כַּאֲשֶׁר אָמַר־לוֹ לָתֵת לוֹ נִיר וּלְבָנָיו כָּל־הַיָּמִים:

In the fifth year of Jehoram, son of Ahab, King of Israel, and Jehoshaphat, King of Judah, Jehoram, the son of Jehoshaphat, King of Judah, became king. He was thirty-two years old when he became king, and he reigned eight years in Jerusalem. He went in the way of the kings of Israel, as the house of Ahab had done, for his wife was the daughter of Ahab. He did what was evil in G-d's eyes. But G-d did not want to destroy Judah, for the sake of David, His servant, as He had said to him, to give a yoke to him and to his sons all the days.

This verse describes the beginning of the reign of Jehoram, King of Judah. He had already begun to share the throne with his father some seven years before, after the battle of Ramoth-gilead. Now, upon his father's death, he became the sole ruler.

During this period, the kings of Judah and Israel both had the same name, "Jehoram," sometimes written without the letter "ה," "Joram." Care must be taken not to confuse them. Sometimes they are identified as "Jehoram, son of Jehoshaphat" and "Jehoram, son of Ahab," or as "Jehoram, King of Judah" and "Jehoram, King of Israel." Elsewhere it is clear from context which is intended.

We will encounter similar confusion with the name "Jehoash" which was also borne by both a king of Judah and a king of Israel. That, too, has two spellings, "Jehoash" and "Joash," both used for both kings.

The words, "and Jehoshaphat, King of Judah" obviously do not mean that it was also Jehoshaphat's fifth year. He did not begin his reign together with Ahab's son, Jehoram. Jehoshaphat had already reigned some eighteen years when Jehoram became king after Ahab's death in the battle of Ramoth-gilead.

Some say that the words "the fifth year" refer only to Jehoram. Jehoshaphat is mentioned here because he ruled the Kingdom of Israel together with Jehoram during those five years.[19]

Others say that Jehoshaphat relinquished his throne entirely to his son for two years after the battle of Ramoth-gilead, because he realized that he too deserved to have died, and it was only by divine mercy that he was spared. Then, when he saw that G-d had forgiven him, he reclaimed it and reigned five more years, the five years mentioned in this verse.[20]

Another interpretation is that Jehoshaphat reigned five years immediately following the battle, but they were considered like a separate reign. Since his life had been saved, it was as if he had died and been born again. After five years he gave the throne over to his son Jehoram, which is the beginning of Jehoram's reign described here. Jehoshaphat lived another two years, a total of seven years after the battle of Ramoth-gilead.[21]

In the Book of Chronicles it says:[22]

> Jehoshaphat lay down with his fathers. He was buried with his fathers in the City of David, and Jehoram, his son, became king in his place. He had brothers, the sons of Jehoshaphat, Azariah, Jehiel, Zechariah, Azariahu, Michael and Shephatiah. All these were the sons of Jehoshaphat, King of Israel. Their father gave them many gifts of silver and gold and precious things, with fortified cities in Judah, but the kingdom he gave to Jehoram, for he was the first-born. Jehoram rose up over the kingdom of his father and strengthened himself. He killed all of his brothers by the sword, and also some of the officers of Israel.

8:20 בְּיָמָיו פָּשַׁע אֱדוֹם מִתַּחַת יַד־יְהוּדָה וַיַּמְלִכוּ עֲלֵיהֶם מֶלֶךְ׃

In his days Edom rebelled from under the hand of Judah, and crowned a king upon themselves.

Edom had lost its independence long ago. Eight kings had ruled over Edom before the first king of Israel, King Saul, as it says,[23] "These are the kings who reigned in the land of Edom before there reigned any king of the Children of Israel." After that, King David conquered them. From then until the time of Jehoram, Edom was ruled by governors appointed by the kings of Judah, as it says,[24] "There was no king in Edom, and they placed governors in Edom."[25] There were eight kings of Israel during that period, corresponding to those eight kings of Edom. They were Ishbosheth, David, Solomon, Rehoboam, Abijam, Asa, Jehoshaphat, and Jehoram.

8:21,22 וַיַּעֲבֹר יוֹרָם צָעִירָה וְכָל־הָרֶכֶב עִמּוֹ וַיְהִי־הוּא קָם לַיְלָה וַיַּכֶּה אֶת־אֱדוֹם הַסֹּבֵיב אֵלָיו וְאֵת שָׂרֵי הָרֶכֶב וַיָּנָס הָעָם לְאֹהָלָיו: וַיִּפְשַׁע אֱדוֹם מִתַּחַת יַד־יְהוּדָה עַד הַיּוֹם הַזֶּה אָז תִּפְשַׁע לִבְנָה בָּעֵת הַהִיא:

Jehoram passed over to Zair, and all the chariots with him. He arose by night and smote Edom that surrounded him, and all the officers of the chariots. The people fled to their tents. Edom continued to rebel from under the hand of Judah until this day. Then Libnah rebelled at that time.

Zair was one of the cities of Edom, and Jehoram chose to start his attack there. The armies of Jehudah and Edom camped opposite each other outside the city, in preparation for a pitched battle the next morning. But instead of waiting, Jehoram attacked during the night. The Edomites were taken by surprise and fled. This defeat, however, was not enough to force them to submit, and they continued to rebel.[26]

Some say it was Jehoram's army that fled after making their initial strike. It ended up being more of a raid than a battle.[27]

Another interpretation is that it was the King of Edom who attacked during the night, killing those Edomite soldiers that remained loyal to Jehoram.[28]

Others say the word "that surrounded him" means that Jehoram attacked all the settlements of Edom that were along the border, but did not venture into the interior.[29]

All Jehoram was able to accomplish was to punish Edom for their rebellion. He couldn't stop them. They saw how weak he was and were encouraged to continue.[30]

As for Libnah, its identity is unclear. Some say it was one of the cities of Edom that was close to Judah and had not rebelled initially.[31] Others say it was a Jewish city close to the border of Edom that rebelled against Jehoram and declared its independence.[32]

8:23,24 וְיֶתֶר דִּבְרֵי יוֹרָם וְכָל־אֲשֶׁר עָשָׂה הֲלֹא־הֵם כְּתוּבִים עַל־סֵפֶר דִּבְרֵי
הַיָּמִים לְמַלְכֵי יְהוּדָה׃ וַיִּשְׁכַּב יוֹרָם עִם־אֲבֹתָיו וַיִּקָּבֵר עִם־אֲבֹתָיו בְּעִיר דָּוִד
וַיִּמְלֹךְ אֲחַזְיָהוּ בְנוֹ תַּחְתָּיו׃

The rest of the things about Jehoram and all that he did are indeed written in the Book of the Chronicles of the Kings of Judah. Jehoram lay down with his fathers. He was buried with his fathers in the City of David, and Ahaziah, his son, became king in his place.

In the Book of Chronicles it says of Jehoram:[33]

> He too made altars in the mountains of Judah. He made the inhabitants of Jerusalem unfaithful, and made Judah go astray. A letter came to him from Elijah the prophet saying, "Thus says the L-rd, the G-d of David, your father, 'Since you didn't go in the ways of Jehoshaphat, your father, and in the ways of Asa, King of Judah, but went in the way of the kings of Israel and made Judah and the inhabitants of Jerusalem unfaithful, like the unfaithfulness of the house of Ahab. And your brothers too, the house of your father, who were better than you, you killed. Behold, G-d will strike a great blow upon your people, upon your children, upon your wives, and upon all your property. As for you, with severe sicknesses, with sickness of your intestines, until your intestines come out from the sickness, day after day.'" Then G-d stirred up the spirit of the Philistines and the Arabs who were next to the Kushites against Jehoram. They came up upon Judah and split it open, and captured all the property that was to be found in the house of the king, as well as his sons and his wives. There was no son left to him but Jehoahaz, the smallest of his sons. After all that, G-d smote him in his intestines with a sickness for which there was no cure. So it was, day after day, until finally at the end, after two years, his intestines came out from his sickness and he died in severe sicknesses. His people did not make a burning for him like the burning of his fathers. Thirty-two years old was he when he became king, and eight years did he reign in Jerusalem. He departed joyless, and they buried him in the City of David, but not in the graves of the kings.

Jehoram was not worthy of seeing Elijah, so Elijah did not appear to him. Instead, he wrote him this message in a letter and sent it by the hand of one of the righteous of that generation, or dictated it to one of the prophets to write in his name.[34]

Note that here Jehoram's single surviving son is called Jehoahaz, "יהואחז," while in other places he is called Ahaziah, "אחזיהו." These are two variations of the same name.

8:25,26 בִּשְׁנַת שְׁתֵּים־עֶשְׂרֵה שָׁנָה לְיוֹרָם בֶּן־אַחְאָב מֶלֶךְ יִשְׂרָאֵל מָלַךְ
אֲחַזְיָהוּ בֶן־יְהוֹרָם מֶלֶךְ יְהוּדָה: בֶּן־עֶשְׂרִים וּשְׁתַּיִם שָׁנָה אֲחַזְיָהוּ בְמָלְכוֹ וְשָׁנָה
אַחַת מָלַךְ בִּירוּשָׁלָם וְשֵׁם אִמּוֹ עֲתַלְיָהוּ בַּת־עָמְרִי מֶלֶךְ יִשְׂרָאֵל:

In the twelfth year of Jehoram, son of Ahab, King of Israel, Ahaziah, son of Jehoram, King of Judah, became king. Ahaziah was twenty-two years old when he became king and he reigned one year in Jerusalem. His mother's name was Athaliah, the daughter of Omri, King of Israel.

Earlier we were told that Jehoram's wife was the daughter of Ahab, Omri's son, but we were not told her name. Since no mention is made of Jehoram having any other wife, we can assume that this was Athaliah, the mother of Ahaziah, who is referred to here. If that is the case, however, she was not Omri's daughter but his granddaughter. Some say that she was called his daughter because she was raised in his house and was particularly close to him. There are many other places in the Bible where grandchildren are referred to as children and grandparents as parents.[35]

The Book of Chronicles gives a similar account, but there Ahaziah's age upon becoming king is given as forty-two rather than twenty-two. It says:[36]

> The inhabitants of Jerusalem crowned Ahaziah, his smallest son, in his place, because all the first ones the band that came to the camp with the Arabs had killed. So Ahaziah, son of Jehoram, King of Judah, reigned. Ahaziah was forty-two years old when he became king, and he reigned for one year in Jerusalem. His mother's name was Athaliah, the daughter of Omri. He, too, went in the ways of the house of Ahab, for his mother used to advise him to act wickedly.

Ahaziah could not have been forty-two years old when he became king, as the Book of Chronicles states. His father, Jehoram, was only forty or forty-one years old when he died, having become king at thirty-two and ruling eight years. Ahaziah couldn't have been older than his own father! Some say the forty-two years mentioned there are not the years of Ahaziah's life, but the time since the establishment of the kingdom of Omri. Omri reigned six years, Ahab twenty-two, his first son, Ahaziah, two, and his second son, Jehoram, twelve. In all, the house of Omri ruled for forty-two years.[37]

Others say that Ahaziah's father, Jehoram, actually ruled about twenty-eight years, but only eight are counted, because those eight alone were good. After that he was defeated by the Arabs, his household was looted, and he fell sick. So, at the age of forty and unable to conduct his kingdom any longer, he turned the throne over to his one remaining son, Ahaziah. Ahaziah was then only twenty-two years old. Jehoram suffered for another twenty years until he finally died. A year later Ahaziah died too. The words, "he ruled one year in Jerusalem" refer to the time that he ruled alone after his father's death.[38]

8:27-29 וַיֵּלֶךְ בְּדֶרֶךְ בֵּית אַחְאָב וַיַּעַשׂ הָרַע בְּעֵינֵי ה׳ כְּבֵית אַחְאָב כִּי חֲתַן בֵּית־אַחְאָב הוּא׃ וַיֵּלֶךְ אֶת־יוֹרָם בֶּן־אַחְאָב לַמִּלְחָמָה עִם־חֲזָאֵל מֶלֶךְ־אֲרָם בְּרָמֹת גִּלְעָד וַיַּכּוּ אֲרַמִּים אֶת־יוֹרָם׃ וַיָּשָׁב יוֹרָם הַמֶּלֶךְ לְהִתְרַפֵּא בְיִזְרְעֶאל מִן־הַמַּכִּים אֲשֶׁר יַכֻּהוּ אֲרַמִּים בָּרָמָה בְּהִלָּחֲמוֹ אֶת־חֲזָהאֵל מֶלֶךְ אֲרָם וַאֲחַזְיָהוּ בֶן־יְהוֹרָם מֶלֶךְ יְהוּדָה יָרַד לִרְאוֹת אֶת־יוֹרָם בֶּן־אַחְאָב בְּיִזְרְעֶאל כִּי־חֹלֶה הוּא׃

He went in the way of the house of Ahab, and did what was evil in G-d's eyes, like the house of Ahab, because he was a son-in-law of the house of Ahab. He went with Jehoram, the son of Ahab, to war with Hazael, King of Aram, at Ramoth-gilead, and the Arameans smote Jehoram. King Jehoram returned to recover in Jezreel from the wounds that the Arameans had given him at Ramah, when he fought with Hazael, King of Aram. Ahaziah, son of Jehoram, King of Judah, went down to see Jehoram son of Ahab in Jezreel, for he was sick.

The Book of Chronicles continues:[39]

He did what was evil in G-d's eyes, like the house of Ahab, for they

> were his advisors after the death of his father, to be the cause of his destruction. He also followed their advice and went with Jehoram, the son of Ahab, King of Israel, to war against Hazael, King of Aram, at Ramoth-gilead. The Arameans smote Jehoram. He returned to recover in Jezreel, because of the wounds that they had given him at Ramah, when he fought with Hazael, King of Aram. Azariah, the son of Jehoram, King of Judah, went down to see Jehoram the son of Ahab in Jezreel, for he was sick.

Azariah, son of Jehoram, is another name for Ahaziah. It could not be anyone else, since all Jehoram's other sons had been killed. The following verses in the Book of Chronicles confirm this, for there he is referred to as Ahaziah. They will be quoted in the next chapter.

II KINGS 9

9:1-3 וֶאֱלִישָׁע הַנָּבִיא קָרָא לְאַחַד מִבְּנֵי הַנְּבִיאִים וַיֹּאמֶר לוֹ חֲגֹר מָתְנֶיךָ
וְקַח פַּךְ הַשֶּׁמֶן הַזֶּה בְּיָדֶךָ וְלֵךְ רָמֹת גִּלְעָד׃ וּבָאתָ־שָׁמָּה וּרְאֵה־שָׁם יֵהוּא
בֶן־יְהוֹשָׁפָט בֶּן־נִמְשִׁי וּבָאתָ וַהֲקֵמֹתוֹ מִתּוֹךְ אֶחָיו וְהֵבֵיאתָ אֹתוֹ חֶדֶר בְּחָדֶר׃
וְלָקַחְתָּ פַךְ־הַשֶּׁמֶן וְיָצַקְתָּ עַל־רֹאשׁוֹ וְאָמַרְתָּ כֹּה־אָמַר ה׳ מְשַׁחְתִּיךָ לְמֶלֶךְ
אֶל־יִשְׂרָאֵל וּפָתַחְתָּ הַדֶּלֶת וְנַסְתָּה וְלֹא תְחַכֶּה׃

Elisha the prophet called to one of the sons of the prophets and said to him, "Gird your loins and take this flask of oil in your hands and go to Ramoth-gilead. Come there and see there Jehu the son of Jehoshaphat the son of Nimshi. Get him up from the midst of his brothers and bring him into an innermost room. Take the flask of oil and pour on his head and say, 'Thus says G-d, "I have anointed you as King of Israel!"' Then open the door and run away. Don't delay!"

When G-d spoke to Elijah at Mount Horeb, He commanded him to anoint three people. Each was to be assigned a part in the punishment of Ahab and his followers. Hazael was to be anointed King of Aram, Jehu King of Israel, and Elisha as Elijah's own successor.

The last of these was the first to be fulfilled. Elijah designated Elisha as his disciple immediately upon his return from Horeb. But he never personally fulfilled the other two. Before the time came, Ahab repented and G-d postponed His vengeance until the the next generation. So Elijah passed on those instructions to his newly appointed successor, Elisha, to be fulfilled when the appropriate time arrived.[1]

No mention is made here or in the previous chapter of G-d commanding Elisha concerning either of these two appointments. It was not necessary, for he had already been instructed in them by Elijah, and that was sufficient.[2]

The opportunity to anoint Hazael had presented itself without

Elisha's effort, but anointing Jehu would require planning. He would have to be approached when he was not with Jehoram. That would be difficult, since, in general, he stayed near the king most of the time. The opportunity came when Jehoram was wounded at Ramoth-gilead, and returned to his capital to recover, leaving Jehu in command in his place.

Even then, Elisha could not risk visiting him in person. Elisha was by now well known, so such a visit would surely be noticed and Jehoram was liable to find out about it. Elisha therefore sent one of his students instead.[3]

The student chosen was Jonah ben Amitai. Later he was to become a prophet in his own right, and his mission to the city of Nineveh would be recorded in the Bible in the book that bears his name. At this time, however, he was yet unknown, so his visit to the officers did not arouse suspicion. Elisha instructed him to anoint Jehu in secret and immediately flee for his life.[4]

The oil with which Jehu was to be anointed was not the special holy oil used to anoint David and Solomon. That oil had been made by Moses in the desert. With it he had anointed the original utensils of the Tabernacle and the first priests, Aaron and his sons. The only kings to be anointed with it were those of the House of David, G-d's chosen representatives, whose kingdom would endure forever. When David was anointed with that oil, royalty was bestowed not only upon him, but upon all his descendants as well. From that time on, the throne of Israel belonged to them.

So no one else would ever be anointed with it to be king over all Israel. Nor did David's descendants need to be anointed after him, since the throne was already theirs. Only when there was a dispute over which of the king's sons was to inherit his throne was the oil used to designate the chosen successor.

Such was not the status that G-d conferred upon Jehu. He was anointed to take vengeance against the house of Ahab, not to found an eternal dynasty. Therefore the oil with which he was anointed was not the holy oil, but Balsam oil, a precious kind of fragrant oil which was a symbol of greatness.

Nor was the oil poured from a horn, as it had been on David and Solomon, but from a flask. A horn, which is long and narrow, indicates a dynasty that will continue on and on forever. A flask is small and round, indicating one that is brief and limited.[5]

9:4,5 וַיֵּ֫לֶךְ הַנַּעַר הַנַּעַר הַנָּבִיא רָמֹת גִּלְעָד׃ וַיָּבֹא וְהִנֵּה שָׂרֵי הַחַיִל

יֹשְׁבִים וַיֹּאמֶר דָּבָר לִי אֵלֶיךָ הַשָּׂר וַיֹּאמֶר יֵהוּא אֶל־מִי מִכֻּלָּנוּ וַיֹּאמֶר אֵלֶיךָ
הַשָּׂר׃

The boy went, the prophet boy, to Ramoth-gilead. He arrived, and behold, the officers of the army were sitting. He said, "I have a word for you, Oh officer!" Jehu said, "To which of all of us?" He said, "To you, Oh officer!"

In this verse, Jonah is referred to by the word "נער," which means a boy. It is also often used to mean a servant. Though he must already have been an advanced student to have been given this mission, he conducted himself humbly as if he were just a boy.[6]

Jehu behaved humbly too. Even though it was fairly clear that he was the officer to whom the message was directed, he made no such assumption, treating the others as if they were his equals.[7]

9:6-10 וַיָּקָם וַיָּבֹא הַבַּיְתָה וַיִּצֹק הַשֶּׁמֶן אֶל־רֹאשׁוֹ וַיֹּאמֶר לוֹ כֹּה־אָמַר ה׳
אֱלֹהֵי יִשְׂרָאֵל מְשַׁחְתִּיךָ לְמֶלֶךְ אֶל־עַם ה׳ אֶל־יִשְׂרָאֵל׃ וְהִכִּיתָה אֶת־בֵּית אַחְאָב
אֲדֹנֶיךָ וְנִקַּמְתִּי דְּמֵי עֲבָדַי הַנְּבִיאִים וּדְמֵי כָּל־עַבְדֵי ה׳ מִיַּד אִיזָבֶל׃ וְאָבַד
כָּל־בֵּית אַחְאָב וְהִכְרַתִּי לְאַחְאָב מַשְׁתִּין בְּקִיר וְעָצוּר וְעָזוּב בְּיִשְׂרָאֵל׃ וְנָתַתִּי
אֶת־בֵּית אַחְאָב כְּבֵית יָרָבְעָם בֶּן־נְבָט וּכְבֵית בַּעְשָׁא בֶן־אֲחִיָּה׃ וְאֶת־אִיזֶבֶל
יֹאכְלוּ הַכְּלָבִים בְּחֵלֶק יִזְרְעֶאל וְאֵין קֹבֵר וַיִּפְתַּח הַדֶּלֶת וַיָּנֹס׃

He got up, came inside, and poured the oil onto his head. He said to him, "Thus says the L-rd, the G-d of Israel, 'I have anointed you as king of G-d's people, of Israel. You will smite the house of Ahab, your master, and I will avenge the blood of My servants, the prophets, and the blood of all G-d's servants, from the hand of Jezebel. The whole house of Ahab will perish, and I will cut off from Ahab every male person*, and all that is guarded and all that is abandoned in Israel. I will make the house of Ahab like the house of Jeroboam ben Nebat, and like the house of Baasa ben Ahijah. As for Jezebel, the dogs will eat her in the portion of Jezreel, and there will be none to bury her.' " Then he opened the door and ran away.

From the first of his words, the prophet made clear that Jehu would be expected to faithfully fulfill the words of the Torah as well as the special assignment which he was given. He could not do with his position as he wished. His subjects were first referred to as "G-d's people" and only afterwards as "Israel." The moment he stopped conducting himself as king of G-d's people, he would lose his right to be king of Israel as well.[8]

The prophet specifically referred to Ahab as "your master." He said, "G-d has not overlooked the fact that Ahab was your master and that you owe him and his descendants your loyalty. Nonetheless, He has commanded you to overthrow them. Do not let your sense of duty and loyalty stop you, for it is the will of G-d, Who is the ultimate master of all men."[9]

He also specifically mentioned Jezebel, lest Jehu hesitate to kill her because she was a woman. He said, "Even though she is a queen and the daughter of a king, show her no deference. It is only under that condition that you are being anointed!"[10]

* The phrase "every male person" can be translated more literally as "all who urinate on the wall."

9:11-13 וְיֵהוּא יָצָא אֶל־עַבְדֵי אֲדֹנָיו וַיֹּאמֶר לוֹ הֲשָׁלוֹם מַדּוּעַ בָּא־הַמְשֻׁגָּע הַזֶּה אֵלֶיךָ וַיֹּאמֶר אֲלֵיהֶם אַתֶּם יְדַעְתֶּם אֶת־הָאִישׁ וְאֶת־שִׂיחוֹ: וַיֹּאמְרוּ שֶׁקֶר הַגֶּד־נָא לָנוּ וַיֹּאמֶר כָּזֹאת וְכָזֹאת אָמַר אֵלַי לֵאמֹר כֹּה אָמַר ה׳ מְשַׁחְתִּיךָ לְמֶלֶךְ אֶל־יִשְׂרָאֵל: וַיְמַהֲרוּ וַיִּקְחוּ אִישׁ בִּגְדוֹ וַיָּשִׂימוּ תַחְתָּיו אֶל־גֶּרֶם הַמַּעֲלוֹת וַיִּתְקְעוּ בַּשּׁוֹפָר וַיֹּאמְרוּ מָלַךְ יֵהוּא:

Jehu went out to the servants of his master, and one said to him, "Is all well? Why did this crazy man come to you?" He said to them, "You know the man and his talk!" They said, "That is a lie! Tell us please!" He said, "Like this and like this he spoke to me, saying, 'Thus said G-d, "I have anointed you as King of Israel!"'" They hurried up, and each one took his garment and put it under him to raise him to the highest level. They blew the horn and said, "Jehu is king!"

The officers thought the sons of the prophets were crazy to begin with, for they shunned the society of men and disdained their politics, spending their time alone instead, praying and studying Torah.[11] Under the influence of prophecy, they sometimes even lost control of themselves and acted as if they were crazy.[12] They were the opposite of soldiers, whose lives are spent in the company of others, dedicated to defending and governing the nation. The behavior of this particular prophet confirmed their opinion, first barging in and singling out Jehu in this strange way, and then dashing out again.

At first Jehu tried to conceal the truth. He thought he might convince them that it was but nonsense. Was the man not, after all, crazy, as they had said themselves?[13] But he did not go so far as to call the prophet crazy, as they had. He would not be so disrespectful.[14]

The officers, however, were not to be fooled.[15] Crazy or not, the man hadn't come for nothing. They knew that, their personal feelings notwithstanding, these prophets were G-d's true messengers. Elisha's many miracles had convinced them of that. The words of the prophets were not to be taken lightly.[16]

So there was no question where their loyalty lay, once they heard what the message had been. They took off their own cloaks to make him a throne, and unanimously declared him their new king. This was by G-d's will, for He had put it into their hearts to facilitate Jehu's mission.[17]

Some say the words "גרם המעלות" mean "like the stone of a sundial."[18] The pile of clothes resembled steps, like the gradations of a sundial. Others say it is not the name of an object, but an expression meaning "the highest level."[19]

9:14,15 וַיִּתְקַשֵּׁר יֵהוּא בֶּן־יְהוֹשָׁפָט בֶּן־נִמְשִׁי אֶל־יוֹרָם וְיוֹרָם הָיָה שֹׁמֵר
בְּרָמֹת גִּלְעָד הוּא וְכָל־יִשְׂרָאֵל מִפְּנֵי חֲזָאֵל מֶלֶךְ־אֲרָם: וַיָּשָׁב יְהוֹרָם הַמֶּלֶךְ לְהִתְרַפֵּא
בְיִזְרְעֶאל מִן־הַמַּכִּים אֲשֶׁר יַכֻּהוּ אֲרַמִּים בְּהִלָּחֲמוֹ אֶת־חֲזָאֵל מֶלֶךְ אֲרָם וַיֹּאמֶר יֵהוּא
אִם־יֵשׁ נַפְשְׁכֶם אַל־יֵצֵא פָלִיט מִן־הָעִיר לָלֶכֶת לגיד (לְהַגִּיד קרי) בְּיִזְרְעֶאל:

So Jehu the son of Jehoshaphat the son of Nimshi conspired against Jehoram. Jehoram had been keeping guard at Ramoth-gilead, he and all Israel, against Hazael, King of Aram. King Jehoram had gone back to recover at Jezreel from the wounds that the Arameans inflicted upon him when he fought with Hazael, King of Aram. Jehu said, "If you agree, let no one escape from the city to go tell in Jezreel."

Carefully, Jehu planned his revolt. He made sure that no news would reach Jehoram before they got to Jezreel, so that he would be taken completely by surprise.[20]

9:16-18 וַיִּרְכַּב יֵהוּא וַיֵּלֶךְ יִזְרְעֶאלָה כִּי יוֹרָם שֹׁכֵב שָׁמָּה וַאֲחַזְיָה מֶלֶךְ
יְהוּדָה יָרַד לִרְאוֹת אֶת־יוֹרָם׃ וְהַצֹּפֶה עֹמֵד עַל־הַמִּגְדָּל בְּיִזְרְעֶאל וַיַּרְא
אֶת־שִׁפְעַת יֵהוּא בְּבֹאוֹ וַיֹּאמֶר שִׁפְעַת אֲנִי רֹאֶה וַיֹּאמֶר יְהוֹרָם קַח רַכָּב וּשְׁלַח
לִקְרָאתָם וְיֹאמַר הֲשָׁלוֹם׃ וַיֵּלֶךְ רֹכֵב הַסּוּס לִקְרָאתוֹ וַיֹּאמֶר כֹּה־אָמַר הַמֶּלֶךְ
הֲשָׁלוֹם וַיֹּאמֶר יֵהוּא מַה־לְּךָ וּלְשָׁלוֹם סֹב אֶל־אַחֲרָי וַיַּגֵּד הַצֹּפֶה לֵאמֹר
בָּא־הַמַּלְאָךְ עַד־הֵם וְלֹא־שָׁב׃

Jehu rode and went to Jezreel, for Jehoram was lying there, and Ahaziah, King of Judah, had come down to see Jehoram. The look-out was standing on the tower in Jezreel, and he saw the troop of Jehu as they were coming. He said, "I see a troop!" Jehoram said, "Take a rider and send to meet them, and say, 'Is all well?' " The rider of the horse went to meet him and said, "Thus said the king, 'Is all well?' " Jehu said, "What is it to you whether all is well? Turn around and follow me!" The look-out reported saying, "The messenger came to them and didn't come back."

Jehu might have simply pretended that he was still loyal to Jehoram and sent the messenger back with some innocent reply, but he had a better plan. He hoped to draw Jehoram out of the city, away from his guards and the forces that were loyal to him. Whatever resistance might be met, the fight would be quicker and less bloody outside the city. In that way, too, he would meet and kill Jehoram in the portion of Naboth, as G-d had decreed. So he said to the messenger, "It is not your concern whether all is well or not. Just come along and do as I say!"[21]

9:19,20 וַיִּשְׁלַח רֹכֵב סוּס שֵׁנִי וַיָּבֹא אֲלֵהֶם וַיֹּאמֶר כֹּה־אָמַר הַמֶּלֶךְ שָׁלוֹם
וַיֹּאמֶר יֵהוּא מַה־לְּךָ וּלְשָׁלוֹם סֹב אֶל־אַחֲרָי׃ וַיַּגֵּד הַצֹּפֶה לֵאמֹר בָּא עַד־אֲלֵיהֶם
וְלֹא־שָׁב וְהַמִּנְהָג כְּמִנְהַג יֵהוּא בֶן־נִמְשִׁי כִּי בְשִׁגָּעוֹן יִנְהָג׃

He sent a second horse rider and came to them and said, "Thus said the king, 'Is all well?' " Jehu said, "What is it to you whether all is well? Turn around and follow me!" The look-out reported, saying, "He came to them and didn't come back, and the driving is like the driving of Jehu ben Nimshi, for he drives crazily!"

As Jehu and his followers came closer, the look-out was able to recognize his wild and careless driving. Jehoram could not wait any longer to find out what was going on. Why had Jehu suddenly returned without sending a message ahead? Though Jehoram had not yet completely recovered from his wounds, he decided to go out to meet him.

9:21 וַיֹּאמֶר יְהוֹרָם אֱסֹר וַיֶּאְסֹר רִכְבּוֹ וַיֵּצֵא יְהוֹרָם מֶלֶךְ־יִשְׂרָאֵל וַאֲחַזְיָהוּ
מֶלֶךְ־יְהוּדָה אִישׁ בְּרִכְבּוֹ וַיֵּצְאוּ לִקְרַאת יֵהוּא וַיִּמְצָאֻהוּ בְּחֶלְקַת נָבוֹת הַיִּזְרְעֵאלִי:

Jehoram said, "Harness up!" and his chariot was harnessed. Jehoram, King of Israel, and Ahaziah, King of Judah, each went out on his chariot. They went out to meet Jehu and found him in the portion of Naboth the Jezreelite.

Jehu purposely stopped in the field that had belonged to Naboth, as a reminder of the sin of Ahab for which Jehoram and the rest of Ahab's family were now to be killed. It was divinely arranged that they meet there.[22]

9:22 וַיְהִי כִּרְאוֹת יְהוֹרָם אֶת־יֵהוּא וַיֹּאמֶר הֲשָׁלוֹם יֵהוּא וַיֹּאמֶר מָה
הַשָּׁלוֹם עַד־זְנוּנֵי אִיזֶבֶל אִמְּךָ וּכְשָׁפֶיהָ הָרַבִּים:

When Jehoram saw Jehu he said, "Is all well, Jehu?" He said, "How can it be well as long as the unfaithfulness of Jezebel your mother and her many witchcrafts continue?"

Some say the words, עד זנוני איזבל אמך וכשפיה הרבים mean "as long as the unfaithfulness of Jezebel your mother and her many witchcrafts continue." Others say it means "until they are destroyed" or "until they are punished."[23] As soon as Jehoram heard these words he knew that Jehu had turned against him. He tried to flee, but it was too late.

9:23,24 וַיַּהֲפֹךְ יְהוֹרָם יָדָיו וַיָּנֹס וַיֹּאמֶר אֶל־אֲחַזְיָהוּ מִרְמָה אֲחַזְיָה: וְיֵהוּא
מִלֵּא יָדוֹ בַקֶּשֶׁת וַיַּךְ אֶת־יְהוֹרָם בֵּין זְרֹעָיו וַיֵּצֵא הַחֵצִי מִלִּבּוֹ וַיִּכְרַע בְּרִכְבּוֹ:

Jehoram turned his hands around and fled. He said to Ahaziah, "It is treachery, Ahaziah!" Jehu drew the bow with all his might and struck Jehoram between his arms. The arrow went out through his heart, and he doubled over in his chariot.

Jehu succeeded in killing Jehoram in one shot. The path of the arrow revealed the sin for which G-d had condemned him to death. It was Jehoram that had demanded interest for the money that he lent Obadiah for sustaining the prophets. That was in direct violation of the prohibition against taking interest from a fellow Jew. But beyond violating the Torah, he had cruelly attempted to enslave Obadiah's children to pay for their father's debt. As he had hardened his heart and reached out with his arms, so the arrow entered his body between his arms and passed through his heart.[24]

9:25,26 וַיֹּאמֶר אֶל־בִּדְקַר שָׁלִשֹׁה שָׂא הַשְׁלִכֵהוּ בְּחֶלְקַת שְׂדֵה נָבוֹת
הַיִּזְרְעֵאלִי כִּי־זְכֹר אֲנִי וָאַתָּה אֵת רֹכְבִים צְמָדִים אַחֲרֵי אַחְאָב אָבִיו וַה׳ נָשָׂא עָלָיו
אֶת־הַמַּשָּׂא הַזֶּה: אִם־לֹא אֶת־דְּמֵי נָבוֹת וְאֶת־דְּמֵי בָנָיו רָאִיתִי אֶמֶשׁ נְאֻם־ה׳
וְשִׁלַּמְתִּי לְךָ בַּחֶלְקָה הַזֹּאת נְאֻם־ה׳ וְעַתָּה שָׂא הַשְׁלִכֵהוּ בַּחֶלְקָה כִּדְבַר ה׳:

He said to Bidkar, his captain, "Pick him up and throw him in the portion of the field of Naboth the Jezreelite! For remember how you and I were riding together behind Ahab, his father, and G-d pronounced against him this decree: 'Surely the blood of Naboth and the blood of his sons have I seen last night,' said G-d, 'and I will repay you in this portion,' said G-d. So now, pick him up and throw him in the portion, in accordance with the word of G-d."

Jehu commanded his highest officer to take Jehoram's body from the chariot. He said, "Don't consider it beneath your dignity to attend to a corpse. He was not an ordinary person but a king and the son of a king.

Furthermore, we were his father's servants, and it is only fitting that we treat the body of our master's son with respect."

"If that is so," Bidkar objected, "why have you commanded me to throw his body in the field? That is certainly not respectful! Nor was it respectful for you to kill him in the first place!"

"True," answered Jehu, "I would never have done these things were it not for G-d's word. That is why it is so important that he be killed here, in this field, and that his body lie here. Everyone must know that it was not to take away his kingdom that I killed him, but to fulfill the prophecy that was pronounced against him."[25]

Another reason that the mission of taking vengeance against Jehoram was given to Jehu and Bidkar was that they had witnessed the decree pronounced against him. It was therefore their responsibility to carry it out, as the Torah says,[26] "The hand of the witnesses will be upon him first, to kill him."[27]

Some say "the blood of his sons" refers to the sons that had not yet been born. Others say that when Jezebel had Naboth killed, she had his sons killed too, so that there would be no heirs left to contest Ahab's claim to his portion.[28]

9:27,28 וַאֲחַזְיָה מֶלֶךְ־יְהוּדָה רָאָה וַיָּנָס דֶּרֶךְ בֵּית הַגָּן וַיִּרְדֹּף אַחֲרָיו יֵהוּא
וַיֹּאמֶר גַּם־אֹתוֹ הַכֻּהוּ אֶל־הַמֶּרְכָּבָה בְּמַעֲלֵה־גוּר אֲשֶׁר אֶת־יִבְלְעָם וַיָּנָס מְגִדּוֹ
וַיָּמָת שָׁם׃ וַיַּרְכִּבוּ אֹתוֹ עֲבָדָיו יְרוּשָׁלָמָה וַיִּקְבְּרוּ אֹתוֹ בִקְבֻרָתוֹ עִם־אֲבֹתָיו
בְּעִיר דָּוִד׃

Ahaziah, King of Judah, saw and fled by way of Beth-hagan. Jehu ran after him and said, "Him too! Smite him in the chariot!" So he did on the ascent of Gur, which is next to Ible'am. He fled to Megido and died there. His servants drove him to Jerusalem and buried him in his grave with his fathers, in the City of David.

In the Book of Chronicles it says:[29]

Ahaziah's downfall was from G-d, that he come to Jehoram, and when he came, that he go out with Jehoram to Jehu ben Nimshi, whom G-d had anointed to wipe out the house of Ahab. When Jehu was carrying out the judgment against the house of Ahab, he found

> the officers of Judah and the sons of the brothers of Ahaziah serving Ahaziah, and he killed them. He searched for Ahaziah and they caught him. He was hiding in Samaria. They brought him to Jehu and he killed him, and they buried him, for they said, "He is the son of Jehoshaphat, who sought G-d with all his heart." There was none left of the house of Ahaziah strong enough to hold the kingdom.

The two accounts differ concerning the details of Ahaziah's death. One says he died in Megido, the other that he survived and was later captured in Samaria and executed by Jehu's orders. One possible reconciliation is that after being wounded, Jehoram fled to Megido. It being clear, however, that Megido would soon fall to Jehu, his servants took him to Samaria, where the remainder of the house of Ahab and those loyal to them had fortified themselves. But soon Samaria too fell, as we will learn in the next chapter, and Ahaziah was captured. Jehu did not disgrace Ahaziah's body, though, as he did those of Ahab's family. It was returned to his followers to be buried with honor.[30]

According to this interpretation, the words, "he died there" are not to be taken literally, but to mean that he fell into a coma in Megido. He was still alive, but it was as if he were dead.[31]

Others say the words "he was hiding in Samaria" refer not to where Jehu found him, but to the sin for which G-d condemned him to death. When Ahaziah visited his brother-in-law in Samaria, he committed a great sacrilege. He scraped off the names of G-d from the Torah scroll and wrote the names of pagan gods in their place. But he was afraid to let his officers see, since they were faithful to G-d, so he did it secretly, and only when he was in Samaria where idolatry was acceptable.[32]

9:29 וּבִשְׁנַת אַחַת־עֶשְׂרֵה שָׁנָה לְיוֹרָם בֶּן־אַחְאָב מָלַךְ אֲחַזְיָה עַל־יְהוּדָה׃

In the eleventh year of Jehoram the son of Ahab, Ahaziah became king over Judah.

The eleventh year here means that Jehoram had reigned ten full years and several months. But his reign extended over thirteen calendar years. He became king at the end of a year and died at the beginning of another. The various methods of reckoning years have already been explained.[33]

Above[34] this is referred to as the twelfth year. Some say Ahaziah began to reign in the last year of his father's life, which was the eleventh year of Jehoram, King of Israel, and and became sole ruler the next year, when his father died.[35]

9:30,31 וַיָּבוֹא יֵהוּא יִזְרְעֶאלָה וְאִיזֶבֶל שָׁמְעָה וַתָּשֶׂם בַּפּוּךְ עֵינֶיהָ וַתֵּיטֶב אֶת־רֹאשָׁהּ וַתַּשְׁקֵף בְּעַד הַחַלּוֹן׃ וְיֵהוּא בָּא בַשָּׁעַר וַתֹּאמֶר הֲשָׁלוֹם זִמְרִי הֹרֵג אֲדֹנָיו׃

Jehu came to Jezreel. Jezebel heard, and she put make-up on her eyes, fixed up her hair, and looked out the window. Jehu came through the gate, and she said, "Is all well, Oh Zimri, murderer of his master?"

Jezebel realized that her husband's house had fallen, but she did not give up. Years earlier, another king, Elah, had been assasinated, but his murderer, Zimri, reigned only a few days before he too was killed. If Jezebel handled the situation right, she might incite the people to avenge her son's death too. First, she had to gain their sympathy. Then she could remind them of the possibility of a successful rebellion.[36]

Like a prostitute, she put on make-up and arranged her hair to make herself attractive.[37] She stood at the window in full view as Jehu entered the city. Let the people choose who would be their leader!

Some say she wanted to entice Jehu to marry her. She felt no loyalty to the memory of her late husband and son, and was ready to join whoever was in power at the moment. According to this, her greeting, "Is all well?" or literally, "Is there peace?" meant, "Is there peace between us?" It was an offer of reconciliation.[38]

9:32,33 וַיִּשָּׂא פָנָיו אֶל־הַחַלּוֹן וַיֹּאמֶר מִי אִתִּי מִי וַיַּשְׁקִיפוּ אֵלָיו שְׁנַיִם שְׁלֹשָׁה סָרִיסִים׃ וַיֹּאמֶר שמטהו (שִׁמְטוּהָ קרי) וַיִּשְׁמְטוּהָ וַיִּז מִדָּמָהּ אֶל־הַקִּיר וְאֶל־הַסּוּסִים וַיִּרְמְסֶנָּה׃

He lifted up his face to the window and said, "Who is with me? Who?" Two or three officers looked out to him. He said, "Throw her down!" They threw her down and her blood splattered on the wall and on the horses, and they trampled her.

But Jehu was more than her match. Quickly, he called out for allies within the palace. He was answered right away, for Jezebel's cruelty had earned her many enemies. They had obeyed her only through fear, and now they took revenge. Before any of her supporters could come to her aid she was dead. Some say it was Jehu himself who rode over her.[39]

Her death was reminiscent of the death of Naboth, for being thrown down and being stoned are variations of the same punishment.[40]

9:34,35 וַיָּבֹא וַיֹּאכַל וַיֵּשְׁתְּ וַיֹּאמֶר פִּקְדוּ־נָא אֶת־הָאֲרוּרָה הַזֹּאת וְקִבְרוּהָ כִּי בַת־מֶלֶךְ הִיא׃ וַיֵּלְכוּ לְקָבְרָהּ וְלֹא־מָצְאוּ בָהּ כִּי אִם־הַגֻּלְגֹּלֶת וְהָרַגְלַיִם וְכַפּוֹת הַיָּדָיִם׃

He came, ate and drank. Then he said, "Please look after this cursed one and bury her, for she is the daughter of a king!" They went to bury her, but they found nothing of her but the skull, the feet, and the palms of the hands.

Jehu left her body there in disgrace' as a further message to any who thought of opposing him. But after he had relaxed and eaten, he decided that his statement had already been made clearly enough. Perhaps she did deserve some respect anyway. Her death and the disgrace her body had already suffered were sufficient punishment.[41]

Even so, it was by virtue of being the daughter of the King of Zidon, not because she herself had been a queen and wife of Ahab. For as queen she had misused her power, nor did she deserve any respect for being Ahab's wife, since she misled him and made him sin.[42]

Three parts of Jezebel's body were spared disgrace: her head, her feet, and her hands. Through them she had performed deeds of kindness, and the merit that she had thereby earned was not forgotten. Whenever a funeral procession would pass by her palace, she would go out, wail, and beat her hands in mourning, as she followed the coffin for ten paces. When a wedding procession passed by, she came out singing and clapping in joy, and followed the bride and groom ten paces too. So when the dogs came to eat her, even though they were fulfilling the decree prophesied by Elijah, those limbs were protected by her good deeds.[43] Thus it is written,[44] "Those who rejoice on happy occasions will be glad when they find a grave."[45]

9:36,37 וַיָּשֻׁבוּ וַיַּגִּידוּ לוֹ וַיֹּאמֶר דְּבַר־ה׳ הוּא אֲשֶׁר דִּבֶּר בְּיַד־עַבְדּוֹ אֵלִיָּהוּ
הַתִּשְׁבִּי לֵאמֹר בְּחֵלֶק יִזְרְעֶאל יֹאכְלוּ הַכְּלָבִים אֶת־בְּשַׂר אִיזָבֶל׃ וְהָיְתָ נִבְלַת
אִיזֶבֶל כְּדֹמֶן עַל־פְּנֵי הַשָּׂדֶה בְּחֵלֶק יִזְרְעֶאל אֲשֶׁר לֹא־יֹאמְרוּ זֹאת אִיזָבֶל׃

They came back and told him. He said, "It is the word of G-d, that He spoke by the hand of His servant, Elijah the Tishbite, saying, 'In the portion of Jezreel the dogs will eat the flesh of Jezebel. The corpse of Jezebel will be like dung upon the face of the field in the portion of Jezreel, that people will not say, "This is Jezebel."'"

The portion of Naboth adjoined Ahab's palace. That was why Ahab had wanted it to make himself a garden, and Jezebel had Naboth murdered so that her husband might have his wish. Now, it was into that very garden that Jezebel fell, and there her body was eaten by the dogs, just as Elijah had proclaimed.[46]

II KINGS 10

10:1-3 וּלְאַחְאָב שִׁבְעִים בָּנִים בְּשֹׁמְרוֹן וַיִּכְתֹּב יֵהוּא סְפָרִים וַיִּשְׁלַח שֹׁמְרוֹן
אֶל־שָׂרֵי יִזְרְעֶאל הַזְּקֵנִים וְאֶל־הָאֹמְנִים אַחְאָב לֵאמֹר׃ וְעַתָּה כְּבֹא הַסֵּפֶר הַזֶּה
אֲלֵיכֶם וְאִתְּכֶם בְּנֵי אֲדֹנֵיכֶם וְאִתְּכֶם הָרֶכֶב וְהַסּוּסִים וְעִיר מִבְצָר וְהַנָּשֶׁק׃
וּרְאִיתֶם הַטּוֹב וְהַיָּשָׁר מִבְּנֵי אֲדֹנֵיכֶם וְשַׂמְתֶּם עַל־כִּסֵּא אָבִיו וְהִלָּחֲמוּ עַל־בֵּית
אֲדֹנֵיכֶם׃

Ahab had seventy sons in Samaria. Jehu wrote letters and sent to Samaria, to the officers of Jezreel, the elders, and the guardians of Ahab saying, "Now, when this letter comes to you, with you are the sons of your master, and with you are the chariots and horses, the fortified city and the weapons. See which is the best and fittest of the sons of your master. Put him on the throne of his father and fight for your master's house!"

How discouraging to the righteous are the blessings of the wicked! Abraham devoted his life to doing G-d's will, yet he was not blessed with even a single son until his old age. But Ahab, who worshiped idols, was granted seventy sons! They were all powerful and wealthy. Each had a summer and a winter palace. Thus the prophet Habakuk said,[1] "Oh, G-d, I heard Your report and I was afraid." He heard of the mercy that G-d showed the wicked and was discouraged by the apparent lack of fairness. He was afraid that there would never be justice. G-d reassured him that there would, and that if the wicked did not repent, in the end all their blessings would come to naught. The prophet Amos alluded to this by the words,[2] "I will smite the winter house as well as the summer house." In their downfall, the suffering of the wicked is all the greater, as they see how much they have lost![3]

Samaria was a well fortified city. It would be very hard to take it by siege. Had it not withstood the siege of Aram just a few years ago? Jehu did not have as mighty an army as Aram, nor was he prepared to inflict such suffering upon his own people. So, rather than attempt to conquer Samaria by force, he devised a plan to take it by cunning.[4]

The "guardians," "אמנים," were the servants of Ahab who had been appointed to care for his children and raise them.[5] Jehu wanted to test them, along with the rest of the supporters of the house of Ahab, to see whether they would remain faithful to their former master or capitulate and join him.[6] This he did with characteristic cleverness, presenting it to them not as a choice but a challenge. If they were planning to resist, let them do it now!

10:4,5 וַיִּרְאוּ מְאֹד מְאֹד וַיֹּאמְרוּ הִנֵּה שְׁנֵי הַמְּלָכִים לֹא עָמְדוּ לְפָנָיו וְאֵיךְ
נַעֲמֹד אֲנָחְנוּ׃ וַיִּשְׁלַח אֲשֶׁר־עַל־הַבַּיִת וַאֲשֶׁר עַל־הָעִיר וְהַזְּקֵנִים וְהָאֹמְנִים
אֶל־יֵהוּא לֵאמֹר עֲבָדֶיךָ אֲנַחְנוּ וְכֹל אֲשֶׁר־תֹּאמַר אֵלֵינוּ נַעֲשֶׂה לֹא־נַמְלִיךְ אִישׁ
הַטּוֹב בְּעֵינֶיךָ עֲשֵׂה׃

They were very very afraid, and said, "Behold, two kings could not withstand him. How will we withstand him?" They sent the one who was in charge of the household, and the one who was in charge of the city, and the elders and the guardians to Jehu saying, "We are your servants. Everything that you tell us we will do. We will not crown anyone. Whatever is best in your eyes, do!"

By this time, however, no one would dare attempt to resist Jehu. Even those who still supported the house of Ahab were not ready to be martyred in its defense.

10:6,7 וַיִּכְתֹּב אֲלֵיהֶם סֵפֶר שֵׁנִית לֵאמֹר אִם־לִי אַתֶּם וּלְקֹלִי אַתֶּם שֹׁמְעִים
קְחוּ אֶת־רָאשֵׁי אַנְשֵׁי בְנֵי־אֲדֹנֵיכֶם וּבֹאוּ אֵלַי כָּעֵת מָחָר יִזְרְעֶאלָה וּבְנֵי הַמֶּלֶךְ
שִׁבְעִים אִישׁ אֶת־גְּדֹלֵי הָעִיר מְגַדְּלִים אוֹתָם׃ וַיְהִי כְּבֹא הַסֵּפֶר אֲלֵיהֶם וַיִּקְחוּ
אֶת־בְּנֵי הַמֶּלֶךְ וַיִּשְׁחֲטוּ שִׁבְעִים אִישׁ וַיָּשִׂימוּ אֶת־רָאשֵׁיהֶם בַּדּוּדִים וַיִּשְׁלְחוּ
אֵלָיו יִזְרְעֶאלָה׃

He sent them a second letter saying, "If you are on my side and listen to my voice, take the heads of the men of the sons of your master and come to me at this time tomorrow to Jezreel." The sons of the king were seventy men. With the great men of the city had they been raised. When the letter came to them they took the sons of the king and slaughtered them, seventy men, and put their heads in baskets and sent them to him to Jezreel.

Now, Jehu tested them further. They would not stand up in defense of the house of Ahab, but would they murder with their own hands their life-long friends and the children whom they themselves had raised? So great was their fear that even this they were willing to do!

But the elders did not bring the heads themselves, as Jehu had requested. They were afraid that he might still be angry and kill them anyway. So they sent them instead, and waited to see what Jehu's reaction would be.[7]

Some say the words, "The sons of the king were seventy men. With the great men of the city they were raised" are part of Jehu's letter.[8] He said, "I know how many there are, so don't think you can fool me and hide any of them!" Others say it is a comment made by the Bible.[9] According to the first opinion, it is to be translated "are seventy men," in present tense, rather than "were seventy men."

Some say the word "דודים" means baskets.[10] The baskets were loosely woven, so the heads would be visible from the outside.[11] Others say it means large pots.[12]

10:8-10 וַיָּבֹא הַמַּלְאָךְ וַיַּגֶּד־לוֹ לֵאמֹר הֵבִיאוּ רָאשֵׁי בְנֵי־הַמֶּלֶךְ וַיֹּאמֶר שִׂימוּ אֹתָם שְׁנֵי צִבֻּרִים פֶּתַח הַשַּׁעַר עַד־הַבֹּקֶר׃ וַיְהִי בַבֹּקֶר וַיֵּצֵא וַיַּעֲמֹד וַיֹּאמֶר אֶל־כָּל־הָעָם צַדִּקִים אַתֶּם הִנֵּה אֲנִי קָשַׁרְתִּי עַל־אֲדֹנִי וָאֶהְרְגֵהוּ וּמִי הִכָּה אֶת־כָּל־אֵלֶּה׃ דְּעוּ אֵפוֹא כִּי לֹא יִפֹּל מִדְּבַר ה׳ אַרְצָה אֲשֶׁר־דִּבֶּר ה׳ עַל־בֵּית אַחְאָב וַה׳ עָשָׂה אֵת אֲשֶׁר דִּבֶּר בְּיַד עַבְדּוֹ אֵלִיָּהוּ׃

The messenger came and told him saying, "They have brought the heads of the king's sons." He said, "Put them in two piles at the entrance of the gate until the morning!" In the morning he went out and stood and said to all the people, "Are you indeed the righteous ones? Behold, I conspired against my master and killed him, but who smote all these? Know, therefore, that no word of G-d that G-d spoke against the house of Ahab will fail to be fulfilled. G-d has done what He said by the hand of His servant Elijah."

Jehu used this as a defense against any criticism he might encounter from the rest of the people. Until then, an opponent might have arisen and accused him of murder. He was in danger of being overthrown in the name of vengeance, just as Zimri had been for killing Elah. But now that the leaders themselves had, albeit unwillingly, become his accomplices, that was no longer possible.

He said, "If I am guilty, you are even more so. No! We have but fulfilled the prophecy of Elijah and punished Ahab and his family as G-d decreed. So let us not think of ourselves as murderers, but as righteous soldiers of G-d."[13] Under the circumstances, they were happy to see things Jehu's way.

10:11-14 וַיַּךְ יֵהוּא אֵת כָּל־הַנִּשְׁאָרִים לְבֵית־אַחְאָב בְּיִזְרְעֶאל וְכָל־גְּדֹלָיו וּמְיֻדָּעָיו וְכֹהֲנָיו עַד־בִּלְתִּי הִשְׁאִיר־לוֹ שָׂרִיד׃ וַיָּקָם וַיָּבֹא וַיֵּלֶךְ שֹׁמְרוֹן הוּא בֵּית־עֵקֶד הָרֹעִים בַּדָּרֶךְ׃ וְיֵהוּא מָצָא אֶת־אֲחֵי אֲחַזְיָהוּ מֶלֶךְ־יְהוּדָה וַיֹּאמֶר מִי אַתֶּם וַיֹּאמְרוּ אֲחֵי אֲחַזְיָהוּ אֲנַחְנוּ וַנֵּרֶד לִשְׁלוֹם בְּנֵי־הַמֶּלֶךְ וּבְנֵי הַגְּבִירָה׃ וַיֹּאמֶר תִּפְשׂוּם חַיִּים וַיִּתְפְּשׂוּם חַיִּים וַיִּשְׁחָטוּם אֶל־בּוֹר בֵּית־עֵקֶד אַרְבָּעִים וּשְׁנַיִם אִישׁ וְלֹא־הִשְׁאִיר אִישׁ מֵהֶם׃

Jehu smote all that remained of the house of Ahab in Jezreel, and all of his great ones, his close friends and his priests, until there was no remnant left of him. He got up and came and went to Samaria. He was at the binding place of the shepherds on the way. Jehu found the brothers of Ahaziah, King of Judah, and said, "Who are you?" They said, "We are brothers of Ahaziah, and we have come down to see how the sons of the king and the sons of the mistress are." He said, "Take them alive!" So they took them alive and slaughtered them into the pit of the binding-place, forty-two men. Not a single one of them was left.

These were not actually Ahaziah's brothers, but his brothers' children. All Ahaziah's brothers had been killed by the Arabs years before, but their children were called brothers too. This use of the word "brother" is found elsewhere in the Bible. Lot, who was Abraham's nephew, was also called his brother. Thus in the Book of Chronicles it says,[14] "When Jehu was carrying out the judgment against the house of Ahab, he found the officers of Judah and the sons of the brothers of Ahaziah serving Ahaziah, and he killed them."[15]

By their answer, Jehu could tell where their allegiance lay. Had they called themselves "the children of Jehoram, King of Judah," Jehu might have spared them.[16] But the respect with which they referred to Ahaziah and Jezebel gave Jehu reason to fear that they would take the side of Ahab's family if they remained alive.[17]

They referred to Jezebel as "the mistress" because she was very powerful. Even while Ahab was alive, her word was law. No one dared disobey her.[18]

"The binding-place of the shepherds," "בית עקד הרעים," was the place where the shepherds gathered to shear their sheep. Some say the word "עקד" refers to the binding of the sheep for shearing.[19] Others say it refers to the gathering of the shepherds for the occasion.[20]

10:15-17 וַיֵּלֶךְ מִשָּׁם וַיִּמְצָא אֶת־יְהוֹנָדָב בֶּן־רֵכָב לִקְרָאתוֹ וַיְבָרְכֵהוּ וַיֹּאמֶר
אֵלָיו הֲיֵשׁ אֶת־לְבָבְךָ יָשָׁר כַּאֲשֶׁר לְבָבִי עִם־לְבָבֶךָ וַיֹּאמֶר יְהוֹנָדָב יֵשׁ וָיֵשׁ תְּנָה
אֶת־יָדֶךָ וַיִּתֵּן יָדוֹ וַיַּעֲלֵהוּ אֵלָיו אֶל־הַמֶּרְכָּבָה: וַיֹּאמֶר לְכָה אִתִּי וּרְאֵה בְּקִנְאָתִי
לַה׳ וַיַּרְכִּבוּ אֹתוֹ בְּרִכְבּוֹ: וַיָּבֹא שֹׁמְרוֹן וַיַּךְ אֶת־כָּל־הַנִּשְׁאָרִים לְאַחְאָב בְּשֹׁמְרוֹן
עַד־הִשְׁמִדוֹ כִּדְבַר ה׳ אֲשֶׁר דִּבֶּר אֶל־אֵלִיָּהוּ:

He went from there and found Jehonadab ben Rechab coming to meet him. He blessed him and said to him, "Is your heart upright as my heart is with your heart?" Jehonadab said, "It is!" "If it is, give your hand!" He gave his hand and he brought him up to him into the chariot. He said, "Come with me and see my zeal for G-d!" So they had him ride in his chariot. He came to Samaria and smote all who were left of Ahab in Samaria, until he had wiped him out, in accordance with the word of G-d that He had spoken to Elijah.

Jehonadab ben Rechab was a descendant of Jethro, the father-in-law of Moses. His descendants, the Kenites, were known for their great scholarship and piety. They were among the foremost students of the first of the judges, Othniel ben Kenaz.

During the time of the judges and the First Temple, most of the Jewish People lived on their ancestral portions, each within the territory of his own tribe. Converts therefore did not assimilate into the general population as readily as they did during later periods. The Kenites remained distinct from the rest of Israel, almost as a separate tribe. Since they did not receive a portion of the land, they continued to live as nomads long after the rest of the Jews had become accustomed to a settled way of life.

Jehu did not know who would support him and who not, so he approached everyone he met with a question. He was pleased with Jehonadab's positive response, and saw it as a sign from heaven that he was doing the right thing.[21]

Jehonadab congratulated Jehu on his victory over the wicked, and was eager to offer his support. He hoped that Jehu would be able to bring about a genuine reform in Israel.

10:18,19 וַיִּקְבֹּץ יֵהוּא אֶת־כָּל־הָעָם וַיֹּאמֶר אֲלֵהֶם אַחְאָב עָבַד אֶת־הַבַּעַל
מְעָט יֵהוּא יַעַבְדֶנּוּ הַרְבֵּה׃ וְעַתָּה כָל־נְבִיאֵי הַבַּעַל כָּל־עֹבְדָיו וְכָל־כֹּהֲנָיו קִרְאוּ
אֵלַי אִישׁ אַל־יִפָּקֵד כִּי זֶבַח גָּדוֹל לִי לַבַּעַל כֹּל אֲשֶׁר־יִפָּקֵד לֹא יִחְיֶה וְיֵהוּא
עָשָׂה בְעָקְבָּה לְמַעַן הַאֲבִיד אֶת־עֹבְדֵי הַבָּעַל׃

Jehu gathered the whole people and said to them, "Ahab served Baal a little, but Jehu will serve him a lot! So now, call to me all the prophets of Baal, all his worshipers and all his priests. Let not one be missing, for I am having a great sacrifice for Baal. Anyone who is missing will not live!" Jehu did this cunningly, to destroy the worshipers of Baal.

G-d had told Elijah that Jehu would not only punish the house of Ahab, but wipe out the cult of Baal as well. Now he prepared to fulfill his second mission. He proceeded with the cunning that he had already demonstrated in foiling the political moves of Jezebel and the other survivors of Ahab's family. This time he used it to devise a plot to wipe out all the adherents of Baal in one blow.

Jehu decided not to immediately proclaim his opposition to Baal, for if he did, many of those who worshiped Baal might feign loyalty to

G-d to escape punishment. Or, worse yet, the followers of Baal might unite and rebel against him. So instead, he pretended to support them.

Now, in general it is forbidden to trick a person into exposing his sinfulness in front of witnesses in order to catch him and have him punished. But, in the case of idolatry it is sometimes permitted, because the sin of idolatry is so severe. If a person tries to persuade others to worship idols, one may pretend to be interested and induce him to present his arguments in front of witnesses. They can then testify against him in court and he will be convicted and punished. There is no other sin for which such deception is permitted.[22] Jehu devised a variation of this scheme to trap the worshipers of Baal.

But Jehu went one step too far. Instead of merely expressing interest, he pretended to already be an adherent of Baal. That was a sin, for a person may not profess support for idolatry, even if in his heart he is solidly faithful to G-d.[23]

He said, "Do you think I killed Jehoram because he worshiped Baal instead of G-d? On the contrary, it was because his dedication to Baal was not complete!"[24]

The words "זבח גדול לבעל" "a great sacrifice for Baal" literally mean "a great slaughter for Baal." When Jehu used them, they had a double meaning. It was the worshipers of Baal themselves that he was planning to slaughter![25]

10:20-22 וַיֹּאמֶר יֵהוּא קַדְּשׁוּ עֲצָרָה לַבַּעַל וַיִּקְרָאוּ׃ וַיִּשְׁלַח יֵהוּא בְּכָל־
יִשְׂרָאֵל וַיָּבֹאוּ כָּל־עֹבְדֵי הַבַּעַל וְלֹא־נִשְׁאַר אִישׁ אֲשֶׁר לֹא־בָא וַיָּבֹאוּ בֵּית הַבַּעַל
וַיִּמָּלֵא בֵית־הַבַּעַל פֶּה לָפֶה׃ וַיֹּאמֶר לַאֲשֶׁר עַל־הַמֶּלְתָּחָה הוֹצֵא לְבוּשׁ לְכֹל
עֹבְדֵי הַבָּעַל וַיֹּצֵא לָהֶם הַמַּלְבּוּשׁ׃

Jehu said, "Dedicate an assembly for Baal!" and they proclaimed it. Jehu sent through all of Israel, and all those who served Baal came. Not a single one was left that did not come. They came to the house of Baal, and the house of Baal was filled from end to end. He said to the one who was in charge of the wardrobe, "Bring out uniforms for all the worshipers of Baal!" and he brought out the uniforms for them.

Once the worshipers of Baal were all assembled, Jehu had them put on their ceremonial garments, which were kept in a special room of the temple. This would make them easier to identify in case any tried to escape after the soldiers began to attack them. It was also an unambiguous demonstration of their participation in the idolatrous rite.[26]

10:23 וַיָּבֹא יֵהוּא וִיהוֹנָדָב בֶּן־רֵכָב בֵּית הַבָּעַל וַיֹּאמֶר לְעֹבְדֵי הַבַּעַל חַפְּשׂוּ
וּרְאוּ פֶּן־יֶשׁ־פֹּה עִמָּכֶם מֵעַבְדֵי ה׳ כִּי אִם־עֹבְדֵי הַבַּעַל לְבַדָּם:

Jehu and Jehonadab ben Rechab came to the house of Baal. He said to the worshipers of Baal, "Search and see, lest there be here with you any of the servants of G-d, for there can only be worshipers of Baal!"

Finally, he asked the idolators themselves to search out anyone that they might suspect of having some loyalty to G-d. This was not a time to change allegiance. No one who was not already a steadfast follower of Baal was permitted to attend. Thus Jehu made sure that he would not be executing any who really worshiped G-d, but had come to worship Baal now because they thought thus to gain Jehu's favor.

10:24 וַיָּבֹאוּ לַעֲשׂוֹת זְבָחִים וְעֹלוֹת וְיֵהוּא שָׂם־לוֹ בַחוּץ שְׁמֹנִים אִישׁ
וַיֹּאמֶר הָאִישׁ אֲשֶׁר־יִמָּלֵט מִן־הָאֲנָשִׁים אֲשֶׁר אֲנִי מֵבִיא עַל־יְדֵיכֶם נַפְשׁוֹ תַּחַת
נַפְשׁוֹ:

They came to perform sacrifices and burnt offerings. Jehu placed himself eighty men outside and said, "The man from whom any of the men that I bring to your hands escapes, his life will be in place of his life."

These instructions must have been given earlier, before the idolaters had gathered, for during the ceremony Jehu was inside the temple. He warned his men, "Any guard who is negligent and lets even a single idolater escape will pay with his own life for the life of that man."

10:25 וַיְהִי כְּכַלֹּתוֹ לַעֲשׂוֹת הָעֹלָה וַיֹּאמֶר יֵהוּא לָרָצִים וְלַשָּׁלִשִׁים בֹּאוּ
הַכּוּם אִישׁ אַל־יֵצֵא וַיַּכּוּם לְפִי־חָרֶב וַיַּשְׁלִכוּ הָרָצִים וְהַשָּׁלִשִׁים וַיֵּלְכוּ עַד־עִיר
בֵּית־הַבָּעַל׃

When he finished performing the burnt offering, Jehu said to the runners and the officers, "Come and smite them. Let not a single one get out!" So they smote them by the edge of the sword. The runners and the officers threw them out of the way, and they went as far as the city of the house of Baal.

Jehu had his men wait until the sacrifice was completed before closing in. By having all these people participate in an act of idolatry, Jehu removed any doubt of their guilt. Even had they never served Baal before, they would deserve to die for this one act. Jehu's soldiers all saw and knew with certainty, so there was no need to bring them before a court and have witnesses testify against them.[27] Perhaps Jehu and his men were considered a Sanhedrin, for there were eighty-one of them, ten more than the required number.

As they killed them, they took the bodies and threw them away from the building so that they would be able to kill those that were farther in.[28] Another interpretation of the word "וישלכו" is that they threw themselves. In their enthusiasm to kill the idolators, they ran to the city of Baal as if they were being thrown.[29]

10:26,27 וַיֹּצִאוּ אֶת־מַצְּבוֹת בֵּית־הַבַּעַל וַיִּשְׂרְפוּהָ׃ וַיִּתְּצוּ אֵת מַצְּבַת
הַבָּעַל וַיִּתְּצוּ אֶת־בֵּית הַבַּעַל וַיְשִׂמֻהוּ למחראות (לְמוֹצָאוֹת קרי) עַד־הַיּוֹם׃

They took out the monuments of the house of Baal and burnt it. They broke down the monument of Baal, and broke down the house of Baal and made it into an outhouse until this day.

After killing those who had served Baal, they destroyed the temple and all the idols. They did everything they could to prevent the cult of Baal from ever being revived in Israel. They were careful to burn every single monument, therefore it says not "they burnt them" but "they burnt it."[30]

10:28,29 וַיַּשְׁמֵד יֵהוּא אֶת־הַבַּעַל מִיִּשְׂרָאֵל׃ רַק חֲטָאֵי יָרָבְעָם בֶּן־נְבָט
אֲשֶׁר הֶחֱטִיא אֶת־יִשְׂרָאֵל לֹא־סָר יֵהוּא מֵאַחֲרֵיהֶם עֶגְלֵי הַזָּהָב אֲשֶׁר בֵּית־אֵל וַאֲשֶׁר בְּדָן׃

Jehu wiped out Baal from Israel. Only from the sins of Jeroboam ben Nebat, who made Israel sin, did Jehu not deviate from following them, the golden calves that were in Beth-el and that were in Dan.

Like his predecessors, Jehu could not bring himself to abandon the golden calves. Though they were a clear violation of the prohibition of making graven images to worship, the kings of Israel claimed that they were justified because they were intended for the worship of G-d alone, not for any other god or power. Jehu knew this cult was wrong, but he continued it. Like the earlier kings of Israel, he was afraid that if the people returned to making yearly pilgrimages to Jerusalem, their allegiance would return to the House of David as well and the Kingdom of Israel would collapse.[31]

Not only was this a violation of a serious prohibition. It was also a demonstration of lack of trust in G-d. Hadn't G-d promised Jehu that he and his descendants would rule over Israel for four generations? He should have felt confident that his kingdom would endure even if the people worshiped together in Jerusalem again.[32]

Some say that Jehu did not originally worship the golden calves, but after becoming king he was corrupted. Having tasted power, he could not bear to risk losing it.[33]

10:30 וַיֹּאמֶר ה׳ אֶל־יֵהוּא יַעַן אֲשֶׁר־הֱטִיבֹתָ לַעֲשׂוֹת הַיָּשָׁר בְּעֵינַי כְּכֹל
אֲשֶׁר בִּלְבָבִי עָשִׂיתָ לְבֵית אַחְאָב בְּנֵי רְבִעִים יֵשְׁבוּ לְךָ עַל־כִּסֵּא יִשְׂרָאֵל׃

G-d said to Jehu, "Since you have done well that which is upright in My eyes, according to all that was in My heart did you do to the house of Ahab, sons of the fourth generation will sit for you on the throne of Israel."

G-d sent the prophet Jonah ben Amitai to deliver this message to Jehu. Earlier, Elisha had chosen Jonah as his messenger to inform Jehu of his mission. Now G-d spoke to Jonah directly, and sent him to commend Jehu for faithfully fulfilling it.[34] This seems to have been before Jehu went astray, as was described in the preceding verse.

As Omri had been rewarded, so would Jehu be. Omri had a son, Ahab, and two grandsons, Ahaziah and Jehoram, who inherited his throne. So too would Jehu be followed by Jehoahaz, Jehoash, Jeroboam and Zechariah. It was a great privilege, but it also involved a responsibility. In that, Jehu failed, and his failure had dire consequences for himself and his people.[35]

10:31-33 וְיֵהוּא לֹא שָׁמַר לָלֶכֶת בְּתוֹרַת־ה׳ אֱלֹהֵי־יִשְׂרָאֵל בְּכָל־לְבָבוֹ לֹא סָר
מֵעַל חַטֹּאות יָרָבְעָם אֲשֶׁר הֶחֱטִיא אֶת־יִשְׂרָאֵל: בַּיָּמִים הָהֵם הֵחֵל ה׳ לְקַצּוֹת
בְּיִשְׂרָאֵל וַיַּכֵּם חֲזָאֵל בְּכָל־גְּבוּל יִשְׂרָאֵל: מִן־הַיַּרְדֵּן מִזְרַח הַשֶּׁמֶשׁ אֵת כָּל־אֶרֶץ
הַגִּלְעָד הַגָּדִי וְהָראוּבֵנִי וְהַמְנַשִּׁי מֵעֲרֹעֵר אֲשֶׁר עַל־נַחַל אַרְנֹן וְהַגִּלְעָד וְהַבָּשָׁן:

But Jehu was not careful to go in the Torah of the L-rd, the G-d of Israel, with all his heart. He didn't deviate from the sins of Jeroboam, who made Israel sin. In those days G-d started to cut down Israel. Hazael smote them on all the borders of Israel. From the Jordan eastward, where the sun rises, the whole land of Gilead, the Gadites, the Reubenites, and the Manassites, from Aroer, which is on the Arnon River, and Gilead and Bashan.

G-d began to bring troubles upon the Jewish People in the time of Jehu. These were a warning of what would happen in the future if they did not improve. But Jehu and his people chose to ignore them. They had taken a big step by eliminating the worship of Baal, but that was not enough. A person must continually improve himself. The moment he becomes complacent and relaxes his efforts, he begins to deteriorate. He may think it is only a matter of not getting better, but really he is getting worse.

Thus was fulfilled Elijah's prophecy,[36] "Those who escape the sword of Hazael, Jehu will kill, and those who escape the sword of Jehu, Elisha will kill." Hazael attacked the Jewish People indiscriminately. He killed the righteous as well as the wicked, and the wicked, too, were among those who escaped. Jehu pursued only those who sinned openly. But Elisha was able to see what was in men's hearts. He cursed the wicked and they died.[37]

10:34-36 וְיֶתֶר דִּבְרֵי יֵהוּא וְכָל־אֲשֶׁר עָשָׂה וְכָל־גְּבוּרָתוֹ הֲלוֹא־הֵם כְּתוּבִים
עַל־סֵפֶר דִּבְרֵי הַיָּמִים לְמַלְכֵי יִשְׂרָאֵל: וַיִּשְׁכַּב יֵהוּא עִם־אֲבֹתָיו וַיִּקְבְּרוּ אֹתוֹ
בְּשֹׁמְרוֹן וַיִּמְלֹךְ יְהוֹאָחָז בְּנוֹ תַּחְתָּיו: וְהַיָּמִים אֲשֶׁר מָלַךְ יֵהוּא עַל־יִשְׂרָאֵל
עֶשְׂרִים־וּשְׁמֹנֶה שָׁנָה בְּשֹׁמְרוֹן:

The rest of the things about Jehu and all that he did and all his might are indeed written in the Book of the Chronicles of the Kings of Israel. Jehu lay down with his fathers. They buried him in Samaria, and Jehoahaz, his son, became king in his place. The time that Jehu reigned over Israel was twenty-eight years in Samaria.

Jehu was a righteous king who sincerely tried to serve G-d. He was rewarded with a long reign and the assurance that his children and grandchildren would inherit his throne. Of such a great man much is expected, so he was criticized for his mistakes even when they were relatively small. Jehu knew that by supporting the cult of the golden calves he was violating the Torah, but he considered this deviation harmless, since his intention was to serve G-d alone.

But no deviation from the Torah, however minute, is harmless. If continued uncorrected, it leads to greater and greater violations, and finally idolatry and denial of G-d. Thus Jehu's mistakes led to more serious ones in the hands of his descendants. Finally, his household deteriorated and was destroyed like those of the kings of Israel who had come before him.

Why did Jehu, who began his reign so righteously, ignore the prophet's warning and worship the golden calves? Some say he condemned himself to eventually go astray by uttering the words, "Jehu will serve Baal a lot." Having proclaimed it himself, he was destined to fulfill it.[38]

Others say he saw the signature of approval that Ahijah the Shilonite had given to Jeroboam, supporting his rebellion against Rehoboam. Ahijah had not intended it as a support of any deviant practices, but Jeroboam took advantage of it to claim the prophet's approval of the cult of the golden calves. The generations that followed continued to be misled by it.[39]

The loss of territory east of the Jordan was the beginning of the exile of the Jewish People, and Jehu was one of the leaders who is held responsible for that exile. It was not until seven high courts served idolatry that G-d permitted the holy land to be destroyed, and Jehu's court was one of them.[40]

II KINGS 11

11:1 וַעֲתַלְיָה אֵם אֲחַזְיָהוּ וראתה (רָאֲתָה קרי) כִּי מֵת בְּנָהּ וַתָּקָם
וַתְּאַבֵּד אֵת כָּל־זֶרַע הַמַּמְלָכָה׃

Athaliah, the mother of Ahaziah, saw that her son was dead, and she got up and destroyed all the descendants of the royal house.

Athaliah was the daughter of Ahab and Jezebel, and she was heir to their wickedness. She murdered her own grandchildren so that she could claim the throne for herself.

It is hard to imagine how a person's craving for power could be so great that it brings him to kill his own children, but history is replete with such cases. One might also wonder how a person could be so shortsighted. Who would inherit her kingdom after she died? Did she not care that her line would be wiped out? Some say that Athaliah had other, illegitimate, children, and it was to these that she hoped to leave her throne and inheritance.[1]

At that moment, the House of David was very nearly wiped out. In three generations, they suffered four terrible massacres First, Jehoram, the son of Jehoshaphat, killed his own brothers. Then all but one of his own children were killed by the Arabs. Although they had children who survived, later those too were killed by Jehu together with Jehoram's son and successor, Ahaziah, as part of the destruction of the house of Ahab. Concerning the death of Ahaziah and his nephews at the hand of Jehu, the Book of Chronicles says,[2] "Ahaziah's downfall was from G-d, that he come to Jehoram, and when he came, that he go out with Jehoram to Jehu ben Nimshi, whom G-d had appointed to wipe out the house of Ahab."

Why had G-d passed such a harsh decree against the children of His beloved servant, David? It was because they united themselves in marriage with the family of Ahab. Asa took the daughter of Omri as a wife for his son Jehoshaphat, and later Jehoshaphat's son, Jehoram, was married to Ahab's daughter, Athaliah. Thus not only were they influenced by the evil ways of the kings of Israel, but actually became part of the house of Ahab. The divine decree of destruction therefore fell upon them as well.[3]

Jehoshaphat thought that by taking Ahab's daughter as a wife for his son he would bring the Kingdom of Israel back under the influence of the House of David. But in the end she tried to seize even the Kingdom of Judah for herself and destroy his rightful heirs. So it is, that if a person marries to raise his status, he ends up only increasing the greatness of his wife's family and weakening his own line. Her family will claim his inheritance, and his own children will be left with nothing.[4]

David was also being punished for inadvertently bringing about the destruction of the families of Ahimelech, the priest, and of King Saul. When David was fleeing from Saul, he came to the city of Nob where he received help from Ahimelech the High Priest. Soon Saul came looking for him, and when he found out that the priests had helped David, he had Ahimelech and his whole family killed. At that time, it was divinely decreed that David's descendants be wiped out too. But one of Ahimelech's son's, Abiathar, managed to escape and join David. It was thereupon decreed that one of David's descendants, too, would escape.[5]

But David had not intended any harm to Ahimelech. Why was he condemned to this terrible fate? Some say it was because he had lied and told Ahimelech that he was on a mission for Saul when he was really running away. Even though a person is permitted to lie to save a life, he must be careful not to thereby endanger the lives of others.[6]

As long as David's descendants were righteous, they were protected from this decree. But when, under the influence of his wife, Ahaziah turned to violence and idolatry, he and his children became vulnerable.

11:2 וַתִּקַּח יְהוֹשֶׁבַע בַּת־הַמֶּלֶךְ־יוֹרָם אֲחוֹת אֲחַזְיָהוּ אֶת־יוֹאָשׁ
בֶּן־אֲחַזְיָה וַתִּגְנֹב אֹתוֹ מִתּוֹךְ בְּנֵי־הַמֶּלֶךְ הממותתים (הַמּוּמָתִים קרי) אֹתוֹ
וְאֶת־מֵנִקְתּוֹ בַּחֲדַר הַמִּטּוֹת וַיַּסְתִּרוּ אֹתוֹ מִפְּנֵי עֲתַלְיָהוּ וְלֹא הוּמָת׃

But Jehosheba, the daughter of Jehoram, the sister of Ahaziah, took Joash, the son of Ahaziah, and stole him from among the children of the king who were being killed, him and his nurse, in the bed room. She hid him from Athaliah and he wasn't killed.

Some say the "bed room" referred to here was a room in the Temple where the priests slept. Those who were not of the tribe of Levi were not generally permitted there, but an exception was made in this case, since it was a matter of life and death.[7]

Jehosheba had access to that room because she was married to Jehoiada, the High Priest, as it says in the Book of Chronicles,[8] "Jehosheba, the daughter of King Jehoram, the wife of Jehoiada the priest." Her familiarity with the outer rooms of the Temple enabled her to bring her nephew there without being noticed, and to come and go without arousing suspicion.[9]

Others say it was the room above the Holy of Holies. Ordinarily, no one was allowed to enter that room. It was only used to gain access to the Holy of Holies from above when repairs had to be made. No one would dare enter to search there. What better place to hide the young king?[10]

Some reconcile the two opinions by saying that in the summer he was kept above the Holy of Holies, but in the winter it was too cold for him there, so he was moved to the rooms next to the sanctuary, which were heated for the priests who slept there.[11] Others say he was brought to those rooms first, but afterwards Jehoiada became afraid that he might be discovered there and killed, so he had him transferred to the room above the Holy of Holies.

King David foresaw that one day his descendants would be in danger of destruction, but would be hidden in the Temple and saved, so he wrote,[12] "He will hide me in His shelter on the day of evil. He will conceal me in the seclusion of His tent. On a rock He will raise me up." "Rock" refers to Jehoiada, who was like a rock.[13] He also alluded to Jehosheba by the words,[14] "For You will light my lamp," and to Jehoiada by the words, "The L-rd, my G-d, will make my darkness shine."[15]

Thus David was repaid for faithfully protecting Abiathar the priest and the line of Ahimelech. Now, it was by the priesthood that his own line was saved.[16]

11:3,4 וַיְהִי אִתָּהּ בֵּית ה׳ מִתְחַבֵּא שֵׁשׁ שָׁנִים וַעֲתַלְיָה מֹלֶכֶת עַל־הָאָרֶץ׃
וּבַשָּׁנָה הַשְּׁבִיעִית שָׁלַח יְהוֹיָדָע וַיִּקַּח אֶת־שָׂרֵי המאיות (הַמֵּאוֹת קרי) לַכָּרִי
וְלָרָצִים וַיָּבֵא אֹתָם אֵלָיו בֵּית ה׳ וַיִּכְרֹת לָהֶם בְּרִית וַיַּשְׁבַּע אֹתָם בְּבֵית ה׳ וַיַּרְא
אֹתָם אֶת־בֶּן־הַמֶּלֶךְ׃

He was with her in the House of G-d, hiding, for six years, and Athaliah ruled over the land. In the seventh year Jehoiada sent and brought the officers of the hundreds to the nobles and to the runners, and brought them to him to the House of G-d. He made a covenant with them and had them swear in the House of G-d. Then he showed them the son of the king.

The officers of the hundreds were the highest officers of the Levites.[17] The "כרי," "nobles," were the upper class of Israel. Since during the period of the kings Israel was surrounded by hostile neighbors and under constant threat, it was the military leaders who had the greatest importance and power. The upper class was therefore a warrior class, who earned their position by their bravery and military skill.[18]

In the Book of Chronicles it says:[19]

> In the seventh year Jehoiada strengthened himself. He took the officers of the hundreds, Azariah ben Jehoram, Ishmael Ben Jehohanan, Azariah ben Obed, Maaseiah ben Adaiah and Elishaphat ben Zichri into a covenant with him. They went around in Judah and gathered the Levites from all the cities of Judah and the heads of the fathers' houses of Israel, and they came to Jerusalem.

11:5-8 וַיְצַוֵּם לֵאמֹר זֶה הַדָּבָר אֲשֶׁר תַּעֲשׂוּן הַשְּׁלִשִׁית מִכֶּם בָּאֵי הַשַּׁבָּת
וְשֹׁמְרֵי מִשְׁמֶרֶת בֵּית הַמֶּלֶךְ: וְהַשְּׁלִשִׁית בְּשַׁעַר סוּר וְהַשְּׁלִשִׁית בַּשַּׁעַר אַחַר
הָרָצִים וּשְׁמַרְתֶּם אֶת־מִשְׁמֶרֶת הַבַּיִת מַסָּח: וּשְׁתֵּי הַיָּדוֹת בָּכֶם כֹּל יֹצְאֵי הַשַּׁבָּת
וְשָׁמְרוּ אֶת־מִשְׁמֶרֶת בֵּית־ה׳ אֶל־הַמֶּלֶךְ: וְהִקַּפְתֶּם עַל־הַמֶּלֶךְ סָבִיב אִישׁ וְכֵלָיו
בְּיָדוֹ וְהַבָּא אֶל־הַשְּׂדֵרוֹת יוּמָת וִהְיוּ אֶת־הַמֶּלֶךְ בְּצֵאתוֹ וּבְבֹאוֹ:

He commanded them saying, "This is what you are to do: One third of you, those who come that week, keeping guard at the king's house. One third will be at the Sur gate, and one third at the gate behind the runners. You will keep guard at the Temple as a barrier. And two thirds of you, all who leave that week, will keep guard at the House of G-d for the king. You will surround the king all around, each one with his weapons in his hand, and whoever comes into the ranks will be killed.

They will be with the king when he goes out and when he comes in."

Since the time of King David, the families of the priests and Levites had been divided into twenty-four shifts, or "watches." Each watch would serve in the Temple for one week, beginning after the offering of the additional sacrifices on Sabbath morning. For that week they would bring all the sacrifices. On the following Sabbath they would conclude their service with the additional sacrifice of that day, and then give the service over to the next watch.[20]

Jehoiada assigned the responsibility of protecting the king to the members of the current watch and the immediately preceding one. Since the current watch would be busy with the Temple service, only half of them would be required to guard the king. The preceding watch, which would otherwise have been free to return home, was now required to stay an extra week. They would all take part in guarding the king, since they had no other responsibilities in the Temple.[21] Therefore one third of the guard was from the current watch and two thirds from the previous one.

The combined group was then divided in three. One third would stand guard at the palace so that none of the king's enemies could get in.[22] The next third would be stationed at the Sur Gate, the gate through which the people passed when coming into the Temple. There were always guards at this gate to warn those who had not properly purified themselves to keep out of the holy area. Whoever came was questioned before he was permitted through, and if he was impure he was sent away, hence the name "Sur," "סור," which means "go away." The expression used in sending away the impure was[23] "סורו טמא," "Go away, Oh impure one!"[24]

In the Book of Chronicles[25] this gate is called the "Gate of the Foundation," "שער היסוד," because the separation between pure and impure is the foundation of holiness.[26] Another explanation of this name is that it means the foundation of the Torah, because there the court would convene to decide questions of law. It was the eastern gate of the Temple, and had seven names: "Sur Gate," "Gate of the Foundation," "שער החרסית," "Sun Gate,"[27] because it faced the rising sun, "שער האיתון" "Arrival Gate,"[28] because everyone entered and left through it, "שער התוך," "Middle Gate,"[29] because it was between the gate of the Sanctuary and the gate of the Women's Courtyard, "שער החדש," "New Gate,"[30] because there the learned men renewed the Law, and "שער העליון," "Upper Gate,"[31] because it was above the Courtyard of Israel and the Women's Courtyard.[32]

The last third were stationed at the "gate behind the runners," so called because the "runners," the foot soldiers, were stationed there.[33] In the Book of Chronicles,[34] they are referred to as "gatekeepers of the thresholds." This gate was in the southern side of the court, and it connected the Temple with the king's palace. Near it was a building called[35] "בית האספים" "the House of Asuphim."[36]

They were especially charged with guarding the places where the wall around the Temple had been broken. These breaks had been made by Athaliah's illegitimate sons, who hoped in this way to weaken the strength of the priests by making their citadel, the Temple, harder to defend.[37]

Some say that the word "מסח" means that they did not take their mind off guarding the king for even a minute.[38] Others say it means "guard it from destruction."[39]

Another interpretation is that only one third, not one half, of the current watch would be diverted from the Temple service to guard the king. They would be divided into three groups, one at the palace, one at the Sur Gate, and one at the gate behind the runners. The larger contingent of the king's guard would come from the watch whose turn had just been completed. Two thirds of that watch would be required to participate. They would accompany the king and protect him wherever he went.[40]

Others say that the current watch would be divided into three groups, one at the palace, one at the Sur Gate, and one at the gate behind the runners. But the previous watch would be divided into only two groups, accompanying the members of the current watch at two of their posts. Half would be at the Sur Gate and half at the gate behind the runners. None would be stationed at the palace.[41]

None of the other watches would be required to help, so no one would have to come before his regular appointed week, or stay more than one week longer.[42] Some say that this was only necessary for one week. Once Athaliah had been killed and her supporters had fled, the king was safe and there was no longer need for special protection.[43]

Although the general plan is clear, the details are not. The structure of these verses makes the description in them difficult to understand, which is why the various interpretations differ so much. The two watches from which the guard was drawn are mentioned separately, "one third of you, those who come that week" in verse 5, and "two thirds of you, all who leave that week" in verse 7. Between them are listed the three places where they would be stationed. This seems to support the interpretation that these were the job of the current watch alone, and the previous watch did not have assigned posts, but rather the general job of protecting the king.

However, the Bible does not always express things as modern western literature would. Within Biblical style, these verses can be interpreted according to the first opinion as well. Jehoiada began by announcing that part of the guard would be taken from the current watch. Since they were involved in the Temple service, he gave them the honor of being mentioned first. Then he went on to describe the various positions. After that, he announced that the rest of the guard would be the whole of the previous watch. It was not necessary to explain that they would be divided in the same way. Finally, he gave general instructions concerning how these duties were to be conducted.

The word "third" in verse 5 may mean that one third of the guard would be taken from the current watch, or that one third would have the job of guarding the palace. According to some interpretations, it seems to be used for both these meanings.

Some say the word "שדרות," "ranks," means the path by which the king would go from the Temple to his palace.[44] Others say it means the rows of guards themselves.[45]

In the Book of Chronicles the division is described this way:[46]

> This is the thing that you will do: One third of you, those who come for that week, of the priests and of the Levites will be for gatekeepers of the thresholds. One third at the house of the king, one third at the Gate of the Foundation, and the whole people in the courtyard of the House of G-d. Let not anyone come into the House of G-d except the priests and the servants, the Levites. They will come, for they are holy. And the whole people will keep the watch of G-d. The Levites will surround the king all around, each one with his weapons in his hand, and whoever comes into the Temple will be killed. They will be with the king when he comes in and when he goes out.

11:9 וַיַּעֲשׂוּ שָׂרֵי המאיות (הַמֵּאוֹת קרי) כְּכֹל אֲשֶׁר־צִוָּה יְהוֹיָדָע הַכֹּהֵן
וַיִּקְחוּ אִישׁ אֶת־אֲנָשָׁיו בָּאֵי הַשַּׁבָּת עִם יֹצְאֵי הַשַּׁבָּת וַיָּבֹאוּ אֶל־יְהוֹיָדָע הַכֹּהֵן׃

The officers of the hundreds did everything that Jehoiada the priest had commanded. Each one took his men, those that were coming for that week with those that were leaving for that week, and they came to Jehoiada the priest.

In the Book of Chronicles it says:[47]

> The Levites and all of Judah did according to everything that Jehoiada the priest had commanded. Each one took his men, those that were coming for that week with those that were leaving that week, for Jehoiada had not let that division go.

11:10 וַיִּתֵּן הַכֹּהֵן לְשָׂרֵי הַמֵּאיוֹת אֶת־הַחֲנִית וְאֶת־הַשְּׁלָטִים אֲשֶׁר לַמֶּלֶךְ דָּוִד אֲשֶׁר בְּבֵית ה׳:

The priest gave the officers of the hundreds the spear and the shields of King David that were in the House of G-d.

Some say these were the shields that David had captured from his enemies. He had put them into the treasury of the Temple.[48] Others say they were the shields that Solomon had made from the gold that David dedicated to the Temple.[49] As for the small shields mentioned in the Book of Chronicles, they are omitted here because they were not the original ones. The gold ones had been taken by Shishak, King of Egypt, in the time of Rehoboam, and these that had been made to replace them were of copper, not gold.[50]

The word "חנית," "spear," is in the singular form, but it can be understood as singular or plural. Context seems to imply that here the plural meaning is intended. There were many spears just as there were many shields, and they were distributed among the guards. But some say that there was indeed only one spear, the great spear of Goliath.[51]

11:11,12 וַיַּעַמְדוּ הָרָצִים אִישׁ וְכֵלָיו בְּיָדוֹ מִכֶּתֶף הַבַּיִת הַיְמָנִית עַד־כֶּתֶף הַבַּיִת הַשְּׂמָאלִית לַמִּזְבֵּחַ וְלַבָּיִת עַל־הַמֶּלֶךְ סָבִיב: וַיּוֹצִא אֶת־בֶּן־הַמֶּלֶךְ וַיִּתֵּן עָלָיו אֶת־הַנֵּזֶר וְאֶת־הָעֵדוּת וַיַּמְלִכוּ אֹתוֹ וַיִּמְשָׁחֻהוּ וַיַּכּוּ־כָף וַיֹּאמְרוּ יְחִי הַמֶּלֶךְ:

The runners stood, each one with his weapons in his hand, from the right side of the house to the left side of the house, from the altar inward, close to the king all around. He brought out the son of the king and put the crown on him and the testimony. They made him king and anointed him, and clapped their hands and said, "Long live the king!"

Only when all this had been arranged and the Temple was secure did Jehoiada reveal the young king. He put the ancestral crown on his head and gave him the "testimony," the Torah scroll that the king was required to have with him at all times.[52]

Some say that the "testimony" was the crown itself. The special crown of the House of David would only fit on the head of one who was divinely chosen to be king. When it was placed on Joash's head and rested comfortably there, that itself was testimony that he was the rightful heir to the throne.[53] This was especially important in Joash's case, since the people did not know him. There were probably many who suspected him of being an imposter, but when they saw that the crown fit, they all knew he really was a descendant of David. Without hesitation they proclaimed him their king.[54]

Others say that the word "עדות" means not "testimony" but "ornaments." It refers to the royal robes and jewels that it had become customary for the Kings of Judah to wear.[55]

As has already been explained, it was not necessary to anoint Joash to confer upon him the status of king. He was a descendant of David, whose dynasty was eternal, and whose descendants would inherit his throne without being anointed. But in times such as this, when the designated king's right to the throne was questioned, the holy oil became a sign of G-d's choice, quieting those who would contest it. Some say that this was not just a practical measure, but a divine law. It was one of the purposes for which G-d had designated the holy oil to be used, for in that way the kingdom would be secure.[56]

11:13 וַתִּשְׁמַע עֲתַלְיָה אֶת־קוֹל הָרָצִין הָעָם וַתָּבֹא אֶל־הָעָם בֵּית ה׳:

Athaliah heard the sound of the runners and the people and she came to the people in the House of G-d.

The words "קול הרצים העם" can be understood in two ways. One is "the sound of the runners and the people," as if it said "קול הרצים והעם." The other is, "the sound of the people running." Thus, in the Book of Chronicles it says,[57] "Athaliah heard the sound of the people who were running and those who were cheering the king, and she came to the people to the House of G-d."[58]

11:14 וַתֵּרֶא וְהִנֵּה הַמֶּלֶךְ עֹמֵד עַל־הָעַמּוּד כַּמִּשְׁפָּט וְהַשָּׂרִים וְהַחֲצֹצְרוֹת
אֶל־הַמֶּלֶךְ וְכָל־עַם הָאָרֶץ שָׂמֵחַ וְתֹקֵעַ בַּחֲצֹצְרוֹת וַתִּקְרַע עֲתַלְיָה אֶת־בְּגָדֶיהָ
וַתִּקְרָא קֶשֶׁר קָשֶׁר׃

She saw, and behold, the king was standing on the platform as befits a king, and the officers and the trumpets were for the king. All the people of the land were happy and blowing trumpets. Athaliah tore her clothes and cried, "A conspiracy! A conspiracy!"

The words "על העמוד," "on the platform," are difficult to explain, because the word "עמוד" generally means a pillar, not a platform. The king certainly did not stand on top of a pillar. One solution is that this verse is an exception, and that here it means "platform."[59] Others say it means "place" or "position." That is, Joash was holding the position that rightfully belonged to him.[60] This interpretation is supported by the corresponding verse in the Book of Chronicles, which reads,[61] "עמודו" "his position," instead of "העמוד" "the position." When the word is in the possessive form, it is clear that it refers to something that was specifically his. The pillars of the Temple did not belong to the king, but his position belonged to him and no one else. Another interpretation is that it means, "next to the pillar," as if it were written "על ידי העמוד"[62]

11:15 וַיְצַו יְהוֹיָדָע הַכֹּהֵן אֶת־שָׂרֵי המאיות (הַמֵּאוֹת קרי) פְּקֻדֵי הַחַיִל
וַיֹּאמֶר אֲלֵיהֶם הוֹצִיאוּ אֹתָהּ אֶל־מִבֵּית לַשְּׂדֵרֹת וְהַבָּא אַחֲרֶיהָ הָמֵת בֶּחָרֶב כִּי
אָמַר הַכֹּהֵן אַל־תּוּמַת בֵּית ה׳׃

Jehoiada the priest commanded the officers of the hundreds, who were appointed over the army and said to them, "Take her out by way of the ranks, and any who follow her, kill by the sword!" for the priest had said, "Let her not be killed in the House of G-d!"

Jehoiada had them take her out through the gate that led to the palace. He was afraid that if she went out in the direction of the city her supporters would come to her aid.[63] According to those who say "שדרות" means the ranks of soldiers, this was to make sure that she would be surrounded by soldiers at all times and not be able to escape.[64]

According to those who say it means the path leading to the palace, she would be trapped inside. The palace was connected with the Temple, and there was no way to leave the royal compound except through gates that Jehoiada's men had already taken.[65]

11:16 וַיָּשִׂמוּ לָהּ יָדַיִם וַתָּבוֹא דֶּרֶךְ־מְבוֹא הַסּוּסִים בֵּית הַמֶּלֶךְ וַתּוּמַת שָׁם׃

They made room for her. She came by way of the horse entrance to the king's house and was killed there.

Rather than arrest Athaliah inside the Temple, they let her turn and flee, as if to escape. But having blocked her path in all other directions, she was forced to run toward the palace. She chose to go out through the gate called "the horse entrance," so they let her, and killed her there.[66]

11:17 וַיִּכְרֹת יְהוֹיָדָע אֶת־הַבְּרִית בֵּין ה׳ וּבֵין הַמֶּלֶךְ וּבֵין הָעָם לִהְיוֹת לְעָם לַה׳ וּבֵין הַמֶּלֶךְ וּבֵין הָעָם׃

Jehoiada made a covenant between G-d and the king and the people, that the people be for G-d, and between the king and the people.

There were two parts to this covenant. The first was "between G-d and the king and the people," that Joash and the people serve G-d faithfully and wipe out idolatry. The second was "between the king and the people," that the people obey their new king, and that he, in turn, take care of them, lead them bravely in war, and treat them kindly.[67]

11:18 וַיָּבֹאוּ כָל־עַם הָאָרֶץ בֵּית־הַבַּעַל וַיִּתְּצֻהוּ אֶת־מִזְבְּחֹתָו וְאֶת־צְלָמָיו שִׁבְּרוּ הֵיטֵב וְאֵת מַתָּן כֹּהֵן הַבַּעַל הָרְגוּ לִפְנֵי הַמִּזְבְּחוֹת וַיָּשֶׂם הַכֹּהֵן פְּקֻדֹּת עַל־בֵּית ה׳׃

All the people of the land came to the house of Baal and broke it down. His altars and his statues they smashed well, and Matan, the priest of Baal, they killed before the altars. Then the priest put appointees over the House of G-d.

During the years of corruption, the organization of shifts of priests and Levites established by King David had been neglected.[68] The righteous priests had tried their best, but there had been little they could do as long as Athaliah was in power.[69] Thus it says in the Book of Chronicles:[70]

> Jehoiada made designated jobs in the House of G-d, to be assigned to the priests, the Levites, whom David had apportioned over the House of G-d, to bring the sacrifices of G-d, as is written in the Torah of Moses, with joy and with song, as established by David. He had the gatekeepers stand at the gates of the House of G-d, so that no impure person would come in for any purpose.

11:19,20 וַיִּקַּח אֶת־שָׂרֵי הַמֵּאוֹת וְאֶת־הַכָּרִי וְאֶת־הָרָצִים וְאֵת כָּל־עַם הָאָרֶץ וַיֹּרִידוּ אֶת־הַמֶּלֶךְ מִבֵּית ה׳ וַיָּבוֹאוּ דֶּרֶךְ־שַׁעַר הָרָצִים בֵּית הַמֶּלֶךְ וַיֵּשֶׁב עַל־כִּסֵּא הַמְּלָכִים׃ וַיִּשְׂמַח כָּל־עַם־הָאָרֶץ וְהָעִיר שָׁקָטָה וְאֶת־עֲתַלְיָהוּ הֵמִיתוּ בַחֶרֶב בֵּית מלך (הַמֶּלֶךְ קרי)׃

He took the officers of the hundreds and the nobles and the runners and all the people of the land, and they brought down the king from the House of G-d. They brought him by way of the Gate of the Runners to the house of the king, and he sat on the throne of the kings. All the people of the land rejoiced, and the land was quiet. As for Athaliah, they killed her by the sword in the house of the king.

In the Book of Chronicles[71] it says that the king entered through the "Upper Gate." Perhaps he went out to the people in the Women's Courtyard, then went back into the Courtyard of Israel, and then through the Gate of the Runners to the palace.

As happy as the people were with their new king, their joy was not complete until Athaliah was dead and they no longer needed to fear her.[72]

II KINGS 12

12:1-4 בֶּן־שֶׁבַע שָׁנִים יְהוֹאָשׁ בְּמָלְכוֹ: בִּשְׁנַת־שֶׁבַע לְיֵהוּא מָלַךְ יְהוֹאָשׁ
וְאַרְבָּעִים שָׁנָה מָלַךְ בִּירוּשָׁלָםִ וְשֵׁם אִמּוֹ צִבְיָה מִבְּאֵר שָׁבַע: וַיַּעַשׂ יְהוֹאָשׁ
הַיָּשָׁר בְּעֵינֵי ה׳ כָּל־יָמָיו אֲשֶׁר הוֹרָהוּ יְהוֹיָדָע הַכֹּהֵן: רַק הַבָּמוֹת לֹא־סָרוּ עוֹד
הָעָם מְזַבְּחִים וּמְקַטְּרִים בַּבָּמוֹת:

Jehoash was seven years old when he became king. In the seventh year of Jehu, Jehoash became king, and he reigned forty years in Jerusalem. His mother's name was Zibiah from Beersheba. Jehoash did what was upright in G-d's eyes all his days, as Jehoiada the priest instructed him. Only the altars were not removed. The people were still sacrificing and burning incense on the altars.

Jehoash's mother, Zibiah, was a righteous woman, and Jehoash followed in her ways.[1] But to his teacher, Jehoiada, goes the real credit for his righteousness. The greatest influence on a person's development comes from those who raise and educate him. The example of his ancestors, though significant, is secondary.

Jehoiada continued to be Jehoash's guide throughout his life. It was his constant presence that kept Jehoash on the path of righteousness. After Jehoiada died, he fell under the influence of the nobles, who had already begun to stray away from Torah. Although he must have realized that they were wrong, without his teacher he could not resist them and became corrupted. Later in the chapter we will read about how this happened.[2] Thus the Bible says not "as Jehoiada taught (למדו) him" but "as Jehoiada instructed (הורהו) him." The word "למוד" refers to training in a way that enables the student to proceed on his own, but "הוראה," means direction or guidance. When his teacher is not there to tell him what to do, the student is lost.[3]

The words "all his days" must therefore mean all the days of Jehoiada, not all the days of Jehoash. Thus in the Book of Chronicles it says,[4]

"Jehoash did what was upright in G-d's eyes all the days of Jehoiada the priest."[5]

Jehoiada was one hundred and thirty when he died, so he was already very old when he took on the job of raising the young king. He was born in the time of King Solomon, when idolatry was first introduced in Jerusalem. G-d saw the people gradually sinking into idolatry, and arranged that a child be born who would eventually help them back to Torah. So it is that whenever Israel sins, G-d prepares a way for them to return.[6]

In the previous chapter, Jehoash's name was spelled "יואש," "Joash," without the letter "ה." The two spellings are variations of the same name, and are used interchangeably. The same is true of Jehoash the son of Jehoahaz, King of Israel. The spelling "יואש" was used in the previous chapter as an allusion to the despair (יאוש) of the nation, for they had given up hope of ever again having a king from the House of David. During the seven years that Athaliah ruled, it seemed as if the last descendants of David had really been wiped out.

12:5,6 וַיֹּאמֶר יְהוֹאָשׁ אֶל־הַכֹּהֲנִים כֹּל כֶּסֶף הַקֳּדָשִׁים אֲשֶׁר יוּבָא בֵית־ה׳
כֶּסֶף עוֹבֵר אִישׁ כֶּסֶף נַפְשׁוֹת עֶרְכּוֹ כָּל־כֶּסֶף אֲשֶׁר יַעֲלֶה עַל לֶב־אִישׁ לְהָבִיא
בֵּית ה׳: יִקְחוּ לָהֶם הַכֹּהֲנִים אִישׁ מֵאֵת מַכָּרוֹ וְהֵם יְחַזְּקוּ אֶת־בֶּדֶק הַבַּיִת לְכֹל
אֲשֶׁר־יִמָּצֵא שָׁם בָּדֶק:

Jehoash said to the priests, "All the money of the holy things that is brought to the House of G-d, obligatory money, each person, the money of his own redemption, all the money that comes upon a person's heart to bring to the House of G-d, the priests will take for themselves, each one from his acquaintance. They will strengthen the repair of the Temple, for all that will be found there to need repair."

In the Book of Chronicles it says,[7] "After that Jehoash had in his heart to renew the House of G-d."

It was not as a result of natural deterioration that the Temple needed to be repaired. It had only been one hundred and fifty-five years since the time of King Solomon when it was built, and it was subject neither to harsh climate nor rough use that would have worn it out. The sad state in which the Temple was found when Jehoash became king was the legacy of the reign of Athaliah, who had intentionally damaged it, as it says in the Book of Chronicles,[8] "For Athaliah the evildoer, her sons made breaks in the House of G-d. All the holy things of the House of G-d, too, did they make into Baalim."[9] The sons mentioned here were not the children of her husband, King Jehoram, since all of Jehoram's sons except Ahaziah had been killed by the Arabs. They were illegitimate children of another man.[10] While she was in power, the people stopped bringing their yearly contribution of a half shekel to the Temple, and some brought it to Baal instead.[11]

The word "בדק," "repair," literally means inspection. It is used here to refer to the places that were broken, and upon inspection were found to need repair.[12]

Some say Jehoash made a special collection for these repairs because he didn't want to use up all the money in the Temple treasury.[13] Others say there was no money left, because Athaliah had taken it all for the Temple of Baal.

Three categories of contributions are referred to here. The first is "obligatory money," referring to the half shekel that each person was required to give every year. The second was "each person, the money of his own redemption," which referred to the pledges that people made. These pledges were made using the expression "I accept my value upon myself," and they were considered a redemption of his soul. The third was "all the money that comes upon a person's heart to bring to the House of G-d." That referred to voluntary contributions that they might make.[14]

The required yearly contribution of a half shekel was given to the Sacrifice Fund, "תרומת הלשכה," which was used to purchase public sacrifices and pay for the operation of the Temple and related public needs. This fund was renewed every year. When the yearly collection was made a new fund was begun, and whatever money was left over from the previous year was used to buy burnt offerings. So too, if a person failed to give his half shekel when it was due and waited until the next year, it would be used for burnt offerings rather than being included with the current contributions.

There were also other funds in the Temple. Some were for money that people had set aside for the purchase of specific sacrifices. They could deposit it in the appropriate box and the priests would take care of the purchase and offering of the sacrifice.

There was also a fund for the repair of the Temple itself. This is the fund that became especially important in the time of Jehoash.[15]

When Athaliah was in power, people had been discouraged from giving contributions to the Temple. During those years many saved their money until a new ruler would arise. Now the time had come, and they brought it all.[16] Jehoash gave the responsibility for these contributions to the individual priests. They were to take the money for themselves, and in return, whenever there was need for money for the Temple, they would be required to provide it. By the decree of the king and the court, all the money that the priests collected became their personal property. Though it had originally been holy, having been dedicated to the Temple, the original sanctity was replaced by the personal responsibility of the priest. Under this system a priest might receive more than he had to give to the Temple, but he might also receive less and have to make up the difference from his own pocket. It was a very simple system, requiring little bookkeeping, but it put a heavy burden on the priests.[17]

12:7,8 וַיְהִי בִּשְׁנַת עֶשְׂרִים וְשָׁלֹשׁ שָׁנָה לַמֶּלֶךְ יְהוֹאָשׁ לֹא־חִזְּקוּ הַכֹּהֲנִים
אֶת־בֶּדֶק הַבָּיִת: וַיִּקְרָא הַמֶּלֶךְ יְהוֹאָשׁ לִיהוֹיָדָע הַכֹּהֵן וְלַכֹּהֲנִים וַיֹּאמֶר אֲלֵהֶם
מַדּוּעַ אֵינְכֶם מְחַזְּקִים אֶת־בֶּדֶק הַבָּיִת וְעַתָּה אַל־תִּקְחוּ־כֶסֶף מֵאֵת מַכָּרֵיכֶם
כִּי־לְבֶדֶק הַבַּיִת תִּתְּנֻהוּ:

In the twenty-third year of King Jehoash the priests had not strengthened the repair of the Temple. King Jehoash called Jehoiada the priest and the priests and said to them, "Why are you not strengthening the repair of the Temple? So now, don't take money from your acquaintances. Give it, rather, for the repair of the Temple."

Some say the king suspected the priests of keeping money for themselves when it was needed for the Temple.[18]

In the Book of Chronicles it says:[19]

> He gathered the priests, the Levites, and said to them, "Go out to the cities of Judah and gather money from all Israel to strengthen the House of your G-d, year by year. Hurry up with this thing!" But the Levites did not hurry up. The king called Jehoiada, the chief, and said to him, "Why didn't you demand of the Levites that they bring from Judah and Jerusalem the tax of Moses, the servant of G-d, and the community of Israel, for the Tent of Testimony?"

The word "משאת", "tax" literally means something that is raised up, and generally means a contribution or a gift. It is similar both in root and usage to the word "תרומה." In this case, however, it refers to the half shekel, which was an obligation, not a voluntary contribution. Jehoash chose to call it "the tax of Moses" because the Torah introduces this commandment with a word derived from the same root, "נשא" in the phrase,[20] "כי תשא," "When you will raise up."[21]

12:9,10 וַיֵּאֹתוּ הַכֹּהֲנִים לְבִלְתִּי קְחַת־כֶּסֶף מֵאֵת הָעָם וּלְבִלְתִּי חַזֵּק אֶת־בֶּדֶק
הַבָּיִת: וַיִּקַּח יְהוֹיָדָע הַכֹּהֵן אֲרוֹן אֶחָד וַיִּקֹּב חֹר בְּדַלְתּוֹ וַיִּתֵּן אֹתוֹ אֵצֶל הַמִּזְבֵּחַ
בימין (מִיָּמִין קרי) בְּבוֹא־אִישׁ בֵּית ה׳ וְנָתְנוּ־שָׁמָּה הַכֹּהֲנִים שֹׁמְרֵי הַסַּף
אֶת־כָּל־הַכֶּסֶף הַמּוּבָא בֵית־ה׳:

The priests agreed not to take money from the people and not to strengthen the repair of the Temple. Jehoiada the priest took one box and bored a hole in its door. He put it next to the altar, to the right as a person would come into the House of G-d. There the priests, the guards of the threshold, put all the money that was brought to the House of G-d.

The priests agreed to the new system. No one would be able to suspect them of misusing the money any more.[22] Perhaps they were also glad to change because they had been losing money under the former system. The demands of maintenance of the Temple were greater than the donations they received.

Some say the "שמרי הסף," "guards of the threshold," were the priests who guarded the gates.[23] Others say that in this verse "סף" means "utensils," rather than "threshold," and they were the general foremen.[24]

In the Book of Chronicles it says:[25]

> The king said, and they made one box and put it at the gate of the House of G-d on the outside. They made an announcement in Judah and in Jerusalem to bring to G-d the tax that had been established by Moses, the servant of G-d, upon Israel in the desert. All the officers and all the people were happy. They brought and threw into the box until it was complete.

Some say there were two boxes, one inside the Temple next to the altar and another outside near the entrance. The Book of Kings describes one and the Book of Chronicles the other. Each served a different purpose. Some say the one outside was for people who were impure and couldn't come into the Temple to bring their contributions. Others say the one inside was for the repair of the Temple building and the one outside was to make new utensils.[26]

12:11 וַיְהִי כִּרְאוֹתָם כִּי־רַב הַכֶּסֶף בָּאָרוֹן וַיַּעַל סֹפֵר הַמֶּלֶךְ וְהַכֹּהֵן הַגָּדוֹל
וַיָּצֻרוּ וַיִּמְנוּ אֶת־הַכֶּסֶף הַנִּמְצָא בֵית־ה׳:

When they saw that there was a lot of money in the box, the king's clerk and the high priest would come up. They would wrap up and count the money that was found in the House of G-d.

So too in the Book of Chronicles it says:[27]

> At the time that they would bring the box to the jurisdiction of the king by the hand of the Levites, and when they saw that there was much money, the king's clerk would come, and the appointee of the high priest, and empty out the box and carry it and return it to its place. So they did every day, and gathered much money.

Every day they counted the money, put it into bags, and labeled each bag with the amount inside.[28]

12:12-15 וְנָתְנוּ אֶת־הַכֶּסֶף הַמְתֻכָּן עַל־יְדֵ עֹשֵׂי הַמְּלָאכָה הפקדים
(הַמֻּפְקָדִים קרי) בֵּית ה׳ וַיּוֹצִיאֻהוּ לְחָרָשֵׁי הָעֵץ וְלַבֹּנִים הָעֹשִׂים בֵּית ה׳:
וְלַגֹּדְרִים וּלְחֹצְבֵי הָאֶבֶן וְלִקְנוֹת עֵצִים וְאַבְנֵי מַחְצֵב לְחַזֵּק אֶת־בֶּדֶק בֵּית־ה׳
וּלְכֹל אֲשֶׁר־יֵצֵא עַל־הַבַּיִת לְחָזְקָה: אַךְ לֹא יֵעָשֶׂה בֵּית ה׳ סִפּוֹת כֶּסֶף מְזַמְּרוֹת
מִזְרָקוֹת חֲצֹצְרוֹת כָּל־כְּלִי זָהָב וּכְלִי־כָסֶף מִן־הַכֶּסֶף הַמּוּבָא בֵית־ה׳: כִּי־לְעֹשֵׂי
הַמְּלָאכָה יִתְּנֻהוּ וְחִזְּקוּ־בוֹ אֶת־בֵּית ה׳:

They gave the money that had been counted to those who did the work, who had been appointed over the House of G-d, and they paid it out to the woodcutters and the builders who worked in the House of G-d. And to the masons and the stonecutters, and to buy wood and hewn stones, to strengthen the repair of the House of G-d, and for all that was spent on the Temple to strengthen it. However, there would not be made for the House of G-d silver pitchers, musical instruments, basins, trumpets, any utensils of gold or utensils of silver, from the money brought to the House of G-d. For to those who were doing the work they would give it, and with it they would strengthen the House of G-d.

In the Book of Chronicles it says:[29]

> The king and Jehoiada gave it to those who did the work of the service of the House of G-d. They would hire stonecutters and woodcutters to renew the House of G-d. And also for the iron and copper smiths, to strengthen the House of G-d. Those who were doing the work did, and the work was restored by their hands. They reestablished the House of G-d in its proper form and strengthened it. When they finished they brought before the king and Jehoiada the rest of the money, and they made of it utensils for the House of G-d, utensils of service, pestles and spoons, and utensils of gold and silver. And they brought burnt offerings in the House of G-d continually all the days of Jehoiada.

Some say the "חרשי העץ," "woodcutters," were the ones who cut down the trees for lumber.[30] Others say they were craftsmen who carved the wood.[31] Some say the "בנים," "builders," were carpenters.[32] Others say they were foremen or master stonecutters.[33] The "גדרים," "masons," were the ones who built the walls.[34] The "חצבי האבן," "stonecutters" cut the stones from the quarry.[35]

The money that was collected was not to be used for making utensils as long as there was work to be done on the building. Only after the building was properly repaired could the remainder of the money be used for new utensils. The restriction in verses 14 and 15 applies as long as there is still work to be done on the building itself. The Book of Chronicles tells what was done with the remainder of the money after the work on the building was completed. Some say this was only possible because the court made a stipulation before the money was collected that if any would be left over it could be used for other purposes, specifically, those for which the "תרומת הלשכה," "Sacrifice Fund," was normally used.[36]

The "מזמרות" were musical instruments, the "מזרקות" were basins to collect the blood of the slaughtered animals, and the "חצצרות" were silver trumpets.

12:16 וְלֹא יְחַשְּׁבוּ אֶת־הָאֲנָשִׁים אֲשֶׁר יִתְּנוּ אֶת־הַכֶּסֶף עַל־יָדָם לָתֵת לְעֹשֵׂי הַמְּלָאכָה כִּי בֶאֱמֻנָה הֵם עֹשִׂים׃

They will not keep accounts with the men into whose hands they give the money to give to those who do the work, for they do it in good faith.

Some say that since only trustworthy men were appointed to distribute the money, no further investigations were made to make sure they were using the money honestly. It is forbidden to suspect one who is known to be trustworthy.[37] Thus, once a person is appointed to collect and distribute charity, he is not required to give account to the community.[38]

Others say that no one was ever suspected of misusing money that had been dedicated to the Temple. Its sanctity was so great that everyone respected it and feared committing such a sacrilege.[39] Under the former system, however, the contributions became the property of the priests, and the sanctity of the money was replaced by a personal obligation on their part to take care of the Temple. Since that obligation was not so clearly defined, they were able to find excuses for their carelessness.

12:17 כֶּסֶף אָשָׁם וְכֶסֶף חַטָּאוֹת לֹא יוּבָא בֵּית ה׳ לַכֹּהֲנִים יִהְיוּ׃

Money for guilt offerings and money for sin offerings will not be brought to the House of G-d. They will be for the priests.

This verse refers to money that had been dedicated for guilt offerings and sin offerings, but was left over after the offerings were purchased. In that generation, the law of what was to be done with that money was forgotten. The people turned to Jehoiada for the answer. Perhaps the extra money should be used for the repair of the Temple? Jehoiada directed them not to use it for the Temple, but to buy burnt offerings instead.

In this way he reconciled an apparent contradiction in a verse in the Book of Leviticus. The Torah says,[40] "It is a guilt offering. He is surely guilty to G-d." The words, "to G-d" are taken to refer to the sacrifice itself, not only to the sin, implying that the sacrifice be given entirely to G-d. This seems to contradict the beginning of the verse, which says that it is a guilt offering. Guilt offerings are eaten by the priests.

Jehoiada explained that the Torah was referring to the extra money. On the one hand, it ought to be no worse than the rest of the money, which had gone for a sacrifice that the priests could eat. But on the other hand, it had been against G-d that the person sinned, so the offering should be given to G-d. Even the meat of the guilt offering itself does not really belong to the priests, but is given to them by G-d as a present. The Torah presented it in this seemingly contradictory way to teach us that it be used for a sacrifice of which more goes to G-d than that of a guilt offering. That is the burnt offering, whose meat was burnt on the altar for G-d, but whose skins were given the priests. Thus it was given partially to G-d and partially to the priests, fulfilling two sides of the verse. The words, "They will be for the priests" do not mean that the money would become their personal property. That would not be possible, since it had been dedicated for sacrifices.[41]

But after the death of Jehoiada, Jehoash began to go astray. In the Book of Chronicles it says:[42]

> Jehoiada married two wives, and he had sons and daughters... Jehoiada became old. He had enough days and he died. He was one hundred and thirty years old at the time of his death. They buried him in the city of David with the kings, for he had done good for Israel and with G-d and His House. After the death of Jehoiada the officers of Judah came and bowed down to the king. Then the king listened to them. They abandoned the House of the L-rd, the G-d of their fathers, and worshiped the Asherim and the idols. There was wrath upon Judah and Jerusalem because of this guilt of theirs. He sent them prophets to bring them back to G-d, and they testified to them, but they didn't listen.

In bowing to Jehoash the officers meant not only to pay him homage as king but to worship him. They said, "No human can enter the Holy of Holies and live. Even the high priest is only permitted to enter on Yom Kippur. But you spent seven years above the Holy of Holies and were not harmed! You cannot be an ordinary person. You must be divine!"

Jehoash found this very flattering, and perhaps he was even convinced by their arguments, so he permitted them to worship him.[43]

Thus, the Kingdom of Judah began to sink back into idolatry, and soon they were punished. Until then, Aram had only attacked the Kingdom of Israel, but now G-d put it into Hazael's heart to attack Judah as well.

12:18,19 אָז יַעֲלֶה חֲזָאֵל מֶלֶךְ אֲרָם וַיִּלָּחֶם עַל־גַּת וַיִּלְכְּדָהּ וַיָּשֶׂם חֲזָאֵל
פָּנָיו לַעֲלוֹת עַל־יְרוּשָׁלָם׃ וַיִּקַּח יְהוֹאָשׁ מֶלֶךְ־יְהוּדָה אֵת כָּל־הַקֳּדָשִׁים
אֲשֶׁר־הִקְדִּישׁוּ יְהוֹשָׁפָט וִיהוֹרָם וַאֲחַזְיָהוּ אֲבֹתָיו מַלְכֵי יְהוּדָה וְאֶת־קֳדָשָׁיו וְאֵת
כָּל־הַזָּהָב הַנִּמְצָא בְּאֹצְרוֹת בֵּית־ה׳ וּבֵית הַמֶּלֶךְ וַיִּשְׁלַח לַחֲזָאֵל מֶלֶךְ אֲרָם וַיַּעַל
מֵעַל יְרוּשָׁלָם׃

Then Hazael, King of Aram, went up and fought against Gath and captured it. Hazael set his face to go up against Jerusalem. Jehoash took all the holy things that Jehoshaphat, Jehoram and Ahaziah, his fathers, the kings of Judah, had dedicated, and his own holy things, and all the gold that was found in the treasuries of the House of G-d and the house of the king. He sent to Hazael, King of Aram, and he went up from upon Jerusalem.

Having permitted himself to be deified, Jehoash's dedication to the Temple waned. Whereas once he had shown such concern for the proper collection of contributions, now he plundered it to buy peace.[44] Nor did he trust G-d and turn to Him for help.

The Book of Chronicles continues:[45]

> The spirit of G-d clothed Zechariah the son of Jehoiada the priest, and he stood above the people. He said to them, "Thus says G-d, 'Why are you violating the commandments of G-d? You won't succeed. For you have abandoned G-d, and He will abandon you.' " They conspired against him and stoned him with stones by the order of the king, in the courtyard of the House of G-d. King Jehoash didn't remember the kindness that Jehoiada, his father, had done for him, and he killed his son. As he died he said, "May G-d see and demand vengeance!"

Next to the king himself, Zechariah was the most powerful and respected person in the kingdom. Not only was he the son of Jehoiada, he was also Jehoash's son-in-law. He thought that no one would dare oppose him, no matter how sharp his rebuke was. To strengthen his position further, he chose Yom Kippur, the holiest day of the year, to deliver his message.[46] Then the people would be in a spirit of introspection and repentance. But they arose against him and killed him anyway, for they could not bear to hear such criticism. They knew they were wrong, but refused to admit it. They wanted desperately to believe that they were righteous.

It was not long before Zechariah's prayer was answered. Aram attacked again. This time Hazael did not lead the army himself, nor did he send as large an army as he had the first time. Nonetheless, he was successful, for the people were not worthy of divine protection. They had committed terrible sins, and finally Zechariah's dying words brought G-d's wrath down upon them. This time Jehoash had nothing left with which to bribe Aram, so he had to fight. Leading the army himself, he was badly wounded and his people defeated.[47]

In the Book of Chronicles it says:[48]

> So it was, that at the end of a year the army of Aram came up against him. They came to Judah and Jerusalem and destroyed all the officers of the people from among the people, and all their spoils they sent to the king, to Damascus. For with only a few men the army of Aram had come, and G-d gave into their hands a very great army, for they had abandoned the L-rd, the G-d of their fathers. As for Jehoash, they executed judgments against him.

Years later, when Jerusalem was conquered by the Babylonians, Nebuzaradan, the chief executioner, entered the Temple and found the blood of Zechariah still wet and bubbling on the ground. He was amazed by such an unnatural sight, and asked the people what it was. "That is the blood of sacrifices," they answered. He suspected that they were lying, so he had them slaughter sacrifices and pour their blood next to it. The blood of the sacrifices behaved like ordinary blood. "If you refuse to tell me the truth," he threatened, "I will scrape off your skin with iron combs!" They were forced to admit. "What can we say?" they answered. "We had a prophet who rebuked us, and we killed him here. Though it has been many years, his blood has never ceased to boil."

Nebuzaradan said, "I will appease him!" He brought the rabbis and judges and killed them all, but the blood kept boiling. He brought the young priests, then the young men and women and killed them, and still it did not stop. Finally he brought the little children and killed them, but even that did not quiet it. Nine hundred and forty thousand were killed. He said, "Zechariah, Zechariah! I have destroyed the best of them! Do you want me to destroy them all?" When he said that, the blood was stilled.

Nebuzaradan was shocked by the divine justice he had just witnessed and began to regret his cruelty. He became very frightened and thought, "If this was the punishment that was decreed on those who murdered one man, what will my punishment be for murdering all of them?" He repented for everything he had done and became a Jew![49]

12:20-22 וְיֶתֶר דִּבְרֵי יוֹאָשׁ וְכָל־אֲשֶׁר עָשָׂה הֲלוֹא־הֵם כְּתוּבִים עַל־ סֵפֶר דִּבְרֵי הַיָּמִים לְמַלְכֵי יְהוּדָה: וַיָּקֻמוּ עֲבָדָיו וַיִּקְשְׁרוּ־קָשֶׁר וַיַּכּוּ אֶת־יוֹאָשׁ בֵּית מִלֹּא הַיֹּרֵד סִלָּא: וְיוֹזָכָר בֶּן־שִׁמְעָת וִיהוֹזָבָד בֶּן־שֹׁמֵר עֲבָדָיו הִכֻּהוּ וַיָּמֹת וַיִּקְבְּרוּ אֹתוֹ עִם־אֲבֹתָיו בְּעִיר דָּוִד וַיִּמְלֹךְ אֲמַצְיָה בְנוֹ תַּחְתָּיו:

The rest of the things about Jehoash and all that he did are indeed written in the Book of the Chronicles of the Kings of Judah. His servants arose and conspired a plot, and smote Jehoash at Beth-milo on the way down to Sila. Jozacar ben Shimeath and Jehozabad ben Shomer, his servants, smote him and he died. They buried him with his fathers in the city of David, and Amaziah, his son, became king in his place.

The Book of Chronicles describes what happened after the Arameans left. It says:[50]

> And when they left him, for they abandoned him gravely ill, his servants conspired against him for the blood of the sons of Jehoiada the priest, and killed him on his bed and he died. They buried him in the city of David, but they didn't bury him in the graves of the kings. These are the ones who conspired against him: Zabad the son of Shimeath the Amonite and Jehozabad the son of Shimrith the Moabite.

Jehoash had a small palace at Beth-milo, and there he was brought to recover. But the people realized that it was his sins and failure to lead them in the way of Torah that had brought their suffering, and his servants arose and murdered him there.[51]

Jehoash was punished according to his sins. His murder was reminiscent of the murder of Zechariah in four ways. The first was location. Just as he had violated the sanctity of the Temple by having Zechariah killed there, so the sanctity of his own palace was violated by his murderers. Secondly, he was killed by his own servants who rebelled against him as he had rebelled against G-d to kill His holy priest. Third, as he forgot the kindness of Jehoiada and killed his son, so they forgot the good things that he and his ancestors had done for the Jewish People. Fourth, as he failed to show respect for the priesthood, they did not respect the status of the king.[52]

In the Book of Chronicles, the names of the two servants are recorded together with the names of their mothers and the nations from which their mothers were descended. There are slight differences between the names as they are rendered in the Books of Kings and Chronicles, but, as we have already seen, many people had more than one name.

The nations of Amon and Moab are infamous for their lack of gratitude. They owed their very existence to Abraham, whose merit saved their forebear, Lot, when Sodom and Gomorah were destroyed. They should have felt some responsibility toward Abraham's descendants and helped them when they were in need, but instead, they coldly refused. G-d therefore chose descendants of these nations to punish Jehoash, who so callously forgot the kindness of his teacher and protector.[53]

Jehoash was punished twice for having committed two terrible sins. He was defeated by Aram as a punishment for making himself a god, and killed as a punishment for the murder of Zechariah.[54]

Thus G-d made clear to all that Jehoash's sorry end was not an accident. By punishing men according to their sins, G-d shows that they are accountable for their actions, and will eventually reap the fruit accordingly.

The Book of Chronicles specifically mentions that, though he was buried in the city of David, Jehoash was not buried in the graves of the kings. Not satisfied with the status of king, he had tried to make himself a god as well. He was punished by being deprived even of the honor that had rightfully been his.[55]

II KINGS 13

13:1-3 בִּשְׁנַת עֶשְׂרִים וְשָׁלֹשׁ שָׁנָה לְיוֹאָשׁ בֶּן־אֲחַזְיָהוּ מֶלֶךְ יְהוּדָה מָלַךְ
יְהוֹאָחָז בֶּן־יֵהוּא עַל־יִשְׂרָאֵל בְּשֹׁמְרוֹן שְׁבַע עֶשְׂרֵה שָׁנָה׃ וַיַּעַשׂ הָרַע בְּעֵינֵי ה׳
וַיֵּלֶךְ אַחַר חַטֹּאת יָרָבְעָם בֶּן־נְבָט אֲשֶׁר־הֶחֱטִיא אֶת־יִשְׂרָאֵל לֹא־סָר מִמֶּנָּה׃
וַיִּחַר־אַף ה׳ בְּיִשְׂרָאֵל וַיִּתְּנֵם בְּיַד חֲזָאֵל מֶלֶךְ־אֲרָם וּבְיַד בֶּן־הֲדַד בֶּן־חֲזָאֵל
כָּל־הַיָּמִים׃

In the twenty-third year of Jehoash the son of Ahaziah, King of Judah, Jehoahaz, the son of Jehu, became King over Israel in Samaria for seventeen years. He did what was evil in G-d's eyes, and followed the sins of Jeroboam ben Nebat, who made Israel sin. He did not deviate from it. G-d's anger was kindled against Israel and He gave them into the hand of Hazael, King of Aram, and into the hand of Ben-hadad, the son of Hazael, all the days.

Jehoash, King of Judah, became king in the seventh year of Jehu. That was counted as his first year. The twenty-third year of Jehoash was therefore Jehu's twenty-ninth year. Since neither Jehu's first year nor his last year were full, his total reign was only twenty-eight years, as was stated above,[1] not twenty-nine. His twenty-ninth year was also the first year of his son, Jehoahaz.[2]

Some say the words "all the days" refer to the days of Hazael and Ben-hadad.[3] Others say it means only the days of Jehoahaz.[4]

13:4 וַיְחַל יְהוֹאָחָז אֶת־פְּנֵי ה׳ וַיִּשְׁמַע אֵלָיו ה׳ כִּי רָאָה אֶת־לַחַץ
יִשְׂרָאֵל כִּי־לָחַץ אֹתָם מֶלֶךְ אֲרָם׃

Jehoahaz prayed before G-d, and G-d listened to him, for He saw the oppression of Israel, that the King of Aram had oppressed them.

Jehoahaz's sin was to worship the golden calves, as his predecessors had done, but he did not worship idols or deny divine providence. So when he and his people suffered, he recognized that it was not an accident but a warning and a call to repent. He admitted his sins and prayed for G-d's forgiveness.

13:5,6 וַיִּתֵּן ה׳ לְיִשְׂרָאֵל מוֹשִׁיעַ וַיֵּצְאוּ מִתַּחַת יַד־אֲרָם וַיֵּשְׁבוּ בְנֵי־
יִשְׂרָאֵל בְּאָהֳלֵיהֶם כִּתְמוֹל שִׁלְשׁוֹם׃ אַךְ לֹא־סָרוּ מֵחַטֹּאת בֵּית־יָרָבְעָם
אֲשֶׁר־הֶחֱטִי אֶת־יִשְׂרָאֵל בָּהּ הָלָךְ וְגַם הָאֲשֵׁרָה עָמְדָה בְּשֹׁמְרוֹן׃

G-d gave Israel a liberator. They got out from under the hand of Aram, and the Children of Israel lived in their tents as in the past. However, they did not deviate from the sins of the house of Jeroboam, who made Israel sin. They followed it. There also stood the Asherah in Samaria.

The liberator that G-d sent was Jehoash, Jehoahaz's son, who succeeded him as king of Israel. During his reign, Israel regained their freedom from Aram and got back the cities that Aram had taken from them.[5]

But there was no relief during Jehoahaz's own time, for, though he prayed for forgiveness, he never gave up his evil ways. It was not by Jehoram's merit but by G-d's mercy that they were saved. Jehoram's prayers directed G-d's attention to the suffering of Israel, and He had pity on them. He would not let the kingdom of Israel be destroyed, because He had promised the forefathers that none of the tribes would ever be completely wiped out.[6] The salvation that was to come in the next generation is mentioned here because it was in response to the prayers of Jehoahaz and the suffering of his people. G-d answered him by giving him a son who would save them.[7]

The people were also guilty of preserving the Asherah and permitting its worship. Though Jehu had eliminated the cult of Baal, the worship of Asherah had continued.[8] Perhaps it was smaller and he did not consider it a serious threat, so he tolerated it.

13:7 כִּי לֹא הִשְׁאִיר לִיהוֹאָחָז עָם כִּי אִם־חֲמִשִּׁים פָּרָשִׁים וַעֲשָׂרָה רֶכֶב
וַעֲשֶׂרֶת אֲלָפִים רַגְלִי כִּי אִבְּדָם מֶלֶךְ אֲרָם וַיְשִׂמֵם כֶּעָפָר לָדֻשׁ׃

For Jehoahaz had no men left but fifty horsemen, ten chariots, and ten thousand foot soldiers. The King of Aram had destroyed them and made them like dust to trample.

Even as G-d prepared for Israel's salvation, He weakened them so terribly that when it came, it would clearly be a miracle.[9]

Their weakened state itself invoked the blessing that G-d had given to Jacob, as it says,[10] "Your descendants will be like the dust of the earth, and you will spread out west and east, north and south." When the Jewish People become humble like dust, they begin to grow and prosper.[11]

13:8,9 וְיֶתֶר דִּבְרֵי יְהוֹאָחָז וְכָל־אֲשֶׁר עָשָׂה וּגְבוּרָתוֹ הֲלוֹא־הֵם כְּתוּבִים
עַל־סֵפֶר דִּבְרֵי הַיָּמִים לְמַלְכֵי יִשְׂרָאֵל׃ וַיִּשְׁכַּב יְהוֹאָחָז עִם־אֲבֹתָיו וַיִּקְבְּרֻהוּ
בְּשֹׁמְרוֹן וַיִּמְלֹךְ יוֹאָשׁ בְּנוֹ תַּחְתָּיו׃

The rest of the things about Jehoahaz and all that he did and his might are indeed written in the Book of the Chronicles of the Kings of Israel. Jehoahaz lay down with his fathers. They buried him in Samaria, and Joash, his son, became king in his place.

There is little else memorable to record about the reign of Jehoahaz. The dynasty of Jehu, that had begun with such bright hopes for the future, was already deteriorating.

13:10,11 בִּשְׁנַת שְׁלֹשִׁים וָשֶׁבַע שָׁנָה לְיוֹאָשׁ מֶלֶךְ יְהוּדָה מָלַךְ יְהוֹאָשׁ בֶּן־
יְהוֹאָחָז עַל־יִשְׂרָאֵל בְּשֹׁמְרוֹן שֵׁשׁ עֶשְׂרֵה שָׁנָה׃ וַיַּעֲשֶׂה הָרַע בְּעֵינֵי ה׳ לֹא־סָר
מִכָּל־חַטֹּאות יָרָבְעָם בֶּן־נְבָט אֲשֶׁר־הֶחֱטִיא אֶת־יִשְׂרָאֵל בָּהּ הָלָךְ׃

In the thirty-seventh year of Joash, King of Judah, Jehoash the son of Jehoahaz became king over Israel in Samaria for sixteen years. He did what was evil in G-d's eyes. He didn't deviate from any of the sins of Jeroboam ben Nebat, who made Israel sin. He followed them.

Jehoahaz became king in the twenty-third year of Jehoash, King of

Judah, so that was his first year, and the thirty-seventh year of Jehoash was Jehoahaz's fifteenth year. The statement above that Jehoahaz reigned seventeen years is therefore difficult to understand. Some say he had his son, Jehoash, crowned during his fifteenth year, while he was still alive, and they reigned together for two years before he died. Thus Jehoahaz was able to see the beginning of the salvation, which began as soon as Jehoash became king, and know that his prayers had been answered.[12]

Others say that the thirty-seventh year in this verse means not the thirty-seventh calendar year, but the thirty-seventh full year of Jehoash's reign. Similarly, the twenty-third year mentioned above was the twenty-third full year. The fifteen years between them covered seventeen calendar years, so it was the seventeenth year of Jehoahaz.[13]

Another explanation is that the kings of Israel did not count their years from the month of Nisan as the kings of Judah did, so a new year could have begun for Jehoahaz while it had not yet begun for Jehoash of Judah.[14]

These two explanations, however, are only able to account for one extra year, not two. For Jehoahaz's reign to have covered parts of seventeen calendar years, it would have to have lasted more than fifteen full years, so it could not have begun in the twenty-third year of Jehoash and ended in the thirty-seventh.

13:12,13 וְיֶתֶר דִּבְרֵי יוֹאָשׁ וְכָל־אֲשֶׁר עָשָׂה וּגְבוּרָתוֹ אֲשֶׁר נִלְחַם עִם
אֲמַצְיָה מֶלֶךְ־יְהוּדָה הֲלֹא־הֵם כְּתוּבִים עַל־סֵפֶר דִּבְרֵי הַיָּמִים לְמַלְכֵי יִשְׂרָאֵל׃
וַיִּשְׁכַּב יוֹאָשׁ עִם־אֲבֹתָיו וְיָרָבְעָם יָשַׁב עַל־כִּסְאוֹ וַיִּקָּבֵר יוֹאָשׁ בְּשֹׁמְרוֹן עִם
מַלְכֵי יִשְׂרָאֵל׃

The rest of the things about Joash and all that he did and his might, that he fought with Amaziah, King of Judah, are indeed written in the Book of the Chronicles of the Kings of Israel. Joash lay down with his fathers, and Jeroboam sat on his throne. Joash was buried in Samaria with the Kings of Israel.

The Bible tells very little about the life of Jehoash here, but some important events will be described shortly. The remainder of this chapter is devoted to the last days of Elisha, his death and his final prophecy, in which Jehoash plays an important role. Some say these two verses really belong at the end of the chapter, but were inserted here to separate between the mention of the sins of Israel in the preceding verse and the sickness of Elisha that follows.[15] Otherwise one might be led to think that Elisha somehow shared the guilt for those sins, and his sickness and death were a punishment.

Describing Jehoash's victories within the context of the prophecy of Elisha rather than in the account of his own reign also emphasizes that credit goes neither to the king's ability nor his merit, but to divine mercy.

The expression "sat on his throne" is an unusual one for describing a son succeeding his father. The Bible usually says that the son "became king in his father's place." Some say it is used here to indicate that Jeroboam had already been crowned during his father's lifetime. As Jehoash had begun his reign before his father, Jehoahaz, died, so did he have his own son, Jeroboam, share his throne.[16]

13:14 וֶאֱלִישָׁע חָלָה אֶת־חָלְיוֹ אֲשֶׁר יָמוּת בּוֹ וַיֵּרֶד אֵלָיו יוֹאָשׁ מֶלֶךְ־
יִשְׂרָאֵל וַיֵּבְךְּ עַל־פָּנָיו וַיֹּאמַר אָבִי אָבִי רֶכֶב יִשְׂרָאֵל וּפָרָשָׁיו׃

Elisha became sick with his sickness from which he was to die. Jehoash, King of Israel, came down to him. He cried on his face and said, "My Father, my Father! Chariot of Israel and its horsemen!"

Three times in his life, Elisha was afflicted with illness. The first was for cursing the children who made fun of him when he left Jericho. The second was for rejecting his follower, Gehazi, who had shown himself unworthy. From both these illnesses he recovered, for they were divine punishments, and once he had suffered, their purpose was fulfilled. But this time he became ill because his time to die was approaching. It was not a punishment, but the vehicle of his death.[17] The three sicknesses are alluded to by the words "became sick," "his sickness," and "from which he was to die."[18]

Elisha was the guide and guardian of Israel. He led them in the way of Torah, and, with his prayers, he interceded in their behalf. As would be expected, he had a particularly close relationship with Jehoash.[19] Though Jehoash and his generation are severely criticized for their faults, they had faith in G-d and Torah and they loved and respected the prophets. Jehu had succeeded in eliminating the worship of Baal, and none of his descendants had reverted to it. So, unlike the house of Ahab, whose relationship with the prophets had been ambivalent at best, Jehoash was wholeheatedly dedicated to Elisha and his followers.

The expression that Jehoash used to address Elisha is the same that Elisha himself had uttered when his teacher, Elijah, was taken up in the fiery chariot. The word "Father" stands for his relationship to Jehoash as teacher, and the expression "Chariot of Israel and its horsemen" for his function as protector of the people.[20]

13:15-17 וַיֹּאמֶר לוֹ אֱלִישָׁע קַח קֶשֶׁת וְחִצִּים וַיִּקַּח אֵלָיו קֶשֶׁת וְחִצִּים׃
וַיֹּאמֶר לְמֶלֶךְ יִשְׂרָאֵל הַרְכֵּב יָדְךָ עַל־הַקֶּשֶׁת וַיַּרְכֵּב יָדוֹ וַיָּשֶׂם אֱלִישָׁע יָדָיו
עַל־יְדֵי הַמֶּלֶךְ׃ וַיֹּאמֶר פְּתַח הַחַלּוֹן קֵדְמָה וַיִּפְתָּח וַיֹּאמֶר אֱלִישָׁע יְרֵה וַיּוֹר
וַיֹּאמֶר חֵץ־תְּשׁוּעָה לַה׳ וְחֵץ־תְּשׁוּעָה בַאֲרָם וְהִכִּיתָ אֶת־אֲרָם בַּאֲפֵק עַד־כַּלֵּה׃

Elisha said to him, "Get a bow and arrows!" so he got him a bow and arrows. He said to the King of Israel, "Rest your hand on the bow!" and he rested his hand. Elisha put his hands on the hands of the king. He said, "Open the window to the east!" and he opened it. Elisha said, "Shoot!" and he shot. He said, "It is an arrow of salvation for G-d, and an arrow of salvation from Aram. You will smite Aram in Aphek until they are finished off."

Though Elisha would not live to accompany Jehoash on his campaigns against Aram, he could at least help him begin them. In that way he might impart some of his merit to the king's efforts. It would also give Jehoash confidence, so he would go out into battle without fear. Elisha had him open the window eastward, toward the land of Aram. Together they shot one arrow, symbolically, beginning the attack.[21]

Aphek was one of the cities of Judah. There, Ahab had defeated Aram years before, killing one hundred thousand soldiers in one day. Elisha predicted that it would again be the site of victory for Israel.[22]

13:18,19 וַיֹּאמֶר קַח הַחִצִּים וַיִּקָּח וַיֹּאמֶר לְמֶלֶךְ־יִשְׂרָאֵל הַךְ־אַרְצָה וַיַּךְ
שָׁלֹשׁ־פְּעָמִים וַיַּעֲמֹד׃ וַיִּקְצֹף עָלָיו אִישׁ הָאֱלֹהִים וַיֹּאמֶר לְהַכּוֹת חָמֵשׁ אוֹ־שֵׁשׁ
פְּעָמִים אָז הִכִּיתָ אֶת־אֲרָם עַד־כַּלֵּה וְעַתָּה שָׁלֹשׁ פְּעָמִים תַּכֶּה אֶת־אֲרָם׃

He said, "Take the arrows!" and he took them. He said to the

King of Israel, "Strike on the ground!" and he struck three times and stopped. The man of G-d got angry at him and said, "You should have struck five or six times. Then you would have struck Aram until they were finished off. But now, three times will you strike Aram."

Jehoash misunderstood Elisha's instructions. He thought that he was to strike just a few times, since it was, after all, only a symbolic act. But Elisha had meant him to continue until he told him to stop.[23] This misunderstanding revealed to Elisha the king's shortcoming. He saw it as a sign that Jehoash's victories would be limited. Some say it had been explicitly revealed to Elisha that if the king struck five or six times the victory would be complete, but if less, not.[24]

Nor could Jehoash remedy things now by striking again. Like the miracle of the flask of oil from which unlimited containers could be filled, this miracle had to be performed without interruption. Once Jehoash stopped striking, he had fixed the limit of his victories.[25]

Were salvation from Aram to be granted by G-d's mercy alone, it would not have mattered how many times the king struck the ground, or whether he struck at all. G-d's decree would not thereby have been altered. But it was by the merit of Elisha and through his prayers that Israel would be saved, so it was dependent upon them. Elisha could not accomplish this by himself. He could only help the Jewish People in their efforts. The king's participation in the prayer was therefore absolutely essential, and the form of that participation would have far-reaching effects on the outcome. That is why Elisha was so angry at Jehoash's mistake. He was disappointed, because now his prayers would not have the effect he had hoped for. Nor could he pray for them again, for that would require more merit than they had.[26]

"Strike the ground" means to shoot the arrows at the ground. Again the king was to shoot, this time without Elisha's help, and not into the air in the direction of Aram, but toward the ground.[27]

13:20,21 וַיָּמָת אֱלִישָׁע וַיִּקְבְּרֻהוּ וּגְדוּדֵי מוֹאָב יָבֹאוּ בָאָרֶץ בָּא שָׁנָה׃
וַיְהִי הֵם קֹבְרִים אִישׁ וְהִנֵּה רָאוּ אֶת־הַגְּדוּד וַיַּשְׁלִיכוּ אֶת־הָאִישׁ בְּקֶבֶר אֱלִישָׁע
וַיֵּלֶךְ וַיִּגַּע הָאִישׁ בְּעַצְמוֹת אֱלִישָׁע וַיְחִי וַיָּקָם עַל־רַגְלָיו׃

Elisha died and they buried him, and bands of Moabites began coming into the land at the beginning of the year.

Some people were burying a man, and behold, they saw the band, so they threw the man into the grave of Elisha. The man went and touched the bones of Elisha, and came alive and got up on his feet.

Some say Elisha performed a total of sixteen miracles, twice as many as Elijah did, thus fulfilling his parting request of Elijah that he receive double Elijah's spirit. Others say he performed eighteen miracles. They were:

1. Splitting the Jordan
2. Curing the water of Jericho
3. Cursing the wicked boys who had mocked him and causing them to be killed
4. Supplying water for the armies of Judah, Israel, and Edom
5. The miracle of the flask of oil
6. Blessing the woman of Shumen with a son
7. Reviving the son after he died
8. Curing the poison in the pot of the prophets
9. Feeding the hundred prophets with only twenty loaves of bread
10. Curing Naaman
11. Afflicting Gehazi with leprosy
12. Recovering the lost axe head
13. Causing his servant to see the armies of angels
14. Capturing the army of Aram
15. Frightening away the army of Aram that had laid siege to Samaria
16. Punishing the officer who had mocked the word of G-d
17. Causing a famine to punish the people for worshiping Baal
18. Reviving the man who touched his bones

The various prophecies that he spoke are not included in this list, for not every prophecy is a miracle.[28]

Another interpretation of Elisha's being granted double Elijah's spirit is that it refers only to the exceptional miracle of reviving the dead. Elijah revived only one person, the son of the woman of Zarephath. Elisha revived two. One was the son of the woman of Shunem. Some say the other was this man, who was revived by touching Elisha's bones. Others say that curing Naaman of his leprosy was considered revival of the dead, because a leper is like a dead person. His skin and limbs die even as his inner organs continue to function.[29]

Elisha died in the tenth year of Jehoash. He had guided Israel for sixty-six years, since the nineteenth year of Jehoshaphat.[30]

According to those who say the salvation started at the beginning of Joash's reign, while his father, Jehoahaz, was still alive, Elisha must have died in the first or second year of Jehoash, for it did not begin until after his death.[31]

But Elisha's death brought trouble too. As long as he was alive, the people were protected by his merit. Only from the army of Aram were they not safe, because he himself had anointed Hazael to be their oppressor. The bands of raiders, however, were afraid to attack, as it says above,[32] "the bands of Aram didn't continue to come to the Land of Israel any more."[33] But once Elisha died they became vulnerable, and the bands of Moab began to attack again.[34]

The "beginning of the year" means the springtime, when the new crops were ripe and being harvested, and there was plenty in the field to steal.[35]

The words, "the man went" mean that the body rolled down from where they threw it.

Some say the man who died was Shalum ben Tikvah, the husband of Huldah, the prophetess. He was one of the greatest men of his time, exceptionally pious and generous. He used to sit at the city gate and give water to all the travellers that came in. It was by his merit that his wife was granted prophecy. He was worthy of living longer, so G-d arranged that he be revived in this way.

When he died, the whole people attended his funeral. As they were accompanying him to his grave they saw the Moabites coming and fled. He returned home and after that a son was born to him, Hanamel ben Shalum, who is mentioned in the Book of Jeremiah.[36]

Others say that he was a wicked man who was not worthy of lying next to the prophet. He lived just long enough to walk out of the cave, and then he fell down dead again. Therefore it says only that he got up on his feet, but not that he went to his house.[37]

G-d performed this miracle for the honor of Elisha, so that his bones not lie together with those of a wicked person. For, though it is the soul that is righteous or wicked and not the body, the body of a righteous person is to be honored for being the home of such a holy soul.[38] Thus King David said,[39] "Don't gather my soul with the sinners."[40] So too, the descendants of the righteous are protected and helped for the honor of their ancestors.

The righteous are even greater after death than during their lives. When Elisha wanted to revive the son of the Shunamite, he had to pray and align his limbs with those of the boy. But now the man was revived simply by touching Elisha's body.[41]

For it was not Elisha who performed the miracle, but G-d. As He had performed miracles for the honor of the prophet during his lifetime, so He did after his death. A prophet has no power to change nature. That power belongs to G-d alone. While Elisha was alive, G-d honored him by fulfilling his words. Now, after his death, He honored him by protecting his bones from disgrace.[42]

13:22,23 וַחֲזָאֵל מֶלֶךְ אֲרָם לָחַץ אֶת־יִשְׂרָאֵל כֹּל יְמֵי יְהוֹאָחָז׃ וַיָּחָן ה׳
אֹתָם וַיְרַחֲמֵם וַיִּפֶן אֲלֵיהֶם לְמַעַן בְּרִיתוֹ אֶת־אַבְרָהָם יִצְחָק וְיַעֲקֹב וְלֹא אָבָה
הַשְׁחִיתָם וְלֹא־הִשְׁלִיכָם מֵעַל־פָּנָיו עַד־עָתָּה׃

Hazael, King of Aram, oppressed Israel all the days of Jehoahaz. G-d pitied them and had mercy on them. He turned toward them for the sake of His covenant with Abraham, Isaac and Jacob. He didn't want to destroy them, and has not cast them from before His presence even now.

Some say the words, "even now" refer to the time of Jehoahaz. It was only until that time that the Jewish People were protected by the merit of the forefathers. Others say that merit protects us forever. It has no limit and is never used up.[43]

13:24,25 וַיָּמָת חֲזָאֵל מֶלֶךְ־אֲרָם וַיִּמְלֹךְ בֶּן־הֲדַד בְּנוֹ תַּחְתָּיו׃ וַיָּשָׁב
יְהוֹאָשׁ בֶּן־יְהוֹאָחָז וַיִּקַּח אֶת־הֶעָרִים מִיַּד בֶּן־הֲדַד בֶּן־חֲזָאֵל אֲשֶׁר לָקַח מִיַּד
יְהוֹאָחָז אָבִיו בַּמִּלְחָמָה שָׁלֹשׁ פְּעָמִים הִכָּהוּ יוֹאָשׁ וַיָּשֶׁב אֶת־עָרֵי יִשְׂרָאֵל׃

Hazael, King of Aram, died, and Ben-hadad, his son, became king in his place. Jehoash the son of Jehoahaz returned and took the cities from the hand of Ben-hadad the son of Hazael that he had taken from the hand of Jehoahaz, his father, in war. Three times did Jehoash strike him, and got back the cities of Israel.

Hazael had been anointed by the word of G-d to oppress Israel, so as long as he was alive there could be no relief. When G-d decreed an end to their suffering, He caused Hazael to die, and immediately Jehoash was able to defeat Aram. However, he was only granted victory over them three times, and never completely destroyed them, as Elisha had foretold.

All these victories were accomplished through Elisha's blessing. It was as if Elisha himself had fought in the battles, for he had begun them by shooting the first arrow together with Jehoash. By his merit G-d was with Jehoash in these campaigns.[44]

II KINGS 14

14:1,2 בִּשְׁנַת שְׁתַּיִם לְיוֹאָשׁ בֶּן־יוֹאָחָז מֶלֶךְ יִשְׂרָאֵל מָלַךְ אֲמַצְיָהוּ
בֶן־יוֹאָשׁ מֶלֶךְ יְהוּדָה: בֶּן־עֶשְׂרִים וְחָמֵשׁ שָׁנָה הָיָה בְמָלְכוֹ וְעֶשְׂרִים וָתֵשַׁע
שָׁנָה מָלַךְ בִּירוּשָׁלָםִ וְשֵׁם אִמּוֹ יהועדין (יְהוֹעַדָּן קרי) מִן־יְרוּשָׁלָםִ:

In the second year of Joash, the son of Joahaz, King of Israel, Amaziah, the son of Joash, King of Judah, became king. He was twenty-five years old when he became king, and he reigned twenty-nine years in Jerusalem. His mother's name was Jehoadan from Jerusalem.

The Bible reckons the reign of Jehoash, King of Israel, from the time that his father, Jehoahaz, died, and he became sole ruler. Even though he had already begun to rule together with his father, those years are not counted toward his reign in this verse. Jehoahaz died in the thirty-ninth year of Jehoash, King of Judah, so the thirty-ninth year of Jehoash of Judah was the first year of Jehoash of Israel. The fortieth year of Jehoash of Judah was the second year of Jehoash of Israel. In that year, Jehoash of Judah died and his son, Amaziah, became king in his place. Thus we read above,[1] that Jehoash, King of Judah, "reigned forty years."[2]

14:3,4 וַיַּעַשׂ הַיָּשָׁר בְּעֵינֵי ה׳ רַק לֹא כְּדָוִד אָבִיו כְּכֹל אֲשֶׁר־עָשָׂה יוֹאָשׁ
אָבִיו עָשָׂה: רַק הַבָּמוֹת לֹא־סָרוּ עוֹד הָעָם מְזַבְּחִים וּמְקַטְּרִים בַּבָּמוֹת:

He did what was upright in G-d's eyes, but not like David, his father. Like everything that Joash, his father, had done did he do. Only the altars were not removed. The people were still sacrificing and burning incense on the altars.

In the Book of Chronicles it says,[3] "He did what was upright in G-d's eyes, but not with a full heart." Amaziah continued the pious practices of his father, but without real conviction. Jehoash lacked deep understanding of Torah, being dependent upon the guidance of his teacher, Jehoiada. He could convey to his son only what he himself had, which was obedience to the laws that Jehoiada had taught him, but not dedication to the principles underlying them. So Amaziah just did what he was accustomed to from his father's time.[4]

14:5,6 וַיְהִי כַּאֲשֶׁר חָזְקָה הַמַּמְלָכָה בְּיָדוֹ וַיַּךְ אֶת־עֲבָדָיו הַמַּכִּים אֶת־
הַמֶּלֶךְ אָבִיו: וְאֶת־בְּנֵי הַמַּכִּים לֹא הֵמִית כַּכָּתוּב בְּסֵפֶר תּוֹרַת־מֹשֶׁה אֲשֶׁר־צִוָּה
ה׳ לֵאמֹר לֹא־יוּמְתוּ אָבוֹת עַל־בָּנִים וּבָנִים לֹא־יוּמְתוּ עַל־אָבוֹת כִּי אִם־אִישׁ
בְּחֶטְאוֹ ימות (יוּמָת קרי):

When the kingdom was secure in his hand he smote his servants who had smote the king, his father. But the children of those who smote he did not kill, as it says in the Book of the Torah of Moses that G-d commanded, saying, "Fathers will not be killed for sons, and sons will not be killed for fathers, rather each person for his own sin will be killed."

Amaziah was referring to the verse,[5] "Fathers will not be put to death because of sons, and sons will not be put to death because of fathers. Each person will be put to death for his own sin." Although it is obviously unjust, at that time it was a common practice among other nations to punish children along with their parents. Thus in the Book of Daniel[6] we find that when Daniel's enemies conspired to have him killed, Darius, the King of the Medes, executed their wives and children together with them. Perhaps it was for this reason that Amaziah quoted the Torah to defend an act that shouldn't have required any special justification.

Amaziah may also have wanted to show that he was relying upon the Torah, not only upon his own judgment. He was not simply a just and merciful person. He accepted G-d's word and obeyed His commandments.

Amaziah used the verse in its literal sense, that children not be punished for the transgressions of their parents. There is, however, another less obvious law that is derived from it. Parents and children cannot be convicted by one another's testimony. A son cannot testify against his own father or a father against his son. If there are no witnesses but these close relatives, the transgressor goes free. Even if there is no doubt of his guilt and the relative who testifies is not suspected of lying, he cannot be punished.[7]

Some say that it is not entirely unjust to punish children for their parents' sins, because children tend to be guilty of the same sort of sins themselves. Thus G-d said,[8] "I count the sins of fathers against sons, against the third and fourth generation of those who hate Me." But when Moses heard these words he objected. He said, "Haven't there been many wicked people whose children were righteous? Even Abraham's father, Terah, was an idolater! Should a righteous child be punished for his father's sins?"

G-d accepted his argument and said, "Now I will proclaim, 'Fathers will not be put to death because of sons and sons will not be put to death because of fathers. Each person will be put to death for his own sin.' Moreover, this principle will forever be remembered in your name." Thus Amaziah referred to it as "the Torah of Moses."[9]

14:7 הוּא־הִכָּה אֶת־אֱדוֹם בְּגֵי־המלח (מֶלַח קרי) עֲשֶׂרֶת אֲלָפִים וְתָפַשׂ אֶת־הַסֶּלַע בַּמִּלְחָמָה וַיִּקְרָא אֶת־שְׁמָהּ יָקְתְאֵל עַד הַיּוֹם הַזֶּה׃

He smote Edom in Gei-melah, ten thousand. He captured the rock in war and gave it the name Joktheel until this day.

In the Book of Chronicles it says:[10]

> Amaziah gathered Judah and stood them according to the houses of the fathers, for the officers of the thousands and the officers of the hundreds, for all Judah and Benjamin. He counted them, from twenty years old and up, and found they were three hundred thousand young men fit to go out to the army, to hold a spear and a shield. He hired from Israel one hundred thousand brave warriors for one hundred talents of silver. The man of G-d came to him saying, "Oh king! Let the army of Israel not go with you, for G-d is not with Israel, all the sons of Ephraim. For even if you arrive and are the stronger in war, G-d will make you fail before the enemy, for G-d has power to help or to cause to fail." Amaziah said to the man of G-d, "What should be done with the hundred talents that I gave to the band of Israel?" The man of G-d said, "G-d has much more to give

They attacked Judah, taking revenge and at the same time proving their superiority.

At first it seems strange that Amaziah suffered for obeying G-d's words, for it was by the prophet's instruction that he had sent them back. Only when we learn about his taking the idols do we understand the reason.

The members of Ephraim had not been worthy of participating in the war because they violated the Torah. They served G-d by worshiping the golden calves. But now Amaziah committed a sin that was infinitely worse, for he worshiped idols. He and his people thereby became even less worthy of victory than Ephraim.[14]

Nonetheless, until he rejected the prophet's rebuke, he could still claim that he had been obedient to G-d's word. The merit of sending them back as the prophet had commanded should have protected him from any repercussions. But when he was given another message and ignored it, he showed his earlier acceptance had not really been a matter of obedience after all. It had not been piety but fear of G-d's threat of defeat.

Amaziah's sin was all the worse given the circumstances. G-d had helped him and granted him victory, yet he abandoned G-d for the idols of the very nation he defeated. Since he had sinned by behaving so foolishly, G-d punished him by making him more foolish yet. He planted in Amaziah's heart the idea of challenging the far superior forces of the Kingdom of Israel, which was sure to lead to destruction. It was this idea to which the prophet was referring by the words, "G-d has advised to destroy you."[15]

14:8 אָז שָׁלַח אֲמַצְיָה מַלְאָכִים אֶל־יְהוֹאָשׁ בֶּן־יְהוֹאָחָז בֶּן־יֵהוּא מֶלֶךְ
יִשְׂרָאֵל לֵאמֹר לְכָה נִתְרָאֶה פָנִים׃

Then Amaziah sent messengers to Jehoash the son of Jehoahaz the son of Jehu, King of Israel, saying, "Let us go and confront one another."

The words "נתראה פנים," literally "see each other's faces," mean to confront in battle.[16]

14:9,10 וַיִּשְׁלַח יְהוֹאָשׁ מֶלֶךְ־יִשְׂרָאֵל אֶל־אֲמַצְיָהוּ מֶלֶךְ־יְהוּדָה לֵאמֹר הַחוֹחַ
אֲשֶׁר בַּלְּבָנוֹן שָׁלַח אֶל־הָאֶרֶז אֲשֶׁר בַּלְּבָנוֹן לֵאמֹר תְּנָה אֶת־בִּתְּךָ לִבְנִי לְאִשָּׁה
וַתַּעֲבֹר חַיַּת הַשָּׂדֶה אֲשֶׁר בַּלְּבָנוֹן וַתִּרְמֹס אֶת־הַחוֹחַ׃ הַכֵּה הִכִּיתָ אֶת־אֱדוֹם

וּנְשָׂאֲךָ לִבֶּךָ הִכָּבֵד וְשֵׁב בְּבֵיתֶךָ וְלָמָּה תִתְגָּרֶה בְּרָעָה וְנָפַלְתָּה אַתָּה וִיהוּדָה עִמָּךְ׃

Jehoash, King of Israel, sent to Amaziah, King of Judah, saying, "The thornbush that is in Lebanon sent to the cedar that is in Lebanon saying, 'Give your daughter to my son for a wife,' and the beast of the field that is in Lebanon went over and trampled the thornbush. Indeed, you have defeated Edom, and your heart has raised you up. Preserve your honor and remain in your house! Why are you starting up with trouble? You will fall, you and Judah with you."

This parable had a double meaning. Obviously, Jehoash was comparing himself to the cedar and Amaziah to the thornbush. His message was that it would have been an insult for Amaziah even to have suggested an alliance between them, so inferior was he. To challenge him was absurd.[17]

It was also an allusion to the attempt of Hamor the Hivite to arrange a marriage between his son and the daughter of Jacob. The lowly Hivites were unworthy of marrying into such a noble family. The destruction that they subsequently suffered at the hands of Jacob's sons was well deserved.[18]

But, though Amaziah's challenge was unforgivable, Jehoash offered to allow him to withdraw without harm.

It was not without reason that Jehoash considered himself superior to Amaziah. During this period, the kings of Israel looked upon the kings of Judah as descendants not of David and Solomon, but of the wicked Ahab and Jezebel, whom their ancestor, Jehu, had been sent to destroy. They considered it a failing on their own part that they had not entirely wiped them out along with the sons of Ahab in Samaria.

The Bible alludes to this above by referring to Jehoash as "son of Jehoahaz, son of Jehu," and later to Amaziah as "son of Jehoash son of Ahaziah." It is unusual for the Bible to mention the name of a grandfather, and when it does, it is always for a reason. Here it is to remind us of the history of enmity between the two royal houses. Ahaziah had followed the evil ways of his maternal ancestors, the house of Ahab, and suffered along with them. Together with his uncle, Jehoram, King of Israel, he was killed by Jehu. Amaziah should have remembered that and been more humble in his dealing with Jehoash.[19]

The fall of the house of Ahab marked a radical change in the relationship between the kingdoms of Judah and Israel, the second such change since the time of Jeroboam ben Nebat. During the first few decades after the nation was split, there was open hostility between the kings of the two countries, but the people of the north were still loyal to the Temple of Solomon, and force was necessary to prevent them from returning there to worship. When Omri became king, however, there began a period of peace and brotherhood between the two kingdoms. At the same time, the Temple had begun to lose its importance for them, and the center of faith and piety shifted to the blossoming school of the prophets, especially the two great leaders, Elijah and Elisha.

The dynasty of Jehu constituted a third period. The idolatry that had plagued the house of Ahab had been purged, but with it, the good relationship with the House of David was destroyed. At first, during the years that Athaliah reigned, Jehu was justified in considering himself the legitimate king of the entire nation, for there was no rightful king in Judah. But when he subsequently failed to recognize Jehoash and appreciate his sincere efforts to restore the Temple, Jehu was reverting to the sins of his predecessors. By the time of Amaziah, the hatred between the two kingdoms had already been well established. Very little provocation was necessary to bring them to war.

14:11-13 וְלֹא־שָׁמַע אֲמַצְיָהוּ וַיַּעַל יְהוֹאָשׁ מֶלֶךְ־יִשְׂרָאֵל וַיִּתְרָאוּ פָּנִים
הוּא וַאֲמַצְיָהוּ מֶלֶךְ־יְהוּדָה בְּבֵית שֶׁמֶשׁ אֲשֶׁר לִיהוּדָה׃ וַיִּנָּגֶף יְהוּדָה לִפְנֵי
יִשְׂרָאֵל וַיָּנֻסוּ אִישׁ לְאֹהָלָו׃ וְאֵת אֲמַצְיָהוּ מֶלֶךְ־יְהוּדָה בֶּן־יְהוֹאָשׁ בֶּן־אֲחַזְיָהוּ
תָּפַשׂ יְהוֹאָשׁ מֶלֶךְ־יִשְׂרָאֵל בְּבֵית שֶׁמֶשׁ ויבאו (וַיָּבֹא קרי) יְרוּשָׁלַםִ וַיִּפְרֹץ
בְּחוֹמַת יְרוּשָׁלַםִ בְּשַׁעַר אֶפְרַיִם עַד־שַׁעַר הַפִּנָּה אַרְבַּע מֵאוֹת אַמָּה׃

But Amaziah didn't listen, and Jehoash, King of Israel, went up and they confronted one another, he and Amaziah, King of Judah, in Beth-shemesh that is in Judah. Judah was beaten before Israel, and each man fled to his own tent. As for Amaziah, King of Judah, son of Jehoash, son of Ahaziah, Jehoash, King of Israel, caught him in Beth-shemesh, and they came to Jerusalem. He made a break in the wall of Jerusalem from the Gate of Ephraim until the Gate of the Corner, four hundred cubits.

As the prophet had foretold, Amaziah's reasoning was clouded and he stubbornly persisted. The Book of Chronicles again explicitly states that this was the reason for his defeat. It says,[20] "But Amaziah didn't listen, because it was from G-d to give them into their hands, because they had inquired of the gods of Edom."

So confident was Jehoash of victory that he agreed to fight at Beth-shemesh, in the territory of Judah. He knew he would win even if the army of Judah had the advantage of fighting in their own territory.[21]

The "Gate of Ephraim" was the gate facing the land of Ephraim, through which members of that tribe would enter when they came to Jerusalem.[22]

14:14 וְלָקַח אֶת־כָּל־הַזָּהָב וְהַכֶּסֶף וְאֵת כָּל־הַכֵּלִים הַנִּמְצְאִים בֵּית־ה׳ וּבְאוֹצְרוֹת בֵּית הַמֶּלֶךְ וְאֵת בְּנֵי הַתַּעֲרֻבוֹת וַיָּשָׁב שֹׁמְרוֹנָה:

He took all the gold and silver and all the utensils that were found in the House of G-d and in the treasuries of the house of the king, and the hostage children, and went back to Samaria.

The "hostage children" were the sons of the kings and lords who were vassals of Amaziah. Each was required to send Amaziah one of his children as a hostage to guarantee that he would not rebel.[23]

Included among the treasures taken by Jehoash were the utensils that had been in the house of Obed-edom when the Holy Ark was there in the time of David. G-d had blessed Obed-edom for being the host of the ark, and he, in turn, had shown his gratitude by donating the utensils that were in his house to the Temple, as it says,[24] "And all the gold and silver and all the utensils that were found in the House of G-d, with Obed-edom."[25]

14:15,16 וְיֶתֶר דִּבְרֵי יְהוֹאָשׁ אֲשֶׁר עָשָׂה וּגְבוּרָתוֹ וַאֲשֶׁר נִלְחַם עִם אֲמַצְיָהוּ מֶלֶךְ־יְהוּדָה הֲלֹא־הֵם כְּתוּבִים עַל־סֵפֶר דִּבְרֵי הַיָּמִים לְמַלְכֵי יִשְׂרָאֵל: וַיִּשְׁכַּב יְהוֹאָשׁ עִם־אֲבֹתָיו וַיִּקָּבֵר בְּשֹׁמְרוֹן עִם מַלְכֵי יִשְׂרָאֵל וַיִּמְלֹךְ יָרָבְעָם בְּנוֹ תַּחְתָּיו:

The rest of the things about Jehoash that he did and his might, and that he fought with Amaziah, King of Judah, are indeed written in the Book of the Chronicles of the Kings of

Israel. Jehoash lay down with his fathers. He was buried in Samaria with the kings of Israel, and Jeroboam, his son, became king in his place.

Jehoash did not live to enjoy his victory long. He died soon after returning to Samaria.[26] Thus he was punished for his arrogance by dying many years before Amaziah.[27] Jehoash had become king two years before Amaziah and reigned sixteen years, so their reigns overlapped fourteen years. Amaziah reigned twenty-nine years, fourteen during the time of Jehoash and fifteen after his death.[28]

14:17-20 וַיְחִי אֲמַצְיָהוּ בֶן־יוֹאָשׁ מֶלֶךְ יְהוּדָה אַחֲרֵי מוֹת יְהוֹאָשׁ בֶּן־
יְהוֹאָחָז מֶלֶךְ יִשְׂרָאֵל חֲמֵשׁ עֶשְׂרֵה שָׁנָה׃ וְיֶתֶר דִּבְרֵי אֲמַצְיָהוּ הֲלֹא־הֵם כְּתֻבִים
עַל־סֵפֶר דִּבְרֵי הַיָּמִים לְמַלְכֵי יְהוּדָה׃ וַיִּקְשְׁרוּ עָלָיו קֶשֶׁר בִּירוּשָׁלַםִ וַיָּנָס
לָכִישָׁה וַיִּשְׁלְחוּ אַחֲרָיו לָכִישָׁה וַיְמִתֻהוּ שָׁם׃ וַיִּשְׂאוּ אֹתוֹ עַל־הַסּוּסִים וַיִּקָּבֵר
בִּירוּשָׁלַםִ עִם־אֲבֹתָיו בְּעִיר דָּוִד׃

Amaziah, the son of Joash, King of Judah, lived after the death of Jehoash son of Jehoahaz, King of Israel, fifteen years. The rest of the things about Amaziah are indeed written in the Book of the Chronicles of the Kings of Judah. They plotted a conspiracy against him in Jerusalem and he fled to Lachish. They sent after him to Lachish and killed him there. They carried him on the horses and he was buried in Jerusalem with his fathers in the city of David.

Like his father, Amaziah began his life righteously and later became corrupted. Both rejected the prophets that had been sent to rebuke them, and both suffered the same fate. They were defeated in war and then murdered by their own servants. The words, "with his fathers" are an allusion to the manner of Amaziah's death. Like his fathers, he died in suffering and shame.[29]

14:21,22 וַיִּקְחוּ כָּל־עַם יְהוּדָה אֶת־עֲזַרְיָה וְהוּא בֶּן־שֵׁשׁ עֶשְׂרֵה שָׁנָה
וַיַּמְלִכוּ אֹתוֹ תַּחַת אָבִיו אֲמַצְיָהוּ׃ הוּא בָּנָה אֶת־אֵילַת וַיְשִׁבֶהָ לִיהוּדָה אַחֲרֵי
שְׁכַב־הַמֶּלֶךְ עִם־אֲבֹתָיו׃

The entire people of Judah took Azariah, who was sixteen years old, and made him king in place of his father, Amaziah. He built Elath and returned it to Judah, after the king had lain down with his fathers.

The next king of Judah, Azariah, is also called "Uziah" in many places.

Some say the rebellion against Amaziah occurred immediately after his defeat by Jehoash, in his fourteenth year. But his escape to Lachish was successful, and he lived there in exile for fifteen years while his opponents ruled his kingdom. They crowned his son, Azariah, in his father's place so that they might present him as the king, but he was really only a figurehead. When they managed to kill Amaziah, fifteen years later, they crowned Azariah again, this time as their real ruler.[30]

The fifteen years that Amaziah spent in exile in Lachish are counted as part of the reigns of both father and son. Thus above we read[31] that Amaziah reigned "twenty-nine years in Jerusalem" and later[32] that Azariah reigned fifty-two years. Together, however, their reigns covered only about sixty-six years. According to this opinion, the reigns of Azariah and Jeroboam both began in the same year.

The statement that Amaziah reigned twenty-nine years is problematic according to this opinion, because it specifically states "in Jerusalem." It is hard to say that this includes fifteen years of exile in Lachish.

Others therefore say that the conspiracy against Amaziah began after the defeat at Beth-shemesh, but he managed to suppress the rebellion for fifteen years. Finally he could suppress it no longer. He tried to flee to Lachish, but was caught there and killed. It was only then that Azariah became king.[33]

The words, "after the king had lain down with his fathers" seem to support the first opinion, implying that there were two periods to Azariah's reign, one before his father's death and one after.[34]

Elath originally belonged to Edom. It was not part of the territory that G-d commanded Moses to conquer.[35] But Israel had access to it in the time of Solomon, as it says,[36] "Then Solomon went to Ezion-geber and to Eloth, on the coast of the sea, in the land of Edom," for David had conquered Edom and it was ruled by his descendants for several generations. Elath may have remained in the hands of Israel even after Edom regained its independence in the time of Jehoram.[37] Until the time of Azariah, however, it had not been fortified and had never become an important city.[38]

14:23,24 בִּשְׁנַת חֲמֵשׁ־עֶשְׂרֵה שָׁנָה לַאֲמַצְיָהוּ בֶן־יוֹאָשׁ מֶלֶךְ יְהוּדָה
מָלַךְ יָרָבְעָם בֶּן־יוֹאָשׁ מֶלֶךְ־יִשְׂרָאֵל בְּשֹׁמְרוֹן אַרְבָּעִים וְאַחַת שָׁנָה׃ וַיַּעַשׂ הָרַע
בְּעֵינֵי ה׳ לֹא סָר מִכָּל־חַטֹּאות יָרָבְעָם בֶּן־נְבָט אֲשֶׁר הֶחֱטִיא אֶת־יִשְׂרָאֵל׃

In the fifteenth year of Amaziah, the son of Joash, King of Judah, Jeroboam, the son of Joash, King of Israel, became king in Samaria forty-one years. He did what was evil in G-d's eyes. He did not deviate from all the sins of Jeroboam ben Nebat, who made Israel sin.

The fifteenth year of Azariah was immediately after the war between Israel and Judah. Joash, King of Israel, died as divine retribution for his arrogance and merciless treatment of Amaziah and his people. Though it was divinely ordained that Amaziah suffer for worshiping the idols of Edom, Joash was not justified in taking advantage of his weakness.

Some say that Jeroboam had already begun to rule together with his father three years earlier, because, while here we are told that Jeroboam reigned forty-one years, later we read that his son, Zechariah, succeeded him in the thirty-eighth year of Azariah, not the forty-first. This opinion is problematic, however, because the statements that Jeroboam began his reign in the fifteenth year of Amaziah and that he reigned forty-one years are mentioned together, implying that the forty-one years be reckoned from this time, even if he had in some way begun to reign earlier.[39]

Others say it was Zechariah who began his reign during his father's lifetime. In the thirty-eighth year of Azariah Jeroboam appointed his son to rule with him. They ruled together for three years.[40]

Unlike the earlier kings of the dynasty of Jehu, who were described as being basically good in spite of their flaws, the description of Jeroboam opens with refence to his wickedness. He followed in the footsteps of his namesake, Jeroboam ben Nebat.[41] It was certainly not by accident that his father had chosen that name for him, and it must have made him identify with the earlier king and everything he stood for. So his life was directed towards strengthening the Kingdom of Israel and insuring its independence from Judah. Serving G-d was no longer primary as it had been for Jehu.

14:25-27 הוּא הֵשִׁיב אֶת־גְּבוּל יִשְׂרָאֵל מִלְּבוֹא חֲמָת עַד־יָם הָעֲרָבָה כִּדְבַר
ה׳ אֱלֹהֵי יִשְׂרָאֵל אֲשֶׁר דִּבֶּר בְּיַד־עַבְדּוֹ יוֹנָה בֶן־אֲמִתַּי הַנָּבִיא אֲשֶׁר מִגַּת

הַחֵפֶר׃ כִּי־רָאָה ה׳ אֶת־עֳנִי יִשְׂרָאֵל מֹרֶה מְאֹד וְאֶפֶס עָצוּר וְאֶפֶס עָזוּב וְאֵין עֹזֵר לְיִשְׂרָאֵל׃ וְלֹא־דִבֶּר ה׳ לִמְחוֹת אֶת־שֵׁם יִשְׂרָאֵל מִתַּחַת הַשָּׁמָיִם וַיּוֹשִׁיעֵם בְּיַד יָרָבְעָם בֶּן־יוֹאָשׁ׃

He got back the border of Israel, from the Approach of Hamath to the Sea of the Plain, in accordance with the word of the L-rd, the G-d of Israel, that He spoke by the hand of His servant, Jonah ben Amitai the prophet, who was from Gath-hahepher. For G-d had seen the affliction of Israel, very adverse. There was nothing guarded and nothing abandoned, and there was no helper for Israel. But G-d had not spoken of wiping out the name of Israel from under the heavens, so He saved them by the hand of Jeroboam the son of Joash.

Jehoash recovered the cities that had been taken by Hazael. Now his son got back the territories that had been taken from Israel by other kings as well. Some say the conquests of Jeroboam included only territories that had already been conquered in the time of Joshua and subsequently lost. Others say he conquered areas that had never been in Jewish hands before.[42]

Some say the prophecy of Jonah referred to here was a special one addressed to Jeroboam telling him to conquer these areas.[43] Others say it refers to the general concept of repentance found in the Book of Jonah. Just as, by their repentance, the people of Nineveh were saved from the destruction that had been decreed against them, so too the generation of Jeroboam was saved.[44]

Another interpretation is that it refers to the earlier prophecies of Jonah to Jehu, when he anointed him as King of Israel, and later, after he had successfully acquired the throne. It was by that divine promise that his great-grandson, Jeroboam, was able to achieve such success, for Jeroboam himself was not worthy of it.[45]

There are various interpretations of the word "מרה." The root seems to be "מרה," which means "to exchange," and generally has a negative connotation. Some say here it means "adverse," that is, the opposite of what is pleasant and desirable.[46] Others say it means "everchanging," that is, unstable. It kept getting worse and worse.[47] And others say it means "rebellious," which is one of the various uses of this root. Even though they rebelled, G-d had mercy on them.[48]

Other interpretations are that it means "bitter," from the root "מר,"[49]

"cast down," from the root "ירה,"[50] or "overpowering," perhaps related to the word "נורא," which comes from the root "ירא" meaning "fear".[51]

Why did G-d favor Jeroboam, granting him such a long successful life and great victories? He was no better than the kings of Israel that came before him, for, like them, he worshiped the golden calves. It was because he refused to believe slanderous reports about G-d's prophets. In the Book of the Prophet Amos we read,[52] "Amaziah, the priest of Bethel, sent to Jeroboam, King of Israel, saying, 'Amos has conspired against you in the midst of the House of Israel. The land cannot contain all of his words! For thus said Amos, "By the sword will Jeroboam die, and Israel will surely be exiled from upon its land."'" But Jeroboam refused to believe him and sent him away in anger. He said, "G-d forbid! Amos is a sincere prophet. He would never have proclaimed such a thing. And if indeed he did, it must be a true prophecy that he received from G-d."

At that moment G-d said, "Even though it is a generation of idolaters and its leader is an idolater, the land that I said to Abraham, Isaac and Jacob 'To your descendants I will give it,' behold, I am giving it into the hand of this one!"[53]

There have been times in history when it seemed that G-d, in His anger, was going to destroy the Jewish People. Twice He told Moses that He would destroy them, once when they made the golden calf and once when the spies returned with discouraging reports about the promised land. But here the Bible tells us that when He uttered those words, G-d had not really intended to destroy them. He said it only to bring Moses to pray for them so that they would be saved. So He told Moses,[54] "Leave Me and I will destroy them, and wipe out their name from beneath the heavens." Moses understood by implication that if he did not leave G-d, Israel would not be destroyed. He understood furthermore that this was G-d's will, even though it seemed to be the opposite.[55]

14:28,29 וְיֶתֶר דִּבְרֵי יָרָבְעָם וְכָל־אֲשֶׁר עָשָׂה וּגְבוּרָתוֹ אֲשֶׁר־נִלְחָם וַאֲשֶׁר הֵשִׁיב אֶת־דַּמֶּשֶׂק וְאֶת־חֲמָת לִיהוּדָה בְּיִשְׂרָאֵל הֲלֹא־הֵם כְּתוּבִים עַל־סֵפֶר דִּבְרֵי הַיָּמִים לְמַלְכֵי יִשְׂרָאֵל: וַיִּשְׁכַּב יָרָבְעָם עִם־אֲבֹתָיו עִם מַלְכֵי יִשְׂרָאֵל וַיִּמְלֹךְ זְכַרְיָה בְנוֹ תַּחְתָּיו:

The rest of the things about Jeroboam, and all that he did and his might, that he fought and that he got back Damascus and Hamath to Judah in Israel, are indeed written in the Book of the Chronicles of the Kings of Israel. Jeroboam lay down with his fathers, with the kings of Israel, and Zechariah his son became king in his place.

II KINGS 15

15:1-4 בִּשְׁנַת עֶשְׂרִים וָשֶׁבַע שָׁנָה לְיָרָבְעָם מֶלֶךְ יִשְׂרָאֵל מָלַךְ עֲזַרְיָה
בֶן־אֲמַצְיָה מֶלֶךְ יְהוּדָה׃ בֶּן־שֵׁשׁ עֶשְׂרֵה שָׁנָה הָיָה בְמָלְכוֹ וַחֲמִשִּׁים וּשְׁתַּיִם
שָׁנָה מָלַךְ בִּירוּשָׁלָםִ וְשֵׁם אִמּוֹ יְכָלְיָהוּ מִירוּשָׁלָםִ׃ וַיַּעַשׂ הַיָּשָׁר בְּעֵינֵי ה׳ כְּכֹל
אֲשֶׁר־עָשָׂה אֲמַצְיָהוּ אָבִיו׃ רַק הַבָּמוֹת לֹא־סָרוּ עוֹד הָעָם מְזַבְּחִים וּמְקַטְּרִים
בַּבָּמוֹת׃

In the twenty-seventh year of Jeroboam, King of Israel, Azariah, the son of Amaziah, King of Judah, became king. He was sixteen years old when he became king and for fifty-two years he reigned in Jerusalem. His mother's name was Jecoliah from Jerusalem. He did what was upright in G-d's eyes, like all that Amaziah, his father, had done. Only the altars were not removed. The people were still sacrificing and burning incense on the altars.

The statement that it was Jeroboam's twenty-seventh year when Azariah became king is very difficult to explain. Above[1] we read that Azariah's father, Amaziah, reigned twenty-nine years. Following that, we read[2] that Jeroboam, King of Israel, became king in Amaziah's fifteenth year, and Amaziah lived another fifteen years.[3] In the Biblical style, with which we are already familiar, the year in which Jeroboam became king is counted in both fifteens, so the total is twenty-nine years, being the length of Amaziah's reign. Thus these verses are all in agreement, indicating Jeroboam's fifteenth year as the one in which Amaziah died and his son, Azariah, became king. All contradict the statement here that it was Jeroboam's twenty-seventh year.

How can this discrepency of twelve years be resolved? We have encountered similar problems before. Sometimes the solution was that a father had his son appointed coregent, and father and son reigned together several years. Some say that Jeroboam had indeed begun to reign with his father, but that was only three years before his father's death, which would make it only his eighteenth year when Azariah became king. It was certainly not his twenty-seventh year, since he would then have had to reign together with his father for twelve years, beginning only five years after his father himself became king.

According to one opinion quoted above, Azariah began his reign in Amaziah's fifteenth year, together with Jeroboam. That would seem to present an additional problem. Not only was it not Jeroboam's twenty-seventh year. It was not his eighteenth or even his fifteenth. It was his first! However, when a son was appointed coregent with his father, his reign could be counted either from the year he was first appointed or the year his father died. So even according to this opinion, had it said that Azariah became king in Jeroboam's fifteenth or eighteenth year it would not have been a problem, since the verse could have been referring to the year of Amaziah's death. But how can we reconcile the statement that it was his twenty-seventh?

It seems, therefore, that this verse cannot refer to the time between the beginnings of the reigns of these two kings, but must refer instead to some other events. One explanation is that it refers to the end rather than the beginning of Jeroboam's reign. It means that when Azariah became king, there remained twenty-seven years to Jeroboam's reign. This is consistent with the above calculation that it was the fifteenth year of Jeroboam's reign and the statement that he reigned forty-one years in all.[4]

This approach, however, is contradicted by the statement later in this chapter[5] that Jeroboam's son, Zechariah, became king in Azariah's thirty-eighth year. If there remained only twenty-seven years to Jeroboam's reign when Azariah became king, then it would be in Azariah's twenty-seventh year that Zechariah succeeded his father.

The statement about Zechariah is a problem even if Azariah's reign is counted from his father's fifteenth year, for if Azariah and Jeroboam began their reigns together and Jeroboam reigned forty-one years, Zechariah would have become king in the forty-first year of Azariah. But since in this case the discrepancy is only three years, it can be explained by the suggestion mentioned above, that Jeroboam had been appointed coregent three years before his father's death. His reign of forty-one years therefore ended in the thirty-eighth year of Azariah.

But what, according to this approach, is the meaning of the statement that Azariah became king in the twenty-seventh year of Jeroboam? The answer is contained in the following verse.

15:5 וַיְנַגַּע ה׳ אֶת־הַמֶּלֶךְ וַיְהִי מְצֹרָע עַד־יוֹם מֹתוֹ וַיֵּשֶׁב בְּבֵית
הַחָפְשִׁית וְיוֹתָם בֶּן־הַמֶּלֶךְ עַל־הַבַּיִת שֹׁפֵט אֶת־עַם הָאָרֶץ׃

G-d afflicted the king with leprosy, and he was a leper until the day of his death. He lived in the house of freedom, and Jotham, the son of the king, was in charge of the house, judging the people of the land.

The Book of Chronicles tells how this happened. It says:[6]

> When he became strong his heart became haughty until it was destructive to him, and he trespassed against the L-rd, his G-d. He came into the sanctuary of G-d to burn incense on the altar of incense. Azariah the priest came after him, and with him were eighty valiant priests of G-d. They stood around King Uziah and said to him, "It is not for you, Uziah, to burn incense for G-d, but for the priests, the sons of Aaron, who are sanctified to burn incense. Go out of the Sanctuary, for you have trespassed, nor is it an honor for you from the L-rd, G-d!" Uziah was enraged, and in his hand was the pan to burn incense. As he raged at the priests, the leprosy shone forth on his forehead, before the priests in the House of G-d, above the altar of incense. Azariah the High Priest and all the priests turned toward him, and behold, he was leprous on his forehead! They hurried him out of there. He too was in a hurry to go out, for G-d had afflicted him. King Uziah was a leper until the day of his death. He lived in the house of freedom, leprous, for he had been cut off from the House of G-d, and Jotham, his son, was in charge of the house of the king, judging the people of the land.

Azariah was not trying to elevate his own status by burning incense. He was king, and there is no higher status than that. He wanted only to serve and honor G-d. His sin was to claim the privilege of honoring G-d in this way. Nonetheless, he incurred this severe punishment. How much more so would one who tried to perform the Temple service to gain honor for himself deserve to be punished![7]

What brought Azariah to make such a terrible mistake? It was because he became too involved with the soil, that is, with earthly matters. There were three people whose involvement with the soil is explicitly stated in the Bible, and all were subsequently corrupted. They were Cain, Noah, and Azariah. Of Cain it says,[8] "Cain was a worker of the soil." Following that we read that his offering to G-d was rejected, and he then killed his brother and was cursed. Of Noah it says,[9] "Noah began to be a man of the soil," which can also be read, "Noah profaned himself by being a man of the soil." Afterwards we read that he became drunk and was disgraced by being found naked by his sons. Of Azariah it says,[10] "he was a lover of the soil." Such great men should have concentrated on Torah and spiritual matters. By becoming involved with mundane affairs instead, they neglected their purpose in life and were thereby profaned.[11]

When Azariah became a leper he could no longer remain in his palace, for lepers are not permitted to enter walled cities such as Jerusalem, where the palace was located. A special house was made for him outside the city in the cemetery. It was called "the house of freedom" because Azariah was now free from the duties of a king. Being a king is a great responsibility, and involves much work. We, who are not kings, see only the privileges and rewards of royalty, but for one who has been a king and taken his position seriously, as Azariah did, it is a great burden. Though he was terribly grieved at being so afflicted, it was nonetheless a relief for him.

The house was in the cemetery because a leper is like a dead person. Like the dead, he is impure, and conveys his impurity to those who touch him. His impurity excludes him from holy areas. And, like the dead who are finally free of the toils of life, as it says,[12] "free with the dead," the leper is involuntarily freed of many of the obligations of live people.[13]

A year after Azariah was afflicted with leprosy, his son Jotham was born. He was not a leper like his father, so he lived in the royal palace and was given some of the status of king. When he was old enough to take responsibility, he began functioning as king as well. Until then, the nobles and ministers conducted the affairs of the kingdom.[14]

We now come to the second explanation of the statement that Azariah became king in the twenty-seventh year of Jeroboam. It is this incident to which that verse is referring. When Azariah was afflicted with leprosy, the nature of his kingship changed. At that point, which was twenty-seven years after he and Jeroboam had ascended the thrones of their respective kingdoms, a new phase of his reign began, for from then on he reigned as a leper. The verse marks the beginning of this new phase.[15]

15:6 וְיֶתֶר דִּבְרֵי עֲזַרְיָהוּ וְכָל־אֲשֶׁר עָשָׂה הֲלֹא־הֵם כְּתוּבִים עַל־סֵפֶר
דִּבְרֵי הַיָּמִים לְמַלְכֵי יְהוּדָה׃

The rest of the things about Azariah and all that he did are indeed written in the Book of the Chronicles of the Kings of Judah.

The Book of Chronicles describes the earlier period of Azariah's reign. It says:[16]

> So it was that he sought G-d in the days of Zechariah, who understood the visions of G-d, and in the days that he sought G-d, G-d gave him success. He went out and fought with the Philistines, and broke through the wall of Gath, the wall of Jabneh, and the wall of Ashdod. He built cities in Ashdod and among the Philistines. G-d helped him against the Philistines and against the Arabs who lived in Gur-baal and the Meunim. The Amonites gave tribute to Uziah and his name spread as far as the approach to Egypt, for he had become exceedingly strong. Uziah built towers in Jerusalem, on the Gate of the Corner, on the Gate of the Valley, and on the end, and strengthened them. He built towers in the desert and dug many cisterns, for he had great flocks, and in the Lowland and on the Plain, ploughmen and vineyard workers in the mountains and the hills, for he was a lover of the soil. Uziah had armies of warriors going out in the army by bands, according to the number of their appointments, under the supervision of Jeiel the scribe and Maaseiah the clerk, under the supervision of Hananiah, from among the officers of the king. All the number of the heads of the families of the mighty warriors was two thousand and six hundred. And under them the warriors of the army, three hundred and seven thousand and five hundred, making war with mighty strength, to help the king against the enemy. Uziah prepared them, for the whole army, shields, spears, helmets, armor and bows, and for the stones of the slings. He made in Jerusalem skillfully designed war machines to be on the towers and on the corners, to shoot arrows and large stones. His name went out afar, for he had been helped exceptionally till he was strong.

15:7 וַיִּשְׁכַּב עֲזַרְיָה עִם־אֲבֹתָיו וַיִּקְבְּרוּ אֹתוֹ עִם־אֲבֹתָיו בְּעִיר דָּוִד וַיִּמְלֹךְ
יוֹתָם בְּנוֹ תַּחְתָּיו׃

Azariah lay down with his fathers. They buried him with his

fathers in the city of David, and Jotham, his son, reigned in his place.

The Book of Chronicles adds,[17] "Uziah lay down with his fathers. They buried him with his fathers in the field of burial that was for the kings, for they said, 'He is a leper,' and Jotham, his son, became king in his place." Instead of burying him in the cave with the other kings, they buried him in the field.[18]

15:8-10 בִּשְׁנַת שְׁלֹשִׁים וּשְׁמֹנֶה שָׁנָה לַעֲזַרְיָהוּ מֶלֶךְ יְהוּדָה מָלַךְ זְכַרְיָהוּ
בֶן־יָרָבְעָם עַל־יִשְׂרָאֵל בְּשֹׁמְרוֹן שִׁשָּׁה חֳדָשִׁים: וַיַּעַשׂ הָרַע בְּעֵינֵי ה׳ כַּאֲשֶׁר
עָשׂוּ אֲבֹתָיו לֹא סָר מֵחַטֹּאות יָרָבְעָם בֶּן־נְבָט אֲשֶׁר הֶחֱטִיא אֶת־יִשְׂרָאֵל:
וַיִּקְשֹׁר עָלָיו שַׁלֻּם בֶּן־יָבֵשׁ וַיַּכֵּהוּ קָבָל־עָם וַיְמִיתֵהוּ וַיִּמְלֹךְ תַּחְתָּיו:

In the thirty-eighth year of Azariah, King of Judah, Zechariah the son of Jeroboam, King of Israel, became king in Samaria six months. He did what was evil in G-d's eyes, as his fathers had done. He didn't deviate from the sins of Jeroboam ben Nebat, who made Israel sin. Shalum ben Jabesh conspired against him and smote him in front of the people and killed him, and reigned in his place.

As has been mentioned above, according to some opinions Zechariah had already reigned along with his father for three years. After his father's death, however, he was not able to hold the kingdom long.

15:11,12 וְיֶתֶר דִּבְרֵי זְכַרְיָה הִנָּם כְּתוּבִים עַל־סֵפֶר דִּבְרֵי הַיָּמִים לְמַלְכֵי
יִשְׂרָאֵל: הוּא דְבַר־ה׳ אֲשֶׁר דִּבֶּר אֶל־יֵהוּא לֵאמֹר בְּנֵי רְבִיעִים יֵשְׁבוּ לְךָ
עַל־כִּסֵּא יִשְׂרָאֵל וַיְהִי־כֵן:

The rest of the things about Zechariah are indeed written in the Book of the Chronicles of the Kings of Israel. That was the word of G-d that He had spoken to Jehu saying, "Sons of the fourth generation will sit for you on the throne of Israel," and so it was.

About the fourth and last of Jehu's successors, the Bible has nothing good to say. He was not worthy of being king, but G-d kept the promise He had made to Jehu.[19] Indeed, had it not been for G-d's promise to Jehu, the people would have rebelled and overthrown his descendants long before.[20]

This promise is not to be understood as a limit. Had Jehu's descendants been worthy, their dynasty could have continued. Had Zechariah abandoned the wicked ways of his father, he would not have been held accountable for them. He too would have enjoyed a long and successful reign and his descendants would have inherited his throne, for he would then have been worthy of it in his own right, not just as a descendant of Jehu. The promise to Jehu was only a minimum.[21]

15:13-16 שַׁלּוּם בֶּן־יָבֵישׁ מָלַךְ בִּשְׁנַת שְׁלֹשִׁים וָתֵשַׁע שָׁנָה לְעֻזִּיָּה מֶלֶךְ
יְהוּדָה וַיִּמְלֹךְ יֶרַח־יָמִים בְּשֹׁמְרוֹן: וַיַּעַל מְנַחֵם בֶּן־גָּדִי מִתִּרְצָה וַיָּבֹא שֹׁמְרוֹן
וַיַּךְ אֶת־שַׁלּוּם בֶּן־יָבֵישׁ בְּשֹׁמְרוֹן וַיְמִיתֵהוּ וַיִּמְלֹךְ תַּחְתָּיו: וְיֶתֶר דִּבְרֵי שַׁלּוּם
וְקִשְׁרוֹ אֲשֶׁר קָשָׁר הִנָּם כְּתוּבִים עַל־סֵפֶר דִּבְרֵי הַיָּמִים לְמַלְכֵי יִשְׂרָאֵל: אָז
יַכֶּה־מְנַחֵם אֶת־תִּפְסַח וְאֶת־כָּל־אֲשֶׁר־בָּהּ וְאֶת־גְּבוּלֶיהָ מִתִּרְצָה כִּי לֹא פָתַח וַיַּךְ
אֵת כָּל־הֶהָרוֹתֶיהָ בִּקֵּעַ:

Shalum ben Jabesh became king in the thirty-ninth year of Uziah, King of Judah, and he reigned one month in Samaria. Menahem ben Gadi came up from Tirzah and came to Samaria and smote Shalum ben Jabesh in Samaria. He killed him and became king in his place. The rest of the things about Shalum and the conspiracy that he conspired are indeed written in the Book of the Chronicles of the Kings of Israel. Then Menahem smote Tiphsah and all that was in it, and its borders from Tirzah, for they didn't open up, so he smote it. All its pregnant women he split open.

Tiphsah was a city of Aram, lying just beyond the border of Israel opposite Tirzah, where Menahem lived. Menahem hoped that since they were neighbors, the inhabitants of Tiphsah would recognize him when he came to power and accept him as their ruler. When they failed to, he was bitterly disappointed and wreaked terrible vengeance.[22]

15:17,18 בִּשְׁנַת שְׁלֹשִׁים וָתֵשַׁע שָׁנָה לַעֲזַרְיָה מֶלֶךְ יְהוּדָה מָלַךְ מְנַחֵם בֶּן־
גָּדִי עַל־יִשְׂרָאֵל עֶשֶׂר שָׁנִים בְּשֹׁמְרוֹן: וַיַּעַשׂ הָרַע בְּעֵינֵי ה׳ לֹא־סָר מֵעַל
חַטֹּאות יָרָבְעָם בֶּן־נְבָט אֲשֶׁר־הֶחֱטִיא אֶת־יִשְׂרָאֵל כָּל־יָמָיו:

In the thirty-ninth year of Azariah, King of Judah, Menahem ben Gadi became king over Israel for ten years in Samaria. He did what was evil in G-d's eyes. He did not deviate from all the sins of Jeroboam ben Nebat who made Israel sin, all his days.

The brief period of reform initiated by Jehu was over. The kings that followed Zechariah were all wicked and violent. They rose by violence and fell by violence. Of them, only Menahem managed to live out his reign and pass on the throne to his son, who held it only two years before he was killed.[23]

Menahem's was the sixth of the seven courts that served idolatry before G-d finally sent the ten tribes into exile.[24]

15:19-22 בָּא פוּל מֶלֶךְ־אַשּׁוּר עַל־הָאָרֶץ וַיִּתֵּן מְנַחֵם לְפוּל אֶלֶף כִּכַּר־
כָּסֶף לִהְיוֹת יָדָיו אִתּוֹ לְהַחֲזִיק הַמַּמְלָכָה בְּיָדוֹ: וַיֹּצֵא מְנַחֵם אֶת־הַכֶּסֶף
עַל־יִשְׂרָאֵל עַל כָּל־גִּבּוֹרֵי הַחַיִל לָתֵת לְמֶלֶךְ אַשּׁוּר חֲמִשִּׁים שְׁקָלִים כֶּסֶף לְאִישׁ
אֶחָד וַיָּשָׁב מֶלֶךְ אַשּׁוּר וְלֹא־עָמַד שָׁם בָּאָרֶץ: וְיֶתֶר דִּבְרֵי מְנַחֵם וְכָל־אֲשֶׁר
עָשָׂה הֲלוֹא־הֵם כְּתוּבִים עַל־סֵפֶר דִּבְרֵי הַיָּמִים לְמַלְכֵי יִשְׂרָאֵל: וַיִּשְׁכַּב מְנַחֵם
עִם־אֲבֹתָיו וַיִּמְלֹךְ פְּקַחְיָה בְנוֹ תַּחְתָּיו:

Pul, King of Assyria, came upon the land. Menahem gave Pul one thousand talents of silver that his hands be with him to secure the kingdom in his hand. Menahem put the burden of the money upon Israel, upon all the brave warriors, to give to the King of Assyria, fifty shekels of silver for each man. So the King of Assyria went back and did not stay there in the land. The rest of the things about Menahem and all that he did are indeed written in the Book of the Chronicles of the Kings of Israel. Menahem lay down with his fathers, and Pekahiah, his son, became king in his place.

Pul conquered the territory east of the Jordan River, and exiled the tribes of Reuben and Gad and half the tribe of Manasseh, as is described in the Book of Chronicles. It says:[25]

> They trespassed against the G-d of their fathers and were unfaithful, following the gods of the peoples of the land that G-d had destroyed before them. The G-d of Israel stirred up the spirit of Pul, King of Assyria, and the spirit of Tilgath-pilnesser, King of Assyria, and he exiled the Reubenites and Gadites and half the tribe of Manasseh, and brought them to Halah, Habor, Hara and the river of Gozan till this day.

Menahem tried to bribe Pul to be his ally, but Pul abandoned him. He had done him enough of a favor by leaving him in peace with the majority of his kingdom still intact.[26]

15:23-26 בִּשְׁנַת חֲמִשִּׁים שָׁנָה לַעֲזַרְיָה מֶלֶךְ יְהוּדָה מָלַךְ פְּקַחְיָה בֶן־מְנַחֵם
עַל־יִשְׂרָאֵל בְּשֹׁמְרוֹן שְׁנָתָיִם: וַיַּעַשׂ הָרַע בְּעֵינֵי ה׳ לֹא סָר מֵחַטֹּאות יָרָבְעָם
בֶּן־נְבָט אֲשֶׁר הֶחֱטִיא אֶת־יִשְׂרָאֵל: וַיִּקְשֹׁר עָלָיו פֶּקַח בֶּן־רְמַלְיָהוּ שָׁלִישׁוֹ
וַיַּכֵּהוּ בְשֹׁמְרוֹן בְּאַרְמוֹן בֵּית־ מלך (הַמֶּלֶךְ קרי) אֶת־אַרְגֹּב וְאֶת־הָאַרְיֵה וְעִמּוֹ
חֲמִשִּׁים אִישׁ מִבְּנֵי גִלְעָדִים וַיְמִתֵהוּ וַיִּמְלֹךְ תַּחְתָּיו: וְיֶתֶר דִּבְרֵי פְקַחְיָה
וְכָל־אֲשֶׁר עָשָׂה הִנָּם כְּתוּבִים עַל־סֵפֶר דִּבְרֵי הַיָּמִים לְמַלְכֵי יִשְׂרָאֵל:

In the fiftieth year of Azariah, King of Judah, Pekahiah, the son of Menahem, became king over Israel in Samaria for two years. He did what was evil in G-d's eyes. He didn't deviate from the sins of Jeroboam ben Nebat who made Israel sin. Pekah ben Remaliah, his captain, conspired against him and smote him in Samaria in the palace of the king's house, with Argob and Arieh, and with him were fifty men from the sons of the Gileadites. He killed him and became king in his place. The rest of the things about Pekahiah and all that he did, behold, they are written in the Book of the Chronicles of the Kings of Israel.

It is not clear whether Argob and Arieh were supporters of Pekahiah who were killed along with him, or whether they were the ones that conspired together with Pekah ben Remaliah.[27] The word "with" can be interpreted in both ways.

Some say "Argob" and "Arieh" are not the names of people but things. Argob refers to the palace and Arieh means "the lion," referring to a golden statue that was there.[28]

15:27-31 בִּשְׁנַת חֲמִשִּׁים וּשְׁתַּיִם שָׁנָה לַעֲזַרְיָה מֶלֶךְ יְהוּדָה מָלַךְ פֶּקַח
בֶּן־רְמַלְיָהוּ עַל־יִשְׂרָאֵל בְּשֹׁמְרוֹן עֶשְׂרִים שָׁנָה: וַיַּעַשׂ הָרַע בְּעֵינֵי ה׳ לֹא סָר
מִן־חַטֹּאות יָרָבְעָם בֶּן־נְבָט אֲשֶׁר הֶחֱטִיא אֶת־יִשְׂרָאֵל: בִּימֵי פֶּקַח מֶלֶךְ־יִשְׂרָאֵל
בָּא תִּגְלַת פִּלְאֶסֶר מֶלֶךְ אַשּׁוּר וַיִּקַּח אֶת־עִיּוֹן וְאֶת־אָבֵל בֵּית־מַעֲכָה וְאֶת־יָנוֹחַ
וְאֶת־קֶדֶשׁ וְאֶת־חָצוֹר וְאֶת־הַגִּלְעָד וְאֶת־הַגָּלִילָה כֹּל אֶרֶץ נַפְתָּלִי וַיַּגְלֵם
אַשּׁוּרָה: וַיִּקְשָׁר־קֶשֶׁר הוֹשֵׁעַ בֶּן־אֵלָה עַל־פֶּקַח בֶּן־רְמַלְיָהוּ וַיַּכֵּהוּ וַיְמִיתֵהוּ
וַיִּמְלֹךְ תַּחְתָּיו בִּשְׁנַת עֶשְׂרִים לְיוֹתָם בֶּן־עֻזִּיָּה: וְיֶתֶר דִּבְרֵי־פֶקַח וְכָל־אֲשֶׁר עָשָׂה
הִנָּם כְּתוּבִים עַל־סֵפֶר דִּבְרֵי הַיָּמִים לְמַלְכֵי יִשְׂרָאֵל:

In the fifty-second year of Azariah, King of Judah, Pekah ben Remaliah became king over Israel for twenty years. He did what was evil in G-d's eyes. He didn't deviate from the sins of Jeroboam ben Nebat who made Israel sin. In the days of Pekah, King of Israel, Tiglath-pileser, King of Assyria, came and took Ijon, Abel of Beth-maacah, Janoah, Kedesh, Hazor, the Gilead and the Galilee, the whole land of Naphtali, and sent them into exile to Assyria. Hoshea ben Elah plotted a conspiracy against Pekah ben Remaliah. He smote him and killed him, and became king in his place, in the twentieth year of Jotham the son of Uziah. The rest of the things about Pekah and all that he did, behold, they are written in the Book of the Chronicles of the Kings of Israel.

The people realized that this defeat was the king's fault, and rose up against him and killed him.[29]

The reference to the twentieth year of Jotham is difficult to explain, since Jotham only reigned sixteen years. Some say that the divine decree of destruction had already been passed against Pekah ben Remaliah during the lifetime of Jotham, so its fulfillment is reckoned in terms of his reign even though it took place after his death. Some say the conspiracy actually began during Jotham's time.[30]

Others say it was to avoid mentioning the name of his successor,

Ahaz. Ahaz was one of the wicked kings, as we will soon learn, so the prophet did not want to mention his name.[31]

15:32-35 בִּשְׁנַת שְׁתַּיִם לְפֶקַח בֶּן־רְמַלְיָהוּ מֶלֶךְ יִשְׂרָאֵל מָלַךְ יוֹתָם בֶּן־עֻזִּיָּהוּ מֶלֶךְ יְהוּדָה׃ בֶּן־עֶשְׂרִים וְחָמֵשׁ שָׁנָה הָיָה בְמָלְכוֹ וְשֵׁשׁ־עֶשְׂרֵה שָׁנָה מָלַךְ בִּירוּשָׁלָםִ וְשֵׁם אִמּוֹ יְרוּשָׁא בַּת־צָדוֹק׃ וַיַּעַשׂ הַיָּשָׁר בְּעֵינֵי ה׳ כְּכֹל אֲשֶׁר־עָשָׂה עֻזִּיָּהוּ אָבִיו עָשָׂה׃ רַק הַבָּמוֹת לֹא סָרוּ עוֹד הָעָם מְזַבְּחִים וּמְקַטְּרִים בַּבָּמוֹת הוּא בָּנָה אֶת־שַׁעַר בֵּית־ה׳ הָעֶלְיוֹן׃

In the second year of Pekah ben Remaliah, King of Israel, Jotham the son of Uziah, King of Judah, became king. He was twenty-five years old when he became king, and sixteen years did he reign in Jerusalem. His mother's name was Jerusha the daughter of Zadok. He did what was upright in G-d's eyes. Like all that Uziah, his father, had done did he do. Only the altars were not removed. The people were still sacrificing and burning incense on the altars. He built the Upper Gate of the House of G-d.

Pekah became king in Azariah's fifty-second year, less than a year before he died. When Pekah's second year began, in the month of Nisan, Azariah was still alive. Thus Jotham became king in the second year of Pekah.

The gate that Jotham built replaced the original one built by King Solomon. In the Book of Chronicles this gate was mentioned in connection with Jehoash. It says,[32] "he came through the Upper Gate to the house of the king." It seems that Jotham strengthened it and made it more beautiful,[33] or perhaps it had fallen and he rebuilt it.[34]

The Book of Chronicles adds:[35]

> He built cities in the mountains of Judah, and in the forests he built fortresses and towers. He fought with the king of the children of Amon and overpowered them. The children of Amon gave him in that year one hundred talents of silver, ten thousand measures of wheat and ten thousand of barley. This the children of Amon gave him, and in the second year and in the third.

15:36-38 וְיֶתֶר דִּבְרֵי יוֹתָם וְכָל־אֲשֶׁר עָשָׂה הֲלֹא־הֵם כְּתוּבִים עַל־סֵפֶר
דִּבְרֵי הַיָּמִים לְמַלְכֵי יְהוּדָה: בַּיָּמִים הָהֵם הֵחֵל ה׳ לְהַשְׁלִיחַ בִּיהוּדָה רְצִין מֶלֶךְ
אֲרָם וְאֵת פֶּקַח בֶּן־רְמַלְיָהוּ: וַיִּשְׁכַּב יוֹתָם עִם־אֲבֹתָיו וַיִּקָּבֵר עִם־אֲבֹתָיו בְּעִיר
דָּוִד אָבִיו וַיִּמְלֹךְ אָחָז בְּנוֹ תַּחְתָּיו:

The rest of the things about Jotham and all that he did are indeed written in the Book of the Chronicles of the Kings of Judah. In those days G-d began to send against Judah Rezin, King of Aram, and Pekah ben Remaliah. Jotham lay down with his fathers. He was buried with his fathers in the city of David, his father, and Ahaz, his son, became king in his place.

Jotham was the only king who did not commit any sin. David sinned with Bathsheba, Solomon permitted the idolatry of his wives, Rehoboam and Abijah abandoned the Torah, Asa hired the King of Aram to fight against the Kingdom of Israel, Jehoshaphat formed a union with the wicked Ahab, Jehoram killed his brothers, Ahaziah served idols, Jehoash killed Zechariah, Amaziah served idols, Azariah entered the Sanctuary to burn incense, Ahaz worshiped idols, Hezekiah disobeyed the court, Manasseh denied the Torah and was very wicked, and Josiah and Zedekiah rejected the prophecies that were sent to them, but nowhere is there mention of any sin committed by Jotham.[36]

Some say "those days" refers to the end of Jotham's life.[37] Others say it was not until after his death.[38]

II KINGS 16

16:1-4 בִּשְׁנַת שְׁבַע־עֶשְׂרֵה שָׁנָה לְפֶקַח בֶּן־רְמַלְיָהוּ מָלַךְ אָחָז בֶּן־יוֹתָם
מֶלֶךְ יְהוּדָה: בֶּן־עֶשְׂרִים שָׁנָה אָחָז בְּמָלְכוֹ וְשֵׁשׁ־עֶשְׂרֵה שָׁנָה מָלַךְ בִּירוּשָׁלָם
וְלֹא־עָשָׂה הַיָּשָׁר בְּעֵינֵי ה׳ אֱלֹהָיו כְּדָוִד אָבִיו: וַיֵּלֶךְ בְּדֶרֶךְ מַלְכֵי יִשְׂרָאֵל וְגַם
אֶת־בְּנוֹ הֶעֱבִיר בָּאֵשׁ כְּתֹעֲבוֹת הַגּוֹיִם אֲשֶׁר הוֹרִישׁ ה׳ אֹתָם מִפְּנֵי בְּנֵי יִשְׂרָאֵל:
וַיְזַבֵּחַ וַיְקַטֵּר בַּבָּמוֹת וְעַל־הַגְּבָעוֹת וְתַחַת כָּל־עֵץ רַעֲנָן:

In the seventeenth year of Pekah ben Remaliah, Ahaz, the son of Jotham, King of Judah, became king. Ahaz was twenty years old when he became king and he reigned sixteen years in Jerusalem. He didn't do what was upright in the eyes of the L-rd, his G-d, like David, his father. He went in the way of the kings of Israel. He even passed his son through the fire, like the abominations of the nations that G-d had driven out before the Children of Israel. He sacrificed and burnt incense on the altars and on the hills, and under every lush tree.

In the Book of Chronicles it says,[1] "He went in the ways of the kings of Israel and also made cast images for the Baalim. He burnt incense in the valley of Ben-hinom, and burnt his children in fire, like the abominations of the nations that G-d had driven out before the Children of Israel."

There were two idolatrous practices involving fire. In one, a person merely passed his children between two fires, but in the other he actually burnt them to death. Ahaz seems to have practiced both. Only by a miracle was his son, Hezekiah, saved. G-d saw that if Hezekiah survived, he would have three righteous descendants, Hananiah, Mishael and Azariah. They would let themselves be thrown into the fiery furnace of Nebuchadnezar rather than profane G-d's holy name. G-d said, "Just as I will save them when that time comes, for they will be worthy of a miracle, so will I save this child now."[2]

Some say his mother rubbed the blood of a salamander on him and it protected him from the fire.[3]

But as for Ahaz, he was punished by being attacked and beaten by his enemies, first by Aram and then by the Kingdom of Israel.[4] The Book of Chronicles continues:[5]

> The L-rd, his G-d, gave him into the hand of the King of Aram. They smote him, took many captives from him, and brought them to Damascus. Also into the hand of the King of Israel was he given, and he smote him a great blow. Pekah ben Remaliah killed in Judah one hundred and twenty thousand in one day, all valiant men, because they had abandoned the L-rd, the G-d of their fathers. Zichri, the mighty man of Ephraim, killed Maaseiahu, the son of the king, Azrikam, the supervisor of the palace, and Elkanah, the second to the king. The Children of Israel took captive from their brothers two hundred thousand women, girls, and boys. They also looted much spoil from them and brought the spoil to Samaria. There, there was a prophet of G-d whose name was Oded. He went out before the army that was coming to Samaria and said to them, "Behold, by the wrath of the L-rd, the G-d of your fathers, against Judah did He give them into your hand, and you have killed them with fury. It has reached the sky. And now, do you intend to subjugate the children of Judah and Jerusalem as slaves and maidservants for yourselves? Is not the guilt to the L-rd, your G-d, yours alone? So now listen to me, and return the captives that you captured from your brothers, for the burning of the wrath of G-d is upon you." Then arose men from the heads of the children of Ephraim, Azariah ben Jehohanan, Berechiah ben Meshilemoth, Jehizkiah ben Shalum, and Amasa ben Hadlai, over those who were coming from the army. They said to them, "Don't bring the captives here, for what you plan to do will become a guilt to G-d upon us, to add onto our sins and our guilt, for we have much guilt, and the burning of wrath against Israel." So the armed men left the captives and the spoils before the officers and the whole congregation. The men who had been designated by name got up and took the captives, and all of their naked ones they clothed from the spoils. They clothed them, shod them, fed them, and gave them to drink. They anointed them and had all the feeble ones ride on donkeys. They brought them to Jericho, the city of the date palms, unto their brothers, and returned to Samaria.

Later, Aram and Israel joined forces to attack again, but this time G-d protected Judah.[6]

16:5 אָז יַעֲלֶה רְצִין מֶלֶךְ־אֲרָם וּפֶקַח בֶּן־רְמַלְיָהוּ מֶלֶךְ־יִשְׂרָאֵל יְרוּשָׁלַם לַמִּלְחָמָה וַיָּצֻרוּ עַל־אָחָז וְלֹא יָכְלוּ לְהִלָּחֵם׃

Then Rezin, King of Aram, and Pekah ben Remaliah, King of Israel, came up to Jerusalem for war. They besieged Ahaz, but they couldn't fight.

In the Book of Isaiah this incident is recorded in detail. It says:[7]

> It was in the days of Ahaz the son of Jotham the son of Uziah, King of Judah, that Rezin, King of Aram, and Pekah ben Remaliah, King of Israel, came up upon Jerusalem for war against it, but they couldn't fight against it. It was told to the House of David saying, "Aram has camped with Ephraim!" His heart and the heart of his people trembled as the trees of the forest tremble before the wind. G-d said to Isaiah, "Go out, please, to meet Ahaz, you and Shear-jashub your son, to the end of the channel of the upper pool, to the path of the field of the washers. Say to him, 'Be calm and quiet. Don't be afraid, and let your heart not soften from these two ends of firebrands, smoking in burning anger, Rezin and Aram and ben Remaliah. Since Aram has counselled evil against you, Ephraim and ben Remaliah, saying, "We will go up against Judah and wear down their resistance. Then we will split it between us and appoint a king in its midst, ben Tabeal." Thus says the L-rd, G-d, "It won't succeed and it won't be." For the head of Aram is Damascus, and the head of Damascus is Rezin, and in another sixty-five years, Ephraim will be beaten down from being a nation. The head of Ephraim is Samaria, and the head of Samaria is ben Remaliah. If you don't believe it, it is because you are not believers.'"

In referring to Ahaz, the prophet mentioned not only his father's name, but his grandfather's as well. This was to indicate that it was by their merit that he was saved. The angels complained to G-d, "Why are you saving Ahaz? He is a wicked man and deserves to be defeated!" G-d answered, "His father and grandfather were righteous, and for their sake I will save him."[8] So too, rather than saying, "It was told to Ahaz," it says, "It was told to the House of David." He himself was not worthy of divine reassurance, but as a descendant of David it was given to him.[9]

16:6,7 בָּעֵת הַהִיא הֵשִׁיב רְצִין מֶלֶךְ־אֲרָם אֶת־אֵילַת לַאֲרָם וַיְנַשֵּׁל אֶת־
הַיְּהוּדִים מֵאֵילוֹת וארומים (וַאֲדוֹמִים קרי) בָּאוּ אֵילַת וַיֵּשְׁבוּ שָׁם עַד הַיּוֹם
הַזֶּה׃ וַיִּשְׁלַח אָחָז מַלְאָכִים אֶל־תִּגְלַת פְּלֶסֶר מֶלֶךְ־אַשּׁוּר לֵאמֹר עַבְדְּךָ וּבִנְךָ
אָנִי עֲלֵה וְהוֹשִׁעֵנִי מִכַּף מֶלֶךְ־אֲרָם וּמִכַּף מֶלֶךְ יִשְׂרָאֵל הַקּוֹמִים עָלָי׃

At that time, Rezin, King of Aram, got Elath back for Aram. He drove out the Jews from Elath, and the Edomites came to Elath and lived there till this very day. Ahaz sent messengers to Tiglath-pileser, King of Assyria, saying, "Your servant and your son am I. Come up and save me from the hand of the King of Aram and from the hand of the King of Israel who are rising up against me."

In the Book of Chronicles it says:[10]

> At that time, King Ahaz sent to the kings of Assyria to help him. Again Edomites came, and smote Judah and captured captives. And Philistines invaded the cities of the Lowland and the South that belonged to Judah, and captured Beth-shemesh, Aijalon, Gederoth, Soco and its villages, Timnah and its villages, and Gimzo and its villages, and took captives there. For G-d had humbled Judah because of Ahaz, King of Israel, for he had made Judah lawless and trespassed against G-d.

Ahaz became more and more wicked as time went on. As he did, he corrupted the Torah and the Temple service and finally abolished them completely. He had a throne placed in the Sanctuary, permitted forbidden marriages, and had the Torah sealed away.[11]

Ahaz is compared to a guardian who was entrusted with the care of a king's son whom he secretly wanted to murder. Knowing that if he harmed the child in any way he would be killed, he instead withheld nourishment from him until he wasted away and died. So too, Ahaz withheld Torah from the Jewish People by closing the study halls. He said, "If there are no kids there will be no goats, and if there are no goats there will be no flocks. If there are no flocks there will be no shepherd, and if there is no shepherd there will be no world." He meant that if the children would not go to school they would grow up to be a generation in which no adults studied Torah. Without a general population that studies Torah regularly there would be no sages, and without sages there would be no prophets. Without prophets there would be no one to receive G-d's spirit of prophecy, and then, hoped Ahaz, G-d would remove His Holy Presence from the Jewish People.[12]

Perhaps it is for that reason that in the passage quoted above, Ahaz is referred to as the King of Israel rather than the King of Judah. He behaved more like the kings of Israel than the earlier kings of Judah, so he was no longer worthy of sharing the title that had been held by his noble ancestors.

16:8,9 וַיִּקַּח אָחָז אֶת־הַכֶּסֶף וְאֶת־הַזָּהָב הַנִּמְצָא בֵּית ה׳ וּבְאֹצְרוֹת בֵּית
הַמֶּלֶךְ וַיִּשְׁלַח לְמֶלֶךְ אַשּׁוּר שֹׁחַד: וַיִּשְׁמַע אֵלָיו מֶלֶךְ אַשּׁוּר וַיַּעַל מֶלֶךְ אַשּׁוּר
אֶל־דַּמֶּשֶׂק וַיִּתְפְּשֶׂהָ וַיַּגְלֶהָ קִירָה וְאֶת־רְצִין הֵמִית:

Ahaz took the silver and the gold that was found in the House of G-d and in the treasuries of the house of the king, and sent a gift to the King of Assyria. The King of Assyria listened to him, and the King of Assyria went up to Damascus. He captured it and exiled it to Kir, and Rezin he killed.

Kir was a city in Assyria.[13] The prophet Amos said,[14] "they exiled the people of Aram to Kir."[15]

16:10-13 וַיֵּלֶךְ הַמֶּלֶךְ אָחָז לִקְרַאת תִּגְלַת פִּלְאֶסֶר מֶלֶךְ־אַשּׁוּר דּוּמֶּשֶׂק
וַיַּרְא אֶת־הַמִּזְבֵּחַ אֲשֶׁר בְּדַמָּשֶׂק וַיִּשְׁלַח הַמֶּלֶךְ אָחָז אֶל־אוּרִיָּה הַכֹּהֵן אֶת־דְּמוּת
הַמִּזְבֵּחַ וְאֶת־תַּבְנִיתוֹ לְכָל־מַעֲשֵׂהוּ: וַיִּבֶן אוּרִיָּה הַכֹּהֵן אֶת־הַמִּזְבֵּחַ כְּכֹל
אֲשֶׁר־שָׁלַח הַמֶּלֶךְ אָחָז מִדַּמֶּשֶׂק כֵּן עָשָׂה אוּרִיָּה הַכֹּהֵן עַד־בּוֹא הַמֶּלֶךְ־אָחָז
מִדַּמָּשֶׂק: וַיָּבֹא הַמֶּלֶךְ מִדַּמֶּשֶׂק וַיַּרְא הַמֶּלֶךְ אֶת־הַמִּזְבֵּחַ וַיִּקְרַב הַמֶּלֶךְ
עַל־הַמִּזְבֵּחַ וַיַּעַל עָלָיו: וַיַּקְטֵר אֶת־עֹלָתוֹ וְאֶת־מִנְחָתוֹ וַיַּסֵּךְ אֶת־נִסְכּוֹ וַיִּזְרֹק
אֶת־דַּם־הַשְּׁלָמִים אֲשֶׁר־לוֹ עַל־הַמִּזְבֵּחַ:

King Ahaz went to greet Tiglath-pileser, King of Assyria, in Damascus, and saw the altar that was in Damascus. King

Ahaz sent to Urijah the priest the design of the altar and its construction, down to all of its details. Urijah the priest built the altar according to everything that King Ahaz had sent from Damascus. Thus did Uriah the priest do before King Ahaz came from Damascus. The king came from Damascus, and the king saw the altar, and the king came close to the altar and brought offerings upon it. He burned his burnt offering and his meal offering and poured his libation, and threw the blood of the peace offering that he had on the altar.

Sometimes a person is so resolved to commit a sin that he will proceed no matter what happens. Thus there were kings like Ahaz and Amaziah who would serve idols no matter what G-d did to them. Amaziah was granted a great victory over Edom. How did he respond? He took the idols of the very nation that he had defeated and worshiped them! Now, rather than granting Ahaz victory, G-d had him defeated. What did he do? Did he see it as a divine warning? No! He took it as an opportunity to introduce idolatry into his kingdom. He said, "G-d is not strong enough to help us."

What can be done for those who are so foolish? Whatever happens to them, they behave the same way. What could G-d do to bring them to repent?[16]

16:14 וְאֵת הַמִּזְבַּח הַנְּחֹשֶׁת אֲשֶׁר לִפְנֵי ה׳ וַיַּקְרֵב מֵאֵת פְּנֵי הַבַּיִת מִבֵּין
הַמִּזְבֵּחַ וּמִבֵּין בֵּית ה׳ וַיִּתֵּן אֹתוֹ עַל־יֶרֶךְ הַמִּזְבֵּחַ צָפוֹנָה׃

As for the copper altar that was before G-d, he brought this one closer than it from before the Temple, between the altar and the House of G-d, and put it on the side of the altar to the north.

The "copper altar" refers to the great stone altar of Solomon that stood in the Courtyard of the Priests.[17] It was called "the copper altar" because it replaced the original altar of Moses, which was a large copper frame filled with earth. Even though this one was not made of copper, they continued to call it by that name.

The words "ויקרב מאת," literally, "he brought it close from," could not refer to the altar itself, since the altar was a permanent structure attached to the ground. Some say they refer to the copper utensils that were dedicated to the service of that altar, the basins that held the water to wash the sacrifices. Ahaz moved them away to make room for his new altar.[18]

Others say they refer to the new altar. Ahaz ordered that this altar be placed closer to the Sanctuary than Solomon's to show that it was more important than the altar of G-d.[19]

Some say he placed it to the north because he sacrificed on it to the constellations and planets, which are stronger when they are in the north. Those constellations that are in the northern part of the sky are above the horizon for more than twelve hours every day. Those in the southern part are above the horizon for less. When the sun and planets are in the north, they are up for more hours of the day.[20]

16:15,16 ויצוהו (וַיְצַוֶּה קרי) הַמֶּלֶךְ אָחָז אֶת־אוּרִיָּה הַכֹּהֵן לֵאמֹר עַל הַמִּזְבֵּחַ הַגָּדוֹל הַקְטֵר אֶת־עֹלַת־הַבֹּקֶר וְאֶת־מִנְחַת הָעֶרֶב וְאֶת־עֹלַת הַמֶּלֶךְ וְאֶת־מִנְחָתוֹ וְאֵת עֹלַת כָּל־עַם הָאָרֶץ וּמִנְחָתָם וְנִסְכֵּיהֶם וְכָל־דַּם עֹלָה וְכָל־דַּם־זֶבַח עָלָיו תִּזְרֹק וּמִזְבַּח הַנְּחֹשֶׁת יִהְיֶה־לִּי לְבַקֵּר׃ וַיַּעַשׂ אוּרִיָּה הַכֹּהֵן כְּכֹל אֲשֶׁר־צִוָּה הַמֶּלֶךְ אָחָז׃

King Ahaz commanded Urijah the priest saying, "On the great altar burn the burnt offering of the morning and the meal offering of the evening, the burnt offering of the king and his meal offering, the burnt offering of the whole people, their meal offering and their libations, and all the blood of burnt offerings. Upon it will you throw all the blood of sacrifices. The copper altar will be for me for occasional use." Urijah the priest did according to everything that King Ahaz had commanded.

The new altar was even bigger than Solomon's. Ahaz had it erected beside the altar of Solomon to show his defiance of G-d. He would sacrifice to the idols in the very courtyard of the Holy Temple! From now on sacrifices would be brought for G-d only when it pleased the king, to show that he considered G-d to be only one among the idols.[21]

16:17 וַיְקַצֵּץ הַמֶּלֶךְ אָחָז אֶת־הַמִּסְגְּרוֹת הַמְּכֹנוֹת וַיָּסַר מֵעֲלֵיהֶם ואֶת־
וְאֶת־הַיָּם הוֹרִד מֵעַל הַבָּקָר הַנְּחֹשֶׁת אֲשֶׁר תַּחְתֶּיהָ וַיִּתֵּן אֹתוֹ עַל מַרְצֶפֶת אֲבָנִים׃

King Ahaz cut up the frames of the bases and removed the wash basins from upon them. And the sea he took down from upon the copper oxen that were below it and put it upon a pavement of stones.

Ahaz wanted to erase the belief that the Temple and all that was in it had been made according to divinely ordained plans. He maintained that King Solomon had not built it according to G-d's word, rather that it had been his own idea to replace the Tabernacle by a building that he himself designed. As Solomon had altered the original design of Moses, so Ahaz altered the designs of Solomon.[22]

Solomon had made special stands for the copper basins. They consisted of square frames on wheels. Ahaz had the frames destroyed and the basins set on stone foundations instead.[23]

Lowering the great Sea of Solomon and the wash basins from their bases and putting them on the ground had divine significance unknown to Ahaz. They were a sign that during his reign the glory of Israel would be brought down by Assyria.[24]

16:18 וְאֶת־מֵיסַךְ הַשַּׁבָּת אֲשֶׁר־בָּנוּ בַבַּיִת וְאֶת־מְבוֹא הַמֶּלֶךְ הַחִיצוֹנָה
הֵסֵב בֵּית ה׳ מִפְּנֵי מֶלֶךְ אַשּׁוּר׃

The Sabbath Pavilion that they had built in the Temple and the outer entrance of the king he turned around to the House of G-d, because of the King of Assyria.

Tiglath-pileser accepted the gifts that Ahaz sent and gladly fought Judah's enemies, for by conquering them he enlarged his own empire. But in the end he was a false friend. When he had finished fighting the other nations he turned on Ahaz himself. In the Book of Chronicles it says:[25]

> Tiglath Pilnesar, King of Assyria, came to him and oppressed him, and didn't support him. For Ahaz had divided the House of G-d and the house of the king and the officers and given to the King of

Assyria, but he wasn't any help to him. At the time that he oppressed him, he trespassed even more against G-d, he, King Ahaz. He sacrificed to the gods of Damascus who were smiting him, and said, "For the gods of the kings of Aram, they are the ones who help them. To them will I sacrifice and they will help me!" But for him, they caused him to fail, and all Israel. Ahaz gathered all the utensils of the House of G-d, and cut up the utensils of the House of G-d. He closed the doors of the House of the L-rd, and made himself altars in every corner of Jerusalem. And in each and every city in Judah he made altars to burn incense to foreign gods, and angered the L-rd, the G-d of his fathers.

Rather than repent and mend his ways after he had been so oppressed, Ahaz became even worse. To make the palace more secure, he had its outer gates sealed up and changed the path from the palace to the Temple so that it would not pass outside the walls, so that access to the palace could be gained only through the Temple. In effect, this turned the Temple into a passageway to the palace, which was a terrible disgrace. Some say this was to make the palace easier to defend.[26] Others say it was to conceal the pomp of the royal procession from the view of Tiglath-pileser and his officers, which might provoke their envy.[27] Finally he had the Temple closed and the doors locked, so that the people would bring their sacrifices elsewhere.[28]

The source of Ahaz's wickedness was his laziness. He exemplified the words,[29] "I passed by the field of a lazy one."[30] He closed the synagogues and study halls so that people would stop studying Torah and not be able to criticize him any more. However, he had one good quality. He was ashamed of his wickedness. When the prophet Isaiah came to deliver G-d's words, he covered his head with a sieve so that Isaiah would not recognize him.[31]

16:19,20 וְיֶתֶר דִּבְרֵי אָחָז אֲשֶׁר עָשָׂה הֲלֹא־הֵם כְּתוּבִים עַל־סֵפֶר דִּבְרֵי הַיָּמִים לְמַלְכֵי יְהוּדָה׃ וַיִּשְׁכַּב אָחָז עִם־אֲבֹתָיו וַיִּקָּבֵר עִם־אֲבֹתָיו בְּעִיר דָּוִד וַיִּמְלֹךְ חִזְקִיָּהוּ בְנוֹ תַּחְתָּיו׃

The rest of the things about Ahaz that he did are indeed written in the Book of the Chronicles of the Kings of Judah. Ahaz lay down with his fathers. He was buried with his fathers in the city of David, and Hezekiah, his son, became king in his place.

II KINGS 17

17:1 בִּשְׁנַת שְׁתֵּים עֶשְׂרֵה לְאָחָז מֶלֶךְ יְהוּדָה מָלַךְ הוֹשֵׁעַ בֶּן־אֵלָה
בְשֹׁמְרוֹן עַל־יִשְׂרָאֵל תֵּשַׁע שָׁנִים׃

In the twelfth year of Ahaz, King of Judah, Hoshea ben Elah became king over Israel in Samaria for nine years.

Here again the Bible's chronology must be reinterpreted. It is clear from the previous chapter that Hoshea became king long before the twelfth year of Ahaz. Ahaz became king in the seventeenth year of Pekah ben Remaliah.[1] Pekah reigned twenty years,[2] after which he was killed by Hoshea ben Elah. So Hoshea's reign must have begun in around Pekah's fourth year. But we need not speculate about the real meaning of this verse as we did about some of the earlier ones. It will become clear in the verses that follow that this refers not to his original coronation, but to the year in which he rebelled against Assyria and declared his independence, becoming a sovereign ruler rather than a vassal.[3]

17:2 וַיַּעַשׂ הָרַע בְּעֵינֵי ה׳ רַק לֹא כְּמַלְכֵי יִשְׂרָאֵל אֲשֶׁר הָיוּ לְפָנָיו׃

He did what was evil in G-d's eyes, but not like the kings of Israel that were before him.

This verse should not be taken to mean that Hoshea was better than all the earlier kings. We have already seen that some of them, such as Jehu, were truly righteous. Even Ahab was described as one whose good deeds and evil deeds were equal until the murder of Naboth. Hoshea was certainly not better than all of them.

There was, however, one sin of which all the earlier kings had been guilty. They prevented the people from travelling to Jerusalem to worship in the Temple, lest they be influenced to return to the House of

David and accept his descendants as their kings. That is why the first king of Israel, Jeroboam ben Nebat, established the cult of the golden calves to replace the Temple service. But some people still preferred to travel to Jerusalem than worship at Jeroboam's shrines, so he set up guards on all the roads to stop would-be pilgrims. This practice was continued by all his successors. The maintenance of these guards was a sin specifically of the kings of Israel, and it was of this sin that Hoshea alone was innocent. He removed the guards and declared that the people were now free to worship at the Temple.[4]

But ironically, this sin of the kings had saved the people from guilt. They were not held responsible for neglecting the Temple as long as their rulers prevented them. Now that the guards were removed, the responsibility was entirely upon the shoulders of the people. But after so many generations, the Temple service had lost its importance for them. Finally free to return, they failed to take advantage of the opportunity. It was this sin of voluntarily abandoning the Temple service that tipped the scales against them, and they were condemned to exile.[5]

See how great is G-d's mercy! Would earlier generations have been any better? Would they have dutifully visited the Temple had they been given the opportunity? Probably not. Nonetheless, G-d gave them the benefit of the doubt. Only now, when the people demonstrated their guilt, were they punished. G-d said, "They will be condemned to exile for the number of years that they did not go to Jerusalem."[6]

Even though Hoshea was not guilty of the sin of the earlier kings, he shared in the guilt of the people. The golden calves and the border guards, the two sins of the kings, had been abolished, but by failing to direct the people to return to the Temple he showed that he did not value the Temple service either. Having initiated the process of reform, he had committed himself to completing it, that is, commanding the people to return. For failing to fulfill that commitment he too was punished. Thus we learn that a person who begins a good deed and doesn't complete it deserves to bury his wife and children and die himself.[7]

The Kingdom of Israel suffered three exiles. The first was in the twentieth year of Pekah ben Remaliah. Together with Rezin, the King of Aram, Pekah attacked the Kingdom of Judah, as we learned in the previous chapter. Ahaz, King of Judah, made a covenant with Tiglath-pileser, King of Assyria, sending him tribute and accepting him as his master in return for saving him from Aram and Israel. Tiglath-pileser attacked the two kingdoms and defeated them. Aram was completely destroyed, and Israel came under the control of Assyria. The northern and eastern territories of Israel were placed directly under the control of the King of Assyria and the population was exiled, as we read above.[8] The spoils brought back to Assyria included the golden calf that had been in Dan.[9] Immediately following that, Hoshea ben Elah conspired against Pekah and killed him, and became king in his place. That was in the fourth year of Ahaz, King of Judah.

For eight years Assyria left Israel in peace. Then, in the twelfth year of Ahaz, Pul, King of Assyria, attacked and conquered the territory east of the Jordan River, exiling the tribes of Reuben and Gad and half the tribe of Manasseh, as is recorded in the Book of Chronicles.[10] This was the second exile. This time the second golden calf, the one that was in Beth-el, was captured, as the prophet Hosea had foretold,[11] "It, too, will be brought to Assyria." Some say that as much as seven-eighths of the population went into exile at that time, as the prophet Amos said,[12] "As the shepherd saves from the mouth of the lion, two legs or the cartilage of an ear, so of the Children of Israel who live in Samaria will be saved the sick on their beds in the corner and the old on their soft bedding." Only one-eighth remained in their land, and the rest were in exile in Damascus and beyond, as Amos warned in another prophecy,[13] "I will exile you beyond Damascus."[14]

It was at this time that the guards were removed from the borders and pilgrims were again permitted to travel to Jerusalem. Now that the golden calves had both been captured, Hoshea saw no point in preventing them any longer. The day on which the guards were removed was the fifteenth of the month of Av, and that is one of the reasons that that day is celebrated as a minor holiday.[15]

17:3-6 עָלָיו עָלָה שַׁלְמַנְאֶסֶר מֶלֶךְ אַשּׁוּר וַיְהִי־לוֹ הוֹשֵׁעַ עֶבֶד וַיָּשֶׁב לוֹ
מִנְחָה: וַיִּמְצָא מֶלֶךְ־אַשּׁוּר בְּהוֹשֵׁעַ קֶשֶׁר אֲשֶׁר שָׁלַח מַלְאָכִים אֶל־סוֹא
מֶלֶךְ־מִצְרַיִם וְלֹא־הֶעֱלָה מִנְחָה לְמֶלֶךְ אַשּׁוּר כְּשָׁנָה בְשָׁנָה וַיַּעַצְרֵהוּ מֶלֶךְ אַשּׁוּר
וַיַּאַסְרֵהוּ בֵּית כֶּלֶא: וַיַּעַל מֶלֶךְ־אַשּׁוּר בְּכָל־הָאָרֶץ וַיַּעַל שֹׁמְרוֹן וַיָּצַר עָלֶיהָ
שָׁלֹשׁ שָׁנִים: בִּשְׁנַת הַתְּשִׁיעִית לְהוֹשֵׁעַ לָכַד מֶלֶךְ־אַשּׁוּר אֶת־שֹׁמְרוֹן וַיֶּגֶל
אֶת־יִשְׂרָאֵל אַשּׁוּרָה וַיֹּשֶׁב אוֹתָם בַּחְלַח וּבְחָבוֹר נְהַר גּוֹזָן וְעָרֵי מָדָי:

Shalmaneser, King of Assyria, came up upon him. Hoshea became his servant and sent him tribute. The King of Assyria discovered a conspiracy of Hoshea, that he had sent messengers to So, King of Egypt, and didn't send up his tribute as every year. The King of Assyria arrested him and bound him in prison. The King of Assyria came up upon the whole land. He came up upon Samaria and besieged it three years. In the ninth year of Hoshea, the King of Assyria captured Samaria and exiled Israel to Assyria. He settled them in Halah, Habor, the Gozan River, and the cities of Madai.

Some say that Tiglath-pileser, Pul, Shalmaneser and Sanherib were all the same person. He had eight names in all.[16]

When Hoshea ben Elah saw that Assyria would not be satisfied having him as a vassal, but was intent upon eliminating his kingdom and turning his country into a province, he broke his covenant and declared his independence. For the first time, Hoshea became a sovereign king. This was the twelfth year of Ahaz referred to in the first verse of this chapter as the beginning of Hoshea's reign. And, realizing that he would not be able to withstand Assyria by himself, Hoshea formed an alliance with Assyria's arch enemy, Egypt.

It was not until the seventh year of Elah's independence that Assyria attacked again, and it took them three years to conquer the land, as we will read in the next chapter,[17] "In the fourth year of King Hezekiah, which was the seventh year of Hoshea ben Elah, King of Israel, Shalmaneser, King of Assyria, came up against Samaria and besieged it. They conquered it at the end of three years. In the sixth year of Hezekiah, which was the ninth year of Hoshea, King of Israel, Samaria was conquered."[18]

Finally Samaria fell, nine years after Hoshea declared his independence. In this verse and in the one at the beginning of the chapter, this is referred to as the ninth year of Hoshea, because his reign is reckoned from the time he became a sovereign king. Even though he spent the end of those years as a captive, he was still the King of Israel. This was the third and last exile of the Kingdom of Israel.[19]

17:7-12 וַיְהִי כִּי־חָטְאוּ בְנֵי־יִשְׂרָאֵל לַה׳ אֱלֹהֵיהֶם הַמַּעֲלֶה אֹתָם מֵאֶרֶץ
מִצְרַיִם מִתַּחַת יַד פַּרְעֹה מֶלֶךְ־מִצְרָיִם וַיִּירְאוּ אֱלֹהִים אֲחֵרִים: וַיֵּלְכוּ בְּחֻקּוֹת
הַגּוֹיִם אֲשֶׁר הוֹרִישׁ ה׳ מִפְּנֵי בְּנֵי יִשְׂרָאֵל וּמַלְכֵי יִשְׂרָאֵל אֲשֶׁר עָשׂוּ: וַיְחַפְּאוּ
בְנֵי־יִשְׂרָאֵל דְּבָרִים אֲשֶׁר לֹא־כֵן עַל־ה׳ אֱלֹהֵיהֶם וַיִּבְנוּ לָהֶם בָּמוֹת בְּכָל־עָרֵיהֶם
מִמִּגְדַּל נוֹצְרִים עַד־עִיר מִבְצָר: וַיַּצִּבוּ לָהֶם מַצֵּבוֹת וַאֲשֵׁרִים עַל כָּל־גִּבְעָה
גְבֹהָה וְתַחַת כָּל־עֵץ רַעֲנָן: וַיְקַטְּרוּ־שָׁם בְּכָל־בָּמוֹת כַּגּוֹיִם אֲשֶׁר־הֶגְלָה ה׳

מִפְּנֵיהֶם וַיַּעֲשׂוּ דְּבָרִים רָעִים לְהַכְעִיס אֶת־ה׳: וַיַּעַבְדוּ הַגִּלֻּלִים אֲשֶׁר אָמַר ה׳
לָהֶם לֹא תַעֲשׂוּ אֶת־הַדָּבָר הַזֶּה:

So it was, that when the Children of Israel sinned against the L-rd, their G-d, who had taken them up from the land of Egypt, from under the hand of Pharaoh, King of Egypt, and they feared other gods. And they followed the laws of the nations that G-d had driven out from before the Children of Israel and of the kings of Israel that they had made. The Children of Israel fabricated things that were not true about the L-rd, their G-d, and built themselves altars in all their cities, from the watchmen's towers to the fortified city. They erected monuments for themselves and Asherim, on every high hill and under every lush tree. They burned incense there on all of the altars, like the nations that G-d had exiled from before them, and did evil things to anger G-d. They served the idols of which G-d said to them, "Don't do this thing!"

After years of defying G-d, the Kingdom of Israel finally suffered the most terrible punishments, destruction and exile. It should have been no surprise. Indeed, they were close to it several times before and were spared only by divine mercy. Nonetheless, the Bible does not report it without reiterating those sins, to leave no doubt that this punishment was just. It was not until seven courts had served idolatry that the kingdom was destroyed. They were the courts of Jeroboam ben Nebat, Baasa, Ahab, Jehu, Pekah, Menahem and Hoshea. As it says,[20] "destitute is she who bore seven." So too, Moses had warned the people[21] "When you bear sons and sons of sons and you become old in the land, and you become corrupted, and make an idol, the form of any thing, and do what is evil in the eyes of the L-rd, your G-d, to anger Him. I have called upon the heavens and the earth to witness against you this day that you will surely be destroyed, quickly from upon the land that you are crossing the Jordan to inherit."[22]

"One good deed brings another, and one sin brings another."[23] At first the Jews went astray by following the practices of the heathens, but they still believed that G-d was the ultimate creator and source of all strength. They acknowledged that He knows everything and can do anything, and no force in the world can resist Him or interfere with Him in any way. They realized, too, that what they were doing was contrary to G-d's will, and that they would eventually have to abandon their evil ways. As they persisted in their idolatrous practices, however, their beliefs began to change too. They became so entrenched in idolatry that they could no longer tolerate the thought that G-d was watching them and disapproved, so they espoused a new doctrine. They said,[24] "G-d doesn't see us. G-d has abandoned the world." They claimed that after sinning so long, G-d had finally abandoned them, and returned them to the status of the other nations, to whom He gives less personal attention and of whom He is less exacting. They maintained that by persisting in their sinfulness, they had gained their freedom. G-d had given up on them.[25]

By adding the words, "that were not so," the prophet declared that they were wrong. A person cannot tell G-d what to do, or trick or force Him. G-d chose the Jewish People as His portion forever. No matter what they do, He refuses to give them up. But, having made these claims, they were punished accordingly. G-d hid His face from them and let them be conquered and oppressed by the other nations as if He didn't see or care. They were removed from G-d's direct control and placed under the control of the forces of nature, represented by the idols, as the other nations are, as it says,[26] "that the L-rd, your G-d, apportioned for all the nations." That does not mean that the other nations are permitted to worship idols. The worship of idols is forbidden for them as it is for Jews. But, unlike Israel, G-d does not respond openly to their deeds. This now temporarily became the portion of Israel as well.[27]

The "watchmen's towers" were the little platforms built in the fields and orchards for the watchmen to stay when they guarded the crops. They epitomized weak, temporary structures. The exact opposite was the "fortified city." From the smallest place to the largest the Jewish People built shrines, so attached were they to idolatry. Not only in the inhabited places, but in the fields and on the mountains as well.[28]

Worse yet, they did this intentionally to defy G-d. They did disgusting things that no rational person would want to do, things that were completely contrary to human nature. What reason could there have been to do them except to show their rejection of G-d's word? That is the meaning of "angering G-d."[29]

They were punished according to their sin. As they had completely filled the land with idolatry, so its destruction would be complete. There would remain neither city, house nor field. All the kinds of places in which they had worshiped their idols would be destroyed. And as they had ignored G-d and refused to listen to His voice, to the pleas of the prophets that He had sent, so He would ignore their cries.[30] As they had accused G-d of injustice that He never did, so He brought upon them suffering from which He had promised to protect them if they would obey the Torah. Thus Moses warned,[31] "Also every sickness and every affliction that is not written in this Torah, G-d will bring upon you until you are destroyed." His mercy was transformed to cruelty, as it says,[32] "They rebelled and antagonized His holy spirit, and He changed into an enemy for them, He fought against them."[33]

17:13 וַיָּעַד ה׳ בְּיִשְׂרָאֵל וּבִיהוּדָה בְּיַד כָּל־נביאו (נְבִיאֵי קרי) כָל־חֹזֶה
לֵאמֹר שֻׁבוּ מִדַּרְכֵיכֶם הָרָעִים וְשִׁמְרוּ מִצְוֹתַי חֻקּוֹתַי כְּכָל־הַתּוֹרָה אֲשֶׁר צִוִּיתִי
אֶת־אֲבֹתֵיכֶם וַאֲשֶׁר שָׁלַחְתִּי אֲלֵיכֶם בְּיַד עֲבָדַי הַנְּבִיאִים:

G-d testified against Israel and Judah by the hand of every prophet of every seer, saying, "Return from your evil ways and keep My commandments and My decrees, in accordance with all of the Torah that I commanded to your fathers and that I sent to you by the hand of My servants, the prophets."

Thus G-d complained afterwards,[34] "What shall I testify against you?" What more rebuke or warning could He have given them? Some say G-d sent two prophets every day, one in the morning and one in the evening. Others say there were four, two every morning and two every evening, as it says,[35] "I sent you all My servants, the prophets, every day, getting up early and sending." "Getting up early" refers to the prophet who was sent in the morning and "sending" refers to the one that was sent in the evening.[36] Thus G-d did for ninety years, because ninety is the numerical value of the word "ויעד," "and He testified."[37]

17:14-16 וְלֹא שָׁמֵעוּ וַיַּקְשׁוּ אֶת־עָרְפָּם כְּעֹרֶף אֲבוֹתָם אֲשֶׁר לֹא הֶאֱמִינוּ
בַּה׳ אֱלֹהֵיהֶם: וַיִּמְאֲסוּ אֶת־חֻקָּיו וְאֶת־בְּרִיתוֹ אֲשֶׁר כָּרַת אֶת־אֲבוֹתָם וְאֵת
עֵדְוֹתָיו אֲשֶׁר הֵעִיד בָּם וַיֵּלְכוּ אַחֲרֵי הַהֶבֶל וַיֶּהְבָּלוּ וְאַחֲרֵי הַגּוֹיִם אֲשֶׁר
סְבִיבֹתָם אֲשֶׁר צִוָּה ה׳ אֹתָם לְבִלְתִּי עֲשׂוֹת כָּהֶם: וַיַּעַזְבוּ אֶת־כָּל־מִצְוֹת ה׳
אֱלֹהֵיהֶם וַיַּעֲשׂוּ לָהֶם מַסֵּכָה שנים (שְׁנֵי קרי) עֲגָלִים וַיַּעֲשׂוּ אֲשֵׁירָה וַיִּשְׁתַּחֲווּ
לְכָל־צְבָא הַשָּׁמַיִם וַיַּעַבְדוּ אֶת־הַבָּעַל:

But they didn't listen. They hardened their necks like the necks of their fathers who didn't believe in the L-rd, their

G-d. They treated with disgust His decrees, His covenant that He made with their fathers and and His testimonies that He testified against them. They followed nonsense and behaved senselessly. They followed the nations that were around them, that G-d had commanded them not to do like them. They abandoned all the commandments of the L-rd, their G-d, and made themselves cast statues, two calves. They made an Asherah, bowed down to the whole host of the heavens, and served Baal.

Originally, their sin had not been the worship of foreign gods, but the improper worship of G-d through the golden calves. By the time of Hoshea ben Elah, however, they worshiped idols too.[38]

The pagan religions are referred to as "nonsense" (הבל) because, though their worshipers took them seriously and believed they had power over human beings, they were really absolutely powerless. The Jews who were impressed by them and began to worship them for fear that there might indeed be some reality in them are compared to a person of means who heard a rumor that a claim was being made against him. He began to worry whether he might be required to pay a hundred gold coins, or perhaps even two hundred. Then the claimant came and reassured him that he had nothing to worry about. The claim against him amounted to no more than a bushel of bran! Thus G-d reassured the Jewish People that they had no need to fear the gods of the pagans. They were powerless and harmless.[39]

Some say the word "מסכה," means "cast statues," statues made by pouring molten metal into molds.[40] Others say it refers to statues made according to special rules, which it was believed would make them function as intermediaries to communicate with the forces of nature. The golden calves were made in this way, so that the kings of Israel would derive power from them that would enable their kingdom to endure.[41]

Of all the idols, Baal is singled out in this verse because it was the god of the sun, and believed to be above the other gods.[42]

17:17 וַיַּעֲבִירוּ אֶת־בְּנֵיהֶם וְאֶת־בְּנוֹתֵיהֶם בָּאֵשׁ וַיִּקְסְמוּ קְסָמִים וַיְנַחֵשׁוּ וַיִּתְמַכְּרוּ לַעֲשׂוֹת הָרַע בְּעֵינֵי ה׳ לְהַכְעִיסוֹ׃

They passed their sons and their daughters in fire, performed sorceries and divinations, and gave themselves over to do what was evil in G-d's eyes to anger Him.

How foolish they were! G-d had sent them the prophets, His true messages, to tell them everything they needed to know about the future. But they ignored them, instead seeking to learn the future by magic and divination. They sinned not only against G-d, but against their fellow men as well. Thus the prophet Amos rebuked them for crimes of promiscuity, murder, robbery and extortion. All of these things were done with the specific intent of defying and angering G-d.[43]

17:18 וַיִּתְאַנַּף ה׳ מְאֹד בְּיִשְׂרָאֵל וַיְסִרֵם מֵעַל פָּנָיו לֹא נִשְׁאַר רַק שֵׁבֶט
יְהוּדָה לְבַדּוֹ׃

G-d was very angry with Israel and removed them from His presence. There remained only the tribe of Judah alone.

Now the Bible turns to the Kingdom of Judah. Included in that kingdom were not only the tribe of Judah, but also Benjamin and many members of Levi and Simeon. There were also members of other tribes whose ancestors had remained faithful to the Temple when the Kingdom of Israel first split away from the House of David. They had given up their homes and land in the north rather than worship the golden calves.

Most of the kings of Judah were righteous, being descendants of the House of David. Even though they went astray, they always returned to G-d and the Torah. But the Kingdom of Judah was not guiltless. It was saved because the good deeds of the people and the righteousness of their kings protected them for the time being. They were also protected by the merit of the Temple which was in their midst and which G-d did not want to destroy.[44]

17:19,20 גַּם־יְהוּדָה לֹא שָׁמַר אֶת־מִצְוֹת ה׳ אֱלֹהֵיהֶם וַיֵּלְכוּ בְּחֻקּוֹת יִשְׂרָאֵל
אֲשֶׁר עָשׂוּ׃ וַיִּמְאַס ה׳ בְּכָל־זֶרַע יִשְׂרָאֵל וַיְעַנֵּם וַיִּתְּנֵם בְּיַד־שֹׁסִים עַד אֲשֶׁר
הִשְׁלִיכָם מִפָּנָיו׃

Judah, too, did not keep the commandments of the L-rd, their G-d, and followed the laws of Israel that they had made. G-d was disgusted with all the descendants of Israel and afflicted them. He gave them into the hand of plunderers until He cast them from before Him.

The Christians claimed that this meant that the Jews had been eternally rejected by G-d and were no longer His holy nation. They maintained that they themselves had replaced Israel as G-d's chosen. But that is clearly a misinterpretation. Throughout the Bible, G-d's eternal commitment to Israel is reiterated. Suffering and exile are always followed by forgiveness and redemption. In particular, the Song of Moses in the end of the Book of Deuteronomy foretold a pattern of sin, punishment and forgiveness that would be repeated many times during the course of Jewish history. The central message of that and many other prophecies is G-d's undying love for Israel, the descendants of Abraham, Isaac and Jacob, whom He promised to guide and protect until they were finally purified from sin and became a completely righteous nation.

The many verses describing the sins of Israel are included here to emphasize that this severe punishment was not unjustified. On the contrary, G-d had been extremely patient with them. In spite of His anger, He did not permit them to be conquered right away. First he caused them to suffer at the hands of their enemies as a warning, to coerce them to turn back to Him and pray for help. Then they might be saved and not suffer defeat and exile. But they persisted until finally there remained no remedy for their wickedness but to be driven out of the Holy Land.[45]

17:21-23 כִּי־קָרַע יִשְׂרָאֵל מֵעַל בֵּית דָּוִד וַיַּמְלִיכוּ אֶת־יָרָבְעָם בֶּן־נְבָט
וידא (וַיַּדַּח קרי) יָרָבְעָם אֶת־יִשְׂרָאֵל מֵאַחֲרֵי ה׳ וְהֶחֱטִיאָם חֲטָאָה גְדוֹלָה:
וַיֵּלְכוּ בְּנֵי יִשְׂרָאֵל בְּכָל־חַטֹּאות יָרָבְעָם אֲשֶׁר עָשָׂה לֹא־סָרוּ מִמֶּנָּה: עַד
אֲשֶׁר־הֵסִיר ה׳ אֶת־יִשְׂרָאֵל מֵעַל פָּנָיו כַּאֲשֶׁר דִּבֶּר בְּיַד כָּל־עֲבָדָיו הַנְּבִיאִים וַיִּגֶל
יִשְׂרָאֵל מֵעַל אַדְמָתוֹ אַשּׁוּרָה עַד הַיּוֹם הַזֶּה:

For Israel had torn away from the House of David and made Jeroboam ben Nebat king, and Jeroboam led Israel astray from following G-d, and made them sin a very great sin. The Children of Israel continued all the sins of Jeroboam that he had done and didn't deviate from it. Finally G-d removed Israel from before His presence as He had said by the hand of all His servants, the prophets, and exiled Israel from upon its land to Assyria till this very day.

Although G-d had appointed Jeroboam ben Nebat and promised him success if he would lead the revolt against Rehoboam, it was not by G-d's word that he was crowned. The ten tribes did not consult the prophets when they chose him, but acted on their own without divine approval. Furthermore, though Jeroboam had been guaranteed the kingdom, and he could have held it securely without violating any commandments, he instituted the cult of the golden calves because he was afraid of losing it. Thus, the establishment of the Kingdom of Israel, which could have been accomplished without the violation of G-d's word, was transformed into sin and rebellion.[46]

17:24-26 וַיָּבֵא מֶלֶךְ־אַשּׁוּר מִבָּבֶל וּמִכּוּתָה וּמֵעַוָּא וּמֵחֲמָת וספרוים
(וּמִסְפַרְוַיִם קרי) וַיֹּשֶׁב בְּעָרֵי שֹׁמְרוֹן תַּחַת בְּנֵי יִשְׂרָאֵל וַיִּרְשׁוּ אֶת־שֹׁמְרוֹן
וַיֵּשְׁבוּ בְּעָרֶיהָ: וַיְהִי בִּתְחִלַּת שִׁבְתָּם שָׁם לֹא יָרְאוּ אֶת־ה׳ וַיְשַׁלַּח ה׳ בָּהֶם
אֶת־הָאֲרָיוֹת וַיִּהְיוּ הֹרְגִים בָּהֶם: וַיֹּאמְרוּ לְמֶלֶךְ אַשּׁוּר לֵאמֹר הַגּוֹיִם אֲשֶׁר
הִגְלִיתָ וַתּוֹשֶׁב בְּעָרֵי שֹׁמְרוֹן לֹא יָדְעוּ אֶת־מִשְׁפַּט אֱלֹהֵי הָאָרֶץ וַיְשַׁלַּח־בָּם
אֶת־הָאֲרָיוֹת וְהִנָּם מְמִיתִים אוֹתָם כַּאֲשֶׁר אֵינָם יֹדְעִים אֶת־מִשְׁפַּט אֱלֹהֵי הָאָרֶץ:

The King of Assyria brought people from Babylonia, Cuthah, Ava, Hamath and Sepharvaim, and settled them in the cities of Samaria in place of the Children of Israel. They took possession of Samaria and lived in its cities. But when they were first living there they didn't fear G-d, so G-d sent lions against them and they killed some of them. They said to the King of Assyria saying, "The nations that you exiled and settled in the cities of Samaria don't know the law of the G-d of the land, so He sent lions against them. Behold, they are killing them, since they don't know the law of the G-d of the land."

There were various beliefs about G-d among the pagan nations. Some worshiped idols but believed in the existence of an omnipotent G-d above them. They did not worship Him because they thought that He was too great to pay attention to human beings. They believed that

He had delegated the forces of nature, represented by the idols, to govern them, and it was therefore to the idols alone that it was appropriate for human beings to pray. They believed, furthermore, that the idols had been given free will, and if they so desired they could respond. Thus G-d said,[47] "My name is great among the nations." Others considered G-d to be only one among the idols, but not above them. Nonetheless, they did not deny His power.

But the people that had settled in the Holy Land did not fear G-d at all. The fear that they lacked was not only respect and reverence, which are considered virtues, but even the simple fear of punishment. When they first arrived they boldly defied G-d. They said, "If He really had power, He would not have let his people be defeated and taken into exile."[48]

These people were known as "Cuthim" because most of them came from Cuth, a city near Babylon. After they settled in Samaria they also became known as "Samaritans."[49] They did not settle in the city of Samaria itself, because it had been destroyed by Assyria, as the prophet Micah foretold,[50] "I will make Samaria a ruin in the field," but only in "the cities of Samaria," that is, the cities that had belonged to it.[51]

Being exiles themselves, they were not happy with their new home and complained to the king, "The land to which we have been sent won't accept us. We are being killed off here!" The king sent for the elders of Israel and said, "You lived in that land many years, yet the wild animals never attacked you. Why will it not accept my servants, whom I have sent to live there now?" The elders discussed the question among themselves. They knew the real reason was that the Cuthim didn't recognize G-d as the Jewish People had.[52] However, they thought this might be an opportunity for their people to be returned to their own land, so they replied, "Oh king, the land will not accept a heathen who is not circumcised and does not study the Torah!"[53]

17:27,28 וַיְצַו מֶלֶךְ־אַשּׁוּר לֵאמֹר הֹלִיכוּ שָׁמָּה אֶחָד מֵהַכֹּהֲנִים אֲשֶׁר הִגְלִיתֶם
מִשָּׁם וְיֵלְכוּ וְיֵשְׁבוּ שָׁם וְיֹרֵם אֶת־מִשְׁפַּט אֱלֹהֵי הָאָרֶץ: וַיָּבֹא אֶחָד מֵהַכֹּהֲנִים
אֲשֶׁר הִגְלוּ מִשֹּׁמְרוֹן וַיֵּשֶׁב בְּבֵית־אֵל וַיְהִי מוֹרֶה אֹתָם אֵיךְ יִירְאוּ אֶת־ה׳:

The King of Assyria commanded saying, "Bring there one of the priests that you exiled from there, and they will go and live there, and he will teach them the law of the G-d of the land." So one of the priests that they had exiled from Samaria came and lived in Beth-el, and he taught them how to fear G-d.

But the king did not respond by sending the Jews back. Instead he said, "Choose two from among you and I will send them back to circumcise the Cuthim and teach them Torah. Then they will be able to remain there!"

The king's decision was final, so they had to accept it. Although the Bible mentions only one priest being sent back, tradition tells us that they sent two wise men, Rabbi Dostai ben Yanai and Rabbi Zachariah. They made up an alphabet that they could teach the Cuthim and made a copy of the Torah for them in it, and they cried as they taught them.[54]

The two fundamental principles that these representatives taught them were that G-d was the absolute power Who controlled the whole world, and that the Land of Israel was His Holy Land to which He paid special attention. The sort of sinful practices that might be overlooked in other places were not tolerated there. They were also taught to keep the seven commandments that G-d gave Noah, by which all humanity is bound.[55] This was certainly not intended as a conversion to Judaism. If anything, they were converted to the status of "גרים תושבים," which is somewhat comparable to the status of resident aliens in modern countries.

Some say they were not even expected to reach that level. All their teachers hoped to achieve was to convince them to recognize G-d as the ultimate power and discontinue the most severe abominations, such as incest, homosexual relationships, and other kinds of sexual perversion. They would be permitted to remain in the Holy Land unharmed even if they continued to practice idolatry, as long as they recognized G-d and thought of the idols as His messengers. That, indeed, was the level of belief of the Kingdom of Israel before it was destroyed.[56]

Whether or not they were told to keep the seven commandments, they did not. They continued to worship idols, only adding the worship of G-d to their other services. On the other hand, they practiced certain stringencies that were not required of them, and tried to claim the status of true converts.

17:29-31 וַיִּהְיוּ עֹשִׂים גּוֹי גּוֹי אֱלֹהָיו וַיַּנִּיחוּ בְּבֵית הַבָּמוֹת אֲשֶׁר עָשׂוּ
הַשֹּׁמְרֹנִים גּוֹי גּוֹי בְּעָרֵיהֶם אֲשֶׁר הֵם יֹשְׁבִים שָׁם׃ וְאַנְשֵׁי בָבֶל עָשׂוּ אֶת־סֻכּוֹת
בְּנוֹת וְאַנְשֵׁי־כוּת עָשׂוּ אֶת־נֵרְגַל וְאַנְשֵׁי חֲמָת עָשׂוּ אֶת־אֲשִׁימָא׃ וְהָעַוִּים עָשׂוּ

נִבְחַז וְאֶת־תַּרְתָּק וְהַסְפַרְוִים שֹׂרְפִים אֶת־בְּנֵיהֶם בָּאֵשׁ לְאַדְרַמֶּלֶךְ וַעֲנַמֶּלֶךְ אֱלֹהֵ
ספרים (סְפַרְוָיִם קרי):

So each nation made its own idols, and put them in the temples of the altars that the Samaritans had made, each nation in their cities in which they lived. The people of Babylonia made Sucoth-benoth, the people of Cuth made Nergal, and the people of Hamath made Ashima. The Avites made Nibhaz and Tartak, and the Sepharvites would burn their children in fire to Adramelech and Anamelech, the gods of Sepharvaim.

Sucoth-benoth was a hen god. The name means "a hen with its chicks." Nergal was a rooster god and Ashima a goat god. Nibhaz and Tartak were dog and donkey gods, Adramelech and Anamelech were mule and horse gods.[57]

17:32,33 וַיִּהְיוּ יְרֵאִים אֶת־ה׳ וַיַּעֲשׂוּ לָהֶם מִקְצוֹתָם כֹּהֲנֵי בָמוֹת וַיִּהְיוּ
עֹשִׂים לָהֶם בְּבֵית הַבָּמוֹת: אֶת־ה׳ הָיוּ יְרֵאִים וְאֶת־אֱלֹהֵיהֶם הָיוּ עֹבְדִים
כְּמִשְׁפַּט הַגּוֹיִם אֲשֶׁר־הִגְלוּ אֹתָם מִשָּׁם:

They feared G-d and made themselves priests of the altars from among themselves, and they would perform for them in the temples of the altars. They feared G-d and they served their own gods, in the manner of the nations from whence they had exiled them.

Some say the word "מקצותם," "from among themselves" means that they chose the priests from the greatest and most respected among them. Others say it means from among the lowest, the outcasts of society.[58]

Some say "the nations from whence they had exiled them" refers to the people of their homeland from which they themselves had been exiled, and refers to the words "they served their own gods." They served the same idols as they had in their original homelands. Others say it refers to the ten tribes that had just been exiled from Samaria. The Cuthim learned the practices of the generation of Israel that lived in the land just before them, which was a mixture of Torah and idolatry.[59]

The Cuthim never completely accepted the Torah or belief in the unity of G-d, so they were not considered proper converts.[60] When the Jews returned from Babylonia, the Cuthim wanted to join them in the rebuilding of the Temple, but the rabbis rejected them. There were one hundred and eighty thousand of them, and they caused great trouble for the Jews, as is described in the Book of Nehemiah. They tried to kill Nehemiah and had work on the Temple stopped for two years. So Ezra the Scribe, Zerubabel and Jehozadak, the High Priest, gathered all the Jews that had returned from Babylonia and declared a ban upon the Cuthim, with three hundred priests blowing trumpets and three hundred children holding Torah scrolls in their hands. It was declared that neither they nor their descendants ever be accepted as converts. It was forbidden to even eat the bread of the Cuthim, and eating thier bread was proclaimed like eating the meat of a pig. Furthermore, it was declared that the Cuthim be denied a portion in Israel even in the world to come, and not be included in the revival of the dead. This ban was upheld and augmented by the Jewish community in Babylonia, and by King Cyrus as well.[61]

17:34-41 עַד הַיּוֹם הַזֶּה הֵם עֹשִׂים כַּמִּשְׁפָּטִים הָרִאשֹׁנִים אֵינָם יְרֵאִים אֶת־ה׳ וְאֵינָם עֹשִׂים כְּחֻקֹּתָם וּכְמִשְׁפָּטָם וְכַתּוֹרָה וְכַמִּצְוָה אֲשֶׁר צִוָּה ה׳ אֶת־בְּנֵי יַעֲקֹב אֲשֶׁר־שָׂם שְׁמוֹ יִשְׂרָאֵל׃ וַיִּכְרֹת ה׳ אִתָּם בְּרִית וַיְצַוֵּם לֵאמֹר לֹא תִירְאוּ אֱלֹהִים אֲחֵרִים וְלֹא־תִשְׁתַּחֲווּ לָהֶם וְלֹא תַעַבְדוּם וְלֹא תִזְבְּחוּ לָהֶם׃ כִּי אִם־אֶת־ה׳ אֲשֶׁר הֶעֱלָה אֶתְכֶם מֵאֶרֶץ מִצְרַיִם בְּכֹחַ גָּדוֹל וּבִזְרוֹעַ נְטוּיָה אֹתוֹ תִירָאוּ וְלוֹ תִשְׁתַּחֲווּ וְלוֹ תִזְבָּחוּ׃ וְאֶת־הַחֻקִּים וְאֶת־הַמִּשְׁפָּטִים וְהַתּוֹרָה וְהַמִּצְוָה אֲשֶׁר כָּתַב לָכֶם תִּשְׁמְרוּן לַעֲשׂוֹת כָּל־הַיָּמִים וְלֹא תִירְאוּ אֱלֹהִים אֲחֵרִים׃ וְהַבְּרִית אֲשֶׁר־כָּרַתִּי אִתְּכֶם לֹא תִשְׁכָּחוּ וְלֹא תִירְאוּ אֱלֹהִים אֲחֵרִים׃ כִּי אִם־אֶת־ה׳ אֱלֹהֵיכֶם תִּירָאוּ וְהוּא יַצִּיל אֶתְכֶם מִיַּד כָּל־אֹיְבֵיכֶם׃ וְלֹא שָׁמֵעוּ כִּי אִם־כְּמִשְׁפָּטָם הָרִאשׁוֹן הֵם עֹשִׂים׃ וַיִּהְיוּ הַגּוֹיִם הָאֵלֶּה יְרֵאִים אֶת־ה׳ וְאֶת־פְּסִילֵיהֶם הָיוּ עֹבְדִים גַּם־בְּנֵיהֶם וּבְנֵי בְנֵיהֶם כַּאֲשֶׁר עָשׂוּ אֲבֹתָם הֵם עֹשִׂים עַד הַיּוֹם הַזֶּה׃

Till this very day they do according to their original practices. They do not fear G-d, and they do not do according to their decrees and their laws, and according to the Torah and according to the commandment that G-d commanded the children of Jacob whose name He made "Israel." G-d made a covenant with them and commanded them saying, "Do not fear other gods, and do not bow down to them! Do not serve them and do not sacrifice to them! Rather G-d, Who brought you up from the land of Egypt with great strength and an outstretched arm, will you fear. To Him will you bow down and to Him will you sacrifice. The decrees, the laws, the Torah and the commandment that He wrote to you will you keep to do all the days, and you will not fear other gods. The covenant that I made with you will you not forget, and you will not fear other gods. Rather, the L-rd, your G-d will you fear, and He will save you from the hand of all your enemies." But they didn't listen. Instead, they continue to do according to their original way. These nations would fear G-d and serve their idols, their children and their children's children. As their fathers did, so do they do till this day.

Some say this last verse refers to the descendants of the Cuthim, explaining clearly the nature of their religion, and how it deviated fundamentally from the Torah. This, then was the reason they were never accepted as true converts.[62] Others say it refers to the descendants of the ten tribes in exile. Even in exile, they continued their deviant practices. Despite the most extreme punishments that G-d brought upon them, they did not repent.[63]

II KINGS 18

18:1-3 וַיְהִי בִּשְׁנַת שָׁלֹשׁ לְהוֹשֵׁעַ בֶּן־אֵלָה מֶלֶךְ יִשְׂרָאֵל מָלַךְ חִזְקִיָּה
בֶן־אָחָז מֶלֶךְ יְהוּדָה׃ בֶּן־עֶשְׂרִים וְחָמֵשׁ שָׁנָה הָיָה בְמָלְכוֹ וְעֶשְׂרִים וָתֵשַׁע שָׁנָה
מָלַךְ בִּירוּשָׁלִָם וְשֵׁם אִמּוֹ אֲבִי בַּת־זְכַרְיָה׃ וַיַּעַשׂ הַיָּשָׁר בְּעֵינֵי ה׳ כְּכֹל
אֲשֶׁר־עָשָׂה דָּוִד אָבִיו׃

In the third year of Hoshea ben Elah, King of Israel, Hezekiah, the son of Ahaz, King of Judah, became king. He was twenty-five years old when he became king and he reigned twenty-nine years in Jerusalem. His mother's name was Abi the daughter of Zechariah. He did what was upright in G-d's eyes, like all that David, his father, had done.

The third year referred to here is Hoshea's third year as a sovereign ruler. Though he had already reigned about nine years as a vassal of Assyria, his reign is counted from the year that he rebelled and declared his independence.[1]

Hezekiah's name, which is composed of the word "חזק," "strong," and G-d's name, "י־ה," alludes to his greatness, meaning both that G-d strengthened him and that he strengthened the people's devotion to G-d.[2]

King David is referred to here as Hezekiah's father, because Hezekiah followed in his righteous ways. Just as Jeroboam and Ahab are mentioned as the originators and models of the sins of the wicked kings that followed them, so David is mentioned here. The righteous receive credit whenever their good example is followed, and the wicked share their followers' guilt.[3]

18:4 הוּא הֵסִיר אֶת־הַבָּמוֹת וְשִׁבַּר אֶת־הַמַּצֵּבֹת וְכָרַת אֶת־הָאֲשֵׁרָה
וְכִתַּת נְחַשׁ הַנְּחֹשֶׁת אֲשֶׁר־עָשָׂה מֹשֶׁה כִּי עַד־הַיָּמִים הָהֵמָּה הָיוּ בְנֵי־יִשְׂרָאֵל
מְקַטְּרִים לוֹ וַיִּקְרָא־לוֹ נְחֻשְׁתָּן׃

It was he who removed the altars, smashed the monuments, cut down the Asherah, and crushed the copper snake that Moses made. For until those days the Children of Israel had been burning incense to it, and called it "Nehushtan."

Until the building of the Temple, it had been permitted to erect altars and offer sacrifices anywhere in the Holy Land. But once the Temple was built such private altars were forbidden, and all sacrifices had to be brought to the Temple. Thus the Torah says[4], "You will not be able to eat within your gates the tithes of your grain, your wine and your oil, and the firstborn of your cattle and your sheep, and your promises that you promise and your donations and the contributions of your hand. Rather, before the L-rd, your G-d, will you eat it, in the place that the L-rd, your G-d, will choose."

By the time the Temple was built, however, the Jewish People had become used to sacrificing on private altars and were reluctant to give them up. Many people could not understand how something that had been acceptable and even praiseworthy for so long could suddenly become forbidden. So they continued to build altars and sacrifice on them throughout most of the period of the First Temple. Even during the reigns of righteous kings, who eliminated idolatry, the private altars were tolerated. They were not seen as a serious offense, since they were for the service of G-d.

Ultimately, it was the kings who were held responsible for this sin. The Bible never fails to mention it whenever their righteousness is described. Thus we find over and over again the words, "the altars were not removed. The people were still sacrificing and burning incense on the altars." It was therefore considered a great accomplishment for Hezekiah to finally eliminate them, and he is duly praised for it.

This was a complete reversal of the decline that his father, Ahaz, had brought about. Ahaz had tried to destroy Torah and the Temple service. Until his time, the private altars had only supplemented the Temple, but Ahaz closed the Temple so that they would replace it entirely. Now his son rectified the corruption he had caused.

Ahaz had also encouraged actual idolatry, in particular, the worship of Asherah and the erection of monuments, which had not been practiced under the kings immediately preceding him, Jehoash, Amaziah, Azariah, and Jotham. These, too, Hezekiah destroyed.[5]

There was no question about destroying any of these things, since they were all clearly forbidden. The copper snake was a different matter.

This was the image of a snake that Moses had made by G-d's explicit command when the Jewish People were bitten by the burning snakes in the desert. Moses was commanded to make this image and hold it aloft on a pole so that the people would look upward, thus directing their attention to G-d. When they did, they were cured. Afterwards, it was kept as a memorial of that miracle, even though it no longer served any purpose. It was kept as a relic, like the staff of Aaron and the jar of manna. These were not just souvenirs, but testimonies to the miracles that had been performed through them, so they were kept to help strengthen the people's faith.

But in time, people began to worship the copper snake. That was exactly the opposite of the original reason for which it was made, to direct the people toward G-d and away from all thoughts of worldly intermediaries. Worshiping defeated the whole purpose for which it was being preserved. Hezekiah decided that it was more important to prevent the people from committing idolatry than to preserve this national relic, so he destroyed it.[6]

But if, indeed, its historical value did not outweigh the spiritual danger it presented, why had the righteous kings before him, like Asa and Jehoshaphat, not destroyed it already? Some say they only addressed the most flagrant violations and left the less serious ones for their descendants, so that they too would have the merit of guiding the Jewish People.[7] Others say that in their time it had not yet been worshiped, so there was no need to destroy it then.[8]

Hezekiah ground it up and threw the dust to the wind. Some say he was required to destroy it because anything that has been worshiped by a Jew even one time is forbidden forever and must be completely destroyed.[9] Others say it had not become forbidden and there was no obligation to destroy it. It had originally been the personal property of Moses, and remained the property of his heirs. It was therefore not affected by the people's worshiping it, since only when a thing is worshiped by its owner does it become forbidden. Hezekiah destroyed it not because it had become forbidden, but to prevent it from being worshiped again.[10]

Some say it was Hezekiah who called it "Nehushtan," which means, "Copper one," to emphasize the fact that it was only a copper image and had no power.[11] Others say this was the name that those who worshiped it gave it.[12] Since they considered it a sort of god or angel, it had a personal identity, so they gave it a proper name.

18:5,6 בַּה׳ אֱלֹהֵי־יִשְׂרָאֵל בָּטָח וְאַחֲרָיו לֹא־הָיָה כָמֹהוּ בְּכֹל מַלְכֵי יְהוּדָה
וַאֲשֶׁר הָיוּ לְפָנָיו׃ וַיִּדְבַּק בַּה׳ לֹא־סָר מֵאַחֲרָיו וַיִּשְׁמֹר מִצְוֹתָיו אֲשֶׁר־צִוָּה ה׳
אֶת־מֹשֶׁה׃

He trusted the L-rd, the G-d of Israel. There was none like him after him among all the kings of Judah, nor that were before him. He clung to G-d and didn't deviate from following Him, and kept His commandments that G-d had commanded Moses.

Hezekiah was the most righteous of all the kings of Judah. Only Jotham surpassed him in purity, for he was completely free of sin, as we learned earlier, but Hezekiah exceeded him in piety.

Some say he was even more righteous than David. Like David, Hezekiah made mistakes, as we will learn shortly. Both were held accountable for their sins and punished, even though they were not due to negligence or lack of dedication, but were the product of misguided piety and zeal. But, unlike David, Hezekiah's sins did not involve severe prohibitions like murder and adultery.

Hezekiah's greatness, though, was not his innocence, but the merit for his many deeds of piety. In this too, he was equal to the earlier kings and perhaps even greater. In particular, he excelled in trust in G-d. No other king had been made to endure such a terrifying experience, yet Hezekiah never lost his faith in G-d.[13]

Others say this statement was not meant to include David and Solomon, who were indeed no less righteous than Hezekiah.[14] Indeed, the statement above that Hezekiah "did what was upright in G-d's eyes, like all that David, his father, had done" can be taken as an indication that he was less righteous than David, since when two people are compared, it is generally the lesser that is compared to the greater.[15]

In the Book of Chronicles it says:[16]

> In the first year of his reign, in the First Month, he opened the doors of the House of G-d and strengthened them. He brought the priests and Levites and gathered them to the eastern plaza. He said to them, "Listen to me, Oh Levites! Sanctify yourselves now, and sanctify the House of the L-rd, the G-d of your fathers. Take out the repulsive idols from the Sanctuary. For our fathers trespassed and did what was evil in the eyes of the L-rd, our G-d, and abandoned Him. They turned their faces away from the Dwelling-place of G-d and turned

their backs toward it. They also closed the doors of the antechamber and put out the lights. Incense they did not burn, and no burnt offering did they offer in the Sanctuary, to the G-d of Israel. The wrath of G-d was against Judah and Jerusalem, and He gave them over to terror, destruction and hissing, as you see with your eyes. Behold, our fathers have fallen by the sword, our sons, our daughters and our wives are in captivity because of this. Now it is in my heart to make a covenant with the L-rd, the G-d of Israel, that His burning wrath will go back away from us. My children, do not be careless now! For it is you that G-d chose to stand before Him to serve Him, and to be servants and burners of incense for Him." The Levites got up, Mahath ben Amasai and Joel ben Azariah from the sons of the Kohathites, and from the sons of Merari, Kish ben Abdi and Azariah ben Jehalelel, and from the Gershonites, Joah ben Zimah and Eden ben Joah. And from the sons of Elizaphan, Shimri ben Jeiel, and from the sons of Asaph, Zechariah and Mataniah. And from the sons of Heman, Jehiel and Shimei, and from the sons of Jeduthun, Shemaiah and Uziel. They gathered their brothers and sanctified themselves and came, in accordance with the command of the king by the words of G-d, to purify the House of G-d. The priests came into the innermost part of the House of G-d to purify it and took all the impurity that they found in the Sanctuary of G-d out to the courtyard of the House of G-d. The Levites received it to take it out to the Valley of Kidron, outside. They began on the first of the First Month to sanctify, and on the eighth day of the month they came to the antechamber of G-d. They sanctified the House of G-d for eight days, and on the sixteenth day of the month they finished. They came inside to King Hezekiah and said, "We have purified the whole House of G-d, the altar of burnt offerings and all its utensils, and the table of the arrangement and all its utensils. All the utensils that King Ahaz threw away in his trespassing when he was king, we repaired and sanctified. Behold, here they are in front of the altar of G-d!" King Hezekiah got up early, gathered the officers of the city and went up to the House of G-d. They brought seven bulls, seven rams, seven sheep and seven goats as a sin offering for the kingdom, for the Temple, and for Judah. He told the sons of Aaron, the priests, to offer them on the altar of G-d. They slaughtered the cattle and the priests received the blood and threw it at the altar. They slaughtered the rams and threw the blood at the altar, and they slaughtered the sheep and threw the blood at the altar. They brought the goats of sin offering close before the king and the congregation, and they laid their hands upon them. The priests slaughtered them and sprinkled their blood at the altar to atone for all Israel, for the king said that the burnt offering and the sin offering were for all Israel. He stood the Levites in the House of G-d with cymbals, harps and lyres according to the commandment of David, Gad, the seer of the king, and Nathan, the prophet. For by the hand of G-d was the commandment that was by the hand of His prophets. The Levites stood with the instruments of David and the priests with the trumpets. Hezekiah said to sacrifice the burnt offering at the altar, and at the same time that the sacrifice began, the song of G-d and the trumpets began, and the music of the instruments of David, King of Israel. The whole congregation was bowing, the song was being sung and the trumpets being blown, all of it until the sacrifice was completed. And when they finished sacrificing, the king and all who were present with him kneeled and bowed. King Hezekiah and the officers told the Levites to sing praises to G-d with the words of David and Asaph the seer. They sang praises with great joy and bent their heads and bowed. Hezekiah raised his voice and said, "Now you have consecrated yourselves to G-d! Approach and bring sacrifices and thanksgiving offerings to the House of G-d!" So the congregation brought sacrifices and thanksgiving offerings, and every generous heart, burnt offerings. The number of burnt offerings that the congregation brought was seventy cattle, one hundred rams, two hundred sheep, all these as burnt offerings to G-d. And the consecrated things were six hundred cattle and three thousand sheep. However, the priests were few and couldn't skin all the burnt offerings, so their brothers, the Levites, helped them until the completion of the work and until the priests sanctified themselves. For the Levites were more upright of heart to sanctify themselves than the priests. There was also much burnt offering along with the fat of the peace offerings and with the libations for the burnt offering, and the service of the House of G-d was established. Hezekiah and the whole people rejoiced over what G-d had prepared for the people, for the thing had happened suddenly.

Hezekiah sent through all of Israel and Judah, and also wrote letters to Ephraim and Manasseh to come to the House of G-d in Jerusalem to make Passover for the L-rd, the G-d of Israel. The king, his officers, and the whole congregation took counsel in Jerusalem about making the Passover in the Second Month, for they couldn't make it at that time because the priests had not sanctified themselves enough, and the people had not gathered to Jerusalem. The thing was proper in the eyes of the king and in the eyes of the whole congregation. They established a decree, to make an announcement throughout all Israel from Beer-sheba to Dan, to come to make Passover to the L-rd, the G-d of Israel, in Jerusalem, for they had not done it as it is written in a long time. The runners went with the letters from the hand of the king and his officers throughout all Israel and Judah, and in accordance with the commandment of the king, saying, "Oh Children of Israel, return to the L-rd, the G-d of Abraham, Isaac and Israel, and He will return to the remnant that is left of you from the hand of the kings of Assyria! Don't be like your fathers and like your brothers who tresspassed against the L-rd, the G-d of their fathers, and He gave them over to destruction, as you see. Do not stiffen your necks now like your fathers. Give a hand to G-d and come to His Temple that He sanctified forever, and serve the L-rd, your G-d. Then the burning of His anger will go back away from you. For by your returning to G-d, your brothers and your sons will be treated with mercy before their captors, and be permitted to return to this land. For the L-rd, your G-d, is kind and merciful. He will not ignore you if you return to Him." As the runners were passing from city to city in the land of Ephraim and Manasseh and as far as Zebulun, they laughed at them and mocked them. However, some people from Asher, Manasseh, and Zebulun were humbled and came to Jerusalem. In Judah, too, there was the hand of G-d to give them one heart to do the commandment of the king and the officers by the word of G-d. There gathered to Jerusalem a numerous people to make the Festival of Unleavened Bread in the Second Month, a very great congregation. They arose and removed the altars that were in Jerusalem, and all the incense altars they removed and threw into the Valley of Kidron. They slaughtered the Passover on the fourteenth day of the Second Month. The priests and the Levites were embarrassed (that they had not prepared themselves on time in the first month) and sanctified themselves and brought burnt offerings to the House of G-d. They stood on their place as was befitting them, according to the Torah of Moses, the man of G-d, the priests throwing the blood from the hand of the Levites. For the congregation that had not sanctified themselves was very great, so the Levites were in charge of the slaughtering of their Passover sacrifices for all who were not pure to sanctify to G-d. The majority of the people, most of those from Ephraim and Manasseh, Issachar and Zebulun, had not purified themselves, but they ate the Passover anyway, which was not in accordance with what was written.

Hezekiah prayed for them saying, "May G-d, Who is good, atone for anyone who prepared his heart to seek G-d, the L-rd, the G-d of his fathers, even though he did not do it with the purity of holiness. G-d listened to Hezekiah and cured the people. The Children of Israel who were present in Jerusalem made the Festival of Unleavened Bread seven days in great joy, and the Levites and the priests were praising G-d day by day, with loud instruments to G-d. Hezekiah spoke encouragingly to all the Levites who understood the service of G-d properly. They ate the festival sacrifices seven days, sacrificing peace offerings and declaring their gratitude to the L-rd, the G-d of their fathers. The whole congregation took counsel about making another seven days, and they made seven days of rejoicing. For Hezekiah, King of Judah, donated one thousand bulls and seven thousand sheep to the congregation, and the officers donated one thousand bulls and ten thousand sheep to the congregation, and priests sanctified themselves in great numbers. The whole congregation of Judah rejoiced, and the priests and the Levites and the whole congregation that came from Israel, and the residents who came from the Land of Israel, and those who lived in Judah. There was great joy in Jerusalem, for since the time of Solomon, the son of David, King of Israel, there had not been like that in Jerusalem. The priests and the Levites got up and blessed the people, and their voice was heard, and their prayers came to His holy dwelling place, to the heavens.

When all this was finished, all Israel who were present went out to the cities of Judah. They smashed the monuments, cut down the Asherim, and broke down the shrines and the altars from all of Judah and Benjamin, and in Ephraim and Manasseh, until they were completely destroyed. Then all the Children of Israel returned, each one to his portion, to their cities. Hezekiah set up the divisions of the priests and the Levites according to their divisions, each one according to his work, for the priests and the Levites, for the burnt offerings and the peace offerings, to serve, to give thanks and to praise, at the gates of the camps of G-d. And the king's portion from his property was for the burnt offerings, for the morning and evening offerings, and the offerings of Sabbaths, New Months and Festivals, as is written in G-d's Torah. He told the people, those who lived in Jerusalem, to give the portion of the priests and the Levites, in order that they be strengthened in G-d's Torah. When the word spread, the Children of Israel brought abundantly of the first of their grain, wine, oil, and honey, and all the crops of the field. They brought a tithe of everything in great amounts. The Children of Israel and Judah who lived in the cities of Judah, they too, brought tithes of cattle and sheep, and tithes of sanctified things that had been sanctified to the L-rd, their G-d, and gave in heaps upon heaps. In the Third Month the heaps began to be piled up, and in the Seventh Month they finished. Hezekiah and the officers came and saw the heaps, and they blessed G-d and His people, Israel. Hezekiah asked the priests and the Levites concerning the heaps. Azariah the chief priest, of the house of Zadok, said to him, "From the time that the contributions began to be brought to the House of G-d there has been eating, being satisfied, and having extra, even very much, for G-d has blessed His people, and the extra is this great amount." Hezekiah said to prepare rooms in the House of G-d, and they prepared. They brought the contributions and the tithes and the sanctified things in good faith, and over it was a supervisor, Conaniah the Levite, and Shimei his brother was the second. And Jehiel, Azaziah, Nahath, Asahel, Jerimoth, Jozabad, Eliel, Ismachiah, Mahath and Benaiah, officers under the supervision of Conaniah and Shimei his brother, by the appointment of King Hezekiah and Azariah, the supervisor of the House of G-d. Kore ben Imnah the Levite, the gatekeeper in the east, was in charge of the donations to G-d, to give the contribution of G-d and the holiest of the holy things. Under him were Eden, Miniamin, Jeshua, Shemaiah, Amariah and Shecheniah, in the cities of the priests, in good faith, to give to their brothers in the divisions, to the great and the small alike. Aside from what was given to the male relatives from three years up, to all who came to the House of G-d, to get something every day, for their work at their shifts according to their divisions. Thus for the relatives of the priests according to the houses of their fathers and the Levites from twenty years up, at their shifts according to their divisions. And all who were related, all their children, their wives, their sons and their daughters for every congregation, for their faithfulness the holy things were sanctified. And so for the children of Aaron, the priests, in the fields of the meadows of their cities, in every single city, there were men who were appointed by their names to give portions to every male among the priests and for every relative among the Levites. Thus did Hezekiah do in all Judah. He did the good, the upright and the true before the L-rd, his G-d. And every deed that he began in the service of the House of G-d, in the Torah and in the commandment, to seek his G-d, he did with all his heart and succeeded.

Hezekiah accomplished a remarkable reform in the Kingdom of Judah. Not only was idolatry eliminated, but the universal study of Torah was established throughout the land. Hezekiah decreed that it was the obligation of every Jew to study Torah. He stuck a sword into the door of the study hall and declared that anyone who did not attend would be killed. This dramatic demonstration of his commitment convinced the people that these were not idle words. They applied themselves to the study of Torah as Hezekiah had decreed, and when his messengers came to inspect, they found that from Dan, the northernmost part of the country, to Beer-sheba, the farthest south, there was not a single man, woman, or child that had not mastered even the most obscure and difficult areas of Torah.[17]

During the period of Hezekiah the Book of Proverbs was completed. Thus it is written,[18] "These, too, are the proverbs of Solomon, that the men of Hezekiah, King of Judah, copied."

18:7,8 וְהָיָה ה׳ עִמּוֹ בְּכֹל אֲשֶׁר־יֵצֵא יַשְׂכִּיל וַיִּמְרֹד בְּמֶלֶךְ־אַשּׁוּר וְלֹא
עֲבָדוֹ: הוּא־הִכָּה אֶת־פְּלִשְׁתִּים עַד־עַזָּה וְאֶת־גְּבוּלֶיהָ מִמִּגְדַּל נוֹצְרִים עַד־עִיר
מִבְצָר:

G-d was with him. In everything that he would set out to do he was successful. He rebelled against the King of Assyria and didn't serve him. He smote the Philistines as far as Gaza and its borders, from the watchmen's towers to the fortified cities.

Some say that Hezekiah never served the King of Assyria at all. His father, Ahaz, had served him and paid him tribute, because Ahaz lacked faith in G-d and did not trust G-d to protect him. But Hezekiah knew that G-d would protect him if he was faithful, so he was not afraid of Assyria. As soon as he became king he discontinued the tribute. This was an act of rebellion even though he himself had never agreed to serve Assyria, because by inheriting his father's position he was bound by all the obligations that his father had accepted.[19] Others say that he served the King of Assyria for a while, but then rebelled against him and refused to pay him the tribute he had promised.

Though it was ultimately G-d's protection upon which Hezekiah relied in rebelling against Assyria, he did not sit idly by and wait for miracles. He waged war against the Philistines, who still held territory along the coast to the south, thus securing and consolidating his kingdom. He trusted that if he did everything humanly possible, G-d would give him success.[20]

18:9-12 וַיְהִי בַּשָּׁנָה הָרְבִיעִית לַמֶּלֶךְ חִזְקִיָּהוּ הִיא הַשָּׁנָה הַשְּׁבִיעִית לְהוֹשֵׁעַ
בֶּן־אֵלָה מֶלֶךְ יִשְׂרָאֵל עָלָה שַׁלְמַנְאֶסֶר מֶלֶךְ־אַשּׁוּר עַל־שֹׁמְרוֹן וַיָּצַר עָלֶיהָ׃
וַיִּלְכְּדֻהָ מִקְצֵה שָׁלֹשׁ שָׁנִים בִּשְׁנַת־שֵׁשׁ לְחִזְקִיָּה הִיא שְׁנַת־תֵּשַׁע לְהוֹשֵׁעַ מֶלֶךְ
יִשְׂרָאֵל נִלְכְּדָה שֹׁמְרוֹן׃ וַיֶּגֶל מֶלֶךְ־אַשּׁוּר אֶת־יִשְׂרָאֵל אַשּׁוּרָה וַיַּנְחֵם בַּחְלַח
וּבְחָבוֹר נְהַר גּוֹזָן וְעָרֵי מָדָי׃ עַל אֲשֶׁר לֹא־שָׁמְעוּ בְּקוֹל ה׳ אֱלֹהֵיהֶם וַיַּעַבְרוּ
אֶת־בְּרִיתוֹ אֵת כָּל־אֲשֶׁר צִוָּה מֹשֶׁה עֶבֶד ה׳ וְלֹא שָׁמְעוּ וְלֹא עָשׂוּ׃

In the fourth year of King Hezekiah, which was the seventh year of Hoshea ben Elah, King of Israel, Shalmaneser, King of Assyria, came up against Samaria and besieged it. They conquered it at the end of three years. In the sixth year of Hezekiah, which was the ninth year of Hoshea, King of Israel, Samaria was conquered. The King of Assyria exiled Israel to Assyria, and settled them in Halah, Habor, the Gozan River, and the cities of Madai. Because they didn't listen to the voice of the L-rd, their G-d, and trangressed His covenant, all that He had commanded Moses, the servant of G-d. They did not listen and did not do.

This short summary of the destruction of the Kingdom of Israel, which was already described in detail in the previous chapter, is repeated here to emphasize the difference between Hoshea, who persisted in his wickedness until he was destroyed, and Hezekiah, who dedicated himself to G-d and was miraculously saved. Both faced the same enemy, whom neither had the military strength to withstand. The only difference was divine intervention.[21]

Thus King Solomon wrote,[22] "G-d's curse is upon the house of the wicked, but the dwelling of the righteous will be blessed." Pekah ben Remaliah was arrogant and self-indulgent. He used to eat a heap of young pigeons just for dessert, but in the end he was defeated. But Hezekiah, who ate just a few vegetables for his meal, was saved.[23]

The repetition also serves to explain why at some times Hezekiah resisted Sanherib and at others was willing to submit, as described in the following verses. At first he had been confident that he could bring his people back to G-d and Torah, and they would be worthy of divine protection. At that time he had resisted Assyria. But in spite of his many successful reforms, he had not been able to completely purify his kingdom. Many Jews had not sincerely dedicated themselves to G-d, and still yearned to return to their old ways. So, when the fortified cities of Judah fell one by one to Assyria, Hezekiah was afraid that it was a divine punishment. He feared that Jerusalem would not be worthy of being saved and would be destroyed like Samaria. Like Jerusalem, Samaria had been a mighty fortress. It had withstood siege for three years, only to be conquered and destroyed in the end. The same might happen to Jerusalem. Hezekiah decided that it would be better to surrender and spare his people the horrible suffering of siege and the risk of total destruction. If defeat by Assyria was the punishment to which G-d had condemned them, then trying to resist would only make things worse.[24] But later, when he saw that Sanherib was bent on destroying him completely, he reversed his policy again and resisted. Though he was still not sure whether or not G-d would save them, he was sure that it was not divine will that he submit under such conditions.

Thus the prophet Isaiah said,[25] "The yoke will be broken by the oil." Normally, the soft fat of an animal's back is worn off by the hard yoke that rubs on it, but this time the strong yoke of Sanherib would be broken by the oil that Hezekiah and the Jewish People burnt staying up late and studying Torah.[26]

Sanherib had forty thousand princes, the sons of kings, under him, and they all rode in golden chariots. He had eighty thousand warriors dressed in armor, sixty thousand swordsmen running before him, and the rest of his army were all horsemen. His camp extended hundred of miles, and when they crossed a river the first soldiers swam across, the middle ones were able to walk with their heads above the water, and the last raised dust with their feet as they walked across the dry river bed. They couldn't even find water to drink.[27]

18:13-16 וּבְאַרְבַּע עֶשְׂרֵה שָׁנָה לַמֶּלֶךְ חִזְקִיָּה עָלָה סַנְחֵרִב מֶלֶךְ אַשּׁוּר עַל
כָּל עָרֵי יְהוּדָה הַבְּצֻרוֹת וַיִּתְפְּשֵׂם: וַיִּשְׁלַח חִזְקִיָּה מֶלֶךְ־יְהוּדָה אֶל־מֶלֶךְ־אַשּׁוּר לָכִישָׁה
לֵאמֹר חָטָאתִי שׁוּב מֵעָלַי אֵת אֲשֶׁר־תִּתֵּן עָלַי אֶשָּׂא וַיָּשֶׂם מֶלֶךְ־אַשּׁוּר עַל־חִזְקִיָּה
מֶלֶךְ־יְהוּדָה שְׁלֹשׁ מֵאוֹת כִּכַּר־כֶּסֶף וּשְׁלֹשִׁים כִּכַּר זָהָב: וַיִּתֵּן חִזְקִיָּה אֶת־כָּל־הַכֶּסֶף
הַנִּמְצָא בֵית־ה׳ וּבְאוֹצְרוֹת בֵּית הַמֶּלֶךְ: בָּעֵת הַהִיא קִצַּץ חִזְקִיָּה אֶת־דַּלְתוֹת הֵיכַל ה׳
וְאֶת־הָאֹמְנוֹת אֲשֶׁר צִפָּה חִזְקִיָּה מֶלֶךְ יְהוּדָה וַיִּתְּנֵם לְמֶלֶךְ אַשּׁוּר:

In the fourteenth year of King Hezekiah, Sanherib, King of Assyria, came up against all the fortified cities of Judah and captured them. Hezekiah, King of Judah, sent to the King of Assyria to Lachish saying, "I have sinned! Go back away from upon me! Everything that you put upon me I will bear." So the King of Assyria put upon Hezekiah, King of Judah, three hundred talents of silver and thirty talents of gold. Hezekiah gave all the silver that was found in the House of G-d and in the treasuries of the house of the king. At that time Hezekiah cut up the doors of the Sanctuary of G-d and the lintels that Hezekiah, King of Judah, had plated, and gave them to the King of Assyria.

As part of his restoration of the Temple, Hezekiah had plated the doors and doorways with gold. The original gold plating of Solomon was long gone, either plundered by one of the wicked kings or removed to pay an earlier enemy.[28] Some say Hezekiah didn't just plate the doors, but replaced them completely with ones of solid gold.[29] Now he was forced to reclaim that gold to buy peace.

When our father Jacob had to face his brother Esau, who was coming to destroy him, he prepared himself in three ways. He sent gifts to Esau to try to appease him, he prayed for G-d's help, and, in case he would be forced to fight anyway, he prepared himself for battle. Hezekiah followed his example. He tried to appease Assyria, he prayed, and he prepared his kingdom to withstand attack.[30]

In the Book of Chronicles it says:[31]

> After these things and truth, Sanherib, King of Assyria came. He camped upon the fortified cities and declared that he would split them open for himself. Jehezekiah saw that Sanherib had come and his intention was for war against Jerusalem. He consulted with his officers and his mighty ones to seal up the waters of the springs that were outside of the city, and they helped him. They gathered a great many people and sealed up all of the springs and the stream that flowed within the ground, saying, "Why should the kings of Assyria come and find plenty of water?" He strengthened himself and built all of the broken wall and raised it up to the towers, and another wall outside. He strengthened the embankment of the City of David, and made many weapons and shields. He put officers of war over the

people and gathered them to him to the plaza of the gate of the city, and spoke encouragingly to them saying, "Be strong and steadfast, don't fear and don't be discouraged because of the King of Assyria and before all the mob that is with him, for there is more with us than with him. With him there is an arm of flesh, and with us, the L-rd our G-d, to help us and to fight our wars." The people relied upon the words of Jehezekiah, King of Judah.

The words, "After these things and truth," refer to Hezekiah's righteousness and his success in bringing the nation back to Torah. It seems wrong that such a righteous generation with such a great leader was made to suffer at the hands of a cruel enemy like Sanherib. Was that the way G-d repaid their righteousness deeds and faithfulness, "these things and truth?" Therefore the chapter in Chronicles begins with this reference to show that it was not because G-d ignored their deeds or forgot them, but, on the contrary, because He remembered them and planned to reward them with a miraculous salvation and great riches and blessing. The siege and threats of Sanherib were but a preparation for that, without which it would not be possible. But G-d knew that Hezekiah would refuse if it were offered to him. He would say, "I would rather forgo this reward than endure such a terrifying experience." So G-d swore to do it anyway, as the prophet Isaiah wrote,[32] "The L-rd of H-sts swore saying, 'Indeed as I imagined, so it will be, as I planned, it will happen, to break Assyria in My land, and on My mountains I will trample it.'" He sent Sanherib without asking Hezekiah or informing him of His plans.[33]

18:17 וַיִּשְׁלַח מֶלֶךְ־אַשּׁוּר אֶת־תַּרְתָּן וְאֶת־רַב־סָרִיס וְאֶת־רַבְשָׁקֵה מִן־לָכִישׁ
אֶל־הַמֶּלֶךְ חִזְקִיָּהוּ בְּחֵיל כָּבֵד יְרוּשָׁלָם וַיַּעֲלוּ וַיָּבֹאוּ יְרוּשָׁלַםִ וַיַּעֲלוּ וַיָּבֹאוּ
וַיַּעַמְדוּ בִּתְעָלַת הַבְּרֵכָה הָעֶלְיוֹנָה אֲשֶׁר בִּמְסִלַּת שְׂדֵה כוֹבֵס׃

The King of Assyria sent Tartan, Rabsaris and Rabshakeh from Lachish to King Hezekiah with a mighty army to Jerusalem. They went up and came and stood at the channel of the upper pool, that was on the path of the field of the washers.

Some say Sanherib took the tribute and immediately attacked again. No payment would have satisfied him, for he was committed to conquering Judah and making it part of his empire.[34] Others say Sanherib took the tribute and left, but in the years that followed, Hezekiah failed to fulfill his demands, so he attacked again.[35]

In the Book of Isaiah[36] only Rabshakeh is mentioned, but not Tartan and Rabsaris. Some say they did not come together. First Rabshakeh came and delivered his demand for surrender. Later, when Sanherib temporarily relaxed his siege to suppress the rebellion in Cush, he sent Tartan and Rabsaris to warn Hezekiah that he would be back.[37] Others say they came together, but Tartan and Rabsaris were not mentioned because they were subordinate to Rabshakeh.[38]

18:18-25 וַיִּקְרְאוּ אֶל־הַמֶּלֶךְ וַיֵּצֵא אֲלֵהֶם אֶלְיָקִים בֶּן־חִלְקִיָּהוּ אֲשֶׁר עַל־הַבָּיִת
וְשֶׁבְנָה הַסֹּפֵר וְיוֹאָח בֶּן־אָסָף הַמַּזְכִּיר: וַיֹּאמֶר אֲלֵיהֶם רַבְשָׁקֵה אִמְרוּ־נָא
אֶל־חִזְקִיָּהוּ כֹּה־אָמַר הַמֶּלֶךְ הַגָּדוֹל מֶלֶךְ אַשּׁוּר מָה הַבִּטָּחוֹן הַזֶּה אֲשֶׁר בָּטָחְתָּ:
אָמַרְתָּ אַךְ־דְּבַר־שְׂפָתַיִם עֵצָה וּגְבוּרָה לַמִּלְחָמָה עַתָּה עַל־מִי בָטַחְתָּ כִּי מָרַדְתָּ בִּי:
עַתָּה הִנֵּה בָטַחְתָּ לְּךָ עַל־מִשְׁעֶנֶת הַקָּנֶה הָרָצוּץ הַזֶּה עַל־מִצְרַיִם אֲשֶׁר יִסָּמֵךְ אִישׁ
עָלָיו וּבָא בְכַפּוֹ וּנְקָבָהּ כֵּן פַּרְעֹה מֶלֶךְ־מִצְרַיִם לְכָל־הַבֹּטְחִים עָלָיו: וְכִי־תֹאמְרוּן
אֵלַי אֶל־ה׳ אֱלֹהֵינוּ בָּטָחְנוּ הֲלוֹא־הוּא אֲשֶׁר הֵסִיר חִזְקִיָּהוּ אֶת־בָּמֹתָיו
וְאֶת־מִזְבְּחֹתָיו וַיֹּאמֶר לִיהוּדָה וְלִירוּשָׁלִַם לִפְנֵי הַמִּזְבֵּחַ הַזֶּה תִּשְׁתַּחֲווּ בִּירוּשָׁלִָם:
וְעַתָּה הִתְעָרֶב נָא אֶת־אֲדֹנִי אֶת־מֶלֶךְ אַשּׁוּר וְאֶתְּנָה לְךָ אַלְפַּיִם סוּסִים אִם־תּוּכַל
לָתֶת לְךָ רֹכְבִים עֲלֵיהֶם: וְאֵיךְ תָּשִׁיב אֵת פְּנֵי פַחַת אַחַד עַבְדֵי אֲדֹנִי הַקְּטַנִּים
וַתִּבְטַח לְךָ עַל־מִצְרַיִם לְרֶכֶב וּלְפָרָשִׁים: עַתָּה הֲמִבַּלְעֲדֵי ה׳ עָלִיתִי עַל־הַמָּקוֹם
הַזֶּה לְהַשְׁחִתוֹ ה׳ אָמַר אֵלַי עֲלֵה עַל־הָאָרֶץ הַזֹּאת וְהַשְׁחִיתָהּ:

They called to the king. Eliakim ben Hilkiah who was in charge of the household, Shebnah the scribe, and Joah ben Asaph the secretary came out to him. Rabshakeh said to them, "Please say to Hezekiah, 'Thus says the great king, the King of Assyria, "What is this trust that you trusted? You spoke, but it was just words of the lips, advice and might for war. Now, upon whom have you relied that you rebelled against me? Now, behold, you have relied upon this staff of cracked reed, upon Egypt, that when a person leans on it, it goes into his hand and pierces it. Thus is Pharaoh, King of Egypt, for all who rely upon him. And if you say to me, 'In the L-rd, our G-d, we have trusted.' Is He not the One whose shrines and altars Hezekiah removed, and said to Judah and Jerusalem, 'Before this altar you will bow down in Jerusalem?'

So now, commit yourself to my master, the King of Assyria, and I will give you two thousand horses, if you can put yourself riders upon them. How can you turn away even one of the smallest of the officers of the servants of my master, and put your trust in Egypt for chariots and horses? And now, was it without G-d that I came up against this place to destroy it? G-d said to me, 'Go up against this land and destroy it!' " ' "

The Book of Chronicles continues:[39]

> After this, Sanherib, King of Assyria, sent his servants to Jerusalem, while he was attacking Lachish and all of his army was with him, against Hezekiah, King of Judah, and against all of Judah that was in Jerusalem saying, "Thus says Sanherib, King of Assyria, 'In what are you trusting and sitting in the fortification in Jerusalem? Isn't Hezekiah misleading you to die of starvation and thirst, saying, "The L-rd, our G-d, will save us from the hand of the King of Assyria?" Isn't Hezekiah the one who removed His shrines and altars and said to Judah and Jerusalem saying, "Before one altar will you bow down and upon it will you burn incense?" Don't you know what I did, I and my fathers, to all the peoples of the lands? Were the gods of the peoples of the lands able to save their lands from my hand? Who of all the gods of these peoples that my fathers destroyed was able to save his people from my hand, that your G-d will be able to save you from my hand? So now, let Hezekiah not mislead you and lead you astray like this. Don't believe him! For every god of every people and kingdom was not able to save his people from my hand and from the hand of my fathers, so even your G-d will not save you from my hand.' "

Rabshakeh was a Jew, perhaps a member of one of the northern tribes that had been captured and taken into exile by the Assyrians. He had become an apostate and a traitor to his people, accepting the religion of his captors and serving them. In that way he rose to a high position. Perhaps Sanherib purposely chose a Jew to send as his messenger because he thought the Jewish People would be more readily persuaded to surrender by one of their own.

Like many others of his generation, Rabshakeh did not understand that it was the Temple service alone that was desireable to G-d. He thought that if the people really wanted to please G-d, they should establish many shrines and altars throughout the land, as they had until then. It could hardly be G-d's will to limit His service by confining it to the Temple in Jerusalem. So Rabshakeh understood Hezekiah's elimination of the other altars as a political move. He accused Hezekiah of trying to increase his own power by consolidating the focus of religion in Jerusalem, thus making the nation religiously dependent upon him.[40] He therefore thought that G-d would not save Hezekiah even if He had the power to.

Rabshakeh argued that there were only three ways that Hezekiah and his people might be saved, and none of them would succeed. The usual thing for a king in Hezekiah's position to do would be to find a powerful ally to face his enemy with him. In this case, it would be Egypt. Both Assyria in the north and Egypt in the south wanted control of the coastal strip in which the Land of Israel was located. Egypt would have liked to annex it to their own empire, but if that was not possible, at the very least they wanted to keep it out of the hands of Assyria.

But Rabshakeh warned that Egypt was not to be trusted. They would risk only as much as it was worth for their own interests. If more was needed they would not hesitate to abandon their allies. Their promises were not to be believed. Defending Jerusalem would require more than they would be willing to give, so in the end they would not save him.

The metaphor of a cracked reed also implies that an unfaithful ally like Egypt is worse than no ally at all. Not only don't they help, in the end they even injure.[41]

As for being saved by a miracle, had not the prophet Isaiah already proclaimed that Assyria would attack them as a punishment for their sinfulness? Thus Isaiah proclaimed,[42] "Since this people has been contemptuous of the waters of the Shiloah, which go slowly, and rejoiced over Rezin and ben-Remaliah. Therefore behold, the L-rd will bring up upon them the mighty and abundant waters of the river, the King of Assyria and all his glory. He will overflow all his channels and overflow all his banks. He will pass over Judah, washing over and passing over, to the neck it will reach. The ends of his branches will fill the width of your land."

The third possibility was that Hezekiah and his army would be able to defeat the armies of Assyria by themselves. That was so unlikely that Rabshakeh did not even mention it, but he alluded to its absurdity by his offer of "two thousand horses, if you can put yourself riders upon them."

So great were the legions of Assyria that they had more horses to spare than Judah had horsemen! How could the Jews even consider resisting?[43]

He said, "The lowest officer of Assyria has two thousand horsemen at his command. Any one of them is greater than your king, for he doesn't even have that many in his whole army! So whom do you choose to serve?"[44]

Rabshakeh's goal was to convince the people to surrender without a fight. He hoped they would be so frightened that they would betray Hezekiah, open the gates and turn the city over to the Assyrians. He belittled Hezekiah, referring to him by his name alone instead of as king. Compared to the King of Assyria, Hezekiah was not a king at all! He had no real power, since he was not able to defend his kingdom. Sanherib could come and take it away from him whenever he liked.[45]

Some say the expression, "just words of the lips" refers to Hezekiah's prayers. Rabshakeh said, "Prayer and piety is all very nice, but when it comes right down to it, they won't help you. The only way to win a war is to be stronger than your enemy, and you can never hope to overcome the mighty empire of Assyria!"[46] Others say it refers to the promise that Hezekiah had made earlier, when he agreed to submit to Assyria and pay the tribute that they demanded. What could he expect to accomplish by empty words? Now that he had broken his promise, he was in worse trouble than he had been before! What is more foolish than to break a promise to such a mighty and terrible enemy as Assyria?[47]

Another interpretation is that Hezekiah's reassurances to his people and his confidence in success were but idle words. Rabshakeh presented himself as if he were advising the people to act rationally for their own good. He warned them not be fooled by Hezekiah, who was nothing more than a demagogue, leading his people to destruction rather than sacrificing his own power for their sake.[48]

"Furthermore," said Rabshakeh, "it was proclaimed by the prophet Isaiah[49] that G-d would bring the King of Assyria upon you. He is therefore acting with divine approval. It is useless for you to look to G-d for help!" Indeed, Sanherib had heard about this prophecy, and believed that he had a divine guarantee of success. He did not understand that Isaiah had prophesied victory for him only over the Kingdom of Israel, not Judah. He thought he was destined to conquer the whole country. Indeed, it had been foretold that he would attack Judah, but not that he would conquer it. On the contrary, his ultimate defeat had also been revealed. But he heard what was agreeable to him and permitted himself to be misled.[50]

18:26 וַיֹּאמֶר אֶלְיָקִים בֶּן־חִלְקִיָּהוּ וְשֶׁבְנָה וְיוֹאָח אֶל־רַבְשָׁקֵה דַּבֶּר־נָא
אֶל־עֲבָדֶיךָ אֲרָמִית כִּי שֹׁמְעִים אֲנָחְנוּ וְאַל־תְּדַבֵּר עִמָּנוּ יְהוּדִית בְּאָזְנֵי הָעָם
אֲשֶׁר עַל־הַחֹמָה׃

Eliakim ben Hilkiah and Shebnah and Joab said to Rabshakeh, "Please speak to your servants in Aramaic, for we understand. Don't speak to us in Judean in the ears of the people that are on the wall."

Hezekiah's ministers were afraid that the people would become frightened by Rabshakeh's threat and betray their king and their city. Some say they did not realize that that was exactly Rabshakeh's intention. They thought that he would have preferred to speak in Aramaic, the language of the Assyrian Empire, and only spoke to them in Hebrew because he thought that otherwise they would not understand him.[51] Had not Sanherib sent him, a Jew, because he would be better able to communicate with his own nation?

Others say they understood full well what Rabshakeh was trying to do, but they thought they could persuade him to stop. They said, "Don't you realize that you are jeopardizing your own position by speaking our language? Remember, you were originally a Jew, and the Assyrians will never really trust you. They are continually watching you for signs of disloyalty. You must be careful not to say anything that might make them think you still believe in G-d. When you speak of Hezekiah's removal of the altars and shrines, it sounds as if you believe that G-d could save us if we deserved it. By speaking in our language you appear to be identifying with your former nation. So speak to us in Aramaic instead, for we will understand and convey your message to the king. After all, it is really for him alone, not for the common people, so it doesn't matter whether they can understand you."[52]

18:27 וַיֹּאמֶר אֲלֵיהֶם רַבְשָׁקֵה הַעַל אֲדֹנֶיךָ וְאֵלֶיךָ שְׁלָחַנִי אֲדֹנִי לְדַבֵּר
אֶת־הַדְּבָרִים הָאֵלֶּה הֲלֹא עַל־הָאֲנָשִׁים הַיֹּשְׁבִים עַל־הַחֹמָה לֶאֱכֹל אֶת־חריהם
(צוֹאָתָם קרי) וְלִשְׁתּוֹת אֶת־שיניהם (מֵימֵי רַגְלֵיהֶם קרי) עִמָּכֶם׃

Rabshakeh said to them, "Is it to your master and to you that my master sent me to speak these words? Is it not to the people who are sitting on the wall, to eat their excrement and drink their urine with you?"

But Rabshakeh was not to be tricked by their arguments. He knew what he had come to do, and from their reaction he knew that he was succeeding.

18:28-35 וַיַּעֲמֹד רַבְשָׁקֵה וַיִּקְרָא בְקוֹל־גָּדוֹל יְהוּדִית וַיְדַבֵּר וַיֹּאמֶר שִׁמְעוּ
דְּבַר־הַמֶּלֶךְ הַגָּדוֹל מֶלֶךְ אַשּׁוּר: כֹּה אָמַר הַמֶּלֶךְ אַל־יַשִּׁא לָכֶם חִזְקִיָּהוּ כִּי־לֹא
יוּכַל לְהַצִּיל אֶתְכֶם מִיָּדוֹ: וְאַל־יַבְטַח אֶתְכֶם חִזְקִיָּהוּ אֶל־ה׳ לֵאמֹר הַצֵּל יַצִּילֵנוּ
ה׳ וְלֹא תִנָּתֵן אֶת־הָעִיר הַזֹּאת בְּיַד מֶלֶךְ אַשּׁוּר: אַל־תִּשְׁמְעוּ אֶל־חִזְקִיָּהוּ כִּי כֹה
אָמַר מֶלֶךְ אַשּׁוּר עֲשׂוּ־אִתִּי בְרָכָה וּצְאוּ אֵלַי וְאִכְלוּ אִישׁ־גַּפְנוֹ וְאִישׁ תְּאֵנָתוֹ
וּשְׁתוּ אִישׁ מֵי־בֹרוֹ: עַד־בֹּאִי וְלָקַחְתִּי אֶתְכֶם אֶל־אֶרֶץ כְּאַרְצְכֶם אֶרֶץ דָּגָן
וְתִירוֹשׁ אֶרֶץ לֶחֶם וּכְרָמִים אֶרֶץ זֵית יִצְהָר וּדְבַשׁ וִחְיוּ וְלֹא תָמֻתוּ וְאַל־תִּשְׁמְעוּ
אֶל־חִזְקִיָּהוּ כִּי־יַסִּית אֶתְכֶם לֵאמֹר ה׳ יַצִּילֵנוּ: הַהַצֵּל הִצִּילוּ אֱלֹהֵי הַגּוֹיִם אִישׁ
אֶת־אַרְצוֹ מִיַּד מֶלֶךְ אַשּׁוּר: אַיֵּה אֱלֹהֵי חֲמָת וְאַרְפָּד אַיֵּה אֱלֹהֵי סְפַרְוַיִם הֵנַע
וְעִוָּה כִּי־הִצִּילוּ אֶת־שֹׁמְרוֹן מִיָּדִי: מִי בְּכָל־אֱלֹהֵי הָאֲרָצוֹת אֲשֶׁר־הִצִּילוּ
אֶת־אַרְצָם מִיָּדִי כִּי־יַצִּיל ה׳ אֶת־יְרוּשָׁלִַם מִיָּדִי:

Rabshakeh stood up and called in a loud voice in Judean, and spoke saying, "Listen to the word of the great king, the King of Assyria. Thus said the King, 'Let Hezekiah not mislead you, for he will not be able to save you from my hand. And let Hezekiah not have you put your trust in G-d saying, "G-d will surely save us, and this city will not be given over into the hand of the King of Assyria!" Don't listen to Hezekiah, for thus says the King of Assyria, "Make a blessing with me and come out to me! Let each man eat his vine and his fig tree, and let each man drink the water of his cistern. Until I come and take you to a land like your land, a land of grain and wine, a land of bread and vineyards, a land of oil-olives and honey, and you will live and not die. Don't listen to Hezekiah, for he will mislead you saying, 'G-d will save us.' Did the gods of the nations indeed save their own lands from the hand of the King of Assyria? Where are the gods of Hamath and Arpad, and where are the gods of the Sepharvaim, Hena and Ivah? Did they save Samaria from my hand? Who of all the gods of the lands saved their lands from my hand, that G-d will save Jerusalem from my hand?' "

Some say the land Sanherib was planning to resettle them in was North Africa. Others say it was in the mountains of Selug.[53]

One might have expected Rabshakeh to promise the people that the land to which they were to be taken would be better than their own. After all, if the new land were only equal to theirs, as he described it, and no better, why should they want to go there? Some say he was foolish to present it that way. He would have made the idea of surrender more appealing to them had he led them to believe that they would not only be saved from siege, but even improve their lot. Others say he was wise not to exaggerate. The people all knew that there was no country better than the Holy Land, so they would have recognized it right away as a false promise.[54]

Some say it was Sanherib himself that had instructed him to speak respectfully about the Holy Land, and not claim that any other land was better. For this he was rewarded by being called "Asnapar, the great and noble."[55]

They must also have known the reason that they would be moved. It would not be for their own benefit, but to strengthen the Assyrian Empire and make its conquests more secure. The Assyrians realized that as long as a conquered nation remained in its own land, it would retain its national spirit and social structures. They would always be there, waiting for an opportunity to be revived. When the time came, the people would arise and rebel against their conquerors. So the Assyrians adopted a policy of removing conquered nations from their native lands and resettling the entire population in another part of the empire. Their former land would then in turn be given to another nation that had been similarly removed from its home. Under the influence of native Assyrians who would govern them and live among them, they would become assimilated into the Assyrian Empire, adopting its customs and knowing no other allegiance or nationality. It was in accordance with this policy that the inhabitants of the Kingdom of Israel had been exiled.[56]

Though this was a clever plan, it ultimately failed. The Assyrian Empire fell soon afterwards, to be succeeded by Babylonia and Persia. Babylonia followed Assyria's example and exiled the Kingdom of Judah, but their empire fell too. It was the Persians, whose policy was just the opposite, whose empire endured the longest. They respected the national cultures and religions of all the countries they conquered, and encouraged the peoples to continue them faithfully while remaining politically loyal to Persia.

At first, Rabshakeh had been careful not to speak against G-d. Though he was a traitor and an apostate, he still had some fear of G-d in his heart. But after hearing the words of Hezekiah's ministers, he decided not leave any doubt about where his loyalty lay. He proceeded to insult G-d by comparing Him to the idols of the other nations, who had been unable to save their worshipers. No longer did he argue, as he had the first time, that they would not be saved because they had not been righteous or faithful. Thus the argument of Hezekiah's ministers, that was intended to subdue his threats, drove him instead to complete blasphemy.[57]

Some say Hena and Ivah were the names of the cities of the Sepharvaim.[58] Others say they were the names of their gods.[59]

The Book of Chronicles records some additional details of this confrontation, making it clear that the source of this blasphemy was Sanherib himself. It says:[60]

> And his servants spoke more against the L-rd, G-d, and against Jehezekiah, His servant. And he wrote letters to insult the L-rd, the G-d of Israel, and to say about Him saying, "Like the gods of the nations of the lands that didn't save their peoples from my hand, so the G-d of Jehezekiah will not save His people from my hand." They called out in a loud voice in Judean to the people of Jerusalem who were on the wall, to frighten them and confuse them, in order that they capture the city. They spoke about the G-d of Jerusalem as about the gods of the peoples of the land, the work of human hands.

How admirable is the humility of the Jewish People at times when greatness was bestowed upon them, and how despicable the arrogance of the heathens under like circumstances! That humility earned them G-d's love, as it says,[61] "It was not for your being greater than all the nations that G-d desired you and chose you, for you are the least of all the nations." This does not mean that G-d chose Israel because they were the smallest nation, for certainly that is not a reason to choose them. It is rather that, of all the nations, they are the ones that act the smallest and most humble at times that they have reason to be proud. G-d said, "Even when I give you greatness, you belittle yourselves before Me!" Abraham said,[62] "I am dust and ashes." Moses said,[63] "What are we?" and David said,[64] "I am a worm, not a person." But the heathen nations become arrogant and boastful as soon as they are granted greatness. Thus Sanherib said, "Who of all the gods of the lands saved their lands from my hand, that G-d will save Jerusalem from my hand?" Nebuchadnezar said,[65] "I will go up on the high places of the people, I will be like the Most High."[66]

18:36 וְהֶחֱרִישׁוּ הָעָם וְלֹא־עָנוּ אֹתוֹ דָּבָר כִּי־מִצְוַת הַמֶּלֶךְ הִיא לֵאמֹר לֹא
תַעֲנֻהוּ׃

The people were silent and didn't answer him anything, for it was the king's command saying, "Don't answer him."

Nonetheless, the Jewish People remained loyal to their G-d and their king.

18:37 וַיָּבֹא אֶלְיָקִים בֶּן־חִלְקִיָּה אֲשֶׁר־עַל־הַבַּיִת וְשֶׁבְנָא הַסֹּפֵר וְיוֹאָח בֶּן־
אָסָף הַמַּזְכִּיר אֶל־חִזְקִיָּהוּ קְרוּעֵי בְגָדִים וַיַּגִּדוּ לוֹ דִּבְרֵי רַבְשָׁקֵה׃

Eliakim ben Hilkiah who was in charge of the household, Shebnah the scribe, and Joah ben Asaph the secretary came to Hezekiah with torn clothes, and told him the words of Rabshakeh.

The king's ministers tore their clothes, as is required of one who hears a Jew curse G-d. Just to witness such an act is a terrible experience, comparable to being present when a human being dies. So, like one who witnesses a death, they were required to tear their clothes.[67]

Some consider this proof that Rabshakeh was a Jew, for when a heathen curses G-d, shocking as it may be, there is no such requirement. Others say there is an obligation to tear the clothes even upon hearing the blasphemy of a heathen.[68]

They had not torn their clothes the first time that Rabshakeh spoke to them because that time he had not blasphemed G-d. That shows that it was because of the blasphemy that they tore their clothes, not because of his threats and the fear of destruction.

As for putting on sack cloth, which is not a requirement in mourning, they did that to afflict themselves, hoping thus to evoke G-d's mercy.[69]

II Kings 19

19:1 וַיְהִי כִּשְׁמֹעַ הַמֶּלֶךְ חִזְקִיָּהוּ וַיִּקְרַע אֶת־בְּגָדָיו וַיִּתְכַּס בַּשָּׂק וַיָּבֹא
בֵּית ה׳:

When King Hezekiah heard he tore his clothes, covered himself with sackcloth and came to the House of G-d.

Hezekiah tore his clothes for two reasons. First, because he heard about the blasphemy of Rabshakeh. Not only are those who actually hear blasphemy from the mouth of a Jew required to tear their clothes, but even one who, like Hezekiah, hears about it from those who were present.[1] The second reason was to evoke G-d's mercy. In this case, tearing the clothes became a mode of prayer, together with the other prayers that he and his people offered.[2]

19:2-4 וַיִּשְׁלַח אֶת־אֶלְיָקִים אֲשֶׁר־עַל־הַבַּיִת וְשֶׁבְנָא הַסֹּפֵר וְאֵת זִקְנֵי
הַכֹּהֲנִים מִתְכַּסִּים בַּשַּׂקִּים אֶל־יְשַׁעְיָהוּ הַנָּבִיא בֶּן־אָמוֹץ: וַיֹּאמְרוּ אֵלָיו כֹּה אָמַר
חִזְקִיָּהוּ יוֹם־צָרָה וְתוֹכֵחָה וּנְאָצָה הַיּוֹם הַזֶּה כִּי־בָאוּ בָנִים עַד־מַשְׁבֵּר וְכֹחַ אַיִן
לְלֵדָה: אוּלַי יִשְׁמַע ה׳ אֱלֹהֶיךָ אֵת כָּל־דִּבְרֵי רַבְשָׁקֵה אֲשֶׁר שְׁלָחוֹ מֶלֶךְ־אַשּׁוּר
אֲדֹנָיו לְחָרֵף אֱלֹהִים חַי וְהוֹכִיחַ בַּדְּבָרִים אֲשֶׁר שָׁמַע ה׳ אֱלֹהֶיךָ וְנָשָׂאתָ תְפִלָּה
בְּעַד הַשְּׁאֵרִית הַנִּמְצָאָה:

He sent Eliakim, who was in charge of the household, Shebnah the scribe, and the elders of the priests, covered with sackcloth, to Isaiah ben Amoz, the prophet. They said to him, "Thus says Hezekiah, 'It is a day of trouble, rebuke and disgrace, this day, for the baby is ready to be born, and the mother has no strength to give birth. Perhaps the L-rd, your G-d, will listen to the words of Rabshakeh, whom the King of Assyria, his master, sent to insult the living G-d, and disprove the words that the L-rd, your G-d, heard. So offer a prayer for the sake of the remnant that is left.' "

Some say the words "rebuke and disgrace" refer to Rabshakeh's challenge to the Jewish People. They are called "rebuke" because he had rebuked them for resisting Assyria and "disgrace" because he intentionally insulted G-d.[3]

Others say they refer to G-d's anger at the people for their sinfulness and lack of faith. Hezekiah understood the terrifying situation into which they had been put as a divine rebuke for their ways, to coerce them to repent.[4]

Hezekiah compared their situation to that of a woman who is giving birth and does not have the strength to push the baby out. Like the baby, the Jewish People could not retreat or return to their former situation. They could never surrender under Sanherib's terms. Hezekiah had been ready to make great material sacrifices to obtain peace, but the demands Sanherib made now were spiritual as well. His proposed exile of the Kingdom of Judah would mean desecration of the Holy Temple, and would make it impossible for the Jewish People to continue to fulfill the many commandments dependent upon the Temple and the Holy Land. By implication, it would also mean the abolition of Torah itself, and the replacement of the service of G-d with idolatry. Under no circumstances could Hezekiah agree to that. There was no choice but to go forward and fight. Yet they had neither strength to fight for themselves nor merit to ask for divine assistance. Only by G-d's mercy could they be saved.

Many Jews, however, did not agree. Shebnah, who had been Hezekiah's prime minister, was the leader of the faction that wanted to surrender. To Hezekiah's dismay, he saw that Shebnah's following was greater than his own. While he had one hundred and ten thousand followers, Shebnah had one hundred and thirty thousand. Hezekiah was afraid that perhaps G-d, too, had agreed to their position, since they were in the majority. If the people chose to go into exile rather than trust G-d, perhaps He would indeed not save them. So G-d sent the prophet Isaiah to reassure Hezekiah that He had not abandoned him. He said,[5] "Do not consider a faction all that this nation considers a faction." The opinion of the wicked, like Shebnah and his followers, is not taken into consideration, even if they are in the majority. There is never real unity among the wicked as there is among those who sincerely adhere to the Torah. Their unity is only temporary, because each has only his own interests in mind. At any moment they may turn on one another. A small but solid group bound together by the common purpose of doing G-d's will can overcome them.

When Shebnah saw that Hezekiah would not yield to the majority, he planned a rebellion. Secretly he sent a message to Sanherib, attaching it to an arrow and shooting it over the wall. He wrote, "Shebnah and his followers want to make peace, but Hezekiah and his followers do not."

The next day, he gathered his followers and prepared to go out and surrender to the Assyrians. He had the gates opened and went out, but before the others could follow, the angel Gabriel came and shut the gates tight again. Shebnah found himself alone among the Assyrians.

"Where are all the followers you told us about?" they asked.

Shebnah had no answer. "They backed out," he said.

The Assyrians were enraged. "Is this some sort of joke?" they said. "No one can make fun of us like that and get away with it."

They pierced his feet and tied him to the tails of their horses. Then they dragged him over the thorns until he was dead.[6]

Some say he was taken prisoner but not killed. Soon afterwards, Sanherib brought him along in chains to witness the Assyrian victory over Cush. But it was only after their return to Jerusalem that Shebnah would learn how foolish his own disloyalty had been, when he saw how Hezekiah was saved and Sanherib defeated.[7]

19:5-7 וַיָּבֹאוּ עַבְדֵי הַמֶּלֶךְ חִזְקִיָּהוּ אֶל־יְשַׁעְיָהוּ: וַיֹּאמֶר לָהֶם יְשַׁעְיָהוּ כֹּה
תֹאמְרוּן אֶל־אֲדֹנֵיכֶם כֹּה אָמַר ה׳ אַל־תִּירָא מִפְּנֵי הַדְּבָרִים אֲשֶׁר שָׁמַעְתָּ אֲשֶׁר
גִּדְּפוּ נַעֲרֵי מֶלֶךְ־אַשּׁוּר אֹתִי: הִנְנִי נֹתֵן בּוֹ רוּחַ וְשָׁמַע שְׁמוּעָה וְשָׁב לְאַרְצוֹ
וְהִפַּלְתִּיו בַּחֶרֶב בְּאַרְצוֹ:

The servants of King Hezekiah came to Isaiah. Isaiah said to them, "Say thus to your master, 'Thus says G-d, "Do not be afraid because of the words that you heard, that the servants of the King of Assyria blasphemed Me. Behold, I am putting a spirit into him. He will hear a report and return to his land, and I will cause him to fall by the sword in his land."' "

G-d said, "Sanherib is indeed a great conqueror, but Hezekiah is a match for him! Sanherib has eight names, 'Tiglath-Pilesar,' 'Pilnesar,' 'Shalmanesar,' 'Pul,' 'Sargon,' 'Asnapar,' 'Raba,' 'Veyakira,' aside from the name 'Sanherib.' But Hezekiah also has eight names, 'Pele,' 'Yoez,' 'El,'

'Gibor,' 'Avi,' 'Ad,' 'Sar,' 'Shalom,' and the name 'Hezekiah' as well. By Hezekiah's merit Sanherib will be defeated."[8]

The "spirit" that G-d put into Sanherib was the desire to interrupt his siege and leave the Land of Israel. First, G-d caused an uprising against Assyria in the kingdom of Cush. That would be a reason for Sanherib to leave temporarily. But Sanherib could have chosen to ignore the Cushites for the time being and finish conquering Israel first. Therefore the prophet points out that it was not the uprising alone, but G-d's instilling in Sanherib the desire to suppress it immediately. This was the second thing that G-d did to save Israel.

In this way the prophet also reminded Hezekiah that it was G-d Who had given Sanherib the desire to conquer Israel in the first place. Some say this was all one desire, the desire to dominate the other nations. The same relentless greed for conquest that made him want to conquer Israel now drove him to subdue Cush. G-d therefore said, "I am putting," in the present tense, rather than "I will put." He had already put it into Sanherib. First it worked to the detriment of Israel, then for their benefit.[9]

By distracting Sanherib in this way, Israel was given temporary relief. They had a chance to go out of the city and harvest their crops so they would have food to withstand another siege should Sanherib return. But Isaiah predicted more than that. This would be followed by a permanent salvation. Sanherib would return to his own country and give up his plans of conquering Israel. By using the singular in reference to Sanherib, "he will hear a report and return to his land," rather than "they will return to their land," the prophet alluded to the terrible plague that would devastate the Assyrian army. When Sanherib and the few survivors at last reached their own country, it would be as if they were returning alone.

Finally, the future would be secured by the assassination of Sanherib. These were four decrees that G-d made to bring about the salvation of the Jewish People: "I am putting a spirit into him," "he will hear a report," "return to his land," and "I will cause him to fall by the sword in his land."[10]

19:8-13 וַיָּשָׁב רַבְשָׁקֵה וַיִּמְצָא אֶת־מֶלֶךְ אַשּׁוּר נִלְחָם עַל־לִבְנָה כִּי שָׁמַע כִּי
נָסַע מִלָּכִישׁ: וַיִּשְׁמַע אֶל־תִּרְהָקָה מֶלֶךְ־כּוּשׁ לֵאמֹר הִנֵּה יָצָא לְהִלָּחֵם אִתָּךְ
וַיָּשָׁב וַיִּשְׁלַח מַלְאָכִים אֶל־חִזְקִיָּהוּ לֵאמֹר: כֹּה תֹאמְרוּן אֶל־חִזְקִיָּהוּ
מֶלֶךְ־יְהוּדָה לֵאמֹר אַל־יַשִּׁאֲךָ אֱלֹהֶיךָ אֲשֶׁר אַתָּה בֹּטֵחַ בּוֹ לֵאמֹר לֹא תִנָּתֵן
יְרוּשָׁלַםִ בְּיַד מֶלֶךְ אַשּׁוּר: הִנֵּה אַתָּה שָׁמַעְתָּ אֵת אֲשֶׁר עָשׂוּ מַלְכֵי אַשּׁוּר

לְכָל־הָאֲרָצוֹת לְהַחֲרִימָם וְאַתָּה תִּנָּצֵל׃ הַהִצִּילוּ אֹתָם אֱלֹהֵי הַגּוֹיִם אֲשֶׁר שִׁחֲתוּ
אֲבוֹתַי אֶת־גּוֹזָן וְאֶת־חָרָן וְרֶצֶף וּבְנֵי־עֶדֶן אֲשֶׁר בִּתְלַאשָּׂר׃ אַיּוֹ מֶלֶךְ־חֲמָת
וּמֶלֶךְ אַרְפָּד וּמֶלֶךְ לָעִיר סְפַרְוָיִם הֵנַע וְעִוָּה׃

Rabshakeh returned and found the King of Assyria fighting against Libnah, for he had heard that he had travelled from Lachish. He heard concerning Tirhakah, King of Cush, saying, "Behold, he has gone out to fight with you!" So he sent messengers back to Hezekiah saying, "Say thus to Hezekiah, King of Judah, saying, 'Don't let your G-d in Whom you trust mislead you saying, "Jerusalem will not be given into the hand of the King of Assyria!" Behold, you have heard what the kings of Assyria did to all the lands to lay them waste. Will you be saved? Did the gods of the nations that my fathers destroyed, Gozan and Haran, and Rezeph and the Children of Eden that are in Telasar, save them? Where is the King of Hamath, the King of Arpad, and the King of the City of Sepharvaim, Hena and Ivah?' "

The first half of the prophecy was fulfilled just as the prophet had foretold. Sanherib heard about the rebellion, and, driven by his desire for conquest and dominion, left to subdue it. Hezekiah should have trusted G-d's promise and not been frightened by Sanherib's threat of returning and completing his conquest of Israel. But again he feared that his people would not be worthy of the promised salvation. He prayed in fear as if he had not already been promised that they would be saved.

19:14-19 וַיִּקַּח חִזְקִיָּהוּ אֶת־הַסְּפָרִים מִיַּד הַמַּלְאָכִים וַיִּקְרָאֵם וַיַּעַל בֵּית
ה׳ וַיִּפְרְשֵׂהוּ חִזְקִיָּהוּ לִפְנֵי ה׳׃ וַיִּתְפַּלֵּל חִזְקִיָּהוּ לִפְנֵי ה׳ וַיֹּאמַר ה׳ אֱלֹהֵי
יִשְׂרָאֵל יֹשֵׁב הַכְּרֻבִים אַתָּה־הוּא הָאֱלֹהִים לְבַדְּךָ לְכֹל מַמְלְכוֹת הָאָרֶץ אַתָּה
עָשִׂיתָ אֶת־הַשָּׁמַיִם וְאֶת־הָאָרֶץ׃ הַטֵּה ה׳ אָזְנְךָ וּשְׁמָע פְּקַח ה׳ עֵינֶיךָ וּרְאֵה
וּשְׁמַע אֵת דִּבְרֵי סַנְחֵרִיב אֲשֶׁר שְׁלָחוֹ לְחָרֵף אֱלֹהִים חָי׃ אָמְנָם ה׳ הֶחֱרִיבוּ
מַלְכֵי אַשּׁוּר אֶת־הַגּוֹיִם וְאֶת־אַרְצָם׃ וְנָתְנוּ אֶת־אֱלֹהֵיהֶם בָּאֵשׁ כִּי לֹא אֱלֹהִים
הֵמָּה כִּי אִם־מַעֲשֵׂה יְדֵי־אָדָם עֵץ וָאֶבֶן וַיְאַבְּדוּם׃ וְעַתָּה ה׳ אֱלֹהֵינוּ הוֹשִׁיעֵנוּ
נָא מִיָּדוֹ וְיֵדְעוּ כָּל־מַמְלְכוֹת הָאָרֶץ כִּי אַתָּה ה׳ אֱלֹהִים לְבַדֶּךָ׃

Hezekiah took the letters from the hand of the messengers and read them. He went up to the House of G-d, and Hezekiah spread them out before G-d. Hezekiah prayed before G-d and said, "Oh L-rd, G-d of Israel, Who sits above the Cherubs, You alone are G-d over all the kingdoms of the earth. You made the heavens and the earth. Turn, Oh G-d, Your ear, and listen! Open up, Oh G-d, Your eyes, and look! Hear the words of Sanherib, that he sent to insult the living G-d. But it is true, Oh G-d! The kings of Assyria have destroyed the nations and their lands! They put their gods in the fire, for they are not real gods, but the work of men's hands, wood and stone, and they destroyed them. So now, Oh L-rd, G-d, save us, please, from his hand, and all the kingdoms of the world will know that You alone are the L-rd, G-d."

Hezekiah argued that G-d save Israel for the honor of His own holy name that Sanherib had insulted. They should be saved even if they were not worthy, for once Sanherib had taken this position it became a matter of defending G-d's own honor. If Israel were defeated, people would think that Sanherib was really more powerful than G-d, as he claimed. Furthermore, the city of Jerusalem was the location of G-d's holy Temple. To let it be defeated would certainly be interpreted as proof of G-d's weakness. He therefore referred to the Cherubs, the figures on the cover of the Ark of the Covenant, representing G-d's love for Israel. It was from above the Cherubs that G-d's voice would emanate when He spoke to the prophets in the Temple. How could the source of G-d's communication with His people be permitted to fall into the hand of an enemy?[11]

Hezekiah spoke of G-d's making the heavens and the earth to emphasize the essential difference between G-d's power and that of a mortal king. G-d is above nature. It is He Who is the source of His own power. It is not derived from the forces of nature. On the contrary, the forces of nature are derived from Him.[12]

19:20-24 וַיִּשְׁלַח יְשַׁעְיָהוּ בֶן־אָמוֹץ אֶל־חִזְקִיָּהוּ לֵאמֹר כֹּה־אָמַר ה׳ אֱלֹהֵי
יִשְׂרָאֵל אֲשֶׁר הִתְפַּלַּלְתָּ אֵלַי אֶל־סַנְחֵרִב מֶלֶךְ־אַשּׁוּר שָׁמָעְתִּי׃ זֶה הַדָּבָר

אֲשֶׁר־דִּבֶּר ה׳ עָלָיו בָּזָה לְךָ לָעֲגָה לְךָ בְּתוּלַת בַּת־צִיּוֹן אַחֲרֶיךָ רֹאשׁ הֵנִיעָה בַּת יְרוּשָׁלָםִ: אֶת־מִי חֵרַפְתָּ וְגִדַּפְתָּ וְעַל־מִי הֲרִימוֹתָ קּוֹל וַתִּשָּׂא מָרוֹם עֵינֶיךָ עַל־קְדוֹשׁ יִשְׂרָאֵל: בְּיַד מַלְאָכֶיךָ חֵרַפְתָּ אֲדֹנָי וַתֹּאמֶר ברכב (בְּרֹב קרי) רִכְבִּי אֲנִי עָלִיתִי מְרוֹם הָרִים יַרְכְּתֵי לְבָנוֹן וְאֶכְרֹת קוֹמַת אֲרָזָיו מִבְחוֹר בְּרֹשָׁיו וְאָבוֹאָה מְלוֹן קִצֹּה יַעַר כַּרְמִלּוֹ: אֲנִי קַרְתִּי וְשָׁתִיתִי מַיִם זָרִים וְאַחְרִב בְּכַף־פְּעָמַי כֹּל יְאֹרֵי מָצוֹר:

Isaiah ben Amoz sent to Hezekiah saying, "Thus says the L-rd, the G-d of Israel, 'That which you prayed to me concerning Sanherib, King of Assyria, I have heard.' This is the thing that G-d said about him, 'She will disgrace you, she will mock you, the virgin daughter of Zion! After you will she shake her head, the daughter of Jerusalem! Whom have you insulted and blasphemed? Against Whom have you raised your voice and lifted your eyes up high? The Holy One of Israel! By the hand of your messengers you insulted G-d, and said, "With my many chariots I have gone up to the heights of the mountains, to the farthest ends of Lebanon. I have cut down the tallest of its cedars, the choicest of its cypresses. I have entered His farthest resting place, the forest of His orchard. I have dug and drunk foreign waters, and I dry up with the sole of my foot all the mighty rivers."'"

In this prophecy, the kingdom of Judah is referred to as a virgin because it had never been conquered, like a virgin who has never submitted to a husband.[13]

As if Sanherib's words were not bad enough, he raised his voice and motioned with his hands and his body. G-d did not overlook any of these things. For each of them he would be punished.[14]

The "heights of the mountains" refers to the Land of Israel, and in particular to Jerusalem and the Temple Mount. "Lebanon," too, has a double meaning. Aside from the mountain of Lebanon and its great forests, it refers to the Temple, where a person's sins are forgiven and he is made clean and white. The "farthest ends" and "farthest resting place" also refer to the Temple, the most holy and most protected. The cedars and cypresses symbolize the leaders and nobles of the Jewish People.[15]

In the Book of Isaiah[16] Sanherib is quoted as saying not "מלון," "farthest resting place," but "מרום," "farthest heights." This reveals

Sanherib's real goal. He imagined that from the earthly Temple, G-d's "resting place," he would be able to proceed to heaven and overcome G-d there as well, in His heavenly Temple, "His farthest heights."[17]

Some say "foreign waters" is a metaphor for the mighty fortified cities that Sanherib conquered. They were so secure that no one imagined they would ever fall. Sanherib boasted that he was able to accomplish anything he set out to do. He compared himself to one who digs a well and doesn't stop until he finds water. Then he enjoys the fruit of his labor. Not so those who are too weak or unskilled and have to give up when they can dig no deeper.[18]

He described the waters as "foreign" or "strange" because no one knew about them until the well was dug and the place of the water reached.[19]

Others say he was referring to the actual digging of wells to supply water to his army, by implication boasting of its size. His soldiers were so numerous that the available water in the countries he conquered was not sufficient for them.[20] According to this interpretation, the words "מצור יארי," mean "mighty rivers" or "deep rivers."[21] A similar interpretation is that as his army forded a river, they carried away so much water on their feet that the river bed was left dry by the time the last soldier crossed.[22]

Others say "יארי מצור" means "the rivers of the fortifications." When they besieged a city, the soldiers and their animals drank so much water that they dried up the rivers or moats surrounding and protecting it and could approach unhindered.[23]

Another interpretation of the word "מצור" is that it is a variation of the name "מצרים," "Egypt." Sanherib boasted that he used up all the water of the Nile.[24]

It was also a mockery of Hezekiah's attempts to protect Jerusalem by diverting the source of water to within the walls. That small amount of water was insignificant for an army the size of Sanherib's!

19:25-28 הֲלֹא־שָׁמַעְתָּ לְמֵרָחוֹק אֹתָהּ עָשִׂיתִי לְמִימֵי קֶדֶם וִיצַרְתִּיהָ עַתָּה
הֲבֵיאתִיהָ וּתְהִי לַהְשׁוֹת גַּלִּים נִצִּים עָרִים בְּצֻרוֹת: וְיֹשְׁבֵיהֶן קִצְרֵי־יָד חַתּוּ
וַיֵּבֹשׁוּ הָיוּ עֵשֶׂב שָׂדֶה וִירַק דֶּשֶׁא חֲצִיר גַּגּוֹת וּשְׁדֵפָה לִפְנֵי קָמָה: וְשִׁבְתְּךָ
וְצֵאתְךָ וּבֹאֲךָ יָדָעְתִּי וְאֵת הִתְרַגֶּזְךָ אֵלָי: יַעַן הִתְרַגֶּזְךָ אֵלַי וְשַׁאֲנַנְךָ עָלָה בְאָזְנָי
וְשַׂמְתִּי חַחִי בְּאַפֶּךָ וּמִתְגִּי בִּשְׂפָתֶיךָ וַהֲשִׁבֹתִיךָ בַּדֶּרֶךְ אֲשֶׁר־בָּאתָ בָּהּ:

Haven't you heard from long ago? That is what I have done! From days of old I formed it. Now I have brought it to pass. Fortified cities will be desolate overgrown mounds. Their inhabitants will be helpless, broken and disgraced. They will be grass of the field, green vegetation, grass of the rooftops, burnt by the wind before it grows to maturity. Your sitting, your going out and your coming in I knew, and also how you provoked Me. Because you provoked Me, your roaring came up in My ears, I have put My hook in your nose and My ring in your lips, and I will bring you back on the way by which you came.

G-d's answer to Sanherib was that, while he imagined himself a mighty conqueror, he was in reality but a puppet in G-d's hands. Thus it is written in the Book of Isaiah,[25] "Oh, Assyria, the staff of My anger." Even before the world was created, the course of history had been revealed and Sanherib's role in it decreed. He had been assigned the task of punishing the nations, and in particular Israel, for their sins. Not only was Sanherib's strength a divine gift for which he could claim no credit, his success was due not to that strength alone, but also to the weakness of his opponents. The nations he conquered had already been condemned to punishment and destruction. They are compared to dried out grass, and to grain that has been burnt by the sun before it had a chance to ripen.[26]

Nonetheless, Sanherib would be held responsible for his deeds of cruelty and destruction. Even though G-d had given the nations into his hands, He had not given him the right to oppress them. Sanherib was not forced by that divine decree to behave as he did. He should have learned a lesson from history. From the time the Jewish People were first enslaved in Egypt, their oppressors were all eventually punished. He should have realized that he would suffer a similar fate.[27]

Sanherib's arrogance would make his disgrace all the greater when the time of his downfall came. The prophet goes on to describe the fate of Assyria once their task would be completed:[28]

> So will it be, that when G-d has accomplished all His deeds, on Mount Zion and Jerusalem, I will attend to the swelling pride of the heart of the King of Assyria, and the glory of the haughtiness of his eyes. For he said, "By the strength of my hand I have done, and by my wisdom, for I am intelligent. I removed the boundaries of the nations, their stores for the future I plundered, and I lowered the mighty of the inhabitants. My hand overcame the armies of the nations like a nest. Like one who gathers abandoned eggs I gathered

the whole land, and there was none that moved a wing, or opened its mouth and chirped." Does the axe pride itself over the one who chops with it? Does the saw consider itself greater than the one that raises it up? As if it were the staff that lifts up the one who holds it high! Indeed, he who raises a stick is not himself wood! Therefore the L-rd, the G-d of H-sts, will send leanness to his fat ones, and in place of his honor a burning will burn like the burning of fire.[29]

But it was not for his cruelty that he would be punished, but for his arrogance and his blasphemy.[30] For failing to acknowledge G-d as the supreme power and for claiming credit that belonged to G-d, he would be reduced to the state of an animal who has no control over his own destiny. It is forced to go wherever its master leads it, even to the slaughter. A hook is put into its cheek or a ring into its nose, and the slightest resistance becomes too painful to endure. The wildest beast submits without a fight. Thus Sanherib would be forced to recognize his own powerlessness.

Isaiah went on in his prophecy to address Hezekiah:

19:29 וְזֶה־לְּךָ הָאוֹת אָכוֹל הַשָּׁנָה סָפִיחַ וּבַשָּׁנָה הַשֵּׁנִית סָחִישׁ וּבַשָּׁנָה
הַשְּׁלִישִׁית זִרְעוּ וְקִצְרוּ וְנִטְעוּ כְרָמִים וְאִכְלוּ פִרְיָם׃

This is the sign for you: Eat this year the wild growths, and the second year shoots. And the third year you will sow and reap, plant vineyards and eat their fruit.

Fulfillment of the prophecy of Sanherib's defeat would be a sign that they would be granted yet another miracle. Though it was already over a year since they had been able to work the land, the plants that grew up without cultivation from the seeds dropped during the previous harvest would flourish, and there would be plenty of food. No enemy would come, and they would be free to harvest them. The next year there would be soft shoots growing from the stumps of the trees that the Assyrians had cut down, and these too they would be able to eat.[31]

Some say the year after Sanherib's defeat was a Sabbatical year, and that was why they would not work the land even though it was already safe. Usually, enough would have been set aside before the Sabbatical year to last until the next year's crops could be planted and harvested. This time, however, it had come after a year of siege, and there would not have been enough had it not been for this special blessing.[32]

Others say that though the downfall of Sanherib would be a sign that all danger from Assyria had passed, it would take years for the people to be convinced. There would be no planting for the next two years, for they would be too frightened to spend time in the fields.[33]

According to another tradition, Sanherib's defeat was in the eleventh year of the Jubilee cycle, the fourth year of the Sabbatical year cycle. It was the night of Passover when the Assyrians were defeated, already too late to plant crops. When they would finally be able to plant again, there would be only one year remaining before the Sabbatical year. The Bible therefore specifically states that they would plant and harvest in the third year, for in the fourth year they would again not work the land. This time, however, it would not be in fear of an enemy, but in observance of the holiness of the Sabbatical year, and with storehouses filled by the blessing of that single harvest.[34]

19:30,31 וְיָסְפָה פְּלֵיטַת בֵּית־יְהוּדָה הַנִּשְׁאָרָה שֹׁרֶשׁ לְמָטָּה וְעָשָׂה פְרִי לְמָעְלָה: כִּי מִירוּשָׁלַםִ תֵּצֵא שְׁאֵרִית וּפְלֵיטָה מֵהַר צִיּוֹן קִנְאַת ה׳ (צְבָאוֹת קרי) תַּעֲשֶׂה־זֹּאת:

The survivors of the House of Judah that are left will again send out a root below and make a fruit above. For from Jerusalem will go out a remainder, and survivors from Mount Zion. The zeal of the L-rd of H-sts will do this.

Again, G-d reminded Hezekiah and his people that this salvation would not come by their own merit, but by G-d's zeal, in answer to the challenge of Sanherib. The Jewish People would be blessed with a complete restoration as a demonstration of his failure to destroy them and the emptiness of his threats.[35]

19:32-34 לָכֵן כֹּה־אָמַר ה׳ אֶל־מֶלֶךְ אַשּׁוּר לֹא יָבֹא אֶל־הָעִיר הַזֹּאת וְלֹא־יוֹרֶה שָׁם חֵץ וְלֹא־יְקַדְּמֶנָּה מָגֵן וְלֹא־יִשְׁפֹּךְ עָלֶיהָ סֹלְלָה: בַּדֶּרֶךְ אֲשֶׁר־יָבֹא בָּהּ יָשׁוּב וְאֶל־הָעִיר הַזֹּאת לֹא יָבֹא נְאֻם־ה׳: וְגַנּוֹתִי אֶל־הָעִיר הַזֹּאת לְהוֹשִׁיעָהּ לְמַעֲנִי וּלְמַעַן דָּוִד עַבְדִּי:

Therefore thus says G-d about the King of Assyria, "He will

not come into this city, nor shoot an arrow there. He will not approach it with a shield, nor throw up a mound upon it. By the way that he will come, by it will he return, and into this city he will not come!" says G-d. "I will protect this city to save it, for My own sake and for the sake of My servant David."

The prophet then turned his attention back to Sanherib. He said, "In your arrogance you left with a threat to return and complete your conquest. You considered it an easy matter that you could interrupt and return to whenever you desired. But it will not happen. Before you have the chance to lay siege again you will be totally destroyed!"

Some say the words "throw up a mound (סללה) upon it" refers to the mounds of earth that besieging armies piled next to the wall of the besieged city so that they would be able to get to the top and climb over.[36] Others say the word "סללה" means a catapult, a machine with which stones are thrown at the wall to break it. The phrase should be translated, "you will not bombard it with a catapult."[37]

This time a second reason was given for protecting Jerusalem. As before, G-d would protect it for the honor of His own name, but also for the sake of David and his righteous descendant, Hezekiah. G-d had promised David that as long as his descendants remained faithful they would be protected and their kingdom would never be defeated.[38]

Sanherib defeated Cush and Egypt as planned. Laden with spoils, he returned to continue his siege of Jerusalem. The fortune tellers advised him to attack immediately. They said, "Today is the last day that you will be able to conquer Jerusalem. Many years ago, David, the ancestor of Hezekiah, incurred guilt by causing the deaths of the priests of the city of Nob. G-d decreed that his descendants would be liable for punishment for it for many years. Today, however, is the last day of that decree. Tomorrow it will be over, as it says,[39] 'There remains yet today to stand in Nob.' If you don't go now you won't succeed!"

Sanherib and his army were still ten days' journey from Jerusalem, but they covered the distance in one day, as the prophet Isaiah said:[40]

> He came upon Aiath, passed through Migron, at Michmash he stores his supplies. They crossed a ford, rested at a resting place at Geba. Ramah trembled, Gibeath-shaul fled. "Raise your voice, Bath-galim! Listen Laish! Respond, Anathoth!" Madmenah wanders, the inhabitants of Gebim strengthen themselves. There remains yet today

to stand in Nob. He will shake his hand at the mountain of the daughter of Zion, the hill of Jerusalem.

They passed through all of these ten places, Aiath, Migron, Michmash, Ramah, Gibeath-shaul, Bath-galim, Laish, Anathoth, Madmenah, Gebim, until they got to the mountain overlooking Jerusalem. There, Sanherib had mats piled up so that he could get on top and view the whole city. When he saw how small it was he said, "Is this the city for which I mustered this great army, and for which I conquered the whole country? It is smaller and weaker than any of the cities and nations that I conquered!"

His advisers said, "Let's attack now!"

But he answered, "Why are you in such a hurry, when we are tired from our long journey?"

"Rest now," he told his soldiers, "and tomorrow each one of you will bring me a piece of stone from the walls and we will demolish it!"[41]

19:35-37 וַיְהִי בַּלַּיְלָה הַהוּא וַיֵּצֵא מַלְאַךְ ה׳ וַיַּךְ בְּמַחֲנֵה אַשּׁוּר מֵאָה
שְׁמוֹנִים וַחֲמִשָּׁה אָלֶף וַיַּשְׁכִּימוּ בַבֹּקֶר וְהִנֵּה כֻלָּם פְּגָרִים מֵתִים: וַיִּסַּע וַיֵּלֶךְ
וַיָּשָׁב סַנְחֵרִיב מֶלֶךְ־אַשּׁוּר וַיֵּשֶׁב בְּנִינְוֵה: וַיְהִי הוּא מִשְׁתַּחֲוֶה בֵּית נִסְרֹךְ אֱלֹהָיו
וְאַדְרַמֶּלֶךְ וְשַׂרְאֶצֶר (בָּנָיו קרי) הִכֻּהוּ בַחֶרֶב וְהֵמָּה נִמְלְטוּ אֶרֶץ אֲרָרָט וַיִּמְלֹךְ
אֵסַר־חַדֹּן בְּנוֹ תַּחְתָּיו:

That night an angel of G-d went out and smote in the camp of Assyria one hundred and eighty-five thousand. They got up in the morning, and behold, they were all dead bodies. Sanherib, King of Assyria, left and went and returned and lived in Nineveh. When he was bowing down in the temple of Nisroch, his god, Adramelech and Sarezer, his sons, smote him by the sword and escaped to the land of Ararat. Esarhadon, his son, became king in his place.

In the Book of Chronicles Sanherib's defeat is described this way:[42]

King Hezekiah and Isaiah ben Amoz the prophet prayed about this, and cried out to heaven. G-d sent an angel and cut off every mighty soldier, commander and officer in the camp of the King of Assyria, and he returned in shame to his land. He came into the house of his god, and his own children killed him by the sword. G-d saved Jehezekiah and the inhabitants of Jerusalem from the hand of the King of Assyria and from the hand of all, and guided them all around. And many were bringing tribute to G-d to Jerusalem and precious things to Jehezekiah, King of Judah. He was exalted in the eyes of all the nations from then on.

There were four kings who prayed for G-d's help, each of them making a greater request than the previous one, yet all were answered. David asked G-d to help him fight his enemies, as it says,[43] "May I pursue my enemies and catch them, and may I not return until finishing them off!" G-d granted his request, as it says,[44] "David smote them from dawn till evening of the next day."

Asa said, "I don't have the strength to kill my enemies. It is all I can do to pursue them. So please, Oh G-d, kill them for me!" His request, too, was granted, as it says,[45] "Asa and the people that were with him pursued them until Gerar. The Cushites fell without any strength to live, for they were broken before G-d and before His camp."

Jehoshaphat said, "I have strength neither to kill my enemies nor even to pursue them. However, I will sing Your praises while you defeat them for me!" And so G-d did, as it says,[46] "When they started with song and praise G-d put ambushes upon the Children of Amon, Moab and Mount Seir who came against Judah and smote them."

But Hezekiah said, "I don't have strength to kill or pursue. I can't even sing! So, while I lie on my bed, please defeat my enemies for me!" G-d granted his request too, as it says, "That night an angel of G-d went out and smote in the camp of Assyria one hundred and eighty-five thousand."[47]

That night was the first night of Passover, as it says,[48] "You will have a song like the night that the festival is sanctified."[49] As the Assyrians stood outside Jerusalem waiting to attack, Rabshakeh looked over the wall and heard the Jews singing Hallel. He was reminded that it was Passover, the time of redemption for the Jewish People, and went to Sanherib and said, "Go back! Miracles were performed for them on this night!" But Sanherib laughed at him and ignored his warning.[50]

The hundred and eighty-five thousand that were killed were all officers who wore crowns on their heads. Some say they were killed by a fire that entered their bodies and burnt their souls, leaving their bodies intact. Others say that their bodies were burnt on the inside, but the outside was undamaged, nor were their clothes burnt. They were thereby spared the disgrace of lying naked after their deaths. G-d showed the

Assyrians this respect even as He destroyed them because they were descendants of Shem, who had taken pains to avoid looking at his father, Noah, when he was naked. By his merit they too were spared this disgrace.[51]

By killing them in this way, G-d also made it clear to everyone that their defeat had been by a miracle, not by human means.[52] Sanherib's personal arrogance had been an implicit arrogance for all mankind, for it meant that a human being could overcome G-d. Only a miraculous defeat would demonstrate that he was wrong. Defeat by another army or by a natural accident would not have been sufficient.

How were they killed? Some say G-d smote them the same way He did the Egyptians at the Red Sea, which is described as "the great hand." Others say it was like the way the Egyptians were smitten by the ten plagues, which is called "the finger of G-d." Others say the angel Gabriel was passing through the land to cause the fruit to ripen. G-d said, "As you pass through, take care of these wicked ones as well!"

Some say G-d blew into their nostrils and they died, some that He clapped and they died, and others that He opened their eyes so that they could hear the singing of the angels. When they heard it they died, as it says,[53] "from the sound of the hosts nations are displaced, from Your loftiness the peoples are scattered."[54]

Unlike Pharaoh, who was punished by G-d Himself, Sanherib was smitten by an angel. Each was punished according to his own sin. Pharaoh had challenged G-d himself, saying,[55] "Who is G-d that I listen to His voice?" G-d therefore repaid him Himself, as it says,[56] "G-d stirred Egypt inside the sea." But since Sanherib did not blaspheme G-d himself, sending his messengers to do it instead, as it says above, "by the hand of your messengers you insulted G-d," G-d, too, punished him by a messenger, as it says, "an angel of G-d went out and smote in the camp of Assyria one hundred and eighty-five thousand."[57]

Even his victory over Cush and Egypt was then turned to a disgrace, for the captives that he had brought along were treated to seeing their oppressor vanquished. They saw as well the greatness of G-d's love for Israel. The mighty enemy that had conquered them was destroyed in a single night.[58]

Not only were the Jewish People saved from destruction, they were also able to claim all the spoils. Thus the prophet Isaiah said,[59] "I have made Egypt your ransom, Cush and Seba I have put in place of you," and again,[60] "The efforts of Egypt and the merchandise of Cush, and the Sabeans, men of measure, they will pass by you and they will be yours."

The downfall of Assyria was also their punishment for destroying the Kingdom of Israel and sending the people into exile. The plunder that they had taken from Israel was now reclaimed by the people of Jerusalem. But they had no obligation to search for the original owners and return it, because they had lost their rights to it when it was in the hands of the Assyrians.[61]

Hezekiah freed the captives, and they all recognized that G-d indeed controlled the whole world, and furthermore, that He cared about people and rewarded and punished them according to their deeds. They recognized the truth of the Torah, and that Israel is G-d's chosen People. They returned home as righteous gentiles and brought thanksgiving offerings in their own lands.[62] Thus the prophet Isaiah said,[63] "On that day there will be five cities in the land of Egypt speaking the language of Canaan and swearing to the G-d of H-sts. 'The City of Heres' will one be called. On that day there will be an altar to G-d in the midst of the land of Egypt, and a monument at its border to G-d."[64]

Some say that of the mighty army of Assyria there were only fourteen left, some say ten, some nine, and some say just five, Sanherib, his two sons, Nebuchadnezar and Nebuzaradan.[65] With them he fled and returned home. When he arrived, he asked his advisers why G-d had performed such a miracle to save the Jewish People. They told him that Abraham, the ancestor of the Jews, had been so dedicated to G-d that he had been ready to sacrifice his son for Him. G-d therefore protects his descendants forever. Sanherib decided that he too would have to earn a comparable merit if he ever wanted to overcome them in the future. Even if he no longer had such ambitions, he was now in danger of being overthrown and killed by his own people, who were enraged over the terrible defeat he had just brought them. The arrogant conqueror was driven to seek divine assistance at any cost. So he went to the temple of his god and promised that if he saved him he would sacrifice his own two sons. His sons, however, were not willing to be sacrificed to save their father's life. When they heard, they fell upon him and killed him.[66]

Some say the idol Nisroch was a board from the ark of Noah. Sanherib believed it was the power of that board that had saved Noah from the flood, so it would be able to save him too.[67]

Thus the wicked are punished according to their evil intentions. As Sanherib had planned to wipe out the Jewish People, so G-d wiped him and his followers out.[68]

G-d wanted to make Hezekiah the Messiah and the attack of Sanherib the war of Gog and Magog, the final tribulation of the Jewish People. The peace that followed would be everlasting, and there would never be an exile or destruction of the Temple. But Hezekiah and his generation failed to show proper gratitude for the wonderful salvation they had experienced. They offered no songs of praise and thanksgiving. It was thereupon argued that by the standards of justice they should not be granted that great favor. After all, G-d had not brought the final redemption in the time of King David, even though he had composed many songs of praise. Would it be fitting, then, to bring it for Hezekiah, for whom so many great miracles had been done, yet who sang no praises at all? There was no answer to this argument. The very earth itself tried to help Hezekiah by singing praises in his place, as it says,[69] "From the corners of the earth we have heard songs, glory for the righteous!" Still, it could not make up for his failure. G-d accepted the argument of justice, and their redemption remained a temporary one.[70]

II Kings 20

20:1-3 בַּיָּמִים הָהֵם חָלָה חִזְקִיָּהוּ לָמוּת וַיָּבֹא אֵלָיו יְשַׁעְיָהוּ בֶן־אָמוֹץ
הַנָּבִיא וַיֹּאמֶר אֵלָיו כֹּה־אָמַר ה׳ צַו לְבֵיתֶךָ כִּי מֵת אַתָּה וְלֹא תִחְיֶה: וַיַּסֵּב
אֶת־פָּנָיו אֶל־הַקִּיר וַיִּתְפַּלֵּל אֶל־ה׳ לֵאמֹר: אָנָּה ה׳ זְכָר־נָא אֵת אֲשֶׁר הִתְהַלַּכְתִּי
לְפָנֶיךָ בֶּאֱמֶת וּבְלֵבָב שָׁלֵם וְהַטּוֹב בְּעֵינֶיךָ עָשִׂיתִי וַיֵּבְךְּ חִזְקִיָּהוּ בְּכִי גָדוֹל:

In those days Hezekiah became deathly ill. Isaiah ben Amoz the prophet came to him and said to him, "Thus says G-d, 'Command your house, for you will die and not live!'" He turned his face to the wall and prayed to G-d saying, "Please, Oh G-d, remember how I went before You in truth and with a whole heart, and what was good in Your eyes I did!" And Hezekiah wept a great weeping.

The words, "In those days" refer to the time of the war with Assyria described in the preceding chapter. Some say the events described here took place three days before the miraculous destruction of Sanherib's army.[1] In G-d's answer to Hezekiah, of which we will read in the following verses, he was promised both that he would recover from his illness and that he and his people would be saved from Assyria. The second promise implies that it took place before Sanherib's army had been destroyed.[2] These events were recorded after the account of the war, however, because they are a separate subject. The account of Sanherib's attack and defeat are completed first, and then the account of Hezekiah's illness and cure.

According to this interpretation, Hezekiah's illness might have been the reason that he did not go personally to meet Rabshakeh, which was some time before this. He was then already ill, although not yet in danger of dying, for he was still well enough to go to the Temple and pray when he heard Rabshakeh's message.[3]

Others, however, maintain that the events occurred in the order in which they are recorded, Hezekiah's illness and cure occurring after the defeat of Sanherib. The assurance of being saved from Assyria that is described in these chapters refers to future attacks.[4] Although Assyria had been defeated, it remained a powerful empire, and Sanherib's successors might soon again try to conquer the Kingdom of Judah. The memory of his disastrous defeat would not deter them long.

The illness from which Hezekiah suffered was not natural. Some say it was because he had not shown proper respect in his prayers. Confident in his righteousness, his posture had been one of a person addressing his equal, not of a human being speaking to G-d. G-d said to Isaiah, "Doesn't a person's whole body tremble when he speaks to a human being who is greater and more powerful than himself? All the more so one who speaks to G-d!"[5]

Others say it was because he refused to marry and have children. It had been revealed to Hezekiah that he would have a very wicked son, who would undo all the reforms he had made. A period of corruption worse than any that the Jewish People had ever known before would follow. So terrible a prospect was this for the pious king that he preferred to die childless than be the cause of such evil. But, though Hezekiah's motives were pure, his decision was wrong. It was Hezekiah's obligation to marry and have children, and, to the best of his ability, to raise them according to the Torah. What would happen after that was out of his hands, and it was not his right to take it into consideration. It is not for a human being to consider what the future will bring in such cases.

However, no one had ever dared rebuke him, so he continued a long time in his error. For he was not only king, but also one of the wisest and most pious men of his generation. The only one who was his equal was his cousin, the prophet Isaiah. Isaiah would surely have rebuked him, but neither Hezekiah nor Isaiah had visited one another in many years. Each felt that it was unbefitting his position to pay such a visit. Hezekiah said, "It is the prophet who must visit the king, as Elijah visited Ahab." Isaiah said, "The king must go to the prophet, as Jehoram went to Elisha." Some say that is why when Hezekiah sought Isaiah's advice earlier, he sent messengers rather than going himself.[6] Others say it was because he was already too sick and weak.[7]

Finally, G-d arranged a compromise between them. He caused Hezekiah to become ill, so that Isaiah would visit him in fulfillment of the commandment of visiting the sick. It was then no longer a matter of a prophet deferring to the honor of a king. He might have done the same for any sick person. There he rebuked him and delivered his prophecy. He said, "Why have you not fulfilled the commandment of marrying and having children? Now you have been condemned to death because of it!"

Isaiah alluded to this by using the expression "house" in telling him to issue his last will. The word "house" includes kingdom, on the one hand, and family on the other. Since Hezekiah had no children, he would not have to decide how his property would be divided among them, nor which of them would be his successor. All that would remain would be his servants, and it would be to them alone that he was now to leave final instructions.[8]

By failing to marry, he not only neglected the commandment of having children, but, also of providing for the future leadership of the Jewish People. This helps explain the severity of his affliction. If, as king, he failed to assure the future of his people, then he was not worthy of a future himself. The double expression, "you will die and not live" means that he would suffer a double death. He would die in this world and not be granted life in the next world either.[9]

Hezekiah defended his decision. He said,"I did it because it has been revealed to me that my children will be wicked. Better, then, to have none at all!"

"The future is G-d's domain, not yours," answered Isaiah. "A person's responsibility is to fulfill the commandments that have been given him. G-d will take care of the future."

Hezekiah accepted Isaiah's criticism, but still he would not resign himself to fate. He knew that G-d's harsh decrees are never final. He answered, "If you will give me your daughter, I will marry her. Then, with your merit and mine together, perhaps my descendants will be righteous."

"Too late!" replied Isaiah, "The decree has already been made against you!"

"Then finish delivering your prophecy and leave!" said Hezekiah, "I know from the teachings of my ancestor, King David, that a person should not refrain from praying for G-d's mercy even if a sword is already touching his neck. King David saw the angel of death with his bloody sword stretched out over Jerusalem, yet he prayed and was answered. Jehoshaphat was about to be killed by the soldiers of Aram, but just before the sword descended upon his neck he cried out and was saved. I too will pray for mercy and perhaps I will be spared." So rather than issuing his last will as the prophet had told him, he turned toward the wall and prayed.[10]

Facing the wall signified several things. It was an allusion to the wall that the woman of Shunem had made for the prophet Elisha. Hezekiah prayed, "Oh G-d, You revived the son of the woman of Shunem by the merit of the little wall that she had made for Your prophet.

Remember, then, the walls that my ancestor, King Solomon, made, for Your own honor. He built You a Sanctuary and a Holy of Holies and covered the walls with gold! Remember that, and for his sake save me, his son, from the death that has been decreed upon me!"[11]

The wall also symbolized the walls of the heart, the innermost thoughts. He said, "I have looked at the walls of my heart and seen that I have not angered You with even a single limb of my body. Should I not therefore be spared?"[12]

It was also an allusion to Rahab, whose home was in the wall of Jericho and who saved the two spies sent by Joshua. Hezekiah said, "Rahab saved just two lives, and in return her whole family was saved. Even those who were married into her family were saved by her merit. Should I, whose ancestors saved so many people and brought countless heathens close to Torah, not be saved?"[13]

Some say the words "what was good in Your eyes I did" refer to his general piety. Others say they refer to the specific act of refraining from marriage. Though he erred, it had been for G-d's sake. He argued that he should therefore be forgiven.[14]

Another interpretation is that they refer to his hiding the book of cures that King Solomon had written. Years before, Hezekiah had seen that rather than turning toward G-d when they were afflicted, people relied upon doctors, who were able to cure them using the knowledge contained in this book. He considered that a failure to take proper advantage of the opportunity that physical affliction offers to come closer to G-d. A person can be cured in different ways, by natural physical means or by divine help. The availability of this book encouraged people to choose the former. Even the righteous king, Asa, many generations earlier, had made that mistake, and he was criticized for it, as it says,[15] "But in his sickness, too, he sought not G-d but the doctors." So, to force the people to rely upon G-d, Hezekiah hid the book. Now, he himself was in that position. He said, "Remember, it is by my own choice that I am praying now rather than seeking a natural cure, for I was the one who brought this situation about. I know that if it is Your will that a person die, being cured of one illness will not save him, for You may kill him in another way. The only ultimate cure is repentance."[16]

Others say the "good" he was referring to was the care with which he had always been accustomed to offer his prayers, even when he was not in grave danger as he was now. He had always been meticulous about prefacing his prayers with mention of G-d's great kindness in redeeming Israel from Egypt. This is considered a very important element of the proper form of prayer, and therefore when the communal prayers were composed, a blessing concerning the redemption from Egypt was instituted immediately before the main prayer. Between these two it is forbidden to interrupt.[17]

20:4-6 וַיְהִי יְשַׁעְיָהוּ לֹא יָצָא העיר (חָצֵר קרי) הַתִּיכֹנָה וּדְבַר־ה׳
הָיָה אֵלָיו לֵאמֹר: שׁוּב וְאָמַרְתָּ אֶל־חִזְקִיָּהוּ נְגִיד־עַמִּי כֹּה־אָמַר ה׳ אֱלֹהֵי דָּוִד
אָבִיךָ שָׁמַעְתִּי אֶת־תְּפִלָּתֶךָ רָאִיתִי אֶת־דִּמְעָתֶךָ הִנְנִי רֹפֶא לָךְ בַּיּוֹם הַשְּׁלִישִׁי
תַּעֲלֶה בֵּית ה׳: וְהֹסַפְתִּי עַל־יָמֶיךָ חֲמֵשׁ עֶשְׂרֵה שָׁנָה וּמִכַּף מֶלֶךְ־אַשּׁוּר אַצִּילְךָ
וְאֵת הָעִיר הַזֹּאת וְגַנּוֹתִי עַל־הָעִיר הַזֹּאת לְמַעֲנִי וּלְמַעַן דָּוִד עַבְדִּי:

Isaiah had not yet gone out of the inner courtyard and the word of G-d came to him saying, "Go back and say to Hezekiah, the Prince of My People, 'Thus says the L-rd, the G-d of David, your father, "I have heard your prayer, I have seen your tears. Behold, I will cure you! On the third day you will go up to the House of G-d! I will add fifteen years to your days, and from the hand of the King of Assyria will I save you and this city. I will protect this city for My sake and for the sake of David, My servant."' "

Indeed, it had never been G-d's will that Hezekiah die, but that he repent and marry. So He answered Hezekiah's prayer immediately, and sent Isaiah back to tell him without delay, before the news spread that Hezekiah was to be punished.[18] This time He referred to Hezekiah as "Prince of My People" both to emphasize his status in G-d's eyes and also to explain why the decree against him had been so severe. As king, he had a responsibility not only to himself but to the whole nation. His mistake could not have been left uncorrected, since it would have had such tragic consequences for the Jewish People. He had therefore been coerced to correct it in this extreme way.[19]

The reference to David in G-d's answer therefore has multiple significance. First, it is a confirmation of Hezekiah's piety. It was the righteous ways of David that he followed, not those of his own father, the wicked Ahaz.[20] G-d had not mentioned David when, several years earlier, He had reassured Ahaz that he would be protected from Assyria. Since Ahaz did not follow in the ways of David he did not deserve to be called David's son.[21] It also alludes to preservation of the line of David as the reason for G-d's insistence upon Hezekiah's marrying and having children.[22]

The cure would be a miracle. Hezekiah's illness was fatal, and there was no natural means by which it could be cured. This too, had been part of G-d's original plan, so that it would be clear to all that both the illness and the cure were of divine origin, not just natural occurrences.

Some say the fifteen years that were added to Hezekiah's life were years that he should have lived anyway, but that would have been taken away from him for neglecting the commandment of having children.[23] Others say he was destined to die at an early age, and the fifteen years he now received were an additional blessing. These extra fifteen years were to enable him to continue his reign until the son that would be born would be old enough to assume the throne. G-d made it a little longer than was absolutely necessary to show that it was not only for that reason, but also for Hezekiah's own merit. Also, these additional fifteen years would bring him to the age of fifty-four. To die at fifty-two or less is considered "כרת," which means, in this context, having one's life cut short. Had Hezekiah died at that age it would have appeared as if he were wicked and his death was a punishment. G-d did not want anyone to say that about Hezekiah after his death, for he was indeed among the most righteous and the greatest of kings.[24]

According to the first opinion, his punishment would have been in accordance with his sin. Just as he was cutting off the line of David, so his own life would be cut off.[25] Others say that even had he not had children, the line of David would not have ended. It would have been continued through someone else, since there were other descendants of David alive in that generation.[26]

The reference to David was also an implicit rebuke to Hezekiah for having referred to his own merit in his prayer, asking G-d to "remember how I went before You in truth and with a whole heart, and what was good in Your eyes I did!" G-d, in His answer, made no mention of Hezekiah's merit. Instead, he spoke of the merit of his ancestor, David. He said, "It is not for your own sake that I am forgiving you, but for the sake of your ancestors and the promise that I made to them." That is not to say that Hezekiah lacked merit and was not worthy of being forgiven, but that he should not have made that the basis of his request. No matter how righteous a person is, to ask to be repaid for his deeds implies that he considers himself pure enough to stand before G-d in judgment and be declared worthy. It also implies that he considers G-d's justice to be unfair, and that he deserves better treatment than he has been given. No one can do that. Everyone has some sin for which he could be held accountable, and most have many. So a person should always pray for mercy rather than justice, and not rely upon his own merit.[27]

One mistake led to another, and the seemingly minor impropriety of mentioning his good deeds in his prayer eventually led to dire punishment. Because he said, "What was good in Your eyes I did" he later said, "What sign is there that G-d will cure me?" Because he asked for and was granted a sign, the news of his miraculous cure spread. That led to heathens, the messengers of the King of Babylonia, eating at his table, as we will learn shortly. The indiscretions that he committed at that time eventually led to his descendants losing their freedom and becoming ministers in the royal palace of Babylonia.[28]

At the same time that G-d promised to cure Hezekiah, He also promised to save him and his people from Assyria. This was therefore a double salvation. The Book of Isaiah records the song of praise that Hezekiah offered at that time:[29]

> The writing of Hezekiah, King of Judah, in his illness, and he recovered from his illness. "I thought that in a fraction of my days I would go through the gates of the grave, that I had lost the rest of my years. I thought I would not see G-d, G-d in the land of the living, I would not look again upon a human being with those who live on the earth. Those of my generation have gone away, they have been exiled from me like a shepherd's tent. I have cut off my life like a weaver, from sickness it will tear me off, from both day and night You will finish me off. I thought I would survive only until morning, for it was like a lion. Thus did it break all my bones, from both day and night You will finish me off. Like a swallow or a crane I will whimper, I will moan like a dove. My eyes lifted up to heaven, 'Oh G-d, snatch me away, take up my cause.' What can I say that would be sufficient praise? He said to me and He did! I will push away all my sleep over the bitterness of my soul. 'Oh G-d, it is by You that all things live. Let the life of my soul be among them. Strengthen me and make me live! Behold, even in peace I had great bitterness, but then You desired my soul from the destruction of being worn out, for You threw all of my sins away as one who throws something behind his body. For it is not the grave that thanks You, nor death that praises You, for those who go down to the pit do not understand Your truth. He who lives, he who lives, he will thank You as I do this day! A father to sons will let Your truth be known! Oh G-d, it is you who will save me, and my music we will play all the days of our lives in the House of G-d.'"

20:7 וַיֹּאמֶר יְשַׁעְיָהוּ קְחוּ דְּבֶלֶת תְּאֵנִים וַיִּקְחוּ וַיָּשִׂימוּ עַל־הַשְּׁחִין וַיֶּחִי׃

Isaiah said, "Take pressed figs!" They took and put on the blister and it was healed.

Some say that G-d's promise was not that Hezekiah would be cured miraculously, but that he would recover in the natural way and not die. But Isaiah saw that Hezekiah was suffering from the blisters in the meantime, so he prescribed this treatment to relieve him. That is why this verse is introduced by the words, "Isaiah said." It was not part of Isaiah's original prophecy, the message that he delivered by G-d's instruction. It was his own idea to give this advice, which he knew by divine insight would be an effective remedy. It is therefore distinguished from the verses that precede it. But the blister was only a symptom of the disease, and relieving it alone would not have cured him. The cure could only come from G-d Himself.[30]

Others say, on the contrary, that the pressed figs were the divine cure that G-d promised. He revealed it to Isaiah, and now the prophet told Hezekiah. It was a double miracle. The nature of fruit like figs is to irritate the skin. Even healthy skin can become sore by prolonged contact with such substances, and certainly skin that is already diseased, yet this time the effect was just the opposite. G-d chose this as the means by which Hezekiah would be cured so that it would be clear that it was a miracle.[31]

20:8-11 וַיֹּאמֶר חִזְקִיָּהוּ אֶל־יְשַׁעְיָהוּ מָה אוֹת כִּי־יִרְפָּא ה׳ לִי וְעָלִיתִי
בַּיּוֹם הַשְּׁלִישִׁי בֵּית ה׳׃ וַיֹּאמֶר יְשַׁעְיָהוּ זֶה־לְּךָ הָאוֹת מֵאֵת ה׳ כִּי יַעֲשֶׂה ה׳
אֶת־הַדָּבָר אֲשֶׁר דִּבֵּר הָלַךְ הַצֵּל עֶשֶׂר מַעֲלוֹת אִם־יָשׁוּב עֶשֶׂר מַעֲלוֹת׃ וַיֹּאמֶר
יְחִזְקִיָּהוּ נָקֵל לַצֵּל לִנְטוֹת עֶשֶׂר מַעֲלוֹת לֹא כִּי יָשׁוּב הַצֵּל אֲחֹרַנִּית עֶשֶׂר
מַעֲלוֹת׃ וַיִּקְרָא יְשַׁעְיָהוּ הַנָּבִיא אֶל־ה׳ וַיָּשֶׁב אֶת־הַצֵּל בַּמַּעֲלוֹת אֲשֶׁר יָרְדָה
בְּמַעֲלוֹת אָחָז אֲחֹרַנִּית עֶשֶׂר מַעֲלוֹת׃

Hezekiah said to Isaiah, "What sign is there that G-d will cure me, and that I will go up on the third day to the House of G-d?" Isaiah said, "This is the sign for you from G-d, that G-d will do the thing that He said: The shadow will go ahead ten degrees or go back ten degrees." Hezekiah said, "It is easy for the shadow to bend ten degrees. No! Rather let the shadow go backwards ten degrees!" So Isaiah the prophet called to G-d, and He made the shadow go back in the degrees that it had gone down, in the degrees of Ahaz, ten degrees backwards.

When the prophet prescribed this remedy, Hezekiah became worried that perhaps he would not really be cured after all, and that Isaiah was just trying to comfort him. So he asked for a sign, a miracle that he could see right away, that would prove that G-d was really helping him and that he would really be cured, not just relieved.[32]

Not long before, there had been a miraculous occurrence. On the day that King Ahaz died there had been only two hours of daylight. The sun set ten hours early, so that his followers would have to bury him quickly and not have time to eulogize him.[33] He had been a wicked king, and G-d did not want him to be praised after his death. Now Isaiah offered to have that miracle repeated as the sign that Hezekiah would be cured. Alternately, Hezekiah could ask that the sun move backwards and set ten hours late. Hezekiah chose the latter, because he considered it a greater miracle. First of all, the other one had already happened once, so it no longer seemed so impressive. No one doubted that it could happen again. Moreover, it involved only an acceleration of the sun's usual motion, not a reversal. Hezekiah asked that the sun reverse its direction, which would be a qualitative change and therefore an undeniable miracle.[34]

As far as Isaiah was concerned, it made no difference. G-d could do one as easily as the other. The important thing was that Hezekiah himself choose the miracle before it was performed, so that afterwards he would be satisfied that it was a convincing proof. Isaiah could have proclaimed from the start that the sun move backwards and it would have happened, but that would not have had as great an effect as letting Hezekiah make the choice.[35]

Even though the miracle really involved the sun, it is described in terms of the shadow because a shadow symbolizes a person's life, as it says,[36] "Our days are a shadow on the earth." Isaiah said, "Your life was nearly over, like the shadow of the day that has passed. You are right to doubt that it can be saved. But if you see the day renewed, will you not be convinced that the same can happen to you?"[37]

Another reason that it is described in terms of the shadow is that it happened gradually, degree by degree, so that Hezekiah and all the other people could watch and witness it. Had the sun suddenly returned to its earlier position, they might had doubted that anything had happened at all. They might have thought that they had been mistaken earlier to think the sun had been higher up. But this way they saw it moving, so there could be no doubt about it.[38]

Another interpretation is that the miracle did not involve the sun at all, but only the light in the area of Jerusalem. There, and only there, had it become dark ten hours early on the day Ahaz died, and there too it remained light an extra ten hours on this day. To postpone the coming of darkness after the sun had set was a greater miracle than causing it to become dark while the sun was still in the sky. The latter could have been accomplished simply by obscuring the light of the sun, but the former required producing light where there was none. Furthermore, it was not only light, but light that cast a shadow like that of the sun, so it must have been shining from where the sun would have been and with similar intensity. While the sun continued in its normal course, its rays were bent so that they appeared to be coming from high up in the sky. In short, even though the sun itself did not actually move backwards, it appeared to the people in Jerusalem as if it had.[39]

G-d had prepared the sun for this miracle from the day it was created, as the Torah says concerning the creation of the sun and the other heavenly bodies,[40] "They will be for signs." G-d used them as signs for Joshua and for Hezekiah.[41]

20:12,13 בָּעֵת הַהִיא שָׁלַח בְּרֹאדַךְ בַּלְאֲדָן בֶּן־בַּלְאֲדָן מֶלֶךְ־בָּבֶל סְפָרִים
וּמִנְחָה אֶל־חִזְקִיָּהוּ כִּי שָׁמַע כִּי חָלָה חִזְקִיָּהוּ׃ וַיִּשְׁמַע עֲלֵיהֶם חִזְקִיָּהוּ וַיַּרְאֵם
אֶת־כָּל־בֵּית נְכֹתֹה אֶת־הַכֶּסֶף וְאֶת־הַזָּהָב וְאֶת־הַבְּשָׂמִים וְאֵת שֶׁמֶן הַטּוֹב וְאֵת
בֵּית כֵּלָיו וְאֵת כָּל־אֲשֶׁר נִמְצָא בְּאוֹצְרֹתָיו לֹא־הָיָה דָבָר אֲשֶׁר לֹא־הֶרְאָם
חִזְקִיָּהוּ בְּבֵיתוֹ וּבְכָל־מֶמְשַׁלְתּוֹ׃

At that time Berodach-Baladan, the son of Baladan, King of Babylonia, sent messages and presents to Hezekiah, for he heard that Hezekiah had been ill. Hezekiah listened to them and showed them his whole treasure house, the silver and the gold, the spices and the good oil, the house of his utensils and all that was found in his treasuries. There was not a thing that Hezekiah did not show them in his house and in his whole dominion.

Some say that until that time no one had ever recovered from such an illness, so the news spread and that was why the King of Babylonia heard about it.[42] Others say it was the miracle of the sun reversing its direction that brought it to his attention. It was his custom to take a nap in the middle of the day and get up in the afternoon. When he arose on the day of that miracle, he found that the sun was shining from the east. He thought that he must have slept through the afternoon and the whole next night, and it was now the following morning. He became enraged at his servants for letting him oversleep and wanted to kill them, until they told him how the sun had suddenly begun to move backwards while he was asleep. He sent messengers to find out the cause of this strange event, and eventually heard about Hezekiah's miraculous cure.[43]

Some say that this king was none other than the King of Assyria, the grandson of Sanherib himself. Once Assyria conquered Babylonia, its king took on the title of king of this ancient and respected country. Berodach's father was Esarhadon, the son and successor of Sanherib. Baladan was his Babylonian name, which he used as King of Babylonia. According to this opinion, this incident took place some time after the defeat of Sanherib, not before.[44]

Others say it took place during the siege, and this king was a vassal of the King of Assyria. He too would have liked to resist Assyria and regain his sovereignty as Hezekiah had, so he was very interested in the recent events in the Kingdom of Judah. Hezekiah saw him as an ally, and also thought that this would be a good opportunity to impress him with G-d's greatness. So, after recounting all the miracles that G-d performed for him and his people, he took the messengers into the Temple and even into the Holy of Holies. He opened up the Holy Ark, which had never been opened since the time it was made by Moses, showed them the Tablets of the Covenant, and said "With these we go to battle and are victorious!" This was a terrible desecration of the Temple and the holy objects, but Hezekiah did it with the best of intentions. HIs enthusiasm that a pagan king had shown interest in G-d's miracles led him to violate the boundaries of propriety.[45]

There are various interpretations of the words "בית נכתה," "his treasure house." Some say it means his secret treasures, some his armory. Others say he had his own wife wait on them and pour their drinks, and others that he showed them a weapon that could destroy other weapons.[46]

Some say "the good oil" was balsam oil, a special kind of fragrant oil made from the fruit of trees that grow only in the area of Jericho. It is from the fragrance (ריח) of this tree that Jericho (יריחו) gets its name. Others say it was the holy oil used in anointing.[47]

20:14,15 וַיָּבֹא יְשַׁעְיָהוּ הַנָּבִיא אֶל־הַמֶּלֶךְ חִזְקִיָּהוּ וַיֹּאמֶר אֵלָיו מָה־אָמְרוּ
הָאֲנָשִׁים הָאֵלֶּה וּמֵאַיִן יָבֹאוּ אֵלֶיךָ וַיֹּאמֶר חִזְקִיָּהוּ מֵאֶרֶץ רְחוֹקָה בָּאוּ מִבָּבֶל:
וַיֹּאמֶר מָה רָאוּ בְּבֵיתֶךָ וַיֹּאמֶר חִזְקִיָּהוּ אֵת כָּל־אֲשֶׁר בְּבֵיתִי רָאוּ לֹא־הָיָה דָבָר
אֲשֶׁר לֹא־הִרְאִיתִם בְּאֹצְרֹתָי:

Isaiah the prophet came to King Hezekiah and said to him, "What did these people say and from where did they come to you?" Hezekiah said, "From a distant land they came, from Babylonia." He said, "What did they see in your house?" Hezekiah said, "Everything that is in my house they saw. There was nothing that I did not show them in my treasuries."

There were four whom G-d tested by asking them a question, and who failed to answer correctly. They were Adam, Cain, Balaam and Hezekiah. When G-d asked Adam whether he had eaten the fruit of the forbidden tree, he should have taken responsibility and admitted his guilt. Instead, he answered, "The woman that You gave me, she gave me and I ate!" He blamed his wife, and even implied that it was G-d's own fault for giving her to him. G-d asked Cain where his brother, Abel, was, and instead of admitting to have killed him, he lied and said he didn't know. G-d asked Balaam who the men were that had come to visit him. He should have said, "Oh G-d, You know!" Instead he boasted "Balak ben Zipor, King of Moab, sent to me."

Hezekiah should have said, "You, Isaiah, are G-d's prophet. You know who they are and what I showed them!" By trying to cover up his mistake rather than admitting it and asking for forgiveness, he made his sin worse and incurred a greater punishment.[48]

Hezekiah knew that it is dangerous to reveal detailed information about a country to foreigners. One day they might become enemies and it could be used against them. For purely practical reasons, therefore, what he had done was foolish. In telling Isaiah about it, he made a point that the people had come from a distant land, so they posed no threat.

20:16-18 וַיֹּאמֶר יְשַׁעְיָהוּ אֶל־חִזְקִיָּהוּ שְׁמַע דְּבַר־ה׳: הִנֵּה יָמִים בָּאִים וְנִשָּׂא
כָּל־אֲשֶׁר בְּבֵיתֶךָ וַאֲשֶׁר אָצְרוּ אֲבֹתֶיךָ עַד־הַיּוֹם הַזֶּה בָּבֶלָה לֹא־יִוָּתֵר דָּבָר אָמַר
ה׳: וּמִבָּנֶיךָ אֲשֶׁר יֵצְאוּ מִמְּךָ אֲשֶׁר תּוֹלִיד יִקָּחוּ וְהָיוּ סָרִיסִים בְּהֵיכַל מֶלֶךְ בָּבֶל:

Isaiah said to Hezekiah, "Listen to the word of G-d! 'Behold, days are coming when everything that is in your house and what your fathers gathered until this day will be taken to Babylonia. There will be nothing left!' says G-d. 'And of your children that will come forth from you, that you will bear, will be taken, and they will be ministers in the palace of the King of Babylonia!' "

But it was not for his practical foolishness that Hezekiah was rebuked. Hezekiah had failed to conduct himself with the proper humility when he met the representatives from Babylonia. Though it was commendable that he tried to impress them with G-d's greatness, he presented it in a way that boasted of the greatness of Israel as well. He made it seem that it was because of their own special qualities rather than G-d's love and mercy that they could always count on Him to help them.

He also committed a serious desecration of the Temple by bringing heathens inside. G-d said, "It was bad enough that you showed them the treasures of the kings of Judah and of the Temple, but you went so far as to open the Ark and show them the Tablets, the work of My hands! As you live, they will come and take all those treasures, and in place of the tablets your descendants will be taken!"[49]

Hezekiah was therefore guilty of three sins. Firstly, he became proud of his success, when the credit was really all due to G-d, not to him at all.[50] Secondly, he should never have shown them even his own personal treasures, much less the inner rooms of the Temple into which it is forbidden for any but the most pure and holy to enter. Thirdly, he failed to properly explain the miracles and the aspect of divine mercy, making it seem, rather, to be the special quality of the Jewish People. Therefore in the Book of Chronicles it says,[51] "But not like the favors had been done for him did Hezekiah answer, for his heart had become high, and there was wrath upon him and upon Judah and Jerusalem."

It should not, however, be inferred from this verse that Hezekiah's sin was the cause of the exile. It was the sinfulness of the Jewish People themselves that was to bring this terrible punishment upon them. G-d would certainly not have punished the entire people for the sins of the king. On the contrary, it was his merit that saved them. Through Hezekiah's righteousness the exile was postponed, and G-d extended His patience toward the Jewish People.[52]

The meaning of this prophecy is rather that Hezekiah's actions would be a sign of the future, an indication of what was to happen to his descendants and his people. As he had refrained from marrying, thereby making himself like one who is incapable of having children, so his descendants would be rendered incapable of having children and be made ministers of the King of Babylonia. As he had welcomed the messengers from Babylonia, so the army of Babylonia would one day come and have free access to the Land of Israel. And as they had seen all his treasures, so they would be able to take them all away. There would be nothing left after their pillage, just as there had been nothing that he did not show them.[53]

The words "everything that is in your house" are an allusion to the holy utensils of the Temple. The extra words "there will be nothing left" are added to include even the most holy of all, the Tablets of the Covenant. These two phrases correspond to the phrases, "Everything that is in my house" and "there was nothing" used by Hezekiah in his answer to Isaiah. In both cases, the second phrase is redundant, so it is understood to refer to something extra that one would otherwise have assumed not to have been included.

But seeing Hezekiah's sincere remorse, G-d rescinded this harsh decree. In place of the Ark and the Tablets He accepted Hezekiah's descendants as an atonement. So the Ark was hidden before the Babylonians came, and Daniel, Hananiah, Mishael, Azariah and other children of the royal family were taken into exile instead.[54] That is why there are two parts to this prophecy, separated by the words "says G-d." In the second, the word "says", (אמר) is used instead of "word" (דבר). "אמר" indicates something said gently, whereas "דבר" indicates something harsh.[55]

The word "סריסים," "ministers," literally means eunuchs, but it is generally used to refer to the servants or ministers of a king or powerful person. Some say that it is in that sense that it is used in this verse.[56] Others say that it is being used literally.[57] The children of the royal household were taken to the palace of the King of Babylonia to be raised there so that they would grow up to be loyal to him. He planned to then appoint them to govern their people in his name.[58]

Another interpretation of the word "סריסים" is that through these children, the idols would be castrated. That is, they would be shown to be powerless, as is described in the Book of Daniel. They would risk their lives by defying the order to worship idols, and be miraculously saved.[59]

Thus, while this was primarily a prophecy of rebuke and punishment, it contained an element of reward and merit as well. Hezekiah understood that he would indeed be granted righteous descendants, for they would be worthy of being an atonement for the Holy Ark, of sanctifying G-d's name, and of refuting idolatry. The divine decree included elements of reward as well as punishment, just as Hezekiah's actions had been a mixture of piety and error. His intention had been to impress the messengers with G-d's greatness, but he had done it improperly. His children were condemned to exile as punishment for his mistake, but within that punishment was the opportunity for great merit. It was therefore also a reward. In exile they rose to greatness by glorifying G-d's name as Hezekiah himself had wanted to do.[60]

Some say that the Ark of the Covenant was indeed taken into exile. According to those who say it was not, there are various opinions of what happened to it. Some say it was swallowed up by the ground beneath the Holy of Holies, for in the description of the building of the Temple it says that the Ark remained there "to this day,"[61] implying that whenever the verse would be read, the Ark would be there. Others say it was removed and hidden by the priests.[62]

20:19 וַיֹּאמֶר חִזְקִיָּהוּ אֶל־יְשַׁעְיָהוּ טוֹב דְּבַר־ה׳ אֲשֶׁר דִּבַּרְתָּ וַיֹּאמֶר הֲלוֹא
אִם־שָׁלוֹם וֶאֱמֶת יִהְיֶה בְיָמָי׃

Hezekiah said to Isaiah, "The word of G-d that you said is good!" He said, "Is it not true that there will be peace and truth in my days?"

Hezekiah's response seems very strange. Did he care only about himself and not his children, that he thought it good that they suffer? Did he have no concern about the future, that he was satisfied as long as he and his generation were spared? Some say that this exclamation was not in response to the prophecy of destruction and exile. Concerning that he was, indeed, deeply grieved. But he realized that it could not be avoided and had already resigned himself to it. In spite of all his reforms, the evil that was seething within the people had not been extinguished. Even among his own descendants it would soon burst into flames again. Rather, he was relieved to hear that this inevitable punishment would be postponed at least until after his death. He had feared that, having been granted extra years, he would live to endure it himself. Perhaps he had even begun to regret having prayed to be cured. It would be better to die than to live to see that.[63] So he was relieved and reassured by the knowledge that the merit of his righteousness would be sufficient to protect his people, at least during his lifetime.

Another interpretation is that Hezekiah was happy to hear that he would have righteous descendants who would be worthy of being an atonement for the Holy Ark. Not only was he not condemned to having only wicked descendants, as he had feared, but that the sin of showing the Ark to the Babylonians would be rectified by his own descendants. He was therefore greatly relieved by Isaiah's prophecy.[64]

20:20,21 וְיֶתֶר דִּבְרֵי חִזְקִיָּהוּ וְכָל־גְּבוּרָתוֹ וַאֲשֶׁר עָשָׂה אֶת־הַבְּרֵכָה וְאֶת־
הַתְּעָלָה וַיָּבֵא אֶת־הַמַּיִם הָעִירָה הֲלֹא־הֵם כְּתוּבִים עַל־סֵפֶר דִּבְרֵי הַיָּמִים
לְמַלְכֵי יְהוּדָה׃ וַיִּשְׁכַּב חִזְקִיָּהוּ עִם־אֲבֹתָיו וַיִּמְלֹךְ מְנַשֶּׁה בְנוֹ תַּחְתָּיו׃

The rest of the things about Hezekiah and all of his might, and that he made the pool and the channel and brought the water into the city, are indeed written in the Book of the Chronicles of the Kings of Judah. Hezekiah lay down with his fathers, and his son Manasseh became king in his place.

Some say that Isaiah gave Hezekiah his daughter as he had requested, and they had two sons. They called one Manasseh and the other Rabshakeh. One day he put the two boys on his shoulders to bring them to school. One said, "Father's head looks good for tanning!" The other said, "Father's head looks good for sacrificing to idols on it!" He could not stand having such wicked children, and he threw them to the ground. Rabshakeh died and Manasseh survived.[65]

Hezekiah is remembered for having made six innovations. Of three of these the rabbis approved and of three they did not. He hid the book of cures, destroyed the copper snake, and defiled the remains of his wicked father, Ahaz, by dragging his bones on a bed of ropes. Of these three they approved. But they did not approve of his diverting the flow of the spring of Gihon and closing up the original outlet, of his cutting up the golden doors of the Sanctuary to send tribute to the King of Assyria, nor of his extending the year during the month of Nisan.[66]

The incident of Hezekiah's extending the year in the month of Nisan is described in the Book of Chronicles, in the section quoted in the preceding chapter. Seeing that the people didn't have enough time to purify themselves, he had the month declared Adar II instead of Nisan, thereby postponing Passover by one month. The rabbis disaproved because this violated the rule that the extra month can only be added while it is still Adar, not once Nisan has begun.

Some say the Temple had become impure because the skull of Araunah, the Jebusite from whom the Temple Mount was purchased by David, was found beneath the altar.[67]

Some say the great accomplishments of Hezekiah in teaching and spreading Torah are alluded to in the Book of Psalms by the words,[68] "Honorable things are said of you." The bringing of water into Jerusalem can also be understood symbolically as bringing in Torah. Thus too, it is recorded in the Book of Proverbs[69] that some of the proverbs of Solomon were collected and recorded under Hezekiah's supervision.[70]

II Kings 21

21:1-5 בֶּן־שְׁתֵּים עֶשְׂרֵה שָׁנָה מְנַשֶּׁה בְמָלְכוֹ וַחֲמִשִּׁים וְחָמֵשׁ שָׁנָה מָלַךְ
בִּירוּשָׁלָםִ וְשֵׁם אִמּוֹ חֶפְצִי־בָהּ׃ וַיַּעַשׂ הָרַע בְּעֵינֵי ה׳ כְּתוֹעֲבֹת הַגּוֹיִם אֲשֶׁר הוֹרִישׁ
ה׳ מִפְּנֵי בְּנֵי יִשְׂרָאֵל׃ וַיָּשָׁב וַיִּבֶן אֶת־הַבָּמוֹת אֲשֶׁר אִבַּד חִזְקִיָּהוּ אָבִיו וַיָּקֶם
מִזְבְּחֹת לַבַּעַל וַיַּעַשׂ אֲשֵׁרָה כַּאֲשֶׁר עָשָׂה אַחְאָב מֶלֶךְ יִשְׂרָאֵל וַיִּשְׁתַּחוּ לְכָל־צְבָא
הַשָּׁמַיִם וַיַּעֲבֹד אֹתָם׃ וּבָנָה מִזְבְּחֹת בְּבֵית ה׳ אֲשֶׁר אָמַר ה׳ בִּירוּשָׁלַםִ אָשִׂים
אֶת־שְׁמִי׃ וַיִּבֶן מִזְבְּחוֹת לְכָל־צְבָא הַשָּׁמָיִם בִּשְׁתֵּי חַצְרוֹת בֵּית־ה׳׃

Manasseh was twelve years old when he became king, and he reigned fifty-five years in Jerusalem. His mother's name was Hephzibah. He did what was evil in G-d's eyes, like the abominations of the nations that G-d had driven out before the Children of Israel. He rebuilt the shrines that Hezekiah, his father, had destroyed, and erected altars for Baal. He made an Asherah as Ahab, King of Israel, had made, and bowed down to the whole host of the heavens and served them. He built altars in the House of G-d, of which G-d had said, "In Jerusalem I will put My name." He built altars for the whole host of the heavens in the two courtyards of the House of G-d.

The name Manasseh was an allusion to his sin. He forgot (נשה) G-d and made the people forget G-d too.[1] His mother was the daughter of Isaiah. She was called "Hephzibah," which means "She is my desire," because she was the only one that Hezekiah desired to marry. He had originally not wanted to marry and have children rather than have a wicked son as had been foretold. But he agreed to marry the daughter of Isaiah, whose virtue he hoped would protect him.[2]

In spite of everything that his father had taught him and the example he had set for him, Manasseh rebelled against G-d and rejected the Torah. He deviated from the Torah in ways that had never been done in previous generations. Earlier generations had worshiped idols together with G-d. None had ever tried to eliminate the service of G-d and replace it with idolatry. They had corrupted the Torah, but not denied it. Manasseh not only worshiped idols, but tried to abolish the worship of G-d. He extinguished the fire on the altar that had come down from heaven when the Temple was dedicated by Solomon and had burnt there ever since.[3] He was therefore compared to the heathen nations rather than to the sinners of Israel.

The only one among the earlier generations to whom Manasseh could be compared was Ahab, King of Israel. Ahab, too, had tried to abolish the Torah and persecuted those who continued to serve G-d. The new level of corruption that Ahab had introduced was continued for several generations after him by his descendants, including his son-in-law, Joram, King of Judah, and then by Joram's son, Ahaziah. Ahaziah went so far as to adulterate the Torah by erasing G-d's name and replacing it with the names of idols.

But in these things, Ahab and his successors had been opposed by their people. During those generations, the people of both kingdoms served G-d and did not question the truth of Torah, deviating only from the manner of service that the Torah prescribed. The people of the Kingdom of Israel worshiped G-d at the shrines of the golden calves, and the people of Judah supplemented the Temple service with sacrifices at local altars. The sort of idolatry introduced by Manasseh was violently opposed by those generations.[4]

These verses describe several stages of Manasseh's wickedness. First, he "did what was evil in G-d's eyes," that is, he personally sinned. Then he "rebuilt the shrines that Hezekiah, his father, had destroyed," thereby influencing others to sin as well. After that he "erected altars for Baal" and "made an Asherah," by which he sank even further, to worship actual idolatry. In that he was like Ahab, King of Israel. But after that he "bowed down to the whole host of the heavens and served them," which even Ahab had not done. Finally he "built altars in the House of G-d," the most severe of all desecrations.[5]

The two courtyards mentioned here were the Courtyard of the Priests and the Courtyard of Israel.[6]

21:6 וְהֶעֱבִיר אֶת־בְּנוֹ בָּאֵשׁ וְעוֹנֵן וְנִחֵשׁ וְעָשָׂה אוֹב וְיִדְּעֹנִים הִרְבָּה
לַעֲשׂוֹת הָרַע בְּעֵינֵי ה׳ לְהַכְעִיס׃

He passed his son in fire, observed auspicious times and omens, and consulted mediums and oracles. He did much that was evil in G-d's eyes to anger Him.

Among the most cruel and unnatural cults was that of Molech. The idol of Molech had the face of a calf and its hands were extended as if to accept a gift. It was made of metal and hollow inside, so that a fire could be made there and the idol would become burning hot. Then sacrifices could be put on its hands where they would roast and burn up. Molech accepted many kinds of offerings, but the most desired were human children. Devoted parents would bring their babies and the priests would place them on the hands of the idol to be burnt alive.

To offer a child to Molech in this way was considered a very noble deed, and attended by commensurate honor. In front of the idol of Molech were seven mesh curtains. If a worshiper brought an offering of fine flour, the first curtain would be moved aside and he would be permitted to enter, but six curtains would still separate him from the idol. For a worshiper who brought a sacrifice of doves, two curtains would be moved aside. One who brought a lamb would be permitted past three curtains, one who brought a ram past four, a calf past five and a bull past six. But only one who brought his child to be sacrificed would be permitted to pass through all seven curtains and stand in the presence of the god. He would kiss the idol and put the child down in front of it. Then the priests would light the fire inside until the hands of the idols became burning hot, and take the child and put it on them. Meanwhile, other priests would beat on drums so that the father would not hear the cries of his child and be overcome by pity and save him.[7]

Perhaps the heathen nations that had practiced this for generations sincerely believed that it was a desirable sacrifice for their god, but for Jews it must have been shocking and repulsive. No god worth worshiping would want a person to do such a thing. The only reason for introducing such an abominable practice was to defy G-d. So intent was Manasseh to rebel and proclaim his independence from G-d that he was ready to mercilessly kill his own children.[8] Some say he eventually sacrificed all of them in this way, and that Amon, who succeeded him, was born after he repented.[9]

21:7 וַיָּשֶׂם אֶת־פֶּסֶל הָאֲשֵׁרָה אֲשֶׁר עָשָׂה בַּבַּיִת אֲשֶׁר אָמַר ה׳ אֶל־דָּוִד
וְאֶל־שְׁלֹמֹה בְנוֹ בַּבַּיִת הַזֶּה וּבִירוּשָׁלַםִ אֲשֶׁר בָּחַרְתִּי מִכֹּל שִׁבְטֵי יִשְׂרָאֵל אָשִׂים
אֶת־שְׁמִי לְעוֹלָם׃

He put the statue of the Asherah that he had made in the House of which G-d had said to David and to Solomon, his son, "In this House and in Jerusalem, that I chose from all the tribes of Israel, I will put My name forever."

Manasseh's grandfather, Ahaz, had already introduced idolatry, but he had not dared to bring an idol into the Holy Temple. He reduced the directness of his confrontation with G-d by placing the idol on the roof. But for Manasseh, the very purpose of idolatry was to defy G-d, and the most extreme defiance he could show was to place the idol in the Temple itself. After a while, even that did not satisfy him. He remodeled his idol, giving it four faces, one in each direction. In that way, symbolically, from whichever direction G-d looked into the Temple, the idol would be confronting him. Therefore, while both here and in the Book of Chronicles[10] it says that Manasseh put a single idol in the sanctuary, later in the Book of Chronicles[11] there is reference to his having made "idols," in the plural. This single idol was considered like several because it had several faces.[12]

In this way Manasseh hoped to drive the Holy Presence out of the Temple, and indeed, G-d's presence left while the idol was there.[13] The idol made the Temple unfit for G-d's dwelling as leprosy on a wall would do to the house of a human being. G-d went to the prophet Jeremiah, who was a priest, to have the Temple declared unclean, as a Jew would do if he discovered leprosy in his house, as it says in the Torah,[14] "He will tell the priest, saying, 'Something like leprosy was seen by me in the house.'" What was it? It was Manasseh's idol! Thus the prophet Ezekiel said,[15] "Behold, north of the Gate of the Altar was this image of jealousy at the entrance." G-d could not stand to remain there together with it, as the husband of an unfaithful wife cannot stand to be together with her lover. Thus the prophet Isaiah said,[16] "For the bed is too short to stretch out, the molten image makes it too crowded to come inside."[17]

Some say that until then, the golden trees that Solomon had engraved on the walls of the Temple miraculously bore golden fruit every year, but when Manasseh put the idol in the Sanctuary they withered.[18]

21:8 וְלֹא אֹסִיף לְהָנִיד רֶגֶל יִשְׂרָאֵל מִן־הָאֲדָמָה אֲשֶׁר נָתַתִּי לַאֲבוֹתָם
רַק אִם־יִשְׁמְרוּ לַעֲשׂוֹת כְּכֹל אֲשֶׁר צִוִּיתִים וּלְכָל־הַתּוֹרָה אֲשֶׁר־צִוָּה אֹתָם עַבְדִּי
מֹשֶׁה׃

"And I will not continue to make the feet of Israel wander from the land that I gave to their fathers, provided that they are careful to do according to all that I commanded them, and the whole Torah that My servant Moses commanded them."

At first, it seems surprising that the promise that the Jewish People would not be made to wander any more was made at the time of the building of the First Temple. At that time they had not yet experienced a complete exile, except for the years of slavery in Egypt. That would not generally be considered an exile, since at that time they had not yet been established as a nation in their own homeland. The two terrible exiles with which we are familiar still lay far in the future. But, as is recorded in the Book of Judges, they had already experienced numerous conquests in which much of their territory was lost. During that period, "the feet of Israel" were indeed forced to wander from portions that they had received. At the time of the building of the Temple much of that territory had only recently been reconquered. The memory of those days was still fresh in the minds of the people, and this promise of national security addressed their fears.

In His promise to Israel, G-d mentioned two catagories of commandments, those that "I commanded them," and those that "My servant Moses commanded them." The first refers to the two commandments,[19] "I am the L-rd, your G-d" and "You will not have any other gods before Me." These two were heard by all Israel directly from G-d at Mount Sinai. The words, "that My servant Moses commanded them" refer to the rest of the commandments, which G-d told to Moses, and which Moses then taught to the people.[20]

21:9-13 וְלֹא שָׁמֵעוּ וַיַּתְעֵם מְנַשֶּׁה לַעֲשׂוֹת אֶת־הָרָע מִן־הַגּוֹיִם אֲשֶׁר הִשְׁמִיד
ה׳ מִפְּנֵי בְּנֵי יִשְׂרָאֵל: וַיְדַבֵּר ה׳ בְּיַד־עֲבָדָיו הַנְּבִיאִים לֵאמֹר: יַעַן אֲשֶׁר עָשָׂה
מְנַשֶּׁה מֶלֶךְ־יְהוּדָה הַתֹּעֵבוֹת הָאֵלֶּה הֵרַע מִכֹּל אֲשֶׁר־עָשׂוּ הָאֱמֹרִי אֲשֶׁר לְפָנָיו
וַיַּחֲטִא גַם־אֶת־יְהוּדָה בְּגִלּוּלָיו: לָכֵן כֹּה־אָמַר ה׳ אֱלֹהֵי יִשְׂרָאֵל הִנְנִי מֵבִיא
רָעָה עַל־יְרוּשָׁלַם וִיהוּדָה אֲשֶׁר כָּל־מעיו (שֹׁמְעָהּ קרי) תִּצַּלְנָה שְׁתֵּי אָזְנָיו:
וְנָטִיתִי עַל־יְרוּשָׁלַם אֵת קַו שֹׁמְרוֹן וְאֶת־מִשְׁקֹלֶת בֵּית אַחְאָב וּמָחִיתִי
אֶת־יְרוּשָׁלַם כַּאֲשֶׁר־יִמְחֶה אֶת־הַצַּלַּחַת מָחָה וְהָפַךְ עַל־פָּנֶיהָ:

But they didn't listen, and Manasseh made them go astray, to do worse than the nations that G-d had destroyed before the Children of Israel. G-d spoke by the hand of His servants, the prophets, saying, "Since Manasseh, King of Judah, did these abominations, he did worse than everything that the Emorites that were before him had done, and made Judah, too, sin with his idols. Therefore thus says the L-rd, the G-d of Israel, 'Behold, I am bringing evil upon Jerusalem and Judah, such that everyone who hears it, his two ears will ring. I will stretch out upon Jerusalem the string of Samaria and the plumb-line of the house of Ahab. I will wipe out Jerusalem as one wipes a plate clean, wiping it out and turning it over.' "

Some say the people of Manasseh's generation were righteous, but they had a bad leader. The generation of the prophet Samuel was the opposite. The people were bad but their leader was righteous. There were other generations in which both the people and their leader were righteous, and others, like that of Zedekiah, where both people and leader were corrupt.

Three prophets, Joel, Nahum and Habakuk, prophesied in the time of Manasseh, but his name is not mentioned in any of their prophecies. So wicked was Manasseh that it would have been an undue honor to have a prophet referred to as having prophesied in his days.[21] Other wicked kings were mentioned in that way, but none were as bad as Manasseh.

The words "string" and "plumb-line" refer to tools used in building. The first is the string that is stretched from the place at which one end of the wall is to be to the place of the other end, so that the bricks or stones can be laid straight. The plumb-line is a string with a weight at one end that is suspended from above the first row of bricks, so that the following rows will all be directly above one another.[22]

Here these expressions are used allegorically to refer to the opposite, to destruction.[23] Jerusalem had been condemned to complete chaos and formlessness. Whereas these tools are used to assure a building will have the proper form, Jerusalem, in its destruction, would be deprived of all form, just as the kingdom of Ahab had been before it.

The comparison of Jerusalem to a plate that has been wiped clean and turned over indicates both the totality of the destruction and how it would take place. Turning over the plate is a sign that it is finished and not to be eaten from any more.[24] First the population would be driven out into exile, like the food that is eaten from the plate. Then, after it was empty, the city itself would be overturned.[25]

21:14,15 וְנָטַשְׁתִּי אֵת שְׁאֵרִית נַחֲלָתִי וּנְתַתִּים בְּיַד אֹיְבֵיהֶם וְהָיוּ לְבַז
וְלִמְשִׁסָּה לְכָל־אֹיְבֵיהֶם: יַעַן אֲשֶׁר עָשׂוּ אֶת־הָרַע בְּעֵינַי וַיִּהְיוּ מַכְעִסִים אֹתִי
מִן־הַיּוֹם אֲשֶׁר יָצְאוּ אֲבוֹתָם מִמִּצְרַיִם וְעַד הַיּוֹם הַזֶּה:

"I will abandon the remainder of My inheritance and give them over into the hands of their enemies. They will be for plunder and trampling for all their enemies. Because they did what was evil in My eyes and have been angering Me, from the day that their fathers went out of Egypt till this very day."

After their defeat, all their enemies would come and plunder them, even those that had not taken part in the conquest itself. Thus in describing the conquest the Bible speaks of their being given over "into the hands of their enemies," but in describing the subsequent plunder it speaks of "all their enemies."[26]

21:16 וְגַם דָּם נָקִי שָׁפַךְ מְנַשֶּׁה הַרְבֵּה מְאֹד עַד אֲשֶׁר־מִלֵּא אֶת־יְרוּשָׁלַםִ
פֶּה לָפֶה לְבַד מֵחַטָּאתוֹ אֲשֶׁר הֶחֱטִיא אֶת־יְהוּדָה לַעֲשׂוֹת הָרַע בְּעֵינֵי ה׳:

And also very much innocent blood did Manasseh spill, until he had filled Jerusalem from one end to the other, aside from his sin that he made Judah sin, to do what was evil in G-d's eyes.

Manasseh committed offenses not only against G-d, but against man as well. He ruthlessly suppressed those who opposed him, and some say that even the great prophet, Isaiah, was killed by Manasseh. Manasseh tried him and sentenced him to death. He said, "Moses, your master, said of G-d,[27] 'No man can see Me and live' but you said,[28] 'I saw G-d.' Moses, your master, said,[29] 'Who is like the L-rd, our G-d, whenever we call to Him,' but you said,[30] 'Seek G-d when He is available, call Him when He is close.' Moses, your master, said,[31] 'The number of your days I will fill,' but you said,[32] 'I will add fifteen years to your days.' "

Isaiah thought, "I know that if I tell him the answers he will not accept them, so it is better that I not tell him. Let his sin remain one of ignorance." So he pronounced G-d's name and was swallowed up into the trunk of a cedar tree. But Manasseh would not let him escape so easily. He had his servants saw the tree in half. When they came to the prophet's mouth he died.[33] The death of this one exceptionally righteous person was considered like filling Jerusalem with blood from one end to the other.

Others say Manasseh really did kill thousands of people. He made an idol that required one thousand men to lift. Every day he had a thousand men carry it and they all died.[34]

The expression "פה לפה," "from one end to the other," literally means "from mouth to mouth." Some say it is an allusion to the rebukes of Isaiah and the retorts Manasseh gave him.[35] Others say it is a reference to Isaiah himself. He was compared to Moses, who spoke to G-d "mouth to mouth." Another interpretation is that Manasseh's sins were so shocking that throughout the city people spoke about them to one another.[36]

The people followed Manasseh's example. Not only idolatry, but violence too, became widespread.[37] Manasseh was held partially responsible for all their offenses.

21:17,18 וְיֶתֶר דִּבְרֵי מְנַשֶּׁה וְכָל־אֲשֶׁר עָשָׂה וְחַטָּאתוֹ אֲשֶׁר חָטָא הֲלֹא־
הֵם כְּתוּבִים עַל־סֵפֶר דִּבְרֵי הַיָּמִים לְמַלְכֵי יְהוּדָה׃ וַיִּשְׁכַּב מְנַשֶּׁה עִם־אֲבֹתָיו
וַיִּקָּבֵר בְּגַן־בֵּיתוֹ בְּגַן־עֻזָּא וַיִּמְלֹךְ אָמוֹן בְּנוֹ תַּחְתָּיו׃

The rest of the things about Manasseh and everything that he did, and his sin that he sinned, are indeed written in the Book of the Chronicles of the Kings of Israel. Manasseh lay down with his fathers. He was buried in the garden of his house, in the Garden of Uzza, and Amon, his son, became king in his place.

In the Book of Chronicles it says:[38]

> G-d brought upon them the officers of the army of the King of Assyria, and they captured Manasseh with hooks. They bound him in chains and brought him to Babylonia. When he was in distress he begged the L-rd, his G-d, and was greatly humbled before the G-d of his fathers. He prayed to Him and He accepted his prayer and listened to his supplication. He returned him to Jerusalem, to his kingdom. Then Manasseh knew that the L-rd is G-d. After that he built an outer wall for the City of David, west of Gihon, in the valley, to the entrance of the Fish Gate. He surrounded the Ophel

> and raised it up very much. He placed officers of the army in all the fortified cities of Judah. He removed the foreign gods and the idol from the House of G-d, and all the altars that he had built on the mountain of the House of G-d and in Jerusalem, and threw them outside of the city. He rebuilt the altar of G-d and sacrificed peace and thanksgiving offerings on it, and he told Judah to serve the L-rd, the G-d of Israel. However, the people were still sacrificing on altars, but only to the L-rd, their G-d.

Some say that when he was a captive, the Babylonians put him into a great copper vat with holes in the sides and began to roast him alive. He cried out to all the idols, but of course he was not answered. Finally he remembered that his father had taught him the verse,[39] "When you will be in trouble, and all these things happen to you, in the end of days, and you will return to the L-rd, your G-d and listen to His voice." He said, "I will pray to G-d. If He answers me, good, but if not, He is no different than the idols!"

When the angels heard his prayers, they closed all the doors of heaven. They said, "Oh, G-d, this is the man who put an idol in the very Sanctuary. There is no repentance for him!"

But G-d said, "If I don't accept him now, the door will be forever locked before all who try to repent." So G-d dug a tunnel through heaven beneath His throne of glory and listened to Manasseh's prayer. He accepted it in mercy, and even though by the standards of justice he in no way deserved to be forgiven. The earth trembled and the vat split open. Then a wind came from between the wings of the cherubim and carried Manasseh away and back to Jerusalem. At the moment that he was saved, Manasseh acknowledged divine justice, and recognized G-d as the judge to whom all are accountable.[40]

Some say Manasseh purposely began by calling to the idols even though he knew they could not help him. It was a trick to coerce G-d to respond when he finally turned to Him. There were three wicked people who succeeded in having their requests granted by presenting clever arguments that could not be refuted. Cain complained to G-d,[41] "Is my sin too great to bear? In the future, when the whole nation of Israel, six hundred thousand people, will worship the golden calf, You will forgive them. Is my sin greater than theirs? I too should be forgiven!"

Esau said,[42] "Have you only one blessing, my Father?" Isaac then agreed to give him a blessing too.

Manasseh deliberately called to the idols before calling to G-d so that G-d would save him to prove His own greatness. Like Cain and

Esau, Manasseh did not pray for kindness or mercy, but presented his demands in such a way that failure to fulfill them would be a disgrace to G-d Himself.[43]

How great is the power of suffering! All Hezekiah's efforts to teach him and raise him properly failed to bring Manasseh to Torah, but when he suffered at the hands of his enemies he repented.[44]

So Manasseh repented for his evil, and some say that the greater part of his life was spent in righteousness. According to this opinion, the comparison to Ahab is understood to mean that just as Ahab had ruled in wickedness twenty-two years, that being the entire length of his reign, so too, for only twenty-two years did Manasseh rebel against G-d. The remainder of his reign of fifty-five years were spent serving Him faithfully.[45] Still, he was never able to completely reverse the corruption of those years. There were many among the people who had wanted to reject the Torah and serve idolatry even before Manasseh. They were encouraged during the years of his wickedness, but did not repent along with him.

Others say he did not repent until near the end of his life. In the few remaining years there was not enough time to bring the people back to Torah.[46]

Some say that it was at this time, too, that the idol that had been made by Micah in the time of the Judges was captured. It had remained in the possession of the Jewish People until then and had never been destroyed, as it says,[47] "The children of Dan set up the idol for themselves, and Jonathan ben Gershom ben Manasseh, he and his sons, were priests for the tribe of the Danites, till the day of the exile of the land." Manasseh, too, had worshiped it, and it was taken into exile with him.[48]

Rav Ashi, one of the greatest rabbis of the Talmud, was once teaching his students about those kings who were so wicked that they were denied a portion in the world to come. One day he announced, "Tomorrow we will begin to learn about our comrade, Manasseh."

That night Manasseh appeared to him in a dream and said, "How do you dare to refer to me as your comrade? Do you even know the proper place to begin cutting a loaf of bread after making a blessing?"

Rav Ashi admitted that he did not. Manasseh said, "You never even learned where to begin cutting bread, yet you dare to call me your comrade?"

Rav Ashi said, "If you tell me, I will teach it to my students tomorrow!"

So Manasseh told him, "From the place that it is baked first!"

"Since you are so wise," asked Rav Ashi, "why did you worship idols?"

"Had you been in that generation," answered Manasseh, "you would have picked up the bottoms of your robes to run there."

The next day Rav Ashi told his students, "Now we will begin to learn about our master, Manasseh!"[49]

It is said that Manasseh knew fifty-five interpretations of the Book of Leviticus, corresponding to the years of his reign.[50]

Some say Manasseh was forgiven for his sins and granted a portion in the world to come. Others say that though he was returned to his kingdom, his portion in the world to come was never regained. His repentance was not sincere enough to earn him forgiveness for the terrible sins he had committed.[51]

Some say it was by his own choice that he was not buried together with the earlier kings. He did not feel himself worthy of lying beside them, and didn't want them to suffer with a neighbor like himself.[52]

21:19-22 בֶּן־עֶשְׂרִים וּשְׁתַּיִם שָׁנָה אָמוֹן בְּמָלְכוֹ וּשְׁתַּיִם שָׁנִים מָלַךְ בִּירוּשָׁלָם וְשֵׁם אִמּוֹ מְשֻׁלֶּמֶת בַּת־חָרוּץ מִן־יָטְבָה: וַיַּעַשׂ הָרַע בְּעֵינֵי ה׳ כַּאֲשֶׁר עָשָׂה מְנַשֶּׁה אָבִיו: וַיֵּלֶךְ בְּכָל־הַדֶּרֶךְ אֲשֶׁר־הָלַךְ אָבִיו וַיַּעֲבֹד אֶת־הַגִּלֻּלִים אֲשֶׁר עָבַד אָבִיו וַיִּשְׁתַּחוּ לָהֶם: וַיַּעֲזֹב אֶת־ה׳ אֱלֹהֵי אֲבֹתָיו וְלֹא־הָלַךְ בְּדֶרֶךְ ה׳:

Amon was twenty-two years old when he became king, and he ruled two years in Jerusalem. His mother's name was Meshulemeth the daughter of Haruz from Jotbah. He did what was evil in G-d's eyes, as his father, Manasseh, had done. He went in all the way that his father had gone, served the idols that his father had served, and bowed down to them. He abandoned the L-rd, the G-d of his fathers, and didn't go in the way of G-d.

Each of the three wicked kings, Ahaz, Manasseh and Amon, was worse than the one before. Ahaz placed an idol on the roof, but he did not dare put it in the Temple. Manasseh put it into the Sanctuary, and Amon put it into the Holy of Holies. Ahaz discontinued the Temple service and sealed away the Torah. Manasseh cut out G-d's name from the Torah and broke down the altar. Amon burnt the Torah and prevented any activity in the Temple, until there were cobwebs on the altar. Ahaz ruled that incest was permitted, Manasseh had relations with his sister, and Amon with his mother. This is a sin for which a person normally has no desire, and indeed finds repulsive. Amon did it only to defy G-d.[53]

21:23,24 וַיִּקְשְׁרוּ עַבְדֵי־אָמוֹן עָלָיו וַיָּמִיתוּ אֶת־הַמֶּלֶךְ בְּבֵיתוֹ׃ וַיַּךְ עַם־הָאָרֶץ אֵת כָּל־הַקֹּשְׁרִים עַל־הַמֶּלֶךְ אָמוֹן וַיַּמְלִיכוּ עַם־הָאָרֶץ אֶת־יֹאשִׁיָּהוּ בְנוֹ תַּחְתָּיו׃

Amon's servants conspired against him and killed the king in his house. The people of the land killed all those that had conspired against King Amon, and the people of the land made Josiah, his son, king in his place.

Amon's reign came to a speedy end because he failed to live up to the standards of a king. G-d had promised the kings of the Jewish People long lives if they would be loyal to the Torah, as it says,[54] "that he not deviate from the commandment right or left, so that his years of his kingdom be long, he and his sons, in the midst of Israel." If, however, a king did not follow the Torah, not only would he be denied this blessing, but his reign would be cut short. Of the kings of the Kingdom of Israel, there were descendants of Jeroboam, of Baasa and of Ahab who each reigned only two years. They were the most wicked of the kings, who lacked any merit to protect them. Now Amon, King of Judah, suffered the same fate.[55]

Amon's death at the hands of his own servants was the appropriate punishment for one who had rebelled against his Master, G-d. But Amon's supporters, the faction that opposed Torah, proved to be stronger than the reformers that had killed him. They avenged his death and crowned his son, Josiah, in his place, expecting that, being only a boy, he would be easily drawn to their side. To their surprise and no doubt, their disappointment, he became one of the most righteous of the kings of the Jewish People.[56]

21:25,26 וְיֶתֶר דִּבְרֵי אָמוֹן אֲשֶׁר עָשָׂה הֲלֹא־הֵם כְּתוּבִים עַל־סֵפֶר דִּבְרֵי הַיָּמִים לְמַלְכֵי יְהוּדָה׃ וַיִּקְבֹּר אֹתוֹ בִּקְבֻרָתוֹ בְּגַן־עֻזָּא וַיִּמְלֹךְ יֹאשִׁיָּהוּ בְנוֹ תַּחְתָּיו׃

The rest of the things about Amon that he did are indeed written in the Book of the Chronicles of the Kings of Judah.

He buried him in his grave in the Garden of Uzza, and Josiah, his son, became king in his place.

In spite of his wickedness, Amon is not included on the list of kings who were denied a portion in the world to come. He was protected by the righteousness of his son, Josiah. Manasseh, on the other hand, was not saved by the righteousness of Hezekiah. The righteousness of a son is a merit to his father, but the righteousness of a father is not a credit for his sons unless they follow in his way.[57]

II Kings 22

22:1,2 בֶּן־שְׁמֹנֶה שָׁנָה יֹאשִׁיָּהוּ בְמָלְכוֹ וּשְׁלֹשִׁים וְאַחַת שָׁנָה מָלַךְ
בִּירוּשָׁלָםִ וְשֵׁם אִמּוֹ יְדִידָה בַת־עֲדָיָה מִבָּצְקַת׃ וַיַּעַשׂ הַיָּשָׁר בְּעֵינֵי ה׳ וַיֵּלֶךְ
בְּכָל־דֶּרֶךְ דָּוִד אָבִיו וְלֹא־סָר יָמִין וּשְׂמֹאול׃

Josiah was eight years old when he became king, and he reigned thirty-one years in Jerusalem. His mother's name was Jedidah the daughter of Adaiah from Bozkath. He did what was upright in G-d's eyes, and went in all way of David, his father. He didn't deviate right or left.

Even as a child, Josiah's piety was evident. His name can be understood to mean "pleasant as a gift for G-d," "יאי שי". He was acceptable to G-d like a pleasant offering on the altar.[1] He didn't follow the example of his wicked father. Instead, he followed the ways of his righteous ancestor, David, and the other righteous kings. The Book of Chronicles tells,[2] "In the eighth year of his reign, when he was yet a youth, he began to seek the G-d of David, his father. In the twelfth year he began to purify Judah and Jerusalem of the shrines, the Asherim, the carved idols and the cast idols." The Bible therefore identifies him with them by referring to King David as his father.[3] Few kings were worthy of being referred to in this way. Noble ancestry alone is not a reason for pride. Only one who follows in the footsteps of his fathers is worthy of being proud of his descent.

22:3-7 וַיְהִי בִּשְׁמֹנֶה עֶשְׂרֵה שָׁנָה לַמֶּלֶךְ יֹאשִׁיָּהוּ שָׁלַח הַמֶּלֶךְ אֶת־שָׁפָן
בֶּן־אֲצַלְיָהוּ בֶן־מְשֻׁלָּם הַסֹּפֵר בֵּית ה׳ לֵאמֹר׃ עֲלֵה אֶל־חִלְקִיָּהוּ הַכֹּהֵן הַגָּדוֹל
וְיַתֵּם אֶת־הַכֶּסֶף הַמּוּבָא בֵּית ה׳ אֲשֶׁר אָסְפוּ שֹׁמְרֵי הַסַּף מֵאֵת הָעָם׃ וְיִתְּנֻהֻ
עַל־יַד עֹשֵׂי הַמְּלָאכָה הַמֻּפְקָדִים בית (בֵּית קרי) ה׳ וְיִתְּנוּ אֹתוֹ לְעֹשֵׂי הַמְּלָאכָה
אֲשֶׁר בְּבֵית ה׳ לְחַזֵּק בֶּדֶק הַבָּיִת׃ לֶחָרָשִׁים וְלַבֹּנִים וְלַגֹּדְרִים וְלִקְנוֹת עֵצִים

וְאַבְנֵי מַחְצֵב לְחַזֵּק אֶת־הַבָּיִת׃ אַךְ לֹא־יֵחָשֵׁב אִתָּם הַכֶּסֶף הַנִּתָּן עַל־יָדָם כִּי
בֶאֱמוּנָה הֵם עֹשִׂים׃

In the eighteenth year of King Josiah, the king sent Shaphan ben Azaliah ben Meshulam, the scribe, to the House of G-d saying, "Go up to Hilkiah the High Priest and complete the account of the money that has been brought to the House of G-d, that the guards of the threshold collected from the people. Give it to those who do the work, who are appointed at the House of G-d. Give it to those who do the work that are in the House of G-d to strengthen the repair of the Temple. To the wood cutters, to the builders and to the masons, to buy wood and hewn stone to strengthen the Temple. However, let account not be made with them of the money that is given to them, for they work in good faith."

The first year of Josiah was a fresh start for the Jewish People. It was the first year of the Jubilee cycle, and was to be a year of sincere repentance. It was more than two hundred years since Jehoash had renovated the Temple, two hundred and eighteen according to some opinions and two hundred and twenty-four according to others. Aside from normal deterioration, it had suffered from the abuses of wicked kings like Ahaz, Manasseh in his early years, and Amon. Josiah therefore ordered another general renovation like the one of Jehoash.[4]

The method of collection instituted by Jehoash was still being practiced. Contributions were collected in a box in the Temple, to be used to pay the craftsmen who were hired to make the repairs. Even an effective system, however, is only as good as those who conduct it. At the time of Josiah the money that was collected was not being used and lay idle in the box. At last, Josiah directed his attention to this problem. He ordered that the money be taken out and used as it was intended.

The phrase "Give it to those who do the work" appears twice in the king's order. The first refers to the officials who supervised the repairs and the second to the craftsmen and workers. The money was to be given to the supervisors, and they, in turn, were charged with engaging and paying the workers.[5]

22:8 וַיֹּאמֶר חִלְקִיָּהוּ הַכֹּהֵן הַגָּדוֹל עַל־שָׁפָן הַסֹּפֵר סֵפֶר הַתּוֹרָה מָצָאתִי
בְּבֵית ה׳ וַיִּתֵּן חִלְקִיָּה אֶת־הַסֵּפֶר אֶל־שָׁפָן וַיִּקְרָאֵהוּ׃

Hilkiah, the High Priest, said to Shaphan, the scribe, "I found the Book of the Torah in the House of G-d!" Hilkiah gave the book to Shaphan and he read it.

The Torah scroll that was found was the original one written by Moses himself, as it says in the Book of Chronicles,[6] "When they were spending the money that was brought to the House of G-d, Hilkiah the priest found the Book of the Torah of G-d by the hand of Moses." Moses had been commanded to write this scroll at the end of his life and put it in the Holy of Holies next to the Ark of the Covenant. He had also made other copies and given them to each of the tribes, and from those all future copies were made. This one, however, remained in the Temple as a holy object, never to actually be opened and read, somewhat like to the small scrolls in Mezuzot and Tefilin.

22:9-11 וַיָּבֹא שָׁפָן הַסֹּפֵר אֶל־הַמֶּלֶךְ וַיָּשֶׁב אֶת־הַמֶּלֶךְ דָּבָר וַיֹּאמֶר הִתִּיכוּ
עֲבָדֶיךָ אֶת־הַכֶּסֶף הַנִּמְצָא בַבַּיִת וַיִּתְּנֻהוּ עַל־יַד עֹשֵׂי הַמְּלָאכָה הַמֻּפְקָדִים בֵּית
ה׳: וַיַּגֵּד שָׁפָן הַסֹּפֵר לַמֶּלֶךְ לֵאמֹר סֵפֶר נָתַן לִי חִלְקִיָּה הַכֹּהֵן וַיִּקְרָאֵהוּ שָׁפָן
לִפְנֵי הַמֶּלֶךְ: וַיְהִי כִּשְׁמֹעַ הַמֶּלֶךְ אֶת־דִּבְרֵי סֵפֶר הַתּוֹרָה וַיִּקְרַע אֶת־בְּגָדָיו:

Shaphan the scribe came to the king. He brought back a report to the king and said, "Your servants have melted down the silver that was found in the Temple and given it to those who do the work, who are appointed at the House of G-d." Shaphan the scribe told the king saying, "Hilkiah the priest gave me a book," and Shaphan read it before the king. When the king heard the words of the Book of the Torah he tore his clothes.

The exact circumstances of this incident are not described clearly here or in any other book of the Bible, so there is much confusion concerning exactly what happened. Some say that at that time there were no scrolls of the Torah available in the entire nation, and the words of the written Torah had been forgotten. This tragic era had begun in the time of the wicked king, Ahaz, who searched for every Torah scroll and burned it. The priests who remained faithful to G-d were afraid that he would go so far as to violate the sanctity of the Temple, enter the Holy of Holies, and destroy the Torah scroll that Moses himself had written, so they removed it and hid it.[7]

But after Ahaz died and was succeeded by his righteous son, Hezekiah, the scroll was not returned to its place. Perhaps those who had hidden it had been killed or died and no one was left who knew where it was. Or perhaps Hezekiah and the priests decided that it would be better off that it remain hidden, lest it be destroyed by another wicked king in the future. So for several generations the Jewish People lived without the written Torah, that is, without the Five Books of Moses. They studied the oral Torah and, during the period of Hezekiah, reached great levels of piety and knowledge. The reading of the written Torah, however, became a neglected commandment. Even the king neglected his special obligation of writing a Torah scroll for himself and keeping it with him at all times. The basic information contained in the written Torah was not forgotten, for it was preserved in the oral tradition. It was still possible to attain a deep understanding of the ideas of Torah. Only the particular holy object, the Torah scroll, was missing. At first there were many who knew the written Torah by heart, so even the words themselves were not lost, but as time went on they died out, and the words were forgotten.

Others say that it was only in the time of Manasseh that the Torah scrolls had been destroyed. According to this opinion, Manasseh had not repented until the end of his long reign. By that time he had successfully eliminated the study of Torah, and in the few years remaining he did not have time to revive it. The reforms that he made during those last years only involved certain fundamental commandments, and the search for a surviving copy of the written Torah and its republication was not among them.

Nor was this problem addressed during the early years of Josiah. The process of reform is a slow and difficult one. The first step was reestablishing the observance of those commandments that were still remembered. Only after that, as the study of Torah progressed, could the practice of more commandments be revived. Perhaps Josiah himself did not know about all the commandments, since he was born after the study of Torah had already been disrupted. He knew only those things about which the prophets had rebuked the people, so that was the extent of his reform. Now, with the discovery of this scroll, he learned of important commandments that were still being neglected, and was understandably dismayed.[8]

Another explanation is that even during the periods of corruption many Torah scrolls had been preserved, hidden by those who remained faithful. By the time the scroll was discovered in the Temple those scrolls had already been copied and distributed under Josiah's direction. All the commandments were known and Josiah was already trying to reestablish them. The great impression made by the discovery of this scroll was not because the words in it were new to them, but because it was found rolled to the section of rebuke. The first words that met their eyes when they opened it were,[9] "G-d will take you and your king that you will set up upon yourself to a nation that you did not know, you and your fathers." They took this as a sign that it was to their own generation that these words referred.[10]

According to these two opinions, the scroll of Moses may never have been hidden at all. It had remained all the while in its place beside the Ark. Only now, when it was removed during the renovations, was it opened and read, making this terrifying impression.[11]

Yet another explanation is that the scroll of Moses was hidden during the time of Manasseh because, like King Ahaziah before him, Manasseh had tried to promote idolatry by erasing G-d's name from the Torah and replacing it with the names of idols. When the priests became aware of this they were afraid that he would dare to corrupt even the scroll of Moses, so they hid it in the wall of the Temple. Josiah knew about it, and for many years he had searched for it unsuccessfully. Now, in the course of renovation, it was accidentally discovered. But greater than Josiah's joy at this discovery was his awe at beholding the words written by the hand of the great prophet himself. All the more so since this scroll was kept completely rolled from beginning to end, so it was the last section, including the rebukes and the Song of Moses, that they read.[12]

Josiah was not required to tear his clothes, since he was not in a state of mourning. It was, rather, an expression of grief and fear of the punishment that had been decreed against them.[13]

22:12-14 וַיְצַו הַמֶּלֶךְ אֶת־חִלְקִיָּה הַכֹּהֵן וְאֶת־אֲחִיקָם בֶּן־שָׁפָן וְאֶת־עַכְבּוֹר
בֶּן־מִיכָיָה וְאֵת שָׁפָן הַסֹּפֵר וְאֵת עֲשָׂיָה עֶבֶד־הַמֶּלֶךְ לֵאמֹר: לְכוּ דִרְשׁוּ אֶת־ה׳
בַּעֲדִי וּבְעַד־הָעָם וּבְעַד כָּל־יְהוּדָה עַל־דִּבְרֵי הַסֵּפֶר הַנִּמְצָא הַזֶּה כִּי־גְדוֹלָה
חֲמַת ה׳ אֲשֶׁר־הִיא נִצְּתָה בָנוּ עַל אֲשֶׁר לֹא־שָׁמְעוּ אֲבֹתֵינוּ עַל־דִּבְרֵי הַסֵּפֶר
הַזֶּה לַעֲשׂוֹת כְּכָל־הַכָּתוּב עָלֵינוּ: וַיֵּלֶךְ חִלְקִיָּהוּ הַכֹּהֵן וַאֲחִיקָם וְעַכְבּוֹר וְשָׁפָן
וַעֲשָׂיָה אֶל־חֻלְדָּה הַנְּבִיאָה אֵשֶׁת שַׁלֻּם בֶּן־תִּקְוָה בֶּן־חַרְחַס שֹׁמֵר הַבְּגָדִים וְהִיא
יֹשֶׁבֶת בִּירוּשָׁלַםִ בַּמִּשְׁנֶה וַיְדַבְּרוּ אֵלֶיהָ:

The king commanded Hilkiah, the priest, Ahikam ben

Shaphan, Achbor ben Micaiah, Shaphan the scribe, and Asaiah, the king's servant, saying, "Go, inquire of G-d for me, for the people, and for all Judah, concerning the words of this book that was found. For great is G-d's wrath that has been kindled against us, because our fathers didn't listen to the words of this book, to do according to all that is written about us." Hilkiah the priest, Ahikam, Achbor, Shaphan and Asaiah went to Huldah the prophetess, the wife of Shalum ben Tikvah ben Harhas, the guardian of the clothes. She lived in Jerusalem within the second wall, and they spoke to her.

Huldah was one of the eight prophets living during that period who were descended from Rahab, the Canaanite woman who helped the spies in the time of Joshua. Joshua married her and they had many illustrious descendants. The other seven prophets were Baruch ben Neriah, Seraiah, Mahsaiah, Jeremiah, Hilkiah, Hanamel, and Shalum.[14]

Huldah's husband, Shalum ben Tikvah, was a very righteous man who excelled in acts of charity and kindness. Though he was respected as one of the leaders of his generation, he did not consider it beneath his dignity to offer help to those in need. Every day he would fill a large container with water and go to the entrance of the city to give water to travellers who arrived thirsty from the road. By that merit his wife was granted prophecy. Some say he was the one who was revived by touching the bones of Elisha, as was related above.[15] Their son was Hanamel, who is mentioned in the Book of Jeremiah.[16]

There were three prophets that prophesied in the time of Josiah. They were Jeremiah, Zephaniah and Huldah. Jeremiah used to prophesy in the marketplaces, Zephaniah in the meetinghouses, and Huldah prophesied for the women.[17] The king's ministers chose to ask Huldah rather than the others because women are more merciful than men, so they hoped she would interpret G-d's words in a favorable way. As for Jeremiah, he was not insulted that they asked her instead of him because she was his relative. Others say that Jeremiah was not available at that time because he had gone to bring back the remnants of the Kingdom of Israel who had been exiled years before.[18]

At that time, the city of Jerusalem had three walls, each one enclosing the other. The innermost part of the city was the most secure, being protected by all three.[19] Some say the word "משנה" refers to the second wall. Huldah lived within the second wall and that was where they found her.[20] Others say it means "study hall,"[21] meaning that she had a permanent place in which she used to teach the people. A third interpretation is that she taught the oral traditions, that is, the Mishnah.[22] A fourth is that she explained all the laws that are mentioned twice in the Torah. She taught what was alluded to by all the extra words, and the punishments and exiles that had been decreed against those who transgressed them.[23] Others say the reference to her living in Jerusalem was meant to explain their going to her rather than Jeremiah or Zephaniah. Of all the prophets, she was the only one present in Jerusalem at that time.[24]

22:15-20 וַתֹּאמֶר אֲלֵיהֶם כֹּה־אָמַר ה׳ אֱלֹהֵי יִשְׂרָאֵל אִמְרוּ לָאִישׁ אֲשֶׁר־שָׁלַח אֶתְכֶם אֵלָי׃ כֹּה אָמַר ה׳ הִנְנִי מֵבִיא רָעָה אֶל־הַמָּקוֹם הַזֶּה וְעַל־יֹשְׁבָיו אֵת כָּל־דִּבְרֵי הַסֵּפֶר אֲשֶׁר קָרָא מֶלֶךְ יְהוּדָה׃ תַּחַת אֲשֶׁר עֲזָבוּנִי וַיְקַטְּרוּ לֵאלֹהִים אֲחֵרִים לְמַעַן הַכְעִיסֵנִי בְּכֹל מַעֲשֵׂה יְדֵיהֶם וְנִצְּתָה חֲמָתִי בַּמָּקוֹם הַזֶּה וְלֹא תִכְבֶּה׃ וְאֶל־מֶלֶךְ יְהוּדָה הַשֹּׁלֵחַ אֶתְכֶם לִדְרשׁ אֶת־ה׳ כֹּה תֹאמְרוּ אֵלָיו כֹּה־אָמַר ה׳ אֱלֹהֵי יִשְׂרָאֵל הַדְּבָרִים אֲשֶׁר שָׁמָעְתָּ׃ יַעַן רַךְ־לְבָבְךָ וַתִּכָּנַע מִפְּנֵי ה׳ בְּשָׁמְעֲךָ אֲשֶׁר דִּבַּרְתִּי עַל־הַמָּקוֹם הַזֶּה וְעַל־יֹשְׁבָיו לִהְיוֹת לְשַׁמָּה וְלִקְלָלָה וַתִּקְרַע אֶת־בְּגָדֶיךָ וַתִּבְכֶּה לְפָנָי וְגַם אָנֹכִי שָׁמַעְתִּי נְאֻם־ה׳׃ לָכֵן הִנְנִי אֹסִפְךָ עַל־אֲבֹתֶיךָ וְנֶאֱסַפְתָּ אֶל־קִבְרֹתֶיךָ בְּשָׁלוֹם וְלֹא־תִרְאֶינָה עֵינֶיךָ בְּכֹל הָרָעָה אֲשֶׁר־אֲנִי מֵבִיא עַל־הַמָּקוֹם הַזֶּה וַיָּשִׁבוּ אֶת־הַמֶּלֶךְ דָּבָר׃

She said to them, "Thus says the L-rd, the G-d of Israel, 'Say to the man who sent you to me, "Thus says G-d, 'Behold, I am bringing evil to this place and upon its inhabitants, all the words of the book that the King of Judah read. Because they abandoned Me and burned incense to other gods in order to anger Me with all the work of their hands. My wrath has been kindled at this place and it won't be extinguished.' " And to the King of Judah who sent you to inquire of G-d, thus say to him, "Thus says the L-rd, the G-d of Israel, 'As for the words that you heard, since your heart was softened and you were humbled before G-d when you heard what I had said concerning this place and concerning its inhabitants, to become a wasteland and a curse, and you tore your clothes and cried before Me, I too have listened,' says G-d. 'Therefore behold, I am going to gather you in above your fathers. You will be gathered into your grave in peace, and your eyes will not see all the evil that I will bring upon this place.' " ' " They brought a report back to the king.

The worst of their fears were confirmed by Huldah's answer. The prophecies that they had read in the scroll were indeed directed toward them. Earlier generations had been spared because, although many had worshiped idols, they had never ceased to worship G-d. The service of G-d in the Temple had never been interrupted. Recent generations, however, had abandoned G-d completely and idolatry had come to replace rather than supplement the Temple service. It was for this that they had been condemned to destruction.

But as for Josiah, he was not guilty of this sin, so he would not be included in the punishment. Not only would he himself be spared, his merit would protect the nation as long as he was alive. Only after his death would this terrible prophecy be fulfilled.[25] Furthermore, his reward in the next world would be even greater than that of the earlier kings. The prophetess therefore described his death as being gathered "above" his fathers rather than "to" them.[26]

No mention was made of the violent death that he would meet. As we will learn in the next chapter, he was killed by the Egyptian army while trying to prevent them from passing through the Holy Land. Huldah carefully concealed this, reassuring him instead that he would be buried in peace with the honor due a great king. The emphasis on his burial, however, can be seen as a hint that his death itself would not be peaceful.[27]

Another interpretation of this prophecy is that he would die while the Jewish People were still in peace, before the destruction started.[28]

II KINGS 23

23:1-3 וַיִּשְׁלַח הַמֶּלֶךְ וַיַּאַסְפוּ אֵלָיו כָּל־זִקְנֵי יְהוּדָה וִירוּשָׁלִָם׃ וַיַּעַל
הַמֶּלֶךְ בֵּית־ה׳ וְכָל־אִישׁ יְהוּדָה וְכָל־יֹשְׁבֵי יְרוּשָׁלִַם אִתּוֹ וְהַכֹּהֲנִים וְהַנְּבִיאִים
וְכָל־הָעָם לְמִקָּטֹן וְעַד־גָּדוֹל וַיִּקְרָא בְאָזְנֵיהֶם אֶת־כָּל־דִּבְרֵי סֵפֶר הַבְּרִית
הַנִּמְצָא בְּבֵית ה׳׃ וַיַּעֲמֹד הַמֶּלֶךְ עַל־הָעַמּוּד וַיִּכְרֹת אֶת־הַבְּרִית לִפְנֵי ה׳ לָלֶכֶת
אַחַר ה׳ וְלִשְׁמֹר מִצְוֹתָיו וְאֶת־עֵדְוֹתָיו וְאֶת־חֻקֹּתָיו בְּכָל־לֵב וּבְכָל־נֶפֶשׁ לְהָקִים
אֶת־דִּבְרֵי הַבְּרִית הַזֹּאת הַכְּתֻבִים עַל־הַסֵּפֶר הַזֶּה וַיַּעֲמֹד כָּל־הָעָם בַּבְּרִית׃

The king sent, and all the elders of Judah and Jerusalem gathered to him. The king went up to the House of G-d, and all the men of Judah and all the inhabitants of Jerusalem with him, the priests, the prophets and the whole people from small to great. He read in their ears all the words of the Book of the Covenant that was found in the House of G-d. The king stood on the platform and made the covenant before G-d, to follow G-d and keep His commandments, His testimonies and His decrees with a whole heart and with a whole soul, to uphold the words of this covenant that are written in this book. The whole people accepted the covenant.

Josiah did not give up hope even after being told that the Jewish People had been condemned to suffer the punishments of which he had read. He knew that the divine decree would be repealed if they repented and mended their ways. It was clearly stated in the Torah that these punishments would come upon them only if they violated the commandments. If they repented and stopped, they would no longer be culpable. So he gathered the people to try to persuade them. They, too, were struck with awe when they heard the words of the Book of the Torah that had been found, and all agreed.

Above, we read that, according to one opinion, the reason the king's ministers had inquired of Huldah the prophetess rather than one of the other prophets was that none of the other prophets were present in Jerusalem at that time. According to that opinion, the reference to "prophets" in this verse cannot be taken literally. It refers, rather, to Torah scholars.[1] But according to the opinion that Huldah was chosen even though there were other prophets available, this verse can be understood in its literal sense. Those prophets were now called by the king to join him in rebuking the people.[2]

As was explained in earlier chapters,[3] the word "עמוד," "platform," refers to the special place in the Temple where a king would stand when addressing the people.

23:4 וַיְצַו הַמֶּלֶךְ אֶת־חִלְקִיָּהוּ הַכֹּהֵן הַגָּדוֹל וְאֶת־כֹּהֲנֵי הַמִּשְׁנֶה וְאֶת־
שֹׁמְרֵי הַסַּף לְהוֹצִיא מֵהֵיכַל ה׳ אֵת כָּל־הַכֵּלִים הָעֲשׂוּיִם לַבַּעַל וְלָאֲשֵׁרָה וּלְכֹל
צְבָא הַשָּׁמָיִם וַיִּשְׂרְפֵם מִחוּץ לִירוּשָׁלַםִ בְּשַׁדְמוֹת קִדְרוֹן וְנָשָׂא אֶת עֲפָרָם
בֵּית־אֵל׃

The king commanded Hilkiah, the High Priest, the secondary priests, and the guards of the threshold to remove from the Sanctuary of G-d all the utensils that had been made for Baal, for Asherah, and for the whole host of the heavens. He burned them outside of Jerusalem in the Plain of Kidron, and carried their ashes to Beth-el.

The most serious offense had been idolatry. Unlike earlier generations that had left the Holy Temple uncorrupted while they built shrines to worship idols throughout the country, recent generations had introduced idolatry into the Temple itself and interfered with the Temple service. The Temple was therefore the first place from which the idols had to be removed. Although Manasseh, in his later years, removed the idols from the Temple, his son, Amon, brought them back. Josiah began to remove them in his twelfth year, but he did not finish until his eighteenth year, after the Book of the Torah was found.[4]

The Kidron Valley lies to the east of Jerusalem, between the Temple Mount and the Mount of Olives. The flat area in the valley that was called "the Plain of Kidron" was probably the southern end, where it joins the Valley of Benhinom, of which we will read shortly. It was to that area that defiled or otherwise rejected things were taken, and, if necessary, destroyed.

From Jerusalem, the holiest place, the ashes of the idols were brought to Beth-el, the city most identified with rejection of the Temple service. Like Jerusalem, Beth-el was a holy city, the site of important events in Jewish history. But, while Jerusalem had been chosen by G-d as the location of His Holy Temple, Beth-el was chosen by Jeroboam ben Nebat as the center of his new cult. It thereafter came to represent idolatry and rejection of Torah. Josiah therefore brought the ashes of the idols from Jerusalem to Beth-el and defiled the shrine of Jeroboam with them. By defiling the altar of Beth-el with those ashes, Josiah made the statement that any deviant mode of worshiping G-d is like idolatry itself.[5]

23:5 וְהִשְׁבִּית אֶת־הַכְּמָרִים אֲשֶׁר נָתְנוּ מַלְכֵי יְהוּדָה וַיְקַטֵּר בַּבָּמוֹת . בְּעָרֵי יְהוּדָה וּמְסִבֵּי יְרוּשָׁלָםִ וְאֶת־הַמְקַטְּרִים לַבַּעַל לַשֶּׁמֶשׁ וְלַיָּרֵחַ וְלַמַּזָּלוֹת וּלְכֹל צְבָא הַשָּׁמָיִם׃

He discontinued the idolatrous priests that the kings of Judah had appointed to burn incense on the altars in the cities of Judah and the surroundings of Jerusalem, and those who burned incense to Baal, to the sun, to the moon, to the planets and to the whole host of the heavens.

The priests of the idols are called "כמרים." Some say the word is derived from the root "כמר," which means black, because they wore black clothes.[6]

This verse mentions five kinds of idolatry, "Baal," "the sun," "the moon," "the planets" and "the whole host of the heavens," which refers to the stars. For worshiping them the Jewish People were later to suffer five punishments mentioned in the Torah,[7] to be "bloated by famine, burnt by fever, cut down by plague," and beset by "the teeth of beasts" and "the venom of those that crawl in the dust."[8]

23:6 וַיֹּצֵא אֶת־הָאֲשֵׁרָה מִבֵּית ה׳ מִחוּץ לִירוּשָׁלַםִ אֶל־נַחַל קִדְרוֹן וַיִּשְׂרֹף אֹתָהּ בְּנַחַל קִדְרוֹן וַיָּדֶק לְעָפָר וַיַּשְׁלֵךְ אֶת־עֲפָרָהּ עַל־קֶבֶר בְּנֵי הָעָם׃

He took the Asherah out of the House of G-d, out of

Jerusalem to the Valley of Kidron. He burned it in the Valley of Kidron, crushed it to dust, and threw its dust on the graves of the members of the people.

The expression "members of the people" refers to the those members of the Jewish People who had worshiped this idol, as it says in the Book of Chronicles,[9] "They demolished the altars of the Baalim before him, and the sun images that were above them he cut down. The Asherim, the carved idols and the cast idols he smashed and ground fine, and threw over the graves of those who sacrified to them." The symbolism of this act is obvious. It was as if to say, "Look at what you used to worship. See how foolish you were! It is powerless even to defend itself, much less those who turn to it for help." It was a disgrace both to the idol and to its worshipers.[10]

23:7 וַיִּתֹּץ אֶת־בָּתֵּי הַקְּדֵשִׁים אֲשֶׁר בְּבֵית ה׳ אֲשֶׁר הַנָּשִׁים אֹרְגוֹת שָׁם
בָּתִּים לָאֲשֵׁרָה׃

He demolished the houses of the monks that were in the House of G-d, where the women wove houses for Asherah.

Some say the "קדשים," "monks," were men and women who had dedicated themselves to the service of the idol. They were similar to priests, but, it seems, of lower rank. They did not conduct the service itself, but assisted in various ways. One such duty was to weave curtains from which a sort of tent was made around the Asherah. This was referred to as its "house."[11] Others say they were prostitutes, which is the usual meaning of the word "קדש."[12] According to the teachings of their religion, such activities were considered pleasing to the gods.[13]

23:8 וַיָּבֵא אֶת־כָּל־הַכֹּהֲנִים מֵעָרֵי יְהוּדָה וַיְטַמֵּא אֶת־הַבָּמוֹת אֲשֶׁר
קִטְּרוּ־שָׁמָּה הַכֹּהֲנִים מִגֶּבַע עַד־בְּאֵר שָׁבַע וְנָתַץ אֶת־בָּמוֹת הַשְּׁעָרִים
אֲשֶׁר־פֶּתַח שַׁעַר יְהוֹשֻׁעַ שַׂר־הָעִיר אֲשֶׁר־עַל־שְׂמֹאול אִישׁ בְּשַׁעַר הָעִיר׃

He brought all the priests from the cities of Judah and defiled the altars where the priests burned incense, from Geba to Beer-sheba. He demolished the altars of the gates, and the one that was at the entrance of the Gate of Joshua, the Officer of the City, that was on a person's left as he entered the gate of the city.

By the time of the later kings, the descendants of Aaron were universally recognized as the priests of the Jewish People. There were none who would consider challenging their position and replacing them with those of other ancestry, as had happened earlier in the Kingdom of Israel. So even when the people strayed into idolatry, it was upon the priests that the duty of performing the idolatrous service fell. Of all the families of the descendants of Aaron, only the family of Zadok remained faithful to G-d and refused to participate. Now, Josiah gathered the errant priests together from all over the country to bring them back to the true service of G-d.[14]

The altars were generally constructed at the gates of the cities. The biggest and most famous of them was the one at the gate called the "Gate of Joshua, the Officer of the City." The Bible therefore mentions this one specifically.[15]

23:9 אַךְ לֹא יַעֲלוּ כֹּהֲנֵי הַבָּמוֹת אֶל־מִזְבַּח ה׳ בִּירוּשָׁלָםִ כִּי אִם־אָכְלוּ מַצּוֹת בְּתוֹךְ אֲחֵיהֶם׃

The priests of the altars were not allowed to go up to the altar of G-d in Jerusalem, but they could eat unleavened bread in the midst of their brothers.

The descendants of Aaron that had participated in idolatrous practices or had served G-d on the altars outside of the Temple did not lose their status as priests. Those that repented retained all the rights and responsibilities of the priesthood. They could even eat the priestly portions of the sacrifices, including the showbread from the table in the Sanctuary. The Bible refers to these portions here as "unleavened bread" because the showbread and most of the other sacrificial bread was unleavened.[16] The only restriction that remained upon them was that they were not allowed to perform the Temple service. That is restricted to those who are pure and unblemished. Just as a priest who is deformed in any way cannot participate in the service, so too, those who had defiled themselves by idolatry were excluded.[17] Their descendants, however, would be unaffected. They would be no different than any other priests, and would be able to perform the Temple service as well.

23:10 וְטִמֵּא אֶת־הַתֹּפֶת אֲשֶׁר בְּגֵי בני־הִנֹּם (בֶן־הִנֹּם קרי לְבִלְתִּי לְהַעֲבִיר
אִישׁ אֶת־בְּנוֹ וְאֶת־בִּתּוֹ בָּאֵשׁ לַמֹּלֶךְ׃

He defiled the Topheth that was in the Valley of Benhinom, so that no one would pass his son or his daughter through fire for Molech.

The Topheth was the place where the idol of Molech stood. It was called "Topheth" because whenever a child was sacrificed to Molech, the priests would beat on drums (תפים) so that the father would not hear his child's cries and, overcome by compassion, grab it away.[18] It was located in a valley near Jerusalem that had belonged to a man named "Hinom," so it was called "the Valley of Benhinom," that is, "the Valley of the son of Hinom," or just, "גי הנם," "Gehenom," "the Valley of Hinom."[19] So frightening was this place that the name "Gehenom" later came to be used for the spiritual place where the souls of the dead suffer as they are purified from their sins before they can enter "Gan Eden," the spiritual place where they enjoy reward for their good deeds.[20]

Others say the name "Benhinom" means "the child sobs," a reference to the cries of the children as they were sacrificed there. The word "הנם" is interpreted as a variation of "נוהם." The name might be translated as "The Valley of Sobbing Children."[21]

Of all the idols, only Molech was located outside of the city. That is an indication of how terrible it was, even for those who worshiped it.[22] They would not dare introduce it in Jerusalem itself. In the Torah, too, Molech is singled out from all other idols as particularly sinful.

Josiah defiled the Valley of Benhinom by designating it as a place for throwing all sorts of unclean things. From that time on it became so disgusting in the eyes of the people that no one could ever consider it holy again.[23]

23:11 וַיַּשְׁבֵּת אֶת־הַסּוּסִים אֲשֶׁר נָתְנוּ מַלְכֵי יְהוּדָה לַשֶּׁמֶשׁ מִבֹּא בֵית־ה׳
אֶל־לִשְׁכַּת נְתַן־מֶלֶךְ הַסָּרִיס אֲשֶׁר בַּפַּרְוָרִים וְאֶת־מַרְכְּבוֹת הַשֶּׁמֶשׁ שָׂרַף בָּאֵשׁ׃

He discontinued the horses that the kings of Judah had

dedicated to the sun from the entrance of the House of G-d to the Room of Nethan-melech, the minister, that was in the fields. The chariots of the sun he burned with fire.

Another idolatrous ceremony that had been introduced by the kings preceding Josiah was the worship of the rising sun. The horsemen waited at the eastern gate of the Temple and rode toward the sun as it rose. When they reached a certain designated spot, they stopped and bowed. At that place there was a building called the "Room of Nethan-melech," where the rites of the sun would be performed.[24]

As was the custom in those days, these horsemen rode in chariots rather than on the backs of their horses. Josiah not only discontinued the service of the sun, but had the chariots destroyed, since they had been used for idolatry.

23:12 וְאֶת־הַמִּזְבְּחוֹת אֲשֶׁר עַל־הַגָּג עֲלִיַּת אָחָז אֲשֶׁר־עָשׂוּ מַלְכֵי יְהוּדָה וְאֶת־הַמִּזְבְּחוֹת אֲשֶׁר־עָשָׂה מְנַשֶּׁה בִּשְׁתֵּי חַצְרוֹת בֵּית־ה׳ נָתַץ הַמֶּלֶךְ וַיָּרָץ מִשָּׁם וְהִשְׁלִיךְ אֶת־עֲפָרָם אֶל־נַחַל קִדְרוֹן׃

The altars that were on the roof of the upper story of Ahaz that the kings of Judah had made, and the altars that Manasseh had made in the two courtyards of the House of G-d, the king demolished. He removed them hastily from there, and threw their dust into the Valley of Kidron.

It is not clear whether this altar was on the roof of the royal palace or of the Temple itself.

Some say the word "וירץ" means "smash" or "destroy."[25] Others say it means "remove hastily."[26]

23:13 וְאֶת־הַבָּמוֹת אֲשֶׁר עַל־פְּנֵי יְרוּשָׁלַםִ אֲשֶׁר מִימִין לְהַר־הַמַּשְׁחִית אֲשֶׁר בָּנָה שְׁלֹמֹה מֶלֶךְ־יִשְׂרָאֵל לְעַשְׁתֹּרֶת שִׁקֻּץ צִידֹנִים וְלִכְמוֹשׁ שִׁקֻּץ מוֹאָב וּלְמִלְכֹּם תּוֹעֲבַת בְּנֵי־עַמּוֹן טִמֵּא הַמֶּלֶךְ׃

And the altars that were opposite Jerusalem, that were to the right of the Mount of Olives, that Solomon, King of Israel, had built for Ashtoreth, the detestation of the Zidonites, for

Chemosh, the detestation of Moab, and for Milcom, the abomination of the Children of Amon, the king defiled.

These altars were not built by Solomon himself but by his pagan wives. He was held responsible for them, however, because he did not interfere. Some say that after the time of Solomon, when those wives had died or no longer had influence, the people appropriated the altars to offer sacrifices to G-d. Others say that idolatry persisted on these altars even though it did not spread throughout the kingdom.

It is hard to understand why these altars had not been destroyed earlier, by righteous kings like Asa, Jehoshaphat and Hezekiah. They, too, had eliminated idolatry. Why had they permitted these to remain? Some say that in their times these altars were being used for the service of G-d, so they did not consider it necessary to destroy them. As has already been explained, the earlier kings did not prevent the people from sacrificing to G-d outside of the Temple, even though it was forbidden by the Torah. Josiah, however, maintained that they had to be destroyed even though they were not currently being used for idolatry, since they had originally been constructed for that purpose.[27]

Others say that those earlier kings would also have liked to eliminate all relics of idolatry. In those times, however, such a task was too great for them to attempt, so they had to be satisfied with discontinuing the actual worship of idols. Though they were not blamed for this, since it might indeed have been impossible for them, the result was tragic. The old shrines and altars remained intact and ready to be revived as soon as the king died. Josiah, however, saw that times had changed and it was now possible. He tried and succeeded.[28]

In this verse, the Mount of Olives is referred to as the "Mount of Destruction." This is a play on words. Its real names were the "Mount of Olives," "הר הזיתים" and the "Mount of Oil," "הר המשחה" because many olive trees grew there from which oil was made. But after it became a place of idolatry, people changed the letters of the word "משחה", "oil", and called it the "Mount of Destruction," "הר המשחית."[29]

23:14 וְשִׁבַּר אֶת־הַמַּצֵּבוֹת וַיִּכְרֹת אֶת־הָאֲשֵׁרִים וַיְמַלֵּא אֶת־מְקוֹמָם עַצְמוֹת אָדָם׃

He smashed the monuments, cut down the Asherim, and filled their places with human bones.

The most impure of all things is the body of a dead person. By making these places into gravesites, Josiah precluded the eventual revival of idolatry there. In the Book of Chronicles it says,[30] "He burned the bones of priests on their altars, and purified Judah and Jerusalem."

23:15 וְגַם אֶת־הַמִּזְבֵּחַ אֲשֶׁר בְּבֵית־אֵל הַבָּמָה אֲשֶׁר עָשָׂה יָרָבְעָם בֶּן־נְבָט אֲשֶׁר הֶחֱטִיא אֶת־יִשְׂרָאֵל גַּם אֶת־הַמִּזְבֵּחַ הַהוּא וְאֶת־הַבָּמָה נָתָץ וַיִּשְׂרֹף אֶת־הַבָּמָה הֵדַק לְעָפָר וְשָׂרַף אֲשֵׁרָה׃

And also the altar that was in Beth-el, the shrine that Jeroboam ben Nebat, who caused Israel to sin, had made, that altar, too, and that shrine, he demolished. He burned the shrine to fine dust and burned the Asherah.

The Book of Chronicles continues,[31] "And in the cities of Manasseh, Ephraim and Simeon, and as far as Naphtali, in their ruins all around. He demolished the altars, crushed the Asherim and the idols fine, cut down all the sun images in the whole Land of Israel, and returned to Jerusalem."

The earlier kings had at most been able to eliminate idolatry within the Kingdom of Judah alone. Now, however, that the Kingdom of Israel had fallen, Josiah was able to enter their former territory and destroy the remains of the cult of the golden calves as well.

23:16 וַיִּפֶן יֹאשִׁיָּהוּ וַיַּרְא אֶת־הַקְּבָרִים אֲשֶׁר־שָׁם בָּהָר וַיִּשְׁלַח וַיִּקַּח אֶת־הָעֲצָמוֹת מִן־הַקְּבָרִים וַיִּשְׂרֹף עַל־הַמִּזְבֵּחַ וַיְטַמְּאֵהוּ כִּדְבַר ה׳ אֲשֶׁר קָרָא אִישׁ הָאֱלֹהִים אֲשֶׁר קָרָא אֶת־הַדְּבָרִים הָאֵלֶּה׃

Josiah turned and saw the graves that were there on the mountain. He sent and took the bones from the graves and burned them on the altar and defiled it, in accordance with the word of G-d that the man of G-d had proclaimed, who had proclaimed these things.

Above, in the thirteenth chapter of the First Book of Kings, we learned about the terrifying warning that Jeroboam ben Nebat had received when he built the altar in Beth-el. As he was performing the first sacrifices on the altar, a prophet came from the territory of Judah.

He proclaimed that one day a king named Josiah would arise from the House of David, who would slaughter the priests of Jeroboam's cult on that very altar and burn human bones upon it. The prophet then left to return to Judah, because G-d had forbidden him to eat or drink in Beth-el. But on the way he was convinced to violate those instructions by a false prophet, originally from Samaria, but who now lived in Beth-el. He returned and ate with him, and as a result was punished by being killed by a lion. The false prophet took the body and buried it in his own grave, so that when he himself died their bones would lie together.

23:17,18 וַיֹּאמֶר מָה הַצִּיּוּן הַלָּז אֲשֶׁר אֲנִי רֹאֶה וַיֹּאמְרוּ אֵלָיו אַנְשֵׁי הָעִיר הַקֶּבֶר אִישׁ־הָאֱלֹהִים אֲשֶׁר־בָּא מִיהוּדָה וַיִּקְרָא אֶת־הַדְּבָרִים הָאֵלֶּה אֲשֶׁר עָשִׂיתָ עַל הַמִּזְבַּח בֵּית־אֵל׃ וַיֹּאמֶר הַנִּיחוּ לוֹ אִישׁ אַל־יָנַע עַצְמוֹתָיו וַיְמַלְּטוּ עַצְמוֹתָיו אֵת עַצְמוֹת הַנָּבִיא אֲשֶׁר־בָּא מִשֹּׁמְרוֹן׃

He said, "What is that marker that I see?" The people of the city said to him, "It is the grave of the man of G-d who came from Judah and proclaimed these things that you did concerning the altar of Beth-el." He said, "Leave him! Let no man move his bones!" So his bones saved the bones of the prophet who had come from Samaria.

Some say that even though the Kingdom of Israel had been destroyed and its people exiled many years before, a few had managed to escape and remain in the land together with the Cuthites that the Assyrians had settled there. Others say they had all been exiled, but later some of them were brought back by the prophet Jeremiah.[32] When Josiah noticed one grave that differed from the others and asked about it, they came forward and told him the story that had been passed down from generation to generation for more than three hundred and fifty years.[33]

It was the grave of the two prophets that Josiah noticed. For all those years the people had kept it clearly marked and distinguished from the rest. Some say that the false prophet had instructed his sons to make a large and distinctive marker on his grave. He knew the prophecy was true, and that in that way his own bones would be saved from disgrace.[34]

Others say it was by a miraculous phenomenon that this grave was distinguished. Some say the miracle was that on one side of the grave the grass grew fresh and green, but on the other it withered and died. Others say that on one side there grew myrtle and fragrant herbs, and on the other thorns and nettles. Josiah noticed this strange phenomenon and inquired about it. The people explained that pleasant vegetation grew on the side where the prophet from Judah was buried, but not on the side of the false prophet who had misled him.[35]

23:19,20 וְגַם אֶת־כָּל־בָּתֵּי הַבָּמוֹת אֲשֶׁר בְּעָרֵי שֹׁמְרוֹן אֲשֶׁר עָשׂוּ מַלְכֵי
יִשְׂרָאֵל לְהַכְעִיס הֵסִיר יֹאשִׁיָּהוּ וַיַּעַשׂ לָהֶם כְּכָל־הַמַּעֲשִׂים אֲשֶׁר עָשָׂה
בְּבֵית־אֵל: וַיִּזְבַּח אֶת־כָּל־כֹּהֲנֵי הַבָּמוֹת אֲשֶׁר־שָׁם עַל־הַמִּזְבְּחוֹת וַיִּשְׂרֹף
אֶת־עַצְמוֹת אָדָם עֲלֵיהֶם וַיָּשָׁב יְרוּשָׁלָםִ:

And also the houses of all the altars that were in the cities of Samaria that the kings of Israel had made to anger G-d, Josiah removed, and did all the same things to them that he had done in Beth-el. He slaughtered all the priests of the shrines that were there upon the altars, burned human bones upon them, and returned to Jerusalem.

The remaining members of the former Kingdom of Israel had persisted in the idolatry of their ancestors even after their kingdom was defeated and destroyed. The shrines remained and continued to function until Josiah destroyed them.[36]

Josiah took nothing from the territory of the former Kingdom of Israel and asked nothing of the people. He wanted no personal gain, but only to bring them back to Torah.[37]

23:21-23 וַיְצַו הַמֶּלֶךְ אֶת־כָּל־הָעָם לֵאמֹר עֲשׂוּ פֶסַח לַה׳ אֱלֹהֵיכֶם כַּכָּתוּב
עַל סֵפֶר הַבְּרִית הַזֶּה: כִּי לֹא נַעֲשָׂה כַּפֶּסַח הַזֶּה מִימֵי הַשֹּׁפְטִים אֲשֶׁר שָׁפְטוּ
אֶת־יִשְׂרָאֵל וְכֹל יְמֵי מַלְכֵי יִשְׂרָאֵל וּמַלְכֵי יְהוּדָה: כִּי אִם־בִּשְׁמֹנֶה עֶשְׂרֵה שָׁנָה
לַמֶּלֶךְ יֹאשִׁיָּהוּ נַעֲשָׂה הַפֶּסַח הַזֶּה לַה׳ בִּירוּשָׁלָםִ:

The king commanded the whole people saying, "Make Passover to the L-rd, your G-d, as is written in this Book of the Covenant." For there had not been made a Passover like this since the days of the judges who judged Israel, and all the days of the kings of Israel and the kings of Judah. Only in the eighteenth year of King Josiah was this Passover made to G-d in Jerusalem.

Passover had certainly been celebrated regularly during the reigns of the righteous kings since David. The celebration of Passover in the time of Hezekiah was described in detail above. The two things that made this Passover of Josiah different was that it was done completely according to the Torah, and that the whole people participated.[38] In earlier generations, there were always some among the people who observed Passover but persisted in idolatry, and others who refused to participate at all. Since the time of Jeroboam, the northern tribes had not gone to Jerusalem, making their pilgrimages to the shrines of the golden calves in Beth-el and Dan instead.[39] Even after the capture of the golden calves, there remained opposition to Jerusalem and the Temple. Thus we read above that when Hezekiah sent messengers to the other tribes inviting them to join him in Jerusalem, they met with scorn in many of the cities of Israel. This time, however, everyone participated.[40] At least for the moment, idolatry had been eliminated, and there was universal acceptance of Torah.[41]

The last time Passover had been observed so completely was in the time of the prophet Samuel, the last of the judges, as is stated in the Book of Chronicles.[42] The statement here, "since the days of the judges," refers to the same time.[43]

The Book of Chronicles also elaborates further details not included here. It says:[44]

> Josiah made Passover for G-d in Jerusalem, and they slaughtered the Passover Sacrifice on the fourteenth of the First Month. He had the priests stand at their assigned positions, and encouraged them for the service of the House of G-d. He said to the Levites who taught all of Israel, G-d's holy ones, "Put the Holy Ark in the Temple that Solomon, the son of David, King of Israel, built. You have no carrying by shoulder. Now, serve the L-rd, your G-d, and His people Israel. And prepare for the house of your fathers according to your divisions, in accordance with the writing of David, King of Israel, and the writ of Solomon, his son. Stand in the holy place according to the divisions of the houses of the fathers, of your brothers, the members of the people, and the divisions of the houses of the fathers of the Levites. Slaughter the Passover Sacrifice, sanctify yourselves,

and prepare for your brothers, to do in accordance with the word of G-d by the hand of Moses." Josiah donated sheep for the members of the people, lambs and goat kids, all for Passover Sacrifices for all who were present to the number of thirty thousand, and cattle three thousand. These were from the property of the king. His officers donated a contribution to the people, the priests, and the Levites, Hilkiah, Zechariah and Jehiel the supervisors of the House of G-d. For the priests they gave for Passover Sacrifices two thousand and six hundred, and cattle, three hundred. And Conaniah, Shemaiah and Nethanel, his brothers and Hashabiah, Jeiel and Jozabad, the officers of the Levites, donated to the Levites for Passover Sacrifices five thousand, and cattle, five hundred. The service was ready, the priests stood at their places and the Levites at their divisions, in accordance with the commandment of the king. They slaughtered the Passover Sacrifice, the priests threw (the blood) from their hands, and the Levites skinned. They removed the burnt offering to give them to the divisions of the houses of the fathers of the members of the people, to offer to G-d, as is written in the Book of Moses. So, too, for the cattle. They cooked the Passover Sacrifice with fire, in accordance with the law, and the other sacrifices they cooked in pots, cauldrons and pans and distributed quickly to the members of the people. After that they prepared for themselves and for the priests, because the priests, the sons of Aaron, (had been busy) bringing the burnt offerings and the fats until night. The Levites prepared for themselves and for the priests, the descendants of Aaron. The singers, the descendants of Asaph, were at their places in accordance with the commandment of David, Asaph, Heman and Jeduthan, the seer of the king. The gatekeepers were at every gate. They didn't have to leave their work, because their brothers, the Levites, prepared for them. The whole service of G-d was ready on that day, to make the Passover Sacrifice and to bring burnt offerings on the altar of G-d, in accordance with the commandment of King Josiah. The Children of Israel who were there made the Passover Sacrifice at that time, and the Festival of Unleavened Bread, seven days. There had not been made a Passover like it in Israel since the time of Samuel, the prophet. None of the kings of Israel had made one like the Passover that Josiah, the priests, the Levites and all Judah and Israel who were there and the inhabitants of Jerusalem made.

23:24 וְגַם אֶת־הָאֹבוֹת וְאֶת־הַיִּדְּעֹנִים וְאֶת־הַתְּרָפִים וְאֶת־הַגִּלֻּלִים וְאֵת
כָּל־הַשִּׁקֻּצִים אֲשֶׁר נִרְאוּ בְּאֶרֶץ יְהוּדָה וּבִירוּשָׁלַם בִּעֵר יֹאשִׁיָּהוּ לְמַעַן הָקִים
אֶת־דִּבְרֵי הַתּוֹרָה הַכְּתֻבִים עַל־הַסֵּפֶר אֲשֶׁר מָצָא חִלְקִיָּהוּ הַכֹּהֵן בֵּית ה׳:

Also the mediums, the oracles, the figures, the idols and all the detestations that were to be seen in the Land of Judah and in Jerusalem Josiah destroyed, in order to establish the words of the Torah that were written in the book that Hilkiah the priest found in the House of G-d.

"Mediums," (אבות), "oracles," (ידענים), and "figures" (תרפים) were kinds of divination and magic.[45]

23:25 וְכָמֹהוּ לֹא־הָיָה לְפָנָיו מֶלֶךְ אֲשֶׁר־שָׁב אֶל־ה׳ בְּכָל־לְבָבוֹ וּבְכָל־
נַפְשׁוֹ וּבְכָל־מְאֹדוֹ כְּכֹל תּוֹרַת מֹשֶׁה וְאַחֲרָיו לֹא־קָם כָּמֹהוּ:

There was no king like him before him who returned to G-d with all his heart with all his soul and with all his might, in accordance with the whole Torah of Moses, and after him there arose none like him.

Some say the expression "who returned to G-d" is not intended to mean that Josiah had sinned and repented for his own sins, but that he returned from the sins of his father and of earlier generations, or from the sins he unwittingly committed as a child under his father's influence, for which he was not really responsible.[46]

Others, however, interpret it to mean that he repented personally, but in a most exceptional way. During the years between the time he ascended the throne and the time the Torah scroll was found, Josiah, as king, had judged many disputes. When he read the words of the Torah he became uncertain whether his decisions had all been in accordance with divine law. Perhaps in some of those cases he had decided in favor of the wrong party. So he returned all the money that had ever been taken from any of the litigants. But since, on the other hand, his original decision might have been correct, he did not take it away from those to whom it had been awarded, but paid it out of his own pocket. There was no other king who did that![47]

Another interpretation is that at first he had only been concerned with his own righteousness and had not tried to correct the sins of the people. Only after Huldah rebuked him did he recognize his responsibility as king to guide the entire nation. He repented for having neglected it until then.[48]

Here the Bible summarizes Josiah's piety to make several points clear, even though they were apparent from the previous verses. First, that it was sincere and wholehearted, not just an outward show. Second, that he was committed to following the Torah, not simply to serving G-d in whatever way he personally felt was right. And third, that in this way he was unique among all the kings. All the rest, even the most righteous, had deviated in one way or another.[49]

A similar statement was made above concerning King Hezekiah. There, however, it says,[50] "There was none like him after him among all the kings of Judah, nor that were before him. He clung to G-d and didn't deviate from following Him, and kept His commandments that G-d had commanded Moses." Josiah and Hezekiah each excelled in a different way. Hezekiah was the greatest in his trust of G-d, for he experienced the greatest test and stood firm. Josiah was the greatest in careful observance of the Torah, in spiritual perfection and in adherence to G-d.[51]

23:26,27 אַךְ לֹא־שָׁב ה׳ מֵחֲרוֹן אַפּוֹ הַגָּדוֹל אֲשֶׁר־חָרָה אַפּוֹ בִּיהוּדָה עַל
כָּל־הַכְּעָסִים אֲשֶׁר הִכְעִיסוֹ מְנַשֶּׁה׃ וַיֹּאמֶר ה׳ גַּם אֶת־יְהוּדָה אָסִיר מֵעַל פָּנַי
כַּאֲשֶׁר הֲסִרֹתִי אֶת־יִשְׂרָאֵל וּמָאַסְתִּי אֶת־הָעִיר הַזֹּאת אֲשֶׁר־בָּחַרְתִּי אֶת־יְרוּשָׁלַםִ
וְאֶת־הַבַּיִת אֲשֶׁר אָמַרְתִּי יִהְיֶה שְׁמִי שָׁם׃

Nonetheless, G-d did not turn back from His great burning wrath, that His wrath burned against Judah, for all the provocation that Manasseh had provoked Him. G-d said, "Judah, too, will I remove from before Me, as I removed Israel. I have rejected in disgust this city that I chose, Jerusalem, and the Temple of which I said, 'My name will be there.' "

It is much easier to bend what is straight than to straighten it again once it has been bent. Although Manasseh repented and spent the latter part of his reign trying to eliminate the idolatry he had introduced, he was unable to bring the people back to Torah. Not all of those that he led astray were willing to repent along with him. His own repentance was therefore never considered complete. That may be why the Bible mentions his repentance only in the Book of Chronicles, but not here in the Book of Kings. It was Manasseh's bad period that was significant for Jewish history, not his good one. Even according to the opinion that he was wicked for only twenty-two of his fifty-five years, it was those twenty-two years that had the more lasting effect.

Some say, furthermore, that Manasseh's repentance was not sincere, being motivated not by true remorse but by suffering. By the merit of his righteous father he had been spared during the years of his wickedness. Rather than being destroyed, he was made to suffer until he repented. So Manasseh's good deeds were not considered to his credit and are not recognized here.[52]

Another possibility is that Manasseh never actively tried to eliminate idolatry among the people. He simply reinstated the service of G-d in the Temple. For that reason his repentance is not mentioned in this book.[53]

G-d's wrath, however, was not in response to the sins of Manasseh alone. Throughout the period of the kings, idolatry and other sins were being practiced among the people. Even during the reigns of the good kings there were always some who continued them in secret. In spite of all the efforts of the prophets and reformers, the tradition of idolatry, which dated from the time of the judges and perhaps even from the exodus from Egypt, had survived and grown stronger. This became evident when the wonderful period of Hezekiah was followed by the disastrous decline under Manasseh.[54]

Even the repentence that Josiah effected in the people was not deep. In the enthusiasm of that moment, they all joined in the Passover celebration. While they did, they felt that they had sincerely become faithful worshipers of G-d and would continue to keep His commandments for the rest of their lives. But once they were home again and the excitement of being in the Temple together with all the other people wore off, they began to revert to their old ways. It is the long-established habits and attitudes of a person that endure. One-time experiences, no matter how intense, have little effect. True change requires altering underlying attitudes and behaviors. That comes slowly.

Thus the prophet Jeremiah wrote,[55] "G-d said to me in the days of King Josiah, 'Have you seen what this errant Israel has done? She has gone on every high mountain and under every lush tree and prostituted there!' " and,[56] "The number of your cities were your gods, Oh Judah!"

During the year that they made the Passover they repented, but afterwards they reverted to their old ways.[57]

23:28 וְיֶתֶר דִּבְרֵי יֹאשִׁיָּהוּ וְכָל־אֲשֶׁר עָשָׂה הֲלֹא־הֵם כְּתוּבִים עַל־סֵפֶר דִּבְרֵי הַיָּמִים לְמַלְכֵי יְהוּדָה׃

The rest of the things about Josiah that he did are indeed written in the Book of the Chronicles of the Kings of Judah.

Some say that Josiah himself realized that the reforms he had achieved would only be temporary. He knew that after him the people would again become corrupted and incur the punishments that had been decreed against them. The Temple would be destroyed and those who survived would be taken into exile, as it says,[58] "G-d will take you and your king that you will set up upon yourself to a nation that you did not know," so he had the Ark of the Covenant hidden away, as it says,[59] "He said to the Levites who taught all of Israel, G-d's holy ones, 'Put the Holy Ark in the Temple that Solomon, the son of David, King of Israel, built. You have no carrying by shoulder.'" He also hid the oil used for anointing, the jar of Manna, the staff of Aaron, and the chest containing the gifts that the Philistines sent when they returned the Ark.[60]

23:29 בְּיָמָיו עָלָה פַרְעֹה נְכֹה מֶלֶךְ־מִצְרַיִם עַל־מֶלֶךְ אַשּׁוּר עַל־נְהַר־פְּרָת וַיֵּלֶךְ הַמֶּלֶךְ יֹאשִׁיָּהוּ לִקְרָאתוֹ וַיְמִיתֵהוּ בִּמְגִדּוֹ כִּרְאֹתוֹ אֹתוֹ׃

In his days, Pharaoh Necoh, King of Egypt, went up against the King of Assyria on the Euphrates River. King Josiah went out to confront him, and he killed him in Megido when he saw him.

Josiah died tragically, not for his own sin, but for the sins of his people. Without his knowledge, they had continued to practice idolatry. They had hidden their idols by painting or carving them on the backs of the double doors, so that when the doors were open and folded back against the wall they would not be visible, but as soon as the doors were closed the two parts of the idol would come together again. Perhaps each half by itself was not even recognizable, so that anyone who saw them while the doors were open would not have suspected what they would become if they were closed. Thus the prophet Isaiah said,[61] "Behind the door and the doorpost you put your remembrance." Josiah suspected nothing, believing his reforms had been successful.[62]

His downfall finally came through the misapplication of the verse,[63] "I will put peace in the land, and no sword will pass through your land." This is one of the promises G-d made to Israel if they would keep the Torah. It refers not only to the swords of enemies attacking, but even the swords of friends and allies. It is a promise of peace and tranquility, not just national security. The Jewish People would in no way be involved with war and violence, even if not directed against them. Josiah thought his generation was worthy of this blessing, so when Pharaoh Necoh entered Josiah's territory with his army on their way to fight Assyria, Josiah met him with his own army and tried to prevent him. Thus in the Book of Chronicles it says:[64]

> After all this that Josiah prepared the Temple, Necoh, King of Egypt, went up to fight against Carchemish that is on the Euphrates, and Josiah went out to confront him. He sent messengers to him saying, "What is there between me and you, Oh King of Judah? It is not against you, (that I am going) today, but to the place of my battle, and G-d has commanded me to hurry. Do not interfere with G-d, Who is with me, that He not destroy you!" But Josiah did not turn his face from him, for he had dressed himself to fight with him. He didn't listen to the words of Necoh from the mouth of G-d, and he went to fight in the Valley of Megido. The archers shot at King Josiah, and the king said to his servants, "Take me away, for I am very weak!" His servants took him from the (battle) chariot and put him in his travelling chariot. They brought him to Jerusalem and he died. He was buried in the graves of his fathers, and all of Judah mourned over Josiah. Jeremiah lamented over Josiah, and all the men and women singers said it in their lamentators over Josiah to this day. They made it a decree upon Israel, and behold, they are written in the Lamentations.

Had Josiah consulted Jeremiah he would have learned the truth about his generation. For them, Pharaoh's offer of peace and friendship was blessing enough. Here was a powerful neighbor fighting Josiah's own enemy for him! But G-d concealed the truth from Josiah so that he would confront him and fall.[65]

Although it had been by divine will that Josiah was killed, Pharaoh Necoh, whose name means "the lame one," was considered guilty and was later punished. After besieging Carchemish unsuccessfully for four years, his army was defeated by Nebuchadnezar, King of Babylonia.[66]

23:30-32 וַיַּרְכִּבֻהוּ עֲבָדָיו מֵת מִמְּגִדּוֹ וַיְבִאֻהוּ יְרוּשָׁלִַם וַיִּקְבְּרֻהוּ בִּקְבֻרָתוֹ וַיִּקַּח עַם־הָאָרֶץ אֶת־יְהוֹאָחָז בֶּן־יֹאשִׁיָּהוּ וַיִּמְשְׁחוּ אֹתוֹ וַיַּמְלִיכוּ אֹתוֹ תַּחַת אָבִיו: בֶּן־עֶשְׂרִים וְשָׁלֹשׁ שָׁנָה יְהוֹאָחָז בְּמָלְכוֹ וּשְׁלֹשָׁה חֳדָשִׁים מָלַךְ בִּירוּשָׁלִָם וְשֵׁם אִמּוֹ חֲמוּטַל בַּת־יִרְמְיָהוּ מִלִּבְנָה: וַיַּעַשׂ הָרַע בְּעֵינֵי ה׳ כְּכֹל אֲשֶׁר־עָשׂוּ אֲבֹתָיו:

His servants carried him by chariot dead from Megido, brought him to Jerusalem and buried him in his grave. The people of the land took Jehoahaz, the son of Josiah, anointed him and made him king in place of his father. Jehoahaz was twenty-three years old when he became king, and he ruled three months in Jerusalem. His mother's name was Hamutal the daughter of Jeremiah from Libnah. He did what was evil in G-d's eyes, like all that his fathers had done.

Josiah left several sons, of whom Jehoahaz was not the oldest. He was, however, popular among the people, especially those who had not supported Josiah's reforms and wanted to return to the days of idolatry. They chose him as the new king, and since he was not the next in line, they anointed him to establish his succession. Some understand the phrase, "the people of the land took Jehoahaz" to mean that they took him by force against the will of his brothers and the other righteous leaders.[67]

The names for the sons of Josiah are given in the Book of Chronicles as:[68] "the first born, Johanan, the second, Jehoiakim, the third Zedekiah, the fourth, Shalum." The name Jehoahaz is not found on this list. However, in one of his prophecies, the prophet Jeremiah says,[69] "Thus says G-d to Shalum the son of Josiah, King of Judah, who reigns in place of Josiah, his father, who went out from this place, 'He will not come back again!' " This description fits Jehoahaz, who, as we will read in the next verses, was taken captive to Egypt, never to return. Some therefore say that Shalum was another name for Jehoahaz. If that is true, then both the omission of the name "Jehoahaz" in this verse and the mystery of who Shalum was and what became of him are explained.

Shalum's position as the youngest among the sons is also consistent with the ages of Jehoahaz and Jehoiakim as recorded here. Jehoahaz was twenty-three when he became king, and Jehoiakim was twenty-five when he replaced him within the same year. Of the four sons of Josiah, it was therefore the eldest, Johanan, who never became king. Perhaps he was righteous like his father and the people did not want him.

The age of Zedekiah, however, is problematic. If he was between Jehoiakim and Jehoahaz, as the order of this list implies, then he must have been about twenty-four. But in the next chapter we read that eleven years later, when he became king, he was only twenty-one years old. That would make him only ten at the time of his father's death, by far the youngest of the sons! Some say that Josiah had appointed him as coregent and successor three years before he died, and it is the time of that appointment that is being referred to as the beginning of his reign. He was then indeed twenty-one.[70]

Others agree with the identification of Shalum with Jehoahaz, but resolve the contradiction of Zedekiah's age differently. They maintain that only two, not three, of the four sons of Josiah eventually became king. The first was Shalum, the youngest, who was called Jehoahaz because he grabbed (אחז) the throne when it was not rightly his. After him came Jehoiakim, the second oldest, who was Josiah's legitimate successor, the oldest, Johanan, having died earlier. But Josiah's third son, Zedekiah, was not King Zedekiah of whom we will read in the next chapters. That was Zedekiah the son of Jehoiakim, as will be explained in more detail in the next chapter, when the succession of those later kings is discussed.[71]

Others say that the verse in Chronicles lists the sons in the order in which they ascended the throne, not in order of age. It is therefore Johanan that is identified with Jehoahaz. According to this interpretation, Jehoiachin, the third king after Josiah, does not appear on the list because he was not a son of Josiah but a grandson. The name Shalum is understood to refer to Zedekiah as well, and the double reference to him in this verse is taken to mean that in age he was the third of the sons, and the fourth to become king after Josiah. Some say he was called "Shalum," "שלום" because he was perfect (משולם) in his deeds, and others because with his reign the kingdom of David was completed (שלמה). No other descendant of David would reign as King of Israel until the final redemption and the coming of the Messiah.[72]

Others agree with this interpretation as far as Johanan, Jehoiakim and Zedekiah are concerned, but differ with respect to Shalum, identifying him with Jehoiachin, the son of Jehoiakin. The reference to him in the Book of Jeremiah as the son of Josiah is explained by the well established practice of referring to a grandson as a son. According to this explanation, the prophecy that Shalum would be taken captive to a foreign land refers to Jehoiachin being taken to Babylonia, not Jehoahaz to Egypt. He is mentioned last even though he reigned before Zedekiah because he was younger and also because he was a grandson, not a son.[73]

23:33-35 וַיַּאַסְרֵהוּ פַרְעֹה נְכֹה בְרִבְלָה בְּאֶרֶץ חֲמָת במלך (מִמְּלֹךְ קרי) בִּירוּשָׁלָםִ וַיִּתֶּן־עֹנֶשׁ עַל־הָאָרֶץ מֵאָה כִכַּר־כֶּסֶף וְכִכַּר זָהָב׃ וַיַּמְלֵךְ פַּרְעֹה נְכֹה אֶת־אֶלְיָקִים בֶּן־יֹאשִׁיָּהוּ תַּחַת יֹאשִׁיָּהוּ אָבִיו וַיַּסֵּב אֶת־שְׁמוֹ יְהוֹיָקִים וְאֶת־יְהוֹאָחָז לָקַח וַיָּבֹא מִצְרַיִם וַיָּמָת שָׁם׃ וְהַכֶּסֶף וְהַזָּהָב נָתַן יְהוֹיָקִים לְפַרְעֹה אַךְ הֶעֱרִיךְ אֶת־הָאָרֶץ לָתֵת אֶת־הַכֶּסֶף עַל־פִּי פַרְעֹה אִישׁ כְּעֶרְכּוֹ נָגַשׂ אֶת־הַכֶּסֶף וְאֶת־הַזָּהָב אֶת־עַם הָאָרֶץ לָתֵת לְפַרְעֹה נְכֹה׃

Pharaoh Necoh imprisoned him in Riblah, in the land of Hamath, that he not rule in Jerusalem. He placed a fine on the land, one hundred talents of silver and one talent of gold. Pharaoh Necoh made Eliakim, the son of Josiah, king in place of Josiah, his father, and changed his name to Jehoiakim. As for Jehoahaz, he took him and brought him to Egypt and he died there. Jehoiakim gave the silver and the gold to Pharaoh. He evaluated the land to give the silver according to Pharaoh. He forced each one of the people of the land according to his evaluation to give the silver and the gold, to give to Pharaoh Necoh.

Jehoahaz gained the throne by force, and by force it was taken from him. Some say that after becoming king he attacked and plundered Egypt to avenge his father's death. He succeeded because Pharaoh and his army were then busy trying to conquer Carchemish, and the country was defenseless. But when Pharaoh heard what Jehoahaz had done he returned and captured him. Thus the prophet Ezekiel compared the Jewish People to a wild lioness and Jehoahaz to her cub. He said,[74] "What is your mother but a lioness? She crouched among the lions. Among the young lions she raised her cubs. She got one of her cubs up and he became a young lion. He learned to tear prey, he ate people. The nations heard him, in their pit he was caught, and brought him with cheek-hooks to the land of Egypt."[75]

Others say that after killing Josiah, Pharaoh Necoh felt he had the right to enter into the domestic politics of Israel and decide who would be their king. Without provocation he removed Jehoahaz and replaced him with his brother. He gave his appointee a new name, too, as a constant reminder of the source of his power. Just as his name was given by Pharaoh, so was his throne. He hoped, thereby, to secure Jehoiakim's loyalty.[76]

The payment that Pharaoh levied on the people was not a yearly tribute but a fine imposed as a punishment for forcefully anointing one who was not fit to be king.[77]

23:36,37 בֶּן־עֶשְׂרִים וְחָמֵשׁ שָׁנָה יְהוֹיָקִים בְּמָלְכוֹ וְאַחַת עֶשְׂרֵה שָׁנָה מָלַךְ
בִּירוּשָׁלָםִ וְשֵׁם אִמּוֹ זבידה (זְבוּדָה קרי) בַת־פְּדָיָה מִן־רוּמָה׃ וַיַּעַשׂ הָרַע
בְּעֵינֵי ה׳ כְּכֹל אֲשֶׁר־עָשׂוּ אֲבֹתָיו׃

Jehoiakim was twenty-five years old when he became king, and he reigned eleven years in Jerusalem. His mother's name was Zebudah the daughter of Pedaiah from Rumah. He did what was evil in G-d's eyes, like all that his fathers had done.

But if Jehoiakim proved loyal to Pharaoh, he was not so to G-d. He followed in the ways of the worst of his ancestors, Ahaz, Manasseh and Amon, as we will read in the next chapter.[78]

II Kings 24

24:1 בִּיָמָיו עָלָה נְבֻכַדְנֶאצַּר מֶלֶךְ בָּבֶל וַיְהִי־לוֹ יְהוֹיָקִים עֶבֶד שָׁלֹשׁ
שָׁנִים וַיָּשָׁב וַיִּמְרָד־בּוֹ׃

In his days, Nebuchadnezar, King of Babylonia, came up, and Jehoiakim became his servant for three years. Then he turned against him and rebelled.

How did Nebuchadnezar become worthy of ruling such a mighty empire? Nebuchadnezar had been the secretary of Baladan, the king about whom we read above, who sent messengers to honor Hezekiah after he was cured.[1] At the time that Baladan was preparing his message, however, Nebuchadnezar was not available, so it was written and sent without him. When he returned, he asked what they had written. They told him: "Peace to King Hezekiah! Peace to the City of Jerusalem! Peace to the great G-d!"

He said, "You acknowledged the greatness of G-d, yet you put Him last? You should have written: 'Peace to the great G-d! Peace to the City of Jerusalem! Peace to King Hezekiah!' "

They answered, "The one who dictates the letter ought to be the messenger!"

So Nebuchadnezar started to run after the messenger to overtake him. But when he had gone only three steps, the angel Gabriel came and stopped him. G-d said, "Since you ran three steps for My honor, I will grant you a dynasty of three emperors who will reign from one end of the earth to the other!"

In fulfillment of this promise Nebuchadnezar became emperor, followed by his son Ewil-merodach and his grandson Balshazar. Had Gabriel not stopped him, the Babylonian Empire would have endured to this day, and the Jewish People would never have been able to become free from its control![2]

As we read in the previous chapter, the prophet Ezekiel compared the Jewish People to a lioness and the wicked kings to her cubs. Of Jehoahaz he said:[3]

> What is your mother but a lioness? She crouched among the lions. Among the young lions she raised her cubs. She got one of her cubs up and he became a young lion. He learned to tear prey, he ate people. The nations heard him, in their pit he was caught, and brought him with cheek-hooks to the land of Egypt.

He continued to describe how Jehoiakim followed in his brother's footsteps and suffered a similar fate:[4]

> She saw that she was despondent, her hope was lost, so she took one of her cubs and made him a young lion. He walked among lions and was indeed a young lion. He learned to tear prey, he ate people. He raped their widows and destroyed their cities. The land and all that was in it became desolate from the sound of his roar. So the nations put themselves upon him all around, from the countries. They spread their net upon him. In their pit he was caught. They put him in a cage in cheek-hooks and brought him to the King of Babylonia. They put him in prison so that his voice not be heard any more in the mountains of Israel.

The Book of Jeremiah and the Book of Chronicles give more details of Jehoiakim's first encounter with Nebuchadnezar. In the Book of Chronicles it says,[5] "Nebuchadnezar, King of Babylonia, came up against him and bound him in copper chains to take him to Babylonia. And Nebuchadnezar brought some of the utensils of the House of G-d to Babylonia and put them in his palace in Babylonia." It was in the beginning of Jehoiakim's fourth year, and Nebuchadnezar himself had just become King of Babylonia. In the Book of Jeremiah,[6] it is referred to as "the fourth year of Jehoiakim, the son of Josiah, King of Judah, which is the first year of Nebuchadnezar, King of Babylonia."

Some say the first chapter of the Book of Daniel also refers to this event. It says,[7] "In the third year of the reign of Jehoiakim, King of Judah, Nebuchadnezar, King of Babylonia, came to Jerusalem and besieged it. G-d gave Jehoiakim, King of Judah, into his hand, and some of the utensils of the House of G-d, and he brought them to the land of Shinar, to the house of his god, and the utensils he brought to the treasury of his god." According to this opinion, it is called the third year because, rather than counting the years from the month of Nisan, the Book of Daniel reckons the actual amount of time that Jehoiakim had been king.[8] Others say Daniel refers to a later defeat at the hands of Nebuchadnezar, as we will read shortly.[9]

Once Nebuchadnezar felt confident that Jehoiakim would remain loyal to him, he sent him back to Jerusalem as his vassal. And to better prepare for the loyalty of future leaders of the Jewish People, he took the most promising children of the royal family to raise and educate in his own palace. Thus in the Book of Daniel we read,[10] "And the king told Ashpenaz, the chief of his ministers, to bring some of the Children of Israel, from the descendants of the royal house and from the nobles, children who had no blemish, of good appearance, intelligent in all wisdom, knowing of thoughts, understanding knowledge, and who had strength to stand in the palace of the king, to teach them the literature and the language of the Chaldeans."

But Jehoiakim's loyalty did not last long. Some say the three years that he was a servant of Nebuchadnezar referred to in this verse were the years that he was imprisoned in Babylonia. As soon as he was freed and returned to his kingdom, he rebelled. Others say he remained faithful three years after he was released.

Nor is it clear how long he was held captive in Babylonia. It could have been as much as four years. Some say that he was returned right away and others that he was never actually taken to Babylonia at all. After capturing him Nebuchadnezar threatened to take him back, but when he promised to be loyal he released him.

There are also different opinions concerning how long he defied Nebuchadnezar. Some say his rebellion was immediately put down, others that it was three more years before Nebuchadnezar defeated him again. In total, however, he reigned eleven years, and since about three of them were before Nebuchadnezar, there remain about eight years between the time Nebuchadnezar first conquered him and the time he was conquered again and killed.[11]

In the Book of Chronicles[12] it says that Nebuchadnezar "bound him in copper chains to take him to Babylonia." It is not clear whether this refers to the first or second conquest, nor is it clear whether the words "to take him" are to be understood to mean that he actually was taken or that it was only Nebuchadnezar's intention to take him, but in the end he did not. Some interpret this to mean that he was not taken even the first time.[13] Others say he was captured alive the second time and not executed, but died before he could be brought to Babylonia.[14]

Some say it was the second conquest, not the first, to which Daniel was referring as being in the "third year of Jehoiakim." It was called his third year because it was the third year after his rebellion, therefore his third year as a sovereign ruler.[15]

24:2 וַיְשַׁלַּח ה׳ בּוֹ אֶת־גְּדוּדֵי כַשְׂדִּים וְאֶת־גְּדוּדֵי אֲרָם וְאֵת גְּדוּדֵי מוֹאָב
וְאֵת גְּדוּדֵי בְנֵי־עַמּוֹן וַיְשַׁלְּחֵם בִּיהוּדָה לְהַאֲבִידוֹ כִּדְבַר ה׳ אֲשֶׁר דִּבֶּר בְּיַד
עֲבָדָיו הַנְּבִיאִים׃

G-d sent against him bands of Chaldeans, bands of Arameans, bands of Moabites and bands of Amonites. He sent them against Judah to destroy it, in accordance with the word of G-d that He had spoken by the hand of His servants, the prophets.

All the bands were sent by Nebuchadnezar to weaken the Kingdom of Judah until it could be destroyed.[16] These nations were traditional enemies of the Jewish People, and they were only too happy to help in its destruction. Some say it was these nations that persuaded Nebuchadnezar to destroy Jerusalem in the first place. He was reluctant to attempt it, remembering the terrible defeat of Sanherib not long before, but the people of Amon and Moab had heard that the prophets of Israel had foretold imminent destruction, and they convinced him that he would succeed.[17]

Nebuchadnezar established his court in the city of Riblah, which in later times was called Antioch. When it was clear that his army would soon conquer Jerusalem, the Sanhedrin went to meet him. They said, "The time has come for this Temple to be destroyed!"

"No!" He answered, "It is only Jehoiakim, who rebelled against me, that I want. Give him to me and I will go away!"

They went and told Jehoiakim, "Nebuchadnezar wants you!"

"Is that the proper thing to do," he replied, "to sacrifice one life for another? Doesn't the Torah say,[18] 'Don't hand over a slave to his master?' "

They replied, "But isn't that what your ancestor, David, did to Sheba ben Bichri?"

Still, he refused to listen to them and give himself up. Finally they took him by force and lowered him over the wall. Some say they bound him and lowered him down alive, others say they killed him. Some reconcile the two opinions by saying that they bound him alive and he died while being lowered down, because he was very delicate and not used to such rough treatment. Others say he was taken alive by the

Babylonians, paraded through all the cities of Judah and then killed.

After that they desecrated his body. Some say they cut open a donkey and stuffed his body inside, as the prophet Jeremiah had predicted,[19] "Therefore, thus says G-d of Jehoiakim the son of Josiah, King of Judah, 'They will not mourn him, 'Woe, my brother! Woe, my sister!' nor will they mourn him, 'Woe master! Woe his glory!' The burial of a donkey he will be buried, dragged and thrown, beyond the gates of Jerusalem.'" Others say they cut his body into small pieces and threw them to the dogs, as is done with the carcass of a donkey, and that is the meaning of "the burial of a donkey."[20]

24:3 אַךְ עַל־פִּי ה׳ הָיְתָה בִּיהוּדָה לְהָסִיר מֵעַל פָּנָיו בְּחַטֹּאת מְנַשֶּׁה כְּכֹל אֲשֶׁר עָשָׂה׃

Indeed, it was by the word of G-d that this happened to Judah, to remove them from His presence, for the sins of Manasseh in accordance with all that he had done.

This does not mean that they were now being punished for the sins that Manasseh committed years before. Why should they be punished for someone else's sins? Nor were they punished for the sins their fathers had done in the early years of Manasseh, nor even for the sins they themselves had committed then. Had they repented they would have been forgiven for them all. Rather, it was the sins that they continued to do. Why, then, are these referred to as "the sins of Manasseh?" Some say it is because they could be traced to the corruption which he began. G-d had forgiven the sins of earlier generations, as bad as they were, but the sins Manasseh introduced were so grave that G-d would not forgive them. He decreed that Jerusalem be destroyed.[21] Others say it was because they did not repent along with Manasseh. They were quick to follow his example when he sinned, but not when he repented.[22]

24:4 וְגַם דַּם־הַנָּקִי אֲשֶׁר שָׁפָךְ וַיְמַלֵּא אֶת־יְרוּשָׁלַם דָּם נָקִי וְלֹא־אָבָה ה׳ לִסְלֹחַ׃

Also the innocent blood that he spilt, and filled Jerusalem with innocent blood, G-d did not want to forgive.

Manasseh's corruption was not limited to rebellion against G-d and violation of religious laws. He had initiated a period of moral and ethical decline as well.

As long as Josiah was alive they had been protected by his merit. Even though the divine decree to destroy Jerusalem had already been made during the time of Manasseh, G-d refrained from carrying it out. But once Jehoiakim became king, G-d did not withhold His anger any more. It was therefore the wickedness of Manasseh, not of Jehoiakim, that is cited as the reason for their destruction. Jehoiakim was responsible only for its coming now rather than being postponed longer.[23]

24:5 וְיֶתֶר דִּבְרֵי יְהוֹיָקִים וְכָל־אֲשֶׁר עָשָׂה הֲלֹא־הֵם כְּתוּבִים עַל־סֵפֶר דִּבְרֵי הַיָּמִים לְמַלְכֵי יְהוּדָה׃

The rest of the things about Jehoiakim and all that he did are indeed written in the Book of the Chronicles of the Kings of Judah.

Jehoiakim's behavior was among the worst of all the kings. Nowhere does the Bible relate the extent of his evil deeds, neither here nor in the Book of Chronicles. Even the prophet Jeremiah alluded to them only obliquely, by the words,[24] "Woe to the one who builds his house without righteousness, and his upper stories without justice, who forces his fellow to work for nothing, and doesn't give to his worker... For your eyes and your heart are only on your profit, on spilling the blood of the innocent and doing violence."

Tradition, however, describes them explicitly. Jehoiakim believed that G-d removed Himself from the affairs of the earth once He created it, and would neither reward the righteous nor punish the wicked. The earth functioned entirely without G-d's interference. The only thing that still came from G-d was the light of the sky. Even that, he argued, could be done without, so there was no need to be afraid of G-d's wrath. He maintained that if necessary it would be possible to produce light here on earth.

He said, "The early generations didn't know how to antagonize G-d! They were afraid to really make G-d angry because they thought they needed Him. But I know we don't! Let Him take His light away! We don't need it! We have shining gold to give us light!"

The people objected, "But doesn't the gold also belong to G-d, as it says,[25] 'Mine is the silver and Mine is the gold' says the L-rd of H-sts."

He answered, "He has already given it to us, as it says,[26] 'The heavens are the heavens of G-d, and the earth He gave to the sons of Man.' "

What did Jehoiakim do? Some say he tattooed G-d's name on a part of his body. Others say he tattooed the name of an idol there.[27] Some say he wore forbidden mixtures of wool and linen. Others say he stretched his foreskin so that he would appear as if he had not been circumcised. Some say he had incestuous relations with his mother, his daughter-in-law, and his father's wife. He killed men to rob their money and take their wives.[28]

Because Jehoiakim disgraced G-d with his body, his body was condemned to disgrace after his death. Hundreds of years later, one of the learned men of Jerusalem found a skull near the gates of the city with the words "This and yet another" written on it. He did not know what to make of this strange inscription, but he buried it respectfully, since, whatever it meant, it was nonetheless a human skull. A short while later, though, he found it uncovered again. He reburied it, and again he found it exposed. Then he concluded that it was the skull of Jehoiakim, and that this was part of the fulfillment of the prophecy, "the burial of a donkey he will be buried, dragged and thrown, beyond the gates of Jerusalem." He said, "Even if he was not worthy of burial, he was still a King of Israel. It is not proper to treat his remains disrespectfully." So he took the skull, wrapped it in silk, and put it in a chest.

A while later his wife came across the strange little bundle. When she saw what it was she went in confusion to tell her neighbors. Of course, her neighbors didn't know any more than she did, but they weren't particularly concerned about honesty, so they said, "That? That's the skull of your husband's first wife. He keeps it because he doesn't want to forget her!"

"Indeed," thought the wife, "so I'm the 'yet another?' I'll show him!" So she threw it into the oven and burned it. When her husband came home and heard what had happened, he understood that this was the final disgrace that had been decreed against Jehoiakim. "Now," he said, "we know the meaning of the words 'and yet another!' "[29] Thus, for disgracing G-d with his body he was denied burial, and for claiming that human beings did not need G-d's light his remains were ultimately burned in fire.[30]

24:6 וַיִּשְׁכַּב יְהוֹיָקִים עִם־אֲבֹתָיו וַיִּמְלֹךְ יְהוֹיָכִין בְּנוֹ תַּחְתָּיו׃

Jehoiakim lay down with his fathers, and Jehoiachin, his son, became king in his place.

The words, "Jehoiakim lay down with his fathers" are simply an expression of death. They do not refer to burial with his fathers, since Jehoiakim was indeed not buried with them, as we just learned.

24:7 וְלֹא־הֹסִיף עוֹד מֶלֶךְ מִצְרַיִם לָצֵאת מֵאַרְצוֹ כִּי־לָקַח מֶלֶךְ בָּבֶל מִנַּחַל מִצְרַיִם עַד־נְהַר פְּרָת כֹּל אֲשֶׁר הָיְתָה לְמֶלֶךְ מִצְרָיִם׃

The King of Egypt did not continue to go out of his land anymore, for the King of Babylonia had conquered from the Stream of Egypt to the Euphrates River, all that had belonged to the King of Egypt.

As for Egypt, it had lost its hold over the region, so Pharaoh no longer had the power to tell the people of Judah whom to crown as their next king. They were completely under the control of Babylonia.

The "Stream of Egypt," also called the "River of Egypt," is the river bed in the Sinai Desert that forms part of the southern boundary of the Holy land. Today it is called "Wadi Elarish." Babylonia had conquered the whole Land of Israel and everything to the north.

24:8,9 בֶּן־שְׁמֹנֶה עֶשְׂרֵה שָׁנָה יְהוֹיָכִין בְּמָלְכוֹ וּשְׁלֹשָׁה חֳדָשִׁים מָלַךְ בִּירוּשָׁלָםִ וְשֵׁם אִמּוֹ נְחֻשְׁתָּא בַת־אֶלְנָתָן מִירוּשָׁלָםִ׃ וַיַּעַשׂ הָרַע בְּעֵינֵי ה׳ כְּכֹל אֲשֶׁר־עָשָׂה אָבִיו׃

Jehoiachin was eighteen years old when he became king, and he reigned for three months in Jerusalem. His mother's name was Nehushta the daughter of Elnathan from Jerusalem. He did what was evil in G-d's eyes, like all that his father had done.

This verse seems to contradict the verse in the Book of Chronicles that says,[31] "Jehoiachin was eight years old when he became king, and he reigned three months and ten days in Jerusalem." Some say that he had been appointed by his father as coregent when he was eight, shortly after his father himself became king. Jehoiakim saw that there were many political forces influencing the succession, and hoped in this way to insure his own choice.[32]

Others say the eight years mentioned in the Book of Chronicles refer not to the age of Jehoiachin but to the reign of Nebuchadnezar. It was the eighth year since the divine decree that Jerusalem be destroyed had been made and since Nebuchadnezar, who had been chosen to carry out that decree, had become king.[33]

Another interpretation is that the words "and ten days" in the Book of Chronicles really mean "ten years," and are not connected with the "three months" but with the "eight years" earlier in the verse. The verse should therefore be understood to mean "Jehoiachin was eight years and ten years old when he became king and he reigned three months in Jerusalem," in exact agreement with the verse here in Kings. There are other places in the Bible where the word "days" is used to mean years, and there are also verses in which a word or phrase is separated from the words to which it refers.[34]

24:10,11 בָּעֵת הַהִיא עלה (עָלוּ קרי) עַבְדֵי נְבֻכַדְנֶאצַּר מֶלֶךְ־בָּבֶל יְרוּשָׁלָם
וַתָּבֹא הָעִיר בַּמָּצוֹר: וַיָּבֹא נְבֻכַדְנֶאצַּר מֶלֶךְ־בָּבֶל עַל־הָעִיר וַעֲבָדָיו צָרִים עָלֶיהָ:

At that time servants of Nebuchadnezar, King of Babylonia, came up to Jerusalem, and came and laid siege to the city. Nebuchadnezar, King of Babylonia, came up upon the city while his servants were besieging it.

After Jehoiakim was killed and Jehoiachin crowned in his place, Nebuchadnezar returned to Babylonia. When he arrived the people came out to celebrate his victory, but upon hearing that he had left Jehoiachin in his father's place, they criticized him. They said, "The saying goes, 'Don't raise a good pup of a bad dog.' Even if the offspring seem good, they are not to be trusted if the parent was bad. All the more so if the pup itself is bad!" Nebuchadnezar listened and immediately turned around and went back.[35]

The word "came up" in this verse is written in the singular, "עלה," but read in the plural, "עלו." First the servants came up and then Nebuchadnezar himself.[36]

24:12 וַיֵּצֵא יְהוֹיָכִין מֶלֶךְ־יְהוּדָה עַל־מֶלֶךְ בָּבֶל הוּא וְאִמּוֹ וַעֲבָדָיו וְשָׂרָיו
וְסָרִיסָיו וַיִּקַּח אֹתוֹ מֶלֶךְ בָּבֶל בִּשְׁנַת שְׁמֹנֶה לְמָלְכוֹ׃

Jehoiachin, King of Judah, came out to the King of Babylonia, he, his mother, his servants, his officers and his ministers. The King of Babylonia took him captive in the eighth year of his reign.

Again the Sanhedrin went to meet Nebuchadnezar, and again they said, "The time has come for this Temple to be destroyed!"

He answered as before, "No! I have not come to destroy Jerusalem. I only want Jehoiachin. Send him out to me and I will leave in peace."

They went and told Jehoiachin. Jehoiachin realized that this was G-d's will, so there was no point in resisting. He gathered the keys of the Temple and said, "Oh, G-d, since we are not worthy of being the guardians of Your House, I return the keys to You!"

Some say a hand of fire came out of heaven and took them from him. Others say he threw them up and they didn't fall back down. The people were so distraught that young men went up to the rooftops and threw themselves down and died.[37]

24:13,14 וַיּוֹצֵא מִשָּׁם אֶת־כָּל־אוֹצְרוֹת בֵּית ה׳ וְאוֹצְרוֹת בֵּית הַמֶּלֶךְ וַיְקַצֵּץ
אֶת־כָּל־כְּלֵי הַזָּהָב אֲשֶׁר עָשָׂה שְׁלֹמֹה מֶלֶךְ־יִשְׂרָאֵל בְּהֵיכַל ה׳ כַּאֲשֶׁר דִּבֶּר ה׳׃
וְהִגְלָה אֶת־כָּל־יְרוּשָׁלַם וְאֶת־כָּל־הַשָּׂרִים וְאֵת כָּל־גִּבּוֹרֵי הַחַיִל עשרה (עֲשֶׂרֶת
קרי) אֲלָפִים גּוֹלֶה וְכָל־הֶחָרָשׁ וְהַמַּסְגֵּר לֹא נִשְׁאַר זוּלַת דַּלַּת עַם־הָאָרֶץ׃

He removed all the treasuries of the House of G-d and the treasuries of the house of the king from there. He cut up all the golden utensils that Solomon, King of Israel, had made in the Sanctuary of G-d, as G-d had said. He exiled all of Jerusalem, all the officers and all the mighty warriors. Ten thousand were exiled, and all the craftsmen and the gate keepers. There remained none but the poorest of the people of the land.

This time, Nebuchadnezar was not content to reduce the kingdom to vassalage and tribute. He ruined the nation economically and socially.

All that remained were the weak and impoverished masses who were incapable of rebelling and establishing an independent country again.

Here we begin to see the terrible cruelty for which the Babylonians were to be infamous. They completely lacked compassion and mercy. Though Jehoiachin submitted without resistance, their hearts were not softened.

Some say it is this exile to which the prophet Jeremiah was referring when he said,[38] "This is the people that Nebuchadnezar exiled in the seventh year, Judeans, three thousand and twenty-three." He referred to it as the seventh year while above it was referred to as the eighth year because it was the seventh year since Jehoiakim was first conquered and the eighth year of Nebuchadnezar.[39] Others say it was the beginning of Nebuchadnezar's eighth year, when he had reigned seven years.[40]

According to that opinion, the ten thousand in this verse is the total number of the exiles. Of those, the three thousand mentioned by Jeremiah were from the tribe of Judah and the remaining seven thousand were from Benjamin and the other tribes.[41]

Others say that Jeremiah was talking about an exile at the time of the defeat of Jehoiakim, several months earlier, which is not recorded here. That one was indeed in the seventh year of Nebuchadnezar, and this one in the eighth. According to this opinion, the Book of Jeremiah discusses only those exiles not recorded here in Kings. The first was after the defeat of Jehoiakim. The one described here was the second. The third was at the time of the destruction of the Temple, ten years later, as it says,[42] "In the eighteenth year of Nebuchadnezar, from Jerusalem, eight hundred and thirty-two people." The fourth was five years after that, as it says,[43] "In the twenty-third year of Nebuchadnezar, Nebuzaradan, the Chief Executioner, exiled seven hundred and forty-five Judean people, the total being four thousand and six hundred."[44]

Some say the words "חרש" and "מסגר" mean the craftsmen and the gatekeepers.[45] Others say they refer to the great Torah scholars. Everyone would gather to learn from them, and their wisdom was so great that when they spoke everyone was quiet (חרש). They were also the ones to conclude (סגר) the discussion, because no one could add to their words.[46] Among them were Ezekiel and Mordechai.

Although they might not have realized it at the time, these pious students of Torah had been granted a great favor by being sent into exile now. They were thus spared the suffering of the siege and the harsh treatment that its survivors were to receive when they were exiled eleven years later. Thus the prophet Jeremiah said,[47] "Don't cry for the one that dies and don't shake your head for him, but surely cry for the one that goes, for he will not come back again and see the country of his birth." The words "the one that dies" are understood to refer in particular to Jehoiakim, and "the one that goes" to Jehoiachin and Zedekiah who would later go into exile.[48]

It was a favor for the whole Jewish People too, because when these scholars settled in Babylonia they established institutions of Torah learning, which were ready there for the others when they arrived later.[49]

It was also a great act of kindness to exile the people at this time rather than postpone the exile any longer. Had G-d waited but two more years, the number of years of Jewish settlement in the Holy Land would have reached eight hundred and fifty-two, the numerical value of the word "ונושנתם." That would have constituted a fulfillment of the prophecy,[50] "When you bear children and children's children, and you become old (ונושנתם) in the land, and you become corrupted... I call the heavens and the earth to witness against you that you will surely be destroyed." Then their wickedness would have become so great that they would have incurred total destruction. Thus Daniel said,[51] "G-d hastened the evil and brought it upon us, the L-rd, our G-d, is righteous."[52]

24:15,16 וַיֶּגֶל אֶת־יְהוֹיָכִין בָּבֶלָה וְאֶת־אֵם הַמֶּלֶךְ וְאֶת־נְשֵׁי הַמֶּלֶךְ וְאֶת־
סָרִיסָיו וְאֵת אולי (אֵילֵא קרי) הָאָרֶץ הוֹלִיךְ גּוֹלָה מִירוּשָׁלַםִ בָּבֶלָה׃ וְאֵת
כָּל־אַנְשֵׁי הַחַיִל שִׁבְעַת אֲלָפִים וְהֶחָרָשׁ וְהַמַּסְגֵּר אֶלֶף הַכֹּל גִּבּוֹרִים עֹשֵׂי
מִלְחָמָה וַיְבִיאֵם מֶלֶךְ־בָּבֶל גּוֹלָה בָּבֶלָה׃

He exiled Jehoiachin to Babylonia. And the mother of the king, the king's wives, his ministers and the nobles of the land he took into exile from Jerusalem to Babylonia. And all the members of the military, seven thousand, and the craftsmen and the gate keepers, one thousand, all mighty ones who could make war, the King of Babylonia brought in exile to Babylonia.

Some say these verses are a more detailed decription of the ten thousand mentioned above. Seven thousand of them were soldiers, one thousand artisans, and two thousand more were officials and other citizens considered important enough to be removed to Babylonia.[53] Others say that these were in addition to the ten thousand above.[54]

Some say the expression "mighty ones who could make war" should not be taken literally. It is not appropriate to refer in this way to helpless captives who are being led away in chains, however strong and skilled at fighting they might be. It is, rather, a metaphor for scholars who were well versed in Torah and can argue effectively with each other.[55]

Nebuchadnezar bound Jehoiachin and imprisoned him in a prison from which no one ever came out. The Sanhedrin said, "It seems that the end of the House of David will come in our time!" Still, they did not give up hope. They went to the queen's nurse and persuaded her to intercede for them, and she went to the queen. Some say the queen's name was Shemirah, others say it was Shemirmoth and others Shemiram. When Nebuchadnezar came to her in the evening she said, "You are a king and Jehoiachin is a king. Just as you want your wife so he wants his!"

Nebuchadnezar ordered that Jehoiachin's wife be sent to him. Some say there was a barred window above his cell through which they lowered her down to him. Others say they made a hole in the ceiling. The first time they did it he found that she was unclean, and refused to have relations with her. She was brought back out and purified herself, and after a week she was lowered back in. G-d said to him, "When you were king in Jerusalem you did not keep the laws of purity, but here in prison you keep them! By that merit you will have a son and you yourself will one day go free!"[56]

24:17-19 וַיַּמְלֵךְ מֶלֶךְ־בָּבֶל אֶת־מַתַּנְיָה דֹדוֹ תַּחְתָּיו וַיַּסֵּב אֶת־שְׁמוֹ צִדְקִיָּהוּ׃
בֶּן־עֶשְׂרִים וְאַחַת שָׁנָה צִדְקִיָּהוּ בְמָלְכוֹ וְאַחַת עֶשְׂרֵה שָׁנָה מָלַךְ בִּירוּשָׁלָם וְשֵׁם
אִמּוֹ חמיטל (חֲמוּטַל קרי) בַּת־יִרְמְיָהוּ מִלִּבְנָה׃ וַיַּעַשׂ הָרַע בְּעֵינֵי ה׳ כְּכֹל
אֲשֶׁר־עָשָׂה יְהוֹיָקִים׃

The King of Babylonia crowned Mataniah, his uncle, in his place, and changed his name to Zedekiah. Zedekiah was twenty-one years old when he became king, and for eleven years he reigned in Jerusalem. His mother's name was Hamutal, the daughter of Jeremiah from Libnah. He did what was evil in G-d's eyes, like all that Jehoiakim had done.

In the preceding chapter we discussed the verse in the Book of Chronicles that lists the sons of Josiah. The four names on that list were Johanan, Jehoiakim, Zedekiah and Shalum. At that time, our primary concern was to explain the absence of the name "Jehoahaz." Jehoahaz was one of the sons of Josiah, not the eldest, but the first to succeed him as king. There we mentioned two opinions. According to one, Jehoahaz is identified with Johanan, and the reference to him in Chronicles as the firstborn is explained to mean that he was the first to succeed his father. According to the other, he is identified with Shalum, the youngest of the sons.

The second name on the list, "Jehoiakim," is unproblematic. He was the second king after Josiah. Whether or not he was the oldest of the sons depends upon the two opinions just mentioned. He was certainly older than Jehoahaz, since he was twenty-five when he became king and Jehoahaz was then twenty-three. If Jehoahaz was Shalum, however, then there was another son, Johanan, who was even older.

In connection with the identity of Zedekiah we encountered new problems, giving rise to four different resolutions. They were discussed briefly there, but now we will consider them again in greater detail. Those who identify Jehoahaz with Shalum can ignore Johanan, since he is not mentioned anywhere else in the Bible. He was the oldest and either died or was rejected for some other reason, but since he is not identified with Jehoahaz, he was not one of the four successors of Josiah. But no one can ignore Shalum. Above we quoted the prophecy of Jeremiah,[57] "Thus says G-d to Shalum the son of Josiah, King of Judah, who reigns in place of Josiah, his father, who went out from this place, 'He will not come back again!'" Those who identify Jehoahaz with Johanan must explain who it is that the prophet is talking about whom he calls "Shalum."

Since the description in this verse clearly does not fit Jehoiakim, there are two possibilities, Jehoiachin and Zedekiah. Each presents its own difficulties. At first it seems that Jehoiachin is in fact the only possibility, since the verse in Chronicles in which the name "Shalum" is found already includes the name "Zedekiah." But if Shalum was Jehoiachin, why is he listed among the sons of Josiah, when he was not a son but a grandson? The practice of referring to grandchildren as children is not a sufficient explanation in this case as it would be in other contexts. The subject of this section of the Book of Chronicles is establishing the geneology of the House of David, listing the generations one after another. Indeed, in the next verse Jehoiachin is mentioned as a son of Jehoiakim. How, then, could he be included in the list of the sons of Josiah?

Those following this approach, however, have already had to deal with a similar problem in the beginning of the verse, where Johanan is called the firstborn even though he was younger than Jehoiakim. The answer given there, that the subject of the list is not really Josiah's sons but his successors, can be applied here as well. Jehoiachin is included because he was both a descendant and a successor to the throne.

But if that is the case, he should have been placed before Zedekiah, since he reigned before him. The answer offered is that he is placed last because he was not a son but a grandson. The verse is therefore a complicated compromise. First of all, although it seems to be discussing the sons of Josiah, it is really about his successors, and lists them in the order in which they ascended the throne rather than birth. But that is only true of those that are really sons. The one who was not a son, although he is included, is placed last. Zedekiah was therefore the youngest son of Josiah. Since he was twenty-one when he became king, he was only ten when his father died eleven years earlier.[58]

This confusion can be avoided by identifying Shalum with Zedekiah instead of Jehoiachin, but then we must deal with a different problem. The name Zedekiah already appears on the list, implying that Zedekiah and Shalum are different people. All the more so since Zedekiah is identified as the third and Shalum as the fourth. Again, the resolution follows from the interpretation of the beginning of the verse. Since the purpose of the verse is not to list the sons of Josiah but to tell their places in the succession to the throne, Zedekiah is mentioned twice, once to tell that he was the third son and again to tell that he was the fourth to become king after Josiah. According to this interpretation he had three names, "Mataniah," "Shalum," and "Zedekiah."[59] "Zedekiah," the name given to him by Nebuchadnezar, was intended to mean, "May G-d pass judgment on you if you rebel against me!"[60]

Those who identify Jehoahaz with Shalum face another kind of problem. According to this interpretation, Johanan, the first on the list, was indeed the firstborn, so the list is understood to continue in order of age. The positions of Jehoiakim and Shalum are consistent with that, since they were twenty-five and twenty-three respectively at the time of their father's death. It is the age of Zedekiah that is now problematic. We just read that he was twenty-one when he became king, but if he was between Jehoiakim and Shalum, then he must have already been twenty-four when Josiah died, eleven years earlier, and have been thirty-five when he ascended the throne.

One answer is that the statement that he was twenty-one when he became king refers to a time fourteen years earlier, when he was appointed by his father as coregent. Zedekiah had been Josiah's own choice as successor, and he had had him crowned as coregent while he was still alive. At that time Zedekiah was twenty-one. But after his father's death three years later, first one brother and then another was given the throne instead. Only now, after eleven years, did his reign begin.

This also explains a seemingly self-contradictory verse in the Book of Jeremiah. It says,[61] "In the beginning of the reign of Jehoiakim, the son of Josiah, King of Judah, this word came to Jeremiah from G-d saying, 'Make yourself harness straps and yokes and put them on your neck, and send them to the King of Edom, to the King of Moab, to the King of the Children of Amon, to the King of Tyre and to the King of Zidon, by the hand of messengers who come to Jerusalem to Zedekiah, the King of Judah." This verse is problematic in itself, because it refers to both Jehoiakim and Zedekiah as king at the same time. If, however, Zedekiah had already been appointed by his father, then he rightfully bore the title of king even though his brother, Jehoiakim, was on the throne. Furthermore, since he had already ruled together with his father, he was recognized by the kings of Tyre and Zidon and they sent their communications to him.[62]

Another answer is that there were two Zedekiah's, one a son of Josiah and the other a grandson, a son of Jehoiakim. It was the second of these that became king after his brother, Jehoiachin. Thus in the next verse in the Book of Chronicles we read,[63] "The sons of Jehoiakim, Jehoiachin, his son, Zedekiah his son." Zedekiah, the son of Josiah, who is the one listed between Jehoiakim and Shalum, was indeed between them in age, but never became king. These two verses, then, can be understood in their literal sense, as lists of sons in order of age, without any need for reinterpretation.[64]

This interpretation is supported by another verse in Chronicles about Jehoiachin that says,[65] "At the end of the year King Nebuchadnezar sent and brought him to Babylonia with the coveted utensils of the House of G-d, and made Zedekiah, his brother, king over Judah in Jerusalem."

There are three points supporting this interpretation. First, it does not require deviation from the literal meaning and order of the verses, as the other interpretations do. Second, it is not dependent upon postulating events not mentioned in the Bible, such as the appointment of Zedekiah during his father's lifetime. And third, that the succession follows the normal order, in which a king is succeeded by his son, not his brother or uncle, and only when a king dies childless is the succession moved back to the previous generation. This follows the same pattern as inheritance of property. Once a son is crowned, the kingdom passes to him and away from his brothers. To the extent that there was deviation from this in that period, it was due to foreign influence.

There are, however, problems with this interpretation too. First is the reference here in the Book of Kings to Zedekiah as the uncle of Jehoiachin, not his brother, as we read, "The King of Babylonia crowned Mataniah, his uncle, in his place, and changed his name to Zedekiah." To resolve this, the word "דוד" in this verse must be reinterpreted to mean not "uncle" but "close friend", and understood to mean that Zedekiah was a friend of Nebuchadnezar, so Nebuchadnezar trusted him and appointed him in place of his brother, Jehoiachin. As for his being called "Zedekiah the son of Josiah", that is explained by the practice of referring to grandchildren as children.[66]

A more serious problem is that the name of King Zedekiah's mother was the same as that of the mother of Jehoahaz, "Hamutal, the daughter of Jeremiah from Libnah."[67] Although Jehoiakim did have incestuous relationships with his father's wives, the product of such a relationship would not have been acceptable for the throne, nor does it seem that the most righteous of all these kings could have been illegitimate.[68]

24:20 כִּי עַל־אַף ה׳ הָיְתָה בִירוּשָׁלִַם וּבִיהוּדָה עַד־הִשְׁלִכוֹ אֹתָם מֵעַל פָּנָיו וַיִּמְרֹד צִדְקִיָּהוּ בְּמֶלֶךְ בָּבֶל׃

For it was because of G-d's wrath against Jerusalem and Judah, to finally cast them from His presence, that Zedekiah rebelled against the King of Babylonia.

During the reign of Jehoiakim it was the righteousness of the people that saved them in spite of the wickedness of their king. In the case of Zedekiah it was the other way around. Zedekiah was righteous but his generation was wicked. He was held responsible for their sins, however, and punished, because he failed to rebuke them. As king, it was his responsibility to control his subjects and not be intimidated by them.[69]

G-d confused Zedekiah's reasoning so that he made the foolish mistake of ignoring the warnings of Jeremiah and rebelling against Nebuchadnezar. He thus brought about both his own destruction and the destruction of his kingdom. The people had sinned for so long and had become so wicked that they were no longer worthy of a king who would lead them wisely and properly. They had already been condemned to destruction for their sins.[70]

In the Book of Chronicles it says,[71]

He did what was evil in the eyes of the L-rd, his G-d. He was not humbled before Jeremiah the prophet by the word of G-d. Against King Nebuchadnezar, too, did he rebel, who had made him swear by G-d, and he stiffened his neck and strengthened his heart not to return to the L-rd, the G-d of Israel. All the officers of the priests and the people, too, transgressed increasingly more transgressions, like all the abominations of the nations, and defiled the House of G-d that He had sanctified in Jerusalem. The L-rd, the G-d of their fathers, sent to them by the hand of His messengers getting up early and sending, for He took pity on His people and on His Dwelling Place. But they mocked the messengers of G-d, belittled His words, and said that His prophets were mistaken, until G-d's wrath against His People rose until there was no remedy.

The names of these kings tell something about them. The name "Jehoiakim" indicates that G-d fulfilled His decree in his days, "Zedekiah," that G-d brought judgment against him and his kingdom, "Jehoahaz" that he held fast to his wicked ways, and "Jehoiachin" that G-d was preparing the exile and the destruction.[72]

The Book of Proverbs alludes to them in the verses,[73] "I passed by the field of a lazy man, and the vineyard of a man who lacked heart, and behold, it was all overgrown with brambles, covered with thorns, and the stone wall was broken down." The lazy man is an allusion to Ahaz, the man who lacked heart to Manasseh, "overgrown with brambles" to Amon, "covered with thorns" to Jehoiakim, and the broken wall to Zedekiah, in whose reign the Temple was destroyed.[74]

II KINGS 25

25:1 וַיְהִי בִשְׁנַת הַתְּשִׁיעִית לְמָלְכוֹ בַּחֹדֶשׁ הָעֲשִׂירִי בֶּעָשׂוֹר לַחֹדֶשׁ בָּא
נְבֻכַדְנֶאצַּר מֶלֶךְ־בָּבֶל הוּא וְכָל־חֵילוֹ עַל־יְרוּשָׁלַםִ וַיִּחַן עָלֶיהָ וַיִּבְנוּ עָלֶיהָ דָּיֵק
סָבִיב׃

In the ninth year of his reign, in the Tenth Month, on the tenth of the month, Nebuchadnezar, King of Babylonia, came, he and all his army, against Jerusalem. He camped upon it, and they built siege towers all around it.

The words, "the ninth year of his reign" refer to the reign of Zedekiah.[1] This chapter is a continuation of the preceding one. Seen together, the juxtaposition of this verse and the one before it makes the reference clear. It was the seventeenth year of Nebuchadnezar's own reign. The Tenth Month is the month of Teveth, and this day is marked by the Fast of Teveth.

25:2 וַתָּבֹא הָעִיר בַּמָּצוֹר עַד עַשְׁתֵּי עֶשְׂרֵה שָׁנָה לַמֶּלֶךְ צִדְקִיָּהוּ׃

The city came under siege until the eleventh year of King Zedekiah.

Although Jerusalem had already been condemned to destruction, G-d spared them for three more years to give them yet another opportunity to repent. Perhaps the sufferings of the siege would move them to abandon their sins.[2]

It is impossible to appreciate what great mercy this was, for we cannot fathom G-d's wrath over the sins of the Jewish People during this period. More than once He had wanted to destroy not only the Kingdom of Judah, but the entire world. Thus Jeremiah began his prophecies with the words,[3] "In the beginning (בראשית) of the reign of Jehoiakim" and [4] "In the beginning (בראשית) of the reign of Zedekiah." Even though these prophecies were not actually given in the beginnings of their reigns, the word "in the beginning" was used to indicate that G-d wanted to return the world to chaos as it had been at the beginning of creation (בראשית).[5]

The Book of Jeremiah[6] records how Zedekiah asked Jeremiah whether G-d had revealed the outcome of the siege to him. The prophet answered that if he continued to resist he would be defeated and captured by the Babylonians. He advised him to surrender, and assured him that if he did he would be treated with mercy. But Zedekiah was afraid to follow Jeremiah's advice, so he persisted.

For a while it seemed that they would be able to repel the Babylonians. Though they were no match for them on the battlefield, with the advantage of their position within the city walls they were able to hold them off.

There was one man in Jerusalem who was so strong that he could catch the stones of the Babylonian catapults in his hands and throw them back. Many of the Babylonians were killed, and they might have been driven away, but G-d caused a great wind to come and blow him off the wall. He fell down and died, and the siege continued.[7]

Hanamel, the cousin of Jeremiah, knew the names of the angels, so he was able to exercise certain powers over them. He called them by name and made them come down onto the wall to fight for the Jews. When the Babylonians saw them they fled. But then G-d changed the angels' names and brought them back. Again Hanamel tried to call them down, but since he did not know their new names he could no longer force them to obey him. He then called the angel of the earth, and it made the whole city rise up into the air. But it was of no avail. G-d pushed it back down.[8]

Jeremiah begged the people to give up before it was too late. He warned them that it was divine will that they be defeated, so nothing they did could prevent it. For a while the siege was interrupted when troops came from Egypt and the Babylonians withdrew. But Jeremiah warned them that the relief was only temporary, and their defeat was inevitable. He said,[9] "Even if you kill the whole army of the Chaldeans who are fighting with you, and there are left of them only wounded men, each one will get up in his tent and burn this city with fire."

When Jeremiah went out of Jerusalem an angel came down and put its foot on the walls of Jerusalem and they split. The angel called out, "Let the enemy enter, for the Master is not in His house!" The Babylonians set up a stage in the Temple court for their generals to meet and decide the fate of the city. They were discussing how to destroy the Temple when four angels came down with torches and set fire to the four corners of the Temple and burnt it.[10]

Nebuchadnezar sent his general, Nebuzaradan, three hundred mules carrying loads of sharp blades to destroy the gates of Jerusalem. The soldiers threw them against one of the gates with great force, but the blades sunk in one by one and still the gate was not broken. Nebuzaradan realized that only by divine protection could it withstand such an attack. He became frightened and wanted to give up and go back. He thought, "If I don't leave soon I will be destroyed as Sanherib was!" A voice came out of heaven and said, "Jumper, son of a jumper! You jumped here once when you accompanied Sanherib, and that time you failed, but this time you will succeed, for the time has come for the Temple to be destroyed and the Sanctuary to be burned!"

He had only one blade left. He went and struck the gate, this time not with the sharp edge but with the back, which was blunt, and miraculously the gate opened! He proceeded to conquer the city and massacre the inhabitants. Finally he reached the Temple. As he was about to destroy it, the building began to rise up to heaven to escape, but the heavens pushed it back down. He plundered it and set it on fire.

Nebuzaradan began to feel that he was indeed a great conqueror, having succeeded where his predecessors had failed. Again a voice came out of heaven, this time to humble him. It said, "They were dead people that you killed! It was a burnt house that you burned!" Thus the prophet rebuked Babylonia,[11] "Take a mill and grind flour!" He did not speak of grinding wheat into flour, but of grinding flour that had already been ground. The Babylonians could claim no credit for their victory, for the Jewish People had already been condemned to defeat and destruction.[12]

25:3 בְּתִשְׁעָה לַחֹדֶשׁ וַיֶּחֱזַק הָרָעָב בָּעִיר וְלֹא־הָיָה לֶחֶם לְעַם הָאָרֶץ׃

On the ninth of the month the famine became severe in the city, and there was no bread for the people of the land.

Weak with hunger, the people could no longer defend the city. The enemy was able to approach the wall and succeeded in breaking through. This verse tells the day of the month, but not which month it was. In the Book of Jeremiah,[13] however, we are told that it was the Fourth Month, which is Tamuz.[14]

Even though it says here and in the Book of Jeremiah[15] that it was on the ninth of Tamuz that the walls were breached, the fast commemorating this tragic event is observed on the seventeenth of the month. Some say the city was entered on the ninth when the First Temple was destroyed and on the seventeenth at the time of the destruction of the Second Temple. After the Second Temple was destroyed the fast was reestablished on the seventeenth because it is from that destruction that we are now suffering.[16]

Another explanation is that in the time of the First Temple as well, the Babylonians did not enter the city on the ninth when the walls were broken. First, they pursued the fleeing soldiers and caught as many as they could. On the seventeenth of the month they returned, enlarged the opening, and entered the city.[17]

Others say that not only the enemy's entrance into the city, but the breaching of the walls as well occurred on the seventeenth. The statement here and in the Book of Jeremiah is a mistake. So distraught were the people during the siege that they could not even tell what day it was! It was already the seventeenth, but they thought it was still the ninth. Rather than correcting their mistake, G-d preserved it in the Bible to show that He was with them in their suffering. He is compared to a king who was busy figuring out his accounts when a messenger came and told him that his son had been taken captive. He became distraught and confused his accounts. Later, he decreed that they remain so as a memorial.[18]

Four other tragic events happened on the seventeenth of Tamuz at different times in history. The first was the breaking of the Tablets of the Law by Moses when he came down from Mount Sinai and saw the golden calf. The second was the discontinuation of the daily sacrifice. Some say this refers to the suppression of the Temple service by King Manasseh. Even though many of the sacrificial obligations were neglected during other periods of corruption as well, the daily sacrifices morning and evening were never interrupted. On this day, however, Manasseh issued a decree forbidding any service in the Temple.[19]

Others say it refers to the end of the Temple service in Roman times. When the Romans were besieging Jerusalem, they were nonetheless willing to sell the Jews animals for the daily sacrifices. Every day the priests would lower two baskets of gold over the wall and the Romans would take the gold and put in two sheep. One day, however, they decided not to cooperate. They took the gold and put in two pigs instead. Before the pigs were half way up, one of them stuck out its feet, dug its hoofs into the wall, and jumped. It landed one hundred miles away and the whole earth shook.[20]

Others say this happened in the time of the Hasmonean dynasty, when the two brothers, Hyrcanus and Aristobulus, were fighting for the throne. Hyrcanus had fortified himself within the city and Aristobulus was besieging him. The two factions cooperated, however, as far as the Temple service was concerned, one lowering down baskets of gold and the other sending up sheep. But there was one unscrupulous old man who had been schooled in the ways of the Greeks. He advised Aristobulus to perform this treachery so that the merit of those inside be lessened and they become vulnerable.[21]

The third event was the burning of the Torah scrolls by Apostimos. Our tradition does not tell who Apostimos was or when he lived.

The fourth was the placing of an idol in the Sanctuary. Some say this too refers to the time of Manasseh. On the very day that he had the sacrifices discontinued he had an idol placed there, as it says in the Book of Daniel,[22] "From the time the daily sacrifice was removed to put a desolate abomination."[23]

25:4 וַתִּבָּקַע הָעִיר וְכָל־אַנְשֵׁי הַמִּלְחָמָה הַלַּיְלָה דֶּרֶךְ שַׁעַר בֵּין הַחֹמֹתַיִם
אֲשֶׁר עַל־גַּן הַמֶּלֶךְ וְכַשְׂדִּים עַל־הָעִיר סָבִיב וַיֵּלֶךְ דֶּרֶךְ הָעֲרָבָה׃

The city was split open. All the warriors fled by night through the gate between the double walls that is next to the King's Garden, with the Chaldeans being all around the city. He went by way of the plain.

The king and his soldiers fled through the gate that was between the inner and outer walls, where they hoped to escape without the enemy noticing.[24] Although this verse speaks of the soldiers, the verb "went," "וילך," at the end of the verse is in the singular. It is the attempted escape of Zedekiah that the Bible is concerned with here, not what happened to the others.

25:5 וַיִּרְדְּפוּ חֵיל־כַּשְׂדִּים אַחַר הַמֶּלֶךְ וַיַּשִּׂגוּ אֹתוֹ בְּעַרְבוֹת יְרֵחוֹ וְכָל־
חֵילוֹ נָפֹצוּ מֵעָלָיו׃

The soldiers of the Chaldeans ran after the king and caught

him on the plains of Jericho. All of his soldiers scattered from him.

Some say there was a secret cave, one opening of which was in Zedekiah's palace in Jerusalem and the other miles away near Jericho. It was through that cave that the king left the city. He would surely have escaped had it not been G-d's will that he be caught. Even the best strategy could not save him. G-d caused a deer to run along the ground above the cave, and some of the Babylonian soldiers, seeing it, began to pursue it. It reached the mouth of the cave just as Zedekiah was coming out, and when the soldiers saw the king they left the deer and caught him instead! Thus G-d told the prophet Ezekiel,[25] "I spread out My net upon him and he was caught in My trap."[26]

25:6 וַיִּתְפְּשׂוּ אֶת־הַמֶּלֶךְ וַיַּעֲלוּ אֹתוֹ אֶל־מֶלֶךְ בָּבֶל רִבְלָתָה וַיְדַבְּרוּ אִתּוֹ מִשְׁפָּט׃

They captured the king and brought him up to the King of Babylonia, to Riblah, and they pronounced judgment upon him.

Nebuchadnezar had not remained with his army during the long siege, but had returned to the city of Riblah, where he had already established his court.[27] Some say he had never bothered to come in person even in the beginning, but had sent his officer, Nebuzaradan, to represent him instead. Nebuchadnezar had his own image carved onto the front of Nebuzaradan's chariot, and all who saw it were overcome with terror as if they were standing in the presence of the king himself.[28]

Nebuchadnezar's accusation was just. Zedekiah had sworn allegiance to him, and now he had broken his oath.[29]

Some say it was a personal promise that he had broken. One day Zedekiah had found Nebuchadnezar eating a live rabbit. Nebuchadnezar was embarrassed and had him swear that he would never reveal what he had seen. But after a while Zedekiah became sick, and he had his oath revoked so that he could talk about it. Nebuchadnezar found out that people were making fun of him and he knew immediately that Zedekiah had broken his promise. He called Zedekiah before the Sanhedrin and accused him of violating the oath that he had taken with G-d's name. They answered, "He had his oath nullified."

Nebuchadnezar asked, "Can such an oath be nullified even when the one to whom it was made is not present?"

"No," they answered, "only in his presence!"

"Why, then, did you nullify it for him? You should have told him that when he requested it of you!"

Realizing that they were guilty and had been caught, they immediately sat down on the ground and began to mourn.[30]

25:7 וְאֶת־בְּנֵי צִדְקִיָּהוּ שָׁחֲטוּ לְעֵינָיו וְאֶת־עֵינֵי צִדְקִיָּהוּ עִוֵּר וַיַּאַסְרֵהוּ
בַנְחֻשְׁתַּיִם וַיְבִאֵהוּ בָּבֶל׃

The children of Zedekiah they slaughtered before his eyes, and the eyes of Zedekiah they blinded. They bound him with copper chains and brought him to Babylonia.

Zedekiah said to Nebuchadnezar, "Kill me first, so that I won't witness the death of my ten children!" His children said, "Kill us first so that we will not witness our father's blood being spilled on the ground!" Nebuchadnezar killed the children and then tore Zedekiah's eyes out and threw them into the furnace. After that he brought him to Babylonia, and wherever he went, Zedekiah cried, "Come, all you people, and see! Jeremiah prophesied to me, 'To Babylonia you will go and in Babylonia you will die, but Babylonia your eyes will not see.' I did not listen to his words, and now they have come to pass!"[31]

Some say this happened on the sixth or seventh day of the month of Marheshvan.[32]

25:8 וּבַחֹדֶשׁ הַחֲמִישִׁי בְּשִׁבְעָה לַחֹדֶשׁ הִיא שְׁנַת תְּשַׁע־עֶשְׂרֵה שָׁנָה לַמֶּלֶךְ
נְבֻכַדְנֶאצַּר מֶלֶךְ־בָּבֶל בָּא נְבוּזַרְאֲדָן רַב־טַבָּחִים עֶבֶד מֶלֶךְ־בָּבֶל יְרוּשָׁלָםִ׃

And in the Fifth Month, on the seventh of the month, that is the nineteenth year of King Nebuchadnezar, King of Babylonia, Nebuzaradan, the Chief Executioner, servant of the King of Babylonia, came to Jerusalem.

The Babylonians entered the Holy Temple on the seventh of the month. On the eighth and ninth they ate and drank there, looted and destroyed. Then, late on the afternoon of the ninth, they set it on fire, and it burned until the end of the tenth. Thus in the Book of Jeremiah[33] it says that the Temple was burned on the tenth of the month.[34]

The Temple was destroyed in the year 3338. The numerical value of the word "שלח" in the verse[35] "Send (שלח) from before Me and they will go out," is an allusion to this year.

Here and in one place in the Book of Jeremiah[36] it is referred to as the nineteenth year of Nebuchadnezar, but later in Jeremiah[37] it is referred to as the eighteenth. Some say it was the end of the eighteenth and the beginning of the nineteenth.[38] Others say it was the nineteenth year of Nebuchadnezar and the eighteenth year since the defeat of Jerusalem under Jehoiakim, which was the beginning of the downfall of the Kingdom of Judah.[39]

25:9,10 וַיִּשְׂרֹף אֶת־בֵּית־ה׳ וְאֶת־בֵּית הַמֶּלֶךְ וְאֵת כָּל־בָּתֵּי יְרוּשָׁלַםִ וְאֶת־כָּל־בֵּית גָּדוֹל שָׂרַף בָּאֵשׁ׃ וְאֶת־חוֹמֹת יְרוּשָׁלַםִ סָבִיב נָתְצוּ כָּל־חֵיל כַּשְׂדִּים אֲשֶׁר רַב־טַבָּחִים׃

He burned the House of G-d and the house of the king, and all the houses of Jerusalem. Every house of a great person he burned with fire. And the walls of Jerusalem all around, all the soldiers of the Chaldeans that were with the Chief Executioner broke down.

The expression "בית גדול," "house of a great person," can also be understood to mean, "house of greatness." When the Babylonians destroyed the Temple they also destroyed all the houses of prayer and study halls where the Torah was studied and made great.[40]

25:11 וְאֵת יֶתֶר הָעָם הַנִּשְׁאָרִים בָּעִיר וְאֶת־הַנֹּפְלִים אֲשֶׁר נָפְלוּ עַל־הַמֶּלֶךְ בָּבֶל וְאֵת יֶתֶר הֶהָמוֹן הֶגְלָה נְבוּזַרְאֲדָן רַב־טַבָּחִים׃

The rest of the people who remained in the city, the surrenderers who had surrendered to the King of Babylonia, and the rest of the masses, Nebuzaradan, the Chief Executioner, exiled.

The Babylonians treated their captives with unusual cruelty. Those who had surrendered earlier and expected to be treated with mercy were exiled along with the rest.[41] In the Book of Chronicles it says,[42] "he killed their young men by the sword in their Temple, and did not take pity on youth and maiden, old and venerable."

There were youths who were so handsome that when the Babylonian women saw them they no longer desired their own husbands. The husbands came to Nebuchadnezar and complained, and he had all the youths killed. But even in their death they remained handsome, and the women could still not resist them, so again the husbands complained. This time Nebuchadnezar had their bodies trampled beyond recognition.[43]

Nebuchadnezar told Nebuzaradan, "The G-d of the Jews is merciful and forgiving. When you capture them don't let them pray, lest they repent. Then G-d will forgive them and destroy us."

Nebuzaradan heeded his master's words and drove his captives relentlessly before him. When one of them stopped he had him torn to pieces and his limbs thrown before the others as a warning. He did not let them stop until they had reached the Euphrates, for then they had already left the Holy Land and the exile had begun. When they stopped, the soldiers ate, drank and rejoiced, while the captives sat and cried, as it says,[44] "On the rivers of Babylon, there we sat, we also cried." There, for the first time, they were permitted to sit down.[45]

25:12 וּמִדַּלַּת הָאָרֶץ הִשְׁאִיר רַב־טַבָּחִים לְכֹרְמִים וליגבים (וּלְיוֹגְבִים קרי)׃

And of the poorest of the land the Chief Executioner left as vineyard workers and diggers.

Some interpret the words "כרמים" as "vineyard workers" and "יגבים" as "diggers" or "ploughmen." They were left to work the land and provide for the soldiers of the Babylonians. Others say they refer to two professions that were unique to the Land of Israel. The כרמים were those who gathered balsam fruit and made it into fragrant oil, and the יגבים were those who caught the special fish used to make the precious blue dye called "techelet" (תכלת).[46] The Babylonians left these craftsmen because they could not be replaced. They were not acting in kindness, but purely in their own self interest, because they did not want to be deprived of these valuable commodities.

25:13-15 וְאֶת־עַמּוּדֵי הַנְּחֹשֶׁת אֲשֶׁר בֵּית־ה׳ וְאֶת־הַמְּכֹנוֹת וְאֶת־יָם הַנְּחֹשֶׁת
אֲשֶׁר בְּבֵית־ה׳ שִׁבְּרוּ כַשְׂדִּים וַיִּשְׂאוּ אֶת־נְחֻשְׁתָּם בָּבֶלָה: וְאֶת־הַסִּירוֹת
וְאֶת־הַיָּעִים וְאֶת־הַמְזַמְּרוֹת וְאֶת־הַכַּפּוֹת וְאֵת כָּל־כְּלֵי הַנְּחֹשֶׁת אֲשֶׁר יְשָׁרְתוּ־בָם
לָקָחוּ: וְאֶת־הַמַּחְתּוֹת וְאֶת־הַמִּזְרָקוֹת אֲשֶׁר זָהָב זָהָב וַאֲשֶׁר־כֶּסֶף כָּסֶף לָקַח
רַב־טַבָּחִים:

The copper columns that were in the House of G-d, and the bases and the copper sea that were in the House of G-d, the Chaldeans smashed, and carried their copper to Babylonia. The basins, the rakes, the musical instruments, the spoons, and all the utensils of copper with which they served, they took. The fire pans and the bowls, whatever was gold, gold, and whatever was silver, silver, the Chief Executioner took.

The descriptions of these various items are found in the seventh chapter of the first volume of the Book of Kings, where the building of the Temple is discussed.

25:16,17 הָעַמּוּדִים שְׁנַיִם הַיָּם הָאֶחָד וְהַמְּכֹנוֹת אֲשֶׁר־עָשָׂה שְׁלֹמֹה לְבֵית ה׳
לֹא־הָיָה מִשְׁקָל לִנְחֹשֶׁת כָּל־הַכֵּלִים הָאֵלֶּה: שְׁמֹנֶה עֶשְׂרֵה אַמָּה קוֹמַת הָעַמּוּד
הָאֶחָד וְכֹתֶרֶת עָלָיו נְחֹשֶׁת וְקוֹמַת הַכֹּתֶרֶת שָׁלֹשׁ אמה (אמּוֹת קרי) וּשְׂבָכָה
וְרִמֹּנִים עַל־הַכֹּתֶרֶת סָבִיב הַכֹּל נְחֹשֶׁת וְכָאֵלֶּה לָעַמּוּד הַשֵּׁנִי עַל־הַשְּׂבָכָה:

The columns two, the one sea, and the bases that Solomon had made for the House of G-d. There was no weight equal to the copper of all these utensils. Eighteen cubits was the height of one column, and there was a crown upon it of copper. The height of the crown was three cubits. There was a network and pomegranates on the crown all around, all of copper. So too, the second column, on the network.

The measurements and description of the columns, too, are found in the seventh chapter of the first volume of the Book of Kings.

In the Book of Chronicles it says,[47] "All the utensils of the House of G-d, both large and small, and the treasuries of the House of G-d and the treasuries of the king and his officers, he brought it all to Babylonia.

They burned the House of G-d and broke down the wall of Jerusalem. All its palaces they burned with fire, and all the coveted utensils were for destruction."

When the Temple was destroyed a cry of anguish went out throughout the whole world, as it says,[48] "The L-rd of H-sts will call out on that day for crying and mourning, for tearing of hair and wearing of sackcloth." The angels said, "Oh G-d, do You permit such a thing? Doesn't it say,[49] 'Splender and glory is before Him, strength and joy in His place?' " He answered, "My house is being destroyed and My children are being led away in chains. How can I not mourn?' " Thus it says,[50] "I am with him in troubles."[51]

G-d has a special place where He cries and it is called "the Hidden Places." What does He cry for there? For the pride of Israel that was taken away from them and given to the other nations, as it says,[52] "In the hidden places My soul will cry because of pride, and My eyes will surely run with tears that the flock of G-d has been taken captive." Outwardly, however, He shows no sign of sadness, but only splendor and glory. For the Temple, however, He even cries publicly, as it says,[53] "The L-rd of H-sts will call out on that day for crying and mourning, for tearing of hair and wearing of sackcloth." And since G-d Himself cries, the angels cry too, as it says,[54] "Behold, His angels cry out outside, the angels of peace cry bitterly."[55]

25:18,19 וַיִּקַּח רַב־טַבָּחִים אֶת־שְׂרָיָה כֹּהֵן הָרֹאשׁ וְאֶת־צְפַנְיָהוּ כֹּהֵן מִשְׁנֶה
וְאֶת־שְׁלֹשֶׁת שֹׁמְרֵי הַסַּף׃ וּמִן־הָעִיר לָקַח סָרִיס אֶחָד אֲשֶׁר־הוּא פָקִיד עַל־אַנְשֵׁי
הַמִּלְחָמָה וַחֲמִשָּׁה אֲנָשִׁים מֵרֹאֵי פְנֵי־הַמֶּלֶךְ אֲשֶׁר נִמְצְאוּ בָעִיר וְאֵת הַסֹּפֵר שַׂר
הַצָּבָא הַמַּצְבִּא אֶת־עַם הָאָרֶץ וְשִׁשִּׁים אִישׁ מֵעַם הָאָרֶץ הַנִּמְצְאִים בָּעִיר׃

The Chief Executioner took Seraiah, the High Priest, Zephaniah, the Second Priest, and the three guards of the threshold. And from the city he took one minister who was appointed over the men of war, five men of those who beheld the king's presence who were found in the city, the scribe who was the officer of the army, who conscripted the people of the land, and sixty men of the people of the land who were found in the city.

Some say that the word "סרים," "minister," in this verse is used in the literal sense, that is, “eunuch.”[56] Others say it means a servant or minister, as it does in most places.[57]

Here it says that the number of men who “beheld the king’s presence,” that is, who sat in his presence continually, was five. In the Book of Jeremiah it is given as seven. The extra two included there were the two scribes who recorded the royal proceedings.[58] Some say these were members of the Sanhedrin.[59]

25:20,21 וַיִּקַּח אֹתָם נְבוּזַרְאֲדָן רַב־טַבָּחִים וַיֹּלֶךְ אֹתָם עַל־מֶלֶךְ בָּבֶל
רִבְלָתָה׃ וַיַּךְ אֹתָם מֶלֶךְ בָּבֶל וַיְמִיתֵם בְּרִבְלָה בְּאֶרֶץ חֲמָת וַיִּגֶל
יְהוּדָה מֵעַל אַדְמָתוֹ׃

Nebuzaradan, the Chief Executioner, took them and brought them to the King of Babylonia in Riblah. The King of Babylonia smote them and killed them in Riblah, in the Land of Hamath, and exiled Judah from upon its land.

Since all these men were among the king’s advisers, they were held responsible for the rebellion and punished.[60]

25:22 וְהָעָם הַנִּשְׁאָר בְּאֶרֶץ יְהוּדָה אֲשֶׁר הִשְׁאִיר נְבוּכַדְנֶאצַּר מֶלֶךְ בָּבֶל
וַיַּפְקֵד עֲלֵיהֶם אֶת־גְּדַלְיָהוּ בֶּן־אֲחִיקָם בֶּן־שָׁפָן׃

As for the people that was left in the Land of Judah, that Nebuchadnezar, King of Babylonia, left, he appointed Gedaliah ben Ahikam ben Shaphan over them.

Even though he had destroyed the city of Jerusalem and the kingdom of David, Nebuchadnezar did not intend to completely eliminate Jewish presence from the Holy Land. He left a small community, too small to be considered a nation, with the official sanction of the Babylonian government. The Book of Jeremiah tells how the prophet Jeremiah was permitted to remain with that community to serve as their adviser and guide.[61]

25:23,24 וַיִּשְׁמְעוּ כָל־שָׂרֵי הַחֲיָלִים הֵמָּה וְהָאֲנָשִׁים כִּי־הִפְקִיד מֶלֶךְ־בָּבֶל
אֶת־גְּדַלְיָהוּ וַיָּבֹאוּ אֶל־גְּדַלְיָהוּ הַמִּצְפָּה וְיִשְׁמָעֵאל בֶּן־נְתַנְיָה וְיוֹחָנָן בֶּן־קָרֵחַ
וּשְׂרָיָה בֶן־תַּנְחֻמֶת הַנְּטֹפָתִי וְיַאֲזַנְיָהוּ בֶּן־הַמַּעֲכָתִי הֵמָּה וְאַנְשֵׁיהֶם׃ וַיִּשָּׁבַע
לָהֶם גְּדַלְיָהוּ וּלְאַנְשֵׁיהֶם וַיֹּאמֶר לָהֶם אַל־תִּירְאוּ מֵעַבְדֵי הַכַּשְׂדִּים שְׁבוּ בָאָרֶץ
וְעִבְדוּ אֶת־מֶלֶךְ בָּבֶל וְיִטַב לָכֶם׃

All the officers of the soldiers, they and their men, heard that the King of Babylonia had appointed Gedaliah. They came to Gedaliah to Mizpah, Ishmael ben Nethaniah, Johanan ben Kareah, Seraiah ben Tanhumeth the Netophathite, and Jaazaniah the son of the Maacathite, they and their men. Gedaliah swore to them and to their men and said to them, "Don't be afraid of the servants of the Chaldeans. Stay in the land and serve the King of Babylonia, and it will be good for you!"

The Book of Jeremiah gives further details of this, the last stage of Jewish settlement in the Holy Land. It says,[62]

> Gedaliah ben Ahikam ben Shaphan swore to them and to their men saying, "Don't be afraid to serve the Chaldeans. Stay in the land and serve the King of Babylonia, and it will be good for you! As for me, behold, I will reside in Mizpah, to stand before the Chaldeans that come to us. As for you, gather wine, figs and oil and put into your containers, and live in your cities that you have taken." Also all the Jews who were in Moab, the Children of Amon, and Edom, and who were in all the lands, heard that the King of Babylonia had given a remnant to Judah, and that he had appointed Gedaliah ben Ahikam ben Shaphan over them. All the Jews returned from all the places to which they had been driven. They came to the Land of Judah, to Gedaliah to Mizpah, and gathered very much wine and figs. Johanan ben Kareah and all the officers of the soldiers that were in the field came to Gedaliah to Mizpah. They said to him, "Do you indeed know that Baalis, King of the Children of Amon, sent Ishmael ben Nethaniah to smite you to death?" But Gedaliah ben Ahikam didn't believe them. Johanan ben Kareah said to Gedaliah secretly in Mizpah saying, "Let me go, please, and I will smite Ishmael ben Nethaniah, and no one will know. Why should he smite you to death, and all Judah that is gathered to you will be scattered, and the

remnant of Judah will be lost?" Gedaliah ben Ahikam said to Johanan ben Kareah, "Don't do this thing, for it is a lie that you say about Ishmael!"

25:25 וַיְהִי בַּחֹדֶשׁ הַשְּׁבִיעִי בָּא יִשְׁמָעֵאל בֶּן־נְתַנְיָה בֶּן־אֱלִישָׁמָע מִזֶּרַע
הַמְּלוּכָה וַעֲשָׂרָה אֲנָשִׁים אִתּוֹ וַיַּכּוּ אֶת־גְּדַלְיָהוּ וַיָּמֹת וְאֶת־הַיְּהוּדִים
וְאֶת־הַכַּשְׂדִּים אֲשֶׁר־הָיוּ אִתּוֹ בַּמִּצְפָּה׃

In the Seventh Month Ishmael ben Nethaniah ben Elishama, from among the descendants of the royal house, and ten men with him, came. They smote Gedaliah and he died, and the Jews and the Chaldeans that were with him in Mizpah.

The Book of Jeremiah provides some additional details of the murder of Gedaliah. It says:[63]

> In the Seventh Month Ishmael ben Nethaniah ben Elishama, from among the descendants of the royal house, came, and the officers of the king and ten men with him, to Gedaliah ben Ahikam, to Mizpah, and they ate bread there together in Mizpah. Ishmael ben Nethaniah and the ten men that were with him got up and smote Gedaliah ben Ahikam ben Shaphan by the sword and killed him, whom the King of Babylonia had appointed over the land. And all the Jews who were with him, with Gedaliah in Mizpah, and the Chaldeans that were found there, the men of war, Ishmael smote.

Gedaliah was killed in the very beginning of the year 3339, less than two months after the Temple was destroyed in the end of 3338. Some say it was on Rosh Hashanah, others say on the seventh of Tishrei. The fast commemorating his death was established on the third of Tishrei. The number of days between Tisha B'Av and the Fast of Gedaliah is fifty-two, which is equal to the numerical value of the name "Gedaliah."

The murder of Gedaliah was a terrible tragedy. Indeed, the murder of any righteous person is a tragedy. It is considered like the destruction of an entire world. It was particularly bitter because he was killed by one of his own people. But above all it was a national tragedy, because with the death of Gedaliah the last vestige of Jewish presence in the Holy Land came to an end. In certain ways it was like the destruction of the Temple itself.

The Book of Jeremiah continues,[64]

On the second day after killing Gedaliah, and no one knew, men came from Shechem, from Shilo and from Samaria, forty men, with shaven beards, torn clothing and scraped skin. There were sacrifices and frankincense in their hands to bring to the House of G-d. Ishmael ben Nethaniah came out from Mizpah to meet them, crying as he went. When he met them he said to them, "Come to Gedaliah ben Ahikam!" When they came into the city Ishmael ben Nethaniah slaughtered them into the pit, he and the men that were with him. There were ten men there and they said to Ishmael, "Don't kill us, for we have hoards in the field, wheat, barley, oil and honey." So he stopped and didn't kill them among their brothers. The pit into which Ishmael threw the bodies of the men that he smote because of Gedaliah was the one that King Asa had made because of Baasa, King of Israel. That one, Ishmael ben Nethaniah filled with bodies. Ishmael took all the remainder of the people who were in Mizpah captive, the daughters of the king and all of the people that were left in Mizpah, that Nebuzaradan, the Chief Executioner, had appointed to Gedaliah ben Ahikam. Ishmael ben Nethaniah took them captive and went to cross over to the Children of Amon. Johanan ben Kareah and all the officers of the soldiers that were with him heard all the evil that Ishmael ben Nethaniah had done. They took all the men and went to fight with Ishmael ben Nethaniah, and they found him at the great waters that are in Gibeon. When all the people that were with Ishmael saw Johanan ben Kareah and all the officers of the soldiers that were with him they rejoiced. All the people that Ishmael had captured from Mizpah turned and went back, and went to Johanan ben Kareah. Ishmael ben Nethaniah escaped from Johanan with eight men and went to the Children of Amon. Johanan ben Kareah and all the officers of the soldiers that were with him took all the remainder of the people that he had brought back from Ishmael ben Nethaniah (that he had taken) from Mizpah after he smote Gedaliah ben Ahikam, mighty ones, men of war, women, children and ministers that he had brought back from Gibeon. They went and stayed in Geruth Kimham, which was near Bethlehem, to go and get to Egypt, because of the Chaldeans, because they were afraid of them, because Ishmael ben Nethaniah killed Gedaliah ben Ahikam, whom the King of Babylonia had appointed over the land.

All the officers of the soldiers, Johanan ben Kareah, Jezaniah ben Hoshaiah, and the whole people from small to great approached. They said to Jeremiah the prophet, "May our supplications be acceptable to you, and pray for our sake to the L-rd, your G-d, for the sake of this whole remnant, for we are left few from many, as your eyes see us. May the L-rd, your G-d, tell us the way on which we should go and the thing that we should do." Jeremiah the prophet said to them, "I have heard. Behold, I will pray to the L-rd, your G-d, in accordance with your words, and every word that G-d answers you I will tell you. I will not keep anything back from you!" As for them, they said to Jeremiah, "May G-d be with us as a witness, true and faithful, if not in accordance with every word that the L-rd, your G-d, will send you to us, thus will we do! Whether good or bad, to the voice of the L-rd, our G-d, to Whom we are sending you, will we listen, so that it will be good for us, because we listen to the voice of the L-rd, our G-d." So it was, that at the end of ten days there was a word of G-d to Jeremiah. He called Johanan ben Kareah and all the officers of the soldiers that were with him, and the whole people from small to great. He said to them, "Thus says the L-rd, the G-d of Israel, to Whom you sent me to present your supplication before Him. 'Surely if you stay in this land I will build you up and not destroy, I will plant you and not uproot, for I regret the evil that I did to you. Don't be afraid of the King of Babylonia, before whom you are afraid. Don't be afraid of him,' says G-d, 'for I am with you to save you and to deliver you from his hand. I will give you mercy and he will have mercy on you, and return you to your land. But if you say, "We will not stay in this land" to not listen to the voice of the L-rd, your G-d, saying, "No! Rather to the Land of Egypt we will go, that we not see war, and the sound of the horn we not hear. We will not be hungry for bread and there will we live." So now, listen to the word of G-d, Oh remnant of Judah! Thus says the L-rd of H-sts, the G-d of Israel, 'If you indeed put your faces to go to Egypt, and come to live there, the sword which you fear, there will it overtake you, in the Land of Egypt. And the famine about which you are worried, there it will cling to you, in Egypt, and there will you die. All the men who put their faces to go to Egypt to live there will die by sword, by famine and by plague. There will be no remnant or survivor left of them from the famine that I bring upon them.' For thus says the L-rd of H-sts, the G-d of Israel, 'Just as My anger and wrath burned against the inhabitants of Jerusalem, so will My wrath burn against you when you go to Egypt. You will be an oath, a desolation, a curse and a disgrace, and you will never again see this place.' G-d has spoken to you, Oh remnant of Judah! Don't go to Egypt! Know surely that I have testified to you this day! For you have deceived yourselves by sending me to the L-rd, your G-d, saying, 'Pray on our behalf to the L-rd, our G-d, thus tell us and we will do it!' I told you this day and you didn't listen to the voice of the L-rd, your G-d, and to all that He sent me to you. And now, know surely that by sword, by famine and by plague will you die, in the place that you desired to go and live there!"

When Jeremiah finished telling the whole people all the words of the L-rd, their G-d, that the L-rd, their G-d, had sent him to them, all these words. Azariah ben Hoshaiah and Johanan ben Kareah and all the rebellious people said to Jeremiah, "It's a lie that you are telling! The L-rd, our G-d, didn't send you to say, 'Don't go to Egypt to live there!' Because Baruch ben Neriah is misleading you against us, to give us over into the hands of the Chaldeans to kill us and to exile us to Babylonia!" Johanan ben Kareah and all the officers of the soldiers and the whole people didn't listen to the voice of G-d to stay in the Land of Judah. Johanan ben Kareah and all the officers of the soldiers took the whole remnant of Judah that had returned from all the nations where they had been dispersed, to live in the Land of Judah. The men, the women, the children, the daughters of the king, and all the souls that Nebuzaradan, the Chief Executioner, had left with Gedaliah ben Ahikam ben Shaphan, Jeremiah the prophet, and Baruch ben Neriah. And they went to the Land of Egypt, for they didn't listen to the voice of G-d, and they arrived at Tahpanhes.

25:26 וַיָּקֻמוּ כָל־הָעָם מִקָּטֹן וְעַד־גָּדוֹל וְשָׂרֵי הַחֲיָלִים וַיָּבֹאוּ מִצְרָיִם כִּי
יָרְאוּ מִפְּנֵי כַשְׂדִּים׃

The whole people arose, from small to great, and the officers of the soldiers, and went to Egypt, because they were afraid of the Chaldeans.

Thus ended the first period of Jewish settlement in the Holy Land. It was not the treacherous murder of Gedaliah that dealt the final blow, but the people's lack of faith in their prophets, the teachers of Torah, whom G-d had sent to guide them. Before long Egypt, too, fell to Babylonia, just as Jeremiah and Ezekiel had predicted. All the Jews that had fled there were either killed or captured and sold as slaves.

25:27 וַיְהִי בִשְׁלֹשִׁים וָשֶׁבַע שָׁנָה לְגָלוּת יְהוֹיָכִין מֶלֶךְ־יְהוּדָה בִּשְׁנֵים עָשָׂר חֹדֶשׁ בְּעֶשְׂרִים וְשִׁבְעָה לַחֹדֶשׁ נָשָׂא אֱוִיל מְרֹדַךְ מֶלֶךְ בָּבֶל בִּשְׁנַת מָלְכוֹ אֶת־רֹאשׁ יְהוֹיָכִין מֶלֶךְ־יְהוּדָה מִבֵּית כֶּלֶא׃

In the thirty-seventh year of the exile of Jehoiachin, King of Judah, in the Twelfth Month, on the twenty-seventh of the month, Ewil-Merodach, King of Babylonia, in the year that he became king, lifted up the head of Jehoiachin, King of Judah, from the prison.

From this verse we can calculate the length of Nebuchadnezar's reign. Since this was in the thirty-seventh year of the exile of Jehoiachin, which was in the eighth year of his reign, the total length must have been forty-four. This is alluded to by the Biblical verse concerning one who offers a sacrifice outside the Temple,[65] "blood will it be considered for that man, for blood did he spill." The numerical value of the word "blood" (דם) is forty-four.[66] Others say it was in the ninth year of Nebuchadnezar that Jehoiachin was taken into exile, so the total was forty-five years.[67]

Here we are told that Jehoiachin was released from prison on the twenty-seventh of the month, but in the Book of Jeremiah[68] the date is given as the twenty-fifth. On the twenty-fifth of the month Nebuchadnezar died, was buried, and was succeeded by his son, Ewil-merodach. But Ewil-merodach was afraid that his father was not really dead and would return and claim his throne. That had happened once before. G-d had caused Nebuchadnezar to become insane as a punishment for his haughtiness. He abandoned his throne and fled to the wilderness, where he lived as a wild beast for seven years.[69] In his absence the people appointed one of his sons in his place. When, after seven years, G-d gave him back his sanity, he returned and killed the son that had replaced him. To make sure that would not happen again, Ewil-merodach had his father's body exhumed the next day and dragged along the ground until it was torn into pieces, thus fulfilling the prophecy of Isaiah[70] "You have been thrown out of your grave like a despised weed."[71]

Already before that time, Ewil-merodach had befriended Jehoiachin. It was Jehoiachin that advised him to take this drastic action to prove that the reign of Nebuchadnezar was really over. The next day he recognized Jehoiachin publicly and gave him the highest position in his kingdom.[72] Some say that when he freed Jehoiachin he freed all the other kings that were in prison too.

Some say it was Ewil-merodach himself who had replaced Nebuchadnezar earlier, and he had not been killed but only imprisoned. It was then that he met Zedekiah. When Nebuchadnezar died the people came to take him out of prison and crown him again, but he was afraid to go, thinking that his father was still alive and would kill him. So they exhumed Nebuchadnezar's body and dragged it in front of him to convince him.[73]

Others say Ewil-merodach wanted to be able to nullify his father's decrees, so he had to establish his own kingdom as a new government that had taken over to replace that of Nebuchadnezar rather than a continuation of it. By treating the body in this way he demonstrated his rejection of the things his father had stood for.[74]

25:28-30 וַיְדַבֵּר אִתּוֹ טֹבוֹת וַיִּתֵּן אֶת־כִּסְאוֹ מֵעַל כִּסֵּא הַמְּלָכִים אֲשֶׁר אִתּוֹ בְּבָבֶל: וְשִׁנָּא אֵת בִּגְדֵי כִלְאוֹ וְאָכַל לֶחֶם תָּמִיד לְפָנָיו כָּל־יְמֵי חַיָּיו: וַאֲרֻחָתוֹ אֲרֻחַת תָּמִיד נִתְּנָה־לּוֹ מֵאֵת הַמֶּלֶךְ דְּבַר־יוֹם בְּיוֹמוֹ כֹּל יְמֵי חַיָּו:

He spoke with him good things, and placed his chair above the chairs of the kings that were with him in Babylonia. He changed the garments of his captivity, and he ate bread before him continually, all the days of his life. His allowance was a continual allowance, given to him by the king, each thing on its day, all the days of his life.

Some say the "good things" that Ewil-Merodach spoke with him were learned discussions, because he recognized the wisdom of the Jewish People.[75]

Jehoiachin was provided with kosher food in his own residence for himself and his family, and was honored with a place at the royal table where he was also served kosher food.[76]

Nonetheless, such an honor is considered more a curse than a blessing. It is better to be a body lying outside in disgrace like Jehoiakim than to dine in honor like Jehoiachin.[77]

Some say the words "all the days of his life" refer to the lifetime of Jehoiachin. Others say it refers to the lifetime of Ewil-Merodach.[78]

As for Zedekiah, he lived just long enough to see Nebuchadnezar die and his evil decrees revoked. He was freed together with Jehoiachin, but he did not live to enjoy that freedom. He died immediately afterwards and was buried in honor. Thus Jeremiah's prophecy[79] that he would "die in peace" was fulfilled. His life had not been spent in peace. It was certainly not peace to see his children killed, to be blinded, and to be taken into captivity. In his last moments, though, he saw the downfall of his oppressor and the beginning of the restoration of his people.[80]

The First Temple stood for four hundred and ten years. The exile following its destruction lasted seventy years, corresponding to the seventy Sabbatical and Jubilee years that had been neglected since the Jewish People had entered the Holy Land.[81] During four hundred and thirty-six of the eight hundred and fifty years from the time of the crossing of the Jordan until the destruction of the Temple, these and many other commandments had been violated. In each hundred years there were fourteen Sabbatical years and two Jubilees, and in the remaining thirty-six years there were five more Sabbatical years, giving a total of sixty-nine. The seventieth is the Jubilee year that should have taken place after they were exiled.[82]

Seven hundred kinds of kosher fish, eight hundred kinds of kosher locusts, and countless kinds of kosher birds were exiled with the Jews to Babylonia. It was not until fifty-two years later, when the Persian King Cyrus permitted the Jews to return, that these creatures began to return as well. This is alluded to by the numerical value of the word "בהמה," which is fifty-two.[83]

When the Temple was destroyed and the Jews were being led into exile, the other nations said, "G-d has finally rejected Israel! They were once His chosen people, but now He desires them no more! Many times He punished them for their sins and then forgave them, but each time they declined a little more. Never did they regain their former level. Now they have sunk so low that He won't forgive them again. They are like a silver utensil that has been broken and repaired. It is never as good as it was before. If it breaks again and again it becomes weaker and less pure each time, for the process of melting it back together introduces impurities. Finally it cannot be fixed any more. It has become too weak to hold together, so it must be thrown into the scrap heap."

Thus the prophet Jeremiah said,[84] "They have been called 'despised silver.' " Jeremiah asked G-d,[85] "Have You indeed despised this people?" He argued, "Why have You treated the Jewish People so harshly? If You really mean to reject them, You should have destroyed them or sent them away and left them to their own devices, like a husband who divorces his wife. If, on the other hand, You intend to take them back, why have You afflicted them with punishments from which they cannot recover?"

G-d answered, "Indeed, I have not abandoned them, as Moses wrote,[86] 'Even when they are in the lands of their enemies I do not despise them and am not disgusted with them to destroy them completely.' "[87]

Thus even after the destruction of the Temple G-d did not abandon His people. Some say the divine presence remained in the place where the Temple had stood, as it says, [88] "My eyes and My heart will be there all the days."[89] The holiness of that location predates the building of the Temple, for G-d had already dedicated it as a place of prayer when He created the world. Even G-d Himself prays there. While the Temple stood He would pray in it, "May My children do My will so that I not destroy My house and My sanctuary." Since its destruction He prays, "May My children repent so that I can rebuild My house."[90]

So too it says,[91] "Behold, This One stands behind our wall." This refers to the western wall of the Temple, which is never destroyed.[92]

Others say that G-d went into exile along with the Jewish People, together with the entire heavenly court.[93] While the Temple stood G-d's presence was there, as it says,[94] "G-d is in His Holy Sanctuary." After it was destroyed it went up to heaven, as it says,[95] "In heaven did G-d prepare His throne."[96]

From the time of the creation of the world G-d foresaw the building of the Temple, its destruction and its eventual rebuilding. This is alluded to by the verses describing the first day of creation. First it says,[97] "In the beginning G-d created." This refers to the building of the First Temple. "And the world was formless and empty"[98] refers to its destruction. "And G-d said, 'Let there be light' "[99] is an allusion to the rebuilding of the Temple in the future, when it will be perfected, never to be destroyed again. Thus the prophet Isaiah wrote,[100] "Arise, My light, for your light has come!" and[101] "Behold, darkness will cover the earth, and dense clouds will cover the nations, but upon you G-d will shine, and His glory upon you will be seen."[102]

G-d revealed this to Adam, to the forefathers, Abraham, Isaac and Jacob, and also to Joseph.[103] When G-d told Abraham that his descendants would sin and be punished, Abraham chose the punishment of exile so that they would gather converts. Abraham's life was dedicated to spreading G-d's truth throughout the world. Ultimately, that task is to be completed by his descendants. Had the Jewish People lived faithfully by the Torah they would have been able to fulfill it without leaving their own land. Having deviated from the Torah, however, it became necessary to be scattered all over the earth to accomplish it.

G-d therefore gave the Jewish People the unique ability to survive in exile. Other nations have only been able to survive as long as they remained in their homelands. Those that left either died out or were absorbed into the peoples among whom they lived. Survival in exile is therefore one of the miracles that G-d performed for His people.[104] Central to it has been the ability to retain the good qualities of the forefathers in spite of the influence of the heathens. Thus G-d's Holy People continues to withstand the sufferings of exile until the time of the final redemption, may it come speedily in our days!

NOTES

Chapter 1 (Pages 3 – 10)

1. Kehilat Yaakov
2. Abrabanel
3. Rashi; Radak; Ralbag
4. Rashi
5. Radak
6. Abrabanel
7. Ralbag
8. Abrabanel
9. Malbim
10. Kli Yakar
11. Kehilat Yaakov; Kli Yakar
12. I Kings 22:52
13. II Kings 3:1
14. Ralbag
15. I Kings 22:52
16. Seder Olam 17; Radak; Ralbag

Chapter 2 (Pages 11 – 27)

1. Abrabanel
2. Genesis 28:17
3. Abrabanel
4. Sifri Vaethanan; Radak
5. Tosefta Sota 12; Abrabanel
6. Yalkut; Radak
7. Rashi
8. Abrabanel
9. Radak
10. Abrabanel
11. Radak; Abrabanel
12. Abrabanel
13. Rashi
14. Abrabanel
15. Abrabanel
16. Thirty-two Midot of Rabbi Eliezar ben Rabbi Yosi Haglili; Rashi; Radak; Abrabanel
17. Rashi; Radak; Ran
18. Rashi; Ran
19. Radak
20. Abrabanel
21. Abrabanel
22. Yerushalmi Brachot 5:1
23. Yalkut
24. Radak
25. Radak
26. Malachi 3:23
27. Abrabanel
28. Yalkut; Pirkei Derabbi Eliezar 31
29. Abrabanel
30. Targum Yonatan; Rashi; Radak; Abrabanel
31. Yerushalmi Avodah Zarah 1:2
32. Abrabanel
33. Sifri Vaethanan; Radak; Abrabanel

34. Abrabanel
35. Moed Katan 26a; Radak; Abrabanel
36. Malbim
37. Abrabanel
38. Abrabanel
39. Abrabanel
40. Thirty-two Midot of Rabbi Eliezar ben Rabbi Yosi Haglili; Rashi; Radak; Abrabanel
41. Abrabanel
42. Radak
43. Rashi
44. Abrabanel
45. Ralbag
46. Targum Yonatan; Radak
47. Tosefta Sota 12; Yalkut; Rashi; Mahari Kara
48. Sota 47a; Rashi; Abrabanel
49. Radak; Abrabanel
50. Radak
51. Abrabanel
52. Exodus 15:22-25
53. Mechilta Beshalah 18c; Yalkut; Rashi; Radak; Abrabanel
54. Abrabanel
55. Rashi; Radak
56. Sota 46b; Abrabanel
57. Sota 46b; Abrabanel
58. Abrabanel
59. Sota 46b; Rashi; Radak
60. Deuteronomy 6:7
61. Abrabanel
62. Sota 47a; Radak
63. Sota 46b
64. Abrabanel

Chapter 3 (Pages 28 – 40)

1. Rashi
2. Radak; Abrabanel
3. Radak; Abrabanel
4. Kehilat Yaakov
5. Malbim
6. I Kings 15:18
7. Malbim
8. Rashi; Radak; Ralbag; Abrabanel
9. Radak
10. Ri de Acosta
11. Radak; Abrabanel
12. Ketubot 96a
13. Rashi; Radak
14. Radak; Abrabanel; Malbim
15. Tanhuma, Pinhas; Midrash Rabah; Abrabanel
16. Radak; Abrabanel; Malbim
17. Malbim
18. Targum Yonatan; Rashi; Radak
19. Radak; Abrabanel
20. Pesahim 66b; Rashi; Radak; Abrabanel
21. Megilah 28a
22. Radak; Ralbag
23. Kehilat Yaakov
24. Deuteronomy 20:19
25. Tanhuma, Pinhas; Rashi; Radak; Abrabanel
26. Deuteronomy 23:7
27. Rashi
28. Tanhuma; Rashi; Radak
29. Radak
30. Rashi; Radak
31. Radak; Abrabanel
32. Radak; Abrabanel
33. Rashi
34. Abrabanel
35. Jeremiah 7:31

36. Taanit 4a; Sanhedrin 39b
37. Rashi
38. Sanhedrin 39b; Abrabanel
39. Amos 2:1
40. Rashi on Jeremiah; Radak; Ralbag; Abrabanel

Chapter 4 (Pages 41 – 59)

1. Tanhuma Ki Tisa 5; Yalkut
2. I Kings 18:4
3. Tanhuma Ki Tisa 5; Targum Yonatan; Rashi; Radak
4. Tanhuma Mishpatim; Rashi; Abrabanel
5. Avot 4:2
6. Jeremiah 49:11
7. Tosephta; Radak
8. Zohar Yitro; Talmud Sanhedrin 92a
9. Ralbag
10. Zohar Lech Lecha
11. Ralbag; Abrabanel
12. Rashi; Rif
13. Rif
14. Radak
15. Bereishit Rabah 35:3; Yalkut; Rashi; Abrabanel
16. Radak; Abrabanel
17. Pirkei Derabbi Eliezar 33; Yalkut; Abrabanel
18. Ralbag
19. Radak
20. Brachot 10b; Radak
21. Brachot 10b
22. Brachot 10b
23. Ralbag; Abrabanel
24. Abrabanel
25. Brachot 10b; Radak; Ralbag
26. Proverbs 15:27
27. Brachot 10b
28. Musar Haneviim; Mikraei Kodesh
29. Rabbi Abraham, son of the Rambam
30. Shabbat 23b; Rif; Kehilat Yaakov
31. Pirkei Derabbi Eliezar 33; Abrabanel
32. Radak; Abrabanel
33. Malbim
34. Rashi; Radak; Abrabanel
35. Zohar Beshalah, Pinhas
36. Zohar Noah
37. Abrabanel
38. Radak
39. Radak; Abrabanel
40. Psalms 145:19
41. Radak
42. Abrabanel
43. Radak; Abrabanel
44. Rashi
45. Bereishit Rabah 53b
46. Pirkei Derabbi Eliezar
47. Rashi; Abrabanel
48. Isaiah 58:11
49. Rashi
50. Yerushalmi, Yevamot; Yalkut
51. Abrabanel
52. Mezudat David
53. Succah 27b; Rosh Hashanah 16b; Radak; Abrabanel
54. Radak; Kli Yakar
55. Malbim
56. Radak
57. Pirkei Derabbi Eliezar 33; Yalkut; Rashi; Abrabanel

58. Abrabanel
59. Pirkei Derabbi Eliezar 33; Yalkut; Abrabanel
60. Radak
61. Yalkut
62. Malbim
63. Taanit 2a
64. Radak; Ralbag; Abrabanel
65. Kritut 6a, Horayot 12a; Radak
66. Kehilat Yaakov
67. Pirkei Derabbi Eliezar 33; Shir Hashirim Rabah 2:5
68. Abrabanel
69. Ketubot 106a
70. Yoma 18b; Abrabanel
71. Rashi; Radak; Ralbag
72. Yoma 18b; Rashi; Radak
73. Radak
74. Targum Yonatan
75. Abrabanel
76. Sanhedrin 11b-12a; Yalkut
77. Abrabanel
78. Abrabanel
79. Rashi
80. Ralbag
81. Radak; Mezudat David
82. Ketubot 106a; Rashi

Chapter 5 (Pages 60 – 73)

1. Midrash Tehilim 78; Yalkut; Rashi; Radak; Abrabanel
2. Musar Haneviim
3. Abrabanel
4. Rif
5. Rashi
6. Tanhuma Tazria; Yalkut
7. Bamidbar Rabah 7:5
8. Ri de Acosta
9. Ralbag
10. Sota 46b; Rashi; Radak
11. Rif
12. Radak; Abrabanel
13. Rashi
14. Rif
15. Abrabanel
16. Abrabanel
17. Radak
18. Kli Yakar
19. Ralbag; Abrabanel
20. Abrabanel
21. Rif
22. Rif
23. Ralbag
24. Abrabanel
25. Rashi; Targum Yonatan; Radak
26. Abrabanel
27. Ralbag
28. Radak
29. Rif
30. Rashi; Radak
31. Abrabanel
32. Rif
33. Rif
34. Kehilat Yaakov
35. Exodus 18:11
36. Joshua 2:11
37. Deuteronomy 4:39
38. Devarim Rabah 2:28
39. Gittin 57b
40. Rashi; Radak; Ralbag
41. Abrabanel
42. Bamidbar Rabah 10:5; Abrabanel
43. Abrabanel
44. Rashi
45. Sifri Vaethanan 6:6

46. Radak
47. Rashi
48. Sifri Ekev 11:25
49. Kli Yakar
50. Sanhedrin 74b
51. Kli Yakar
52. Rashi
53. Bamidbar Rabah 7:5
54. Targum Yonatan; Rashi
55. Proverbs 6:18
56. Vayikra Rabah Mezora 16
57. Mezudat Zion
58. Rashi
59. Arachin 16a; Rashi
60. Radak; Ralbag; Mezudat David
61. Targum Yonatan; Rashi; Radak
62. Ralbag
63. Yerushalmi Sanhedrin 10:2
64. Abrabanel
65. Targum Yonatan; Radak
66. Ralbag
67. Sota 47a, Sanhedrin 107b, Sanhedrin 100a; Avot Derabbi Natan 9
68. Arachin 16a; Abrabanel
69. Yerushalmi Sanhedrin 10:2
70. Sota 47a, Sanhedrin 107b
71. Radak; Abrabanel
72. Ralbag; Kli Yakar
73. Exodus 21:6

Chapter 6 (Pages 74 – 86)

1. Sanhedrin 107b, Sota 47a; Rashi; Radak; Ralbag; Abrabanel
2. Yerushalmi Sanhedrin 10:2
3. Minhah Ketanah
4. Sanhedrin 107b; Rashi; Radak; Ralbag; Abrabanel
5. Abrabanel; Kehilat Yaakov
6. Abrabanel
7. Ralbag
8. Rashi
9. Radak; Ralbag
10. Abrabanel; Malbim
11. Abrabanel
12. Minhah Ketanah
13. Minhah Ketanah
14. Abrabanel
15. Tanhuma Tazria 9; Yalkut; Kli Yakar
16. Targum Yonatan; Rashi; Radak
17. Ralbag; Mezudat David
18. Rashi; Radak; Abrabanel
19. Ralbag
20. Radak; Abrabanel
21. Mezudat David
22. Ralbag; Abrabanel; Mezudat David
23. Rashi; Abrabanel
24. Rashi
25. Tanhuma Tazria; Yalkut
26. Yalkut
27. Malbim
28. Ecclesiastes 9:18
29. Eliyahu Rabah 7
30. Ralbag
31. Rashi
32. Isaiah 9:19
33. Taanit 5a; Radak; Abrabanel
34. Minhah Ketanah
35. Rashi; Abrabanel
36. Deuteronomy 28:53
37. Radak; Ralbag
38. Sanhedrin 74a; Abrabanel
39. Pesikta; Yalkut; Rashi; Radak; Abrabanel

40. Rashi; Abrabanel
41. Taanit 14b
42. Abrabanel
43. Ri de Acosta
44. Abrabanel
45. Abrabanel
46. Abrabanel
47. Radak; Ralbag
48. Ralbag
49. Radak; Ralbag; Abrabanel
50. Abrabanel
51. Abrabanel
52. Rashi; Radak

Chapter 7 (Pages 87 – 94)

1. Proverbs 19:3
2. Rif
3. Sanhedrin 107b; Sota 47a; Rashi; Radak; Ralbag; Abrabanel
4. Seder Olam 18
5. Leviticus 13:46
6. Vayikra Rabah Zav 6
7. Minhah Ketanah
8. Avodah Zarah 27b
9. Abrabanel
10. Minhah Ketanah
11. Ri de Acosta
12. Joshua 10:11
13. Algarish
14. Radak; Ralbag; Abrabanel
15. Kli Yakar
16. Rashi; Ralbag; Abrabanel
17. Ri de Acosta
18. Targum Yonatan; Rashi; Abrabanel
19. Ralbag
20. Abrabanel
21. Abrabanel
22. Malbim
23. Kli Yakar; Minhah Ketanah

Chapter 8 (Pages 95 – 108)

1. Brachot 55a
2. Rashi
3. Abrabanel
4. Psalms 50:16
5. Yalkut; Vayikra Rabah 16:4
6. Sota 47a, Sanhedrin 107b; Rashi; Radak; Abrabanel
7. Radak; Abrabanel
8. Abrabanel
9. Genesis 45:18
10. Isaiah 1:19
11. Abrabanel
12. Abrabanel; Musar Haneviim
13. Rashi; Abrabanel
14. Abrabanel; Minhah Ketanah
15. Abrabanel
16. Abrabanel
17. Radak; Ralbag
18. Targum Yonatan; Rashi; Radak
19. Ralbag; Abrabanel
20. Seder Olam 17; Rashi
21. Radak
22. II Chronicles 21:1-4
23. Genesis 36:31
24. Samuel II 8:6
25. Rashi

26. Radak
27. Abrabanel
28. Radak; Ralbag
29. Rashi
30. Abrabanel
31. Radak
32. Rashi; Abrabanel
33. II Chronicles 21:11-20
34. Radak; Abrabanel
35. Radak; Abrabanel
36. II Chronicles 22:1-3
37. Seder Olam 17; Ralbag; Abrabanel
38. Radak; Abrabanel
39. II Chronicles 22:4-6

Chapter 9 (Pages 109 – 121)

1. Abrabanel
2. Abrabanel
3. Abrabanel; Homat Anach
4. Seder Olam 18; Yalkut; Rashi; Radak; Abrabanel
5. Horayot 11b; Megilah 14a; Radak; Abrabanel
6. Kli Yakar
7. Minhah Ketanah
8. Abrabanel
9. Abrabanel
10. Abrabanel
11. Radak; Abrabanel
12. Radak
13. Rashi; Abrabanel
14. Minhah Ketanah
15. Rashi; Radak
16. Ri de Acosta
17. Radak; Abrabanel
18. Targum Yonatan; Rashi; Radak
19. Radak; Ralbag
20. Radak
21. Abrabanel
22. Abrabanel
23. Mezudat David
24. Shemot Rabah 31:4
25. Abrabanel
26. Deuteronomy 17:7
27. Pirkei Derabbi Eliezar
28. Sanhedrin 48b; Bereishit Rabah 22:9; Radak
29. II Chronicles 22:7-9
30. Radak; Abrabanel
31. Radak
32. Sanhedrin 102b; Rashi
33. Radak
34. II Kings 8:25
35. Rashi
36. Abrabanel; Kehilat Yaakov
37. Abrabanel
38. Rashi
39. Radak; Abrabanel
40. Radak
41. Abrabanel
42. Radak
43. Pirkei Derabbi Eliezar 17; Yalkut
44. Job 3:22
45. Homat Anach
46. Abrabanel

Chapter 10 (Pages 122 – 133)

1. Habakuk 3:2
2. Amos 3:15
3. Yalkut
4. Ri de Acosta
5. Rashi
6. Abrabanel
7. Kli Yakar
8. Rashi
9. Radak
10. Targum Yonatan; Radak; Ralbag
11. Ralbag
12. Rashi
13. Rashi; Minhah Ketanah
14. II Chronicles 22:8
15. Radak; Abrabanel
16. Minhah Ketanah
17. Ri de Acosta
18. Radak
19. Radak; Ralbag
20. Rashi; Targum Yonatan
21. Ri de Acosta
22. Sanhedrin 67a
23. Sanhedrin 102a; Abrabanel; Kli Yakar
24. Minhah Ketanah
25. Kli Yakar
26. Abrabanel; Kehilat Yaakov; Malbim
27. Kli Yakar
28. Targum Yonatan; Rashi; Ralbag
29. Radak
30. Radak
31. Abrabanel
32. Minhah Ketanah
33. Tana Devei Eliyahu Zuta 7; Yalkut
34. Seder Olam 19; Rashi; Radak; Abrabanel
35. Radak; Abrabanel
36. I Kings 19:17
37. Abrabanel
38. Sanhedrin 102a
39. Sanhedrin 102a; Yalkut
40. Gitin 88a

Chapter 11 (Pages 134 – 145)

1. Rashi; Radak; Abrabanel
2. II Chronicles 22:7
3. Seder Olam 17
4. Eliyahu Zuta 3
5. Sanhedrin 95a,b
6. Musar Haneviim
7. Radak; Abrabanel
8. II Chronicles 22:11
9. Rashi; Abrabanel
10. Shir Hashirim Rabah 1:16; Rashi
11. Shir Hashirim Rabah 1:16
12. Psalms 27:5
13. Seder Olam 18; Yalkut; Rashi
14. Psalms 18:29
15. Midrash Tehilim
16. Sanhedrin 95a,b; Yalkut
17. Abrabanel
18. Rashi; Radak; Ralbag
19. II Chronicles 23:1,2
20. Taanit 26a, 27a; Rashi; Radak
21. Radak; Ralbag
22. Radak
23. Lamentations 4:15
24. Ralbag; Abrabanel
25. II Chronicles 23:5
26. Abrabanel

27. Jeremiah 19:2
28. Ezekiel 40:15
29. Jeremiah 39:3
30. Jeremiah 26:10; 36:10
31. II Chronicles 23:20
32. Yerushalmi Eruvin 5; Radak; Ralbag
33. Rashi; Abrabanel
34. II Chronicles 23:4
35. I Chronicles 26:15
36. Rashi; Radak; Ralbag
37. Ralbag; Abrabanel
38. Targum Yonatan; Rashi; Mezudat Zion; Mezudat David
39. Radak
40. Abrabanel
41. Rashi
42. Abrabanel
43. Rashi
44. Rashi
45. Radak
46. II Chronicles 23:4-7
47. II Chronicles 23:8,9
48. Radak
49. I Kings 11:10
50. I Kings 14:25-27; Malbim
51. Kli Yakar
52. Rashi; Ralbag; Abrabanel
53. Avodah Zarah 44a; Rashi; Radak
54. Musar Haneviim; Targum Rav Yosef on Chronicles 23:11
55. Radak; Abrabanel
56. Radak; Ralbag; Abrabanel
57. II Chronicles 23:12
58. Radak
59. Targum Yonatan; Radak
60. Rashi; Radak; Abrabanel
61. II Chronicles 23:13
62. Radak; Ralbag; Abrabanel
63. Rashi
64. Radak
65. Rashi
66. Abrabanel
67. Rashi; Radak; Ralbag; Abrabanel
68. Kehilat Yaakov
69. Abrabanel
70. II Chronicles 23:18,19
71. II Chronicles 23:20
72. Minhah Ketanah

Chapter 12 (Pages 146 – 158)

1. Abrabanel
2. Bamidbar Rabah 23:13; Rashi; Radak
3. Malbim
4. II Chronicles 24:2
5. Abrabanel; Malbim
6. Seder Olam 18; Yalkut
7. II Chronicles 24:4
8. II Chronicles 24:7
9. Seder Olam 18; Radak; Abrabanel
10. Radak
11. Rashi on Chronicles; Radak; Abrabanel
12. Rashi; Radak
13. Radak
14. Rashi; Radak; Abrabanel
15. Ketubot 106a,b; Mishneh Torah Shekalim 4:4
16. Radak; Abrabanel
17. Rashi; Radak
18. Radak
19. II Chronicles 24:5,6
20. Exodus 30:12
21. Abrabanel
22. Radak
23. Targum Yonatan; Rashi

24. Radak; Ralbag; Abrabanel
25. II Chronicles 24:8-10
26. Yerushalmi Shekalim 6:4; Malbim
27. II Chronicles 24:11
28. Rashi; Abrabanel
29. II Chronicles 24:12-14
30. Radak
31. Ralbag
32. Radak; Ralbag
33. Targum Yonatan; Rashi
34. Rashi; Radak; Ralbag
35. Rashi; Radak; Ralbag
36. Ketubot 106a,b; Yalkut; Mishneh Torah Hilchot Shekalim 4:4; Radak; Abrabanel
37. Radak; Abrabanel
38. Baba Batra 9a
39. Ralbag
40. Leviticus 5:19
41. Mishnah Shekalim 6:5; Yerushalmi Shekalim 6:4; Rashi; Radak; Abrabanel
42. II Chronicles 24:3,15-19
43. Rashi
44. Minhah Ketanah
45. II Chronicles 24:20-22
46. Eicha Rabah; Targum Yonatan; Rashi
47. Radak; Abrabanel
48. II Chronicles 24:23,24
49. Gitin 57b; Sanhedrin 96b
50. II Chronicles 24:25,26
51. Abrabanel
52. Abrabanel
53. Rashi; Radak; Abrabanel
54. Musar Haneviim
55. Shemot Rabah 8; Musar Haneviim

Chapter 13 (Pages 159 – 169)

1. II Kings 10:36
2. Radak; Abrabanel
3. Malbim
4. Mezudat David
5. Rashi; Radak; Abrabanel
6. Ralbag
7. Abrabanel
8. Radak; Abrabanel
9. Abrabanel
10. Genesis 28:14
11. Shemot Rabah 25:8
12. Radak
13. Abrabanel
14. Ralbag
15. Rashi
16. Seder Olam 19; Radak; Abrabanel
17. Sota 46b; Baba Mezia 87a; Abrabanel
18. Maharsha
19. Abrabanel
20. Abrabanel
21. Rashi; Radak; Abrabanel
22. Radak; Abrabanel
23. Abrabanel
24. Radak
25. Abrabanel
26. Abrabanel
27. Targum Yonatan; Rashi; Radak
28. Abrabanel
29. Hulin 7b; Abrabanel
30. Seder Olam 19; Radak; Abrabanel
31. Radak
32. II Kings 6:23
33. Tosefta Sota 11:5
34. Radak
35. Rashi

36. Pirkei Derabbi Eliezar 33; Yalkut; Radak
37. Midrash Tehilim 26; Sanhedrin 47a; Abrabanel
38. Abrabanel
39. Psalms 26:9
40. Midrash Tehilim 26
40. Hulin 7b
42. Abrabanel
43. Vayikra Rabah 36:6; Yerushalmi Sanhedrin 10:1
44. Abrabanel

Chapter 14 (Pages 170 – 181)

1. II Kings 12:2
2. Seder Olam; Radak; Ralbag
3. II Chronicles 25:2
4. Malbim
5. Deuteronomy 24:16
6. Daniel 6:25
7. Sanhedrin 27b, 28a; Radak; Abrabanel; Malbim
8. Exodus 20:4
9. Bamidbar Rabah 19
10. II Chronicles 25:5-16
11. Jeremiah 31:28; Ezekiel 18:2
12. Rashi
13. Radak
14. Ralbag
15. Seder Olam 19; Rashi
16. Rashi; Radak; Ralbag
17. Radak; Ralbag
18. Bereishit Rabah 80:3; Yalkut; Rashi
19. Ralbag
20. II Chronicles 25:20
21. Ralbag
22. Radak; Ralbag
23. Targum Yonatan; Rashi; Radak
24. II Chronicles 25:24
25. Targum Rav Yoseph
26. Seder Olam 19; Radak
27. Abrabanel
28. Seder Olam 19; Yalkut; Abrabanel
29. Seder Olam 19; Radak; Abrabanel
30. Seder Olam 19; Rashi
31. II Kings 14:2
32. II Kings 15:2
33. Radak
34. Seder Olam 19; Rashi
35. Deuteronomy 2:8
36. II Chronicles 8:17
37. II Kings 8:20
38. Radak; Abrabanel
39. Rashi
40. quoted by Radak
41. Abrabanel
42. Radak; Abrabanel
43. Radak; Abrabanel
44. Yevamot 98a; Yalkut; Radak
45. Mahari Kara
46. Rashi
47. Radak
48. Ralbag
49. Menahem ben Saruk
50. Mahari Kara
51. Targum Yonatan
52. Amos 7:10,11
53. Eliyahu Raba 17
54. Deuteronomy 9:14
55. Shemot Raba 44:10

Chapter 15 (Pages 182 – 193)

1. II Kings 14:2
2. II Kings 14:23
3. II Kings 14:17
4. Radak; Abrabanel
5. II Kings 15:8
6. II Chronicles 26:16-21
7. Sifri; Yalkut
8. Genesis 4:2
9. Genesis 9:20
10. II Chronicles 26:10
11. Bereishit Rabah 36:3
12. Psalms 88:6
13. Horayot 10a; Rashi; Radak; Abrabanel
14. Radak
15. Seder Olam 19; Rashi; Radak
16. II Chronicles 26:5-15
17. II Chronicles 26:23
18. Rashi
19. Rashi; Abrabanel
20. Malbim
21. Eliyah Raba 17
22. Rashi; Radak; Ralbag
23. Abrabanel
24. Gitin 88a
25. I Chronicles 5:25,26
26. Radak
27. Abrabanel
28. Rashi
29. Abrabanel
30. Seder Olam 22; Radak; Abrabanel
31. Seder Olam 22; Rashi; Radak
32. II Chronicles 23:20
33. Radak; Abrabanel
34. Radak
35. II Chronicles 27:4,5
36. Rashi on II Chronicles 27:2
37. Rashi
38. Radak

Chapter 16 (Pages 194 – 202)

1. II Chronicles 28:2,3
2. Targum Rav Yosef
3. Sanhedrin 63b
4. Abrabanel
5. II Chronicles 28:5-15
6. Abrabanel
7. Isaiah 7:1-9
8. Bereishit Rabah 63:1; Rashi; Radak
9. Rashi; Radak
10. II Chronicles 28:16-19
11. Sanhedrin 103b; Rashi
12. Yerushalmi Sanhedrin 10:2
13. Radak; Abrabanel
14. Amos 1:5
15. Radak
16. Sanhedrin 103a
17. Radak
18. Rashi
19. Radak; Ralbag; Abrabanel; Malbim
20. Abrabanel
21. Rashi; Radak; Abrabanel
22. Abrabanel
23. Rashi; Radak
24. Abrabanel
25. II Chronicles 28:20-25
26. Rashi; Radak
27. Rashi
28. Radak

29. Proverbs 24:30
30. Sanhedrin 103a
31. Sanhedrin 104a

Chapter 17 (Pages 203 – 218)

1. II Kings 16:1
2. II Kings 15:27
3. Seder Olam 22; Rashi; Radak
4. Gitin 88a; Seder Olam 22; Rashi; Radak
5. Gitin 88a; Seder Olam 22; Rashi
6. Gitin 88a; Abrabanel
7. Tana Devei Eliyahu; Yalkut
8. II Kings 15:29
9. Seder Olam 22; Rashi
10. I Chronicles 5:26
11. Hosea 10:6
12. Amos 3:12
13. Amos 5:27
14. Seder Olam 22
15. Taanit 30b; Seder Olam 22
16. Sanhedrin 94a
17. II Kings 18:9,10
18. Abrabanel
19. Seder Olam 22; Rashi
20. Jeremiah 15:9
21. Deuteronomy 4:25,26
22. Gitin 88a; Abrabanel
23. Avot 4:2
24. Ezekiel 8:12
25. Abrabanel
26. Deuteronomy 4:19
27. Abrabanel
28. Abrabanel
29. Abrabanel
30. Abrabanel
31. Deuteronomy 28:61
32. Isaiah 63:10
33. Tanhuma Behukotai 2
34. Lamentations 2:13
35. Jeremiah 7:25
36. Eicha Rabah 2:17; Yalkut
37. Yalkut
38. Abrabanel
39. Pesikta Derav Kahana, Shimu
40. Mezudat David
41. Abrabanel
42. Abrabanel
43. Abrabanel
44. Abrabanel
45. Abrabanel
46. Abrabanel
47. Malachi 1:11
48. Rashi
49. Pirkei Derabbi Eliezar 38; Tanhuma Vayeshev; Abrabanel
50. Micah 1:6
51. Radak; Abrabanel
52. Abrabanel
53. Pirkei Derabbi Eliezar 38; Tanhuma Vayeshev; Yalkut
54. Pirkei Derabbi Eliezar 38; Tanhuma Vayeshev; Yalkut
55. Radak; Abrabanel
56. Radak
57. Sanhedrin 63b; Yalkut; Rashi; Radak; Abrabanel
58. Kidushin 75b
59. Abrabanel
60. Rashi
61. Pirkei Derabbi Eliezar 38; Tanhuma Vayeshev; Yalkut
62. Rashi; Radak
63. Radak; Abrabanel

Chapter 18 (Pages 219 – 241)

1. Rashi; Radak; Abrabanel
2. Sanhedrin 94a
3. Minhah Ketanah
4. Deuteronomy 12:17,18
5. Abrabanel
6. Abrabanel
7. Hulin 6b,7a; Yalkut; Radak; Abrabanel
8. Radak; Abrabanel
9. Avodah Zarah 44a; Abrabanel
10. Avodah Zarah 44a; Radak
11. Rashi; Radak
12. Targum Yonatan; Radak
13. Abrabanel
14. Radak
15. Minhah Ketanah
16. II Chronicles 29:3-36; 30:1-27; 31:1-21
17. Sanhedrin 94b; Abrabanel
18. Proverbs 25:1
19. Radak; Ralbag; Abrabanel
20. Abrabanel
21. Abrabanel
22. Proverbs 3:33
23. Sanhedrin 94b
24. Abrabanel
25. Isaiah 10:27
26. Sanhedrin 94b
27. Sanhedrin 95b
28. Radak; Abrabanel; Mezudat David
29. Rashi
30. Kohelet Rabah 9
31. II Chronicles 32:1-8
32. Isaiah 14:24
33. Sanhedrin 94b; Yalkut
34. Mezudat David
35. Radak; Abrabanel
36. Isaiah 36:2
37. Rashi
38. Radak
39. II Chronicles 32:9-15
40. Rashi; Radak; Abrabanel
41. Kehilat Yaakov
42. Isaiah 8:6-8
43. Abrabanel
44. Rashi
45. Abrabanel
46. Radak; Abrabanel
47. Rashi; Abrabanel
48. Ibn Ezra
49. Isaiah 8:7
50. Sanhedrin 94b; Yalkut; Rashi
51. Rashi; Radak
52. Abrabanel
53. Sanhedrin 94a; Yerushalmi Seviit 6:1; Yalkut; Rashi
54. Sanhedrin 94a; Yalkut; Rashi
55. Ezra 4:10; Sanhedrin 94a
56. Brachot 28a; Rashi; Radak; Abrabanel
57. Abrabanel
58. Rashi; Radak
59. Radak
60. II Chronicles 32:16-19
61. Deuteronomy 7:7
62. Genesis 18:27
63. Exodus 16:7
64. Psalms 22:7
65. Isaiah 14:14
66. Hulin 89a
67. Moed Katan 26a; Sanhedrin 56a, 60a; Rashi; Radak
68. Moed Katan 26a; Sanhedrin 60a; Abrabanel
69. Radak

Chapter 19 (Pages 242 – 258)

1. Sanhedrin 56a, 60a; Yalkut
2. Radak; Abrabanel
3. Rashi; Radak; Abrabanel
4. Radak
5. Isaiah 8:12
6. Sanhedrin 26a,b
7. Yalkut
8. Sanhedrin 94a
9. Yalkut; Radak; Abrabanel
10. Abrabanel
11. Mezudat David
12. Abrabanel
13. Radak; Ralbag
14. Abrabanel
15. Targum Yonatan; Rashi; Radak; Abrabanel
16. Isaiah 37:24
17. Sanhedrin 94b
18. Rashi
19. Rashi; Radak
20. Radak
21. Targum Yonatan
22. Sanhedrin 95b
23. Rashi
24. Radak; Ralbag; Abrabanel
25. Isaiah 10:5
26. Rashi; Radak
27. Targum Yonatan
28. Isaiah 10:12-16
29. Rashi; Radak; Abrabanel
30. Abrabanel
31. Rashi; Radak; Abrabanel; Mezudat David
32. Ralbag; Abrabanel; Mezudat David
33. Abrabanel
34. Seder Olam 23; Shemot Rabah 18:5; Rashi on Megilah 31a; Radak
35. Abrabanel
36. Targum Yonatan; Rashi; Radak
37. Abrabanel
38. Abrabanel
39. Isaiah 10:23
40. Isaiah 10:28-32
41. Sanhedrin 95a
42. II Chronicles 32:20-23
43. Psalms 18:38
44. II Samuel 30:17
45. II Chronicles 14:12
46. II Chronicles 20:22
47. Eichah Rabah 4:15
48. Isaiah 30:29
49. Shemot Rabah 18:5; Radak; Abrabanel
50. Yalkut
51. Sanhedrin 94a; Shemot Rabah 18:5; Rashi; Radak
52. Abrabanel
53. Isaiah 33:3
54. Sanhedrin 95b
55. Exodus 5:2
56. Exodus 14:27
57. Sanhedrin 94a,b
58. Radak
59. Isaiah 43:3
60. Isaiah 45:14
61. Sanhedrin 94b
62. Seder Olam 23
63. Isaiah 19:18,19
64. Yalkut
65. Sanhedrin 95b
66. Sanhedrin 96a; Rashi; Radak; Abrabanel
67. Sanhedrin 96a
68. Eliyahu Rabah 7
69. Isaiah 24:16
70. Sanhedrin 94a

Chapter 20 (Pages 259 – 275)

1. Seder Olam 23; Rashi
2. Seder Olam 23; Radak; Abrabanel
3. Abrabanel
4. Ralbag
5. Eliyahu Rabah 8
6. Maharsha
7. Abrabanel
8. Abrabanel
9. Brachot 10a; Eliyahu Rabah 8; Rashi; Radak
10. Brachot 10a; Eliyahu Rabah 8; Yalkut; Abrabanel
11. Brachot 10b; Abrabanel
12. Yerushalmi Brachot 4; Yalkut
13. Yerushalmi Brachot 4; Kohelet Rabah 5; Yalkut
14. Abrabanel
15. II Chronicles 16:12
16. Brachot 10b; Yalkut; Radak
17. Brachot 10b
18. Rashi; Radak
19. Abrabanel
20. Bereishit Rabah 76:4
21. Musar Haneviim
22. Abrabanel
23. Yevamot 50a; Bereishit Rabah 61:4; Radak
24. Abrabanel
25. Abrabanel
26. Yevamot 50a
27. Brachot 10b; Yalkut
28. Sanhedrin 104a; Eliyahu Rabah 8
29. Isaiah 38:9-20
30. Abrabanel
31. Mechilta Beshalah; Tanhuma Beshalah 18; Yalkut; Rashi; Radak
32. Radak
33. Sanhedrin 96a; Rashi
34. Sanhedrin 96a; Radak
35. Abrabanel
36. Job 8:9
37. Abrabanel
38. Abrabanel
39. Abrabanel
40. Genesis 1:14
41. Hizkuni on Genesis 1:14
42. Pirkei Derabbi Eliezar 52; Rashi
43. Sanhedrin 96a; Yalkut; Rashi; Radak
44. Radak; Abrabanel
45. Pirkei Derabbi Eliezar 52; Rashi; Abrabanel
46. Sanhedrin 104a; Radak
47. Rashi; Radak; Abrabanel
48. Bereishit Rabah 19:11; Rashi
49. Pirkei Derrbbi Eliezar 52
50. Rashi
51. II Chronicles 32:25
52. Abrabanel
53. Rashi; Abrabanel
54. Pirkei Derabbi Eliezar 52; Yalkut; Rashi; Radak
55. Rif on the Abrabanel
56. Targum Yonatan
57. Sanhedrin 93b; Pirkei Derabbi Eliezar 52
58. Rashi; Radak; Abrabanel
59. Sanhedrin 93b; Radak
60. Rif on the Abrabanel
61. I Kings 8:8
62. Yoma 53b,54a; Shekalim 15b,16a; Yerushalmi Shekalim 6:1
63. Abrabanel
64. Rif on the Abrabanel
65. Hagaot Habah on Brachot 10a; Kohelet Rabah 5:6

66. Pesahim 56a; Brachot 10b
67. Yerushalmi Pesahim 9
68. Psalms 87:3
69. Proverbs 25:1
70. Shoher Tov

Chapter 21 (Pages 276 – 288)

1. Sanhedrin 102b; Yalkut
2. Or Hazevi
3. Radak
4. Abrabanel
5. Malbim
6. Mezudat David
7. Yalkut Yirmiah 277; Eichah Rabah 1:36; Abrabanel
8. Abrabanel
9. Malbim
10. II Chronicles 33:7
11. II Chronicles 33:22
12. Sanhedrin 103b; Yalkut
13. Kli Yakar
14. Leviticus 14:35
15. Ezekiel 8:5
16. Isaiah 28:20
17. Vayikra Rabah 17:6
18. Yerushalmi Yoma 4:4
19. Exodus 20:2,3
20. Abrabanel; Mezudat David
21. Seder Olam 20; Yalkut; Rashi; Radak; Abrabanel
22. Rashi; Ralbag; Mezudat David
23. Rashi; Radak
24. Malbim
25. Radak
26. Kli Yakar
27. Exodus 33:20
28. Isaiah 6:1
29. Deuteronomy 4:7
30. Isaiah 55:6
31. Exodus 23:26
32. II Kings 20:6
33. Sanhedrin 103b; Yevamot 49b; Yalkut; Radak; Abrabanel
34. Sanhedrin 103b; Yalkut
35. Kli Yakar
36. Minhah Ketanah
37. Mezudat David
38. II Chronicles 33:11-17
39. Deuteronomy 4:30
40. Sanhedrin 103a; Pesikta; Targum Rav Yosef on Chronicles; Yalkut
41. Genesis 4:13
42. Genesis 27:38
43. Sanhedrin 101b
44. Sanhedrin 101b
45. Seder Olam 24; Sanhedrin 101b; Yalkut
46. Abrabanel
47. Judges 18:30
48. Seder Olam 24; Yalkut
49. Sanhedrin 102b; Yalkut
50. Sanhedrin 103b
51. Sanhedrin 102b; Yalkut
52. Kli Yakar
53. Sanhedrin 103b; Yalkut; Abrabanel
54. Deuteronomy 17:20
55. Abrabanel
56. Abrabanel
57. Sanhedrin 104a

Chapter 22 (Pages 289 – 296)

1. Pirkei Derabbi Eliezar 32
2. II Chronicles 34:3
3. Abrabanel
4. Seder Olam 24; Yalkut; Radak; Abrabanel
5. Abrabanel
6. II Chronicles 34:14
7. Rashi; Mahari Kara; Mezudat David
8. Radak
9. Deuteronomy 28:36
10. Yoma 52b; Seder Olam 24; Radak; Abrabanel
11. Radak
12. Abrabanel
13. Mezudat David
14. Yalkut; Radak
15. II Kings 13:21
16. Pirkei Derabbi Eliezar 33
17. Yalkut; Radak
18. Megilah 14b; Yalkut; Rashi; Radak; Abrabanel
19. Abrabanel
20. Rashi; Mezudat David
21. Targum Yonatan
22. Rashi
23. Rashi
24. Radak; Kli Yakar
25. Abrabanel
26. Abrabanel
27. Abrabanel
28. Moed Katan 28b; Rashi; Radak

Chapter 23 (Pages 297 – 318)

1. Targum Yonatan; Abrabanel
2. Radak
3. II Kings 11:14
4. Radak
5. Rashi; Radak
6. Radak; Abrabanel
7. Deuteronomy 32:34
8. Baal Haturim on the Torah
9. II Chronicles 34:4
10. Abrabanel
11. Rashi; Radak; Abrabanel
12. Rashi
13. Ralbag
14. Abrabanel
15. Abrabanel
16. Radak
17. Menahot 109a; Rashi; Radak; Abrabanel
18. Yalkut Yirmiah 7:277; Rashi; Radak; Abrabanel
19. Radak
20. Aruch Hashalem ““Gei Ben Hinom’’
21. Yalkut Yirmiah 7:277
22. Yalkut Yirmiah 7:277; Abrabanel
23. Radak; Abrabanel
24. Rashi; Radak; Abrabanel
25. Radak
26. Targum Yonatan; Rashi
27. Radak
28. Abrabanel
29. Rashi; Radak
30. II Chronicles 34:5
31. II Chronicles 34:6,7
32. Megilah 14b; Yalkut; Rashi; Radak; Abrabanel
33. Radak; Abrabanel
34. Radak; Abrabanel
35. Rashi; Radak
36. Radak

37. Abrabanel
38. Rashi; Radak
39. Rashi
40. Rashi
41. Radak; Abrabanel
42. II Chronicles 35:18
43. Radak
44. II Chronicles 35:1-18
45. Rashi; Radak
46. Radak; Abrabanel
47. Shabat 56b; Yalkut; Radak
48. Ralbag
49. Radak
50. II Kings 18:5
51. Abrabanel
52. Abrabanel
53. Abrabanel
54. Abrabanel
55. Jeremiah 3:6
56. Jeremiah 1:12
57. Abrabanel
58. Deuteronomy 28:36
59. II Chronicles 35:3
60. Seder Olam 24; Horayot 12a; Yoma 52b
61. Isaiah 57:8
62. Taanit 22b; Rashi; Radak
63. Leviticus 26:6
64. II Chronicles 35:20-25
65. Taanit 22b; Abrabanel
66. Radak
67. Horayot 11b; Rashi; Radak; Abrabanel
68. I Chronicles 3:15
69. Jeremiah 22:11
70. Ibn Ezra
71. Abrabanel
72. Horayot 11b
73. Radak on I Chronicles 3:15
74. Ezekiel 19:2-4
75. Radak
76. Radak
77. Abrabanel
78. Radak

Chapter 24 (Pages 319 – 336)

1. II Kings 20:12
2. Sanhedrin 96a; Yalkut
3. Ezekiel 19:2-4
4. Ezekiel 19:5-9
5. II Chronicles 36:6,7
6. Jeremiah 25:1
7. Daniel 1:1,2
8. Radak; Abrabanel
9. Rashi on Daniel
10. Daniel 1:3,4
11. Seder Olam 25; Radak; Abrabanel; Ralbag on II Chronicles 36:6
12. II Chronicles 36:6
13. Ralbag on II Chronicles 36:6
14. Seder Olam 25
15. Seder Olam 25; Rashi; Radak; Abrabanel
16. Radak; Abrabanel
17. Sanhedrin 96b
18. Deuteronomy 23:16
19. Jeremiah 22:18,19
20. Vayikra Rabah 19:6; Seder Olam 25
21. Radak
22. Sanhedrin 102b; Abrabanel
23. Abrabanel
24. Jeremiah 22:13,17
25. Hagai 2:8
26. Psalms 115:16

27. Sanhedrin 103b; Yalkut
28. Vayikra Rabah 19:6 Yalkut; Abrabanel
29. Sanhedrin 82a; 104a; Yalkut
30. Maharsha
31. II Chronicles 36:9
32. Radak
33. Seder Olam 25
34. Abrabanel
35. Seder Olam 25; Vayikra Rabah, 19:6; Radak; Abrabanel
36. Radak
37. Vayikra Rabah 19:6
38. Jeremiah 52:28
39. Seder Olam 25; Megilah 11b
40. Radak
41. Seder Olam 25; Rashi; Radak
42. Jeremiah 52:29
43. Jeremiah 52:30
44. Malbim
45. Targum Yonatan; Rashi; Radak
46. Seder Olam 25; Sanhedrin 38a; Gitin 88a; Rashi; Radak
47. Jeremiah 22:10
48. Rashi; Mahari Kara; Radak
49. Gitin 88a; Tanhuma Noah
50. Deuteronomy 4:25
51. Daniel 9:14
52. Gitin 88a
53. Seder Olam 25; Abrabanel
54. Radak
55. Seder Olam 25; Sifri; Radak
56. Vayikra Rabah 19:6; Yalkut
57. Jeremiah 22:11
58. Radak here and on I Chronicles 3:15
59. Horayot 11b
60. Horayot 11b; Radak; Abrabanel
61. Jeremiah 27:1-3
62. Ibn Ezra on Daniel 1:1
63. I Chronicles 3:16
64. Abrabanel
65. II Chronicles 36:10
66. Abrabanel
67. II Kings 23:31
68. Malbim
69. Sanhedrin 103a
70. Radak; Abrabanel
71. II Chronicles 36:12-16
72. Abrabanel
73. Proverbs 24:30,31
74. Sanhedrin 103a

Chapter 25 (Pages 337 – 358)

1. Rashi; Radak
2. Yalkut Eicha 1009
3. Jeremiah 26:1, 27:1
4. Jeremiah 28:1
5. Sanhedrin 103a
6. Jeremiah 38
7. Yalkut Eicha 1009
8. Yalkut Eicha 1009
9. Jeremiah 37:10
10. Yalkut Yirmiah 20
11. Isaiah 47:2
12. Sanhedrin 96b; Yalkut
13. Jeremiah 39:2, 52:5
14. Radak; Abrabanel
15. Jeremiah 39:2, 52:6
16. Taanit 28b
17. Abrabanel
18. Yerushalmi Taanit 4:5
19. Rashi on Taanit 25b
20. Yerushalmi Taanit 4:5; Rabenu Hananel and Maharsha on Taanit 26b

21. Baba Kama 82b
22. Daniel 12:11
23. Rashi on Taanit 26b
24. Radak
25. Ezekiel 12:13
26. Rashi; Mahari Kara; Radak
27. Radak
28. Sanhedrin 96b; Yalkut; Radak; Abrabanel
29. Rashi; Radak
30. Yalkut
31. Yalkut
32. Shulhan Aruch Orah Hayim 580
33. Jeremiah 52:12
34. Taanit 29a; Yalkut; Radak; Abrabanel
35. Jeremiah 15:1
36. Jeremiah 52:12
37. Jeremiah 52:29
38. Radak; Abrabanel
39. Megilah 11b; Radak; Abrabanel
40. Megilah 27a; Rashi
41. Abrabanel
42. II Chronicles 36:17
43. Sanhedrin 92b
44. Psalms 137:1
45. Eichah Rabah 5:5
46. Shabat 26a; Radak
47. II Chronicles 36:18,19
48. Isaiah 22:12
49. I Chronicles 16:27
50. Psalms 91:15
51. Yalkut Tehilim 91:15
52. Jeremiah 13:17
53. Isaiah 22:12
54. Isaiah 33:7
55. Hagigah 5b; Yalkut Yirmiah 13; Yalkut Eichah 1009
56. Targum Yonatan; Radak
57. Mezudat Zion
58. Radak
59. Yerushalmi Sanhedrin 1:2
60. Abrabanel
61. Jeremiah 40:6
62. Jeremiah 40:9-16
63. Jeremiah 41:1-3
64. Jeremiah 41:4-43:7
65. Leviticus 17:4
66. Abrabanel
67. Seder Olam 28; Megilah 11b
68. Jeremiah 52:13
69. Daniel 4:29-34
70. Isaiah 14:19
71. Vayikra Rabah 18:2; Abrabanel
72. Seder Olam 28; Abrabanel
73. Vayikra Rabah 18:2; Radak
74. Seder Olam 28; Rashi
75. Kli Yakar
76. Abrabanel; Homat Anach
77. Sifri Ekev
78. Agadat Shmuel; Yalkut; Radak
79. Jeremiah 34:5
80. Seder Olam 28; Moed Katan 28b
81. II Chronicles 36:21
82. Seder Olam 26; Rashi on Leviticus 26:34, Ezekiel 4:5, Habakuk 2:3, II Chronicles 36:21
83. Yalkut Yirmiah 9
84. Jeremiah 6:30
85. Jeremiah 14:19
86. Leviticus 26:44
87. Yalkut Yirmiah 14; Shemot Rabah 31:10
88. II Chronicles 7:16
89. Shemot Rabah 2:2
90. Brachot 7a; Yalkut Tehilim
91. Song of Songs 2:9
92. Bamidbar Rabah 11:2; Shemot Rabah 2:2
93. Zohar Shemot 9
94. Habakuk 2:20
95. Psalms 103:19

96. Shemot Rabah 2:2
97. Genesis 1:1
98. Genesis 1:2
99. Genesis 1:3
100. Isaiah 60:1
101. Isaiah 60:2
102. Bereishit Rabah 2:5
103. Bereishit Rabah 56:10, 69:7
104. Maharal

THE FOURTH WOMAN

ROSELYN TEUKOLSKY

This is a work of fiction. Names, characters, places, and incidents either are the product of the author's imagination or are used fictitiously. Any resemblance to actual events, locales, organizations, or persons living or dead, is entirely coincidental and beyond the intent of either the author or the publisher.

Graveyard Press
112 S Orange Grove Blvd
Apt 110
Pasadena, CA 91105

Graveyard Press paperback ISBN-13: 978-1-967036-03-5
Graveyard Press e-book ISBN-13: 978-1-967036-04-2

Visit our website at www.graveyardpress.com

First Graveyard Press Printing: November 2025
Printed in the United States of America
0 9 8 7 6 5 4 3 2 1

FOR DOMINIQUE

What if the imagination oversteps its bounds?

—Anonymous

CHAPTER 1

The reflection staring back at me is a stranger. *Red lipstick?* Give me a break. I grimace at my image and a serial killer grins back. What was I thinking? My date tonight is supposedly someone intelligent, so why am I preening for him? With a swipe of tissue and a quick application of gloss, my normal self reappears. Even without slasher lips, I can be formidable—six feet tall with a black and gray buzz cut for starters. Silver Fibonacci spirals dangling from my ears.

It's a Tuesday evening in October, my jacket is on, and I'm about to step out when my desktop computer vibrates with red flashing lights.

ALERT! YOUR COMPUTER HAS BEEN LOCKED! ALL YOUR DATA ENCRYPTED! TO REGAIN ACCESS, YOU MUST PAY 10 BITCOIN WITHIN 72 HOURS! FAILURE TO PAY MEANS WE THROW AWAY THE KEY AND YOU LOSE ALL YOUR FILES!

A ransomware attack. *Goddammit.*

Obviously I can't deal with it now, or I'll be late for my date with Vincent. We're supposed to meet in half an hour at a local bar in Cambridge, Mass. My first date from Professionals.com—first date in years, to be honest—and it's already a bust.

For a few seconds I'm paralyzed, hyperventilating, my eyes darting to the four bare walls of my office.

Focus.

I flirt with the idea of abandoning everything, locking up, and going to meet Vincent anyway. *Postpone the flak until tomorrow.* But the sane personality, the one that always takes charge, banishes the thought immediately. *Forget it. You'd be a basket case.*

My business always takes precedence. *Damn.*

I send a hurried message to Vincent. *Sorry: emergency at work. Reschedule for Friday?*

Fat chance. He probably has ten other suitable women—*matches,* in the lingo of the dating site—all lined up, ready to go. My inbox isn't exactly brimming with matches. I already said no thanks to an engineer who sent me two hearts and five emoji winks. I'm sure he's perfectly lovely, but I'm just not a winky, happy-clappy type of person.

This computer hacking would be a disaster for anyone, but it's especially bad for me. I'm supposed to be a crackerjack cybersecurity expert. My company—Madeline Geiger Cyber Solutions—motto is: *Your computer is my business.* People pay me big bucks to protect their networks, so if it becomes known I'm a victim of ransomware, it's goodbye to the lovely old house in Cambridge, the suite of offices in Harvard Square, and my full-time office manager, Shawna.

That's Shawna Robinson, my vivacious young employee who waved goodbye about an hour ago. She too has a big date tonight, with her boyfriend, Lonnie.

"Madeline, go whoop it up tonight with that new man of yours," was her parting shot. My proposed rendezvous with Vincent has blossomed in her imagination. She'd be outraged if she knew I'd canceled my date. Shawna's superpower is her charm, a bubbling brew of dimples and inner radiance. She is someone who'll never have to resort to online dating.

I, on the other hand, am not a slayer of men. The best one could say is my looks are *striking*, with my tall, skinny bod and aristocratic nose. Only a mother would call me beautiful, and mine does with regularity.

Some more fun facts about me: thirty-three-year-old widow, destined to be single and sex-starved forever because there's never enough time to put effort into my social life. Goal with this online dating gig: to recapture the romantic happiness of my early marriage, though probably futile. I've really been looking forward to meeting Vincent, who is no film star either, but has an eye-popping scientific resume. I'm intrigued. He seems promising, but thinking about him now is self-defeating.

Instead, I must figure out how a lowlife infiltrated my computer and got past my so-called impenetrable firewall. Their demand: ten bitcoin. Today that's about $900,000. But cryptocurrency is volatile—it could be a million dollars next week. I won't pay a cent, because if there's one thing I've learned in this job, it's that paying is the kiss of death. Those jerks always come back for more.

How did I get caught? I never go phishing, which means I *never* click on unsolicited links. Shawna and I have unassailable fortifications on our computers, encrypted software I myself wrote and continue to market and license. There hasn't been a problem with it in the three years since I started the business. Any person—*wetware* in computer lingo—who comes into the office is carefully monitored and not allowed near our computers. Definition of wetware: irrational gray matter floating in the squishy confines of human flesh. It is always the weakest link in a computer network. I'm basically suspicious of wetware, which probably explains the deficiencies in my social life.

So with all these precautions, how did I get hacked?

My brain processes this while I copy the malware code from the infected desktop to my laptop. Then I wipe the desktop clean by deleting everything on it and painstakingly restore all my files from backup. This is my reward for being diligent—okay, *obsessive*—and backing up every keystroke to storage.

The time creeps by. It's almost 9:00 p.m.

If I can't neutralize the ransomware, the hacker will attack me again and again until I pay up or lose my business. That's how they operate.

Since I trust my software, the source of my problem must be hardware—the gadgets that connect me to the internet. The only way someone got into my computer is through the Ethernet cable, my connection.

My office is in an old Cambridge building, where I rent a suite of three rooms. The cable is attached to the back of my computer, an inelegant blue snake that is stapled to the bottom of the wall and winds around the room to one of the far corners, where it disappears through a small hole in the floor. My office is on the first floor, so there must be a basement underneath me. I'm still settling in here and have yet to explore it.

I grab a flashlight, secure my office with a double lock, push through a heavy door at the end of the hallway, and go down a staircase to the underground room that houses my cable connection. The stairs are steep and poorly lit, the air frigid as I descend into the bowels of the building. A sweep of my flashlight shows there's not a soul around.

I check my phone. No response from Vincent. *Damn!*

The downstairs is dark, dank, and unfinished, with a dull cement floor, pipes and gray stone walls. There's also a furnace making a godawful clattering noise.

In the corner under my office, my cable emerges from the basement ceiling and enters my router box, which is connected to a panel on the wall labeled Verizon. That's their fiber-optic network. All good, except there's something mighty puzzling about my router box, which sends internet connections to each of my three rooms on the first floor. Instead of being safely secured in my office, where it belongs, it's directly *under* my floor, in the basement, accessible to every hacker and their mother.

And some freeloader has taken advantage of the faulty setup.

A fourth cable that doesn't belong to me extends from my box and disappears into the cover panel of the furnace. No router of its own. It looks like the villain is the heating company, which remotely monitors the furnace system. The jerk who set up the furnace piggybacked on my connection; they're getting a free internet ride, paid for by me.

It takes about two seconds to figure out how I got hacked. The heating company made itself part of my network, one of their employees fell into a phishing trap by clicking on a malign link (the bait), and the malware smoothly traveled into my computer. *Unbelievable.* This is embarrassing. I should have checked my hardware on moving-in day. Shame on me.

If my theory is right, the heating company is also dealing with a ransomware attack. The same hacker who ensnared me would have caught them too.

The furnace panel has a phone number. After I've punched in the digits, a stern voice tells me it's after hours, then the phone goes dead in my hand. It'll have to wait until tomorrow. Damn! Thieving assholes. The heating company deserved to be hacked.

I take note of their address, then use my Swiss Army knife to slice through their illicit cable. Let them figure out why they've lost their ability to monitor the furnace. Before leaving this awful room, I make a mental note to install a small surveillance camera that will keep an eye on my Ethernet cable. And tomorrow I'll move my router box into my office.

Back upstairs, I fidget with my phone. Still no indication Vincent received my message. *Shit!* Perhaps he's at the bar right now with a soul full of hope, keeping his eye out for a tall woman in a navy-blue business suit with a nice buzzy haircut. And then I realize how late it is—almost 10:00 p.m. He probably went home in disgust long ago and crossed me off his list.

This is my first foray into online dating. I met my husband Mike in college and married him when we were computer science graduate students. Children. I was a virgin.

Focus on the hacking attack!

My next goal is to track down the IP address of the computer that sent the ransomware. Find the computer, access it, destroy it. The hacker is probably using a spoofed IP address (namely fake) he assumes can't be traced back to his actual location. He's mistaken. This hacker doesn't realize he's messed with the wrong person. I can find his real address if I get him to chat to me from his actual source address. Revenge will be sweet, but it may keep me here all night.

The malware code is straightforward and I plunge right in, spurred on by adrenaline. There's a button that says PAY NOW! My entry ticket. In the comment box, I write: *Can't pay. Can you lower your price?*

Another screen of bile pops up.

YOU NOW OWE 20 BITCOIN! PRICE DOUBLES FOR EACH DELAY! GET YOUR ACT TOGETHER! PAY NOW TO UNLOCK FILES!

I write down the new spoofed address.

Our exchanges become more and more heated as I insist I can't pay.

ALL YOUR PERSONAL FILES WILL GO ON THE INTERNET IN ONE HOUR! ALL PERSONAL EMAILS! ALL YOUR PRIVATE DATA AND PORN! YOURE TOAST!

Each time he yells at me from a new spoofed address, it narrows down the path and gets me nearer to his computer. *Yes!*

My phone jangles on my desk. Mom. *Not now, please.*

With a shaking hand, I kill the call.

Speed is crucial. I dare not lose him. Yet it's maddening how slow this algorithm is, working backward on the branches of a tree, limb by limb, to get to the root, the source computer, eliminating all but a handful of networks. Time drags, grinding on, testing my patience.

My phone pings. I glance at it. *Vincent.* It's 1:30 a.m. Why is he only writing now, at this ungodly hour? *Do I really want to date an insomniac?*

The computer address of the hacker pops up on my screen. *I've got him!*

Mom and Vincent will have to wait.

With a murderous heart, I send a stream of malware speeding to the hacker's computer.

Turn off the internal thermal protection sensor inside the guts of his computer, disabling the fan that cools down the hardware. Let loose a barrage of infinitely looping algorithms that will pierce the brain of his computer, his nerve center, his central processing unit. Grind away until his computer is smoking in front of him, literally fried to death.

He'll need a new computer. Vengeance is sweet.

I breathe deeply for a second, then call my mother, who doesn't reply. *Why did Mom call so late?* When I try again, a humanoid voice apologizes because Mom's voicemail is full. God I'm tired. I drop my head in my hands and let out a cry.

My spine is knotted with anxiety by the time I click on Vincent's message.

His response, sent through Professionals.com, is brief.

Can't meet on Friday. How about tomorrow, same time same place?

CHAPTER 2

In the pale light of an October moon, I hurry through darkened streets to my house in Cambridge.

Please let Mom be home and safe.

The outside light is triggered by my step on the garden path. I push through the front door, breathing heavily, hit by a smell of burning plastic. *What the hell?*

The smoke alarm starts its earsplitting siren. Fire in the kitchen?

Dropping my computer, purse, and jacket, I run, stumbling past the breakfast nook to get to a frying pan that seems to be melting on the stovetop. The electric burner is on—low heat, thank God—and the contents of the pan are like charcoal. I turn off the burner and, with an oven mitt, grab the frying pan and lower it into the sink, where it sends up a noisy sizzle. Next, the alarm must be defanged, windows opened and the house aired out.

This is an old Victorian house that could have burned down in minutes.

Mom, in her nightgown, comes into the kitchen. "What's going on, Mads? Why are you cooking so late at night?"

My mother is beautiful, with golden-brown hair that frames her face with a feathery softness. But her eyes are vague and unfocused, a window to the dementia that has started to afflict her in her late sixties. It seems to have advanced in the past few weeks, though this is beyond anything she's done before.

It's 2:00 a.m., and in every sense of the word, I'm running on fumes. *What am I to do?*

It's unthinkable that Mom would go into a nursing home. I want her living here with me, in this lovely house. But she can't be on her own. Nor can I deal with this now.

I put my arm gently around my mother's shoulders and rest my cheek on her head. "Come, Mom. Let's go to bed."

My first piece of business on Wednesday morning is to send Vincent a text. Like a teenager, I agonize over the wording, then give up. Less is more.

Tonight is fine. Waldo's at 6:15.

Task number two is easier—call Shawna and let her know I'll be in late to the office. She's more interested in how my date with Vincent went.

"Couldn't go," I say. Curt. Unwilling to spend time on this call. "Emergency at the office. Tell you about it later."

As expected, she's outraged. "You missed your date last night because you had to *work*?"

"Don't worry, my date is still on, for tonight."

"Gosh darn, Madeline, go and have *fun*," she says. "You know, F-U-N?"

Task three is the one I'm dreading. I seek out Mom in the sitting room, where she and Tosca, our large ginger and black tabby cat, are sharing a chair, sunning themselves at the window.

My mother is bright-eyed this morning. When she smiles at me, a sharp sensation pierces my chest, like premature grief.

"Mom, do you know you left a frying pan on a hot stove last night?" I put my hand out to stroke Tosca while she ponders her reply. She can't win. If she says she wasn't the one who did it, I can justify my efforts to get us live-in help. Which of course I can also do if she confesses that, yes, she did it.

She hangs her head.

"It's okay, Mom." My voice is soft. "I know you wouldn't ever intentionally hurt us. But you have to let me hire an assistant for you. It would set my mind at rest."

She nods miserably, then purses her mouth. "You know I manage fine on my own most of the time, Madsy. I promise I won't use the stove while you're out."

My heart yearns to believe her, like it has before.

I've become expert at advertising for a housekeeper. The actual job description is harrowing, something I can't explicitly put in writing. *A woman who will live with us and prevent my mother from burning down the house, or wandering into traffic, or precipitating disasters not yet in my imagination.*

Mom always resists the implication that she needs help. So far, she has systematically worked her way through three valiant women who were pushed out the door by Mom's antics. Despite her lapses, she's become sly and indomitable in her resistance.

My speech, this time, is prepared. *Mom, because I love you, I'm willing to try again and find us a housekeeper. If you make her life impossible, like you did with the others, you'll have to go live in River View, where they'll take care of you. This time I mean it. I've put down a deposit and reserved a spot for you.*

When I start to speak, the first sentence trips me up—*because I love you*—and my voice falters. Mom grips the arms of her chair, and tears that have glistened at the corners of her hazel eyes spill out down her cheeks. I can't push out another word. All the emotions wrapped up in the threats to my fragile business and fear for my bighearted mom, who's departing from me more and more each day, all those feelings coalesce, and I weep silently.

How is it possible I'm as smart and hard as nails when I deal with computers, but a pile of mush when it comes to my mother?

She homes into my weakness straightaway and puts the cat down. "Oh, my darling girl, come here." And she tries to gather up her six-foot baby, long legs, dangling arms and all. *Ridiculous.*

My mother's love is not enough. I'm lonely. On a cold Sunday last month, walking with my chocolate Lab Torvill in the icy light of a Boston sun, I realized the dumb, unconditional love of my pets and sporadic warmth of my mother left me bereft, not comforted. I craved male companionship—love, romance, sex. Not necessarily in that order. Even getting married again flitted through my mind as a possibility.

I decided to dip my ungainly toes into the online dating pool.

My past experiences with men haven't been the best, and there's still pain in my heart when I think back. My late husband was unfaithful; my computer science colleagues in academia had been dismissive; and my former boss here in Boston was an asshole, a "shut up and go make coffee" kind of guy.

Because I'd been preoccupied and curt with my mother the past few weeks, and had brought up the topic of River View Nursing Home more times than necessary, I decided to cheer us both up by including her in my dating project. At the dining table in our kitchen, having one of our favorite lunches—creamy tomato soup and buttered toast—I told my mother. Her reaction was entirely predictable.

"Oh, hallelujah! It's about time you got yourself a boyfriend. I'll help you. Maybe we'll get a smile on your face."

After lunch, we found a dating site that seemed suitable, Professionals.com, and I had a first go at setting up my profile. It was painless and easy, like taking a quiz.

Mom swiveled around my laptop to see what I'd written, her glasses low on her nose.

"*Forbrydelsen*?" she said. "Your favorite TV series is *Forbrydelsen*?"

"Yes, why? It's that Danish murder mystery—*The Killing*. You loved it too."

"Oh, Madsy, you can't put that in your profile. You'll cut out two-thirds of American men."

"Maybe I want the other third," I said indulgently.

She laughed, her eyes sparkling, all signs of dementia banished.

The more she read of my profile, however, the more disapproving her face became. "You can't say you're a cybersecurity expert. My God, Mads, *think* about it—you'll scare men off."

There was a time my mother bristled with pride at my computer smarts. All that seemed to have melted away.

"It's just one of those things, Mom," I said sadly. "I work with computers. I want programmers, not poets."

She examined me thoughtfully for a while, rotating my head and giving me her eagle eye. "Maybe you should grow your hair a bit. You know, to soften your face. That weird haircut makes you look like you'll eat a man for lunch." When my mother gets going she can be relentless.

"It's stylish, Mom. I'm a businesswoman. It's the image I want to project."

I don't look as bad as she makes out. When viewed from the right angle, my haircut flatters my face. Super short, super soft dark chop on the sides, with a #7 clipper guard silvery taper on top.

Eventually, Mom said, "Fine. Go and put on some makeup for your photo. Maybe we'll pose you with the animals to soften you up, give you some personality."

"You know I don't wear makeup," I said. "The last thing I need is for my date to think he's getting a babe and then find himself with me."

My mom finally chuckled. She loved the challenge of this project, trying to sell me to a new man.

I decided not to use the word "widow" in my dating profile because it is a sad word, best spoken in private, with the right person. For once, my mother agreed with me.

For the all-important profile photo, we shifted operations to the living room, where I could pose in front of the Victorian fireplace. Mom arranged me in an armchair, then dropped the cat onto my lap. Tosca, however, being old and grumpy, wasn't interested in participating. My goofy dog, Torvill, with his kind face and tongue hanging out, scrambled up and allowed Mom to arrange him. He was more than an armful.

"Woof woof," Mom said. "Come on, Madsy, try smiling for God's sake."

Torvill did the trick. He licked my face, colluding with Mom. Between the two of them, we ended up with a quirky photo in which it looked like I just kissed the dog.

There was a section for filling in my pronouns, and I wrote *she* and *her*. When asked about the pronouns of the person I'd like to meet, on a whim I checked *any*.

"Madsy, you can't do that. You have to say "he" and "him," otherwise who knows what you'll get."

"Maybe I'm open-minded Mom, willing to play the field. What could go wrong?"

My mother sighed. "Darling Mads, always trying to get a rise out of me." She grabbed for the mouse, but for once I was quicker than she was, and with one final click, we launched me into cyberspace.

To my astonishment, I scored a promising early match: Vincent. His profile said "neurobiologist with his own lab," which had the same heft as "cybersecurity expert with her own business." There was a cosmic symmetry to it. During our digital chats, he said he enjoyed his work and would like to talk about science and life with a like-minded companion. When he suggested meeting at a bar, I accepted with alacrity. I'm a brisk decision maker, and the directness of his approach appealed to me.

When I showed Vincent's profile to Mom, she immediately said, "He's not for you."

I thought she'd be thrilled. "How can you say that without reading a word about him?"

"Anyone who can't find it in himself to smile for his profile photo is going to be a loser. Try someone else, Madsy."

Like they were lining up in droves and I should go down the list.

"His face is thoughtful and serious, Mom. He appeals to me."

Other points in his favor, which I declined to mention to my mother: his straight-arrow personality, like mine, and no hint in his profile of being "fun-loving," a phrase that raises images of heavy-drinking adults who party deep into the night.

On Wednesday morning, after I've confirmed my date for tonight with Vincent and let Shawna know I'll be late, I disable the fuse for the stove.

Today my mother will be on her own—again.

"Take good care of Mom," I tell the animals, who are playfully batting each other about.

There's one more challenge to deal with before I head to the office: the person who had the gall to hijack my internet connection for his heating company.

CHAPTER 3

Memorial Drive along the Charles River is clogged with traffic on this chilly fall day. I'm headed across the river to Allston Village where Nicholson's Heating and Appliances is located. Some jerk on the phone this morning declined to give me an appointment with the boss, so I'm just going to muscle my way in and confront them about using my Ethernet cable. My guess is they're struggling to cope with the ransomware attack. I asked, but he wasn't telling.

The air is restless, and the river is churning, in sync with me. Maybe someday soon I'll pass by a peaceful scene that triggers a feeling of hope for the future. Perhaps my date tonight will be a knockout. *Ha ha.*

On this Wednesday morning, it seems all of Boston is parking in Allston. Miraculously, I score a prime spot just a few blocks from Nicholson's, backing my Jeep Wrangler in between two fat SUVs with one sweep of the wheel.

A more laid-back personality might slow down and take in the sights—a quirky mix of restaurants, thrift shops, and secondhand bookstores. For me, it all registers on the periphery as I hurry along, trying not to overthink my mission to confront those weasels about their cable in my router, check if they really had a ransomware attack, and see what they're doing about it.

Nicholson's is an eclectic place, hawking everything from food mixers and microwaves to appliance repair. It has a touch of seediness that fits right in to the quaintly run-down feel of the neighborhood.

I've given some thought to my appearance; a dark-burgundy pantsuit and crisp white shirt. With my height and close-cropped hairstyle, I want them to pay attention.

When I enter the store, things are calm and no one appears to be freaking out over locked files.

"May I speak to the owner?" I ask at the service department counter.

"Mr. Nicholson is in a meeting," the assistant says, "but perhaps I can help you."

"No, thanks." I tap my knuckles on the counter. "What time will his meeting be over?"

He pulls up a calendar on a computer that appears to be just fine. Did I miscalculate the source of my office attack?

"Why don't I set up an appointment for you and Mr. Nicholson sometime next week?"

We're both being awfully courteous, so I dial it up a notch by raising the volume. "Thank you, but no. I need to see your boss now—like yesterday—to talk about how my business got hacked because of your company's illegal furnace monitoring on my premises."

The man, who is after all just a very polite flunky, stares at me with his mouth open. His unctuous demeanor dies on his face, and he scurries away, presumably to talk to the owner. While I'm waiting, I wonder whether they've detected that their cable is no longer functioning in my office building. Perhaps there's been a red alert somewhere.

Either way, I predict Mr. Nicholson will show up in the next five minutes.

And here he is. A large grizzly bear, probably a former football player who's not the man he used to be. Scowling, he marches toward me. "Who are you, and what's our furnace monitoring to you? Are you from the cable company?"

I can just picture his poor employee a minute ago at the receiving end of his scorn. *A woman? You couldn't get rid of a woman?*

"Could we talk in your office?" I say pleasantly.

He's sweating profusely, damp stains near his armpits. "I don't have time to talk. Tell me what you want, miss."

His tone of voice has attracted some eyeballs. Well, I can make a few heads swivel too.

"I'm here about your ransomware attack yesterday," I say, loud and clear for all to hear.

There's a sudden quietness in the room.

His head snaps around, and after a few seconds, he says, "Okay. Come into my office."

Why thank you, don't mind if I do.

He leads me to a pokey, windowless room at the back.

"Are you Mr. Nicholson?" I ask when I'm facing him across his cluttered desk. "Madeline Geiger." I hand him my card.

He tosses it aside. "You've pulled me out of a meeting. What do you want?"

Fair enough. "I work at 102 Mount Auburn Street in Cambridge, where your company installed the furnace. You—your business—monitors the furnace remotely."

"Are you having heating problems?"

"No, not directly. But I bet your company is, as we speak, having problems checking the carbon monoxide levels in our building." I give him a hard stare and am rewarded by his shifty eyes. "Did *you* install the monitoring cable, Mr. Nicholson?"

"Maybe I did, maybe I didn't. A lot of cables pass through here." Then, abruptly, he picks up my card and changes his tune. "Maddie—may I call you Maddie?—tell me what happened to our cable. I already got a complaint today that our data was wrong."

I lean forward, palms on his desk. "No, you may not call me Maddie; I'm Ms. Geiger. And in answer to the question about your cable, it got cut. By me, with my Swiss army knife."

His arms, which were folded across his belly unfold and he glares at me. Then, unexpectedly, he laughs. "Come again? Seriously?" For a moment, he looks human.

"How much did you pay Verizon this year for that connection in our building?" I ask.

"That's none of your damn business, *Mizz* Geiger." The smile on his face is strained.

"The reason it is my damn business, *Mister* Nicholson, is that your company has been using my Verizon connection, which I have actually been paying them for. I should report you to Verizon for theft."

He opens his hands in a placating gesture. "Wait a minute, slow down. Scout's honor, I didn't know. I have an employee who handles accounts and another one who deals with furnace set up. I'm just the boss who pulls the strings here."

I soften toward him, despite my antagonism. I believe him. He's being frank about his ignorance. He just has a business to run, like me. He's nothing but a Grand Poobah, not smart enough to have figured out how to piggyback on my internet connection.

"How did you deal with the ransomware attack?" I ask. If Nicholson didn't have an attack, then I've misdiagnosed the source of my system's weakness. While he's debating how much to lie, a teenager enters the room.

"Uh, Mr. Nicholson, about the internet and those missing files."

"Not now, Buck," Nicholson says sharply.

The guy, who looks to be about sixteen, grunts and departs, his long, biblical hair flowing behind him. *Is he their tech department?*

"He helped us out yesterday—knows a bit about computers."

"Did you pay the ransom?" It had taken me hours to neutralize the threat.

"Hell, no," Nicholson says. "We fixed the problem, chop-chop. No more demands for money. That ransom guy knew he met his match. No sirree, no payments from here."

"What's, uh, Buck's position in the store? A salesperson?"

He laughs. Then frowns. "Now that would be telling. Let's just say he's a high school dropout, weird as hell. You know the type. Good at hooking up furnaces. Not so keen to put him on the floor with that hair and all." *Earring, nose stud, and eyebrow piercing.*

My visit has elicited what I needed to know. Yes, they did have a ransomware attack. And no, Nicholson wasn't the one who fixed it. Nicholson unlocking computer files is like me writing romantic poetry.

I stand and say cordially, "Mr. Nicholson, thank you for your time." *Now run along back to your meeting.*

"Are we good?" He licks his lips, reluctant to go now.

"Sure, we're fine."

"I'll get someone to show you off the premises."

"No, don't let me keep you." *Go already.*

He doesn't move. For sure his eyes are on me as I walk through the store, out the door and along the sidewalk. Out of his sight, eventually.

In the frosty air, a brisk walk around the block is called for, taking in the sights and enjoying the genteel, slightly run-down ambience of the neighborhood.

After at least twenty minutes, I slip back into Nicholson's store, standing in the shadows of refrigerators, surveying the room. The tech wiz is nowhere to be seen. Mr. Nicholson, too, is out of sight.

I move swiftly to the service counter. "Is Buck around?" I ask softly.

"Buck does his own thing," the clerk replies. "But I'll look in back."

I linger on the floor, making myself scarce against a wall.

My luck is in. Buck reappears.

He flicks his bangs to the side and surveys me through long-lashed brown eyes. "Jeffrey the HackMeister Buck Who are you?" His voice is pure adolescent geek.

"Madeline the ByteBeast Geiger." That name takes me back a few years.

The HackMeister extends a skinny arm, and we shake on it.

"Cool hair," he says.

"Thanks. You too." I look around. "Is there any place other than here we can talk?"

He stands silently like a statue, staring at me and perhaps converting me into digital bits.

"Why?" he says eventually, with more curiosity than aggression.

"Because of yesterday's ransomware attack. I also got hacked by the same hacker as you." I pause to let it sink in. "I want to know how you resolved it and"—looking around, I lower my voice—"I want to talk somewhere more private."

"Okay. Furnace lab." He spins on his heel, executing a U-turn, motioning me to follow him. He's a beanpole like me, with a long T-shirt that has an elongated skull and bones on the back, including a vertical bone through the skull's chin.

The furnace lab is a nerd-tool paradise, complete with large, heavy, metal fire pokers and medieval implements. Moving machinery. Controlled fires.

"You like it here?" We're in a concealed corner, and no one will hear us over the noise.

"It's cool." He regards me, trying to decode me.

"How'd you fix the ransomware thing?" I ask.

"Negative, no fix. The problem went away. Like the hackman got cold feet or something." *That's me, frying the hacker's computer.*

"How did you unlock the data? Restore the files?" I'm very curious.

He's fidgeting. Wants to get back to his nerd tools. "Secret decrypt protocol. Garbage in garbage out."

"You decrypted their locked files?" The bad leg from my skydiving accident is getting sore from standing still. I lean against the wall, which feels like it's being heated by a furnace on the other side.

"Affirmative." He treats me to a lopsided smile—knows I'll be impressed.

"Where'd you learn to do that?"

"Here 'n there. AP computer science. Whatever. School sucked, big time. Much better here." He makes a broad gesture around the hellhole lab.

"They pay you well?" He's obviously low on the totem pole. Probably loves his ten bucks an hour.

"Maybe." His body language says he's suspicious. Or perhaps he's being cagey.

"Come work for me, Buck. I have a cybersecurity business. My office is in Cambridge. You'd be working on computers all the time. Ransomware. I'll show you how to burn the bastards at the other end." I hand him my card.

He pockets the card without looking at it and studies me frankly. "Negative."

So he likes his furnace toys down here. Or he dislikes the look of me.

"How much would you like to be paid?" I'm still crisping myself against the hot wall, arms folded.

He walks in a circle, his eyes closed.

"You'd have your own office," I say. "Your own den."

He stops pacing and scratches his head. "Dunno. Definitely overtime?" he says, his voice cracking on "time."

Sounds to me like they're getting him for nothing. But he's not saying.

I take a stab. "Okay, how about forty an hour. How does that sound to you?"

Eyes wide open. Flying saucers. "Forty dollars?"

He really is just a kid.

But then his eyes narrow and he licks his lips. "How about fifty?"

Fast learner. Thinks on his feet.

I do a quick calculation. "Why don't we say forty per hour for a month's probation while I check you out. Then $100K per year if I hire you. Will that buy me your services?"

"Affirmative," my new HackMeister says.

CHAPTER 4

Vincent Cantley, the man I'm meeting tonight, has grown in my mind. Even though I've learned that anticipation often exceeds the actual event, I'm looking forward to our date.

The clinical efficiency of his profile on the dating site appeals to me. He's a scientist who studies brainwaves. No hyperbole or extraneous adjectives. And no distracting embellishments on his photo, either. He's actually quite hard to describe—a generic man with dark hair and a blocky face, strong chin, and serious expression. Kind of nondescript. When I squint slightly at his photo, he looks handsome.

"I'm a man who gets what he wants," he writes under *Work Ethic.*

Since I'm not big on small talk, there's a question in my mind about which personal details I should share at our meeting. Safe topics: my secondhand, red Jeep Wrangler, which, more than three years ago, transported me, my mother, dog, and cat from Upstate New York to Boston. My prior academic life as a computer scientist at Cornell. How I love living among smart people in a college town. Is that offensive? If so, he's probably not the guy for me. When he asks about my work, I'll describe my business, but I won't tell him about my previous job in Boston, where I had an insufferable, sexist boss. My date doesn't need to know I was fired for "insubordination and personality incompatibility." *No, I don't make coffee, and no thanks, I try not to sleep with assholes.*

I'll have to find an opportune moment to tell Vincent I'm a widow. Safe subtopics: my deceased husband, Mike (but not his infidelities), the awful skydiving accident, and my replaced right knee.

After a swipe through my hair and a dash of lip gloss, I'm good to go. Mom pats my rear end and removes an imaginary piece of lint. "Don't worry, darling. Everything will work out. Be nice to Vincent. Sit back and don't frighten him."

She's forgotten her earlier antipathy toward him.

Torvill knows I'm going out and thinks he's being taken for a walk. He starts panting at the door, waiting for me to get the plastic poop baggy, which is always a happy sign for him. No luck tonight, though. By now, I'm used to how his body droops and his eyes become baleful pools of resignation. I ruffle his velvety ears, squat down to hug him goodbye, then I'm out the door.

It's a clear fall night with a half-moon that lights my way to Harvard Square. Fallen leaves have started to crackle underfoot. Walking in the chilly air, I'm grateful for my heavy leather jacket and tight cords.

With a sense of apprehension and hope, I enter the noisy bar and cast my eyes about for a rectangular head that matches the small photo on my phone. He's probably been looking out for me too, because a man who seems promising is edging toward me through the crowd.

"Madeline? Hi, I'm Vince."

A nice baritone voice, quite mellifluous, and a man as tall as I am. It shouldn't be important, but it sure doesn't count against him. We shake hands, which feels right too, so we're off to a good start. A firm handshake, not a rock crusher.

He's much better looking than his profile photo, more animated. Surprising blue eyes.

"Shall we sit at a table?" he says. "Less noisy than at the bar."

We probably should have met in a nicer setting with quiet ambience for an intimate conversation, but I didn't want to be stuck with a jerk in a restaurant. At least here I can bail and run if needed.

We end up at a small table squeezed into a crowded corner. From a vintage poster on the wall, John Wayne gives me a stern, manly eye as we order drinks above the din. They have specialty cocktails—my weakness—and I ask for a concoction with vodka, sprite, mint, and cucumbers in a tall glass. He wants scotch on the rocks. Of course he does.

Steer clear of alcohol on your first date. One of the admonitions from our dating site. But these are the same people who suggested I use wink emojis as an ice breaker with a stranger.

"What should I call you?" Vincent says, a strong point in his favor. He doesn't assume I'm a Maddie.

So we are Madeline and Vince.

For a while, he studies me frankly, without embarrassment.

God. Should I smile at him?

I'm not well-practiced in the dating game, so I stare back and examine him too. Striking face with strong, symmetrical features. Good hair. Clean-shaven, with no overpowering aftershave. Black turtleneck, brown pants and a leather jacket. It occurs to me that he's well-preserved—forty is definitely in his rearview mirror.

He's made an effort, and I warm to him and relax.

"So tell me, Madeline, are you divorced?" he asks after our drinks arrive with a bowl of fragrant popcorn.

His directness surprises me. So the "W" word has come up earlier than I anticipated. Might as well get it out of the way.

His face becomes suitably grave and sympathetic when I describe how my husband died during a skydive. He reaches across the table and touches my hand briefly. No electric sparks, but hey, nice gesture.

"How about you?" I ask.

"Unmarried," he says brusquely. When he sees my raised eyebrows—because surely I deserve more—he says, "A couple of long-term relationships that didn't work out." His tone says it all: he wasn't the one who terminated those relationships. Smoothly, he switches topics. "Tell me about your work, Madeline. Cybersecurity, huh? You must be in huge demand."

His interest appears to be sincere, and I unbend. This I can talk about without any self-consciousness. I *love* my work. He gets an earful—encryption, security licenses, firewalls—and when he still seems captivated, I give him a second earful.

He sits back. "Wow. Brilliant and beautiful. You're the real deal."

I don't think of myself as a blusher, but warm waves of heat spread across my neck and cheeks. I'd be lying if I said I wasn't flattered, maybe even turned on a bit.

"Perhaps I should hire you to check my security systems," he says languidly.

I laugh, defusing the moment. "I don't come cheap."

"I use computers, too," he says. "In my lab. Manipulating brainwaves in rodents."

Using complicated hand gestures, he describes his experiments with mice and rats, starting with tiny lights implanted in their heads. He studies behavioral stuff. Mind control. He's proud of his results and is about to submit a paper to a prestigious journal.

He inserts lights and chemicals in their bodies.

"Does your research get you into trouble?" I ask.

He pauses in apparent surprise. "What kind of trouble?"

A trickle of sweat runs down my back. It's warm in here, and noise is bouncing from the rafters. I raise my voice. "Experimenting on animals. Violating their bodies."

"Mice? Rats?" He signals at a passing waitress for another scotch on the rocks and more popcorn. "They're hardly warm and fuzzy pets."

"No, but they are fellow creatures."

Raucous laughter at an adjacent table.

It's an awkward moment. I sound like a sanctimonious jerk.

He puts his drink down and leans closer. Intense. "Mice and rats are used in thousands of labs. My research aims to help *people*. Brainwaves are brainwaves, no matter which creature they're in."

In the dark light of the bar, his face has become lit from inside. He sure is passionate about his rodent experiments and wants to convert me. I nod and take another sip of minty cocktail. It's not my goal to change his worldview.

It's time to call it a night.

We've consumed two bowls of popcorn. I'm nursing one drink, which is enough. No question it's been an interesting interlude, but I'm ready to head home.

He, however, is not. While he's working on his second drink, he signals vigorously for more snacks, studying me, invading my airspace. If I weren't an amateur at this dating game, I'd say he's staring at me with too many stars in his eyes.

"You're a fascinating woman, Madeline."

God. What's the right response? Thank you? You too? To be honest, he's coming on a bit strong, and what I really want to say is *Sit back!*

He picks up his glass again. "I work just a few blocks away from here. We could walk there right now. I'd like to show you my lab."

Thanks, but no.

My phone jangles in my purse. *Mom.*

I jump up from my chair. "Vince, excuse me for a minute. I must take this." I ignore his startled face and push my way through the crowd. Outside, the cold air cools me down in an instant.

"Mom, is this really necessary? You know I'm meeting Vince."

"Vince? Who's Vince?" she says.

My throat squeezes shut. "Mom, I'm in the middle of a date, remember? Online dating?" The words come out in a futile croak, lost to the wind.

"Come home now, Madsy, I'm really frightened," she says in a wan, little voice. Who has hijacked my mother? I must escape. *Okay, Mom, I'll be home really soon and please don't call again when I hang up and kiss kiss kiss.*

I hurry back inside, my nerves strumming, stumbling recklessly past moving bodies to reach our table.

Vince looks up at me, concerned. "Everything okay?"

Someone squeezes past me, and I must scrunch myself toward him as I sit down. I'm as taut as an E string.

"I must go home to check on my mother." Rasping. Breathless. Not what Professionals.com had in mind for mature adults on their first date.

"Your mother," he says. Not judgmental, but definitely processing the new development. Somewhere in the turmoil, I'm grateful for his reaction, that his demeanor is serious and concerned, not annoyed.

"My mother has Alzheimer's," I say, my voice raw with phlegm. "I worry about her all the time."

"Oh, Madeline, how horrible for her—and for you." Hs face creases with sympathy as he lightly squeezes my arm.

And just like that, he unleashes a flood. With his face barely eighteen inches away from mine, I tell him all about her. That this Alzheimer's thing came out of the blue. That she's alone and untrustworthy. It spills out in its pathetic details, the sad tales of all our previous housekeepers and my futile struggles to hire someone new. On and on, same old story.

It makes me feel better in the way you feel better when you've just thrown up.

Unbelievable that I'm using Mom as an escape valve.

I gulp down the last of my drink. The lovely minty cucumber cocktail, which was sweet and innocuous as I sipped it, turns out to have a powerful punch as it fizzes through my bloodstream. With my head buzzing, the man in front of me doesn't seem so bad. At the very least, he has compassion, and he's intriguing. Eyebrows that announce themselves and blend into one when he talks about his work. He seems genuinely interested in my company. Right now, he's regarding me with open curiosity, showing a personality that extends beyond himself. Perhaps my original judgment about his use of animals was too hasty.

"Okay, Vince, I'll go see your lab sometime, but not now." Carefully, so I don't tip it over, I place my empty glass on the table.

"Great. How about Saturday night? Dinner first. At a real restaurant with nice atmosphere and white tablecloths." When I don't immediately answer, he adds, "My treat."

I consider it while munching on the last vodka-soaked cucumber slice. How about that; he wants to see me again, in spite of my mother. Mom—the other mother, the lucid one—will take the follow-up invitation as a good sign, especially the white tablecloths. And here I was, thinking of ditching him because he experiments on animals. Maybe he treats them like pets and has cute names for them. I'm floating above my chair, never a good place to be when making decisions.

"Okay, thank you, yes to dinner," I say. "Yes to a nice restaurant, but we'll get separate checks, thank you." *Stop thanking him.* Just clarify the parameters.

The walk home clears my head, but leaves me with a feeling of optimism tinged with degradation. When I arrive at the house, it's quiet, except for Torvill, who scratches on the door and woofs hello. I drop to my knees to give my amiable, good-natured dog some undiluted love, which he receives blissfully, eyes closed.

"Did she treat you well tonight?" I whisper. He won't tell, he's too kind.

When I go to the kitchen to forage, I realize the place is ominously still. No TV.

"Mom," I call out. "I'm home." The house is old, and my voice echoes back against the old wood floors. I find my mother in the sitting room at the window, in the dark. Dear old Tosca is on her lap. Two ladies of a certain age, staring at the house across the road.

"Hey, Mom." I drop down next to her and hug her, examining her face.

"Sometimes this place gives me the chills," she says.

"Aren't you going to ask about my date?"

"Don't need to ask. No walking you home, and no sleeping together."

I laugh with relief. She has some of her wits back, for now. "Maybe he didn't invite me to sleep with him," I say.

"Nonsense. You could have charmed him."

"He did, however, invite me to see his lab. He respects my brain."

She chuckles. "Baloney. Men don't go for women because they respect their brains."

"He likes me, Mom. He wants to show me his most intimate place: his work."

CHAPTER 5

First thing on Thursday morning, Shawna corrals me as I walk into the office. Her sharp, animated face is in full interrogation mode.

"Don't you dare leave out even one thing. I want details. Was he a sexy dude? Was he totally in awe of your amazing awesomeness?"

"Put it this way," I say, laughing. "His looks and personality improved after I fortified myself with vodka."

"And?"

"I'm having dinner with him on Saturday. And the answer to all your other questions is no."

I ask her to reschedule my afternoon appointments because, unexpectedly, Boston Family Services has a prospective companion for Mom, a former nurse. Her interview, which is scheduled for 2:30 p.m. today, takes precedence over everything.

Luckily, I can leave the office with Shawna in charge. Shawna, who is studying to become a computer support specialist, is an expert with spreadsheets, data entry, and software installation. She also happens to be a crackerjack administrator who knows my business inside out.

Today is Jeffrey the HackMeister Buck's first day on the job. It's not a good sign when he rocks up half an hour late. I'm massively irritated with him.

"You telling me you already hired this guy?" Shawna says.

To enter my office, he calls from the outside callbox so we can unlock the exterior door. He must then travel down a hallway to reach the actual door of my suite. Shawna and I refer to this empty corridor as "No Man's Land." There are hidden cameras installed in No Man's Land so we can inspect the wetware headed to see me.

Shawna and I watch Buck, who is wearing headphones and bopping to a beat in his head. He hesitates in the corridor and swivels around to study the walls and ceiling, where a smoke alarm conceals a camera. After peering at it for a good few seconds, he unsheathes an imaginary sword and performs an elegant fencing routine before moving to the entrance.

Shawna clutches her chest. "Lord that's disturbing."

A keypad on the door requires a code, which I've given him to memorize. He punches it in with jaunty attitude and enters the reception room that doubles as Shawna's domain.

My assistant gives him a dimpled smile, her beaded hair framing her face,.

He seems dazzled by her, and stares with his mouth open.

"Buck, this is Shawna, our office's Command Center. If you have any problems, she's the one to see."

"Cool." He has not removed his headphones, and the beat of drums is clearly audible. My new employee spins around, then bops in place.

"Uh, paging Mars," Shawna says. "We have some forms for you to sign after you've settled in."

He acknowledges her by doing an exaggerated head bop in her direction.

I don't say a word, because I want him to feel at home. Today is probably not the best time to talk about punctuality, headphone use, office dress code (clean clothes), and projecting a professional look (clean hair).

I lead him to the adjoining room, which will be his domain.

"Okay, Mr. HackMeister, welcome to your new workspace."

It's pretty bleak—bare white walls, a generic desk and chair, laptop and desktop computers, and a microwave. Shawna will need to take him shopping.

"You're welcome to get whatever you want to improve the décor," I say to Buck, motioning to the walls.

"You da best," he says.

During the morning, I give him some low-hanging fruit to try. Is he good enough to retrieve lost files from a crashed hard drive? He is. Can he take apart a keyboard and fix the space bar? He can. His expertise, however, doesn't extend to interpersonal interactions. Just before lunchtime, he uses salty language to tell a customer it's time to buy a new computer. The customer isn't happy and feels bruised after his encounter with my apprentice.

"Don't blame me," Buck says to me afterward, rubbing the earlobe that doesn't have an earring.

"Next time, try apologizing to the client that the computer isn't fixable and tell him to have a nice day," I say mildly.

He kicks the leg of his desk. "Why? His computer was a pile of crapola, and he was being an asshole."

I lock my teeth together and let it go. I'm determined not to have a dustup with him on his first day. On top of her other skills, Shawna will have to learn to manage my difficult new employee.

Back home in the afternoon, my doorbell chimes at 2:30 p.m. sharp. My pulse quickens—a lot is riding on this encounter. Torvill runs to the door, barking his head off.

The woman on my doorstep is of indeterminate age—though not young—and radiates a nervous energy in her gray and black pantsuit and rubber-soled shoes. Her dark hair, shot through with gray, is pulled back into a loose bun, revealing a faded bruise on the side of her cheek. Even with Torvill giving her his melting-chocolate look, her face is unsmiling. She's tense. I could imagine her perhaps once being attractive. Now, she's a formidable presence, vaguely unsettling.

"Madeline Geiger?" she asks, a faint hint of Europe in her voice.

"You must be Gretchen Auerbach. Come in."

With a glance back over her shoulder before I shut the door, she ignores the baleful pleading of my dog and only idly touches his head.

Not a dog person. Which doesn't immediately disqualify her.

The aura of a migraine starts to hover over me.

"Let me show you your rooms," I say. "Upstairs."

There's no luggage since it's not settled that Mrs. Auerbach will take the job. Her circumstances are mysterious. She's a single woman with no mention of a husband or significant other. She has the vibe of someone who's fleeing from some domestic situation.

If she thinks it's peculiar my mother is missing in action, she keeps it to herself. She's been briefed about the delicacy of the situation.

We now must confront going up two flights of stairs to her quarters. Starting at the ornate wooden pillar that anchors the railing, dark oak handrails ascend and twist to the upper floors.

The stairway is steep. We climb in silence, broken only by the creaks of the old house. On the first landing, muted beams of light filter through a stained-glass window. I lead the way, holding my breath. She must agree to live with us—that part of her job offer is nonnegotiable.

"You'll have this floor to yourself." I gesture to the suite of two rooms at the top of the stairs with an old-fashioned bathroom and claw-foot bathtub. For a certain type of person, it could be charming.

Her inspection of the rooms is almost cursory—as if it's a formality, almost pre-ordained—but she pauses at a window to examine the curtains and the rope-pull mechanism that draws them with a gravelly slide.

"Does it get cold up here?"

In the newly darkened room, I shiver. "The heating is fine."

My head is starting to throb. Not even the hint of a smile has crossed her face. How will I tolerate such a dour presence in my house?

My legs drag as we descend to meet my mother.

Her room is on the ground floor, and I knock softly. "Mom? Come and meet Gretchen." Not a sound.

Mrs. Auerbach, who is tall like me, stands to the side, her arms crossed and her face impassive. I knock again. When it's clear we're not going to get an answer, I turn the doorknob and stick my head around the door. The room is empty.

My mother is already causing a provocation.

We find her in the garden under the oak tree with Tosca. The October afternoon bristles with cold, and my mother isn't dressed warmly enough. I run up to her and put my arms around her. "Mom, Gretchen is here."

Mrs. Auerbach, who was watching from the kitchen door, steps carefully into the yard and approaches us, extending her hand. "Hello, Janet."

"Please call me Mrs. Geiger," Mom says icily, turning away from the outstretched arm.

Gretchen's face remains impassive, except for an almost imperceptible narrowing of her eyes. "Of course, Mrs. Geiger. I am Mrs. Auerbach."

Later, back inside the house and out of Mom's hearing, I apologize. "She's sensitive. Doesn't want anyone keeping tabs on her. But I'll feel so much better to know you're here. I need you to assure me—promise me—you'll keep her in your sight as much as possible, just in case ..." I'm unable to finish the sentence because the lump in my throat is too big. *In case she sets herself alight, or slips in the bathtub, or walks in front of a car.* I can't bear the thought of Mom trapped in a burning house. I don't have any children, and she's as close to one as I'll ever know.

"Madeline, it's fine. I understand the situation completely." Gretchen already knows what happened with the pan on the stove.

"I'd like you to start as soon as possible," I say, uncharacteristically wobbly. Lights spiral in front of my face, a full-on migraine obscuring Gretchen's features. Will she take the job? *Please.*

"I can move in today," she says.

Relief flows over me. I want to take this unsmiling woman in my arms.

"Thank you," I say quietly.

I don't ask about the domestic situation that drove her out of her current home. I don't want to hear about it or cause her to think of the implications of this radical move. I don't want to give her the opportunity to change her mind. After meeting my mother, I would.

The deal is Gretchen will get free room and board and a generous monthly salary. In return, she will cook, take Mom shopping, do some light cleaning, help with the animals and—this is the part whispered out of Mom's presence—keep a constant eye on Mom. Perhaps befriend her. That's not a requirement but would be nice. The indications so far are not good. There's ice that must be chipped away.

After Gretchen leaves to pick up her belongings, I finally exhale.

My mother is still outside, her face bristling with dissatisfaction. I pull up a chair, real close. She is sulking and doesn't look at me.

"I don't like her. Not my type."

"Mom." I touch her arm. "You've barely spoken a word to her, except to be rude."

"She's like that evil housekeeper in *Rebecca*. Do you remember her, Madeline?"

"Mom, Gretchen *will* be moving in today, even if she reminds you of Satan. I need help with the house." I reach across and gently ruffle Tosca's beautiful fur. She leans into the touch and stares at me, her yellow eyes sharp as ever.

"Tosca's getting old," Mom says. "She can't jump up on my lap like she used to."

"Be nice to Gretchen. She seems competent. She has good references."

Mom shrugs. "Fine, Madeline. Do what you have to do."

My phone pings. A new message. *Vince*. I'd forgotten about him.

The Farris House Tavern on Brattle Street, 7 pm, Saturday. Looking forward to it.

Another ping follows immediately afterward.

Sorry I didn't consult you about the restaurant. I'm a take-charge kinda guy.

CHAPTER 6

Mrs. Auerbach moves in that afternoon, lugging two large suitcases to her suite of rooms. I help, carrying boxes, hampers of clothing, CDs, knickknacks, and lamps, the two of us negotiating our way up the twisty stairs. Mom stays hidden in her room. My headache wanes as our loads lighten, leaving a queasy aftermath of distant throbbing. My new housekeeper is blessedly silent, preoccupied with her own troubles.

I show her where to find clean linens and how to operate the washing machine. None of it is trivial, including a faulty dryer door that needs a bit of a kick before it grinds into action.

Expecting to sleep like the dead after so much exertion, I instead spend the night tossing with insomnia, juggling work and home schedules in my head. When I drift off, it's already early dawn of Mrs. Auerbach's first day with us, the Friday before my dinner date with Vince.

At breakfast, when Mom appears, Mrs. Auerbach says, "Good morning, Mrs. Geiger." My mother is stone-faced and doesn't respond to the greeting.

Instead, Mom turns to me. "Hello, Madeline."

I have no patience with her unpleasant demeanor. To have some privacy, I ask Mrs. Auerbach to take Torvill for his walk. It's a pleasant task, walking in our neighborhood in the early light, yet my enigmatic new helper sighs as she tentatively approaches my big dog. Perhaps he senses her nervousness, because he steps back and growls. Why is everything so hard? Why can't they all get along?

"Put out your hand so he can sniff it and befriend you," I say. When I put out my own hand to illustrate, my brown darling looks at me with accusatory eyes and sadly licks my hand. Poor Mrs. Auerbach trembles as she approaches. Why, I wonder, did she want to move from her home and hide in this house with us?

After they've left, Mom says, "She hates me. It's dangerous to leave me alone with her."

"It's a simple equation, Mom. If Gretchen Auerbach is forced to leave, then you will have to go too. She's all you have standing between you and River View."

This threat is horrible, raising acid in my throat. All it has going for it is truth.

I move to sit next to my sad mother and lean sideways so we're cheek to cheek. Her warm tears roll down my face. "You don't have to love her, Mom. Just cooperate. I need her to help me with cooking and cleaning. I can't do it all."

"I can do it," Mom cries, stabbing a tissue at her eyes. "Let me cook and clean."

"This is a big house, Mother. And a boring conversation, because we've had it before."

When I finally leave for work, the instructions are clear. Mrs. Auerbach will accompany my mother to the supermarket and help do the week's shopping. Mom doesn't raise objections, because for now, I've browbeaten her into submission.

A miracle occurs at work. Buck arrives on time, hair washed, bangs cut, wearing a new T-shirt. Shawna winks at me, from which I infer she has worked on Buck, who is now under her spell.

When I hear a deep bass beat reverberating from his cave, I go to have a chat with him. Realization dawns that Shawna has taken him shopping, and he has taken my offer to heart to buy anything he wanted for his office. I had imagined a few posters and perhaps a framed print of a computer. Instead, he has banished the bland white walls, completely covering them with—wall paper? Curtain fabric?—fiery orange dragons writhing in combat and breathing fire. *Star Wars* posters with giant images of R2-D2 and C-3PO. The strong bass beat that drew me to the office booms from two large speakers on the bookcase. Colored lights are revolving on the ceiling, glinting on my assistant's nose stud. I absorb all this in a glance, including a greenish-blue lava lamp burping oil bubbles to the beat.

He's turned his office into a disco, spending much more money than was reasonable. How did he get Shawna to go along? *Men!* But this one is barely out of diapers.

When he sees my face, he says, "Hey, boss lady. I can change the ceiling to a night sky if you'd prefer."

"Buck, please come and talk to me in my office." My high school principal used to sound like that. When did I get to be so *old*?

He comes bounding in. "Cool, huh?"

"Yeah, all totally cool, except we're not in a disco." I hate myself.

His eyes open wide—did he think I'd love it?—and he gets the same baleful look as my dog. Am I really so awful that I'll take away his toys?

"Tell you what," I say, and his face brightens. "Lose the ceiling lights—they give me a headache—and turn down the music. Okay?"

He gives me a wide grin. "Yeet yeet."

I've caved.

After lunch, I escape from everyone, driving my Jeep to the Upper Charles off-roading trail about forty minutes from Cambridge. This Jeep suits me fine, embracing all six feet of me, as well as providing a nine-speaker audio system through which I can blast opera with no one nearby telling me to turn it down. It's ironic, I know, but I'm the boss.

My Jeep, with its slanted back window and strange symmetry, is rugged, clambering over rocks and branches and through muddy streams that lead into the woods. I open the convertible top and relish the shock of cold air around my naked ears, bringing back memories of skydiving, before the terrible accident that brought me down. Here, on the off-road trail, I've found a different way to commune with nature, breathing in the rich, complicated smells of vegetation and watching chinks of light fading and filtering through the trees to Wagner's "Ride of the Valkyries."

With a shiver of anticipation, I think about my date tomorrow tonight. Will Vince and I click? It's been a long time since I had a real dinner date.

When I arrive home, the place is ominously quiet.

My housekeeper is alone in the living room, concentrating fiercely on something she's knitting.

"How were things?" I say. "Where's my mother?"

Mrs. Auerbach quits clicking her needles and looks up at me with her steely, brown-black eyes. "Your mother fired me this morning."

Even the animals, who have padded into the room, are riveted to the spot, staring.

I sink into a chair facing her. The exertions of the week have worn me out.

"Mom doesn't have the authority to fire you. I'm so sorry you had to go through that."

She nods. "Your mother and I have worked out an accommodation concerning the house."

God. "Where is she?"

Mrs. Auerbach misses about five beats as she resumes her knitting. It occurs to me she resembles a painting of John Whistler's mother, *Wall Furniture.* I may fire her myself if she keeps me in suspense while she knits the next stitch.

"Mrs. Geiger is somewhere in her half of the house. I'm not allowed to follow her," she says in her strangely inflected voice. Clack go the needles. The pattern is some kind of Fair Isle with incongruously bright colors.

"But that's the main part of your job, to keep tabs on her. If she moves out of your sight, please do stay alert to where she is."

Ugh. I hate having to rebuke her, especially since she has put up with Mom's nonsense and hasn't quit her job. I'm paying her generously in addition to the free rent, but that's not the point. I truly fear for my mother.

Without waiting for a reply, I haul myself up and find Mom in her bedroom. She appears to be dusting her dresser with a tissue.

"Hey, Mom."

"That woman must go. She gives me the creeps."

"Mom, do you remember I'm going out to dinner with Vince tomorrow night? Are you going to force me to cancel my date?"

"Madsy, take me with," she says. "I'd leave you alone. I could sit at a different table. Have dinner on my own."

And we both collapse on her bed, hysterical, because she's such a ridiculous riot.

CHAPTER 7

Vince has chosen a fancy restaurant on Brattle Street, and we've agreed to meet there at seven o'clock. Not my usual scene, but my mind is open.

In sleek brown cords, orange sweater, and a tan leather jacket, I'm a vision of fall when I set out to the restaurant on Saturday evening. It's cold and blustery, the wind carrying a faint tang of the ocean.

My feelings about Vince are ambivalent—the date could go either way. No instant attraction to him on Wednesday, but he wasn't a definite no either. He was an attentive date, leaning in, listening to my story of starting a cybersecurity business, observing me with open curiosity and admiration. At times, he seemed genuinely interested. No condescension in his manner at all. He was kind about my mother, and I had warmed to him.

He's punctual—a small but significant point in his favor—standing at the bar when I enter. My short hair has blown about in the wind, and I suspect my cheeks and ears are bright red. His dark hair is barely ruffled, combed to the side. He looks suave in a dark-blue shirt, jacket and pale-blue tie. I wonder where he lives. He knows I live somewhere in Cambridge.

"My dear Madeline."

A vague alarm goes off because I barely know him and already I'm his "dear." He sounds like Cary Grant in a bowtie from an old black-and-white movie. Do people still talk like that?

"Hey, Vince," I say.

He grasps my hands warmly. "These are two blocks of ice. Let's warm you up." His voice is smooth and his touch jolts me. No surge of electricity, just a stirring of some long-buried feelings. Vince senses it and holds on for a minute.

We're led through an enchanted place of burgundy carpets and leather chairs. In the muted light from rose-colored lamps, the tablecloths are pale pink. Vince wasn't kidding when he said he'd pick an upscale restaurant. This isn't one of my regular haunts.

When we're seated, I request vodka with lime and seltzer water, and Vince gets scotch on the rocks. The dollar signs weigh heavily on the menu as I feel the leather heft of it. There's something decadent about eating here. Thank goodness I insisted on paying for myself; I won't need to feel embarrassed when I order obscenely expensive items. I request six oysters Rockefeller—gold-plated shells, obviously—followed by baked cod with rice and mushrooms. I barely ate during lunch today, and my stomach rumbles.

Vince orders garlic soup and an entrée of lamb tartare. I pause in mid-sip. Garlic and raw lamb. *No kisses tonight!* He interrogates the waiter about the freshness of the meat, and something about his exuberant carnivorousness turns my stomach. My reaction is odd because I'm not a vegetarian. And somewhere a fish was killed so it could lie on a platter for me, smothered with wine-based sauce.

"This place is known for its lamb tartare," Vince says, perhaps noticing my interest. "One of my favorite dishes."

"And you have it with ... French fries?"

"Hand-cut fries with herb salt," he says, smiling.

"Fit for a professor."

He throws back his scotch. "I'm not a professor." Puts the glass down with an emphatic clink of ice. "Not anymore." Signals for a refill.

"Were you fired?" The vodka warming me. Trying for a droll, I-can-handle-anything tone. I discovered a bit of his history online, but I want to hear it in his own words.

He gives a low chuckle. Light falls on the planes of his face, the ridge of his brow, his blue eyes in shadow. "I study brains. How they react to various stimuli." He accepts a refreshed drink from a bowing waiter.

"I could tell you which part of your brain would light up right now if I hooked you to a computer," he says in a low voice.

Eerie. "Really?"

Creases at the sides of his mouth. He's amused. "I was a professor at MIT in their neurobiology department. Invented a chip to implant in the brains of epilepsy patients to control seizures."

"I've heard of that. It was successful, wasn't it?" I learned this from googling him. Lots of awards for his work.

"That wasn't the best thing I did, though." He leans forward. "I got a patent for my invention, quit academia, and became the CEO of a startup."

"Ah. Made piles of money, huh?"

He nods. "You got it. I sold the business at a very good price and now have my own lab here in Cambridge."

"You're still studying brains?"

"Oh yes. Lots of people have brain chemistry that goes haywire. Kids with ADHD who can't learn. People with depression, anxiety, bipolar disorder. All fixable with just a small manipulation of their brain waves." His face is animated, his eyes gleaming.

"Who funds your research?"

"Great question. You're a smart cookie. No one pulls my strings. That's the beauty of it. No proposals for funding needed. I pay for everything myself. That way, I don't need excuses, rationalizations, or permission for using vermin in my experiments."

A party of six leaves the restaurant, and a blast of cold air reaches me.

Something in the way he says *vermin* ...

Oysters and garlic soup are delivered to our table with an elegant sweep from the waiter, who produces a pepper grinder that's half as tall as me. The oysters are dollops of heaven, smothered in a buttery herb sauce. I swallow ninety dollars in two minutes, while Vince spoons his soup at a more leisurely pace. He observes me with a bemused expression as I sip oyster juice from the shells.

After an interlude of sipping and slurping, plates of browned fish and glistening lamb are ceremoniously placed in front of us.

"Just like my mother used to make," Vince says. I can't tell whether he's being ironic.

If I keep my eyes off Vince's lamb, the cod is delicious. *Hypocrite. You should have ordered the mushroom burger.* Nevertheless, it all slides down like butter.

In between bites, I tell Vince about my own recent patent—software to block out cyber lurkers.

He leans in, listening intently. "You're one scary woman," he says, reaching across the table to jiggle one of my knuckles. What am I to make of him? He's part gentleman and part ghoul.

The dessert menu arrives with a flourish of gold lettering and silk tassels.

"I would like bananas Foster with flambé at the table," Vince tells the waiter.

So he's an exhibitionist, trying to impress me with his—what?—something he doesn't quite have.

"Madeline, you could order some dessert flambé too." He waves an airy arm. "Go on, live dangerously."

Oh, please.

"Raspberry sundae," I say demurely.

Later, the lamps dim to a flicker, setting off Vince's dessert with an orange-blue flame, and mine with a dark slash of raspberry sauce on vanilla ice cream. *Blood on snow.* If they make the room any darker, the man across from me will resemble Frankenstein.

My head spins suddenly, and I rest my spoon on the saucer.

"Coffee or tea?" The waiter is at our table again.

"No thanks." The Earth tilts slightly, and I shut my eyes for a moment.

"What you need," Vince says, "is a good, bracing walk to my lab. It's not far from here."

He orders espresso. "As it comes, please, that's how I like it—strong and lethal."

He turns to me and beams. "My coffee and my women."

God. I shake my head at everyone. *No thanks.*

"I'd prefer to get home sooner rather than later," I say when the waiter disappears. "I have a situation at home." *Mrs. Auerbach and Mrs. Geiger.*

Vince says. "I really would like you to see my work in the lab." He brushes the top of my hand with his fingers. "You promised, remember?"

His pound of flesh.

Obviously, I don't owe this man a thing. I could say flat out that I have no desire to see his lab. And yet, some odd sense that a deal has been made tells me it's too late to pull out now.

CHAPTER 8

The wind has come up when we step outside, threatening to sweep me off the sidewalk. I zip up my jacket and pull a winter hat down over my head and ears. Vince buttons his woolen coat all the way to the bottom. We turn into the icy wind, leaves blowing around us, and set off at a rapid pace.

He hooks his arm through mine, which feels entirely natural, keeping each other on the ground. I lean into his bulk, which is as solid as a rock.

"Where are we going?" I ask.

"Over the hills and far away. Actually, through Harvard Square and a few blocks past. It's a healthy walk."

His hair is blowing against the grain, exposing his scalp. He'll be bald before he knows it.

We don't chat much, mainly because it takes energy to stay firmly on the sidewalk. Eventually, we're on a dark street in front of a two-story building. A sign on the front says *Eastman Enterprises.*

"The realtor," he says. He removes a bunch of keys from his pocket, without relinquishing his hold on me. "I like you, Madeline," he says quietly.

I don't tell him I find him weird.

He unhooks himself from my arm and riffles through the keyring. It takes two keys to unlock the front door, and a key pad with a code to enter an inner door. We have this much in common.

"I approve," I say as he punches in his code. He makes no effort to hide what he's doing, and by force of habit, I commit his passcode to memory. I'm hypervigilant with numbers, always parsing sequences for patterns. Once, soon after my husband died, I worked as a spy.

The inner sanctum—the lab—is a rectangular room with an assortment of glass tanks and containers. A whiff of Lysol and excrement. An aquarium bubbles softly in the corner. At the edges, some buzzing and scuffling hovers.

When Vince clicks on a wall switch, fluorescent lights blossom above, with one of the bulbs flickering and fizzing. "Piece of junk," he says. "That's practically new."

The room is inadequately lit. Perhaps Vince feels it too, because he says, "I'm afraid I'm going to have to change that light bulb now. The animals are very sensitive to light." *Me too.*

It's clear he's done this before. In a minute, he's on top of a ladder, detaching the dead white tube, which he balances expertly as he hands it down to me. It really does feel like flimsy garbage. I set it onto an empty counter and hold aloft the replacement. *May the force be with you.* In a few seconds, the new bulb glows with a cool white luminescence.

"Let me introduce you to my little friends," he says after the ladder and debris have been removed. "They need several minutes to acclimate before I run the experiment."

"What are you going to do to them?" I'm shivering even though there's central heating and I haven't removed my jacket.

"Oh, my dear Madeline," he says, crossing the room and touching my arm. He's solicitous. "You must know I'd never hurt them."

I know no such thing. Coming here was a mistake. Nevertheless, I must calm down, let him show me his precious experiment, politely say goodbye, then go home. No obligations, end of story.

He's disappeared into a back room and returns with a deep tray of mice, squealing and chattering together.

I take a chair near the lab bench.

"These are all males," Vince says, lifting two mice with one hand and plopping them into a glass cage.

The small creatures seem curious, running to all four corners of their glass box, sniffing and putting their cute little paws up on the wall. It's not until they've fully explored their prison that they pay attention to each other. There's mutual dislike, that much is clear. Fighting is a strong word, more like smacking each other about with puffball hits. One of the mice is more aggressive than the other and tries to headbutt his cellmate, who retires to his corner and takes a break. Then the cycle of aggression starts again.

I'm queasy. "Are we going to sit here all night until one mouse bites the other's head off?"

"Oh, no, this is a computerized experiment. Watch what happens when I give them a signal." He hurries to remove a large Dell laptop from a drawer, and after a few clicks, says, "Now, watch."

The mice freeze for a few seconds as if lightly zapped by Tasers, then they're moving again, clinging to each other like long-lost friends, all animus gone. After a minute or two, they are grooming each other gently, then lying together in a corner.

"What did you do to them?" My mouth is dry, the rich dinner churning in my stomach.

He's completely absorbed by his mice. "They each have a tiny light implanted near their brain," he says, "which I can activate with my computer. The light causes neurons to fire—"

"And that makes them love each other?"

"Don't be so cynical." He laughs, pulling up a chair near to mine. "Listen to how it works. It's a neat experiment. I zapped them with light of the same frequency so their brains are in sync." He's hyped up and walks to the glass cage. "Take a look, they're still big buddies."

"What happens if their brains aren't in sync—different light frequencies."

"Clever woman. I *knew* you were a clever woman." He goes back to his computer. "You asked exactly the right question. Watch."

I want to cover my eyes. His hands are poised above the keyboard like a pianist's. *Lord of the mice.* Click-click-click, and the mice are at each other's throats, miniature warriors throwing punches and kicks. It's not pleasant to watch. These little creatures may bite each other's faces off. I don't care if the whole scientific world uses "vermin" in their experiments, I don't have to be a witness.

"Thank you, Vince, I've seen enough," I say. "I'd like to go home." My voice is neutral and polite.

But he wants to convert me, his face animated. "Can't you see the possibilities, being able to manipulate the brain with wireless technology and tiny bits of hardware?" He turns to the enclosed tray of extra mice, lifts two of them by their tails and tosses them into the glass cage with the two fighters. They go down squealing.

I recoil.

A few more clicks on his computer, and they're having a group hug.

"What's the point?" I say, my voice barely audible.

He's in his own zone, his face incredulous. "Think about the real-life applications. Like treating anxiety with light therapy. Clinical depression." He pulls his chair nearer to mine. "Imagine a group therapy session for loners and depressives where their brains are all in sync."

"What? The therapist controlling them with a wireless router box?"

"Exactly, you got it!" He has no irony about his research. He talks an altruistic game, *but he lifted little creatures by their tails and threw them into the cage.*

The air in the room has become oppressive and constricts my chest. His universe of squealing creatures with implants in their heads. Where is the mice cemetery for those who don't survive the implant surgery? Out back? A little crematorium? I understand I'm being unreasonable, hypercritical of fascinating—maybe even ground-breaking—research, but my date's callousness toward his living subjects repels me. *I need fresh air.*

He's oblivious to my revulsion as he transfers the mice from the experiment to their tray.

"Thanks, Vince, this sure has been interesting." I'm still wearing my jacket and scarf, and start edging away. Slow. No rush. Date over. *No thanks, don't need companionship on the way home.*

"But, Madeline, we've barely begun." He's back at the bench, after shuttling trays of experimental subjects in and out of the back room. A new batch of noisy creatures scuffles about energetically.

He tips the tray toward me so I can see the large rodents.

"My experiment works across species," he says.

CHAPTER 9

"Rats." Presented with a flourish.

Oh God, no. If I leave right now—step through the door of the lab and keep on walking—will he follow me? For sure that will end our acquaintance on a sour note, which I'm strangely reluctant to do.

So here I stand, motionless.

He places a large, gray rat in a glass tank with a squealing mouse cowering in fear at the opposite corner. The precondition for his experiment. That rat could swat the mouse and put it away for good.

I'm one of his mice, wondering what the giant rat will do next.

"Vince, please, no animal fights. I get the point of your experiment."

"The mice aren't in mortal danger," he says. "Not ever." He sits close to me and gestures to the glass container. "I think of the rats and mice as components of my experiment, no more, no less. They're not cute little creatures in some Beatrix Potter book. My goal is—and always has been—to help people in psychological distress."

"That's great, Vince—noble. But if animals are hurt in the production of your device, no one will be interested in your product."

He listens carefully, his eyes hardening. "Please notice the rat isn't aggressive. If the mouse stays in its corner, it's completely safe."

But does the mouse know that?

Despite myself, I watch, fascinated. The animals have obviously both been fed and don't want to eat each other. But mad Dr. Strangelove here could turn this experiment into hunger games if he wanted.

"Guess what happens if I put their brains in sync." He's back in his element, showing me his tricks, seemingly unmoved that the experiments turn me off.

"What?" I say. "They spread-eagle themselves and rub noses?"

On the way to his computer, he walks past me and squeezes my shoulder. "Madeline, you're funny."

Cringe. I really want to leave without a scene. Just a normal end to the date where we part ways. No melodrama, just a quiet thank you for this interesting evening.

"Watch," he says, clicking on the computer. "Their brains are now in sync."

Both rodents lift their heads, as if hearing a distant bell. The tension in their interaction dissipates. No apparent fear on the part of the mouse. When they meet in the middle of the tank, they seem to embrace, burrowing and gentle with their snouts and little paws, circling the cage in a strange communion.

"Isn't that totally amazing?" Vince says. "They get along even though they're different species."

The odor of animal droppings is heavy in my nose. "I'm ready to leave," I say without looking at him.

He leans in, removes the mouse by its tail, and plops it in the mouse tray before clicking off his computer. Involuntarily, I shudder, already planning a smooth goodbye and getaway.

"I'll walk you home," he says when we're finally outside the lab on the sidewalk. He takes my arm again. "This sure has been a great evening."

Gently, I move free of him. "Vince—"

"Don't say a word. Let it sink in for a while." He puts his gloved finger on my lips and holds it there. "You're an intriguing woman, Madeline."

"No! Vince—" Alarm causes my voice to rise in pitch, exactly what I wanted to avoid.

We're on a side street, which is deserted and dark at this time of night. Windows shine in the headlights of occasional cars, but no pedestrians. Harvard Square, just a few blocks away, seems an infinite distance from where I stand. Surreptitiously, I touch my pocket that has the Swiss Army knife.

His hands are still on me, holding me at arm's length. Tenderly. "I'm not young, Madeline." His voice is soft "I've been waiting a long time for someone like you. So much disappointment. I nearly didn't try this new dating site."

Breathe. Evenly. "Vince, thank you for the compliment, but I'd like to take a break."

He doesn't respond; nor does he move away.

If I were at a computer, I could fix the problem immediately, find an algorithm and hit *Delete*. But standing with a human, a man saying terrifying things, I'm at a loss. This is not ransomware, which I could deal with. It is toxic wetware.

Surely this happens to most people who date online—it doesn't work out, you shake hands, and go on to the next match.

I shut my eyes and process the problem. In that second, his arms are around me and his garlicky mouth is on my lips. I stiffen. *Permission denied.*

I don't push him off me, but I turn my face away and say, "Vince, please—no!" Not too loudly. I don't want the situation to escalate into a physical tug-of-war. How can I dump him and get back to Harvard Square? Stabbing him in the jugular seems too extreme.

He drops his arms and steps back. "Madeline, I'm sorry. I got ahead of myself. It's just—you're so beautiful." He falters. Looks down at his shoes. The less threatening he appears, the faster my heart beats.

"Vince, I'm flattered. But *please* don't contact me again." I'm being too polite. Still trying to defuse the situation.

"Let me at least walk you home."

He tries to link his arm through mine, but I step back sharply.

"No, Vince. Let me go."

"Are you going home?" He's still in my space, not moving away.

We've not shared home addresses, just phone numbers.

"Drop it, Vince." More sharply.

He nods, sighs, and turns away from me. "Will you at least walk with me to Harvard Square?"

"No, you go on ahead." I force my voice to be calm. Thinking clearly. "Go *now*—without me."

And, finally, he does, becoming a shadow disappearing down a darkened street.

I take a circuitous route to my house. The streets are unlit, with large trees on the sidewalks. Every now and then, I duck behind a thick tree trunk and hold my breath. Am I being followed? I case out the surrounding area, checking. He's made me paranoid. The wind has died down from its earlier fury and all I hear now is the rustling of leaves and the distant bark of a dog.

Slow down.

Three nights ago at the Cambridge bar when I first met Vince, with his good looks and aura of success, the atmosphere vibrated with possibility. Now, I'm in spilt-milk territory—too late for me to wish I hadn't agreed to a second date. *Stupid!* Mom's first instincts were right. He is so not for me.

I can try again. Surely Boston is teeming with eligible men?

When I finally approach my house, it's all but indistinguishable in the dark. No silver moon to light the way.

My phone pings with a message.

Dearest Madeline, thank you for indulging me and visiting my lab. When can I see you again?

CHAPTER 10

The next morning—Sunday, my phone has two new messages from Vince.

Lunch next week? Pick a day and a place.

Then, two hours later. *We have so much in common, Madeline. Let's try again.*

Perhaps I should have spelled it out for him: *I'm repelled by your callousness toward your animals and won't go out with you again.*

Men seldom pursue me, so this is a strange new feeling. How can I stop him? It confounds me, and I shove my phone deep into my pocket. I'm a problem solver; it's what I do every day at work. Surely it's just a matter of finding the key to an encrypted file?

Breakfast is silent. I'm preoccupied. Mom, Mrs. Auerbach, and I circle each other like planets.

"Bad date?" Mom says eventually.

I decide, unwisely, to explain the Vince situation and ask for advice. Mom gets the executive summary, including some details about the rodent experiments. "He's a ghoul, Mom. He drills holes in their heads and implants lights." Why did I say that? I have no idea how he does it.

My mother takes it all in with a long face. I can read her mind. *Another man down the drain.*

"Men!" Mrs. Auerbach bursts out from her corner. "Tell him to get lost. Threaten him with police action if he doesn't stop bothering you."

My mother freezes her with a glare that would vanquish a lesser woman.

"Don't be so fast," Mom says, turning her back on Mrs. Auerbach. "Remind me, Madeline—how many other men—matches—did you get for your profile?"

"None that I liked." Now is not the time to tell her about Wanda Hargraves, the woman who's just popped up as a match.

"Okay, then," Mom says. "Tell Vince you'll meet for coffee after Halloween. Tell him you're busy until then. That gives you time to think about it."

Mrs. Auerbach, who is peeling something at the sink, turns to face me. "That won't work. He'll be back to pester you, I know the type. Best to pull out the weed by the root—now."

Mom is on her feet. Mrs. Auerbach is treading on her turf, namely my dating life. I can't bear to watch the hissing and spitting that ensues and leave the kitchen. Way past time to go upstairs and do some work.

I block Vince from calling and texting my phone and send him a message through Professionals.com. *Please don't contact me again.*

The next morning, I have an appointment in Boston to inspect a client's work premises. When I get to my own office after eleven o'clock, the thrum of rock music welcomes me in.

Shawna grimaces. "We have evaluations from a couple of customers this morning. Our Buck the HackMeister sure is a mixed bag of goods."

I sit across from her. "Let's hear it."

"Rave review from customer number one. Files restored from a crashed hard drive."

Only the best of the best can do that. I clutch my chest. "Is he a brilliant hire or what?"

She makes a sad face. "Customer number two—not so happy."

"Tell me."

"The guy's computer was kaput and our boy wasn't able to fix it."

"And? Did Buck explain that sometimes a computer is fried and you have to buy another one?"

"I didn't hear the convo, but I did go investigate when that boy's stereo suddenly blasted the office at top volume." She rolls her eyes. "Here was the customer, going on a rant, demanding to see 'the boss instead of this moron,' and our guy cranking up the volume and letting loose the strobe lights, telling the customer he was"—she consults her notes—"a dumb womp rat."

It hangs in the air for a second.

"Womp rat?" we scream, dissolving.

"Guy sure was a womp rat," Shawna says, wiping away tears.

I have to clamp it down and use my stern face when I reach Buck's den.

"Hiya, ByteBeast." He waves as I enter through the open door.

The strobe lights and music are off, the regular light is on, and my employee is on his best behavior, hard at work at his computer. Who am I kidding? He's probably playing video games or online poker.

I unplug the lava lamp and smack down the console of his laptop.

"Do I need to fire you?" I ask.

A paperweight I've owned since I was ten has disappeared. I notice it's gone as soon as I come into my bedroom after work. It's an exquisite artifact, with a delicate glass polyhedron suspended inside as if floating on air. It was given to me by my father, who recognized my mathematical bent at an early age. The small paperweight has been in the same place in my various bedrooms—on the window sill.

My first thought is that Vince has been in my room and is collecting mementos. I shake my head, aghast at my irrationality. His persistence is driving me bonkers.

I survey the room. Mrs. Auerbach has cleaned it today—desk and night table dusted, the rugs vacuumed, and my various odds and ends straightened. Perhaps in her cleaning zeal Mrs. Auerbach misplaced the paperweight. A quick look around dispels that notion. It's nowhere to be seen. My spirits sink. I love that miniature polyhedron—a rare tangible reminder of my father—and hate the prospect of confronting Mrs. Auerbach.

When I've kicked off my work clothes, I find my mother in her bedroom, watching television.

"How's it going, Mom?" I say, flopping onto her bed.

"Auerbach had a man in today," she says, giving me a meaningful rise of her eyebrows.

Cold trickles down my back. *Vince?*

"What do you mean?"

"I was in my room, Madsy, and I heard bang, bang, bang. A woman of her age, imagine."

If Mom didn't have dementia, it would have the ring of truth. Relief makes me dizzy. I sit at the edge of the bed and drop my head down between my knees. "She's entitled to her private life," I say. "She lives here."

"What was I supposed to do? Put on noise-canceling headphones? Remind her she should be watching me?" There's triumph in her voice.

"New topic, Mom." It's been a long day. I move nearer to her so I can speak softly. "Have you seen my paperweight—you know, the one Daddy gave me?"

"No. Why?"

"I noticed just now it was gone."

Without missing a single beat, my mother says, "Obviously, *she* took it."

I stand to leave and she gets up too. She walks to me and envelops me in an unexpected hug. "My darling Mads, having to worry about all of us. You're a saint."

I hug her back, resting my chin on the top of her soft hair. How different we are. I'm my father, all bones and jutting angles, strong chin and a nose that makes a statement. Mom, on the other hand, is a sine curve of pillowy softness. Pregnant with me, she must have resembled a Renaissance Madonna. She tells the story that when I was born, there was no dainty baby girl for her, but a long-boned screamer who overflowed the scale.

Mrs. Auerbach is nowhere to be seen. Stew simmering in a pot on the stove, and the living room empty and dark. "Mrs. Auerbach," I call out softly. She's not in the sitting room either.

The silence is dense as I climb the winding stairs to her apartment. The door at the top of the stairs is shut, which of course she's completely entitled to do—it's now her home, after all. I rap on the door. "Mrs. Auerbach—Gretchen."

No reply.

Tentatively, I turn the doorknob. Locked. I knock again, and the sound reverberates. Why wouldn't she go out? She knows I'm in for the night. So why am I so annoyed?

I love that paperweight.

She opens the door and stands framed in the doorway, her brown-gray hair released from its bun, flowing to her shoulders, her feet in slippers. Casual slacks and a sweatshirt. She looks human and normal in a way she hasn't before. Perhaps it's my imagination, but in the dark at the top of the stairs, her eyes seem glazed. *Drugs?*

Strains of a cello emanate from inside, soft and haunting. Mrs. Auerbach doesn't invite me in, and I realize how soul-destroying this job with my mother must be. *What's in it for her?* I wish Mom were nicer.

"What can I do for you, Madeline?" Flat voice. Not unpleasant, but not pleasant either. I don't relish what I must do.

"My mother complained that you and your visitor made noise this afternoon." I clear my throat. "She heard banging from upstairs that disturbed her."

She gives a dry laugh. "I didn't have any visitors, but I did use a hammer and nails on the bed frame, which is old and needed reinforcing. It was threatening to fall apart. So—guilty. I did what needed to be done, short of asking you to buy a new bed. I'll apologize to Mrs. Geiger for the noise."

The air between us is thick, and I can't judge whether she's telling me the truth. There either was a visitor or there wasn't. I don't trust either of the women in the house. I let it go. Decide to monitor the situation. I've been through this before—Mom and her shenanigans, getting rid of the hired help.

"Will that be all?" Mrs. Auerbach says, her hand on the door, ready to shut me out.

"Just one more thing." I sigh, almost involuntary. We could cut the atmosphere with a knife. "Thank you for cleaning my room so well—"

"I know you didn't come up here to thank me." Quiet. Hostile. Her hand is still on the door, and I wonder if there's a man in the other room now.

"My glass paperweight has disappeared." *And so has my diplomatic tone.* "Did you take it?"

She laughs again, that same dry hack. "No, Madeline, I did not. But I suspect you knew that. I suggest you speak to your mother about it. Now, if you'll excuse me ..."

She shuts the door firmly, and I hear a key in the lock.

A cutoff of the light.

My phone pings with a new message from the dating website. *Vince.*

I clutch the wooden handrail on the top step, paralyzed. It's cold up here and I'm shivering. My eyes take in the screen.

I visited your house this afternoon.

Vince at my house, violating my space, helping himself to a memento from my bedroom. He must have found my address online somehow. Was he really in my house? Did he ring the doorbell? Surely Mrs. Auerbach or Mom would have mentioned it.

What does he think he's doing?

I can't go to the police because his actions don't quite rise to the level of a crime.

I'm reluctant to tell Vince to stop sending me messages through the dating site because I'm still using the site. But I don't want to communicate with him. What should I do? Standing at the top of the stairs in a state of frustration, I consider the problem.

I've already blocked him from calling and texting my phone.

I've said no to him at least ten times.

In a sense, I've been through this before—men who ignore me and continue to make demands. *I thought I'd moved past taking shit from men.*

A solution comes to me right there on the stair, stunning in its symmetry. I could fight back by intruding on his space. *Keep an eye on him in his lab.* The more I think about it, the more this option appeals to me. Fight fire with fire.

Men always underestimate me.

CHAPTER 11

The next night, I set out at 10:00 p.m. heading toward Vince's lab, armed with a tiny high-tech digital surveillance camera and a flash drive containing spyware. The night is clear, with a yellow moon lighting my path to the building. Vince had mentioned that occasionally he worked late on weeknights. I hope tonight is not one of those nights.

Fallen leaves crunch under my shoes as I walk briskly along the Cambridge streets. The route is imprinted in my memory. Within twenty minutes I'm at the outside door, armed with my special little implement to gain entry. My fingers are dexterous.

I survey the street. Not a soul in sight.

I'm through the first door in a minute, peering through the second to check that the lab is in darkness. All good. I click in Vince's codes to defang the alarm and take me through the second door. It was almost too easy to get in, and I bask in a kind of evil under-glow of satisfaction.

Don't do this, it's illegal, my conscience says.

Screw that, he's harassing you, the rationalizing under-glow retorts.

Moonlight streams through the slats in the blinds as I sweep the room with a strong flashlight. No surveillance cameras as far as I can tell. Not everyone is a security maniac like me. Carefully,

I make my way to the center of the lab, then stop and listen. The place seems deserted. Nothing but the soft bubbling of the aquarium and far-off scuffling of small animals.

Hurry! Get his laptop from the drawer. I'm assuming this computer stays at work, in the drawer I observed, to record his experiments. It's an older model. Perhaps he has a more up-to-date computer at home.

When I have my bearings, I creep to the drawer and open it. Yes! There is the computer. Carefully, I lift it out and place it on the workbench. I recall how sloppy he was, going right in without a password. Using his internet browser, I scan his searches. Move on, I urge myself, but satisfying my curiosity is irresistible. A name appears—*Madeline*—Madeline Geiger! My website. The professional photo with an enigmatic smile like Mona Lisa.

Reluctantly, I stop gazing at myself and insert the spyware flash drive in a USB port. In a few seconds, I've hit the Install button. It's not completely clear what I'll be looking for, but I'm set up to watch his keystrokes, observe his experiments, and keep an eye on anything to do with me.

Stealth software. Invisible. Undetectable.

He's stalking me, so I'm taking precautions.

I relax and shut my eyes while the clunker of a laptop grinds away at a slow download.

Now for the next tool in my arsenal—a surveillance camera. After some reconnaissance, I find a perfect spot on the ceiling at the top of a pillar that faces Vince's workbench. The ladder I'll need for installation is stored nearby, which I remember from when Vince changed a light bulb.

So far so good. With the lab deserted, I'm like a cat burglar, stealthy and swift under cover of darkness.

With my flashlight in my teeth, I begin to climb. On the third step, my head starts spinning and I'm hit with an attack of vertigo so sudden my flashlight clatters to the ground. Clutching the ladder to keep my balance, I take a deep breath to fight the nausea that rises like bile in my throat.

Stop. Listen. The noise unsettles something in the animals' room, a brief skittering and rattling of cages.

It takes all my strength and willpower to make it down the ladder without falling. I lower myself to the ground and hang my head between my knees. *Shit!* I can't leave without installing the damn thing, nor can I lift my head, let alone climb a ladder.

Sheer willpower drags me up that ladder again. My hands tremble as I insert the small, white device in the crease between pillar and ceiling. It is well camouflaged, and the camera is computerized, so I'll be able to observe Vince in his lab from the comfort of my laptop.

The ladder vibrates with the stress of my descent. At the bottom, I rest my damp forehead on the pillar. A clicking sound at the entrance freezes my blood. At this late hour, someone is coming into the lab. *I must get out of here.*

The download is complete. I snatch the flash drive, shove it into my pocket, bang the computer shut, slide it back in its drawer. But it's too late. I don't have time to hide the ladder. As the inner door opens, I grab my flashlight and hotfoot it into the little room that houses his animals—those mice and rats—and sink down on the floor. My presence sets up a squealing and scampering among them. I've disturbed their slumbers, or whatever it is they do at night. The stench of their excrement mixes with my anxiety.

Already I'm preparing my story, what I'm doing here. I'll show him the camera. I'm intrigued by his work and want to watch him insert little lights in the creatures, all so fascinating I just couldn't resist. Please forgive me, Vince, my motives were pure. I intended you no harm. I should have asked your permission.

My heart drums in my chest as I wait to be discovered. The damning evidence—that ladder—standing to accuse me in the middle of the floor.

I wait ... and wait. Nothing happens. Everything is still in darkness.

I peer through a crack in the door and see the shape of a person, crouched down, moving to the back of the room and disappearing from my view. Someone other than Vince has entered the lab, obviously intent on his own nefarious mission. Two intruders in Vince's lab on one night? Another person who knew the passcodes and could unlock the outside door?

It's nearly midnight. I've sat for at least fifteen minutes without moving. The animals have calmed down and are watching me with their beady little eyes.

Slowly, I emerge from the back room. Except for the fish, nothing is stirring in this section of the lab. While I'm calculating the wisdom of returning the ladder, a distant sound of pounding comes from below. Hammering on metal. Banging on wood. The ladder makes its own soft clank as I release the catch and pull shut the metal legs. The noise echoes in the room, hopefully submerged by the action downstairs.

After I've stashed away the ladder, common sense orders me to leave immediately; but of course I don't. Curiosity about what's going on draws me inexorably to the back of the lab. The events happening underground may be just the thing I need to get an edge.

Staying in the shadows against the wall, I find a door at the far end that leads to a staircase. It's pitch-dark in the stairwell, but I daren't use my flashlight. As I feel my way down the stairs, the noises become closer, until I'm at the door of the room where this activity is taking place. The door is shut. Across from it is another closed door with the words HAZARDOUS MATERIALS. DO NOT ENTER.

While I'm crouching like a cat in the dark, contemplating my next move, the door to the banging slams open, almost knocking me over, and a man strides across to what I think is a bathroom. My crouch against the wall pays off. He doesn't see me. But I get a good look at him, backlit from behind. A bald head, thick glasses, lots of sweat. Heavy. Needs his exercise.

There's mayhem in the room. Open boxes, tools, and a tangle of wires and electronic gadgetry spread all over the floor. What the heck is he doing?

After a few seconds of fruitless contemplation, it's really time to leave. I've pushed my luck, and this guy will be back at any moment. Taking advantage of the faint light from the room, I climb the stairs two at a time and get myself out of the lab—fast. My guard doesn't come down until I'm on my way, out of breath.

Who is that guy hammering in Vince's basement at midnight?

CHAPTER 12

The following day, Mrs. Auerbach produces a dinner of beef stir-fry with overcooked beef and undercooked broccoli. It actually tastes quite good, and I'm grateful I didn't have to make it. Torvill pants expectantly under the table, snapping down the beef treats I send his way.

Mom pushes away her plate. "This is horrible."

Mrs. Auerbach, at the sink, says nothing. I've instructed her to ignore Mom's provocations, and I've increased her pay. Hazard pay.

My mother slams the fridge door open and helps herself to cheese and an apple. It's her choice. I refuse to engage with her while she's being impossible. It's been a long day and the last thing I need is flak at home.

After dinner, I find Torvill and Tosca dozing on the living room couch, lying head to head, their paws entwined. They've become adorably inseparable, but my dog needs his walk. When I gently extricate Torvill from the cat, Tosca objects loudly, batting away my hand.

It's dark outside, with dense clouds in the sky. Torvill is sluggish in the frosty night.

When we return to the front path of our house, someone—barely a shadow—scurries past us down the road. Did I imagine that? Was someone tracking me? I shake my head to clear it. *Ridiculous.*

Torvill follows me upstairs to my study, where we stand together at the window in the unlit room. Surreptitiously, I pull back the curtain to survey the street in front of the house. The trees are black silhouettes, their leaves blowing in the wind. It's close to Halloween, and I imagine ghosts flitting through those branches.

A shadowy figure is leaning against a tree on the sidewalk, quite motionless. He appears to be in profile, and distant enough in the darkness for me to be unsure about whether he's facing my window, watching me. I edge back, barely breathing, waiting for the phantom to move, but it doesn't. *This is your life 24/7 from now on if you can't get rid of your stalker.*

The shadow has been so still, I begin to think it's just that, merely a shadow, until a phone screen flickers like a firefly in the night.

Is Vince watching the house?

Using the faint gleam from my phone, I navigate to my desk and open my laptop. I can certainly find out if Vince is at his computer. The spyware I installed will tell me. My screen glows bluish-green until I fire it up.

Someone is at Vince's keyboard.

In that case, who's outside my house?

The typist, probably Vince, is writing a lab report about mice, rats, and larger mammals. *Move on! Don't get waylaid by the gruesome details.* A scan of his internet activity from today is like looking in a funhouse mirror. *Madeline Geiger on her website. Madeline Geiger at Cornell University. Madeline Geiger on her wedding day. Madeline Geiger, miraculous survivor of a skydiving crash.* Like drifting through a nightmare of my life. I go back a week. His keystrokes reveal he's been googling my name every day. He knows my home address. Why am I not surprised? He's already told me he tracked me down. White pages

My back has tensed up and is so rigid it could break.

I check the window. The lurker outside hasn't moved.

Without overthinking, I rush downstairs, pulling my jacket back on, and go out into my yard through a back door. I whisper to Torvill to *stay* in the kitchen, so I can creep around noiselessly to the front and move swiftly to the tree. Unfortunately, I don't have a gun, but I do have my trusty Swiss Army knife and flashlight. I'll surprise him. *Who the hell are you? What do you want?*

But there's no one there. Of course there isn't. We're playing hide-and-seek.

My phone pings with a chat message from Professionals.com.

Vince.

Damn! He's got to me through the dating site.

Happy Halloween week, he writes.

When I appear at breakfast on Thursday morning, the dynamic between Mom and Mrs. Auerbach has deteriorated to the point they can't have a meal in the same room. So while Mom and I sit at the kitchen table, Mrs. Auerbach is in the living room with a TV tray of tea and toast. This is a situation I'll have to confront eventually, but not now.

I decide instead to raise the topic of my upcoming date this Saturday afternoon.

"There's another match for me on Professionals.com," I say casually.

Mom frowns. "What's wrong with the guy Vince that you met? I thought you liked him."

She's forgotten everything I told her.

"He didn't work out well, so I'm going out with someone else."

"Good-looking guy? What's his name? Show me his picture."

"It's a she, Mom, and her name is Wanda," I say, my voice falsely bright.

"Oh God, no. *Why*? You like *men*. You were married to a man for ten years. You dated men up until last week." She emphatically puts down her mug. "You know me, Mads, I have nothing against gay people—*lesbians*—"

"Maybe I just want a new friend, *Mother*."

She picks up her coffee and, without sipping, puts it down again. "You don't use a dating site to get a new friend."

I'm indulgent with my mother. There was a time we would have banged heads and she would have imposed her will, but now it's all amicable because I do what I like.

"Wanda is accomplished, Mom. She has a PhD in math and is a professor at MIT. And, she looks a bit like you. Very beautiful." I sit back and enjoy my tea, strong and black with a squeeze of lemon.

"So what? Forget about Einstein and Miss Universe. Just find an ordinary man. The clock is ticking."

For someone with dementia, she sure speaks well. Must be all those years as an English teacher.

"Oh, for heaven's sake. I don't need a man to have a baby."

"Of course you do! Who's going to change the diapers?"

At work, when I go into Shawna's office, she says, "The HackMeister wants to date me."

"Don't do it," I say, laughing but half serious. "It'll add too much intrigue at the office to have romantic attachments."

Her face is pensive. *Does she want to date him? Surely not.*

"Tell him you have a boyfriend. What happened to Lonnie?"

“We’re cooling off for a bit,” Shawna says, her eyes downcast. “Basically because I can’t date someone whose only goal is to be a writer.”

“But Lonnie is lovely. And besides, what’s wrong with writers?”

“He doesn’t have any money, and I don’t want to be supporting another man. So I said no to the serious stuff.”

She doesn’t look me in the face. Instead, she straightens a pile on her desk, which is already perfect. “And don’t worry about Buck. I already told him to get lost. He’s not shaving yet, and I’m twenty-eight.”

“Oh hell. Hope you were nice and didn’t scare him away from us.” Again, half serious.

This time she chuckles. “Of course. I’m always nice. And I have lots of experience telling guys off.”

Maybe I should consult her about my Vince problem.

*****

After lunch, Shawna pops her head around the door of my office. “We got wetware with slow internet waiting outside to see you. Made the appointment this morning.”

“New customer?” I ask.

“No one I’ve seen before. Good-looking guy.” She consults her notebook. “Says he knows you. Vincent Cantley.”

CHAPTER 13

Deep breath. Remove jacket slowly and fold it over back of chair.

Shawna, who reads me with complete fluency, moves swiftly into the room, shuts the door, and sits across from me. She says softly, "Should I get rid of him, Madeline? You gone a little gray in the face."

I put my head on my hand. "Give me a minute."

"Why not send Buck to fix the guy's internet?" Shawna says. "Win-win. You get the client outa your hair, then charge him the big bucks. Assuming our whiz kid can do it. That Vincent needs to be going to his cable company for slow internet. What we got here is luxury service."

My first inclination is to give Vince the boot and tell him not to sully the premises with his presence again. It dawns on me, however, this is a perfect opportunity to build on the skills of my new employee and train him to work with clients. At the same time, I can show I mean business. My charge for house calls is $600 per hour.

He comes into No Man's Land and, like all other clients, pauses on the threshold. Dressed in a casual turtleneck and jacket. His blocky head trapezoidal in the distorting camera angle.

"This your boyfriend?" Shawna asks.

"Heaven forbid." Terse. "It's my date that didn't work out."

She knows the story. Her mouth forms an O.

"Beep-beep." Buck glides between us into Shawna's territory, ostensibly to look at the camera image of the an incoming client.

"Buck, come into my office," I say. "Help me diagnose the problem for this client."

"A-OK, boss lady."

"Time to go, Shawna. Show the guy in."

As Buck and I move to my office, I say, "Do you need to take notes?"

He appears stymied. Fiddles with his dangling silver earring.

"You know, Buck? Pen? Paper? Laptop?"

"Negative," he says.

After a few minutes, Shawna announces, "Mr. Cantley."

He follows her in, beaming.

"Madeline. What a pleasure." Like I'm an old friend and all is Zen in the universe. He puts out his hand, but I'm already behind my desk.

"Take a seat, Mr. Cantley." *Cool and professional. Face expressionless.* "This is my associate, Jeffrey Buck."

"Hey, dude," Buck says, extending his fist for a bump.

"Madeline, could we have some privacy?" Vince says, tilting his head at Buck.

I've anticipated this. "Buck will be assisting me in diagnosing your internet problem." I lift my chin slightly and make strong eye contact. "Tell us what's going on?"

He's not happy and regards me through narrowed eyes, then gives a curt nod. "This problem has been ongoing for about a month. Internet slowing to a crawl in the lab, completely unusable. Webmail, research—all impossible. People in my office have been complaining nonstop."

"Have you called your cable company?" I ask, maintaining my neutral, crisp tone.

"They've sent a couple of guys to the lab, with their tool belts and beards. Shouldn't be a problem, they say, the cable is perfect. Everything plugged in where it should be, nothing interfering with service, yada yada. The bottom line is, on some days we can't use the damn internet. Bunch of incompetents." This is about as agitated as I've seen him. His problem seems to be insidiously genuine.

"Alert! Need to inspect your premises," Buck pipes up.

Vince rotates his body so he can see my apprentice, who is bopping to his own beat.

"Who are you? Remind me." Hostile.

"Mr. Cantley, to diagnose your internet problem, we'll need to visit your lab." I give him a few seconds to process that, then make firm eye contact. "Buck accompanies me on client house calls, and my charge is $600 dollars an hour. I'll require a $300-dollar deposit before we proceed. If that's unacceptable, we can quit right now and charge you for one hour."

There. My price is on the table. I'm not interested in playing footsie with you, mister.

He stares at me, quite speechless. Eventually, he nods his head. "Must he come along?" He jerks his thumb at Buck, who's in another world, his eyes closed.

"Yes, Mr. Buck will accompany me." Then to Buck. "Are you okay with walking to the lab, Buck?"

"Affirmative."

Vince stands abruptly, knocking his chair to the side. "We'll do it your way then. As you know, it's a good walk." He pauses. "And stop being ridiculous. Call me Vince."

"Okay, Vince, we'll meet you in your lab in about an hour."

He frowns. "Why can't you come with me right now?"

I cross my arms and stare him down. "Do you want your internet fixed or not, *Vince*?"

His lab is brighter than it was last night, less like a morgue. Two lab workers sit at benches, wielding pipettes and test tubes. No squealing animals in sight. Buck heads straight to the fish tank, sinks to the floor, and goes eyeball to eyeball with a tropical fish.

Vince says softly, "How have you been, Madeline?"

Moving toward his lab bench, I act as if I didn't hear him. My health is not up for discussion.

He touches my jacket. "We had a wonderful dinner on Saturday. Why are you avoiding me?"

I shake him off. "Let me examine a computer on your network. Something as simple as malfunctioning firewalls could be the cause of the problem."

"Firewalls? I doubt it." He doesn't like being dissed and is curt, which is fine by me.

"Let me rule the obvious things out, at least," I say evenly.

He produces the laptop that has my spyware on it, the machine he uses to control lights in rodents' heads. Suppressing my distaste, I go to work. Vince stands just behind me, closer than I would prefer. The back of my neck prickles.

His internet is working perfectly today. No glitches at all. The response pages for Google come up like lightning. The anti-virus firewall is doing its thing. His files are well protected. Every item on his control panel is fine. Nothing malign lurking in the bowels of the computer, except for my spyware, which, of course is a secret between me and his computer. The spyware is not the culprit, because his problem started before its installation, and everything is working well right now.

I move away from his computer and instruct him to test his web mail. It appears to be fine.

"This is what's driving me insane," he says. "The problem isn't continuous. It comes and goes. But when it comes, everyone gets pissed off because they can't work."

I return to his computer. My peripheral vision tells me his attention is wandering. He's checking on his employees in the lab. In a flash, I examine my spyware to see if it's functioning properly. *Perfect.*

"Everything I've checked is good. You take your security seriously," I say. The dramatic irony is irresistible.

"Madeline ..."

I tune him, and everything else, out. The lab, Buck, the fish tank—all background noise. What's left is a tantalizing puzzle: what's messing with his internet? It would be a lie if I said I didn't want to impress him. After charging a hefty fee, it's unthinkable not to find the answer.

"I wish you'd see me again," he says softly and suddenly, laying a heavy hand on my arm.

I smack his hand away. "If you touch me again, Buck and I are leaving."

He backs off.

"Now about your internet problem. The only explanation consistent with the evidence is someone is intermittently using more than their fair share of internet, draining bandwidth from everyone else."

"So how do I fix it?" His voice is gruff.

"Lead me to the downstairs office where they're having the worst problems," I say stiffly.

He shrugs. "Everything's going to hell down there—the internet, the air conditioning, my accountant."

"Why do you need air conditioning? It's almost winter."

"Mainly because it gets hot. It's a stuffy room. No outside air. And guess what. The air conditioning tech expert? Another useless jerk. Said the AC was working just fine. Problem was the room's too hot."

On the way to the downstairs lab, I detour to collect Buck from the fish tank. "Earn your keep, Buck," I hiss to him. "Interact with the client."

"Be right down," he says, hitting the wall with flattened palms. "Need to check something first."

On the wall?

The downstairs room—the same one I observed last night—is full of clutter, a different universe from the pristine lab upstairs. A damaged bookcase leans precariously against the wall, its angled shelves supported by jagged old books. All emerge out of a jumble of boxes, broken computers, and discarded glass tanks. Wild guess—the boss seldom ventures into this hothouse of a room where the hired help simmers in the heat.

There's something wrong with this picture. The gadgets and wires that were strewn over the floors last night are gone.

The room is oppressive. A loud fan whirs and coughs, its power aimed at the chair occupied by a balding middle-aged man, who jumps out of his sneakers when he sees us. He jabs at a button that shuts down—without saving—whatever he was doing on his computer.

I recognize him immediately as the midnight intruder.

Vince introduces him as his accountant and general assistant, Leo Metzger. He's nondescript, slightly overweight, and has a naturally scowling face, as if he frowned once and the clock struck twelve.

"What's the purpose of this room?" I ask Vince. "Other than being Mr. Metzger's office." I'm stalling, furiously trying to figure out the man's story.

"Mainly to house the computer servers and our uh—non-living—lab equipment," Vince says.

"Tell me about your problems with the internet, Mr. Metzger," I say. "Can you be specific?" *Where's Buck?*

Leo doesn't seem to be thrilled at being interrupted and interrogated by a strange woman. He shrinks away from me and looks at Vince, who nods.

"I, um, do the payroll, order stuff, feed the animals, pay bills."

He's dodging the internet question.

With a flash of insight, I understand that he's the cause of the problem.

At this moment, Buck slips into the room, his eager eyes taking in the mess. A yellowing poster held up with masking tape catches his attention. "*Star Wars*, yeah!" Undeterred by any protocol, he heads to the wall and sets up a drum beat in the center of the poster. Rat-a-tat-tat. He gives another knock on the poster, and it goes clank. *Metal.*

"What's under the poster, Vince?" I ask.

"I have no idea. What does it matter?" He makes no attempt to hide his annoyance.

"Uh-oh." Buck, with no clue about propriety or boundaries, rips the masking tape, lifts the poster, and reveals a metal panel.

Leo is on his feet, waving his arms. "Hey, you can't do that."

"What's in the panel, Vince?" I say.

"Nothing, that's what. It's an old electrical panel. Hasn't been used for years. What does that have to do with anything?" He's angry, sweat glistening on his brow.

With a twist of Buck's screwdriver, the panel is open, revealing a black metal box with wires extending from it. The contraption looks like a bomb.

An integrated circuit attached to Leo's computer. The source of Tuesday night's hammering becomes clear.

"We need to get under the floorboards, Vince," I say. "Then you'll see what's causing your internet problem."

Leo is soaked with sweat, his eyes bulging. "Now, wait a minute—"

"Go ahead, why don't you?" Vince says. "Rip up the floor boards."

As he says this, Buck sinks onto his hands and knees and starts knocking on the wooden boards. Barely a sound. Probably cement underneath the wood veneer. As he moves, the knocking gets louder, then becomes hollow, reverberating through the room.

"Score!" Buck springs up from the ground and approaches me for a fist bump. I put out both fists in self-defense, and Buck does a double bump, jab-jab. Does he know what's going on?

Vince watches the scene with narrowed eyes. The meter is ticking.

"By the way, dude," Buck says to Vince, "About your internet problem? I got it solved. Piece of cake."

He tries a fist bump with Vince, but Vince isn't playing. "If you're so smart and have it all figured it out, wouldn't it be great if you'd let me in on the secret?" He says this with a twist of his mouth.

The irony is lost on Buck, who curls his fists into a telescope that he holds aloft. With exaggerated slowness, he lowers it to his eye.

"Spyware on your upstairs computer, dude."

CHAPTER 14

Tightness in my chest, like a heart attack. I take a sharp step back. *Think!* Process what just happened and neutralize it.

Buck's error #1: He waited until we left the lab, then examined the client's computer.

Error #2: He gave the client an assessment without consulting me.

Error #3, the kicker: He's so damn smart, he detected spyware that's virtually invisible. Shit! Sabotaged by a pipsqueak batting above his paygrade.

Vince, who's shown no love for my assistant, turns on him and says, "If the problem is on my computer, why the hell are you digging up the floor?"

Buck opens his mouth to respond, but I shut him down by saying, "Mr. Cantley, please forgive my apprentice, Mr. Buck. He's a new employee who's learning on the job. He should not have touched your computer without permission."

I turn my back on Vince and face Buck. I mime a quick gesture zipping my mouth. *Zip the lip.* "From now on, Buck, please follow my instructions," I whisper furiously.

"Big yikes," Buck says mildly.

Damn, double damn!

"We're good," I say softly. "Now pull up those floorboards."

"What about the spyware?" Vince says, moving near to me. "Does he know what he's doing?"

Buck is lying on the floor again, his ear on the hollow-sounding floorboard.

"Screwdriver. Hammer." *Talking to himself.* He's wearing his tool belt, a throwback to his furnace-fixing days.

"There's no spyware," I murmur to Vince. His hip has inched closer to touch mine—*Creep!*—but I must stay close. "Buck is incorrect. It's actually your firewall, which is keeping tabs on what comes into your computer. Be patient, Vince. In a minute you'll find out what's been slowing your internet."

He puts his hand on my back. I edge away.

Buck is on his knees, a screwdriver under a floorboard, banging with a hammer, prizing it, getting right under it. Like a trapdoor with a spring, it pops right up.

Leo is gaping at him. "Are you going to let this weirdo tear up the room?" he implores Vince, his voice cracking on "room."

"Can you explain in English what's going on?" Vince seems fed up with Buck—his self-assurance, his tools.

"Have your electric bills been high recently?" I ask Vince.

"Too high—bunch of crooks." He's toned down the hostility and edges toward me again.

Another floorboard comes up, revealing a hardware universe of devices and wires. Vince goes down on his haunches and gawks. All of us stare at this electronic city. I now understand what Leo was doing last night: expanding and rearranging his vast, secret subterranean domain.

Buck, pushing back his hair, moves toward Leo. "Sorry, dude. Bitcoin party is over."

Leo crumples in his chair and starts to sob like a baby. Buck sits on the floor and awkwardly tries to pat him. It's time for me to wrest some control.

I turn to Vince. "Leo has been doing bitcoin mining here on your dime. You're looking at thousands of dollars of computer equipment that's been overheating this room."

Vince moves closer to me. "Madeline—"

"Listen!" I speak in a fierce whisper and move sharply away. "Your accountant, Leo, has been stealing from you—time and energy. When you shut down his little enterprise, I predict the temperature in this room will go down, as well as your electric bill and your internet problems."

He moves toward me again. "Madeline, you're incredible. How can I thank you?"

"Vince, back off! I'm not doing this out of kindness. It's my business. I expect to be paid in full, now, and to not be contacted again by you unless it's to engage my professional services."

A flash of anger in his eyes directed at me.

"I suggest you call the police," I say coldly. "Get them to confiscate this expensive equipment. Lots of computing power—at least forty devices, I would say. Because if you don't involve the police, your accountant will go rip off someone else."

Vince doesn't respond straightaway, barely registering Leo's betrayal and the fact he'll need a new employee. Instead, he says, "Why are you being so cold, Madeline?"

"Vince, this is a professional gig for me. No more, no less."

"Could we wipe the slate clean and start again?"

How do you tell someone to back off for good? That you find him repulsive? The intensity of his look gives me chills. Is he trying to hypnotize me?

I can't soften it and say this relationship isn't working, because he'll twist it around and say we can make it work. If I say I'm not attracted to him, he'll say give it time. It has to be a definitive no.

"I'm sorry, Vince," I say. "You must stop contacting me. The answer is no, there's no starting again."

His face hardens. His neck too; the tight, powerful cords above the collar of his shirt. When I first met him, I thought him quite handsome. But today his features are sharp and icy, his blue eyes a shade too pale.

Without a word, we move upstairs to settle accounts. He gives me no flak on the bill, which is a hefty one, because I don't want him sitting in my office next week with a space bar that doesn't work.

Afterward, I go downstairs to retrieve Buck. Leo is nowhere to be seen. Is he in the bathroom or has he taken off? *Not my problem.*

Buck, on the other hand, is sitting at Leo's computer, clicking away. He has no moral qualms about making a move on someone else's computer. All problems for him are abstract, rearranged into bits and bytes that can be rejiggered until a solution is found. It's uncanny how he caught on about the bitcoin mining, how he knew where to look and what he'd find. Starting upstairs, tapping the walls and floors, playing hide-and-seek with the devices. Then coming down here, sussing out the oppressive steam bath of a room, knowing where the computing power had to be.

Finding the spyware on Vince's computer.

When we get back to the office, I'll read him the riot act about protocol with clients.

Jeffrey the HackMeister Buck is a dangerous employee.

Roselyn Teukolsky

CHAPTER 15

On Saturday morning, my mother shows up in the kitchen looking disoriented. She's half-dressed, wearing sweatpants, sneakers, and her pajama top. Her hair is a bird's nest, untouched since yesterday.

Gently, I take her arm and steer her upstairs to her room. The animals accompany us. I guess they don't fancy being alone with Mrs. Auerbach. Tosca has put on weight and is struggling on the stairs. She's been sluggish lately, a far cry from the will-o'-the-wisp sprite who once sprinted to the top of our tree. Torvill stands behind her on the stairs, nudging her up with his snout, patiently waiting while she drags herself to the next step. Carefully, I lift her, hugging her against me. She meows in protest, but doesn't try a jump, which she would have done in the old days. Up we go to the top of the stairs, Tosca's luxuriant ginger-black fur soft against me.

"Okay, Mom, let's pick a good top to go with these pants," I say cheerfully, hating my false voice. I'll throw myself off the roof if someone ever speaks to me like that.

She's obedient and fumbles at her closet. In a few minutes, with my help, she's respectable, her hair brushed. It breaks my heart.

"Madsy," she says on the stairs, "who's that strange woman in the kitchen? I don't like her."

Before leaving for my date with Wanda, I pull Mrs. Auerbach aside, out of Mom's hearing. "My mother isn't having a good day, so please don't let her out of your sight until I get home."

She nods, her face impassive. "I will do my best, Madeline. Mrs. Geiger can be very difficult." She lowers her eyes and folds her arms. Defiant.

There was a time I would have canceled my plans and stayed home with Mom myself, but I've made this deal with the devil to keep my mother close and also live my life. I can't cancel my plans every time she loses her compass.

A wintry mix is rattling on the window panes, a sleety rain that could turn into snow if the temperature drops. I'm insulated against the weather, with tights, cords, and a long puffy coat that hugs my body and keeps me warm. I tug a waterproof winter hat low over my ears, and I'm ready for a walk to Harvard Square, where I've arranged to meet Wanda at 2:00 p.m. She's driving in from Boston, and our plan is to play it by ear and choose a place to go.

On a wet day like today, it would have made sense to give Wanda my home address and have her pick me up. But I've become cautious with strangers, and until I meet her, that's what she is.

Luckily, there's more rain than ice, and the walk is not as hazardous as it might have been. I have a wide umbrella and am happy to escape the oppressive atmosphere at home. There aren't too many people out and about, so the splashy clomp of boots behind me give me pause. *Ignore them,* I tell myself. *It's normal to hear people on a Cambridge street.* As I resolutely ignore the footsteps, they follow me into Harvard Square. I speed up, my replaced knee aching in the cold.

Wanda and I have arranged to meet in front of the Coop Café. *I'm here,* I text. Around me are no likely candidates. I pull off my snug hat, shake out my hair, and survey the scene. Being punctual is one of my things—she has ten minutes or so before I take off.

I scan the people nearby, half-expecting Vince to appear and offer himself. *Stop it!*

Then I see a familiar face staring into a window, shading his eyes to cut down glare. I recognize the hunched posture, the shape of his head as he peers forward. *Leo Metzger, the bitcoin miner. Vince's man. What the hell is he doing less than ten feet away from me?*

I clutch my purse and hold it close. *Where's Wanda?*

"Madeline?"

The voice is husky, assertive. I swing around, and my impression is of a solid woman in heavy boots with lots of brown hair coiled up and held precariously with a small stick through it. I had imagined someone petite like my mother, but this woman is anything but.

"Hi. Is your car nearby?" I say softly, turning around, watching Leo.

"Yes, why? I had trouble parking and then got lucky." Green eyes, looking at me quizzically.

Leo hasn't moved. Still peering. Too long to look in a shop window. *He's following me. Did Vince fire him? Is he pissed at me and seeking revenge?*

"Let's go." I put my gloved hand on Wanda's arm and pull her away from Leo, in the opposite direction.

"Where we going?" She opens her umbrella, and we hurry away together until we reach her Camry.

"I'm really sorry," I say. "I think I'm being followed by someone. Can we just get out of Cambridge? Drive across the river?"

Amazingly, she seems unfazed. Inside the car, she leans toward me and pecks my cheek. "Hi, I'm Wanda. Nice to meet you."

"Do you mind if we just go?" My breathing is ragged.

"Yes, ma'am," Wanda says, with a nonchalant sweep of the wheel that swings the car out of a tight spot and into traffic.

I sink against the comfy leather seat and put my head back against the headrest.

"I'm Madeline," I say tersely. "Madeline, not Maddie."

Wanda gets the wipers going, and before too long, we're watching the rain pelting the Charles as we cross the bridge into Boston.

"What's going on, Madeline not Maddie?" my date says.

A car has been behind us since we pulled out of our spot in Cambridge. If I crane my neck, I see it clearly in the side mirror. The driver is obscured by the rain, but I could swear it's him.

"Quick, turn onto a side street. I want to shake the car behind us."

Screeching the car, she hangs a right and picks up the pace.

"Now park. I want to see if he follows us."

She gives me a strange look, but says, "Okay! Done." Another crunch of wheels as she maneuvers expertly into a no-parking zone. "Can you explain what we're doing here?"

Wanda has a nice profile, calm and beautiful. I decide to tell her about Vince. The abbreviated version. "He's stalking me," I say. "I think—"

"Vince is in the car that's following us?" Her voice is incredulous.

"Not exactly. It's complicated." I despise the tension in my voice.

The car that was behind us drives past us. Same car, without a doubt. Same distinctive head on the driver.

Definitely Vince's man, Leo.

CHAPTER 16

Wanda is watching me. Impassive. "Do you want me to lose him?" She gestures to the car that just passed, then leans across and puts a gloved hand on my arm. "Hey."

"Yes, please," I say softly.

She grins. "Buckle up."

With a screech of wheels, she executes a perfect U-turn, and before long, this lovely stranger is taking me on a joyride through rainy Boston. She seems perfectly relaxed, giving me a running commentary, taking a circuitous route, pointing out the Boston Common, the Frog Pond, and the crazy people splashing about through the muck.

I keep looking back, and a pulse starts jumping in my neck. I'm so spooked by Vince that I don't even question the logic of being followed by Leo on foot from my house, and then chased again on wheels into Boston. For example, where did Leo park his car?

Wanda finally slows down in Beacon Hill, pointing at Acorn Street, with its cobblestones and old gas lamps, ghostly in the rain. "The Underground Railroad operated here in the 1800s," she says, as if we're on a museum tour.

"Where are we going?" My voice is unnatural, still tense.

She pulls over, parking illegally on a narrow road. "I live a few blocks from here, on Joy Street. I'm taking you to my home. Where no one can grab you off the street."

"But—"

"Don't argue. No one's following you now. We lost that car many miles ago. Calm down and relax." She smiles at me, and for the first time during this rainy trip, I smile back.

One of my pet peeves is dealing with irrational people, and I'm being a moron. Do I really believe that Leo, the bitcoin-mining thief, is following me on behalf of Vince? In what universe would Vince be paying Leo to keep tabs on me? For all I know, Vince fired Leo. When I actually start thinking clearly, I conclude it's too bizarre to be a coincidence. I just can't figure it out.

The rain is tapering off, and the day is brightening. My tour guide points out a quaint store, Rouvalis Flowers, with its bright-green, striped awning, and windows displaying antiques and garden ornaments. A golden Buddha winks at me, and suddenly I'm charmed by my date.

She has a *Resident* parking sticker and finds a spot near the entrance to her condo. I watch her surreptitiously as she focuses on a perfect parallel parking maneuver. Some of her hair has sprung loose from her careless hair style, and she looks like a woodland tree creature in a fairy tale.

The apartment is in a red-brick house, whose entrance is quite close to the road but obscured behind a row of trees. This street is off the highway, with no more than an occasional passing car. It seems like a place I may feel safe, far away from Cambridge.

"Hey, look. The sun is coming out," she says as we get out of the car. And it is, beams of it filtering through the trees and lighting her up. My spirits lift.

Wanda's condo is miraculous, starting with the variegated stone steps leading to a heavy mahogany door. Inside, we shed our coats, scarves, and boots, and I can finally exhale. She appraises me frankly, while I take in the casual elegance of her living room and the big bay window that floods the place with light. Hanging plants, creeping vines, clay pots, and African prints. Colored triangles on the rug. How different Wanda and I are. My Persian rugs are as ancient as my house.

Did Wanda design all this? I've never given much thought to the interior design of my house. Just a comfy old couch, a few ancient chairs thrown in, some gauzy landscapes on the walls, and loaded-down bookcases haphazardly arrayed around the room. But in my defense, it's a happy clutter that I've lived with all my adult life.

Wanda has been watching me take in the gorgeousness of this room, enjoying my appreciation. She moves toward me. "Gosh, Madeline, you're so—" She cuts herself off and inspects me. "You know you could be a model."

How does one respond? It's the kind of comment that makes me tongue-tied. Isn't she a mathematician? Why aren't we talking about something less threatening, like number theory?

She pulls the stick out of that tower of a hairdo letting her hair tumble down, then combs her hands through, making it symmetrical. Fine wrinkles are visible at the corners of her eyes. For a second, she seems weathered and comfortable, like my couch at home.

"Can I make you coffee? Nespresso? Strong? Weak? Decaf? Tea?" Then, in a deep *Young Frankenstein* voice, "Ovaltine?"

I grin despite myself, the rustiness of my social skills on full display.

"People can see in. Can we close the curtains?"

"Sure thing." In a blink, she steps to the window and pulls a cord, releasing the beige curtains to curve around the bay window. The room is suddenly dark and cozy. She moves to the door and closes the dead bolt with a loud click. "All secure," she says. "No one can get at you in here." She looks at me and laughs. "Except me."

She's really nice.

When I put out my hand and touch her cheek, her skin is smooth. "Thank you," I say.

"It's okay now, he's gone." She gives me a reassuring hug, and I tighten my grip, because the solid warmth of her is so unexpectedly comforting, and enticing.

She's almost but not quite as tall as me, and must stand on her toes to reach up and kiss me. It's a chaste kiss, her lips just resting on mine while she strokes my neck and hair. I don't know what I thought we'd do on this date. Talk about our work, I reckoned, assess if we liked each other, perhaps decide to be friends. How strange it's turned out like this, standing in a horny clinch with a female mathematician. I've never been with a woman.

"Mmm, lots of tension here," she says. "I'm an expert masseur. I could loosen you up in a minute." Her touch on my neck is light and probing.

She reaches up to kiss me again, and this time, I yield to let her in.

I haven't felt like this in a long while.

She takes my hand and leads me to her bedroom, where I sink down on pillows and softness. A gentle whir of curtains gliding shut. I lie passively and watch her while she removes my sweater and folds it, places it on a chair, rolls me onto my front and unclasps my bra, her hair on my back and her mouth slowly kissing me down my knotty spine.

She's right—it *is* a good massage, one that makes me forget Vince and Leo and everyone else. Eventually, I relax against her and wonder what the hell I'm doing in a stranger's bed.

My phone rings. Sharp, urgent bursts from my purse in the living room.

"Leave it. Whoever it is can wait." She nibbles my ear. Keeps me enfolded in her arms.

But of course I'll jump up and answer it. I always do.

"I must get that. It may be my mom." I extricate myself from Wanda and am suddenly shy in my nakedness. I pull on my clothes before running to the living room. Wanda's right. I probably shouldn't drop everything whenever she calls.

When I finally reach my phone, the name I see is Gretchen Auerbach. That can't be good news. Mrs. Auerbach has never called me.

The phone is still ringing. There's no help for it, this can't be postponed.

"Hello," I say.

"Oh, thank heavens. Madeline." She's breathing heavily.

I collapse onto the rug, white fingers gripping the phone. "What's wrong?" I'm curt and furious with her for bringing me yet more trouble.

"Your mother has disappeared," she says. "I can't find her."

CHAPTER 17

Wanda appears in the living room, fully clothed. "What's happening, Madeline?" She drops down beside me and rubs my back. Her kindness sends a deep sadness through me.

Where to start?

She gets a quick summary because we must leave right now. "My mom has dementia and has left the house, alone." I don't have the emotional energy to explain about Mrs. Auerbach, who has committed a fireable offense—losing Mom. But of course I won't fire her because suckers aren't knocking down my door to take her job.

Wanda accepts the situation for what it is, and in a few minutes, we are back in her car, speeding down Storrow Drive. To my relief, she doesn't tell me things will be fine. What she does say is, "I'd like to see you again, so we can get acquainted with clothes on."

Why would she want to be anywhere near me again? So far, I've revealed myself as paranoid about being stalked and having an unstable mother who disrupts my life. Both trips in her car have involved a screech of tires.

The rain and sleet have stopped, and a pale sun is shining through the clouds. Rays glint off the bridge as we speed into Cambridge.

“Where are we going?” she says.

I lead her on a circular path, up and down the roads near my house. Trawling the streets for a petite woman wandering aimlessly. *Where are you, Mom? She could be stepping in front of a car right now.* A pulse beats in my cheek as we wind down the search without success.

Eventually, I direct Wanda to my house.

She’s wistful as she pecks me goodbye. “Take care of yourself, Madeline. And good luck with your mom.”

Mrs. Auerbach is distraught. “A man rang the doorbell and asked for your mother. I didn’t think I had the right to ask him to leave.”

“Did he give a name?”

“I don’t remember—wait. Vincent.”

Oh God, no.

“What did he want?” I’m like a machine gun, shooting one question after another because I’m so frightened. How is it possible that Mrs. Auerbach, after all my admonitions, lost track of my mother?

“He asked to see the house, very politely.” She’s calmed down a bit but is anxious.

“So what happened?” My voice is shrill.

“Madeline, I’m not the boss of your mother. She invited the man inside and showed him around. They went into the kitchen and played with the dog and cat. He was really taken with those animals.”

He put his hands on my pets. Those rodent-cutting hands.

“And where were you while all this playing was happening?” I sound like a shrew.

Her lips are set in a line. “Watching your mother from a distance. Or, as you would say, ‘keeping tabs.’”

"What did he want?"

She looks at me with a steady gaze. "To find out about you and your life." Her flat, unemotional voice sends ice up my spine.

"What?"

"He asked to see your bedroom, so your mother took him upstairs. I waited at the bottom of the staircase."

It takes my breath away—his gall, her stupidity.

"Why didn't you follow them? He could have harmed her!" She just doesn't get it, my fear about Mom.

"I had to make a judgment. She had a visitor who seemed charming, so I gave her space."

Your job isn't to give her space. It's to keep her safe.

Mrs. Auerbach is fed up with my interrogation and pushes stray gray hairs out of her face. Her forehead is lined in a way I haven't noticed before. This business of watching my mother is a minefield.

The air in my house is cool, but the kitchen where we're standing feels too warm, suddenly short on oxygen. I sit down at the table.

Mrs. Auerbach sits across from me, her face defiant. "From where I was, I could hear him clearly, saying, 'Tell me everything about Madeline.' And Mrs. Geiger started talking about you. She told him about your skydiving accident, your wheelchair, how she came to live with you and nursed you. He wanted to know about your husband, and Mrs. Geiger said he wasn't good enough for you, that you were much smarter than him."

"Why didn't you text me that a strange man was in the house?" The ground is shifting, and I shut my eyes to regain equilibrium. *Not happening.*

"He didn't seem threatening," she says in that maddening monotone of hers.

I put my forehead in my hand and signal her to go on.

"They came downstairs. He told your mother how lovely she was—just like her daughter—and invited her to go out for coffee with him."

"You let her go out with him?" My breath catches in my throat.

"Of course I didn't!" Contempt in her voice. "I explained to him that if Mrs. Geiger went out, I'd need to accompany her. That it was my job." She looks at me. "I couldn't very well come out with it and say your mom is senile and I must stay close to her."

Your mom is senile. I want to grab her neck and squeeze the callousness out of it. *But what the fuck did I expect her to say? That Mom has a neurocognitive disorder?*

"So then what?" I ask evenly.

"He nodded, said they'd do it another time. Mrs. Geiger announced she was going to have her usual afternoon nap."

Why didn't you watch her?

"I couldn't exactly invade her bedroom." Mrs. Auerbach, reading my mind, has become increasingly red in the face. "They played me. When I checked in her room about half an hour later, it was empty."

I want to kill Mrs. Auerbach with my bare hands, even though I know she's blameless. My anger should be directed at that jerk, Vince.

I fumble at my phone to call the police, while simultaneously debating whether to search nearby coffee shops or enlist everyone I know to help.

I tried, Mom, to keep you safe.

A car crunches on the road outside, then stops. I stumble in a rush to the door.

Mom is on the front walkway, and a dark-gray car is pulling away from the curb. She's rosy-cheeked, her eyes sparkling.

"Hello, Madsy," she says pleasantly, as if she's returning from a lovely, brisk walk. She shuts the door and says, "You'll never guess where I've been this afternoon." She offers her cheek to be kissed, and I dumbly oblige.

A surge of light-headedness hits me, and I sag against the wall. "Where'd you go, Mom?"

She smiles. "Today I met your boyfriend, Vince."

CHAPTER 18

"I don't feel well," Mom says, rubbing her haunches with both hands. "My back hurts. And my head too." My mother never complains about aches and pains, and momentarily I think she's trying to escape the interrogation she surely knows is coming.

"Mrs. Auerbach, please take the rest of the day off," I say softly. When our housekeeper's face registers alarm, I add, "No, please don't misunderstand me. You've been under stress. I'll be with my mother this evening."

As I say it, I realize the truth of it. Mrs. Auerbach has a wrung-out look to her. She turns toward the foot of the stairs.

"Gretchen, wait." I put my hand on her arm. "Thank you."

Too little too late. She barely breaks stride, nods at me, and is gone.

"Let's go to your room," I say to Mom, trying to smile sympathetically.

Unclench.

In her room, she climbs onto her bed and half-sits against the pillows. When I move to turn on the light, she says, "No, Mads, no light."

The remnants of today's storm have left thick gray clouds in the sky, and the room is in near-darkness.

I'm the one who breaks the heavy silence. "Vince is not my boyfriend. You need to be very clear on that."

"He's nice, Mads, and he's crazy about you. You sure could do worse."

"That's not fair, Mom, and I don't have to tell you. It's intrusive." I turn away from her. *Why am I being so reasonable?* My response is always rational. It never includes rushing to her bedside and shaking her shoulders until there's sense in her head.

"Vince asked me to put in a good word for him. He can't understand what he did to upset you."

"Mom—"

"He loves animals. You should have seen him playing with our two, rolling them onto their backs, petting them."

"None of it matters. He repels me. And you need to respect my feelings."

She sits up straight. "Next thing you'll be telling me is you're attracted to the woman you met today. When Vince asked if you'd found another man, I couldn't help laughing. I told him about her."

"How dare you!" It comes spitting out of me. A final indignity. Mom's dementia has tipped into dangerous territory, and I don't know how much longer I can live with her. Slipping out the house to go God knows where with Vince. Her antagonism toward Mrs. Auerbach. She's grinding us down, just as she did with the other housekeepers.

"You need to respect my feelings too," my mother says. "I'm a prisoner here. And it shouldn't cause a"—she gropes for a word—"*crisis* because I went out for an afternoon to have coffee with a nice man."

"You took him into my bedroom. What's happened to you that you can't tell it's beyond the pale? Do you understand how creepy that is, the thought of this man seeing *my stuff*?" My voice cracks on "stuff." I'm so angry with her for letting herself be manipulated, for not understanding how insidious the situation has become.

She's still gesticulating. "He loves you, Mads, and wants to be close to you. I sympathize with him. I know how ... difficult you can be."

There's no response for her disloyalty, so I shake my head. I'm flushed, as if I have a fever. Is this what Alzheimer's does, steals away the person you know, leaving an imposter in her place?

When I don't reply, she barrels on. "Since we're having this honest little chat, I should fess up that I gave Vince a little something of yours." Even in the dark, she can't meet my eyes. She knows she's crossed a line. "Those little twisty earrings you like."

My silver Möbius strips!

"You what?"

"He held them as if they were sacred," Mom says. "I was so moved, I told him to keep them. Spur of the moment. I'm sorry, Madsy, that's one thing I really regret."

"I'm so angry with you, Mom—you've betrayed me. I'll be having dinner on my own while I figure out how to deal with everything."

"It's fine, Mads. I have a really bad headache and don't feel like eating."

I get up to leave—we've probably said it all—but something holds me back. At the door I turn around to face Mom. "Did he hurt you? Physically, I mean."

"Of course not," she says. "What would make you think that?"

When I'm in my room, I call Wanda.

"Madeline, I've been thinking of you all afternoon. Did you find your mom?"

Her lovely, calm, rippling voice.

"Yes, thank you, she's fine," I say. "Can we meet tomorrow evening? I want to clue you in on a few things."

"Oh, yes, please. Tell me where and when." She's smiling at me through the phone.

I lower my voice. "Slide that bolt on your door and watch your back."

On Sunday morning, my mother, Mrs. Auerbach, and I are all in the kitchen, preoccupied with our own problems. Mom winces when she gets up to prepare her breakfast. "Still sore," she says sharply.

A better daughter would go and hug her and offer to make her oatmeal and tea, but I haven't gotten past the events of yesterday. My anger is tempered with grief for the person my mother once was. I can barely recognize her. *Rise to the occasion,* I berate myself. *Be kinder.*

Mrs. Auerbach leaves the kitchen with a tray to have her breakfast in another room. She and my mother haven't spoken one word to each other this morning, but that's nothing new. A loose hinge outside is creaking in the late October wind, and the tension in the house is palpable. The animals feel it too, snipping and snapping at each other, Torvill growling when Tosca bats his food bowl, and Tosca baring her claws at him. Her claws! Certainly not best friends like they usually are.

I need to escape for a while.

"I'm going to the supermarket." Softening a tiny bit toward my mother. "I'll wait if you'd like to come with me."

She's sipping her tea and doesn't look up. "No, thanks." Curt. Aggrieved, like me.

At the store, I buy a plump rotisserie chicken and a loaf of freshly baked French bread—Mom's favorite—as a kind of peace offering. We can't fight forever, and I, of course, must forgive her.

When I return home, the television is on in the living room, so I head for the sitting room, where my mother usually sits. She's not there.

"Mom!" I call down the hallway. Nothing. More games?

With a sigh I head to her room. When I knock, there's no reply. I turn the door handle and look in. Gone. *Has she snuck out with Vince, her new best friend?*

Onward again, the rigmarole of interrogating Mrs. Auerbach. It's getting tedious.

Down the echoing hallway to the living room I go. There's some kind of drama playing on TV, a gale howling above the squawk of birds.

"Mrs. Auerbach," I say as I come into the room.

What I see stops me cold.

"Hello, Mads," Mom says. She is sitting next to Mrs. Auerbach on the couch, their arms linked and knees touching.

"Gretchen and I are watching *The Raven*," she says.

CHAPTER 19

Vince has gotten to them.

It's warm in the house, but I shiver as realization dawns.

He's controlling my family until I capitulate. He will make them injure each other if I won't have him.

Even as I think those thoughts, I comprehend their absurdity. To be correct means he performed surgery on the animals and Mom yesterday, and fitted in Mrs. Auerbach too.

And yet, Torvill and Tosca have always gotten along—loved each other—and now they're at each other's throats. Spitting and hissing in their separate corners. Like the mice and the rats.

Vincent has disturbed my household, and it is freaking me out.

My experiments work across species.

At lunch, Mom invites Mrs. Auerbach—who is now *Gretchen*—to join us at the kitchen table. I pick at my lunch, observing the creepy geniality between them and hearing the snarling of our pets at their food bowls.

"Were you with Vincent yesterday when he ... played with the animals?" I ask Mom, my voice strained.

"I was at the kitchen table," she says. "Gretchen watched from the door."

"Can you remember what he did to them—exactly?"

"His back was to me, but he was on the floor, fluffing up their fur." Mom looks at me sternly. "He was lovely with them, Madsy. Nothing wrong with that."

"He had toys with him," Gretchen says thoughtfully. "He took some stuff out of a bag."

Scalpel?

A strange vibe pervades the house, either in the air or my imagination.

After lunch, I go to my mother's bedroom, where she's reclining on her bed. Quietly, I shut the door behind me.

"How come you made friends with Gretchen?" My voice is soft, trying to sound non-accusatory.

She thinks for a while, then her lip quivers. "Tosca threw up this morning, and Gretchen cleaned it up."

"That's it? You bonded over Tosca?"

Mom looks confused and shakes her head. "I'm not sure. I think I took some photos of them." She reaches for her phone.

So suddenly she's friends with Mrs. Auerbach. I can't fathom it.

My theory is irrational—nuts, actually—but there's a logical way to rule it out. In order to control the animals and humans remotely, Vince needs a Wi-Fi router box in our house to receive his computerized signals. Where would he conceal such a box? In a minute, I'm furiously ransacking the kitchen, pulling open drawers and cabinets, inspecting the pantry, and poking into all the nooks and crannies. *Where is it, goddammit!*

It's not in the kitchen.

In the living room, where Mrs. Auerbach is sitting and knitting in an armchair, I pull up the couch cushions, revealing crumbs and other debris, but not a little black box.

My housekeeper rests her needles on her lap and stares. "What are you looking for, Madeline?"

"A small box—looks like the cable box. Have you seen one around? May I look under the cushions of your armchair?"

After a long, probing look at me, she stands up under sufferance, gathering her pattern, knitting needles and yarn. "May I sit on the couch?" she says sotto voce.

I gesture *of course* and pull up her armchair, setting off a puff of dust from under the cushion. I search among the cabinets and old furniture, but it's futile. Perhaps he's put it in one of the bedrooms, or the middle level of the house, to have a greater range. I barely know where to begin.

Like a woman possessed, I tear through all the rooms, breathing in dust and dead spiders in my quest to find that box.

Mom watches me in her room, her eyes wide. "Are you looking for your paperweight?"

"I'm searching for something Vince may have left in the house. Metal boxes. Recording devices. Bugs. He was very intrusive."

"Oh, Mads."

"I need to look in your drawers and closets, Mom, just to be sure."

She sits up and sniffs. "Do what you have to do."

When I crawl out from under her bed with dust bunnies in my hair, she says, "Madeline, you're frightening me, you're not yourself."

In my bedroom, I survey everything through his eyes. My closet, with its jumble of shoes and casual clothes mingling among my business suits and shirts. Did he put his face in here and breathe me in? Nothing lurking under the bed or in my desk. He wouldn't place it in my underwear drawer—*surely not?*—

which isn't to say that I don't check and imagine his hands rummaging through my Jockey French-cuts. *Ugh.*

Eventually I've searched the entire house, except for Mrs. Auerbach's quarters. Down the stairs I go, finding her where I left her on the couch, thin-lipped and knitting like a demon.

It's a little awkward, because I can't exactly come clean about what I'm looking for. *A little Wi-Fi box that's controlling lights in the heads of our pets, my mother, and you.*

"Gretchen, may I go into your rooms?" I ask politely. "I'm searching for something personal that may have been there before your time here."

Just a little white lie to make her say yes.

"Oh, what is it?" she says. "I may have seen it."

I sigh. "A small metal box, probably black. Looks like the router box in our broom closet."

Her eyes narrow, and she thinks for a second or two. "I'd rather you didn't go into my living space. But I'll look for it and report back to you."

So that's where it must be. Up there in her rooms. Is she in cahoots with Vince? She did, after all, let him into the house. Did he charm her too?

For now, even though I'm fully within my rights as an employer, I don't push the issue. I will search Mrs. Auerbach's quarters when she's out. I must confess I'm reluctant to antagonize Mom's assistant and new best friend.

My spirits lift at the sight of Wanda waiting for me at Waldo's. Punctually. Six o'clock. Her jacket is off, but she's still wearing a long, wooly scarf wound around her neck. When she embraces me, I want to lose myself in the solid feel of her. That's how fragile I've been all day.

She orders a Coors Light, and I go with a small glass of Chablis. Then her hand is covering mine and she's looking at me quizzically. Beautiful gray-green eyes and long lashes that I barely noticed last time. Graceful hands, too, with soft fingers.

"Okay, Madeline, tell me what's going on. Who's coming for my back? Why must I watch it?"

I tell it like an algorithm—short, sharp and accurate. No embellishments. Online dating, Vince, mice, rats, revulsion, stalking.

"You won't believe it, but Vince wheedled himself into my house, spirited away my mother, and leaned on her to say nice things to me about him."

"Oh, poor you." She gives my hand a sympathetic shake.

"Not just that—you're part of the story. Mom told Vince about you."

Wanda blinks and shakes her head. I feel awful, disloyal to my mother. "We've always had each other's backs," I say sadly. "Mom's old self would never have said these things to a stranger I dislike."

"Don't worry. I can handle myself."

"It gets worse." I put down my wine glass.

Keeping it dispassionate, I try to lay out my theory of Vince's experiments and how those light implants have affected the behavior of my entire household. It's no use. Before I'm halfway done, Wanda is squirming in her seat, and her eyes are squeezing together and squinting at me.

"Lights? Really? In the heads of your mother and pets?"

Her incredulity is unbearable and I look away. "You think I'm crazy."

"Put it this way—you've had quite an insane weekend so far," she says. "You're right about one thing—he sure is messing with your head."

It's hopeless. If Wanda doesn't buy it, who will?

I drop the subject and allow our conversation to drift in other directions. We settle on safe topics, this and that and getting rid of unwanted men. *Men! Who needs them?* I gather Wanda never dates men, but she can't avoid them in her line of work. She steers me toward an interesting theorem she's trying to prove using a devilish new technique. If she can pull it off, she'll publish and maybe move ahead of the sexist Neanderthals in her field.

I walk home in the frosty dark.

Our meeting has unsettled me further. Nothing has been resolved. It's after nine when I arrive at my doorstep, drained. My key is out, ready to unlock the front door, when I almost tread on a letter near the welcome mat.

Just one handwritten word on the envelope: *Madeline.*

I've never seen Vince's handwriting, but I know it's his.

CHAPTER 20

I'm reluctant to touch the envelope. Nor do I want to bring it into the house. What if it contains some kind of poisonous powder, or a lethal dose of something to exact revenge? Vince is insane and may be ramping up his game.

I leave the letter lying like a coiled little snake on the doormat while I go and search for a pair of latex gloves and a face mask to cover my nose and mouth.

"Madeline, what are you doing?" Mom is standing near the door holding dear old Tosca. Both are staring at me with big eyes.

Getting ready to open a letter from Vincent.

"Don't worry about it, Mom. I'm dealing with something—just being careful."

I grab a letter opener and flashlight from the hallway. A morbid curiosity draws me back onto the porch, and in a minute, I'm standing in the dim light contemplating the thick, white envelope. As I pick it up gingerly, holding it at the corner, my mother comes outside, followed by Mrs. Auerbach and Torvill.

"A letter?" Mom says. "I thought you caught a skunk or something."

"Stand back," I say sharply. "I don't know what's in this, and I'm being careful."

Shaking the envelope does not produce any rattling or loose powder. When I squeeze the contents, all I feel is the heft of paper, no more, no less.

Torvill makes a happy bark and heads toward me.

"Stay!" I command, and he drops to the ground, whimpering.

I slit the envelope and shine my light inside. A simple letter, and here I am standing like a ghost in a mask and white gloves, a sharp little spear in my hand.

When did I last receive an actual personal letter?

"Good God, Madeline, what's wrong?" Mom says, advancing. "You're being Halloween crazy."

Mrs. Auerbach puts her hand on Mom's arm. "Let her read it, Janet."

Big buddies, those two. They creep me out.

The thick, creamy paper crackles sharply as I unfold it. In the skeletal glow of the flashlight, I see handwriting with tall, impatient letters bursting off the page.

My Dearest Madeline,

What I'm about to say may take you by surprise because we haven't known each other very long. Our acquaintance has, however, been intense, certainly from my side. Listening to you speak about your work and observing your brilliance up close, meeting your lovely mother, and seeing your home and pets, has made me realize you are the right woman for me. If I were a poet, I'd try and say something like woman of my soul.

Before you tear this up, hear me out. I'm proposing marriage to you, with the understanding that you do not love me now, but that love will eventually grow. I would make no demands on you, physical or otherwise. You would be completely independent, conducting your life as you usually do. All I would offer is love and support, and I'd help you as much as I can. It would be a joy and privilege for me to be by your side and watch you thrive.

This proposal comes with the assurance that Janet, your dear mother, would live with us, and her assistant too, as well as your delightful pets. I am charmed at the thought of welcoming your family into my life. I promise to do all I can to nurture Janet and keep her safe, including finding a replacement for Gretchen Auerbach if she turns out to be unsuitable.

Please know that I'm not motivated by your wealth. I myself have a small fortune that is waiting to be lavished on you.

Here are some intangibles that I'll bring to the table. A mutual love of science and math, and a shared obsessiveness about our respective endeavors. The joy of investigating serious topics. A contempt for trivialities. I'm an articulate man who can also—occasionally—be eloquent. A tall, reasonable-looking, virile man who appreciates your beauty. I will always be faithful to you.

Madeline, I'm not a young man. I've spent many years searching for the right person. Now that I've found you, I cannot let you go.

I have no false modesty, and am truthful about my strengths and weaknesses. Please know that my major strength is perseverance in the face of obstacles.

My main weakness right now is I haven't succeeded yet in winning you over.

Please don't dismiss this marriage proposal out of hand. I urge you to set it aside and think about it. It is not an offer you can refuse.

Madeline, I await your response, serene in the knowledge you will do the right thing.

Be aware you have in your hands my future happiness. It's a fragile thing. Handle it very carefully.

Love and, dare I say, kisses?

Vince.

I sink down against the pumpkin Mrs. Auerbach has carved and, still holding on to the letter, hang my head between my knees.

Oh hell.

The dangling skeleton knocks in the eaves as a sudden gust blows through its bones.

"What is it, Madsy? Is he threatening you?" Mom cries. Relinquishing the cat and dropping down next to me, she hugs me close. Her desire to get her hands on the letter is stronger than the wind.

Mom and Mrs. Auerbach cannot be allowed to see it.

"Yes, he's threatening me," I say, folding the letter, inserting it in the envelope, and shoving it down the front of my sweater and into my bra.

I don't want their advice. And the last thing I need is Mom saying yes to Vince on our collective behalf. No, I'll hold these radioactive words close, sleep with them under my pillow if necessary.

In the privacy of my study, I scan the letter into a safe backup space on the cloud.

It's my first tangible evidence.

CHAPTER 21

The Cambridge Police Department is about eight miles from my office, an imposing redbrick and glass building on Sixth Street. It takes me less than half an hour on Monday morning, aggressively threading the Jeep through traffic and going head-to-head for a good parking spot.

I'm in no mood to be tangled with.

The CPD has walk-ins, and I announce myself at the front entrance. A woman in a crisp uniform asks me to state my business. There are other people at the counter, and I lower my voice. "I'd like to file a complaint. I'm being stalked."

"Are you in immediate danger?" she asks.

"I don't know," I whisper. "Could I speak to someone in private?"

She pushes a form toward me and says, "Fill this out in the waiting room, and you can speak to the next available officer."

Five other women are sitting in a small, generic waiting room, all fidgeting and probably in some state of trauma. I suspected there'd be a wait, and I munch listlessly on my emergency lunch apple.

The piece of paper in front of me requires my name, address, age, occupation, and complaint. Two inches of white space to state my grievance. How can I possibly convey how Vince has invaded my life? The phrases I use are awkward and melodramatic, bad writing in a daytime soap opera.

Won't take no for an answer. Intrusion into my house. Following me.

Officer O'Connell, sitting across from me in a tiny room, has a haircut much like my own. He actually looks a bit like me, with a thin, prominent nose and a face that discourages bullshit. He appears to be somewhere around my age. After reading my complaint, he says, "How long has this alleged stalking gone on?"

"Excuse me, Officer. The stalking is not alleged, it's real. And it's been going on since Saturday, October 19th."

He raises his eyebrows. "By my calculation, Ms., uh, Geiger, that's a little over a week."

"You got it, Officer O'Connell. He's been harassing me for more than a week."

He narrows his eyes ever so slightly.

He's not in my corner.

"What evidence do you have?"

I scroll down my phone and lean across the desk to show the cop the texting stream from Vince. *When can I see you again? Lunch next week?* And then my replies. *Sorry, can't make it. No, no, and no.*

"Dude really likes you," O'Connell says. Then, without permission, he scrolls further up. "I see you guys made a dinner date for last Saturday."

I lean across and take my phone back. "He's not a dude, Officer, he's a stalker. After that date, I asked him not to contact me again, but he ignored me."

"That's hardly stalking, Ms. Geiger. Red-blooded men persevere with women they like. You should be flattered."

I sit back and stare at him. Every ounce of self-control goes into staying in my chair and keeping my hands off the officer's neck.

He lifts his palms toward me in surrender. "Tell me about this, uh, stalking." He studies my complaint again, shaking his head as if he's missing something.

"This past Saturday, he kidnapped my mother," I say, the pitch of my voice rising.

Stay calm.

His head snaps up. "Did he use violence? What happened?"

"My mom has dementia. He came into my house while I was away and somehow convinced her to get into his car. When I got home, she was gone. No message." The memory is harrowing, and my hands are shaking.

Officer O'Connell is finally showing interest. "How did your mother get back home?"

"Vince brought her back after several hours."

"Was she harmed? Could she talk to you?"

I must thread the needle carefully.

"I don't know if he harmed her. When she got home, my mother felt ill, had a backache, and would not eat dinner, which is uncharacteristic."

He's shaking his head again.

"There's something else," I say. "On the day he took my mother, he came into my house uninvited—I've never given him my address—interfered with my pets—who have since not been themselves—and he went into my bedroom, handled my personal belongings, and convinced my mother to give him a pair of my earrings."

At last the cop has started listening.

"The man is intruding in my life, Officer O'Connell, after I've asked him not to contact me again."

"I get it, Ms. Geiger, that you don't want to see this man again. But it sure seems to me that your mother, who is an adult, willingly consented to his activities in your house, and also accepted his invitation to go out with him." He sighs heavily.

Officer O'Connell is pissing me off big time.

"Have you heard what I just said? My mother has Alzheimer's. She's unable to make rational decisions. Vince knew she was unwell and took advantage of her, invading our privacy, taking my jewelry."

"I've noted the dementia," Officer O'Connell says mildly.

I place Vince's letter on the desk and move it toward the officer. "Read this. It was on my front doorstep last night, which means this man was at my house again uninvited. It's the final straw after I've repeatedly asked him to stop contacting me."

He's immediately suspicious and doesn't touch the envelope, sitting back, away from it. "What's this?"

"Don't worry, there's nothing inside but a letter from him."

O'Connell removes the creamy stationery and lets his eyes rove down the first page. His face creases in what looks like disbelief.

"Ms. Geiger, most women would kill to get such a proposal. This guy really loves you. He doesn't want to harm you, he wants to marry you."

This is one obtuse cop. Or is he himself a stalker?

"Can't you see the *threat*, Officer, after I've expressly told him I don't want to see him again? Look at some of the wording—*an offer I can't refuse?*"

"I'm sorry, ma'am, I don't see any evidence of stalking in what you've told and shown me. It's been less than two weeks, and all

I see from this man is love and kindness. What has he done to explicitly threaten you?"

He's actually *indignant*on my stalker's behalf.

I know I'll regret it, and take a deep breath before plunging in. "His area of expertise—professionally—is mind control. I believe he's experimenting on my pets, my mother, and our housekeeper."

"Wait a minute."

"Hear me out, Officer." I lean toward him with all the force of my tall-strong-woman personality.

Officer O'Connell stares at me in a way I've seen before. *God help the men who marry women like this.*

I say, "Since the Saturday my mom was taken, the behavior of all living creatures in my house has changed. Radically. I know without doubt Vince harmed them physically and is controlling what they do."

O'Connell has put his pen down. He's not recording any of this. His whole demeanor is saying, *time to call in the next crazy woman from the waiting room.*

"And is he controlling *your* mind too, Ms. Geiger?"

Jerk.

"If the answer were yes, I wouldn't be here, would I, Officer O'Connell? But I think it's only a matter of time before he tries."

"I'm struggling to take this complaint seriously," he says. "We deal in reality here—beatings, bruises, injuries, threats."

He's confident in his toxic smugness, so I say something in language he understands.

"Is there a female officer I can speak to? Someone who understands the implicit threat in everything I've shown you? I'm willing to wait." I try to maintain an edge of civility in my voice.

He shrugs. "It doesn't matter who you talk to; we all follow the same playbook. You'd be wasting our resources."

"It's only a matter of time, Officer, before this man escalates the threat and leaves bruises or worse on me. I'm filing this complaint preemptively. If he doesn't get a restraining order now—or at least a strong warning—I'll be in trouble. And your name will be on the report that recommended I wait and see." My knees are knocking together under the desk. I want to land a kick on him where it hurts.

His mouth is set in a thin, slightly slanted line as he rises to dismiss me.

I have no choice but to stand too. "Please note on your summing up that I fear for my safety, Officer O'Connell."

This is how we leave things: O'Connell will open a digital file for me and scan my complaint into it. "If you feel threatened, Ms. Geiger, please don't hesitate to call us." He says it completely straight with no sense of irony at all.

The futile conversation spins in my head as I drive along Memorial Drive back to my office.

No, Ms. Geiger, not enough substance to issue a warning to Mr. Cantley.

So he's free to continue stalking me unhindered?

We need more ammunition, I'm afraid.

His turn of phrase gives me an idea.

Time to order a ghost gun online.

CHAPTER 22

After arriving home, I go inside to check on my mother. She's in the kitchen with Mrs. Auerbach, who is helping her grease cake pans. Mom is not as deft as she used to be, dropping globs of Crisco onto the countertop.

"Torvill isn't himself today," Mom says. "He peed on the living room floor."

He's never done that before, not since I've known him. I find him in his nook near the pantry, lying on his side. Tosca, his constant companion, is nowhere to be seen.

I drop to the floor and put my arm on Torvill's warm, furry neck. "What's up, pal?"

He summons the energy to lick my cheek, but his ears are down and there's an uncharacteristic lethargy about him. Since the Saturday Vincent "played" with my guys in the kitchen, they've been hostile to each other and listless when on their own.

Time to schedule a vet appointment.

At my office, Buck is making sheep's eyes at Shawna. I wish he wouldn't. Since my world is off its axis, I'd like the people in my orbit not to tilt it more.

"Go fix that computer, Bucky-Ball," Shawna says, as Buck scampers away.

"Bucky-Ball?"

Shawna chuckles. "That boy needs so much help. We're gonna hang after work today so I can set him straight."

"What about Lonnie?"

"What about him?" she says, miffed. "Buck and I just going for a drink after work. You know, like friends? Colleagues?"

"Don't encourage him. You're going to break his heart and then he'll have to leave."

"I got it, Madeline. Don't worry your head about it."

Another thought is uppermost, and I sit across from her. "Shawna, if that guy Vincent Cantley comes by, please don't let him in the front door."

"He still bothering you?" She gives me her sympathetic look that says *tell me more.*

"Look at this." The marriage proposal. "Keep it confidential. I need advice."

When Officer O'Connell read the letter this morning, my heart was in my stomach. With Shawna it's different. I trust her totally, a feeling that's reinforced when she turns to page two and says, "Oh shit." I wait for her to finish reading.

"How do I respond without provoking him? I'm terrified that just by writing back he'll take it as a positive development. Should I ignore this and not reply? I'm tempted—"

"You can't not reply," she says, slapping the pages onto her desk. "It'll give him a reason to hound you more. He'll feel mad at you and justified. I know men. They go for the smallest excuse to hassle you. And I bet your man will be"

"He's not my man, okay?"

"Ok-ay." She gives me the dimples and reaches across the desk to pat my hand.

I say, "I'm going to ask Jessica to send a cease and desist letter." That's Jessica Kim, my man-eating lawyer who sets up business contracts with my clients. "I should have told her about this long ago."

"Brilliant idea," Shawna says, "but you can't use it as a copout. You need to write a personal response."

"Type, not write. The last thing I need are odes to my beautiful handwriting from him."

"Don't worry, I've seen your writing. Ain't gonna happen, darlin'." She grins.

"So what do I say? Hi, Vince, thanks for your proposal, but no thanks?"

"No, Madeline, that's exactly what you don't say. Don't use provocative words like thanks and proposal. It'll sound like you considered it and then rejected it. He'll tell you he can wait forever." She drums the table for a few seconds, then says slowly, "I wouldn't go with the 'Hi Vince' opening because hi sounds too cutesy. How about Mr. Cantley, followed by something like: fuck off, get the hell out of my life, and don't come onto my property again." She looks at me with a quizzical stare to check that I'm following her drift. "You can even say you've contacted your lawyer, who'll be in touch with him too."

That's Shawna, my on-site social genius.

In my office, I load some business stationery into my printer and draft a business letter. The address I type on the letterhead is his lab's. I don't know—or care—where he lives.

Mr. Cantley,

The answer to your offer is no.

I am stating unequivocally that I do not want to hear from you or see you again.

Stay off my property and away from my place of work. Do not text, email, or call me. Do not write to me either. I will not respond.

And do not contact my mother, who, as you know, has diminished mental capacity due to Alzheimer's.

Sincerely,

Madeline Geiger

After *Sincerely,* and before my typed name, I sign: *M. Geiger.* Crisply, I fold the letter in three and slide it into an envelope that is addressed to Dr. Vincent Cantley and has his lab address typed on the front. There are two Forever stamps available to me, an American flag or a Halloween stamp with a black cat. I select the flag—less provocative—and make sure all is sealed and square. Then I go out immediately to drop the letter into a mailbox on the street.

Done and dusted.

Jessica Kim, whose law offices are in Cambridge, stops by to see me in the afternoon.

"Is that *Star Wars* I hear?" she says as I shut the door.

I tell her about the HackMeister and his music. His essence.

Standing next to Jessica, I'm the giant who ate the princess. She's petite, about five feet tall, and favors five-inch heels and tight black skirts. She's the stereotype of the killer Korean action character, with her short, black bangs and bob hairdo. She has taken care of my legal needs since I've been in Boston. That includes getting a nice settlement from the sexist boss who fired me.

Right now, Jessica is sitting, knees crossed, speed-reading my marriage proposal.

She's already processed Vince's text messages, a transcript of his emails, and a description of Leo, who's been tracking me. The "incident" with my mother was a little trickier to describe. Also, the "playing with" my pets, and the mice, rats, and lights. It was a relief for me to move onto more solid ground—the obnoxious ubiquitousness of Vince in my life since those ill-fated dates.

"He googles me every day. He's obsessed."

"How do you know this?" Jessica came to the US from Korea when she was five. She's now about forty-five but retains a hint of an accent. Her speech is charming. She has a golden voice that is eloquent in the defense of her clients.

I confess to the spyware I installed on his computer.

"Unsay that, I don't want to hear it," she says, removing her dark-framed glasses and fixing me with a direct stare. "To win these cases, everything we do must be aboveboard."

I tell her about Officer O'Connell and his digital folder.

"You got a dud cop. Repeated harassment, even if the stalker claims romantic interest, is a crime in every state."

"Yeah, he said the dude sounded very nice. You know, like what's the matter with me?"

"Yeah, bad male cops are a problem when it comes to stalking. They're probably channeling the guy and thinking that's how they would act."

"So what am I supposed to do?"

"Listen, Madeline, everything you've described—the texts, visits, house invasion—are illegal. They intrude on your privacy. And here's the other thing. You don't have to wait for a physical attack to happen to get a protective order. The crime is harassment without assault. And you qualify."

Some weight comes off my shoulders as she speaks. I love her.

"Don't respond to his latest salvo, the marriage proposal," she says. "It'll just egg him on." She inserts Vince's letter into her briefcase.

"Too late. I already mailed him a response." I slide a copy of my letter toward her.

"This is fine, as long as you understand it won't deter him." She adds it to her briefcase. "He'll respond for sure. I know this type. They feel justified by their so-called love and the fact they haven't physically harmed you."

"So what's next?"

She crosses her small hands with their manicured red nails on my desk. "I'll compose a cease and desist letter, which I'll share with you to get your approval. Then we'll wait and see if it does the trick."

My package from someplace on the dark web containing the kit for a small Glock-19 ghost arrives the next day after lunch.

Guns and I have an unhappy history, which means I'm a persona non grata when it comes to background checks. A tenant of mine in Ithaca committed a gun crime in my house, leading to my name on a black list in New York State. When I applied for a gun permit in Massachusetts, I failed the background check. Good old innocent me. *Permit denied.*

That was during the time of my obnoxious boss in Boston.

So now I'm looking at an illegal ghost gun kit from a dodgy website. I'm good at tinkering, handy with tools, always the one who can put together anything from a box. After a really fun hour or two of drilling, sanding, and lubing, I have an elegant black gun that's a dead ringer for the real thing.

On Tuesday afternoon, I hop in my Jeep with my gun and take myself to the Boston Firearms Training Center, which is no more than fifteen minutes away from Cambridge. My beefy instructor holds me tight during our session, teaching me how to aim, pull the trigger, and steel myself against recoil. Mr. Beef tells me I'm a natural.

Every time I point and shoot, Vince's head explodes off his shoulders.

CHAPTER 23

They know the pet carrier for Tosca means one and only one thing: a visit to the vet. As soon as I bring it to the kitchen, Torvill collapses onto his tummy and gives me the frantic Halloween eyes, while Tosca, in a great burst of energy, tries to escape from the kitchen. We're a good team, Mom and I, capturing our spitting, fighting cat, shoving her headfirst into the carrier and snapping the flap shut.

When we walk outside on this overcast Wednesday morning, Mom carries the yowling cat, while I drag about a hundred pounds of squirming dog out of the house.

They hiss and growl at each other, Tosca on the back seat and Torvill refusing to go anywhere near her. He hurls himself onto the front seat, whining and generally out of sorts. We are headed along the tree-lined Craigie Street toward Cambridge Veterinary Services on Massachusetts Avenue. The farther away from home we get, the calmer the animals become.

Out of range of the router.

Dr. Karl Kovacs, who's a cross between Santa Claus and a Cavalier King Charles Spaniel, greets us jovially. "Well, well, well, what have we here?"

The room is like a kiddie paradise, with fuzzy blankets, chew toys, and tasty treats on the doctor's desk. Torvill is first up on the steel table, his paws clicking on the shiny surface, his eyes wild with agitation. The doctor scratches and snuggles him into submission.

"What's up with this big feller?" he asks.

"Please hear me out because my theory is really weird." I've decided to plunge right in. I don't want him to send us home with a blessing and multivitamins.

"Ah, Madeline, these walls have heard everything."

"A man—a bad actor—talked his way into my house about ten days ago while I was out and spent time with Torvill and Tosca. My mother says he played with them."

Dr. Kovac's face, which is normally creased with smiles and humor, is frowning.

"This man has a lab where he controls the brains of rats and mice by inserting tiny lights in their heads and varying the light frequency. I believe he somehow implanted lights in the heads of my dog and cat, because they haven't been the same since then."

The doctor, with his right hand stroking my dog's flank, sits heavily on a chair next to the table. He motions that I take the chair across from him.

"What evidence do you have of this? What are their symptoms?" His voice is even, but his skepticism shines through.

"Ever since I've known these animals, they've been best friends. Since the home invasion, they can't stand being in the same room together."

He sighs with a sound that echoes through his cavernous chest. "I've known you for a while, Madeline, and you seem like a very sane person. So I'm sure you can accept that sometimes when animals age, their personalities change."

My body slumps in frustration.

Dr. Kovac says, "Can you tell me what on earth this man's motive could be?"

"He's been pursuing me, trying to get me to date him. I've had to send a cease and desist letter through my lawyer."

Dr. Kovac whistles long and loud, and both animals snap to attention. "So tell me, what exactly do you want from me?"

"When you examine them, check their heads, faces—maybe necks—for signs of microsurgery." Briefly, I lower my eyes. *God, did I just say that?*

The amiable doctor stares at me, his bushy eyebrows raised.

I exhale. "Find those lights, Doctor. Or tell me definitively there are no lights."

"I can't do that without a CT scan."

"Then order one." Again, I must use the force of my personality to impose my will.

He inclines his head. "There's a long line of sick animals waiting to get scans," he says.

"My guys have been tampered with in a way that makes them sick. They need to get in the queue for treatment." I approach Dr. Kovacs and put my hand on his arm. He's such a nice man. "Please, Doctor, do this for my babies." My voice catches.

Torvill is lying on his side. With infinite gentleness, Dr. Kovacs probes his face, head, eye sockets, and the bridge of his nose. He flashes a light in my dog's eyes. By now, Torvill is hypnotized and will give himself up as a sacrifice to this shaggy creature with white, curly hair and a bushy beard.

"Okay, no signs of facial surgery," Dr. Kovacs says in a quiet voice. "Come along, feller, we're gonna flip you on your back." He leans over my dog, who licks his face. With a deft movement from the vet, Torvill is plopped onto his back.

He emits a shriek, a high-pitched bark that chills my blood. Still barking sharply, he scrambles to his feet, his paws slipping on the table in his frenzy. His eyes roll in his head. It all happens so fast and unexpectedly, the doctor and I are momentarily paralyzed.

The sound of my dog's distress is terrible in that room.

Within a few seconds, Dr. Kovacs has gathered Torvill into his lap and is holding him tenderly, his head on the dog's head, his nose rubbing the dog's nose, and his big hands stroking his fur. The barking stops, but Torvill is breathing heavily when Dr. Kovacs places him tummy down on the table. Slowly, Dr. Kovacs works his way along Torvill's spine, parting the fur of his neck and back and peering at patches of exposed skin under a magnifying glass. Everything is sore—I don't need a vet to tell me that. I can barely watch while my darling boy whimpers and cries during the examination.

"Normally I would say it's mysterious, these tender spots on the back. There's nothing visible. But given your story and the big guy's obvious distress, perhaps we should investigate with some imaging."

I hate that my dog is hurting. "That evil man is responsible, I know it."

"Let's check Tosca," Dr. Kovacs says.

My big, beautiful cat, freed from her cage, is trying to get the better of a ball of string on the carpet. When I place her carefully on the table next to Torvill, she rubs her head on his leg.

"No hostility at all," Dr. Kovacs says.

"Because we're out of that man's signal range," I say. It's completely logical—no signal, no weird behavior. As soon as we get back home, the hostility will resume. *I must find that router box.*

"Come here gorgeous girl," Dr. Kovacs says. She purrs under his touch, a deep vibration.

Carefully, the vet strokes her back, pressing gently along her spine. Several spots make her jump, but she endures the examination with more equanimity than Torvill.

"Our Tosca also has a tender back," Dr. Kovacs says.

I expected no less.

Dr. Kovacs has completed his examinations and administered the necessary routine shots. Lots of crying and yelping from my babies, and two pairs of baleful eyes.

"I'll order CT scans for both of them," Dr. Kovacs says. "The pain in their backs is abnormal, and we should take a look at what's going on."

"Thank you."

"However, there's a long wait. So many animals and afflictions." He shakes his head sadly.

The earliest available appointments are after next week. I have no choice.

I need proof.

CHAPTER 24

On Wednesday afternoon, Shawna pops her head around my office door. “There’s a woman outside. Wanda Hargraves. Says she’s a friend of yours. Should I buzz her in?”

We haven’t been in touch since Sunday, when things were strained between us. I didn’t give her my work address, which means she must have googled my business expressly for this visit.

A premonition of bad news settles over me. “Show her in.”

With a strange kind of preemptive heartache, I take in her luminosity and self-possession as she walks in—thick brown hair swept up at a jaunty angle, and the whole package of her in power sneakers, blue jeans, and an elegant navy jacket.

I shut down my desktop and invite her to join me on the couch. “Coffee? Tea?” The offer comes out sounding like gravel, and I clear my throat. I’ll need steel in my spine.

“No, thank you.” Precariously perched on the edge of the couch, she looks down at her hands, then up at me. “I’m so sorry, Madeline.”

“What’s up, Wanda?” But of course I already know. She’s giving me the heave-ho, and we barely know each other.

“I came to tell you in person, because I like you so much.”

"Please cut the sweet talk and tell me the punch line." I'm a bottomless pit when it comes to pain, but I'm not a masochist. I don't want to draw this out.

She nods. "Everything in my world—math—is logical, Madeline, and I thought that would be your thing too. You know, rational thinking? Right now, I can't deal with ramped-up rodents and lights in peoples' heads and car chases around Boston." Her face is sad, and she doesn't look away. "On the dating site, you seemed so perfect for me. And at my apartment. But I was wrong. I can't relate to this *tension* you're caught up in." She takes out a tissue and blows her nose, honking at me like a goose. "I feel awful. I'm not the brave, gutsy woman you need right now."

"I'll figure out what I need, thank you. But I appreciate that you delivered the message in person."

A cold bitch, that's what I'm being. To protect myself.

We stand. Awkwardly. There's nothing to say, and I can't trust an embrace.

We haven't even had a proper date, so why should I care?

I move to open the door. "My assistant will see you out."

"Madeline—"

But I'm already at my desk, rebooting my computer, ready to go, a lucrative new contract waiting in the wings. I blink back the tears because, really, they're such a waste of time.

The young man I'm negotiating with is a bit in awe of my whip-sharp tongue and two-tone buzz cut. They adore me, these babies and their startups. I'm the zany Tech Mother who will keep their computers protected. My business is thriving, but I'm driving on empty.

I really liked her. The thought nibbles around the edges and I push it away. If I let it, the sadness about Wanda will engulf me.

The loneliness never goes away, and I must double down. What makes me think I need to find love with a man or a woman or anyone else? Right now, all I want is to go back to my normal life.

Later in the afternoon, Jessica Kim calls to inform me that Vince has received her cease and desist letter. "This is always the most dangerous time," she says. "They never believe the letter. They always think their personal magnetism will win the day. Sometimes they become threatening."

"What will we do if he threatens me?"

There's a pause. "Document everything, Madeline. We'll march right back to the police department and shove the threat under their noses."

As soon as I cut the call, I open my laptop to spy on Vince and his lab computer. One capability of my spyware is to follow keystrokes in real time, and at this very minute, he's typing on it. In fascination, I watch him compose an email to me.

Dearest Madeline,

I'm hurt and baffled by your curt, dismissive response to my marriage proposal. I'm offering you everything—all my possessions, lifetime care for your mother, and undying love for you. And in return, I get a kick in the teeth—your horrible message and a lawyer's letter. A lawyer's letter! I can't believe you felt you had to resort to that.

I know you well, dear Madeline. You would never intentionally be cruel. Don't reply in haste. I beg of you to reconsider. Take all the time you need.

Yours lovingly,

Vince

I sit in suspense, waiting to receive this in my inbox, but he surprises me. He deletes the message. *Breathe.* He's taking Jessica's letter seriously.

But then he starts again.

Madeline,

You're a fucking cunt, just like the others. You're all the same.

He deletes this so fast, I can't believe my own eyes. I slam down the lid of my computer and wait for the icy shivers down my back to subside.

First Wanda, now this.

I'm being stalked and I've been dumped. And yet, perversely, it's a day I've been able to land two big contracts for my business. No one is better at compartmentalizing than me.

That nasty message from Vince doesn't even count as a communication from him, because he deleted it. Technically, he didn't say it because I haven't received it. It wouldn't be allowed as evidence in a court of law because it was illegally obtained. Nevertheless, I transcribe the horrible words from memory, put a date on the note, and add it to my list of Vince transgressions.

My phone pings with a message from Wanda.

I'm being followed by that creepy guy Leo. Could you contact your boyfriend and ask him to call off his goon?

Will this day of horrors never end?

He's not my boyfriend, and I don't control him. So sorry, Wanda, that I've caused problems for you.

P.S. Drive carefully.

I'm so brittle that if I bend, I'll break.

Shawna comes in to say goodbye. It's after five. "The HackMeister and I are leaving."

"Seriously, you and Buck?"

"It's not what you think. I gotta set that boy straight on why it's inappropriate for me to go out with him."

"I thought you did that last week. Remember, I told you that you could blame me? No office romances—*please*. The last thing

I need here is an undertow, or to lose a heartbroken employee. I have enough problems as it is."

"Who's heartbroken, Madeline? You see me crying my eyes out over that baby boy?"

Despite myself, I laugh. "No, Shawna, but I sure can see him bawling and breaking the sound barrier with his stereo over you."

My phone pings again as they're leaving the office. *Wanda.*

That asshole forced me off the road. I guess he's trying to scare me off you. Just so you know.

While I'm deciding if and how to respond, my desktop starts flashing with red lights.

RANSOMWARE ATTACK! THIS TIME IS DIFFERENT! THERE'S NO ESCAPE! ALL YOUR FILES ARE LOCKED! YOU HAVE EXACTLY 48 HOURS FROM NOW TO OPEN THE DIALOGUE BOX. IGNORE THIS AT YOUR PERIL! ALL FILES WILL BE DESTROYED. NAMES AND PERSONAL DATA OF CLIENTS WILL BE PUBLISHED ONLINE!

"Nooo!" I wail to the empty office, jerking to my feet and sending my chair crashing into the bookcase. Where can I find the bandwidth to deal with this? Why is my office computer so vulnerable?

Why are the gods surrounding me saying *Smite!* at every turn?

I pick up my chair and shove it back behind my desk.

Another cliché message pops up on the screen.

YOU HAVE BEEN WARNED! THE CLOCK IS TICKING!

CHAPTER 25

It feels like a full-body Novocain injection. Every part of me is numb.

Brain still operational. Think!

When there's no bitcoin amount, it's especially ominous. An open-ended threat for one of my clients usually means they end up paying more than they could imagine.

My first move is to call Mom. Now, of all times, there's no reply.

Mrs. Auerbach, however, answers on the first ring. "Madeline?"

"Gretchen, I have an emergency at the office and will be home very late. Please tell Mom not to wait up. Where is she? Can I speak to her?"

After a long pause, Mrs. Auerbach says, "Janet isn't feeling too well."

I try to tamp down the ever-present dread. "What's wrong?"

Another silence. "Headache. She's asleep. I'll keep her company until you get home."

Why do I find her so creepy? It's irrational. I must remind myself that whether or not she has lights in her head, I'm really grateful to Gretchen Auerbach.

After the call, I let myself into Shawna's and Buck's offices and fire up their desktops. Clean. No ransomware attacks. So it's just me being targeted, not a network thing. From my laptop, I check the video camera I installed in the basement. It's gone dark. Which means someone has disabled it.

I grab my phone and flashlight and hurry downstairs. The good news is no one is piggybacking on my switch like last time. The bad news is someone has put a strip of duct tape over the lens of the camera.

Will I really have to go through the whole rigmarole of wiping my computer and restoring from backup? And what about finding the perp? The real question is why do I have this weakness?

Resigned to a night of drudgery, I trudge back upstairs to access my backup drive.

It's empty.

Someone has cleared out my backup!

Keeping my head cool, I access my alternative backup on iCloud. A few quick passwords and I'm in!

Nothing but hieroglyphics.

All my backup files have been corrupted.

The air becomes clogged with the odor of my sweat. Unlike the first attack, I'm in real trouble, completely at the mercy of the hacker.

Is it Vince?

Be rational. He's not a programmer. Stay calm. We'll get through this.

That's what I say to clients who come to me to fix their ransomware attacks.

I remove my suit jacket, fold it neatly, and drape it over the edge of the couch. Then I sit on a comfortable cushion and think.

The hacker has to be Buck.

The thought has hovered at the edge of my mind from the start. There's no way a bad actor from outside my office could infiltrate my computer, because my firewall is like reinforced steel. The hacker is therefore someone local, who got into the building and used duct tape in the basement. He knew our passwords. He was computer savvy enough to wipe my backup.

Jeffrey Buck, the HackMeister, checks all the boxes.

Why the hell would Buck hit me with ransomware? He knows I'd figure it out in a minute and fire his ass. He loves his job and his zany office and his dragons and stereo and lava lamp. And he loves Shawna too, because every person who meets Shawna loves her. Buck follows her around like a tomcat. So why would he risk losing his cushy job and the object of his lust? Is it a prank? Buck is incorrigible enough to run something like this through his adolescent brain.

No, I discount that theory. I didn't even know Buck when the first attack happened, and this second attack is clearly from the same person.

Therefore, Buck is not the hacker.

None of it computes.

The decision to call Buck to help me restore my locked files is a mark of desperation, but my business is at stake. My heart is fluttering like a caged bird, and it feels as if my very life is at risk. The call goes straight to voicemail.

Hey, dude, leave a message, beep de beep.

Damn! "Buck, pick up!" I yell at my phone.

I return to my computer screen and click on the dialogue button of the hack page. I type two brief sentences.

Good evening. We've received your message.

Acknowledging the ransom note is always step one. Use plurals to make it sound like you have a battalion of geeks and lawyers at your side.

They reply straightaway.

We have your files. Deposit 100 bitcoins in the wallet below within two days.

So they're asking for about ten million dollars, which is from outer space. Obviously, they expect me to negotiate.

I type, *You're a talented hacker, but we can't pay you that much.*

It's important to compliment the hacker on his computer skills. Irate victims who insult the perp usually cause the price to be jacked up. Telling them how smart they are is a crucial step in bringing down the temperature, and the price. I say this from bitter experience with clients who cursed at the hacker and ended up paying double.

Because I've been polite and obsequious, I expect a sharp reduction in price, right about now.

Shut the door of your office and turn on the camera at the top of your computer.

My eye twitches. What? This is *not* in the negotiators' handbook.

Why?

Your price just went up to 200 bitcoins. Turn on your camera.

A small toggle at the top of my monitor activates the camera. Am I really going to do this?

Turn on yours so I can see who I'm talking to.

My identity is irrelevant. Open your shirt and move the camera so I can see your chest.

My hand freezes on the mouse. It's hard to breathe suddenly.

Is this the price for getting my files back? Is this how you operate? Like a pervert?

Open those buttons. Then we'll talk price.

What is this? A striptease? Tell me the plan, then give me back my files.

I roll my shoulders in a futile attempt to release some of the tension and exhale slowly. He's holding all the cards, and I'll have to debase myself to get back my files. Trying to decrypt locked files without a key is a nightmare. Therefore, telling him to fuck off isn't an option.

Except ... I know my brain is fried, because giving hackers what they want is a loser's strategy.

Slumping and miserable, I open the top button of my shirt. The shrill ring of my phone echoes in my office. *Buck!* I flick the camera switch to off, and say, "Buck, I'm in a ransomware situation. Can you get here?"

"On my way, ByteBeast. Don't give away the store."

Is it possible to love Buck? At that moment, I do.

Price now at 300 bitcoins. Turn on that camera to reduce to 200.

Reduce to 10 for 2nd shirt button.

Christ. Did I just type that? Don't judge me, I tell the imaginary universe, until you're sitting in my shoes. It's hard to think clearly.

10 bitcoins for bare chest. Turn on the camera.

Down to one million. I chew an end off my thumbnail and my hand throbs with pain. Where does this negotiation end? My fingers are trembling so badly, I struggle with the buttons. A drop of blood from my thumb stains my shirt. If there were sounds in this ghastly negotiation, I would probably hear heavy breathing from the other side. Ugh.

My chest is grotesquely bare, with my nipples erect in the cold. I turn on the camera, bow my head and shut my eyes.

The door of my office swings open, and Buck charges into the room.

"Holy crap!" he says.

The world spins.

I grab at my shirt to cover myself, then turn off the camera. "He emptied my backup." I gesture at the screen so Buck can see the dialogue so far. I'm choked up, unable to speak. Completely mortified and at a loss. It's not clear what Buck can do to help, but I'm oddly comforted by his presence.

I move to the window and put myself together while the HackMeister takes my chair and studies my screen.

"At the very worst, we can ignore him and try to decrypt your files. Start with the ones you need tomorrow, because it'll take a shitload of time."

"How did I get hacked, Buck? You know how good our firewalls are."

"If a dude wants to hack you, they find a way. Maybe you got an ex-boyfriend with a grudge who hired a geek to get revenge."

I stare at him. *Vince? Not his style.* But what is his style? I haven't forgotten his recent obscene outburst at his computer.

Another line has appeared in the dialogue box.

Where are you? Right now 10 bitcoins is final offer to get your files back.

"What should I do? I don't want to pay this jerk."

Buck, with his nose stud and glittery earring, contemplates me with a very serious look, his head to one side. "How much can you afford to pay? He's not going to come down to zero. Like, 10 bitcoins is about a mil. Can you do that?"

"I can do it. But I hate to pay an asshole like that in cold blood."

"Know what I think you should do, boss-lady?" He's come up with a plan and bops his head from side to side. He's going to suggest something ridiculous, I know it. He often thinks outside the box and comes up with nutburgers. His word.

"What should I do?" I say.

"Tell him you can't afford his price, but if he comes down to five bitcoins, you'll meet him in person."

"Buck, that's seriously nuts. The guy's a pervert."

"It would be a business decision, not a date or anything. I'd come with you. Have your back. Like in the gangster movies."

"What, you're going to bring a gun?"

"No, I'd just be a threatening male presence." He grins. He's serious. It's an amazement to me that even the weediest weed of a guy thinks he's Macho Man.

He's back to frowning, massaging the problem. My nutty employee is warming to his idea and scheming further.

"Wait, there's a better plan," he says slowly. "You should offer to meet him indoors somewhere if he'll restore your files. No bitcoin payment. That would be your negotiating position."

If things weren't so dire, I'd be rolling on the floor with laughter. What cartoon multiverse does he live in?

"So let me see if I understand what you're saying. I should give him an address where I'd be waiting, and then I'd—what—climb into his car and let him drive me to some grubby room where we'd have a nice chat, I'd do a striptease, and then at some point I'd tell him we're done, get dressed, and could he please, pretty please, restore my files now and drive me back to Cambridge? Is this your plan?"

"You got it," he says. No humor. Straight face. "Obviously, I'd get in the car with you. Then wait outside the room. Kind of like your personal firewall."

His idea for saving my business hangs in the air.

"What do you have to lose?" he says.

The strange logic of my predicament means I'm going to do it. Or something like it. Meet this hacker in person. The alternative is to lose a mountain of money, with no guarantee. There's a sense of all rational thought slipping away while the hacker squeezes me into submission.

The sentence I type in the dialogue box is brief.

In person meeting in Cambridge in return for my files?

Price raised to 100 bitcoins for wasting my time.

I throw my hands up in frustration. "I could have predicted that. What you suggested is ludicrous." What am I doing, taking ass-headed advice from an underdeveloped brain?

"ByteBeast, be cool. Don't give up just because he rejected your first offer." When my consultant pushes his hair off his forehead, he reveals a new outbreak of acne. Oily little spots that he's tried to conceal with beige makeup.

"Let me type something," he says. "You can change it."

I relinquish my seat. This won't end well.

In person meeting in Cambridge, indoors, in return for my files?

I'm listening.

Buck and I stare at the screen. "Holy crap, he's gonna do it," Buck says. He types quickly, before I can veto the plan.

In person meeting in Cambridge, you choose the place, in return for my files?

"This is insane," I say. "If they really do send a car to pick me up, don't come with me. Make sure you get the license plate number, and also track my phone so you know where I am if something goes wrong."

His face loses some of its animation. He wanted to be in on the action. He just doesn't sense the danger to me.

"You're the boss," he says.

"This whole thing doesn't make sense," I say. "Why would he say yes?"

Deal accepted.

I grab the mouse from Buck. "Move over."

What guarantee do I have you'll give me back my files?

The answer flashes back instantaneously.

None.

My knife is in my pocket and pepper spray in my purse, along with my phone, water and an apple. My teenage protector is at my side, anxiously scanning the street. We're outside Cooper Gallery on Mount Auburn Street, near my office building—my choice of meeting place.

My tormentor is late. We have no information about what make of car we're looking for or what the driver looks like. I'm trying to fathom the type of moronic adolescent mentality that would agree to a plan that didn't insist I come alone.

The longer I wait, the less I like the scheme.

A nasty wind blasts us with frigid air. Thank heaven I have my jacket. Buck has one of those ubiquitous, thin windbreakers, and he's doing a little jig next to me, blowing on his hands to stay warm.

One minute he's there by my side, the next minute he's gone. *Where did he go?*

"Buck!" I call out, looking around frantically through the people on the sidewalk.

Something sharp—a bee sting?—pierces my thigh and distracts me, at the same time a rough arm encircles me and presses a rag on my face from behind. Chloroform? I didn't see any of it coming.

The air is filled with purple streaks.

A faraway pain, then lights out.

CHAPTER 26

When I regain consciousness, I have no idea how long we've been driving. I'm lying on the back seat of a well-upholstered car with a rough canvas bag over my head, secured at the back of my neck. Sitting up is impossible, with something attached to my wrist yanking me down, forcing me to stay prone. The cold reality shocks me.

I didn't expect to sit like a princess in the front seat of the car enjoying the scenic route—obviously my hacker doesn't want to disclose his identity and location. But I didn't think I'd be trapped on the back seat with a hood over my head and my arm handcuffed to the door. That wasn't part of the deal.

This is a serious lapse of judgment on my part. I don't even know what the deal is. But what choice did I have?

The back seat was not built for tall people, and my limbs must contort into a pretzel to give me any semblance of comfort. My weak knee is aching. I remind myself firmly that I'm a rational being, doing this crazy thing to get my business back. The personal information of my clients. My entire professional life.

Beyond the stale odor of the hood, I try to get a sense of where we're going. No sounds and smells of the river, so I think we're still in Cambridge.

Did Buck get the license number? And is he tracking my phone?

With my free hand, I grope around on the seat. My phone is gone!

"Hello," I say to the driver. "Did you take my phone?"

"Shut up," he says.

Not a voice I recognize. Hoarse, like he has a cold.

Damn!

I'm getting cramps in my legs and arms, but refrain from complaining. I didn't bargain on being a handcuffed prisoner, but now that I think about it, it makes perfect sense from the hacker's point of view. Will he stick to his side of the bargain? Why would I expect him to be honorable? I'm still deluded that there's some kind of transactional deal here.

What exactly did I agree to? My legs are becoming numb, and with them, my brain. *Focus.* The breathing of my driver, an uneven sibilant rasp, intrudes on my thoughts. What will be the real price of releasing my files? And who will believe my story if I'm physically attacked? It's barely credible to me.

The sounds of traffic have died down and our speed has slowed. It feels like we're in a residential neighborhood.

When the car stops and the engine is off, I say, "Are you the person I've been negotiating with?"

"I'm no one," he says, getting out of the car and slamming the door.

My knife is folded in my pants pocket. It presses on my thigh.

The driver unlocks the door on my unfettered side and leans a sweaty, odiferous body across me to unlock the handcuff. If I wanted to, I could stab him in the groin. But what would that achieve?

He grunts with exertion, but eventually I'm free.

"Get out the car," he says brusquely.

"Can you take this hood off so I can see where I'm stepping?"

"Get out first. There's no curb."

"Seriously? You're going to make me walk blindfolded?"

Tentatively, I feel my way out of the car. The perfume of trees and foliage is strong.

While I'm trying to assess my situation—garden or forest?—the driver yanks the hood off my head, grabs me around my waist and shoves another dose of chloroform into my face. The move is fast and unexpected. It doesn't knock me out entirely, but it does disorientate me further.

I have the impression of a brick façade.

A curse on my tongue, as again I pitch forward into darkness.

I'm having a nightmare. Vince is in my bedroom, invading my space, sitting on my bed, holding my hand. I'm in that shady region between sleeping and wakefulness, a twilight world in which the bad dream continues.

He's on my bed! Except it's not my bed, not even my bedroom.

"Madeline?" he says. "Can you hear me?"

Yes, I can. But I'd rather not speak to you.

My head is in a clamp, and I can't move. The prongs of the vise press in, holding me horizontal, my head on a rough pillow. I keep my eyes shut, control my breathing, and try to process my predicament.

Did I spend the night? How many days have passed?

I try to pull myself upright but the pressure is too great, drawing me back. My eyelids droop again. Some of yesterday comes back. Ransomware. Buck, Harvard, chloroform, darkness. Riding in a car with a blindfold, a thug at the wheel who ignores my groans. More darkness. Being led into an unknown house. Oblivion.

Then the nightmare.

I open my eyes, and he's sitting nearby.

"Happy Halloween, Madeline," Vince says. "I'm so pleased to see you.

CHAPTER 27

In the soft light of Halloween morning, with sun filtering through the blinds, he doesn't look so bad. Relaxed in an armchair, calmly watching me.

A fly is buzzing overhead with a stereo sound that emanates from its wings and a speaker in my head.

There's a strange disturbance in my eyesight, reducing the items in the room to two-dimensional objects, their shapes flattened out as if projected onto a plane. The contours of Vince's face seem sketched onto cardboard, his blue eyes painted more or less in the right place, like bad paint-by-numbers.

I shake my head to clear it. At least the clamp is gone.

How can I stop my body from spilling out its edges?

Everything is confusing. Where's the hacker?

"Vince, do you have my phone?" I say.

"Coming right up, ma'am." He digs into his jacket pocket and gets up to give it to me. "You dropped it on the floor of the car."

Reaching out to take it, I grasp at empty space, the phone tumbling onto the bed. Is my depth perception scrambled too? Not so hard to see the phone has been switched off. Nothing accidental about that. A phone can't be tracked if it's off. So no one could contact me.

I'm off the grid.

"Where's the hacker, Vince?" I say. "What's going on?"

"That's all behind us," he says, settling back in his chair. "All the problems have been ironed out." His voice has a melodic thrum to it, turning something soft and loose in me.

But events are moving much too quickly, floating in the air. When I shut my eyes, I recall fleetingly but vividly how my head was held at the perfect angle. How a faint hissing sound and wafting of antiseptic were followed by a short sharp pain, and someone said *anesthesia amnesia.* Afterward, a strange lassitude flowed through my body, a sensation of tranquility. I'm seldom at peace, so this was a pleasant change. I slept like a newborn.

My clothes are on a nearby chair, neatly folded, and I'm in a feather bed wearing soft flannel pajamas. Did Vince arrange all this? How was he connected to the ransomware and that horrible driver who brought me here?

"How did you fix the problem?" I ask, genuinely curious. I know I should be asking more piercing questions, being more aggressive, but why don't I just ... let it go?

"Which problem are you talking about, Madeline?" His face is politely curious, with no malice at all.

It's too difficult to explain, too challenging to clear the fog in my head. I say, instead, "I'm hungry. I haven't eaten since lunchtime yesterday. Could you fix me some tea and toast?" *Do I even like tea?*

He smiles a lovely smile. "Madeline, of course. This makes me so happy. We'll have breakfast together and then I'll drive you home."

A pair of fluffy slippers, open-toed, are on the rug near the bed—perfect for my big feet. When I swing my legs around, I'm hit with pain that stops me cold.

Legs? Back? Head? An everywhere pain.

"Wait! Let me help you, Madeline." He hurries to my side, links his arm through mine, and eases me up with a combination of patience and gentleness that brings a lump to my throat. When was the last time someone treated me with such care?

He drapes a satiny robe about my shoulders, patting it down. Then, slowly, he leads me through the house. *Is it his?*

The kitchen is large and modern, with shiny pans hanging from a wooden beam.

A feast is laid out for me—pineapple slices and blueberries, followed by fried eggs and thick buttered toast. Only one thing is clear. Vince has a definitive algorithm for frying eggs, crisping the whites, poking away the goop, and serving the eggs sunny side up with orange yolks still soft and shimmering on the plate. Ravenous, I plunge the toast into an egg yolk and savor it. Manna from heaven. An egg drop dribbles down my chin, and Vincent walks around the table, picks up a snowy napkin, and tenderly wipes it off my face.

"We're going to start again, Madeline," he says. "Take it slow. This time get to know one another a little better."

I'm not sure how I feel about that. Confusing signals are clogging my brain.

So I nod. "Sure."

"May I come to your house? Visit with you and your mom? Have a drink with you all?" He pauses. "Would this Sunday work?"

I try to wrap my mind around this request, while sopping up the rest of the egg with my toast, cleaning my plate. My head is confused.

Wait! Not my head—my body.

I'm at a loss for words.

"Sunday, yeah, why not," I say eventually.

CHAPTER 28

Where the hell am I?

I think it's the garden of Vince's house. Bits and pieces of falling leaves, swirling around my head like insects. My eyesight is blurred, so maybe they *are* insects.

Vince said he'd bring the car around to the front.

Focus. There's no number visible on the house, so I'll have to memorize the route home. Part of my documentation.

He kidnapped me. Then fucking kept me overnight.

It feels like the middle of the morning, and I'm not at work. Also, I didn't come home yesterday. Mom will be a basket case, and Shawna will be freaking out.

I power on my phone to a blizzard of messages, everyone yelling at me in capital letters.

Mom: *Where are you, Madsy? Did you run away from home? CALL ME!!!!!*

Mrs. Auerbach: *Madeline? What's going on? Janet is REALLY upset.*

Shawna: *Hey, woman, where are you? What's happening?? Buck said it was OK, you'd taken a little trip. That boy sounds like he's on a trip. I don't trust him. CALL ME NOW!*

Buck: *Hey ByteBeast! That slimy dude restored all files! You rock!! PS. YOU OK??*

Vince smiles at me and opens the passenger door to let me in. It hurts my back to stoop down. He leans across to help with my seatbelt, but I put my hand on his chest and give him a strong shove. "It's okay, Vince. I know how to put on a seatbelt."

He grins and shuts the car door. “My spunky Madeline,” he says.

Puke.

I text everyone. *Coming home now. I’m fine. Will explain later.*

But I’m not fine. Of course I’m not fine.

“I need some answers, Vince. Number one. Were you the person I was negotiating with yesterday?”

He hesitates long enough for me to understand that the truth will be obfuscated.

“Yes and no,” he says.

When I slump my shoulders, he continues.

“I subcontracted to someone. The bottom line was he had to get you here.”

“So you weren’t the one who ordered me to undress in front of my camera?”

He slows the car and jolts to a stop at the side of the road. “Oh, Madeline, I’m so sorry. You know me, I’d never do that. It’s so low class.”

“And you didn’t instruct this subcontractor to inject me with a drug, then stick chloroform in my face—twice—and handcuff me to the door of the car?”

He puts his forehead in his hands. “I’m so embarrassed. Of course I didn’t.”

“Why go through the whole charade of the ransomware? Why couldn’t your goon just snatch me off the street and bring me to your house? It would have been simpler.”

I expect him to protest that such a thing is below his dignity, but instead he says, “I considered it. But that would be kidnapping, a crime.” His voice is matter-of-fact.

“You don’t think what you actually did is kidnapping?”

"The difference is subtle, my dear Madeline. You gave your consent to meet in person."

"I was coerced." His gall is breathtaking. "You really think that would hold up in court?"

He touches my arm in a placating gesture. "Dear Madeline, calm down. No one's going to court."

How else will I get rid of him?

We're now in a part of town I'm familiar with, driving along Memorial Drive. For a while it's too difficult to speak, but I have to say it and gird myself with a deep breath.

"At your house, you undressed me against my will. It's a felony—assault."

"I'm a gentleman, Madeline, and would never do such a thing. You *asked* me to help you. I was very respectful. I didn't touch you, if that's what you're worried about."

"What *did* you do to me? Why was my head in a clamp?" An edge of hysteria in my voice. *Unbearable.*

"Whoa," he says. "What are you talking about? Head in a clamp? Are you hallucinating? Aftereffects of the drug, maybe? Or it might have been a nightmare. When we got you into your pajamas, you were asleep in a minute."

"Who's we? Was your thug also helping me into my pajamas?"

He puts his foot down and the car speeds up, jolting my aching back. "This is counterproductive, Madeline. Let's get you home."

For a minute or two, we ride in silence, the outrage thick in my head.

"Was it Leo—your goon—who drove me? That bitcoin-mining guy? Was he the one who set up the ransomware attack?"

"What does it matter? You have your files back." He takes his eyes off the road. "It's over, Madeline. Let's move forward."

I clasp my shaky knees together.

"If it's over, what was it all about? The ransomware and negotiation and kidnapping? Was it so you could make me a nice breakfast then take me home?"

"I wanted us to start again, Madeline. I care for you. It's really as simple as that."

When he drops me at home and tries to have a little farewell in the car, I click open the passenger side and heave myself out, groaning inwardly at my aching back. I don't intentionally slam the car door, but it shuts with a bang. Good riddance.

As soon as the car has pulled away, I call Wanda.

It makes no sense—she doesn't want to see me, but I want her anyway. Her solid-as-an-oak-tree presence. That's the only thought in my head. A distant version of myself recognizes I'm not functioning rationally.

When she accepts my call, I say, "Are you okay? You know, being forced off the road by Leo?"

"I'm fine now."

"Wanda, I need your help. A huge favor." *No begging, please. We're strong women.*

A silence ensues.

"Wanda?"

"What do you need?" Her voice isn't hostile. Just wary.

"I've been injured by Vince, the guy who's stalking me. I'm asking ... would you come to my house and take close-up photos of my head, back, neck. I don't know—bruises, scratches, cuts. Anything that shows signs of violence. I'm documenting his actions."

Another pregnant silence occurs.

"Why can't you ask your mother to do this for you?" she says eventually, her tone reasonable.

"My mother would freak out." *She will no matter what.*

My request is crazy, asking her to drive to Cambridge for a photo session that's vague at best and off-the-wall insane at worst. I myself would say no to me.

But she doesn't immediately say no. Instead, she asks softly, "Madeline, what did he do to you?" Something in the tone of her lowered voice tells me Wanda isn't alone.

She's replaced me.

My brain, still cloudy from my ordeal, comes up with exactly the reply I'd told myself to avoid. "He gave me an anesthetic and somehow—" My voice catches and cracks with strain. *Breathe.* "He has inserted something in my body—maybe a small light—so he can control me." *Don't break down now.* "Please, Wanda, I need your help."

"Oh, Madeline, really? I know you're stressed out from this guy, but honestly—*surgery?*"

She doesn't believe me. Who's to blame her? I barely believe myself.

She says, "I can't do what you're asking. I'm at work having office hours with my students. Leaving now is out of the question."

I clutch my phone tightly, the tension white in my knuckles. "How about afterward, after work?" Desperate and begging. Despicable.

I'm not myself. I need your support.

But my phone emits two low beeps. Wanda has terminated the call.

CHAPTER 29

Lifted by the breeze, the Halloween porch skeleton flops its bones from side to side, its skull in a death grin.

My hands are trembling with apprehension. The house, where Vince has tampered with my family, is pulling me in like a magnet.

The immediate problem facing me is my mother.

I follow the faint drone of appliances into the kitchen, where Mom is making chocolate-covered strawberries for Halloween. She seems sharp in her movements, no shakiness with the dipping and arranging. To break the ice, I pop a strawberry in my mouth, a burst of milk chocolate and tart sweetness on my tongue.

"Don't touch those!" Mom snaps, slapping my hand away. "You treat me like dirt, disappearing, not caring enough to let me know."

"Aren't you at least going to ask me what happened?"

"It's always something different, some new excuse. I'm sick of your selfishness."

The old version of Janet Geiger would have been full of concern. Right now, I can't deal with her new personality and float away from my body, blocking out the sound, watching my mother's red mouth complaining and distorting her face into a repellent blur. Backing away, out the door, I say, almost to myself, "Where's Mrs. Auerbach?"

A shrill voice follows me out. "If you're referring to Gretchen, missy, find her yourself."

The pressure in my head lessens on the stairs, and to my relief, Mrs. Auerbach is on her way down.

"You're home," she murmurs, ghostlike.

She's also acting weird, but perhaps it's just me.

"Gretchen." I pause. "Could you come to my bedroom for a minute? I'd like you to check something."

A curtain falls behind her eyes and she hesitates, her hand lingering on the banister. I sense hostility, even though her face is deliberately impassive.

When we're in my bedroom, I shut the door, wavering, not quite remembering all that transpired. A web has woven itself around my memory and I'm vague on the details. I know, however, what I feel—I'm in pain, and I'm being manipulated. I had thought I wanted to be enveloped by a loving man. I was wrong.

I pull out my phone, select the camera, and after a few clicks, go and hand it to Mrs. Auerbach, who is keeping her distance. "I'd like you to take a close-up or two of my back."

She stares at me for a few beats, holding the camera at arm's length. "Why, did he hurt you?" she asks eventually.

Did I mention Vince to her? Ever?

"I need evidence before I go to the police." I pull up my top, roll down my pants, and lie stomach down on the bed. "Start taking pictures, Gretchen. Thank you."

"What am I looking for?"

"Bruises, scratches, stitches, needle marks. Please zoom in. I want the photos to be as clear and unambiguous as possible." I don't hear her move. "Gretchen?" I say. "Take as many pictures as you need. Use the flash if it's too dark."

For a few seconds, we're in a state of suspended animation, with just the hum of the heating in the house.

Then at last, a soft footfall near the bed, a faint click-click of the camera, disapproving eyes on my back, and goosebumps rising up and down my arms.

The presence behind me is malevolent.

A feeling of lightheadedness comes over me. What the hell am I doing? Having photos of a bruised back doesn't prove a thing.

"How bad is it, Gretchen?" I whisper.

"Nothing, Madeline. No scratches or bruises anywhere."

Her dead voice lands with a thud. What game is she playing? *Of course there are marks on my back. It's killing me.* While I'm lying there, I try to recreate the strange interlude at Vince's house. The featherbed in the darkened bedroom. Vince in his chair, watching me.

After we're done and I've murmured my thanks and rearranged my clothes, I'm ready to be rid of her gray presence. She lingers in the room, watching me.

"Gretchen?"

She takes a deep breath, revealing gaunt collarbones. "Madeline, I hope you remember that I'm going out this evening—no Halloween for me."

I had forgotten. Something about a pagan holiday that was against Mrs. Auerbach's religion.

"That's fine, Gretchen. But I'll be out during the day. Please don't leave before I get home."

When the door snaps shut, I examine the photos. No bruises. Just some close-ups of the fine hairs on my back, the skin smooth and unbroken, no hidden incisions to be seen.

An urge to get out of the house *now* pulls me through the kitchen door into the backyard, squelching through wet leaves sucking at my sneakers into the small courtyard where the garbage cans are kept, into air that smells of skunk. I slide down the back wall, leaning against the brick, my head in turmoil, gray spots floating in my vision.

I must report this latest outrage to the cops, but where to begin? *Kidnapped, handcuffed, blindfolded, drugged?* How can I describe the latest crimes perpetrated on me without sounding like a paranoid schizophrenic?

At the Cambridge Police Department, the woman at the front counter has a witch's hat and a green face. Is this a rogue cop, or CPD Halloween policy?

"I would like to request that someone other than Officer O'Connell (*that male chauvinist sexist pig from last time*) hear my complaint," I say when I finally make it to the front of the line.

"You'll be assigned the next available officer," the green witch says, sliding toward me the form for my complaint and shunting me aside to take care of the man behind me.

Hopelessly, I contemplate the bland-looking form with its two-inch space for my "concise" complaint. *Ransomware, blackmail, kidnapping, surgery.* That's in the first sentence. *Stalking, chloroform, handcuffs, assault* goes in the second line. I add, *Second complaint against Vincent Cantley! This man has been stalking me since our second date and has now implanted lights in my head so he can manipulate me from afar until I say yes to his advances.*

When I read this sentence aloud to myself—just to try it out—a woman sitting near me moves to a seat across the room.

I wait in an uncomfortable metal chair, my back aching, while the clock inches toward 3:00 p.m. It occurs to me I should have asked Jessica to accompany me. Too late now.

More evidence of scrambled-brain syndrome.

Officer Larry Corbett reads my complaint with concern on his crinkled brown face. He has the aura of a man who has seen it all and is unfazed. He places the form on his desk, both hands palms down on it, and emits a deep sigh.

"These are serious allegations," he says, watching me, shaking his grizzled gray head. "Way out there, to be honest."

Even though I feel anything but strong and assertive, I meet his eyes firmly and say, "Please don't dismiss this. It's all true."

"Okay, let's go through everything in detail, starting yesterday afternoon." He types something into a computer and says, "Go ahead."

It's painful to describe, especially my humiliation in front of my computer, my open shirt buttons, my acquiescence in agreeing to meet my tormentor.

"I was desperate to get my files back," I say.

"Will this, uh, Mr. Buck, confirm your story?"

"Of course he will! He was there. He helped me negotiate with the hacker."

"Now here comes a painful question, Ms. Geiger." He laces his fingers together, still with his eyes on me. "Were you sexually assaulted during your ordeal?"

"No. I don't think so." *But of course I don't know if they touched me. I was under anesthetic.* It's hot in this room, and I'm sweating.

"Have you seen a doctor?" he says. "Check for assault and, uh, lights in your head, ma'am." He says it straight—at least I think so—just the slightest edge of something in his voice.

"I have an appointment for tomorrow morning," I say. "It was the earliest I could get."

I leave Officer Corbett with a promise that he'll check it out, my strange story. He doesn't come right out and say he doesn't believe me. He just rechecks that he has the right addresses of Buck's workplace and Vince's lab.

How will Vince explain his actions?

The small ghosts and witches that come to the door scream in fright at the billowing sheet-draped bushes and the dark creatures that sway and loom above them. Some tiny princesses with gossamer wings stretch out plump fingers for the candy and send an unfamiliar pang of longing through me, a broody message that's entirely new.

Babies.

Vince comes unbidden into my head. Does he want children? Is that what this is all about? These thoughts are terrifying. With unfocused eyes, I miss the treat bag of a short, plump monster, who lets out a cry as he drops to the ground to find an errant Kit Kat.

My phone alerts me that Gretchen is out, and I must search her digs for the router that's controlling the lights Vince has planted in all our heads.

As I think about it now, my suspicions seem absurd, and I debate whether to cancel that search and just get on with my life. Something in the house is making me lethargic, and I'm struggling to regain the anger, to clarify what it is about Vince that made me so dead set against him. *He's not so bad, is he?*

The note I've written to myself is firm. *Search Mrs. A's rooms from top to bottom. Find that damn router. Turn off the signal!*

Why am I so agitated?

My mother revels in this night, the ringing doorbell and the trick-or-treaters. I leave her to it.

Despite my torpor, I slip away and climb the stairs. The trek up is uncharacteristically arduous, and I clutch the banister at the top. I peer down into the darkness. All clear.

I can do this.

Gretchen's door unlocks with my spare key, even though I fumble a bit, my hands unsteady. But I'm in soon enough, pulling the door silently shut behind me. Not a sound inside.

I wait for a beat or two then turn on the light. The lamp in the corner flickers anemically, casting the sitting room into a gray and colorless blur, as if Mrs. Auerbach has leached all the brightness out of it. And it's freezing in here, no heat on, with the curtains billowing at an open window.

The place is in disarray. Clothes are strewn about and containers have spilled their contents everywhere. For an absurd moment, I imagine that Gretchen too has been searching for the signal box, frantic to find where Vince has hidden it. I then have another thought. *That man is messing with all of us.*

For a few seconds, I'm at a loss where to begin. Where would he hide a small box in here? Certainly not in the dresser among her underwear and personal effects. Still, the faded walnut chest beckons me. I step gingerly among the obstacles, then open the top drawer. It gives off a musty smell. This morning I accused Vince of violating my privacy, and here I am, with my hands on the inelegant, serviceable cotton underwear of Gretchen Auerbach.

I pause, trying to remind myself of my mission.

The drawer is already disturbed, the bras and panties in a haphazard tangle. A black bra with wire and firm uplift cups sits like a Halloween prank among the puritan cotton. Some literature about Jehovah's Witnesses. It's none of my business what Mrs. Auerbach keeps in her dresser. It occurs to me that my housekeeper may be involved in a deeper way than I know. She's harboring a key piece of hardware, participating in Vince's plan.

None of it makes sense.

I pause, reluctant to abandon the tantalizing drawer. Screams float up from the street and boots clatter on the porch. Despite the cold, I'm flushed, and this place is full of shadows. I listen intently for the telltale creak on the stair, Mrs. Auerbach returning home.

At the back of the drawers my hands alight on something hard inserted in the dark woolen socks. I squeeze. There's no give. Carefully, without disturbing a thing, I lift a stuffed sock from the drawer, insert my hand as if into a sock puppet, and draw out a large bottle of pills, filled to the top. The bottle has no name on it, nor any dosage. Instead, it has a makeshift white label with the word *Morning* scrawled across it.

Further investigation shows more pills and cans of white powder. Every sock is a container. There are pills in the medicine chest and the bathroom cupboard.

Jumbled thoughts collide in my head. *How can I trust this woman with my mother? Where would a drug addict hide a signal box? Perhaps the signal box is on the floor in plain sight.*

I paw my way through the night table, closet, cabinets, and even the bed, feeling revulsion with myself as I pat Mrs. Auerbach's pillow and palpate her mattress. There are enough nooks and crannies in these rooms to keep me here all night, but I'd better move along. Mrs. Auerbach could come home at any time.

I turn off the bedroom light and return to the sitting room. The artifacts scattered about seem random. One item catches my eye and shimmers through my faintly blurred vision. A small flash of glass stirs in my line of sight as I narrow my eyes to focus. There's something achingly familiar about it. I reach for it and lift it off the floor.

My missing glass paperweight!

At that moment, a floorboard creaks outside, and a key clicks in the lock at the door. I am up off the ground, killing the light, and taking a dive behind the couch before my brain even registers the response of my reflexes. I hold my breath, clutching the paperweight against my galloping heart.

Mrs. Auerbach pauses on the threshold, possibly sensing a disturbance in the air. The pale light flickers on. I hear the clatter of debris being kicked aside as she makes her way to the couch, where she sits down heavily. She's so close, I can smell the soapy fragrance of her hair, almost touch it. She rummages in her purse, followed by the clatter of pills and the glug of water.

Next, the sound of texting—tick tick tick.

Ouch. I'm in a cramped position and hope she's not planning to stay on the couch all night.

Mrs. Auerbach's voice, soft and seductive, speaks to her phone. "Everything's good to go. Don't worry about a thing." *Click.*

Finally, she rises from the couch, turns off the light, and goes into the bathroom. I wait until I hear the latch of the bathroom door before I drag myself up off the dusty floor. Slowly, in the dark, I creep to the apartment entrance.

Once outside, I can breathe again.

The Halloween mayhem has died down, and all is quiet. On the stair, I sidestep the floorboard that creaks. My phone pings with a message, startling me.

The sender is Gretchen Auerbach.

Did you find what you were looking for? Be sure to lock the door behind you.

CHAPTER 30

The following morning, Mrs. Auerbach and I avoid each other's eyes. Not a word passes between us about the paperweight or my visit to her apartment. She's jittery at breakfast, pacing back and forth in the kitchen.

Threatening her, interrogating her, firing her—all have occurred to me, but none of them will happen. We both know how desperately I need her to help with my mother.

Torvill stays away from the table and barks sharply at Tosca when she dares to approach.

"Torvill, quit that!" I say, lifting and stroking my jittery cat.

Mom has forgotten about our quarrel yesterday, and before I leave the house, we share a hug. I don't explain to her what happened with Vince on Wednesday night.

I'm on my way to see a doctor, someone who would see me this morning. I will instruct him to find the foreign object in my head and get rid of it. If he gives me flak, I'll move on to the next doctor.

As soon as I leave my house, the fog in my mind recedes. And the farther I walk, the clearer my predicament becomes. The house is poison.

Dr. Patel is in a medical complex not far from where I work. He's a courteous, dignified gentleman of a certain age—old school—who may do what I ask. He clasps his perfectly manicured hands on his desk and asks what has brought a lovely lady like myself to his office.

"I think I have a brain tumor," I say.

He studies my face for a while. "Ms. Geiger, be assured there are many conditions between tension headache and brain tumor. Please do tell me the symptoms you're experiencing." He lifts a Parker pen, ready to write on a blank pad. None of this modern medicine where the doctor types what you say into his computer while failing to size up the real you.

"I've been having severe headaches—always acute, sometimes debilitating."

"Do you have a headache now?" He's monitoring me with disconcertingly piercing black eyes that can probably see right through my dissembling.

I think about how my head ached last night. "I do." *It was held in a clamp. It's still sore.*

"And your other symptoms?" His voice is kind and coaxing.

"My vision has become blurred, my memory isn't as sharp as it was, leg pain and weakness and—here's the worst—mental confusion. *An evil man is messing with my head, and I need you to find the implant. Please.* I blow my nose with a tissue and wipe away tears that are threatening. "I'm under a lot of strain, Dr. Patel."

He does not invite me to hop up onto the examination table. He shakes his head.

"Tell me about the strain, Ms. Geiger, so I have a better idea of the situation here."

He has picked up some wrong notes and wants to solve the problem. And just like that, I change tack and tell him everything.

The truth. He expresses neither outrage nor disbelief. His eyes don't roll when I say "clamp" or "light in my head."

Finally, he says, "Why don't you put on the gown, and I'll do some tests."

The tests are obnoxious, but I seem to come through with flying colors. Scraping the undersides of my feet—yes, I felt that. Needles in my fingers—yes, that too. Knee reflexes, elbows, all perfect. *Jesus Christ!* Jumping when he thumps his hammer on my knees. The doctor stares into my eyes with his little light and says all good. He flips me over to examine my spine.

"Some bruising here," he says, pressing gently.

"Ow!" The pain makes me see stars, like in the cartoons. *Auerbach is a liar.*

"Sorry about that," Dr. Patel says. "How did this happen? Were you hit on your back?"

Whatever happened, my stalker is the perpetrator. Hurt by a clamp? Too outlandish.

"I don't know," I say.

The doctor takes pictures of my back and documents what he sees. He studies my scraped wrist and writes it's consistent with being roughly handcuffed for a period of time. He examines my head, neck, and behind my ears and says there's no evidence of puncturing or a surgical procedure. He orders a urine test to check for any drugs in my system.

Dr. Patel drapes me in a modest paper blanket and asks my permission to check for signs of sexual assault. The gentle doctor assures me that discomfort will be kept to a minimum. While he snaps on a fresh pair of gloves, I mentally escape from the table by composing new software for my business.

"No signs of assault," Dr. Patel says casually, like he's remarking, *No signs of rain today.*

When I'm dressed and back at his desk, he says, "First of all, I'd like to put your mind at rest. You don't present as having a foreign object in your brain."

His words cause my heart to drop to the floor.

"Dr. Patel, there's something in my head that doesn't belong there. I need you to find it and remove it." *Calm. Assertive.*

"Ms. Geiger—Madeline, if I may—you're a software engineer. You have your own security business. You seem like a very together person who is hurting in a way I don't quite understand. I will order an MRI for you."

I exhale with relief. I had feared he was going to recommend a good psychiatrist.

Being away from my house has clarified a few things, and there's something I must do right now.

The lucid version of my mother answers her phone immediately. "Madsy. Where are you?"

Oh, Mom. "I'll be home in fifteen minutes. Please meet me in the garden, under the tree, with the animals."

"But it's cold outside."

"Put on your coat. I won't keep you long."

"Okay, I'll chat to Gretchen while we wait for you."

"No," I say, a little too sharply. "Just you and the animals."

"Madeline, you're acting weird again," she says.

I hurry into the garden and throw my arms around my mother. "Mom!" She's standing—a short little woman—and I hold on to her for dear life. "I'm so sorry for everything," I say. "I wasn't myself yesterday."

She hugs me back without saying a word. She's probably forgotten our awful exchange, which doesn't make me feel any better.

The animals are antsy when I crouch down to embrace them, one in each arm. Tosca squirms away, and Torvill isn't his usual loving self. They want to go back inside. Of course they do, it's freezing out here. I let them go.

"I'm so happy things are okay with you and Vince," Mom says. "He called me this morning."

A blackbird explodes out of the oak tree and caws overhead.

"What are you talking about?" I demand, my voice shrill.

Mom smiles benevolently. "Vince told me you invited him over for a drink on Sunday evening."

"No, I didn't." *Did I?* My time at his house is a blur. I sit on the wet grass, my head in my hands.

Mom stares at me. "Anyway, too late now. I was embarrassed to have him come for just a drink, so I invited him for dinner."

CHAPTER 31

Damn!

"Oh, Mom, I wish you'd asked me first."

My mother's face sags. "But, Madsy, he was so nice on the phone. He says he has a wonderful surprise for us on Sunday."

"He's *not* my boyfriend, and I don't want to see him again." I'm grinding my teeth, and it takes an effort right now to be kind to my mother. I stand and lead her back inside. "Please get this man out of your mind and delete him from your contacts." *How did he weasel himself into her phone?*

It's probably the only thing Mom will remember this weekend—that Vince is supposed to come for dinner on Sunday night.

Somehow, he's using my mother to seep back into my life.

On Friday afternoon, I step through the entrance of my office building, only to find that even here his presence engulfs me, my hairs rising as soon as I come through the door. A fan is whirring nearby, and I shiver.

How is he doing it?

"Mizz Madeline! It sure is good to see you again." Shawna's pure happiness buoys my spirit, but as I move to hug my assistant, my legs are like wood.

"Shawna. Hi."

Don't stand there like a moron. Look lively. Say something brilliant.

"Wowza, I hope you're okay." Shawna inclines her head, scrutinizing me head to toe "You look kinda like a zombie."

I'm fine, is what I want to say, but my speech mechanism falters. *A zombie? Really?*

A flash of dimpled smile lights up Shawna's face. "In case you're worrying, that creepy guy Vincent didn't come anywhere near here while you were gone."

But she's wrong. Vince's power is everywhere.

Come on, be happy about Sunday's dinner. Do it for your mother.

My heart is fluttering with agitation. Did I speak aloud? Shawna is looking at me weirdly.

I ask, "Is Buck in his office?" Something is missing—the familiar beat of his music.

"Yeah, that boy's around."

"Good. I need to speak to him."

Her eyes burn holes in me as I glide by.

Buck's office door is closed but not locked. The knob turns easily. He's hunched at his desk, a keyboard in pieces around him, a screwdriver lodged under the spacebar.

"Hey, ByteBeast," he says without looking up.

He doesn't want to meet my eyes.

Normally, I don't need to muster the authority to command his attention, but today is difficult. The scrim in my brain is making me slow to anger, when I know I should be yelling at him, *Put the fucking screwdriver down and look at me, Goddammit!*

"Where did you disappear to on Wednesday afternoon?" I say. Instead of blasting him off his seat with my accusations, the words come out mild and faintly curious.

He's still tinkering with a piece of the keyboard. "I came here—helped you with the ransomware."

"*After* that. Outside the gallery. When I was abducted."

His face goes into a contortion to manufacture a lie. Still looking down, he mumbles, "One minute I was standing next to you, then you were gone."

Oh, sure.

At about four-thirty, Buck comes into my office and asks if he can leave early. He's done with his projects for the day.

"Sure, go ahead and have a nice weekend." *Catch up with you later.*

As soon as he's out the office, I seek out Shawna, who is typing up a storm. Her hairdo is different today, scraped back into a perky topknot.

"Would you walk outside with me for a minute?"

She looks up, surprised. "Sure. Where we going?"

"Away from here." *Out of range.*

Again, Shawna tilts her head sideways, as if trying to get a handle on this new, strange version of her boss.

Outside on the sidewalk, my head clears. I put my hand on Shawna's arm. "This is confidential, so don't say a word to Buck."

"What's he done?"

"I think he's hiding a router box somewhere in our offices, and I'd like you to help me find it."

Shawna gapes at me, her face screwed up into a frown. "Madeline, are you okay? Why would he do such a thing?"

"I don't yet know, but I'm being harmed at work by the signal coming from that router."

She stares at me as if I've just come out of a cuckoo clock.

I plow on. "I have a key to unlock his desk drawers."

"Can we do that—legally, I mean?" Her normally animated, happy voice is subdued.

"Yes, it's legal—he's harming me and it's my office."

"I'm really worried," she says. "If you're being harmed, why aren't I also being harmed?"

"Because you're not susceptible," I snap. *Why is she being so difficult?* I force myself to take her hand and squeeze it. *Smile.* "One of these days, I'll explain."

Back inside the building, in Buck's office, my head floats off again.

Christ. What am I doing here?

Shawna isn't into the search, half-heartedly riffling through Buck's desk drawers. "Look, a photo of me," she says. "In his top drawer. It breaks my heart."

Right next to it sits a big mug with the words *Code Breaker.*

I fight the impulse to give up the search. *Why not give in to Vince? Just accept him?* There's something dreamy about being in someone's signal, like receiving cool messages from a strange planet, ceding control to another being. Isn't that what I wanted when I joined Professionals.com?

Stop!

Horrified, I fight to submerge the feeling of surrender and smack my palms on the dragons on Buck's wall, and the posters. Nothing. No strange boxes, nothing plugged into the power strip under the desk.

Where would he hide it?

"Madeline?" Shawna says.

It has to be nearby, but Buck is crafty, an outside-the-box creature like me, who would take pleasure in outthinking me.

Laptop computers in various stages of disrepair line the bottom shelves of Buck's bookcase. In a kind of frenzy, I drop down to examine them, pulling each one off the shelf to get to the next one. They clatter onto the floor.

"Oh shit, Madeline, get ahold of yourself," Shawna says, slamming Buck's drawers shut. "This is *so* not okay, you going all paranoid on me."

With an upside-down computer on my lap, my hands freeze. Shawna has never been sharp with me before.

"You too, Shawna?" Sad. "Is Vince using you too?"

She gets down on the floor beside me and hugs me close, her skin soft on my cheek. "Madeline, I'm so sorry about the devils in your head. Wanna tell me about 'em?"

"Shawna—" Tongue-tied and teary-eyed. "It's *my* problem. Please go—leave. I'll tell you soon. Not now."

"But Madeline ..."

We stand awkwardly, and I touch her arm. "Don't worry about a thing. Please go."

She shrugs and heads to the door, pauses with her hand on the door frame, turning toward me. "I sure hope you find what you're looking for and feel better on Monday."

"Shawna ..." But I'm moving through molasses, and she's gone.

A while after she leaves, I call my mother. "Mom, I won't be home for dinner. I must work late."

There's a scrambling on the phone line, a murmur of voices out of earshot.

"Madeline, this is Gretchen," says Mrs. Auerbach in her colorless voice.

I can hear Mom's aggrieved tone in the background, coaching her helper on what to say.

"Janet is asking you to make a special effort to come home for dinner because we're trying out a new recipe for Sunday night."

Oh shit. Abruptly, I cut the connection. The fog in my brain causes a tremble of doubt. *What's the harm in it? Let Vince visit, do it for Mom. He's not so bad, he's not so bad ...*

A stronger voice, my own, says, *Find the damn box.* I drag myself to the front office, pulling my legs out of the quicksand that threatens to sink me.

A movie reel of Buck's actions this afternoon plays through my mind. *Pay attention.* Buck had no fear when I entered his office, not even a swivel of his eyes. Therefore, the signal box is not in his office. Something else. When Buck exited our suite of rooms, his eyes studiously avoided the front area that doubles as Shawna's office.

Come to think of it, because it's easy to access, Shawna's domain is the most likely place. *Is she involved too? Don't be absurd.*

In a burst of lucidity, I survey the room, pulling my entire being into focus. The box I'm searching for needs a power source. The easiest solution, of course, would be to plug it in somewhere, but Vince—or Buck—would surely be more creative than that. I wonder, not for the first time, about Buck's involvement.

Under Shawna's desk is a power strip that takes care of the various electrical needs of the office. I follow a wire to a lamp in the corner that sits on a triangular coffee table whose right-angled vertex fits snugly against the wall. The cord of the lamp emerges from a large circular base and snakes along the wall to the power strip.

By this time, it's dark outside, and the lamp's spherical globe is casting a soft yellow light in the office. As I approach it, I'm quaking with anticipation, my brain urging me forward, while a force field pulls me back. Vince and his soft, seductive voice.

Don't do it, Madeline, we'll be so good together.

A kind of lassitude makes me pause.

I clench my fists, dig my nails into my hands, and command myself to move forward.

The box is right there in front of your face. You just need to see it.

Reach for the switch, kill the light, tinting the room in fluorescent blue from the overhead office illumination.

Every atom of my being resists as I turn the lamp onto its side, using infinite care not to damage it. The base is hollow. A white box about four-inch square is inscribed in the circle of the base, engineered into the lamp, held by some mechanism, its cord entwined with the cord of the lamp, emerging from the base as a single wire, and plugged into Shawna's power strip.

Hot damn! This is it—the source of the signal.

CHAPTER 32

The victory is so sweet that for a while I cradle the lamp in my lap, like a baby. Adrenaline courses through me, igniting my dormant self. I could lose myself in this surge of joy, and—

Put the lamp back. Turn on the light. Let it go, sweet Madeline. The beguiling voice in my head, making me mellow, sapping my aggressiveness, soothing my brain. How easy it would be to float along with Vince's plans, saying yes to everything he wants.

Abruptly, I stand and shove the lamp onto an armchair, lunge toward the power strip and yank the cord out of the socket.

All noise stops.

The vibrating buzzing whirring droning hissing whispering—gone. Silence, like a vast tide surging onto the beach, washes away the debris and clears my mind. I'm free!

Holding the lamp upside down, firmly gripped between my knees, I'm in a stupor of happiness as I study the signal box. The words *Squid.link Gateway* are written in a corner. I know what this is! It's not Wi-Fi, it's a cellular communicator, the technology used to connect appliances to the internet. Speaking to one's phone, saying things like, *Turn off the fridge. Disarm the alarm.*

Activate the light in Madeline.

He's been treating me like an appliance!

It's unbearable to think about it, the way he's controlling me. Why would I ever want to be controlled? Am I really looking for love, marriage—*subjugation?* The joy with my husband, Mike, has grown in my memory since his death. But sitting here in semi-darkness, grasping this control box, I confront the reality that I submerged my career so Mike could succeed in his, geared my research to what he wanted, and ultimately, sat home nights alone while he betrayed me.

What was I thinking?

With a small screwdriver, I stab the lid off the gateway rectangle, leaving the box in the base of the lamp. Inside is a little electronic world, the circuit board of a miniature computer. With my Swiss Army knife, I sever some of the connectors, then for good measure, squeeze a dollop of super glue inside, all invisible damage that will render the gateway useless. Vince will find out soon enough, and my only regret is I won't be there to see his face. Gently, I press the lid of the box back on and it's as if no one touched it. In a minute, I've plugged the lamp back in and switched on the light.

So, it's cellular technology that's been controlling me.

Buck is certainly smart enough to have set up the gateway box in the lamp. But why would he do it? And the whole ransomware thing that wiped out my backup? Buck has the smarts to have done that too. But why, oh why, would he chew off the hand that's feeding him? Was he the one who eventually restored my files? What hold does Vince have over him? Now that I can think clearly, I understand that solving these mysteries is key to getting rid of Vince.

In my office, I fire up my laptop and move to spy on Vince. The software on his computer has been disabled. Of course it has.

This means Vince followed up with Buck and enlisted his services. *Damn!*

And what about the surveillance camera I hid in Vince's lab pointed at his workbench? Did Vince discover that too? I can find out right now.

I activate it, and it's working. As expected, the lab is in darkness—it's after hours. I picture Vince at home, issuing commands and trying to exert mind control. Well, this particular fridge is out of order.

As I sit and ponder the possible whereabouts of a *Squid.link* gateway in my house, a shadow crosses the bench in Vince's lab. It's not Vince, because he'd turn on the light. It must be Leo, Vince's henchman. The bitcoin miner. The goon who followed me and Wanda on the day I met her. He, too, is an expert programmer, operating in the shadows. I wonder if he's the oaf who kidnapped me and handcuffed me to the car. Is he the one who set up the ransomware? What hold does Vince have over these geeky men?

Why don't I ask Leo right now, tonight?

CHAPTER 33

Newly liberated from Vince in my office, I grab a couple of items for my trip to his lab. A small canister of pepper spray attached to a key ring. It may look like a puny pink Pez dispenser, but is a potent pepper spray/tear gas combo that packs an unpleasant punch for any thug who tries to find out if it's for real.

I also retrieve from my office safe my Glock-19 ghost gun, which is locked and loaded. Hopefully no one will test *its* authenticity. A separate compartment of my handbag is perfect for the gun, and I slide it right in.

It's surprising how dark it is on this moonless November night, the bare-branched trees barely visible as I tread my way carefully toward Vince's lab. No crackle of leaves under my boots, the sidewalks cleared and waiting for winter. I pull my jacket tight around me and shove my hands deep into my pockets. I must devise a plan of action.

There's no reason in the world Leo should answer my questions—like, are you the moron who incapacitated me and shoved me into a car to kidnap me? Or, are you the perverted asshole who sent me ransomware and made me strip in front of my computer?

So I must somehow convince him it's in his interests to tell me what his stake is in this story. For example, why Vince didn't fire him after finding out about the bitcoin mining.

But first I must get myself into Vince's lab.

Since Vince invaded my workplace, his is fair game.

There's good news and bad news. My makeshift key gadget works perfectly and gets me in through the outside door with barely a squeak. But when I type Vince's old pin number into the keypad, it beeps and flashes red. He's changed the four-digit code. I know a thing or two about password cracking, enough to tell me that my chance of success is lower than the lowlife I'm pursuing.

The number of four-digit permutations is 10,000, but there are some tricks to lower that number. For example, most people don't create pins that start or end with zeroes. Also, given that you know the previous code—which I do—you can try numbers that keep the same two end digits. People are lazy and forgetful, and often use something to help them remember the new pin. I try my idea on Vince's door pad and go clicking my way through the various possibilities. No luck. My expectation of success was low to begin with, and I'm already planning my stakeout—to wait outside for Leo—when another flash of an idea hits me.

Vince knows my birthday date, because he had this quaint notion he'd memorize it and surprise me on the day. At the time he asked, he hadn't yet turned into Enemy #1, so I happily gave him the date—December 29th. He told me he'd commit it to memory forever, which at the time I thought was bizarre. I certainly didn't play cute and ask him for his birthday.

The conversation comes back to me now, and I immediately dismiss the possibility. *Surely not?* Would he really be that stupid? With stiff, cold fingers, I type in 1229, and the light flashes green.

After staring at it in disbelief, I glide right in. It's amazing how often garbage like this works.

The lab is quiet and deserted, nothing but a low bubbling from the aquarium in the corner. Was I mistaken? Was the shadow in the lab a phantom?

The strange odors of air freshener and disinfectant waft around me as I contemplate my next move. Suddenly, there are footsteps coming up the stairs at the far end of the lab. Leo? Confronting him in this open lab will be futile, because he can duck and hide among the lab benches. The key is to lure him into a confined space.

An obvious solution is the back room that houses the animals. Inside, I play my flashlight over the walls and ceiling, revealing ghostly shadows, but no cameras. Perfect. Breathing through my mouth to avoid the stench, I run my nails lightly over the tops of the cages, setting up a great stir and squealing of rodents.

The door of the room is open, and I crouch in wait behind it in the darkness. Footsteps approach in a slow, wary manner. On the threshold, someone stops and says, "Anyone in here?"

The room is windowless, its only illumination from ambient light in the lab. The animals continue to be agitated, scurrying about and banging against their cages.

The man flips on the light and walks in.

I give the door a shove with my foot, and it slams shut. "Freeze!" I shout.

He stops, standing motionless with his back to me. I wonder if he's armed, since he too is an intruder in Vince's lab.

"Put your hands up and turn around slowly," I say.

"Who the hell are you and what do you want?" He complies, then drops his arms to his sides. It's Leo alright. Chubbier and balder than I remember, but the same familiar raspy voice and sweaty demeanor.

He glares at me. "You!"

I'm pointing the container of pepper spray at his face. "I'm not going to harm you. I just need some information. Like you can start by giving me some details of what Vince did to me on Wednesday night."

"How the hell would I know?" Shifty eyes.

"You're telling me you weren't there?" I jiggle the pepper spray at him. "That you weren't the one who shoved chloroform in my face and handcuffed me to the car?"

"You're fucking crazy, you know that?" He moves toward me, where I'm standing with my back against the door. "No more questions until we get out of this room. It stinks."

"If you take another step, I'll spray chemicals in your face." *God help me, I will.*

"You think I'm scared of that pink little girly weapon?" He laughs and moves to shove me away from the door. He's almost on top of me when I squeeze the cap and spray a mist into his eyes.

"Shit!" He springs away, covering his face and falling to his knees. His eyes are streaming. "Water," he gasps. "I need water."

I reach into my bag and throw him my plastic water bottle. Crouching not too far away, I say, "Why did you run my friend Wanda off the road last weekend?"

He pours water on his face and, in a quick move, throws the uncapped bottle at me and lunges for the door.

In an instant, the Glock ghost is in my hand and pointed at his back. "Freeze or I'll shoot you!"

He turns around, and the sight of my gun wipes the contempt from his face. "Christ. Put that away."

"Get back in here." I gesture with the gun toward the animal room. The last thing I need is this weasel loose in the lab. What I *do* need is answers.

"Please. I hate those pests," he pleads with the same whiny voice he used during the bitcoin mining incident.

"Move back!" The gun is pointing squarely at his chest. "Now tell me why you forced Wanda off the road."

He licks his lips. "Didn't wanna hurt her, just scare her away from you."

"Vince's instructions?"

He nods.

Of course. "Did Vince instruct you to send ransomware to my computer?"

He stares at me, then rubs his eyes, which are still red and streaming. "I swear on my mother's life—" *Poor woman.*

"So you didn't force me to ... negotiate in front of my computer?"

He licks his mouth again. "I would have if I could."

He takes some steps toward me and I shake the gun at him. "Stay where you are. I'm not done. Can you explain to me why you do it, Leo? Vince's dirty work. What power does he have over you? Or is it really just for money? Is it on a per job basis? How much to stand under a tree for two hours and watch my house? How much to track me on a Saturday afternoon? How much to snatch me off the street and deliver me to Vince? That must have been a biggie, what with the injection and chloroform and handcuffs. How much, Leo? What's in it for you?"

His face cracks wide open. "You really don't get it, do you?" His voice is almost wistful. "Like, sometimes guys just help each other out."

"You're right, I'm mystified. What did Vince ever do for you?"

A rat squeaks and Leo jumps to the side. "Shit. *Please* can we go in the other room?"

"Just tell me, Leo. Help me understand."

"Is that even a real gun?" he says.

"Do I really have to prove a point by getting off a shot in this room?" I get into a crouch position and aim at his shoe.

He takes a smart step back. "Jesus! Wait! Okay. When I was in trouble after my girlfriend dumped me, Vince lifted me up, gave me a place to stay and a job. So now I help him out with ... stuff."

"What kind of stuff? Kidnapping stuff? Handcuffing stuff? Running people off the road stuff?" Actually, what he's saying has the whiff of truth. But there's a missing piece. "How did you guys meet?" *How did a rat like you find a so-called high-class guy like Vince?*

"Online. Bunch of guys with women troubles. Bitches—excuse me, *girls—women*—even high-and-mighty chicks like you—always saying no. So we get together. Bitching about bitches. Help each other out."

I begin to see the outlines of something new about Vince, Leo, and even Buck. A deeper understanding of what's animating these men in my orbit. Guys with nothing in common but the inability to attract women. It's as if my eyes are slowly adjusting to the darkness. I've heard about men like this, men who are involuntarily celibate.

Incels.

"What else do you do for Vince?"

He pauses for a minute, like he's sizing me up, or perhaps staring at me with loathing. "What makes you think you're so special?" he says. "I've helped him with all the other women."

Is Vince stalking others?

My world tilts, and I brace myself on a floor that's no longer solid. In that split second, Leo rushes toward me and hits my right arm upward, grabbing at the gun and setting off a gunshot that ricochets off a metal beam and lets loose a screaming and clattering of rodents and a howl from Leo, who is clutching his shoulder with blood everywhere.

This is the price I have paid to find out Leo is mostly telling the truth. But he's unleashed a kaleidoscope of chaos—red, brown, and gray. Utter turmoil among the animals and in my mind. *Did anyone hear the gunshot?*

Leo, pale as a ghost, has sunk to the ground. For now, he's out of commission. I crouch down on the floor and, with shaky hands, place the gun back in my handbag. Everything is receding into the background as I absorb the revelations of the past few minutes and understand one glaring new fact.

The traitor in my office, the source of both ransomware attacks and the destroyer of my backup files, is Buck.

I can hardly believe it, but there's no other logical conclusion. Buck is playing a double game. For some reason, he's become involved in Vince's diabolical plan to control me.

At the instant I think of Vince, it's as if I've conjured him up at the door.

"What the hell's going on?" he says.

CHAPTER 34

He moves toward me until he's violating my space, as if the mere fact of my presence in his lab entitles him to pollute my personal air. He's so close I can smell him—his coffee breath, the sweat, the fabric of his jacket. My spine freezes. I dare not move and dare not speak first.

"Boss, she shot me," Leo whines.

"Must I call an ambulance or will you survive without one?" Vince gives Leo a look of such contempt that he shrinks back as if he's been shot again. The rodents scamper and squeal, re-traumatized by this new presence in the room.

Vince turns his gaze on me, his pale-blue eyes almost translucent behind wire-rimmed glasses. "What are you doing here, Madeline?" His voice is soft with menace.

How the hell did he know I was here?

My story is ready. It has the advantage of being true. "I came to your lab hoping to find Leo. I wanted answers about Wednesday night. The ransomware. The horrible negotiation, the kidnapping."

"And did you get answers?" Neutral. Unemotional.

"No, not really." My voice is steady.

"Why the gun?"

I could tell him any number of reasons, including the true one—for my protection against the jerk who kidnapped me. Perhaps subconsciously I intended to have it go off, to assert some kind of power in this malevolent place.

"Let me set the record straight," I say. "I didn't shoot him. Leo hit my arm and caused the gun to fire. If I'd wanted to harm him, I wouldn't have missed."

"I don't doubt it. So, I repeat. Why the gun?"

"How else would I get Leo to talk?" It sounds true, and I run with it.

Vince looks at me with his cold, noncommittal face. "So what am I to do about this situation? Call the police?"

"No! No cops," Leo whimpers.

"Why wouldn't I? Two people breaking into my lab. Gunshots on my property. Disruption of my experiments. Is that gun even legal? Where in Massachusetts did you manage to get a gun?"

Part of my success in business is knowing when to fold. I'm not holding too many cards on this particular hand, but that doesn't mean I can't play my meager holdings well.

"I've been observing some of these rodents," I say. "I would bet that those against the right wall are the control group, the ones with no lights implanted."

He takes the bait. "What makes you say that?"

"They didn't react well to the disturbance in here. They're still super-agitated. But look at these on the left." I walk to a cage and crouch down. "They're unperturbed. Some of them are half asleep."

My breath is ragged. I'm not out of danger. The power of his eyes on my back is palpable. He's coming for dinner at my house on Sunday. I had planned to cancel, but now, with tonight's debacle, I may have to suck it up and endure his company. I need his forgiveness and must be docile as a lamb.

"You're correct in your observations," he says.

I stand and look him in the eye. *Lie to his face.*

"I'm interested in your research. Would you be willing to show me how you do the light thing—implant the lights in their heads?"

"What do you take me for, a fool?" he says. "I could call the cops right now and report you for possessing and firing an illegal gun."

"But you're not going to do that because my mother is cooking up a storm for you for Sunday night."

He stands and considers it, doing the calculation. All pretense of amicability gone.

"Take one of those rats and show me now," I say.

Inwardly, I apologize to all the critters in this lab.

Leo will be fine. The bullet ricocheted off the ceiling and grazed his shoulder on its way down. It turns out he's a world-class martyr, wallowing in his victimhood.

For Vince, Leo is a distraction in this drama. A flunky. "Clean yourself up, then take care of this room. Later, you can tell me what the hell *you* were doing here."

Vince's scorn confirms my suspicion that Leo is the hired help, paid to do the boss's dirty work.

Fluorescent lights buzz on the ceiling of the lab when Vince flips the light switch. The lab seems seedy, marred by paint bubbles at the edges of the benches. From one of the cabinets, he removes a rectangular white pad, two syringes, and various sterilizing paraphernalia. To my surprise, there are no cutting implements—no blades, knives or scalpels.

My stomach heaves with squeamishness.

He hangs his jacket on a coat tree in the corner and retrieves a clean lab coat from a cabinet.

"This process may surprise you with its simplicity," he says. "Let's go select a rat. Why don't we name him MR, for Madeline's rat?"

We go into the back room together, complicit.

Leo is mopping the floor and scowls when he sees us. "I don't appreciate this," he says.

"Did you or did you not break into my lab?" Vince says.

"But so did she." He indicates me by jabbing a thumb.

My best strategy is to hold my tongue, and I do.

"Yes, but she's not irritating the shit out of me," Vince says.

I shudder. What can I do? I'm in deep.

When offered the choice, I select a smallish rat who seems shy and reluctant, not an alpha, that's for sure. Vince sticks his latex-gloved hand into the cage, and the creature whimpers, backing itself against the wall. *I'm sorry, Mr. rat, I'm cornered just like you.* With a skillful maneuver, Vince tosses the rat into a sort of butterfly net and carries the flailing little guy into the lab, where he places the net on the white pad.

The net is deceptively open—the more the rat tries to escape, the more tangled in its fronds he becomes. Vince discards his gloves and dons another pair. In a minute, he has filled a syringe with liquid and given MR a quick jab in his haunch. Instantly, MR rolls over onto its side, unconscious. Was this the drug injected into my thigh?

"He won't feel a thing," Vince says.

The rat looks dead.

With great dexterity, Vince untangles the creature from the net and spread-eagles him, stomach down on the pad, the front paws and back legs stretched out in an X.

"Rest easy, MR," Vince says, stroking the animal's back, honing in on an area at the base. "This is where I'll insert the light. Amazing new technology."

Vince's laptop is open on the bench. Syringe #2 is attached to a cable that he plugs into a USB port. He fills the syringe from a small ampule, swabs the rat's lower back, and inserts the needle.

Images swirl on the screen.

"This tells me when the needle is perfectly positioned," Vince says. "What I'm injecting is a tiny electronic chip that is so flexible it can travel in the spinal fluid and lodge near the brain." He pauses. Waits for it to sink in. "Light pulses sent to the chip can then control the animal's mood."

The computer image shows a pulsating mass, like an ultrasound in a horror movie. I can't look away. "Where's the chip?" I clear my throat.

"So tiny it's not visible in this image. It's a microchip. Neat, huh?"

I look away and nod. *Yeah, really cool.*

"Where will this rat go now?" The air is dense, making it hard to breathe. A weight pressing on my chest.

"Into a rehab cage." He's dismissive about the fate of the creature, ready to move on. "We have an understanding now, Madeline, am I right?" Again, his cold, rectangular face. When I don't immediately acquiesce, he spells it out. "No one saw a gun tonight, if ..."

"I understand perfectly, Vince." My face is feverish.

I now know how he inserted lights into all of us.

CHAPTER 35

A police cruiser is parked outside my house on Saturday morning. Torvill and I have been out walking, and both our ears prick up when we see the car.

The gun? Or the lab break-in? Or the spyware?

We stand motionless on the sidewalk, dredging up all kinds of trouble that I may be in.

Eventually, the two of us—me wearing my game face, and my dog hanging his head—push on into the house.

Officer Larry Corbett is on the living room couch with my mother, and she's regaling him with details about the Sunday night dinner she's preparing for Vince. All hope of credibility drains from me.

Officer Corbett says, "Ms. Geiger, I interviewed Vincent Cantley at length about your allegations—all of 'em—and he denied everything."

I sit heavily on a chair across from him.

His face is furrowed. "When I asked about the kidnapping, he said you just showed up on his lawn on Wednesday night, drenched from the rain and high on drugs."

"What?" The house pulsates around me.

"He said he took you in, washed and dried your clothes, gave you pajamas, let you sleep it off in his spare room, made you breakfast, then drove you home on Thursday morning. When I asked about, uh, implanting lights, he laughed. Told me not to waste his time."

It's a punch in my gut.

"Obviously, he's lying," I say, winded. "Why would I show up on his lawn? I didn't even know his home address. The truth is I was violently thrown into a car, brought to his house as a prisoner, and undressed by him without my consent." My fury saps my strength, superseding any signal flowing through me in the house.

"Mr. Cantley says that during the night you had hallucinations about being attacked, and it was tough to quiet you down." Corbett is reading from his notes in a fast monotone, as if he's embarrassed. He should be.

"I was there against my will, Officer. This man's story makes no sense. I'm a respected businesswoman. I have no history of being a deranged drug addict who suddenly disappears and shows up raving on someone's lawn."

"I'm not disagreeing, ma'am. Just telling you his side of things."

"There is no his side of things. Just the truth of what happened." Outrage drives me out of my chair. "What about the stalking? What bullshit answer did he have for that?"

"Oh, Madeline, quit that," Mom says, suddenly in the middle.

Officer Corbett sniffs and shakes his head. What's the matter with him that he can't see the outrageousness of Vince's replies? He looks up at me then continues. "Mr. Cantley got his computer open and showed me all those friendly messages between you and him, making dates to meet. He said all contact was consensual."

On and on, all those lies, all this craziness dragging me down.

"Officer Corbett, those messages were early days, before I told him not to contact me again."

Corbett licks his thumb, turns a page, and consults his notes. Clears his throat. "There's more, Ms. Geiger."

"Can we do this outside, Officer? I'd like some privacy." *I'd like some fresh air to dilute the stench.*

He looks up, surprised, and his grizzled face comes back into focus. "Why, sure thing."

We walk outside toward the police cruiser. The blessed cold air helps restore my equilibrium.

Corbett continues. "Mr. Cantley says he didn't know about the ransomware attack. I'll quote him here: 'I'm not a computer expert. Couldn't ever do it. That whole business of blackmail and negotiating with her blouse open is a crock.' Cantley then suggested maybe you faked the ransomware attack just to implicate him."

We're at his car, and I lean on it. "Why would I do such an insane thing, Officer? I'm not a perpetrator here. I'm caught up in some *game* this criminal is playing." Something else strikes me. "Did you speak to Jeffrey Buck about Wednesday night? He was with me when I was grabbed off the street."

Corbett sighs with the full weight of his job. "Buck claims he didn't see what happened to you. Says you just disappeared."

Fucking hell. Fits with my new suspicions.

"Please add to the record that he was standing right next to me at the time of my abduction. And there's another thing I want to add."

The officer nods. "Go ahead."

"I saw a doctor yesterday, as you suggested. He documented bruises on my back, suggesting some kind of recent assault. He noted stress marks on my wrist, consistent with a handcuff restraint." I pull up my sleeve and show Corbett my wrist, which still has marks. He shakes his gray head with confusion. Like maybe I scraped up my wrist to implicate an innocent man.

My phone pings. The patient portal of Dr. Patel's office with results of my urine test.

The words pop out at me—LSD and Oxycontin in my urine on Friday morning, the day after the kidnapping! I enlarge the image and hold it out to Corbett.

"I don't use drugs," I say. "The truth is I was abducted, assaulted, undressed, and drugged by this man, who forced me to spend the night in his house."

"I hear you," Officer Corbett says sadly. "But I'm afraid this test result is consistent with Mr. Cantley's story too—that you showed up drugged on his lawn."

I'm lost in some alternate universe where there are no absolutes of true and false, and the cops are on the side of the bad guys. How will I prove my case?

Corbett changes the subject abruptly. "What about your dinner invitation to Mr. Cantley—your alleged stalker—for tomorrow night? What am I to make of that?"

This is where I tell him about Mom's illness. How she's forgotten about my breakup with Vince. How this dinner—which he wheedled out of her—has become a *huge event* in her life and has been foisted on me. Canceling at this late stage when the curry is prepared and the fancy cake is in the freezer will be a terrible blow. I'm struggling with how to be cruel to my mom in the kindest way possible. It's hopeless.

He listens carefully and nods sympathetically. Then he says, "But cancel you must, Ms. Geiger, to have any credibility concerning this man."

I am not one of his rats. I'm a rational human being with the power of comprehension.

I know what he did to me and what he wants.

Even in the house, with his signal blasting at full tilt, I can fight back. I'm a problem solver, that's my strength. All I have to do is figure out how to get rid of him for good without committing murder.

After lunch, I head to my study to cancel our dinner date for tomorrow. Strangely, I have difficulty composing a suitably cold message and fall into a state of lethargy, struggling to remember Officer Corbett's urgency.

The thrum of the dishwasher floats upstairs and hums in my brain.

Only the ring of the doorbell startles me out of my reverie. My first thought is that Vince is a day early, and we've somehow confused the dates. I'm not appropriately dressed, with my turquoise sweats and old sneaks. And Mom will have a fit after all that cooking for a special occasion. She will have to defrost the chicken curry and make do with a sprinkle of coconut and South African mango chutney.

Torvill is barking like a demon.

I take my time at the front door, dropping to the floor, hugging my big furry dog, admiring his energy, which isn't bad at his age. Seven years?

My mother comes into the hallway and stares, her face wrinkling in disgust. "What's the matter with you? You're like a big slug. Would it kill you to get up and open the door?"

This is vintage Janet, having one of her rare lucid afternoons, stepping purposefully around me and flinging open the door. A flower arrangement in a rectangular ceramic vase is sitting on the welcome mat, a blaze of pink and white roses, red tulips, and sunflowers. I scoot back from it sharply, as if it were radioactive, at the same time Janet swoops down as if to embrace it.

"Oh, it's for you," she says, not quite able to hide her disappointment. "There's a card—Madeline."

"Should I bring it in?" Gretchen asks, stepping outside, touching my mother's arm, standing for a minute to contemplate the blooms, the excess of it all.

Finally, I rouse myself, lean in, and remove the little stick that holds the card. It's bulky, the card, as if it contains a lucky charm.

"Open it," my mother commands, like she doesn't have all day to wait and see what their Important Visitor has sent.

There's no note inside, just a small flash drive. A fashionable one, gold-plated.

"He's sent me a private message," I say.

A chill wind blows across the porch. I hurry indoors and, clutching the flash drive, climb the stairs to my study. The flowers are over the top, the cloying fragrance making me queasy. I shut the study door and turn the key in the lock.

Vince's presence is everywhere. Upstairs and downstairs, I sense his watching eyes as I steel my nerves and insert the flash drive into my computer.

There are two files: one pdf called *Just so you know*, and the other a video called *The Rodent Room*. Despite my resolve, my hands tremble as I click on the movie. A pale shadow is creeping around in the dark. It takes a few seconds to realize I'm looking at myself. Ultraviolet light illuminates my sly moves—running my fingernails over the cages and crouching in wait. The weasel Leo licks his lips and advances toward me in a shower of violet pepper-spray mist, like an art-house fantasia, then cuts to the gun—that selfsame gun now locked in this desk—held steady in my hand, aimed at Leo's heart.

There's no sound in the video. It's like watching a sinister pantomime, with myself as the villain and soft, pathetic Leo an amorphous blob of victimhood. In the spooky light, I look like a killer, tall and lithe and deadly.

Where was the camera?

I don't need to read Vince's pdf note to understand the threat. I read anyway, of course.

My Dear Madeline,

Please understand that I was in no way spying on you. Just last week I installed state-of-the-art cameras in the cages so I could check on the animals. They are, after all, living creatures who often have special needs. Because they are in close proximity to each other, their equilibrium is occasionally disturbed.

I now have a monitor at home, and when there is more agitation than usual, I investigate. This is what brought me to the lab at an ungodly hour last night.

The video you're watching is between the two of us, and will probably go no further.

Please enjoy the flowers. I selected the blooms with great care and love.

I'm so looking forward to tomorrow evening.

Lovingly yours,

Vince.

P.S. I located the bullet in a rat cage. The rat was unhurt.

"What did he say," Mom asks later.

"Just what you'd expect. He's looking forward to tomorrow night and hopes we enjoy the flowers."

"Such a gentleman," my mother says wistfully.

The formal dining room is seldom used. It's a stuffy Victorian room, with a floor-to-ceiling mahogany sideboard displaying cut glass bowls and liquor glasses inherited from my grandfather.

The crystal chandelier hasn't been dusted for years, and the job of spit and polish falls to Mrs. Auerbach.

Mom is insistent. "What's the point of having a beautiful dining room if we never use it?"

"The room is gothic, Mom. Please don't tell me you're going to serve food on the silver platters." This is a token protest. The dinner is my mother's party, so she has the final say on all arrangements.

Besides, I'm distracted by Vince's threat, which has settled in my gut like a stone.

The video is between the two of us, and will probably go no further ...

Dread drags me down on Sunday morning. Stepping outside to pick up the newspaper, I'm greeted by a pale-white light, the type that can trigger a migraine; the cloudy Boston sky of November.

The inevitable progression of events follows me, and Wanda comes into my mind—her sweet, intelligent face and her body curled up on the couch with her hands cradling a steaming mug. My chest swells at the thought of her. It pierces me, alone in the kitchen, that Vince has interfered with my life and driven my new friend away.

Wanda is in my *Favorites* list on my phone, and on impulse I hit the button to call her. Seven in the morning on a Sunday. For all I know, she's been up since five and is on her morning jog. I know next to nothing about Wanda. Is she a morning person? Does she stream mysteries on television? Will she hang up when she sees my name?

"Hey, Madeline. What's up?" Her voice is groggy. She's either been sleeping or has a hangover.

"My mother's having a dinner party tonight. She invited Vince, and our housekeeper, Gretchen, and I'm trapped in the middle of this and, oh God, Wanda, will you come and save me? Join us? Six o'clock." It comes out garbled and rushed as I realize I *really* want her to be there.

"Whoa, Madeline." The voice is sharper. Waking up.

"Please," I say quietly.

Time ebbs away while Wanda thinks about it.

"Okay, Madeline," she says faintly. "I'll be there."

CHAPTER 36

"Why are we outside in the cold, Madsy?" Mom says.

Sunday morning has dawned beautiful, the fake sun trying hard on this crisp day. We're taking a walk with Torvill, who is frisky and tugs on the leash.

Away from the house, my mind is crystal clear, heightening my understanding of how trapped I am by Vince's blackmail. And now I've drawn Wanda into Vince's sights, using her as a buffer to diffuse the danger.

Mom is confused, asking me repeatedly which day Vince is coming and smiling happily when I tell her today is the day. "Are you excited to see him?" she asks.

I'm a wimp and a coward who gave in to his threat.

"I've asked Gretchen to set another place at the table," I say casually. "My friend Wanda will be joining us."

"Who?" Mom says. She stops walking. "Do I know her?"

"I want you to meet her. She's a special friend of mine."

"Oh no, no, Mads, that's not a good idea, spoiling Vince's night." Comprehension dawns. "Isn't she that woman you met on the dating site?"

"Think of it this way, Mom. You're making a special dinner for me and my friends tonight, and I love you for it." While Torvill is sniffing something in the grass on the sidewalk, I kiss the top of my mother's head. She too is a pawn in Vince's game.

"You're buttering me up," she says, teary-eyed.

At 6:00 p.m. sharp, he arrives in his dark turtleneck and blue jacket uniform. He's changed his look a bit, with a dark shadow of stubble, like he thinks he's a male model in *GQ*. His chin is sandpapery when it brushes my cheek in greeting. I feel his allure straightaway and understand it's his special signal to my implant, and I must climb above it.

Back off!

His voice, earlier, in my head. *I was in no way spying on you.*

I've taken no special care with my appearance, and am decked out in my usual outfit of skinny pants, sweater and sneakers; the scuffed ones that disappoint my mother.

Mrs. Auerbach and Mom are gaga over Vince, chattering around him, ooh-ing at his gift of wine—one red, one white—relieving him of his jacket, and leading him to the living room.

"Janet, you are even more beautiful than your daughter, if such a thing were possible," he says, taking a seat in Mrs. Auerbach's favorite armchair and casting his eyes about with a sigh.

"Oh, you," Mom says, openly flirting, which she would never do on a lucid day. My heart squeezes.

I've written on my palm, *Fight back!!*

Mrs. Auerbach, who has on an elegant blouse, has made a fire in the grate, and for once, the poor lighting is perfect, casting a glow on us and creating a cozy atmosphere. An Agatha Christie setting where the wine is ruby red in the firelight and the honored guest is about to keel over with a knife in his throat.

Where's Wanda?

Vince raises his glass. "To Madeline and Janet, I'd like to propose a toast for providing this lovely evening." Mom swoons with pleasure, while Mrs. Auerbach, who did most of the work, barely blinks in the muted light.

Why am I resisting? Some women would kill for a guy like this.

I force myself to focus on his blackmail. *I located the bullet in a rat cage.*

At 6:30, after we've polished off the cheeseballs and two glasses of wine, Mom says, "Why are we waiting? It's time for dinner."

No call or text message from Wanda. *Where is she?*

My mother, in consultation with Mrs. Auerbach, has devised a seating plan that places her at the head of the table, where she has easy access to the kitchen. Vince is at her right, and I am seated opposite him, so I can't escape the laser of his gaze.

"Oh, wonderful," he says when Mrs. Auerbach steers Mom to place him across from me. "What a joy." He's laying it on thick, but I'm clinging to the flower arrangement and the threat buried deep in its blooms for some sanity.

Mrs. Auerbach is seated next to Vince, and a place is laid for Wanda to sit beside me. Her empty seat is a bleak reminder of how fragile life is. Too bad. I was depending on having her here as an ally against the dark forces playing out against me.

The magnificent chandelier has a dimmer switch, and a soft rose light glows on the rich mahogany wood that has been polished to a shine. I could almost succumb to the allure of the atmosphere that's been set up by my mother and her helper. Tonight they are not in my corner.

Resist him!

Chicken curry, a spicy blend of Cape Malay and India, embellished with coconut, chutney, creamy cucumber raita, and bananas. One of Mom's divine specialties, which Vince, Mom, and Mrs. Auerbach attack heartily, while I push a small helping around on my plate.

Vince is extravagant in his praise, and my mother is radiant.

"I'll cook for you anytime," she says. "Notice how our Madeline eats like a bird."

No one says a word about the empty chair beside me.

When we all have coffee and apple cake in front of us, and my heart is heavy because Wanda broke her promise, Vince says, "I think this is the perfect time to make an announcement."

I shiver.

A small velvet box materializes in front of him. He opens it, walks around the table, and places his hand on my shoulder. "Take this, dear Madeline. It's a token of my love and good intentions. Marry me. Please say yes."

The speech sounds stilted and rehearsed, as if he practiced in front of a mirror. He knows how I feel about him. Is he really going to blackmail me into marrying him?

A pear-shaped, blue-white diamond twinkles at me from a soft fold of dark velvet. An engagement ring. I sit up, lightheaded. My silence grows to encompass the whole house. I'm sweating under my clothes. The vibes in the room bend toward me.

Say yes.

Isn't this what I wanted? Love and romance? A strong man who'd climb mountains to have me?

"May I see it?" Mom lifts the little box away from me.

In that moment, Mrs. Auerbach gives me a look of sharp intensity and an almost imperceptible shake of her head. Then it's gone, a veil coming over her eyes. Something passes between her and Vince, then Mrs. Auerbach shrinks, like an animal fearing to be struck. All happening in the blink of an eye.

All at once I'm alert to something in the air, my past experience as a spy clicking in like a reflex. I've learned to keep my face blank—no alarm—take a sip of water, smile.

Who is she?

Mom has put the ring on her finger, and we're all mesmerized by its brilliant sparkle.

"Since my daughter is so tongue-tied," my starry-eyed mother says, "I accept this generous proposal. Yes, yes, a million times yes."

What? No! My chest constricts with anguish, and everything fades out except the vibrations in the air and Mom's elegant hand and the diamond floating in front of my eyes.

As if on cue, the doorbell rings.

CHAPTER 37

"Oh, for heaven's sake, let Gretchen get that," Mom snaps. But I'm already up from my chair and out the room, my heart thudding, my hand turning the doorknob and pulling open the door.

Wanda is dressed for the occasion—cords, cashmere, real shoes, and an X of bamboo sticks in her hair. My breath catches with every cliché of longing as I grasp her hands and tug her inside.

"Thank God you're here," I say.

Wanda pecks my cheek. "I almost didn't make it—a break-in at my apartment this afternoon."

"Oh no."

My mother appears at the door, all frosty smiles and perfect hostess. "You're Madeline's friend. Do come inside and tell me your name. I'm Janet."

And my darling girl gathers my mother into a hug, saying, "I'm Wanda, and what a joy it is to finally meet you, because Madeline adores you and speaks about you often."

"Yes, well ..." Mom extricates herself. "Why don't you come in and have something to eat? Celebrate with us. Vince—our guest of honor—just gave Madeline a diamond engagement ring."

Wanda's mouth is an O, her thick eyebrows up, before I say, "But my mother is jumping the gun because I haven't accepted it."

Such an exquisite diamond.

Wanda snaps her fingers in front of my face. "Madeline! Wake up! Where are you?"

I shake my head and blink rapidly. It's as if I blacked out momentarily to escape the awkwardness.

When we move to the dining room, I hope Wanda's smart enough to cope with the situation. She walks right up to Vince and says, "Hi, I'm Wanda. And you must be Vince." She puts out her hand to shake his, but he grasps it instead between both of his.

"How great to meet you. Any friend of Madeline's is a friend of mine." His voice is charming, and he's oozing clichés, but he knows about Wanda and can't be happy.

My mother sends Mrs. Auerbach to the kitchen to heap a curry plate for Wanda. Mom probably wants to control the diamond ring situation and won't let me out of her sight.

"I'm so sorry I'm late," Wanda says.

"Oh, no problem. Food coming right out," Mom says in her most gracious voice.

Wanda inclines her head in thanks, and her hairdo teeters in a way I love. "I was out this afternoon, and when I got home, my condo had been broken into."

"How did they get in?" I ask. She had pretty substantial locks on her door.

"They somehow evaded the alarm." She strokes my hand under the table, then squeezes it. "I'll have to come see you for a security consultation."

I squeeze back. "Was anything missing?" Her beautiful decor comes into my mind. So much for a thief to take.

"Here's the thing. Nothing was taken. The theft was in progress. The guy was in my bedroom, pawing through my night table drawer."

Vince is alert, sitting straight up in his chair.

His flunky, Leo?

"What did you do?" he says gruffly.

"I pushed a panic button. You know, a woman living on her own in Boston? Then I talked him down—he was very agitated—and told him I wouldn't press charges if he left quietly and promised not to come back."

"You didn't!" I'm shocked. My whole business model is built on the idea that we'll catch and prosecute the intruders.

Vince, looking more relaxed, reaches to the center of the table and helps himself to a morsel of dark chocolate. "So you let the guy go?"

"Sure did," Wanda says. "Then I gave his license plate number to the cops, who picked him up very easily and arrested him. That's why I'm so late to this party; dealing with the cops in my condo."

Is it my imagination that Vince is uneasy?

"Who was the thief?" I ask.

"Look at this diamond," Mom says abruptly, moving the little box across to Wanda. It sparkles at us, brilliant under the chandelier.

Without touching it, Wanda says, "*Magnifique*. Someone spent the big bucks."

"The price is nothing." Vince flicks his wrist. "The main question is whether Madeline will have me. What do you say, Mads? Should we say yes to this grand adventure?"

Trapped in a vise. Vince leaning forward, beaming a laser into my eyes. Did he request to sit across from me so he could reinforce the light frequency and hypnotize me? Mrs. Auerbach looking away, not meeting anyone's eyes. Mom grinning like the Cheshire Cat, ready to bring out the champagne.

At that instant, looking at Vince's frigid blue eyes, I know that if I say no to his proposal, all the looming threats—the gun, implanted lights, spyware, Buck's treachery, Mrs. Auerbach's brooding presence, and Vince, most of all Vince—will finally coalesce into a giant wave, taking me down. I could go to prison if he reports the gun. Buck has access to everything in my office. He could destroy my business. Mrs. Auerbach knows all the nooks and crannies of my house. She could cause mayhem.

Wanda grabs my hand under the table with such force that it hurts.

Snap out of it!

Sweat trickles under my clothes.

Malevolent thoughts rush through me in a wave of nausea. Then, a strange clarity as I fight them off and the fuzziness evaporates. I know what I must do.

Climb above that damn signal.

I shake Wanda's hand off and stand up. "Vince, the answer is no. It was no last week and the week before. It'll never be yes, no matter how many jewels you buy me."

"Madeline! Quit that," Mom says, her chest heaving. "Vince, I'm so sorry."

"I'm going to the bathroom," I say. "I need some breathing space."

"I have to go too," Wanda says. "Is there another bathroom I could use? Come, Madeline, show me."

I almost trip over my feet to leave. In the poor light, Vincent's face appears purple.

Wanda follows on my heels. Up the stairs we go, and in my bedroom, she moves to embrace me. But I shoo her away and pull down a small suitcase.

In the end, you have to choose; you must trust someone.

CHAPTER 38

Like burglars in my own house, Wanda and I creep out through a back entrance. My need to escape is so intense that I don't say goodbye to anyone—not my mother, my housekeeper, nor my pets. As for Vince, what kind of bizarre alchemy did he use to convince me and my household to invite him in?

It's raining, and by the time we step into Wanda's car, we're wet and shivering.

"I'm driving the getaway car," she says.

I relax against the seat, breathing in the feeling of freedom.

My phone pings. Mom. *Where are you?*

It's not so hard to be truthful. *Out for the night. Make my excuses.*

Another ping. This one from Professionals.com. They have a new match for me, one with 95 percent compatibility. A pediatrician. Not a particularly good-looking man, but with a lovely smile. *Dare I try again?* With a fluid movement, I hit delete and throw my phone into my purse.

Wanda doesn't ask. She's alert, driving carefully in the poor visibility, cars flashing distorted headlights into our eyes.

"Why didn't you call me tonight? Let me know you'd be late?" I ask.

Briefly, she takes her eyes off the road. "Because, up until the very last minute, I wasn't sure I would come."

The brittle rubber of the car's wipers shudders on the windshield.

"What changed your mind?"

We're across the bridge and in Boston. Wanda doesn't respond. While my question hangs in the air, she flicks the right-turn signal and pulls over in some unidentifiable illegal parking spot. Her seat whirs as it moves back from the steering wheel.

"I could say that I came to your house because you're gorgeous and smart and irresistibly sexy."

I'm still shivering, damp and goose-bumpy in the seat. "But?"

"What you actually are is stubborn and weird, you and your wine-colored suits and aggressive haircut. Being with you is like living in a B-movie, science fiction, spy thriller, with car chases, thugs, kidnappings, stalkers, Frankenstein, mad scientists—you name it."

"I thought you didn't want all that stuff." The rain is coming down, clattering on the car. I hug myself tightly.

"I didn't. That's why I had a hard decision. Everyone else I meet is so ordinary compared to you." She leans across and touches my cheek. "Now I guess I'm stuck with you. I assume you're planning to stay at my place for a while?"

I take her hand and kiss it, then hold it against my cheek. "Just for a few days, Wanda. I can't go back to my house right now."

"Say no more. It's done. Come here."

We lean together, and she puts her hand inside my shirt and under my bra. "I lied," she whispers in my ear. "I came to your house tonight because you have the sexiest boobs in Boston."

The immensity of what I'm doing weighs on me as we approach Wanda's condo. I understand, yet again, how dependent I am on Mrs. Auerbach. I could never pack up and leave Mom on her own; my mother, who oscillates between sanity and dementia.

Wanda shows me the damaged lock on the front door. It looks like someone took an axe to it. The doorknob is gone, and we get inside by pushing the door.

"You left it unlocked and came to my dinner party?" I ask.

"I reckoned it was safe now. Leo, your little thug friend, is in jail as we speak, and one of those bystander pedestrians on the street is actually a cop guarding my door."

"So we *are* in a spy thriller."

Inside, there's evidence of the invasion—side tables upended and furniture rearranged. Nothing was stolen, as far as Wanda can tell, but a message was sent.

Later, while we're drinking tea on the couch, Wanda goes very quiet and pensive.

"I should call my mother," I say.

"May I give you some advice?"

A cue in her voice, a hardening. It puts me on alert. "What?"

"If we weren't sipping tea, I'd come and sit next to you, take you by the shoulders and shake you until your brain rattles." Her green eyes are sharp and direct.

"What?" I say again.

"For someone so brilliant, you sure act stupid." The tea has gone tepid, and she takes a gulp. "How do I knock some sense into you? Your current situation is untenable."

A pulse starts in my neck. "I'm listening."

She puts the cup down and comes and sits next to me. "It's time for your mama to go into an assisted-living facility where she can get proper care."

"Wait." She doesn't have a clue about our history. How dare she be so presumptive?

"And it's time to get the creepy housekeeper out of your house."

"Oh, Wanda."

"And it's also time to sic the cops on your stalker and get him out of your life."

"You have no idea."

"Enlighten me then." Her eyes are cold.

"First of all, my life can't be reduced to a set of bullet points. So stop with the simplistic solutions."

"Madeline, none of it is simple." Finally, she softens. "I too once had a mother. I get it, I really do."

"It's not just love for my mom; we have a huge bond. It's been just the two of us since I was ten. And I also have an infinite debt of gratitude. She gave up her life—months of it—to care for me at home after a skydiving accident. So I owe her. Being thrown into a nursing home is her worst nightmare, and she told me this long before her illness struck."

"You don't have to throw her anywhere. You have enough money to find a nice place in Boston where you could visit her every day if you wanted."

"And the creepy housekeeper, as you call her, is the first caregiver for my mom who has actually befriended her. I can't ask her to leave. She's more valuable than anything in my house. As for siccing the cops on Vince ... Well, I've been to the cops—twice—and it's gotten me precisely nowhere. It's my word against his, and they sympathize with Vince."

Wanda shakes her head, and her mouth is set in a thin line. "I assume you've contacted a lawyer, who has sent Vince a cease and desist letter?"

I nod miserably.

"Well, have you followed up with his violations, which seem to be multiple and ongoing?" she demands.

I listen patiently while Wanda lays out the steps of my incompetence like some damning mathematical proof. Then, agitated, I tell her my own sequence of events, including the skepticism of the Cambridge Police. I confess to her about the scene in Vince's lab on Friday night—my illegal break-in, the gunshot, and the hold Vince now has over me.

"Tiny electronic chips injected into the spines of my household," I whisper. "Now can you see why I can't go back to the cops? They'll never believe me. Jessica, my lawyer, will think I'm deranged."

"No, that's not true, Mads." Wanda puts her hand on my thigh and presses her fingers into my flesh. "Just scream blue bloody murder at the cops every time Vince bothers you, and eventually, they'll get sick of you and do something about it. Jessica is in your corner. Document everything, and she'll go after Vince." Wanda's lovely face is stern. "And about that gun? You can always justify it as something you got in self-defense when the cops wouldn't do anything to help you."

I love her for her seriousness and for not saying I'm nuts and for being so passionately rational.

I think she receives the love vibe, because she gets up, stretches her arms languorously. "It's late. Let's go to bed. Take your mind off all this crap."

"Will I sleep on the couch?" I ask, suddenly shy.

"Don't be silly," Wanda says, laughing. "My bed is plenty big enough for both of us."

After some delicious preamble on the way to bed, followed by high jinks under the covers, Wanda lies back sideways on her elbow, watching me. Then she breaks the mood. "Here's another bullet point, Madeline. It's time to hire a bodyguard who'll protect you when that godawful Vince shows up again."

CHAPTER 39

I wake up to small, unfamiliar noises and a lacy sun trickling into the bedroom. An aroma of freshly brewed coffee wafts in my direction.

The mirror in the bathroom does not bring good news. I'm fed up with Vince, Buck, and Leo—not in any particular order—and my truculence shows. There's fur on my tongue, and I glare at my image.

Wanda will be staying home this morning, setting her apartment back in order and getting her door fixed. She seems so Zen about everything, giving me a crinkly eyed smile when I show up in the kitchen in my burgundy suit. She moves to me, arms outstretched, but I don't linger. I'm off to work early, to take charge.

I Uber to my house, straighten my spine, and go inside. "Mom?"

My mother and Mrs. Auerbach are at the kitchen table eating pancakes.

"Hiya, Madsy," Mom says. "Why are you all dressed up for breakfast?"

She's forgotten.

I give her a brief hug. "I'm off to work and won't be here tonight."

Then some meaningful eye contact with Mrs. Auerbach, who nods.

Up the creaking stairs and into my bedroom I go, breathing deeply. Concentrating, my mind focused, I keep my back straight, head up, and brain sharp. I will not allow myself to be warped by electronic signals in this house. I'm here to pick up more stuff—blue suits and blouses, my laptop and precious little paperweight—and all of it happens easily, without a problem.

Perhaps Vince has turned off the signal. But then again, maybe not.

Before I leave, I have a big mutual slobber-fest with Torvill and a quiet head-to-head cuddle with Tosca, then back to my mother for a teary-eyed farewell kiss on her cheek.

"Go already," Mom says.

Shawna welcomes me back to the office with open arms that fold me in a warm embrace. "Which Madeline is here today? My tough old boss or the Zombie invasion?" She examines me critically. "Zombie's gone, praise the Lord."

She makes me laugh. "I should fire you," I say.

"You're gonna hafta tell me the story of who took you on Wednesday, woman. Bucky-Ball and his shifty eyes wouldn't even give me one clue."

I signal she should follow me into my office and shut the door.

"So many messages for you," she says. "And lots of walk-ins for Buck. He's the Man."

"Don't say one word to Buck." I'm keeping my voice very low. "He's involved in what went down with me. I'll tell you everything, but not now."

Her eyes widen, and she nods.

We go back out to the front, and I don't relish my next move.

Buck knows something is up because his music is low and subdued.

"Hey, boss lady," he says, quizzing me with his eyes as I step up to his desk. His eyebrow stud is gone.

"In my office, Buck."

"Okay, just let me finish—"

"*Now.* Drop everything." I wait until he's out of the door, then turn around smartly and follow him.

In my office, I sit behind my desk and let Buck stand facing me. I don't invite him to pull up a chair.

"ByteBeast ..." he says.

I sit back and plant both feet on the floor. "Is there something you want to tell me, Buck?"

His body language—hunching his shoulders in defeat—starts the ball rolling without him saying a word. But he actually says, "I feel bad about what happened to you."

"That's a good start, because you should feel bad. What about your part in it?"

His eyes open wide at me. "What part? I didn't have any part in it."

"No?" I cross my arms and stare him down. "For starters, what about the ransomware attacks? The emptying and destruction of my backups? Luring me outside where I could be kidnapped?"

"Madeline, no! I didn't do any of that. Why would I?" Skinny arms, long hair; a scarecrow pose, rigid with indignation.

"I don't know exactly what your motive was, Buck, but I intend to find out."

"Can I go back to work now?" Completely disingenuous, playing me for a fool.

Not today, buddy.

"What you can do, Buck, is go home. I'm suspending you—with pay—until I get to the bottom of this." My voice is low and perfectly controlled.

"Wait! No fair—"

"*And* I am impounding your computers—the desktop and the laptop."

"No! You can't take my laptop." He lunges toward my desk and leans his clenched fists on it.

I sit forward into his space. "Buck, both of those computers belong to my business. They're perks of employment here, something you should have thought about before betraying me."

He looks like a child about to cry. "Am I fired?"

He has no idea how hurt and angry I am. He's so young and vulnerable, and despite all he did, I like him. I can't help myself. He's part of my programming tribe. Nevertheless, I have to harden my heart.

There's steel in my voice when I reply. "You're not officially fired. You're temporarily suspended while I investigate the attacks on me. If you assist in my investigation, I may reconsider. Everything is up in the air right now."

"I didn't do it!" he cries, letting lose a small shower of tears.

I accompany him to his office, where he puts his meager belongings in a box. His grubby water bottle, square tin of thumb drives, some kind of kitchen towel, a chipped mug and stack of small paper plates. Slowly, he shrugs on his pathetic thin jacket.

Like an ice queen, I stand and watch. None of his cute-kid act melts me.

"Keys." I hold out a rigid palm. He reaches in his pocket and, after disgorging a few gum wrappers, hands me a keyring. I'm not taken in by his show of reluctance—for sure there's another set or two under his belt.

"Can I take the lava lamp?" he says in a weak voice.

I'm on the verge of saying no, it's part of the office décor, when a devil or saint in me says, "Sure, be my guest."

He moves to type something on his desktop, but I stay his hand. "Don't touch the computers."

He pulls his arm away and uses it to wipe snot from his nose. Then he lifts the box, and hugging it to his body, says, "ByteBeast, I didn't do it."

"If you come clean with everything, I won't file criminal charges."

He looks shocked, but I don't buy the look. I add, "Ransomware attacks can put you away for a lot of years, kid. Think of it. Best years of your life, rotting in jail."

"But not unless you prove it," he says, the old gleam in his eye briefly back.

CHAPTER 40

The HackMeister walks out through the front area, where Shawna is typing furiously at her computer. She gasps when she sees our little procession and puts her hands on her cheeks. "Bucky-Ball?"

"Bye, Shawna. Guess I won't be bothering you anymore."

An odd silence pervades the office after he leaves. I've gotten used to the Afrobeats and the cosmic blast of *Star Wars*. For a while, it seemed that my business was a cool place—security software with a hipster vibe.

"What did he do?" Shawna asks.

I tell her about the ransomware attacks and my suspicion. "I know Buck did it and Vince gave him instructions. But I have to prove it."

"I hear you." She gives a wry smile. "I like the dude, but he sure is a sly one, that Buck."

I ask Shawna to bring in a locksmith *today*, so we can change the locks on all office doors and, in particular, secure Buck's office.

"What? You think that boy is coming back here for a nighttime visit?" she says, incredulous.

"I don't think it, I know it. We have similar blood in our veins, and it's what I would do in his situation."

"You think he's gonna try steal his laptop?" She shakes her head, her beads clacking.

"No. He's going to try and get rid of the evidence. He knows I'm onto him."

"Uh, Madeline, can't that boy do it from home?" Shawna has learned a thing or two over the years, and she's savvy about many aspects of my business.

"Good thinking. But luckily we have a closed network here, so he must be in the office to access it." I tap my head. "Security decision."

With Buck out of the office, I now must catch up with my clients and complete Buck's work for the walk-ins. Shawna helps me get up to speed, and within a couple of hours, I'm back in my well-ordered world of hardware and software, unencumbered by male wetware.

Toward late afternoon, Shawna comes into the office. "Sorry, Madeline, no locksmith takers for today. Earliest appointment I could get was for 8:00 a.m. tomorrow morning, so I grabbed it. The Keys to Happiness."

"Say what?"

"The name of the locksmith company, darlin'." She waves at me from the door, ready to get back into her world of normal people.

It may not be such a bad thing to allow Buck back into his office. That way, perhaps I can catch him red-handed trying to access his computers. Confront him. Demand to know how he did it—the latest attacks on my computer. I'll wait and watch. Lull him into thinking I forgot to change the entry codes and locks.

Wanda isn't thrilled that I may be staying in the office overnight.

"We've lived together for less than a day, and already you're making excuses to be away from home." The phone crackles, and my blood warms in a way it hasn't for some time.

"I've got an emergency," I say regretfully.

"Just kidding, Mads. I know your life's crazy. Will you be crouching in the dark with your gun, waiting for the bad guys to come and getcha?"

I laugh. She's not so far off the mark.

"See you tomorrow, sweetheart," she says. "Not in the morgue, I hope."

I roll it on my tongue: *sweetheart.*

Inside Buck's office, I discover he has modified his light switch to produce a spectrum of colored lights. I try blue and find myself in an opium den of dueling dragons and *Star Wars* creatures. For a moment, I miss him.

His desktop computer is as he left it, open and accessible.

As I suspected, there's no sign of ransomware code. The files must have been deleted. No hints of the "negotiation" with me or any instructions to access my backup files. No communications with Vince. I inspect all his directories, and they're clean. I expected no less from Buck. If I'd found those files, he wouldn't be the brilliant techie I hired. He knows how to cover his tracks.

What can I do to nail him, if all the evidence is invisible? Despite my distaste for what I'm doing, this is my sweet spot, being in the thick of an intractable problem. One part of my mind is—despite myself—admiring him for the technical feats he achieved, while another is shuffling around variables, then showing me a snapshot of what I should do.

Of course. The backup log!

He emptied the backup server. If I could retrieve the backup log, I'd have him. The log keeps a record of everything to do with backing up, and it never lies.

I think I'm onto a simple, elegant solution. If it works, it'll cut through all the other things. If he emptied the backup, he engineered the ransomware. If he sent the ransomware, he set up the negotiation with Vince. And if he really was in on the negotiation, he was up to his ears in cahoots with Vince.

My solution depends on the small possibility Buck didn't empty the backup as thoroughly as he could have. Does he know, I wonder, that deleting all files is not the same as erasing those files? The answer is yes, of course he knows. One has to wipe the computer completely clean in order to erase the files from the face of the earth, and it's a pain in the neck to do. It's time consuming.

I'm counting on the hope Buck was lazy and arrogant and had some vague intention of coming back to wipe his computers, but hadn't yet done it. And if I'm right, I know some magic to restore our backup log, which is floating somewhere in the software soup of the computer.

It's complicated and must wait until I have some fuel in me.

There's a good take-out restaurant nearby. I lock up the office, set the alarm, and head out to get dinner. A thunderstorm is brewing, with bruised gray clouds gathering in the sky, and a witches-on-broomsticks kind of wind. I zip up my jacket. After the warmth indoors, the air is frosty.

I'm famished and order three fried chicken thighs, with a giant baked potato and Diet Coke. It seems to take forever to get the chicken ready, but through the window I have a perfect view of the front of my office building. Unless he's very well disguised, no one resembling Buck goes near it.

The rain starts pelting down as I approach the entrance, dinner intact, but hair soaked. It's Monday after 6:00 p.m., and the place seems deserted. A crack of thunder and lightning jolts me for a second, as the light in the No Man's Land hallway flickers and threatens to blow.

Back in my office, with the storm raging outside, I tear into my dinner and wash it all down with the diet soda, which leaves a saccharine taste on my tongue.

I don't relish what I must do now—examine my backup server for traces of Buck's guilt.

The log file keeps a record of every action for my business's private backup system, including users and times. Shawna, Buck and I all have passwords to this server. My goal right now is to find evidence my arrogant little shit of an employee removed all the backed-up files on Wednesday night before the second ransomware attack. I suspect Buck not only emptied my backup, but also destroyed the log file, thus hiding his criminal activity.

My big question is: did he wipe the file or simply hit the "delete" command, which gives me a shot at recovering the file?

At my desktop, I fire up *Foremost*, a nifty tool for undeleting files. It's a new little toy I mastered for my clients who hit "delete" by mistake or have a crashed hard drive. My clients think I'm a wizard, but the magic is in the software.

Since the file I want to restore is called the *audit log file*, I enter "audit" as the search string. The software will bring up any deleted files containing this word. I hold my breath, listening to the sheets of rain strafing the window while the software scours the disk.

Within seconds, there's a hit, and the file I'm searching for, *audit.log*, pops onto the screen. Success! My hands shake as I open the file and scroll through it, right to the bottom, to the final entries before it was deleted. It's there in black and white. User 3 logged on at 16:45 on Wednesday, October 30, and executed the command to delete the backup files.

Jeffrey Buck is User 3. I have him!

While I'm savoring this sleuthing victory, a crash of thunder and lightning hits right in front of me, and the lights go out.

CHAPTER 41

As the storm clatters on, my eyes strain to adjust to the darkness, causing an unfamiliar tightness in my neck.

Chill. No one is coming to attack me tonight, and besides, I'm a woman with a loaded gun. I slide my hand along the ridge of my desk, groping for the top drawer, making sure.

When I look up, a person has entered my building and is slouching through No Man's Land. A gray ghost, beamed to me from the surveillance cameras, which have backup batteries and can see in the dark. The shady figure has somehow broached the locked entrance and is headed toward the inner door with its waiting keypad, also on backup battery.

He has not looked up. A cap on his head conceals his hair, and a bulky jacket conveys nothing to me about his identity. Nevertheless, I have no doubt I'm looking at Buck, headed toward his office to erase the evidence against him.

He has no problem at the keypad, and glides through the door.

I sit in my office like a mouse, while surveillance cameras throughout my suite allow me to track his progress. Pausing in Shawna's territory, he looks around, moves to her desk, and sits in front of her computer. Completely at home in front of it, typing a password, trying to get in. No luck.

Of course this is Buck, always in hacker mode. He can't help himself.

Through the camera lens, I watch him pull open Shawna's desk drawer and riffle around. I know exactly what he's looking for—a Post-it note with her passwords or some kind of written reminder. I myself always do that as step two when trying to crack a computer. But it's not going to be his lucky night, which he should know, because in a business that deals with security issues, we keep our passwords secure. That was one of the first things I taught Shawna.

Eventually he gives up, kicks the chair and, in the darkness, moves swiftly to his office. As I suspected, he has a spare set of keys, and within seconds, he's at his desktop, his fingers flying over the keys trying to gain entry.

I've anticipated this move, and type a command on my computer that allows him in. I want to test my theory he's here to wipe the backup log. It's a creepy battle of wits, played silently in the dark.

He must be relieved to have access to his computer. Perhaps he feels on top of things, because he tugs off his jacket and cap, tossing them onto the floor. I sense a relaxation up and down his spine, a false sense of security, as he does a full-body motion of shaking loose his hair. When his hair tumbles down, this shadowy avatar morphs into Jeffrey Buck.

A camera trained on Buck's computer shows me he's attempting to access the backup server. But, of course, I've disabled his password and the monitor flashes an *Access Denied* message. Frustrated, he bangs his hands down on the desk. As if by magic, the lights come back on. His office is still blue, and he looks like a ghoul at his computer.

I make a swift, silent move. "Hello, Buck."

"Holy crap!" He jumps up from his chair and hugs his arms, staring at me with panic in his eyes.

"Am I going to call the cops, or are you going to tell me everything that happened—right from the beginning, starting with that illegal cable from the heating company."

"It's not what you think," he says, his voice pleading.

Lying traitor. "Let's go in my office, and you're going to sing a different tune, starting with what 'it' is."

He walks, slumping, ahead of me. Inside, I gesture to a chair for him, and, as I activate the recorder of my phone, he says, "I didn't know that switch in the basement was yours. I just saw a neat way for the heating company to monitor the furnace without paying Verizon."

"Did it occur to you it was criminal?"

He lowers his eyes. "I wasn't this big mastermind or anything. It was fun to figure it out."

"And the ransomware attack? Was that fun too?"

He shakes his head, like I'm being unfair. "I did it to impress my boss at the heating company, not to get money. As soon as that guy—Nicholson—got the attack on his computer, I offered to fix everything, to make it all go away. I wanted to be their techie guy, so the attack was a way to make them notice me."

"And what about me? No one made it go away for me."

His face looks pained. "Honest, ByteBeast, I swear I didn't know you'd get hit too. I didn't realize the heating cable would carry the ransomware to your computer. I was shocked."

"Oh yeah? So how did you find out?"

"When this person from outer space sent me a message that they couldn't pay 10 bitcoins. Scared the crap out of me, and I realized some other person had been hit with the same ransomware. I figured out the person whose switch I used—you—was now on the heating company's network."

"So what did you do about it, huh?"

He leans forward, full of grievance. "Before I could do a thing, this person—you—had destroyed my computer! It started frying on my desk. Total wreckage. I had no money, and you trashed my new computer. It pissed me off."

So my method worked. Perversely, I feel a brief stab of job satisfaction. But the moment passes fast. "I don't get it. You were so angry at me that you engineered another ransomware attack? The one that happened last week."

He jumps up, shivering, running his hands up and down his arms, his face flushed.

"No, ByteBeast, you got it wrong. What *really* pissed me off—you know, like major heartbreak type of pissed off—was you told Shawna not to go out with me. My Princess Leia said no because she didn't want to lose her job."

I stare at him. "You're serious? You and Shawna?" But I don't need to ask. Of all the stuff he's told me so far, this is the one thing that's obviously true. He hasn't been able to take his eyes off her, not from the first day he came into the office.

"That same afternoon, your guy—Vince—was hanging around outside the office waiting for me to come out the building."

Goose bumps rise on my neck. "Vince was waiting for you?"

"Yeah, he was like, 'Can I take you for a hamburger?' Dude wouldn't let me say no. Told me how crazy in love he was with you and you wouldn't even speak to him, and could I help him out—get your attention so he could just *talk* to you. And I said, yeah, I knew a good way to get your attention. And I could even set it up so he could talk to you."

I lower my head and rub my eyes with the heels of my hands. Suddenly, it's been a really long day. "I can't believe you didn't tell me any of this."

His chin is at an angle, defiant. "I already said I was pissed off at you. Here was this cool dude talking to me, man to man, both crazy in love, and you were being more than a bit of a bitch, if you don't mind me saying."

"Why couldn't you just do the ransomware? Why did you have to empty the backup?"

But I already know the answer. His personal honor was at stake. I had defeated him the first time by restoring my files from backup. This time, with no backup files available, he'd be the winner, and we'd be even. Teenage computer games with immature geeks. I'd seen enough of them at school to know the syndrome.

"I'm really sorry, ByteBeast," he says, flopping back. "It got out of hand with the negotiations and stuff. That's why I came to help you out and put the files back."

"So Vince was the one negotiating?" Again, I know the answer.

"Yeah. I set it up with dialogue capability on his computer. When I saw he was making you take off your clothes in front of the camera, I wanted to punch his face off. That wasn't part of the deal."

"So tell me the stuff that *was* part of the deal."

"I had to get you to agree to come and talk to him, and wait with you in front of the art gallery." He lowers his eyes, embarrassed by all of this. "Vince was sure you would trust me."

I nod. I can see exactly how I got sucked in. I did trust Buck. Anger swells in me. *God, how well I was played.* "You betrayed me." I say it softly. A statement of fact.

He hangs his head, but his regret is too little too late.

"Two more things." I harden my face. "Did you remove the spyware from Vince's computer, and did you tell him I was the one who'd installed it?"

"Yeah, I got rid of it. But when he asked who installed it, I told him I didn't know."

"Thanks for nothing."

"Wait." He digs into his pocket and takes out a flash drive. "I wasn't sure if this would be useful, but at the same time, I downloaded his hard drive."

Really? "Why?" I ask. "I thought you hated me."

"No, I didn't hate you. I was pissed off with you. And I thought it might help me keep my job." He looks around wistfully. "I love it here."

"Too late to suck up now," I say, taking the flash drive and pocketing it. *Probably full of malware.* "But I do have one more question."

"Shoot."

There are tears and snot on his face. I hand him a tissue. "Wipe your nose and tell me about the Squid Link Gateway box. The one you installed in the base of the lamp in the other room. Was that also because you were pissed off with me?"

He honks into the tissue. "No, it was also part of the deal. But there's something real weird about it."

"Yeah, I'd agree. Definitely something screwy about setting me up like an appliance to receive signals, wouldn't you say?"

But he's frowning, my tone of voice lost on him. "Here's the strange thing," he says. "Vince told me to put it in an obvious place in the office, like the base of a lamp."

"Why?"

Buck shrugs. "He wanted to make sure you found it."

Roselyn Teukolsky

CHAPTER 42

Vince wanted me to know how effortlessly he could control me.

Not for the first time tonight, I stare at Buck in disbelief. In Vince's cat-and-mouse game, I'm the chief mouse and clueless Buck is one of his disposable flunkies.

"Am I still suspended?" he says, like an errant schoolboy mired in the muck of his childish pranks.

I'm unmoved by his plight. He's proved he's a weasel of the lowest order. Yet I'm reluctant to fire him outright, because he may still be useful.

"I need time to think about it," I say, the ice in my voice genuine.

Sniveling, he gets on his knees and puts his palms together, praying to me. "Please, ByteBeast, let me stay. I thought Vince would get to sweet-talk you, then I'd restore your files, and we'd be even. Things got out of control. I'm sorry."

Naïve idiot. "Buck, get up."

He staggers backward and collapses into his chair, keeping his doe eyes fixed on me.

"Stay away from here until I email you." What I don't say is that one condition of his re-employment will be that he testify against Vince. The next time my lawyer and I go after Vince, it'll stick. When Buck's head slumps onto his chest, I add, "One other thing. No more break-ins to this office. All the surveillance cameras are activated, including some you don't know about. If I see you anywhere near here, I'll report the ransomware attack to the police. You and your job will be history."

He sits there in a dejected heap, probably plotting his next break-in. I have no illusions about baby-face Buck.

I wave my hand in front of him. "Do you roger me loud and clear?"

"I won't let you down again," he says, getting up to leave.

After he's gathered his cap and jacket from his office and had one last look around, I stop him at the door. "One more thing. Vince may contact you again, right? And, you know, ask for another little favor."

"From now on, I'm yours, ByteBeast." He holds up the peace sign and smiles through his tears. "I'll let you know if he contacts me, like straightaway. Jedi's honor."

All of his garbage "confession" goes into my documentation for Jessica Kim.

I call Wanda before heading "home," but after two rings, I'm thrown into her voicemail. I text her instead. *Found and killed Vince's mind-control signal! So, I'm not as crazy as you thought. See you soon. xxx*

I've always been able to pan back and think outside the box. Gather the puzzle pieces and shift them around until they fall into place. And if they don't, come at them from a different angle, stir and repeat, until the problem is solved.

My current task is to unravel the mystery of Vince. His bizarre pursuit of me.

During the next several days, I make some disturbing discoveries.

Dr. Patel calls and informs me I don't have a brain tumor. *Hooray.* In the next sentence, however, he says, "Madeline, the radiologist detected a miniscule shadow in your cerebrospinal fluid that could conceivably be a piece of metal, which would tend to support your story of a spinal implant."

His voice is so matter-of-fact, it takes me a few seconds to absorb this. "Oh God, what do I do now?"

"Nothing to do, Madeline. I spoke at length to the radiologist—who, I might say, is one of the best in Boston—and he agreed with me the risks of exploratory surgery exceed the benefits. I will refer you to a neurologist for a second opinion."

I thank him and don't ask about the margin of error for these tests. In a way, I'm grateful to have a tangible piece of evidence.

The vet report for Torvill and Tosca is similarly vague, yet encouraging in terms of my case against Vince. Dr. Kovacs tells me there are "tiny shadows" on their scans, suggesting electronic foreign bodies at the base of their skulls. No tumors, just lights. Hello world, I'm not crazy.

"These findings are consistent with the strange story you told me, Madeline. The radiologist suggested we do nothing other than keep an eye on your pets. Brain or spinal cord surgery—especially at their age—could be much more dangerous."

The report, which should upset me horribly, buoys me up. It all means there's a Squid Link signaling box in the house that I haven't yet found.

Another missing piece is the relationship between Mrs. Auerbach and my mother. They hated each other until Vince took my mother out. Now they're best friends. During this interlude of living with Wanda, I've been home every day to visit Mom and have found her happily cooking or watching TV with Mrs. Auerbach. What's puzzling to me is this: If Vince were controlling them with light frequencies, surely it would be in his interest to make them hostile toward each other. Because then I wouldn't be able to stay with Wanda.

Conclusion: he *isn't* controlling them with lights in their heads. Which is not to say he isn't trying. What does all of this mean?

One thing I know for sure: my desire for a new man—love, romance, marriage—is, for the moment, dead. It was a fairy tale based on magical thinking. It didn't include Wanda, who swept into my bloodstream like a miracle. And yet, I think what I really want now is to get the hell back to my normal independent existence. Then I will reassess.

But first I must solve the Vince puzzle and figure out once and for all how to kick him out of my life.

Slowly, I unspool the whole Vince experience in my mind, starting with the day I placed a profile on Professionals.com.

Vince was impatient to meet me and dismissive of the private chat feature offered by the dating site. He was a man in a hurry, with no time for trivialities.

Me too. Let's get the meeting part done and over with. Cool and efficient, a good start.

He introduced me to the idea of his lab before the end of our first drink at the bar. *I mustn't judge him for it. I spoke about my work too, ad nauseam.* Then he pushed the lab idea, harped on it, until he extracted a promise from me. *Yes, I'll go to your lab and observe your experiments.*

What if I'd said no? A definitive no, as in *I won't watch experiments that involve animals.*

Would he have dumped me? A strange thought, but I can't shake it.

As soon as I agreed to see the lab, he nailed down a second date.

How clearly I remember my sense of unease in his lab under the parallel bars of fluorescent light. The orderly arrangement of sterile equipment and dull lab surfaces. The *creepiness* of it all. The sliver of malice in his gleeful face.

On our second date, the talk about his research. *Brainwaves are brainwaves, no matter which creatures they show up in.* Grinning, leaning toward me. *I could tell you which part of your brain would light up now if I hooked you to a computer.*

Did he already have the idea of hooking me to a computer?

And then his comments in the lab, with rats and mice laid out before my eyes. *My experiment works across species. If the mouse stays in its corner, it's completely safe.*

On the day of the bitcoin mining revelation at his lab, Vince invaded my airspace. *I work with brains. My thing is mind control.* Watching him observe me was hypnotic. Even then I sensed his power.

He came to my house and collected my mother. Effortlessly. Was he trying to threaten me? Show me how easily he could control us?

Then tampered with my pets. He could control them too.

After that day, the behavior of every creature in my household changed.

He kidnapped me and drugged me. Hallucinogens? Opioids? A bruise on my back and a strange kind of hypnosis.

He knew I was smart and would follow the breadcrumbs if he laid them out. *Lights in our heads. Electronic signals controlling us.* Stupid! How susceptible I've been.

Summary. He took me to his lab. He showed me the rodent experiments. He came to my house and messed with my pets. He somehow (loose end) convinced my mother and Mrs. Auerbach to be friends so I could see his experiments worked on humans. He wrote me a marriage proposal, which he knew wouldn't succeed. He kidnapped me and implanted a light in my body. He got Buck to install a signal box in my office, which I was sure to find.

Vince *wanted* me to think he was controlling my mind. And of course he was. So far I've done everything he set me up for. I've been a sitting duck. *I allowed him to come for dinner.*

I recall the intensity of our first date, the way he stared at me—studied me—without embarrassment. I assumed he was assessing me as a love interest, even though there wasn't an iota of sexual chemistry between us. I thought he was doing all this to get me to go out with him. Because he was attracted by my powerful pheromones. But now, I suspect he was doing it to see how susceptible I'd be to having my mind controlled.

He was calibrating me as a lab subject.

His words: *the mice and rats are components of my experiments, no more, no less.*

And of course, the lab is another component. Window dressing.

Slowly but surely, this new knowledge unfolds inside me, until the final puzzle piece drops into place. As soon as I see it, I know—*right down to my core*—I am right.

The animals are not the subjects of his experiments.

I am.

CHAPTER 43

What makes you think you're so special? I've helped him with all the other women.

That's what Vince's flunky, Leo, said.

Vince experiments on women. Plural.

So. I've joined the crowd.

His lab subjects probably come from the same place he found me: a dating site.

What led him to such a dark experiment? I imagine the Vince of the past, an eminent research scientist, unsuccessful with women, a nondescript man without charisma or sex appeal.

My guess is on a day not too long ago, he hit on an idea to modify his research so as to make women he dated more compliant. More receptive to his limited charms. Single women were plentiful, easy to find online. But the man was fussy about his choices, specifying he wanted a particular type of woman. A mathematician or scientist. A professional. Someone who'd understand all too well his research with rodents. Someone with a fertile imagination who could extrapolate to humans. In other words, someone susceptible to the power of suggestion.

Someone like me.

How gullible I was, succumbing to his strange combination of mind games and alchemy.

Nothing between Vince and me has been real. His interest in my work? Feigned. His effusive compliments—perfect woman, brilliant soulmate? Part of the script. That cold marriage proposal deposited on my doorstep? Probably a pivotal piece of his diabolical experiment. What if I'd said yes? Would he have dumped me, checked me off on his spreadsheet, marked me as a success, and said *next?*

I haven't heard a peep from him since Sunday night's rejection.

Has he moved on?

Not a chance. Somehow, this is all part of his plan.

At work on Friday, Shawna sidles up to me in that irresistible way of hers. "Show-and-tell time, darlin'. What's up with your stalker? He in jail yet?"

Today, Shawna's hair is an elaborate up-do of braids and beads set at a jaunty angle and enhanced by gold hula hoop earrings.

It's a long story. The gun, blackmail, dinner, diamond ring. I give her an abbreviated version. "Maybe I've scared him off finally," I say, ready to get back to work.

"Dream on, Madeline." She steps back and examines me. "I don't care how many smarts you have, they sure don't help you with men."

"Hey, I work with men all the time and do just fine."

"See what I mean?" she implores the heavens. "Clueless."

It's time to change the topic. "How many walk-ins today?" The whole load is on me now, which means I'll be staying late.

"Lots. What's the latest on Bucky-Ball? Are we letting that boy back in so you can go back to having a sort-of life?"

"It sure would be nice to have an extra pair of hands on these computers," I say, "but I haven't forgiven him yet." It's my turn to scrutinize her. "Why? Do you miss him? Do you want him here?"

But I don't need to ask. Of course she does. We both miss his music and his antics and the hip vibe he gives the place. I miss his expertise. All it'll take is a phone call, so what's stopping me?

At 5:00 p.m., Shawna comes into my office to say goodbye. She's meeting her boyfriend, Lonnie, for dinner to talk about their non-relationship.

"If it's not serious, how come you go out with him all the time?" I like to jerk her chain about Lonnie, who is cross-eyed madly in love with her.

But she's not biting. "How're things with Wanda? You still staying in her house or what?"

This particular topic is harder to discuss. I've not gotten into it with Shawna.

"Yeah," I say. "I'm not back at home yet."

What's left unsaid is: *I'm still in her house, and also in her bed.*

It's complicated. I wouldn't know where to start.

Wanda fills me up with love and softness, a sense of safety I've never felt before. Nights of warm embrace and loving sweetness.

Living with her is strange and thrilling.

It's been quite a week.

Shawna is still studying me quizzically, while I am blushing to my roots. She gives me the wicked Shawna twinkle, until she sees my narrow-eyed look and lets it go.

"Be nice to Lonnie," I say.

Today I have Wanda's parking permit, and I get lucky straightaway.

There are complex aromas when I let myself in. Curry and oregano. In the kitchen, I find her squeezing honey from a squeeze bottle into a large pot. "New recipe," she says, stirring furiously. It doesn't quite resemble shark-infested tar, but it does look like we may be having peanut butter sandwiches for supper.

The kitchen is steamed up, and Wanda's hair has sagged, hanging listlessly on her back. I encircle her waist and kiss a small beauty spot on her neck.

I love her culinary adventures. I love her Zen attitude toward them. And I love that ineffectual stick in her hair. "Mmmm." I nuzzle into her warmth.

After our peanut butter dinner, I share with her my theory about Vince and how I'm surely one of the subjects of his mind-control experiment.

"Well, he's succeeding with you, big time," she says. "He's on your mind a lot."

She shrugs on her coat, because snow is forecast, and she's off to a public lecture at the university. It's another nasty late-fall day in Boston. Through the living room curtain, the sky is a brooding menace spitting rain at the window. November darkness rolling in.

I kiss Wanda goodbye, a lingering caress. "I'm going to work on solving the puzzle of that man so I can put him away," I breathe into her ear.

"Lock the door and don't do anything stupid," she says, sounding like my mother. "If the weather holds, I'll bring ice cream to make up for the dinner flop." And out she goes, slamming the door behind her. Sometimes she's a whirlwind, and I love that about her too.

Before I move to the study, I check the new front door. Locked and bolted.

Wanda's study can accommodate two desks, and this is where I've worked these past several evenings. Moving in bit by bit, making myself at home. It's as if I've known her forever.

Tonight I will study Vince's lab computer from the illicit flash drive Buck gave me. See if I can confirm my theory about his research. Solving the Vince conundrum is a tantalizing puzzle, one I'm unlikely to let go until I have the complete answer.

I settle down at my temporary desk and start by running the contents of the flash drive through a virus detector. It's clean, no malware. Next, I begin the search for results of Vince's experiments. A strange anxiety grips me, a pulse behind my eyes. The light in the study is too bright, and I get up to find the dimmer switch.

Outside, the night is making threatening noises.

Back to Vince's computer. No cute little rodent names appear—somehow I'd pictured Henry, Joey, Chico. Instead, there are vast arrays of mice and rat variables, a huge sample set spread over pages and pages of spreadsheets. Like me, Vince is a number cruncher. By every parameter, we should have suited each other well. *Cold bastard.*

A lot is missing. There are no units for the numbers, nor any explanations of the experiments. *No documentation.* These results are incomplete, which leads me to believe he has a more secure computer at home where he keeps the incriminating data—names, places, *details.*

A gust of wintry mix rattles the window frames, startling me. What a horrible night for Wanda to be out.

I shiver as I skim over the spreadsheets, when suddenly something different appears in front of me. A single page. A table with precisely four subjects—w1, w2, w3, and w4. *Four women. I'd bet my life on it.* There are six columns in the table, labeled Phase 1, Phase 2, Phase 3, and so on, up to Phase 6.

Here it is in black and white—sort of. Vince's experiment reduced to variables and phases. What if all the women in Vince's experiment were subjected to each of six phases, a weird kind of control group? My mind races ahead. Based on my own experiences, I sure could speculate about those phases.

Phase 1—the first date, his song and dance about seeing his lab. Phase 2—the lab visit, forcing me to watch the creepy rodent experiments. Phase 3—controlling my pets and household, and testing me with a written marriage proposal. Phase 4—implanting a light in my spine. Phase 5—testing the experiment: the dinner party at my house and the diamond ring.

All of this is pure speculation—nothing explicit on the page—which means I'm in trouble, because no sane person will buy this bizarre theory.

I examine Vince's table. The first three rows for women 1, 2, and 3, have numbers filled in for phases 1–6. The experiments have been completed. Mysterious, meaningless numbers without a key.

For woman #4, the data are in for phases 1–5. Phase 6 is blank.

The empty rectangle on the chart rises and swells in front of me. It's waiting for a value.

I have no doubt I'm w4, the fourth woman.

And Phase 6, the final phase of Vince's experiment, is about to begin.

CHAPTER 44

A table of undefined variables and numbers isn't evidence. I've imposed my own evil narrative on the data, and all the hackles and goose bumps rising on my arms tell me I'm right.

Vince has gone quiet on me this week, but he has a master plan and will be back.

I'm in a lonely place. Wanda flat-out won't believe me, and my lawyer will cleverly finesse the theory and steer me in a saner direction. Cops will tell me to stop wasting their time. Shawna will raise her eyes to the heavens and tell me to stick to cybersecurity.

I'm in trouble.

Some more searching produces no further information. Conclusion? Vince keeps his descriptions of the experiment—names, places, specifications—well hidden. My best guess is his home computer. Which means I must figure out a way to gain access without being flagrantly illegal. My motive is pure—*find proof and shut down the experiment*—but the method will probably involve some kind of hack. Welcome to my life.

The air in Wanda's study is stifling, not enough oxygen for me to think clearly. The noise of the weather is muted through the window panes, beckoning me.

Before leaving, I shut down the computer and pocket the flash drive.

Within a few minutes, I'm at the hallway closet grabbing my jacket, boots, gloves, and woolly hat, throwing back the bolt on the door, and navigating the snowy front steps to the sidewalk. The pavement is buried under a layer of powder, which sparkles in the ambient light.

The snow has mostly abated, soft flurries swirling around me.

I can't inhale enough of the cold fresh air that burns my lungs as it buoys me up. The road is a sheet of white. Pristine and as yet unplowed. It's after nine. Where is Wanda? She'll have a slippery ride home. Just thinking *Wanda* raises in me an ache of longing. She's so capable in navigating her environment—everywhere—I shouldn't worry about her.

The road is deserted. Like a kid, I plow through the snow on the sidewalk, kicking up powder and making boot angels. A new snowfall is a benediction, before it becomes sullied by the muck and mush of the city.

After a spin around a few blocks, my equilibrium is restored, and I head back to Wanda's condo. To my relief, the front steps now have two sets of prints, my own coming down and another pair going up. Whew! Wanda's home. She must have come in while I was briefly off this street. Why didn't she text me to say she was on her way? Why am I suddenly paranoid?

I pause and examine the prints, whose edges are blurring in the snow. *Too large.*

As I slot my key into the lock, it strikes me that surely she would have texted me to ask where I was. I turn the key and stand motionless at the door, sweating under my jacket, checking my phone. No messages.

There's someone in the condo, waiting for me.

Perhaps he's waiting for Wanda.

He may not be waiting for anyone, another thief who is cleaning out the place while I stand here having a debate with myself. In my haste to get out, did I leave the door unlocked?

Shit. Think.

Well, there's no sense in dithering on the threshold. I turn the doorknob, shove the door open and flood the hallway and living room with light. A strange pair of boots is on the shoe mat in the hallway, leaving a small puddle of melting snow. *Not Wanda's.*

"Hello, Madeline, so lovely to see you, as always," Vince says. He's on the living room couch, shoes off, making himself at home.

Sweet Jesus, how did he get in?

He inclines his head toward the sofa. "Why not take off your boots and join me?"

I don't move a muscle. "How dare you come here?"

"Since you've blocked me from your phone, I can't speak to you or text you. Therefore, I must surprise you."

Wanda will have a fit. She'll think I opened the door for him.

"What do you want?" I say it roughly, and it comes out sounding rude and uncouth.

"I'd like to show you something, if you don't mind." He stands and holds up a flash drive. "I know you'll be very interested in this—it concerns your family. Let's go into the study."

He's been in her study!

His previous incriminating flash drive was a video of me with my gun in his lab. What kind of blackmail does he have in store for me now? If this were a movie, the audience would be screaming, *Turn around and get yourself outta there! Call 911!*

Every rational nerve ending tells me to do just that, but with his threat about my family, he's sucked me in to play his game to the bitter end. If I don't, he'll be back, again and again, seeing what it takes to wear me down. I know it with certainty.

The experiment with me is not over. And when he's done, he'll go on to the fifth woman.

Almost in slow motion, I remove my coat, gloves, scarf, and boots, and stuff my feet into indoor shoes.

He watches me silently, then says, "Thank you, Madeline. I didn't want our relationship to end the other night with you storming out of your mother's dinner party."

"We don't have a relationship." Fists clenched.

"She was very perturbed, your mother. The housekeeper too." He has on a dark turtleneck and a well-worn navy sweater. His socks are black with diagonal, thin red stripes; a ridiculous sight. And he's not as relaxed as he would like me to think. A tic is jumping at the corner of his mouth.

I give a curt nod. That's how I play it, but my knees are turning to water. The movie audience is yelling, *Tell him to leave. Smash him with a poker.* But the intrepid, stupid woman is accompanying him to the study, doing his bidding, because she wants to solve the mystery and find out what he has in his hand.

Thank goodness I powered off my computer and removed the incriminating evidence before I went for a frolic in the snow. Force of habit. Protect your data. You never know when there's danger lurking.

He has set up his computer on Wanda's desk. The gall of him, invading her study.

"I took the liberty," he says. "Your friend seems nice. I don't think she'll mind."

Your friend.

A trickle of sweat runs down my face, salty on my mouth. I lick my lips. "If she walks in, she'll throw you out of her home and call the police."

He has set up a video on his screen, a right arrow waiting for activation. "You may have seen it already," he says. "It's from your surveillance camera in my lab."

This time I stare at him, my shock undisguised. "How did you get the video?"

"You're not the only tech expert on the block." His voice is contemptuous, and I'm quaking so badly I must sit down.

"Did you really think I was so dense that after I neutralized your spyware I wouldn't check for bugs or hidden cameras in my lab?" He doesn't look at me when he says this, because he's casting about for an outlet where he can plug in his computer's power source. Brazenly, he removes the plug for Wanda's lamp, casting the room into semi-darkness.

When he's all plugged in, he straightens up, stretches, and gives me a look that could freeze blood. "You have a dark heart, Madeline, and I've learned not to underestimate you."

This was a mistake. How can I make him leave?

As soon as I think it, a key turns at the front entrance, then the door slams shut, as clear and sharp as a gunshot.

CHAPTER 45

"Madeline," she calls from the hallway, stomping her boots as she changes into indoor gear. "Ice cream in the kitchen."

She breezes into the study, then backs off to take in the scene. "Whoa." Nodding toward Vince. "What the fuck?"

"Vince broke in," I say.

"Get the hell away from my desk," she says to him.

When she glares at me, I add, "He came in while I was out for a walk."

Vince extends his hand to Wanda. "*Enchanté.* We meet again."

"What am I missing here?" Wanda says to me, ignoring Vince and his outstretched hand. "This is the creep who's been stalking you, right?"

He smiles at her—actually *smiles*—showing perfect teeth. "Well that's a little strong, but yes, you could say I've been ardent in my pursuit of Madeline. I'm the first to admit it."

This is why I can't get rid of him. He oozes into all the empty spaces.

Wanda gives a dry laugh, and her eyes are flashing in the muted light. "Why don't you get your big-boy boots on and leave," she says. "And just so you know, as soon as you're outta here, I'm calling the cops and lodging an unlawful entry complaint."

For the briefest instant, a look of menace crosses his face, but he's smiling as he says, "But, Wanda, your friend invited me to visit. Do you really believe I'd come all this way on a night like this if I weren't invited? Breaking and entering? That's not my style. Your door was unlocked when I arrived, and I made myself at home until Mads came back from her spin in the snow."

The irony is she's never looked more beautiful as she turns to me, confused, and says, "Is that right, Madeline? You left the door unlocked?"

"He's lying. The door was locked. And no, I wasn't expecting him."

But, actually, I was. Phase 6.

Vince says, "You're a grown-up, Mads, you shouldn't have to justify yourself to anyone. Let me show you the surveillance video you asked to see. Wanda"—he swivels to face her—"you're welcome to stay and watch."

Her gaze in his direction is pure loathing. "Sure. Since it's my study and my desk, why don't I accept your invitation to watch."

In one manly stride, he's in front of his computer and has pressed *Play*.

Is it going to be a dead rat being dissected? My stomach heaves.

What I see is a scene of two women sitting at Vince's lab bench. The picture is blurry, and I don't immediately recognize them. Or perhaps my brain is reluctant to accept what I'm seeing. One of the women is my mother, animated and happy. The other is Gretchen Auerbach.

In his lab.

They are linking arms and chatting amiably with Vince, who is seated across from them. The time stamp is Saturday, October

26th, the day I first met Wanda, and the afternoon Mrs. Auerbach called me with a frantic phone call to say Mom was missing.

"Madeline, what's wrong?" Wanda says.

Blood drains out of my head as I lurch toward the side of the room and slide down the wall until I'm on the floor. I'm hot, cold, sweaty, dizzy all at once, and numb in the soles of my feet. It's as if my head is weighed down by cement blocks, spinning off my neck. Vertigo.

Echoes from far away.

Madeline, are you okay?

Madeline? Come back.

Wanda on the floor, her arms cradling me.

Vince across the room, his face inscrutable.

Slowly, Wanda helps me up, and I walk back to face him, with Wanda like a rock by my side.

"Good God, Madeline," he says. "I would hope I'd never react like that at the sight of *my* mother."

The attack of vertigo slowly passes, and my head clears. "What are you trying to do, Vince? What was that scene about?"

"Madeline," Wanda says, her hand on my arm.

"I invited your lovely mother to see my lab," Vince says. "That witch of a housekeeper insisted on accompanying her. But, as you can see, we had a rip-roaring time together. Those girls were loads of fun. You could learn a thing or two from your mother."

"Get out." I slam his laptop shut and yank the plug out the wall. "Go!"

"I can see I've outstayed my welcome," he says, standing abruptly and taking his computer. He pats his pocket, removes an envelope, and drops it on the desk. "Look at this at your leisure, Madeline. You can respond through Professionals.com."

At the door, as he's about to leave, he turns to Wanda. "You're a fascinating woman. I'm afraid I've ignored you. I'd like to hear about *your* work one of these days."

"Leave!" Wanda says.

He puts up his hand and touches her cheek. "If you're interested in my research, I'll take you to see my lab."

She slaps his hand away and stands watching him until he's gone, those big boots crunching in the snow.

Waiting near the door in a state of queasy horror, I relive the scene on Vince's computer. Mom and Mrs. Auerbach in his lab the Saturday before Halloween; the day my mother disappeared and my household changed. Another improbable puzzle piece lands in place.

He took them to his lab, gave them amnesia-inducing anesthetics, and implanted synchronized lights in their spines.

CHAPTER 46

"What was that all about?" Wanda says, her tone like frost.

"He kidnapped my mother and implanted a light in her spine. My housekeeper too, I think."

"Well, that's surreal. But I meant the break-in tonight."

"I've already told you. He must have jimmied the lock. I found him waiting for me in the living room."

My friend's face is like thunder.

A nearby spider catches my eye, and I watch its leisurely walk on the couch pillow. I decide to let it live. "Is this an interrogation?"

"Here's what I don't understand. You claim this man is stalking you, and yet you didn't scream at him to get the fuck out or you'll call the cops." She inhales sharply. "If he refused to leave, you could have stood outside and screamed for help. We're not isolated here. I have neighbors. You could have raised a ruckus and people would have come to help you get rid of him. Why, Madeline? Why didn't you make him leave?" Her voice has risen and become shrill. "I don't goddamn understand you and your passive reaction to this man."

My dear friend and lover Wanda, whose normal essence is tranquil bedrock, is yelling at me like I burned down the building.

Yet I respond quietly. "Because he had information about my mother. And what he's doing is evil, and I want to make him pay."

We're at opposite ends of the couch, separated by a chasm.

"Also, if I'd gotten rid of him the way you suggested, he'd be back next week on some different pretext."

"Then go to the police. Get your lawyer to slap a restraining order on him for God's sake, Madeline!"

"Wanda, stop yelling at me to do stuff and *listen*."

She throws both arms into the air, as if to say, *There's no hope. I'm done.*

"I'm going to find proof of his criminal actions and file charges." And before she can interrupt or contradict, I tell her what I found on his laptop—numerical scores for phases one through six, and my theory he's experimenting on women without their consent. It comes out fast and garbled, because I don't know how to cut through the conflict that thickens the air like sawdust.

"I'm one of his experimental subjects," I say. "Not a love interest."

Wanda's hand is clammy when I move over and cover it with mine. It's unthinkable that she wouldn't hear me.

"So this man implanted lights in your pets," she says. "He punctured their backs."

"Yes. Shadows that resembled small electronic chips were detected on their CAT scans."

"And lights in you, your mother, and housekeeper?" Her eyes are like steel. No crinkles at the corners today.

And so we go, wading through the marshes, drowning in the murky water of what I suspect Vince has and hasn't done. Heartbreak settles on me slowly as I realize she'll never accept any of this. It's too fantastical for her hardcore mathematical mind. I myself can barely believe it. My knuckles are white as the sharp edges of my fingernails dig into my palms.

If she can't understand what's driving me, I must leave her before she's exposed to even greater danger. My darling Wanda, soulmate and confidante, who's offered nothing but love, support, and a safe haven.

Torvill, my faithful dog, with his big baleful eyes, pops into my head. He's probably missing me. And Tosca, too, my beautiful girl. I think of my carefree mother having a laugh with her friend Gretchen while sitting at Vince's workbench, and it's too much to bear. He's using them with evil intent, as he's using me.

It's time to go home to my family.

This business with Vince has changed me. It pains me—pisses me off, actually—that Mom will surely see I've become a grim, unsmiling woman in these past several weeks, one with too much negative karma. There's a softening and blurring of who I am, and I loathe this false version of myself.

I stand up heavily from the couch.

"Madeline, wait." Wanda gets up too, and a smile finally flickers on her face. She flaps the envelope from Vince in front of me. "Let's try something radical. Why don't we run this through the shredder in my study without opening it? Why don't we totally ignore him? We could solve this problem right now."

For a few seconds, I hover on the edge. How inviting it is, the thought of burrowing into her sexy warmth and just wishing the problem away.

And yet ...

She hasn't heard a word I've said about wanting to find proof and putting Vince behind bars. Nothing. No acknowledgment or affirmation. At this moment, she's taking charge, managing me, treating me like a subordinate. One with a regrettable mental illness that can be cured by her shredder.

I snatch the envelope from her hand and stride to the bedroom to pack my suitcase.

Wanda appears in the room as I'm zipping the case shut. How pathetic—such a small case—the sum total of my possessions at her house.

"I'm sorry, Madeline," she says. Her fury has subsided, her face lined with regret. "I tried, I really did. I don't know how to break this terrible spell you're under."

It's not a spell. It's resolve.

I say nothing as I brush past her.

Tonight, I'll sleep in the living room and will head home in the morning. By then, I hope the roads will be plowed.

Vince's invitation is on a crisp, white card. The word *Invitation* scrolls across the top in a slanted calligraphic font. The card is printed, except for the blue-black signature *Vince*, written with a flourish at the bottom.

Before reading, I take a photo and send his words into safe backup on the cloud.

Dear Madeline,

Dinner at my house on Saturday evening, November 17th, a week from tomorrow. A time of your choosing.

Bring your laptop.

Please respond using the chat feature on Professionals.com.

Dress: Business formal.

This will be a business meeting. I hope to engage your professional services.

Warmly,

Vince.

CHAPTER 47

It's a dazzling Saturday morning when I arrive home. The porch has been cleared of Halloween debris and is now littered by leaves that have blown from the nearby trees. Melting snow drips from the eaves as I approach the front door and hear my dog hurl himself against it in a frenzy.

When he sees me, he jumps up and down on two legs like a basketball player, almost overpowering me. Together, we collapse onto the porch furniture, and I hold him in a long, tight embrace while he gives me wet kisses on my face.

"Did you miss me?" I say in my doggy voice while we rub noses. "Yes you did, yes you did."

A meow below and a soft paw on my leg. Tosca wants in too. I lift her up and hold her and Torvill squashed together. Have I really been away for almost a week? I adore my furry guys with their uncomplicated love.

"Will you rub noses with me too?"

Mom has appeared on the porch, her auburn hair shiny and full of bounce. She smiles benevolently, no recriminations or grievances about the dinner party that took a turn.

She settles into one of the ancient wicker chairs facing me. "You look pale, Madsy, like you need a day on the beach."

I lower my babies to the ground and squat down next to my mother. Her hair warms my hand as I run my fingers through the thick waves. "I'm jealous. Why didn't I get your hair?"

She ruffles my spiky head. "Just be grateful you got his brain."

She seems so lucid. But I know the previous version of my mom would be berating me for abandoning her and our dinner guest.

Cold air seeps through the cracks in my old house, and I hug myself for warmth as I climb the steps to my bedroom. There's something I should have done long ago. I shut the door and call Jessica. Apologizing for disturbing her weekend and not returning her calls.

"Has he left you alone since I sent the letter?" she asks, dispensing with all niceties.

Yes, other than the fact he orchestrated a ransomware attack against me, kidnapped me, kept me overnight against my will, saddled my family with a wedding proposal dinner party, and invaded my friend's house last night.

I do my best to update her like an intelligent being, but the events are outlandish and I can barely believe them myself. Jessica doesn't interrupt me. She listens in silence to my theory about his research, the phases of his experiment, and my resolve to track down his other women to help me uncover the truth.

"The next time I go to the police with a complaint, I want it to be airtight, backed up by actual corroborating evidence."

"Why don't we go to the Cambridge Police Department *right now* and file a complaint." She's deathly serious.

"Because I've already made two complaints that went nowhere. And because there's more to the story, and I want to know it all."

"Madeline, have you made another date with this ... stalker?" She's working hard at maintaining her cool professionalism.

I choose my words carefully. "I'm convinced the evidence I need is in his house. So I'm going to his house to find it next Saturday."

During the silence that ensues, there's typing and ticking in the background. I picture her phone, wedged between her sleek head and raised shoulder, while she furiously documents my insanity.

"Madeline," she says eventually in a slow, measured voice. "I urge you in the strongest terms to rethink the visit to this stalker's house. The action you're proposing exposes you to unpredictable danger I can't protect you from. As a lawyer—and a friend—I'm asking you not to do it."

Jessica always gives me sterling advice, sometimes saving me from my own impulsiveness. That's why I pay her a fat retainer. Now, however, I've become involved in something bigger than myself, and clawing out the truth has become a personal imperative. If I don't give the police complete information, there will be future victims.

She senses I'm wavering. "Stay away from him, Madeline. This man is dangerous. We have enough ammunition to go after him right now."

"But we don't have enough to stop him. I guarantee there'll be a fifth woman."

"Oh, Madeline."

She's not hearing me. I might just as well have been talking about the phases of the moon. If nothing else, this conversation clarifies my goal. Still holding tight to my phone, I formulate a compromise.

"Give me a chance to interview some of his previous women. I'll probably need a couple of days. If I hit a dead end, I'll cancel Vince's Saturday dinner and go with you to the police station to file a final complaint."

Her sigh quivers through the phone. "If you can't stay safe, Madeline, stay in touch."

In the afternoon, I tell Mrs. Auerbach to take the rest of the day off. She stares at me as if she hasn't quite understood, then she nods as if, yes, she'll do it for me.

Mom and I go for a spin along Memorial Drive, then cross the bridge into Boston. The roads have been plowed, and with the blue sky and snowy sidewalks, we luxuriate in the magnificence of a New England late-fall day.

After some fumbling, my mother rolls down the window and turns her face up to the sky. "Hello, sun."

I drive all the way to the Waterfront, to Abigail's Tea Room, where we order a pot of their special blend, with scones, raspberry jam and whipped cream. Mom is as happy as I've seen her in a while, scarfing down the scones, gazing out the window at the water, and having another cup of the potent tea.

Wistfully, she says, "Madsy, I so wish you'd find someone."

At home after dinner, I shut the door of my study and go to Professionals.com. In the private chat feature, I type to Vince: *I'll be at your house on Saturday at 7:00 p.m.*

This is necessary, if only to give him a false sense of smugness and keep him at bay.

Before hitting *Send*, I pause to think about what I'm doing. Disregarding dire warnings from Wanda and Jessica, allowing a strong necessity to drive me on. When I signed up for Professionals.com, I imagined I was searching for a long-lost notion of romantic love; but what I'm finding instead is a truer version of myself. Stubborn. Reckless. *Fearless?* Willing to do what it takes to fight back against a relentless foe.

And yet, what I'm doing is dangerous. Vince is not going to roll over and play dead.

I take a deep breath and forge ahead with my plan, clicking on Vince's profile page and probing for access to his dating history. No luck.

Step 2 is to create a fake profile that will allow chats to Vince from someone he can't identify as me. Not as hard as it sounds. Just a tiny text string added to the code of an unsecure server turns me into a *Premium user* who can get a new membership for free.

I'm in!

I fashion a profile photo with a random cat photoshopped onto a distorted old snapshot of my mother and name her *Cat Girl.* Thirty-eight years old, Vince's sweet spot. Then, with renewed purpose, I set up a profile that will make Vince drool.

Love everything science. Searching for a lab guy who'll do experiments while I watch over his shoulder. Mmmm.

I can't bring Cat Girl to say she's fun-loving, but she does enjoy physics, reading, and creative foreplay. I send Cat Girl into cyberspace and wonder if she'll hook Vince.

Almost immediately, my computer pings with several matches for Cat Girl. It seems too easy. Vincent Cantley shows up as a match. Of course he does; I've created a perfect research subject for him.

Cat Girl accepts him as a possibility, and without much time elapsing, she receives a message from him in the chat. *Hey, Cat Girl, let's get together so I can show you my lab.*

Phase 1.

A small surge of venal pleasure passes through me at how easy it was to reel Vince in.

Back to reality, the silence in the house that tells me Mom has long gone to bed. Still, there are footfalls on the stairs that pause near my room. A creak outside my door.

When I look out into the hallway, it's deserted.

My arms tremble, mainly because it's freezing in my study. I go to my bedroom for an extra sweater, and this time I'm not mistaken—there are footsteps near my room. No one to be seen but Mrs. Auerbach, ascending the stairs. It's a long trek up to her apartment. She's climbing in the dark, like a ghost. *Are the landing lights broken?*

"Goodnight, Gretchen," I say, flipping the switch.

She flinches in the sudden light and scampers up without a word. She too lives in her own remote, lonely world.

Back I go, filled with a restless energy, to search for a way to hack into Vince's Chat Messenger without a password. There has to be a way to find his previous women from Professionals.com. I tease the problem, turning it over in my mind.

After an hour of mental tinkering, a brainwave strikes. Of course! An obvious solution. I'll send him some malware in a photo. This technique—steganography—is frequently used to conceal data in an innocent, non-secret message.

I grab my phone and pull up the selfie I took of Mom and me at Abigail's today, an adorable picture, our heads together, mouths full of scone, and holding our teacups aloft. Mom has a dab of whipped cream on her nose. I transfer the photo to my computer. It takes just a few minutes of coding to embed an invisible message in the image, a piece of encrypted malware.

Back in Professionals.com, I open my chat stream to Vince. *Check this out: Mom and me having high tea at the site of The Boston Tea Party.* I include a link to the photo and hit *Send.*

While I'm wondering whether he's likely to be up this late, his reply pings back.

My two favorite girls.

He's taken the bait and opened the picture, launching my subliminal instructions. *It worked!* Vince's entire chat history on Professionals.com is now mine.

CHAPTER 48

My new hacked status allows me to see both Vince's entire chatting history and his dating stats on the site. He's a low-activity user, who doesn't reach out to all of his matches. But he always makes the first move and perseveres to make a date.

With jaded equanimity, I'm able to confirm I'm not the great and glorious love of his life. He's currently chatting up more than a few women. If the vulnerable side of me feels a brief glimmer of rejection, the dominant problem solver puts a lid on that and feels vindicated. I'm just one cog in the array of his diabolical mind-control experiment.

My mission now is to find the other cogs.

Susan Buffington lives in Somerville, two miles north of Boston.

When she opens the door to my ring, I'm struck by how like me she is. Tall, lanky, short dark hair. Sharp eyes, which examine my business card, then my skinny cords, then my face, which is trying to look intelligent.

"Thanks for seeing me on a Sunday," I say.

She nods, moves aside for me to come in, and says, "I was curious. It's been a while since I went out with Vince, and he was one strange bird."

She's wearing blue jeans and a summery tank top, the muscles of her arms rippling.

"Cold doesn't get to you, huh?" I say conversationally. It's about sixty degrees in the house. She doesn't offer to take my jacket.

"Been through menopause yet?" she says. Snappish and rhetorical. "Want some iced coffee?"

"Sure, why not?" Put some ice in my veins.

The living room is well lived in, parts of the Sunday newspapers strewn around on every surface. John Coltrane oozing honey through the speakers. I've thought about my opening gambit ahead of time and decided honesty—well, 95 percent honesty—is likely to elicit what I want.

"I'm being stalked by Vince," I say, "and I'm investigating other women he dated."

"How did you find me?" she asks.

I've obviously anticipated this question, and here's where my little white lies come in. "He mentioned you when I first met him." I can't exactly tell her I hacked into Professionals.com and have access to all of her conversations with Vince.

She stops in mid-step. "Mentioned how?"

"Um, said he admired women surgeons." *God. Would he really say that?* I'm not a good liar and follow up quickly. "Do you mind telling me what went wrong with you and Vince?" I'm stabbing in the dark. Something must have gone wrong. She's not seeing him anymore.

She gives a short, barky laugh. "It's not that anything *went wrong*, it's that he was unsexy as hell and I broke up with him.

Story of my life––men who become impotent when I tell them I'm a brain surgeon."

We both laugh. She's pretty scary, even without a scalpel.

"Did he accept you breaking up with him?" I sip my icy drink, which chills my marrow.

"If you're asking whether he made a pest of himself, the answer is no. But you may be interested to know that I contacted him about a month after our breakup."

Not exactly what I'm waiting to hear. "Really?" I say politely.

"I had seen his lab, where he experimented with rats and mice."

"I've seen his rodent experiments," I say, trying to speed things along.

She hesitates, then says, "I had an old dog, Salt, who sadly is no longer with us. I got an adorable puppy, Pepper. You know, Salt and Pepper. But it was more like chalk and cheese. They hated each other. It came to the point where Pepper tormented Salt constantly, and Salt started fighting back. I was scared they'd kill each other."

I stare at her. "Don't tell me you asked Vince to implant lights in their heads so they would love each other." But of course, that's exactly what she did.

"I'm a believer in science," she says, "and his experiments seemed miraculous."

She delivered her dogs to his lab, where he injected some anesthetic right under their eyeballs. Then he performed a little surgery on them. She shudders. Rubbing her arms, reliving it. "You're right, it *is* cold in here."

So he's improved his technique. Now it's insertion through the spinal fluid.

"Did it work?"

"Salt didn't survive the surgery," she says, her voice terse. "He died that night."

"I'm so sorry." The thought of my two babies, so trusting of human monsters. "Was Pepper okay?" I ask.

"I didn't wait to find out," she says, avoiding my eyes. "I gave him back to the shelter, because I didn't deserve to keep him. Disgusted with myself for asking Vince to torture Salt and Pepper to make my life easier."

"And Vince?"

"He said I owed him another date."

"Did you go out with him again?" Suddenly, I'm back in familiar territory.

She laughs. Heartily this time. "Are you serious? The man's a ghoul. I told him I'd made a mistake and didn't want to see him again."

"And that was it?" I'm incredulous.

"I think he was scared about me reporting the thing with the animals. I didn't see him again." She knocks the table. Throws back her drink. Crunches loudly on the ice. "Now you've resurrected him. Sounds like he's changed, though it could be he finds you really sexy in a way he didn't find me."

Not bloody likely.

We part on good terms. My takeaway from our conversation is that Vince has been rejected a lot since his relationship with Susan. I think it made him change his technique—if he can't find a woman who'll have him, he'll damn well work on her until she says yes.

The whereabouts of the next woman are not entirely clear. I call a phone number I picked up through the White Pages.

"Who is this?" a sharp woman's voice says. She's using the same voice I use for suspected junk calls.

"This is Madeline Geiger. I'm not selling anything and would like to speak to Kay Fornato."

The person on the other end does not terminate the call, but nor does she respond to my request.

"Hello?" I say.

"Kay is dead," the voice says.

By now I'm quite practiced in speaking to strangers—running my business has helped with that. Social situations, however, are not my superpower.

"I'm so sorry," I say lamely. *Think!* "May I come and see you? I'm—"

"In regard to what?"

"I'm investigating someone on the dating site Professionals.com. Kay used that site."

"I curse the day she signed up. I warned her no good would come of it."

Mrs. Fornato is Kay's mother, a youthful woman who reminds me of my own mother. Sadness is in the creases of her face. She allows me to come in. Suspicious, but gracious enough. I sink into an armchair upholstered with flowers and remove my jacket, because it's about ninety degrees in here.

"I have information that Kay dated Vincent Cantley," I say after giving Mrs. Fornato my business card and activating my *Record* button.

"She more than dated him. She was engaged to marry him."

I shift in my chair. *Really?* The heat is oppressive, and I'm aware of sweating unpleasantly through my sweater. "What went wrong?" I say softly.

"First, let me tell you I didn't like that man. He was cold and phony, and something hard to describe."

I hear you, lady.

She digs a tissue from her pocket and wipes her eyes. "Kay had never had any luck with men. She was forty, unmarried. Very depressed. Wanted a normal life, a child or two, and so accepted his marriage proposal. She wasn't madly in love with him. She was pragmatic."

I lean toward her, this small, sad woman. "So the marriage didn't happen?"

"Two months before the wedding, he told her he could help with her depression—some kind of hypnosis he was studying through his research."

"What happened?" My voice is hardly a whisper.

She stands up abruptly and paces around the room, angry. "He turned her into a zombie is what happened. I don't know what he did to her, but she just couldn't snap out of it. Quit her teaching job." She stops near to me. "He destroyed her life. That's what he did."

I stand and put my arm around her shoulders. "He's horrible," I say. "He's hurt other women."

"Kay seemed to go totally under," her mother says. "Three weeks later, she had a fatal car accident, hit a tree. The investigators said the tire tracks showed she aimed for the tree, and I believed them."

"Had Vince taken Kate to his lab, shown her his experiments?" I probably shouldn't ask, but I want to document all the phases.

"Oh yes. She was massively impressed. Brought her AP Physics students to his lab for a field trip."

Phase 2. Done and dusted.

There's a horror to the parallels.

Phase 3, the marriage proposal. Phase 4, inducing the "zombie" stage. Phase 5, screwing with her mind, nailing down the control.

Was Phase 6 death?

"Can you remember if she complained of back pain after the hypnosis?" I ask. I'm barely breathing.

Mrs. Fornato puts her head in her hands. "Now that you mention it, I think she did."

A light injected into her spinal cord? I'll never know.

I shift in my chair, reluctant to cause more pain, but driven to nail down this one last thing. "There's a suspicion Vince drugged some of his dates. Were drugs found ... in Kay's body?"

"Let her rest," Kay's mother says sharply and moves away from me then.

I probably have all the information I'm going to get.

But then she surprises me, turns to face me again. "Sure there were drugs, a whole damn pharmacy of garbage. You name it, he'd given it to her."

"And you didn't go to the police?"

She looks at me for a second. "Of course I went. But they couldn't figure out what to charge him with."

I find a small place nearby for lunch. While I sip tea, I debate about what to do next. These searches are tedious, and I reckon I more or less have the gist of Vince's dating life. He's looking for research subjects not wives or sexual partners. No sex mentioned anywhere by anyone.

Idly, I scroll through the next sequence of his Chat Messenger, pages and pages. This third woman is halfway in love with Vince's profile, complimenting his photo, telling him she loves tall, dark, handsome men. She accepts a first date with alacrity and writes she can't wait to see his lab, science in action with a brilliant scientist.

Who *is* this obsequious person?

I find her profile, with a small picture of a striking, auburn-haired woman grinning at the camera, full of *joie de vivre*. She looks vaguely familiar, and I scroll up to find her name. There it is, in black and white.

The third woman is Gretchen Auerbach!

CHAPTER 49

I signal for the check, then with hands shaking, call my mother. After a few rings, it goes to voicemail. Mom's perky voice says, *This is Janet, thanks for calling. I'll get back to you.*

Where is she? She always picks up.

I hesitate, then call Mrs. Auerbach. *Is Vince monitoring her phone?*

"Hi, Madeline." A thump sounds in the background. "Could you give me a minute?" Two clicks on my phone, and the call ends. I grip my throat and squeeze the skin on my neck. Everything feels wrong.

For fuck's sake, it's just a dropped call.

When my phone jangles a minute later, two academic types at an adjacent table glare at me through skinny glasses. I drop $30 next to my plate, grab my stuff, and run out the door, knocking over a chair that blocks the aisle.

"Gretchen," I say, sinking down to the sidewalk. "Can I speak to Mom?"

"Janet is having a bad day. She's resting in her bedroom. Can I give her a message when she wakes up?"

That's insane. My head smacks against the brick wall of the coffee shop, short-circuiting my brain.

"Madeline?"

"Gretchen, sorry. Please go into her room. I need to speak to her now. Would you ask her to call me?" My breath is coming in gasps, short and painful—hyperventilating—which I recognize is an overreaction.

"I'm afraid that's not possible," Mrs. Auerbach says.

"Wake her up, for God's sake!"

Again, my phone clicks off.

I drive home like a maniac, my Guardian Angel protecting me from other Boston drivers. When I finally turn left at the *No Left Turn* sign, my body is one churning mess. Every nerve and tendon tells me Mom is gone—dead or missing—and I can barely maneuver my key into the lock at the front door.

She's in the living room with Mrs. Auerbach, watching tennis on TV.

A player serves an ace, and there they are, Mom and Mrs. Auerbach, screaming with joy and pumping their fists in the air. As for me, I throw off my jacket and gloves, drop everything to the floor, storm into the living room, and jab a finger at the TV power button.

A devastating silence fills the room.

Mom turns to Mrs. Auerbach. "Prima donna time."

Calm. Breathe. She's okay.

I say, very quietly, "Where were you, Mom? I called and Gretchen said you couldn't come to the phone."

She looks down, guilty, and says in a small voice, "I stepped out with the animals. Took them for a walk."

"You went out on your own?" I glare at Mrs. Auerbach.

"I told Gretchen I wanted to be alone," Mom says, defiant. "We agreed we wouldn't tell you, because you'd have a hissy fit like right now."

I shut my eyes. Briefly. "Okay. I understand perfectly what happened, including Gretchen dropping my calls."

I force myself to amble over to my mother and squeeze her shoulders. "Mom, I'm relieved everything is fine, and you had a lovely walk with our guys. Gretchen and I will go upstairs and … plan for the coming week."

"You can talk in front of me," Mom says. "I want to hear how you'll punish her for being my friend."

It stops me cold, her clarity of mind in this instant. "There are some things you don't know about, Mom, that may be hurtful."

"Here's what I know." Her face crumples into softly weeping sobs. "That lemon face you have on now is exactly why you can't find anyone to love. You make yourself unlovable, and it tears me up inside."

How did we get to this?

Mrs. Auerbach has been watching with a taut, unreadable face. I look at her until her eyes lock on mine.

"Gretchen, I'm sorry, but I must terminate your employment here."

"No!" Mom shouts. "That's not okay, Madeline. Blame me, not Gretchen."

I hate that my mother will be hurt. My heart is literally aching. I'll have to explain everything to her when all this drama has passed.

Reluctantly, I turn to face Gretchen again. "I'll book you into a Boston hotel for two weeks, starting tomorrow night. This gives you time to pack."

"Why, Madeline?" Mom cries. "All this cruelty because I wanted to walk on my own for a bit?"

I inhale deeply and gird myself. "Mom, Gretchen has been spying on us."

I set Mom up in her bedroom to watch the rest of the tennis match. Then, with the TV on high volume, I remove my shoes and creep silently up the stairs. The creaky floorboards are well-known to me, and I negotiate my way around them, like a lynx stalking its prey.

At the top of the stairs, I pause and listen at the entrance of Mrs. Auerbach's apartment. A murmuring of her voice is audible, but it's too muted for me to distinguish words. Swiftly, I use my master key to unlock the door and step into her living room.

Her phone is at her ear, and she gasps when she sees me. She types quickly with her thumbs, shoves her phone into her pocket, then says dully, "It's illegal for you to burst in like that. This is still my home." Her eyes are dead pools.

"You were speaking to him, weren't you?"

"He knows everything," she says, throwing some books into an empty box on the floor.

Fear propels me to follow her into her bedroom, where she reaches for an old suitcase whose wheels are missing. Why is she living like a pauper?

She pauses and turns her sullen face toward me. "He knows you made two frantic calls this afternoon, and he heard the conversation we just had in the living room."

I sit down heavily on the faded armchair. "Is the house bugged?" I whisper.

She shakes her head no and points to her phone on the bed.

Spyware on her phone. Vince has the app and can see every keystroke, hear every word.

Mrs. Auerbach is strangely passive when I reach for her phone and power it off. I make sure mine is on, recording everything.

"He told you to come and work for us, didn't he?" I say. How clear it is now—she showed up for an interview the day after our first date at the bar, when I told Vince about my troubles with my mother. He saw an opportunity and grabbed it. Install Gretchen Auerbach and enlist her help in landing Madeline.

"How did you—or Vince—convince Boston Family Services to take you on so fast? Didn't they check your references?"

"They were desperate for full-time aides, and Vince made me say I had experience working with dementia patients. They sent me here straightaway, without any vetting."

Vince made me say.

"Why, Gretchen? What power does he have over you?" This is the missing piece of the puzzle I can't completely fathom.

"I'm older than him," she says simply. "I wanted to find someone."

A cloud passing over the setting sun darkens the room. No warmth in here at all.

"Tell me about Vince. You met him on the dating site?"

She nods. "I liked him. I'm bipolar, and his strangeness suited me."

I'm curious about what went wrong. So far, everything sounds true. "I take it you saw his lab, and he followed up with more dates?"

"Yes."

"Did you give him any resistance?"

"Not in the beginning, no."

Her story is different from mine, and I want to know everything, so I can slot her into my narrative of Vince. "What happened next? What made you resist?"

She's being very weird, her eyes drifting away as if she's not quite here. She slumps down on the bed.

"Gretchen, wake up! Are you drugged?"

Her eyes are rolling around in her head, slipping up out of view, like some kind of seizure pulling the spirit from her body. It creeps me out. I grab Mrs. Auerbach by the shoulders and shake her. She's the key to everything. I won't leave this room until I know.

"Get off me! Don't touch me." She smacks me away with a blow that causes me to stumble backward and step heavily on a floorboard that echoes with a hollow sound. The dresser stops my fall, and I clutch it to remain upright. Another look at the floorboard shows it's slightly raised—different from the others. Kneeling down, I use my hands to pry it up.

Gretchen runs toward me. "Wait, Madeline!"

But she's too late. Underneath the board is the small, Squid Link Gateway device I knew existed *somewhere* in this apartment. A green light is blinking. *It's in use.*

"He's controlling lights in me and Mom and our pets," I say, lifting the small, white square.

Gretchen lunges forward, but this time I'm ready for her and step aside. She sprawls onto the floor and seems winded, lying there motionless.

"Please don't take it away, I'm begging you," she says. "There's an implant. Helps control my illness."

Holding tight to the device, I go back to the armchair. Her story explains a lot, and despite everything that's happened, I feel sorry for her.

"Tell me about it," I say softly.

She sits across from me, sighs, and shuts her eyes. Her body is slack and resigned. "After I saw his experiments with the mice, he offered to put a light in me to help my bipolar depression."

This immediately makes sense. I've seen with my own eyes her melancholy.

"How did he insert it? Through your spine?" Despite my sympathy for her, there's steel in my voice. She's put us through a lot.

She nods. "Yes, a spinal injection. He also gave me a drug he was developing, kind of a combination of LSD and painkillers." She gives a wry smile. "At first it was like a miracle, the drug plus the light. I almost fell in love with him because of how much he helped me. Then we started living together."

Total mind control.

"Gretchen, I think you know he's been stalking me, kidnapped me. Could you tell me if he was—is—violent with you?"

"He's a monster."

The vehemence in her voice surprises me.

"He threatened to withhold the light if I wouldn't let him experiment with the frequencies. I didn't really have a choice—didn't realize what torture it would be. When we had sex, he couldn't ... perform if the light wasn't at a high frequency that made me crazy. High-pitch ringing in my ears, feeling like my eardrums would burst. And he wouldn't stop. I was trapped."

I recoil from her, even as I believe her. Her story is consistent with my theory. She has been through Phase 6 and come out the other side in a state of complete subjugation. My experience is different from hers in so many ways, but I can't shake the fear I'm looking at my future self if I can't shut this man down.

Gretchen lets loose her faded, gray-brown hair and runs her hands through it. In that moment, I see the beautiful woman she once was.

"Did you go to the police?" I ask.

"No. He promised to leave me alone if I would take this job with you and your mother. I agreed to it to get away from him." She looks at me weirdly. "And now he's dating you."

"Uh, not exactly," I say. "What will you do now? Will you go back to him?"

"I'll do whatever he says." She's like a zombie. Her lips pinch together in a zigzag of wrinkles.

I press my elbows to my sides. "While you were here—in this house—what else did you do for him?"

She looks away and I brace myself, watching the rolling black clouds of late fall through the blurry window.

"I sprinkled Vince's drug powder on your food," Gretchen says. "Just a tiny amount, according to his instructions."

She says it so *sotto voce,* I don't immediately comprehend it.

Something in the attic thuds above us. A giant rat, perhaps, dropping dead.

"You drugged me?" But of course she did. It explains my mental fog in this house since I was kidnapped. Through sheer willpower, I overcame the light in my head. But against the drugs, I was powerless.

"So everything went according to his plan," I say bitterly. "You reported back, and he knew where I was at all times, and who I'd be meeting. What a good soldier you've been."

Darkness has fallen in the apartment, and she gets up to turn on a lamp. "There's just one thing he didn't plan for," she says. "I fell in love with your mother."

Her face softens in the lamplight with the truth of this. But it's too late to cue the violins. There's no way she can stay here.

My phone pings. A chat message to my fake persona, Cat Girl, from Vince.

All set for our date at Lulu's on Wednesday night.

See ya then, Cowboy, I type back. Phase 1 for Cat Girl.

My phone pings again. This time a message for Madeline, the real me. He's a busy little bee this evening.

7 pm Saturday night is perfect. How can I bear to wait until then?

Here's what I'd like to reply: *Deal with it, asshole.* But of course I don't.

For now, the date, and Phase 6, are on.

CHAPTER 50

I'm still in Mrs. Auerbach's apartment, clutching the Gateway control box that sends light signals into all the heads in my house. "I'm taking this and disabling it," I say.

"No!" she cries. "Please, Madeline."

"I'm sorry, Gretchen, I really am. But I can't let Vince mess with all of us."

Again, she lunges toward me, but I'm nimble in evading her, and grab her phone off the bed "I'm holding onto this too, because I don't want you to contact him again while you're in my house." I pocket her phone next to mine.

"I depend on that control box," she says, an edge of hysteria in her voice.

"Take some of those drugs you told me about," I say, hardening my heart.

The hatred in her eyes is naked, and she makes no effort to hide it. "Am I a prisoner in this apartment tonight?"

"Not at all. You can leave or stay. Just don't plan on sleeping here tomorrow night."

My interaction with Mrs. Auerbach takes the stamina out of me, and I retire to my bedroom, locking the door. *Who is this person, the one without an ounce of compassion?*

The first thing I do is disable the Gateway control by prizing it open and removing its innards. The hum in my head that has been so all-encompassing in my life is suddenly and dramatically stilled. A quiet peacefulness flows through me, like a benediction. It's a moment to savor despite the turmoil.

The dead box goes into my safe, which is concealed in my closet. *Evidence.*

Next, I check the recording of Auerbach on my phone. To my frustration, her voice is muffled and inaudible, probably because the phone was under my backside on a cushioned chair. *Damn!* Irrationally, I want to throttle her.

Now I must transcribe it all for Jessica.

My heart seems to be skipping beats, and I put my feet up on my bed. I was once kinder, softer, and more vulnerable. Since widowhood, I've had to envelop myself in a veneer of strength, which by now has hardened into a shell. I'm not cruel by nature, and Mrs. Auerbach's situation doesn't sit well in my gut. She has bonded with my mother, but has harmed us and my pets and has violated my trust. She has to go.

The Vince situation has become more urgent, my lawyer's warning uppermost in my mind. "You don't need to expose yourself to more danger. We have enough to bring a case." And this was *before* the shocking revelations from Mrs. Auerbach.

What I understand, however, is the tenuousness of the evidence. Most of the damning facts are hearsay, accusations from women with questionable mental stability. Any competent lawyer representing Vince would rip this testimony to shreds. They would accuse me of suffering from delusions. I've experienced too many raised eyebrows when I mentioned my suspicions.

My analytical brain says I need proof. Hard, cold facts, clearly documented as Exhibit A and Exhibit B in court. Names, addresses, dates, and details of the women who are Vince's subjects. The phases of each experiment. Having witnessed how he writes up his rats and mice, pure analogy dictates he has similar write-ups for his women.

And I'm the one who must find it. It's a very simple logic exercise for me. The document is in Vince's house. I need to get my hands on that document. Therefore, I must go to Vince's house.

It's late, so I send Jessica a text.

My hunch is correct, other women are involved. Saturday night is still on. Stay tuned.

Much like the woman with the candelabra, descending the dark staircase into the lair of the monster.

Dinner is a quiet event. Mrs. Auerbach doesn't come downstairs, and Mom, like a piece of ice, sits at the table nibbling on something unidentifiable and refuses to speak to me. I forage for leftovers in the fridge and make myself an omelet with cooked shrimp that still seem to be okay. Torvill declines to take a shrimp under the table.

I give some more thought to the Vince problem. During the day he works in his lab, using the computer there. This is the laptop whose data and files I've examined. There has to be another computer in his house that he uses to write up his "women experiments." Since some of the details are damning, he probably keeps that computer well hidden.

A sudden brainwave hits me, and I grab my phone. At Professionals.com, I go in as Cat Girl and send Vince a message.

Hey, Vince, what are you doing, right now, at this minute?

Almost instantaneously, he replies.

Wow, Cat Girl. Boring answer. I'm working at home. Wanna come join me?

From the speed of his reply, it seems like he's working on his home computer.

Why don't I go to his house right now and do some reconnaissance? I accept his offer as Cat Girl, and he sends "her" the address.

"Stay warm, Mom," I say. "Be back soon."

Vince's address is easy to find. I turn onto a nearby side street and cut the headlights. Everything is dark and still, but for the faint chirp of insects. No outside lamp lights my way. Vince's house is distinctive, with wrought iron grilles on the windows. I'm nervous to look into the front window because my intent isn't innocent, and any snoop watching me from a neighboring house will surely raise the alarm. So I creep along the side to peer into windows of lit rooms.

Tentatively, I lift my head. Some kind of a living room. It's empty.

Another lit room is at the far side of the house, and that's where I tiptoe next. Crouching at the window, lifting my eyes, I see him. Vince is at a table working on a computer I haven't seen. He's intent on his task.

This is it! The computer I must access. Somehow.

For a while, I'm motionless, starting to devise a plan for Saturday night.

Just as I turn to leave, I catch a lucky break. Vince rises from his chair, removes a painting from the wall, and reveals a safe behind the picture. An honest-to-goodness safe with a combination dial embedded in a recess of the wall. He stands in front of it, so I don't see the combination, but the steel door swings open. From the safe, he removes a small item, which, from where I stand, resembles a flash drive.

Bingo! I'm gratified how pure deduction brought me to this moment.

My nemesis inserts the drive into his computer and resumes typing, following my playbook. If I had spyware on this laptop, I would be able to see it all. I would bet the data on that flash drive is the Holy Grail, his description of experiments on women.

Is he writing about me, the fourth woman? Is he documenting how docile I've been so far? That I've barely raised a ruckus? Does he mention how willing I've been to play along?

The parameters of the Vince problem are becoming clear. Get into his safe, gain custody of the flash drive, and access his home computer. When the problem is well-defined, it's simply a matter of solving it. This has been a productive evening.

I'm about to call it a night when his phone rings. I hear the faint jangle through the window. He lifts it to his ear and abruptly looks up at me. I drop down like a brick and breathe heavily against the wall. Did he see me?

The shrill ringing of a phone goes off in my pocket. Not my ring tone. It's Mrs. Auerbach's phone! I yank it out to silence it, and *Vince* shows on the screen. *He's trying to call her.*

It's time to get out of here.

The moon slides behind a cloud plunging the landscape into darkness. In my panic, I step badly and twist my ankle, causing my body to pitch forward. As I fall, my knee hits the concrete wall, sending a shock of pain up my leg through my hip and into my jaw.

A bat flaps out from under the eaves and brushes my cheek. I stifle a cry as I bury my face in the dirt. I must get up and leave, but I'm temporarily immobilized. On the muddy ground, I breathe in leaves and twigs, waiting for the boom to fall—Vince's heavy hand on me, or a neighbor's shotgun, or wailing police sirens.

There's nothing but silence, however, and the throbbing pain down my leg.

Time passes, and by some miracle, I'm still lying here undisturbed.

In my other pocket, my own phone starts ringing. *Wanda.* I swipe it fast.

"Madeline?" she says, from the planet of normal people. "Am I disturbing you?"

My heart lifts with pain. I clear my throat and speak very softly. "Hi, what's up?"

She hesitates. "You okay, Mads?"

I can't exactly tell her I'm lying outside Vince's window with a sprained ankle and banged-up knee. "What's happening?" I whisper.

"Your boyfriend—stalker—whatever—just called and asked me for a date."

He must have lifted her phone number when he was in her condo. I'm in such a state of distress that I can't quite process this. "Did you say yes?" I ask stupidly.

"Are you kidding me, Madeline?" Her voice is gravelly with outrage. "I told him he was a sick fuck, then I ended the call and blocked his number. What a jerk."

I shift my position and continue to speak softly. "I'm going to nail this guy, put him away. As we're speaking now, I'm outside his house. Spying on him."

A pause. "Christ, Madeline. Do you have a death wish?"

"I'm doing what I must do to end things."

The moon slides out from behind its cloud, and Vince's garden is suddenly sheathed in silvery moonlight.

"Will you do something for me, Wanda?" My mind is running on ahead.

"Nothing to do with that asshole. I don't want to see him again."

She never swears. But she's still listening.

"I'm going to Vince's house on Saturday night."

"Oh, Madeline. Why would you do such an insane thing?" She doesn't want to hear the answer and clicks off.

This is what our relationship has disintegrated into—a series of disconnected calls and long-distance weirdness.

I text her Vince's home address, and a message.

If I can't be found on Sunday morning, please come get me.

CHAPTER 51

At this moment, there's nothing to be done about the pain in my leg. It's simply a matter of clawing myself into a standing position and hobbling to my car. So why am I still horizontal and immobile? No sense in salivating about that tantalizing flash drive in his computer. If I could teleport myself into that space, the little piece of evidence would soon be in my pocket, but I can't, so I must be patient and focus on getting home.

While I'm contemplating the problem of getting myself vertical, there's a crackling of foliage nearby, someone walking on the lawn.

"Anyone out here?"

Vince's voice, approaching the side of the house.

I burrow into the mud and hold my breath. Through peripheral vision, I see a beam of light playing on the wall above me. I'm well-camouflaged, dressed to look like mud.

"Cat Girl, are you there?"

I reckon he's about six feet away from me, with a massive, industrial-strength flashlight. But he's not shining it down. He doesn't expect his visitor to be flat on her face underneath the bushes against the wall.

My hands are clammy, and my twisted ankle is throbbing.

"Don't be shy, come inside. Have some tea. Tell me about yourself." He's still speaking to Cat Girl, fixating on the narrative she was so attracted to him she couldn't stay away. He stands, unmoving, while I sweat hail stones that he'll discover me.

Miraculously, the light subsides, and I hear the blessed sound of receding footsteps.

I wait for eons before placing a tentative hand on the brick and gritting my teeth to put weight on my sore ankle. Eventually, I'm up, uncoordinated and clumsy, debris falling from my hair.

Carefully, I limp back to my car in the dark.

During the drive home, I think about my mother, alone in the house with the zombie housekeeper. Did Mrs. Auerbach exit her room and prevail on Mom to use her phone? *Mom.* I'm certain Mrs. Auerbach won't harm her. Would she?

I sprinkled some of his drug powder on your food.

She had no qualms about hurting me.

I put my foot—the unhurt one—hard on the gas, suddenly anxious to get home.

My house is in pitch darkness, no welcoming porch light outside, which is ominous.

When I insert my key in the lock, Torvill's paws scrape the door in a subdued welcome. I sit down and rest my cheek on his chocolate haunch, feeling the steady beat of his heart.

"Why so gloomy?" I whisper to him.

It's very late; Mom and Tosca are probably in bed.

Why no lights? Did Mom forget?

A possible reason hits me suddenly, like a blow to the head.

Mom has gone away with Gretchen Auerbach.

But that's ridiculous. Would Mom really leave?

I'm frozen at the foot of the stairs, standing with my hand on the newel post, my swollen ankle refusing to take a step. My other foot is shaking, and I don't know how long I linger on the staircase before finally turning around to go check on my mother.

If Mom is hurt, I'll die.

The door to her room is shut, as usual. Infinitely slowly, I turn the knob, praying to a God I don't believe in. Quietly, I enter the room. The curtains aren't drawn and billow gently at the windows. The room is faintly lit by the night sky, enough to show the bed is unslept in, and my darling mother is not in her room.

A sudden gust sighs through the trees. *Don't panic yet.*

Because of Gretchen's firing, I was in Mom's dog-box today. The most logical explanation for Mom's empty room is that she and her friend are both upstairs in Gretchen's suite of rooms, giving me the finger. *Of course, that must be it!*

Fearfulness turns me into a puddle, and I weep softly as I take the steps two at a time, on my sprained ankle, to reach Auerbach's front door. At the top of the stairs, I listen for sounds of talking, but all I hear is silence. They must be sleeping.

I rap sharply on the door. When there's no reply, I use my key to enter. I don't care if I'm muscling in on their sleep, they have no right to frighten me like this.

The room is in darkness, and I punch at the light switch.

Yesterday's debris has gone. Everything's been cleaned out, even the bedroom. The apartment is empty. What am I to do? I can't call the police and report that my mother, an adult, has been missing for two hours. Alzheimer's changes the equation, but I'm certain Auerbach won't harm Mom. At this moment, I'm the loneliest person on the planet.

Back downstairs, my eyes sweep the hallway, kitchen, and other spaces for evidence of a message, a hastily written note, an envelope—something—but there's just the usual debris of my life.

Auerbach's phone is in my pocket, so I can't call her. My mother, however, may have her phone with her. After two rings, I'm tossed into her voicemail.

"Call me, Mom, anytime tonight. I'm crazy worried about you."

Next, I contact the hotel where I've booked a room. "Has Gretchen Auerbach checked in?" I ask.

"No one of that name has shown up yet," a clerk informs me.

This is Auerbach's revenge for cutting her light frequency, firing her. I have no doubt she has taken an all-too-willing Janet to punish me.

I drag my bruised, mud-caked body to the bathroom, and before long, I'm under the stinging hot needles of the shower. With the layer of grime, some scales are washed from my eyes. *Vince. Phase 6. Mind control.* This is his doing—using Auerbach to send me a message. If I don't play along on Saturday night, my family will be harmed further.

On Monday morning, before I can gear up into action, there's a click at the front door, and my mother, shiny as a new penny, shows up in the kitchen and joins me at the breakfast table.

Relief makes me lightheaded, and I don't know whether to hug or throttle her. I set down my coffee mug and put my head in my hands. "Why, Mom? Why must you scare me like that?"

My mother drops her purse and looks at me intently. "Can you find it in your heart, Madsy, to reconsider your decision and let Gretchen stay on?" She speaks as lucidly as the English teacher she used to be.

Breathe. Slowly. "I can't do anything until you tell me where you disappeared to last night. Were you with her?"

"I was helping with her stuff."

"Where's the note telling me where you went? Or did you intend for me to sweat and worry?" My voice is shrill and ugly with relief.

My mother gets up and moves to sit beside me. To my surprise, she relieves me of my cereal spoon and takes my hand. "I'm sorry. I didn't think of leaving a note."

I've forgotten how soft her skin is.

Still holding hands, she says, "Being single has made you harsh, Mads. I know Gretchen isn't perfect. She told me about the drugs she takes for depression, and some of the other stuff."

"Mom—"

"No, let me finish." She wipes her eyes. "Gretchen and I have become friends. I tell her stuff, too—confide in her. My life isn't easy, with my memory problems."

"She did some really creepy things to me, Mom. She helped Vince stalk me."

But my mother's not hearing, already shaking her head. "Mads, the best thing you can do for me now is invite Gretchen back. Let her stay."

Have I become too harsh?

My mother pats my hand. "Even if you're against it, do it for me."

"And if I refuse, will you disappear again to punish me?" I say bitterly.

My situation is impossible. I love Mom and sympathize with Gretchen, but after everything that's happened, how can I keep her under our roof?

To be honest, without Gretchen Auerbach's dark presence, the house breathes a sigh of relief. I feel it in the lightness of my step and renewed energy of the animals. Even Mom, despite her entreaties, embraces the sudden freedom, lifting Tosca high into the air for a grand embrace, kissing the cat's fluffy head as she meows in protest. Torvill and I go out for a bracing walk, and not even the bite of the November wind can subdue our spirits.

Somehow there's promise in the day, and for now, I'm liberated from the malevolence that blew through my house.

Unfortunately, Mom must stay alone in the house during the day. I tell her to call me if there's a problem, and she assures me there won't be a problem. Well of course there won't—not for her. Yet again, I must suffer through the rigmarole of hiring a new housekeeper.

When I arrive at work, Shawna and Buck are having a heated conversation in the front office. My presence puts a lid on it, and there's an uncomfortable silence. Not a smile or dimple to be seen on Shawna's face, which surprises me, because she really likes Buck.

"Hi, everyone," I say brightly. "Buck, let's go into my office."

We have an appointment, which I have initiated.

He too is unhappy, glancing at me with shifty eyes and fiddling with a dangling earring.

"Whazzup, Madeline?" he says gruffly.

He knows he's toast. He never calls me Madeline. I guess our ByteBeast and HackMeister days are over.

"I've thought about everything that happened, Buck, and I just can't invite you back. I have to be able to trust my employees."

"I made a mistake, ByteBeast."

He chews at an end on his fingernail and looks very young.

I feel very old.

"Please take the posters and dragons from your office," I say, standing to dismiss him. "And one more thing, Buck. Don't even *think* about retaliating. Because if you do, I'll bust your ass to the police department, heating company, and cable company with every illegal thing you've done. It's a long list. They'll put you in a dark little dungeon somewhere and throw away the key."

When he slumps out the door, I have a brief pang of regret. My conscience, however, is clear. Buck will easily make his fortune, with or without a reference from me.

The way I see it is this: today is a good day. I've gotten rid of Vince's spy in my house, and now I've said goodbye to his spy in my office.

All that remains is for me to get rid of Vince.

CHAPTER 52

On the Thursday before our dinner date, Cat Girl receives a message from Vince.

Why did you stand me up last night?

The Phase 1 date.

Cat Girl has served her purpose, and without reply, I delete her profile from Professionals.com. Let Vince chew on that for the rest of the week.

Clarity of mind has not been my strong suit since the start of the Vince era. The light and drugs have taken a toll, leading me to this juncture.

All is crystal clear now, except the final knowing. To that end, I start putting into action a plan that begins with a message to Vince through Professionals.com.

Hi Vince, I'd like to bring my mom with me to dinner on Saturday night.

I imagine him frowning—not many women bring their mothers along on a date.

Late Thursday night, his reply is cool but polite.

Since we'll be having a private business dinner, could Janet make other arrangements? A lab assistant of mine is willing to spend the evening with her. We could, of course, on a future date have a dinner for the three of us.

I respond immediately. *Vince, please do reconsider. My mother becomes disoriented with strangers and would prefer to accompany me. She won't disturb us, I guarantee you.*

I can picture his reluctant fingers on the keys.

Of course. Please, do bring Janet along.

Step one.

As if on cue, my phone rings. *Wanda.*

Interestingly, she too offers to babysit my mother on Saturday night. Specifically, she says, "Would Janet like to go out to a movie with me?"

I blow kisses through the phone. "Mom is going to be my chaperone."

She pauses. "You're telling me that not only will you be in danger, your mom will too? Seriously, Madeline?"

"He won't harm Mom. Besides, I need her to help me." I don't feel as confident as I sound. If my mother is having a bad night, she won't remember a thing, and I'll have to resort to my inferior backup plan—playing it by ear.

"What's your goal? What's the point of it all?" Wanda says.

Oh, Wanda, I've already told you. To vanquish him once and for all, that's what.

On Friday, I think carefully before sending a message to Vince through Chat Messenger.

Will I find out the point of all this tomorrow night?

After Friday dinner, he responds.

Madeline, it's always been about my obsession with you. You dazzle me.

Baloney! I know about the other women. Tomorrow night is truth night.

I'm always truthful. Bring your computer.

BTW Vince, ground rule: No drugs or alcohol for me tomorrow night.

His response jumps back. *Drugs???*

This is what I'd like to reply: *Do me a favor—cut the crap.*

It's at my fingertips, but I don't send it.

Mid-November in Boston can spit up any kind of nasty weather, though thunderstorms are rare. On Saturday the temperatures are cold, but relatively mild, which means the dark storm clouds gathering in the late afternoon will probably bring rain, not snow. Tosca is Zen about the weather, always has been. Torvill is frightened and bristles at the distant thunder. Mom's answer to his anxiety is to add extra kibble to his food bowl. He's becoming chunky, my big old dog.

I watch Mom as she dresses for dinner, making herself gorgeous in pale-green cashmere and a skinny silk scarf. When I wear green, I look like I just threw up, but she can wear anything.

"You're a babe, Mom," I say. "You put those Hollywood stars to shame."

She blushes darkly, lowering her eyes, and I realize this dinner has become an *event* for her. She's just as solitary as I am. So far it's been a good day for my mother, and I'm relieved to be able to clarify this is not a romantic date for me.

"Too bad," she says wistfully. "He sure is keen on you."

Now is the time to explain my plan. "Maybe you can help me tonight, Mom."

My wardrobe choice is a no-brainer; a royal-blue pair of cords with deep pockets—literally. I recharge my phone, which will be set to record everything, and place it in a pocket. Pepper spray, in a small, flat container, goes into the other pocket, together with two flash drives of different sizes and shapes. Both pockets are concealed by a flattering skinny sweater that comes down to the middle of my thighs.

Vince's requirement that I bring my laptop is mysterious, but I don't press the issue, because my sleek Dell fits right into my plans too.

In further preparation, I take a solidly frozen bottle of water from the freezer and put it in my purse. The gun, which I brought home from the office, goes in next. A precaution.

By the time we leave at 6:30 p.m., rain is coming down steadily. A mist has arisen, causing the headlights to reflect back in our eyes, slowing the traffic to a crawl.

"I don't know how you can drive in this," Mom says loudly, talking above the windshield wipers that are thwacking away at top speed.

I pat her leather jacket. "Trust me."

She laughs, her wonderful deep, throaty cackle that I haven't heard for ages. "That's what you always say."

Miraculously, Vince's house emerges from the scrim of darkness, its exterior lit by floodlights. I could swear these weren't here before when I snooped around outside. There's something sinister about these sweeping lights, which scour the outside terrain like searchlights in an old spy movie.

I help Mom from the car, sheltering her with my wide umbrella, and like two refugees huddled together, we splash through the rain to the front door.

The doorbell chimes in the house. Darling Torvill would go berserk to hear such bells at the door. Footsteps approach, sounding like more than one person; a confident tread and a shuffling following behind. *Other guests?*

Vince opens the door and beams at us. "Welcome, Madeline. Janet—here, let me get you out of the rain." He takes her hand, and in we go.

"I have a surprise for you, Janet," he says, stepping aside.

Standing in the hallway—hollow-eyed, unsmiling, and in a flowery apron—is Gretchen Auerbach.

CHAPTER 53

Mom squeals with happiness and drops everything to hug her friend.

"Gretchen! Are you joining us for dinner?"

Vince beams at them with unsettling high wattage. He's a despot, who no doubt has leaned on Mrs. Auerbach to be the maid. He says, "Gretchen has very kindly offered to cook for us."

Sure.

Mrs. Auerbach, a zombie in a weird apron, says, "Janet, after dinner we will stream something in the family room."

I get it. Her mission is to cook, clean, and spirit Mom away, so Vince and I can be alone.

Mom casts a glance at me, and I smile and nod. "How lovely," she says.

No need to change the plan.

Vince has made a fire in the living room and ostentatiously prods it with a poker, making it spit and crackle. The lights are low, and if it weren't for the bizarre circumstances of our gathering, the room would be a cozy, romantic setting.

I take a seat away from the fire and drop my handbag and computer case at the side of my chair.

"May I take all that and put it in the hallway closet or the study?" Vince says, heading toward me to grasp my stuff.

Hands off! I slam a protective hand over the straps. "No!" It comes out more sharply than I intended.

Vince backs away, but he recovers fast. "Can I offer you ladies a cocktail?" he says. "Wine?"

"I'm old-fashioned," Mom says, "but I'd love a sherry if you have it."

This surprises me; I haven't seen my mother drink sherry for a long time.

"Sherry coming right up," Vince says. "Madeline? Vodka? Martini?"

"I'm good," I say pointedly, opening my handbag and removing the bottle of water. Some of the ice has melted, so I can take cold sips of tap water. *Perfect. No drugs for me tonight, thank you.*

"Oh, Madsy," Mom says. She turns to Vince, whose smile has slipped a little. "You have to forgive my daughter."

I raise the bottle to Vince, unscrew the cap, and take a sip. "I'm on the wagon," I say.

"All part of the charm." He pours a generous sherry for Mom.

Mrs. Auerbach disappears, presumably to the kitchen, and we sit and spout inanities for some interminable minutes that stretch into the dinner hour. I detect an almost imperceptible buzz, the hint of a Gateway signal, pulling at my mind.

Sorry, mister, I've got this.

The dining room is dimly lit, a ghostly light that casts a pall over the table, exacerbated by the strange presence of Mrs. Auerbach, who seems to be floating in some fantasy netherworld. Wordlessly, she brings out a large wooden bowl of salad.

What has he given her?

Vince seats himself at the head, with my mother to his left and me at his right. It's not clear that Mrs. Auerbach will be included as a guest at this dinner, but my purpose here tonight is not to get justice for this particular woman, so I hold my tongue.

My computer bag goes under my seat, and I hang my purse, with its long strap, on the knob of the straight-backed chair.

After Vince helps himself to salad, he passes the bowl to Mom. At my turn, I take the communal bowl and heap my plate. This salad may be all I eat tonight. In the poor light, the cherry tomatoes are a deep and wonderful red, and the lettuce varied and plentiful. Red-leaf and Boston green, fresh and crisp and appetizing.

Vince ladles on salad dressing from a communal glass bottle—not bought—and I gratefully do the same.

Mom stands abruptly. "Where's Gretchen? I'm going to keep her company." And out she marches, taking off in the direction of clattering dishes and running water.

"Alone at last," Vince says. "How are you tonight, my dear Mads, ravishing and nonchalant as always." His face is unreadable.

"I'm not your dear Mads," I say coldly. "I never was."

He feels free to extend an index finger and touch my arm. "Give it time," he says softly.

A pungent sizzle comes from the kitchen, and despite myself, my mouth waters.

"Sautéed shrimp—stir-fry—with broccoli and rice," Vince says. "Ah, here it comes."

Like a nineteenth-century maid from the British Empire, Mrs. Auerbach comes bearing a large silver tray, which she sets down at the vacant end of the table. Separate plates, all seemingly identical, steaming and fragrant. This is what I expected to receive—a special plate set down in front of me by Mrs. Auerbach.

I sprinkled Vince's drug powder on your food.

Of course I won't touch it.

When Mrs. Auerbach moves out of the dining room, Mom is still in the kitchen.

I lift my fork to the sound of a giant crash and Mrs. Auerbach's anguished voice screaming, "Vince!"

His face pales. He jumps up and dashes out of the room. In a flash, I've swapped plates, and the food destined for me is now in front of him.

Mom's voice, distraught. "I don't know what happened! The pitcher was there on the countertop and then it was— Oh, Vince, I'm so sorry. Your beautiful glass in pieces on the floor."

I go to the kitchen and find Gretchen and my mother in a flurry of brooms and dustpans, sweeping and mopping and crunching on bits of glass. Vince's face is flushed with annoyance, but he tries to be gracious. It's an axiom: If he's still trying to woo me, he has to be nice to my mother.

"It's just a jug, Janet. Don't worry about a thing. Let's go eat before the rice congeals. Gretchen will fix this mess."

And so, with Cinderella in the kitchen, the three of us return to the dining room. Even lukewarm, the stir-fry dinner is delicious, the shrimp seasoned with a zing of hot paprika or tabasco. Mom, who generally likes milder food, guzzles it down, seemingly recovered from her mishap.

It'll be hours before I can debrief her. I certainly didn't instruct her to break kitchenware, but I did ask her to get Vince out of the dining room after the entrée was served if—and that was a big if—the opportunity arose. It wasn't clear I'd get a chance to swap our food, but here I am, with a divine dinner in front of me. Yum.

Mom came through!

Vince devours his—strictly speaking, *my*—plate of food with relish. I watch with interest as the rain clatters rhythmically on the roof. Is his mouth, like mine, on fire from the peppers and spices?

Without a doubt, they were used to conceal the taste of drugs.

CHAPTER 54

He's a fastidious eater, meticulously cutting each shrimp into three pieces before switching his fork into his right hand.

How are you feeling, Vince?

He notices I'm watching, which seems to throw him off his rhythm. His fork clatters down. "Madeline?"

I smile at him. "All delicious. Every morsel."

He looks at me narrowly, his eyes in a cross-eyed squint.

Mrs. Auerbach, like a pre-programmed robot, produces a cake with buttercream frosting and pink icing rosettes. Store-bought, with lots of sugar per cubic centimeter. Silently, she gives me the cake cutter—it appears I'm to play mother. I help myself to a giant slice. *The communal cake is safe.*

"Tea or coffee?" Mrs. Auerbach asks in a monotone.

Mom requests caffeinated tea, Vince caffeinated coffee, and I wave my water bottle at them and say, "I'm good." *No drugs plopped into my tea, thank you.*

Dinner is over. Mom seems embarrassed by her friend's servitude, and sure enough, she heads to the kitchen to help with the dishes. When Vince and I rise to leave the table, I'm gratified to see my host is sluggish in his movements. The drug is taking effect.

We move to the living room, where he makes a half-hearted attempt to stoke the fire before sinking down on the couch. The large picture window is streaked with rain, which continues to pelt down, rattling the panes.

I arrange my computer and purse near to my chair, as before. The room is hot and stifling, the damp wool of my sweater prickling against my skin.

How effective are his drugs, I wonder? Will they make him compliant? I take a stab. "What's in the drugs, Vince?"

He puts his head in his hands, then shakes it as if to clear it. Opens his eyes wide with the effort, followed by rapid blinking. A shock of recognition sluices through me, sharpening my focus. *I know exactly how he feels.*

He says, "My unique mixture—opioid, hallucinogen, and anti-depressant." He grins. "Irresistible combo, huh?"

Without any great show of urgency, I dig into my pocket, glance at my phone, and make sure it's still recording.

"Why?" I ask. "What's the drug for? Does it have a name? Where can I buy it?"

Take advantage of him and his compromised brain.

He laughs. Unsteadily. "Oh, Madeline, Madeline. How little you know."

"Enlighten me, Vince."

A shadow crosses his face. "Why wouldn't you go out with me, Madeline?"

Another rumble of thunder, and the light flickers. Despite the fire, I shiver.

Because you're creepy, Vince.

I say, "After seeing your lab, I was turned off by the animals—the experiments."

"And what about the others? Why did *they* say no?" Vince is wild-eyed. The drug is loosening his tongue and making him unpredictable.

"Whoa, Vince. What others?"

"There's always some excuse. They like their independence, it's nothing personal, they want to stay single, their boyfriend's upset, they've met someone else, they don't want to date a colleague, my mother doesn't like you, Vince, you're not my type. No, no, no, always no."

He gets up and walks to me, grabs my shoulders, and shakes me. Hard.

I shove him away and stand up. "Vince, stop!"

"I offered you marriage. Security for your mother. A diamond ring worth thousands. But all I heard was no! What would it take for you to say yes?"

"Step back," I say softly.

He thinks and then he moves away, collapsing in a chair.

"Is that what the drug is for?" I say. "To make women compliant?"

"Well, yes and no. Its *raison d'être* is to help pay for my research, which has a stiff price tag. But the effect of the drug is to make women *compliant.* Good word." He looks up at me. "You were the perfect subject."

Rumblings and lightning in the distance. His garden is probably a lake by now.

"Were?" The muscles in my neck are tense, down through my back and aching knee.

He stares, his normally sharp blue eyes blurry and unfocussed. That was some dose he intended for me. "You haven't ... cooperated recently."

"How do you make the drug?" I say, barely breathing.

"I'm a biochemist by training. Use your imagination."

The mysterious room in his lab, the one with the danger sign? So he's manufacturing illegal drugs that make people—women—compliant. How much will he tell me before the drug wears off?

I lean toward him and force my face into an encouraging smile, the way he sometimes does. "Who buys the drugs, Vince? How do you market them?"

"There are lots of men who can't get bitches like you to say yes. Ever."

Bile rises in me, an acid gush like heartburn. I swallow it. I have no desire to change him.

"Do you find them—the men—in a private Facebook group?"

"Used to. Facebook kicked us off. Too much misogyny." He says it without irony.

I shudder at the thought of the dark web with a bunch of lunatics masturbating to handcuffed women and assault rifles. The crucial question hanging over the evening can no longer be put off.

"What is Phase 6?"

His face darkens, then lightens with that terrible smile. "Ah, Phase 6, the final test. Thought you'd have figured it out by now, Madeline, smart girl like you."

I roll my shoulders, the tension in them threatening to knock me down. "What?"

He stands up again and moves toward me. "Doing whatever it takes, obviously, to get to yes."

CHAPTER 55

"Stop, Vince!" I stand my ground and whip out the pepper spray.

He slows, but doesn't stop. "Just a hug, Madeline, for God's sake. What must I do to get one drop of warmth from you?" He falters about two feet away from my outstretched arm.

Nothing, Vince, don't do a thing. Ain't gonna happen.

What *is* going to happen are the next two parts of my plan. I'll need luck.

After staring him down for a beat, I say, in a softer voice, "Show me the diamond ring, Vince. I never really got a chance to look at it."

His blue eyes open wide and bore into me with suspicion and hope. "Why? Are you going to marry me?" He steps back, still facing me.

I shrug my shoulders as if thinking about it. "I'm going to try the ring on for size." I splay the fingers of my left hand and examine them front and back, while my other hand holds the pepper spray steady.

He hesitates a good while, but eventually his vanity comes through for me. "The ring is in the study," he says slowly. "I'll go get it."

I pick up my purse and computer and follow right behind him.

"Oh, you can wait in the living room." He waves his hand at me, shooing me back. "I won't be long."

Not a chance, mister.

The sounds of gunshots ring out. Mom and Mrs. Auerbach must be deep into their thriller.

Vince's mind is scrambled by the drug, because he doesn't seem bothered that I'm at his side as he accesses his safe.

Yes! I knew he'd keep the diamond here.

When the heavy safe door swings open, I drop my stuff at my feet and shove the pepper spray back into my pocket. Now, both my hands are free.

The interior of the safe is black. I'm almost cheek-to-cheek with Vince as I peer inside, getting a whiff of the fake woodsy fragrance of his aftershave and a close-up of his stubbly chin.

"Hey, wait a minute!" he says.

"I see it!" Before he can react, I reach in, grasp the velvety box, and draw it out. "Here it is."

Gingerly, he takes the box from me, opens it, and together we gaze at the splendor of the blue-white diamond. My other hand, like lightning, pockets the flash drive from the safe and replaces it with a similar one. The hand is quicker than the eye. *Ms. Twinkle-fingers.* Mission accomplished.

And what about the ring, which has served its purpose? I do what any red-blooded woman would do—take it out the box and slide it onto my ring finger, where it sparkles like a demon. Mesmerizing. For a brief minute, I think back to my early expectations from Professionals.com, how I dared to imagine an ending like this; a ring on my finger and a man declaring his love. That's what I thought I wanted.

Vince notices the subtle shift in my gaze. "Are we're getting to yes?" he says quietly.

Some kind of magnetism still operating. I shake my head. Force myself out of it.

Hell no. Move on!

"Why did you ask me to bring my computer?" I ask.

He fumbles with the ring box and blinks rapidly, as if he's confused and events are moving too fast. After snapping the empty box shut, he says, "I want to watch you ... interact with other men."

Seriously? This man is pathetic. "What do you mean?"

"Go onto Professionals.com and chat to a guy who's a match. Talk sexy. Try and turn him on."

The drug has made him crazy. I search his face for a hint of humor, but he's unsmiling.

What about Phase 6? Is this it?

"Just to clarify," I say. "You want to watch me have a sexual conversation with a strange man?"

"Honest to God, Madeline, you sound like a schoolteacher. But yes, you have it right. Let's hear some warmth—heat—which is something I've never gotten from you."

I stifle an urge to laugh at him. *How addlebrained is he?* Maybe—just maybe—I can use his crazy suggestion to achieve my second goal of the evening. "Okay," I say, my mind going at full speed.

During a pause in which I devise a new scenario, Vince becomes all business and bustle, clearing a table in an alcove of the living room, shoving papers onto a nearby chair. His feverish plan is that we'll sit side by side while he watches me play screen hooker.

"Wait, I have a better idea," I say, setting down my laptop at one end of the table.

"What?" He squints at me. "This is my call."

Which it may well have been if *I'd* ingested the drug, but unluckily for him, I'm the one whose brain is clear and he's the one seeing sex bubbles in the sky.

"Get your computer," I say. "Set it up. We'll sit at opposite ends of this table."

"Deal breaker. I want to be next to you while you're typing."

"Sorry, Vince. Talking dirty with strange men isn't something I normally do. The last thing I need is your heavy breathing down my neck. You'll cramp my style."

"No fun if I can't watch," he says. Peevish. "You said you'd do it."

"Maybe there's a way I can swing it. How about I put spyware on both our computers so you can watch me *from your computer?*"

He shakes his head, trying to clear it. "Huh? Why do that when I can watch you live?"

"That's the deal, take it or leave it." I shut the lid of my laptop with a definitive *thwack.*

"Wait." He moves to get his computer and returns swaying slightly, unsteady on his feet. He's wavering. "What if I say no to your plan?"

"Then I'll give you back your diamond, get my mother, and go home right now." I shrug. "It's all the same to me."

For my plan to have a chance, he has to take the bait. I'm banking on his computer illiteracy, grogginess, and sleaziness of mind. I'm also depending on his total self-absorption where it comes to me. I stand motionless, watching him.

But he clutches his laptop to his chest like it's a teddy bear. "No way." He seems to shrink before my eyes, this shriveling man who's instilled so much fear and loathing in me. That drug he's taken is potent, sending the evening in a surreal direction.

He's wavering, I sense it and lean in to close the deal. "Think about it, Vince. I'm willing to go along with your night games and am offering you the ability to spy on me. Right now. I'll install the software, then show you my secret, mind-blowing erotic life. You've convinced me—maybe we'll enjoy it." A naughty, fun-loving smile lights up my face. Thank God Wanda isn't around. She'd go batshit.

Miraculously, he slowly relinquishes his computer, smiling back at me, seeming grateful.

God.

Moving swiftly, I'm at his keyboard, inserting a nondescript gray flash drive into one of the USB ports, shutting down Windows, and rebooting the operating system to Linux. Vince is at my side, breathing heavily.

He peers at the screen and at me, then frowns. "What the hell are you doing?"

"Installing your spyware, Vince." I give him an honest, earnest smile. "Isn't this what we agreed to?"

He grunts and nods, still nervous.

"It'll take a while. Let's go see how the weather is doing." I stand and stretch, the diamond up in the air, a little flash of fire.

His computer grinds away as we move across the room. Through the window, the rain shows no sign of abating, pounding down and rumbling with thunder.

"Let's get going here," he says when we're back at the table.

A glimpse at his computer screen reveals mission accomplished. It's time to extricate myself and Mom and get the hell out of here.

"Let's test this," Vince says.

His words are punctuated by a loud thud in the house. *Mom?* I jump up. "Be right back. I'm going to check on my mother."

"Wait!"

But I'm not asking for permission, and I run from the study in the direction of the noise.

The hallway is dark and sparks a memory of this house when I was held captive. I'm near the room where on Halloween eve I slept in a drugged stupor and woke to find Vince sitting across from me. This place does not have the creaks and ghosts of my Victorian house, but the old terror slows me down, puts a crimp in my step, and intensifies the ache in my bad knee.

I limp to the family room and put my ear to the door. Silence. No TV. "Mom?" I knock and enter. A flash of lightning blinds me momentarily, then the room is in darkness, empty.

Panicked, I find Mrs. Auerbach in the kitchen. She's washing dishes.

"Where's my mother?"

In that maddening dead-eyed way, she turns slowly, looking at me as if to say, *I don't work for you anymore.*

"Janet is in the bathroom," Mrs. Auerbach says, and before I can react, a toilet somewhere flushes. Mrs. Auerbach dries her hands. "Now we're going to go finish watching our show."

I catch Mom emerging from the bathroom. "Get your stuff and come to the living room. We're leaving."

"But, Madsy—"

"Just do it!"

Back in the alcove, I pop out and pocket the gray flash drive from Vince's computer. It's done its work.

"What's that gray drive about, Madeline?" Vince says. Even with the drug, he's tense.

"The software for the spyware. What else would it be?"

"You tell me."

A really nasty malware called Symbiote. Very new. Just about impossible to detect. I now own your computer, Vince. I could steal your identity and empty your bank accounts, but I won't, because that's not what I'm after. All I want is access to your files, including notes about every woman you've ever harassed, your lab results for all your phases and your women. And I want to read about your greatest failure—me.

My mission is over. It's time to go. I pack my laptop in its case. "Actually, Vince, I'm worried about the weather, so we're leaving."

"Hey, wait, Madeline!" Abandoning his open computer at the table, he follows me out the alcove. "You promised—"

"The weather made me change my mind."

The fire in the grate has died down, but the heat has not.

Vince pokes at the embers.

"You do know, Madeline, that my experiment didn't work with you. The effects of the light I implanted wore off. Then I found I couldn't be objective about the data. You've gotten under my goddamn skin. I despise myself for letting feelings get in the way. What a useless thing this so-called love is." He takes out a handkerchief and mops his brow.

"It's over, Vince." I remove the diamond ring and place it on the coffee table by his chair, looking at him firmly, eye to eye. "And I mean *really* over. I don't want to see you again. Not ever."

As if to punctuate it, another flash strikes at the window, followed by a sharp crack of thunder. When the lights flicker, I pick up my stuff and move to gather up my mother so we can get out of this infernal place.

The concept of Phase 6 has receded into the background of my mind. I have no idea what the final reckoning was supposed to be, nor any desire to find out. I feel complacent—superior even—because I've outwitted my host at every turn. Vince's strange compliance in the past hour has softened my edges, lowered my vigilance.

Something stops me as I step away. A different quality to the air, a degree or so colder, as if the outside chill has pierced the house. Realization dawns one split second before Vince speaks again. He's standing close behind me, and prickles rise on my back.

"There's nowhere to run, Madeline. The roads are flooded, and Janet and Gretchen are locked in."

I spin around to face him, the sudden sinister cast of his brow. "What do you mean, locked in?" He's been in the same room as me since I saw Mrs. Auerbach in the kitchen and Mom outside the bathroom, not five minutes ago.

Light flares and flashes at the window, illuminating the clouded sky.

A different voice says, "Don't move! The night is young, dude."

I know him, of course I do. I just don't recognize the clean-cut young man with a skinhead haircut who has suddenly materialized out of the shadows. He resembles a Mormon on a mission, except for the gun he's pointing at my heart.

CHAPTER 56

Buck!

I gape at him. Where did the HackMeister go, and who is this stranger with his voice?

I stumble backward. "What the hell are you doing here, Buck? Put the fucking gun down." Full of bravado, but my legs are quaking.

Buck waves the gun about like an amateur, but doesn't lower it. My stomach heaves.

Vince, even with his drugged aura, looks bemused. "Forgive him, Madeline, he's young. Wants to be Master of the Universe. I told him to start by cleaning up his act—lose the hair and jewelry if you want to work for me."

I do the calculation—how many steps to reach him if I charge—and I reject it. Too risky.

"Sit on that chair," Buck says, gesturing with his head, as if he's read my thoughts.

I move, my bad knee wobbly but holding up. "Can anyone tell me what's going on," I say. "And what's with the gun?"

"Very conveniently left in your purse," Buck says. "Vince knew you'd bring your gun."

Shit! I dropped my stuff to go and check on Mom. Buck must have gone through my bag, grabbed the gun, somehow locked the women in the family room, then surreptitiously made his way back.

"I invited Buck this evening to come and observe," Vince says. "He's now my research partner and also my tech rep."

"What? He's helping with those rats and mice?" I can't picture it. "What's he doing, cleaning cages? I thought that was Leo's job."

"Shut up!" Buck wrestles with himself for about a second, then can't resist telling me. "I've invented a new kind of microchip, one that has an embedded computer on it."

"Wow. Impressive. Is that to replace the lights in the animals' heads?" I keep my eye on the gun, which is still pointed at me.

"My chip is much better," Buck says. "Easy—it can go anywhere under the skin. That's my big breakthrough."

"Gosh, Buck, that's fantastic." *You egotistical little bastard.* "What's in it for you?"

Buck, perhaps realizing he's saying too much, abruptly turns to Vince. "I thought tonight was going to be the big night. What happened? Did she get—you know?"

Did I get the drug? Did I get raped?

Vince rubs his eyes with the heels of his hands. "She's difficult. But the night isn't over."

"Just give me the word, boss man," Buck says, his voice cold. No sentimental memories about me and the lovely job he had.

Rat fink.

"First, I want you to check my computer," Vince says. "She sat in front of it and installed spyware for me to watch her, but I don't trust her."

"*Hello.* I'm still in the room. We tested it, Vince. It worked just fine, remember?"

"You're a demon," he says, then turns to Buck again. "Go check that she didn't screw something up. I'll keep an eye on her."

Before Vince's techie henchman disappears into the alcove, he hands Vince the gun. In his drug stupor, Vince lets it dangle between his legs. Almost in reach. This isn't the time to get bogged down by thinking. I rise out of the chair and lunge for the gun, but my bad leg betrays me and buckles, causing me to trip over the coffee table. I stretch out to grab the weapon from Vince's hand, but I'm too late.

"Get back to your chair!" he shouts, waving the gun at me. "Goddammit, Madeline."

Buck charges in. "Everything A-OK, partner?"

"Go and check the computer," Vince says as I pick myself up and ease my winded body back into the chair.

Shit! Will Buck detect Symbiote? For anyone else, I'd bet against them. But not Buck. I've seen him in front of a computer, I know what he'll try. I inserted special lines of code just to specifically evade *him*. But he's clever. I've learned not to underestimate him.

Sweat trickles down my front underneath my sweater. All my grand plans for tonight have worked like charms, but everyone who warned me about the danger was right—I was too cavalier, too arrogant, and too confident I could handle Vince. *Yeah, Superwoman. Now look at me.*

To ease the tension in the room, I say, "Is Buck really your business partner, Vince? You're trusting that little weasel with your lifelong research?"

His blue eyes wander from my face in a way that tells me he's still fogged up. He seems to be fighting the urge to tell me more than is wise.

"We're creating the whole package, Buck and I. With his microcomputer and my special drug, we can make ... animals completely docile." He smiles at me—a Satanic smile—like he's letting me in on a big secret.

"In other words, you could get women to sleep with you," I say. "Right, Vince? That's what this is really about, isn't it? Women."

Buck comes back into the living room. "Your computer is perfect," he says to Vince. "No problems. You can still spy on her if you want."

Not a chance. I can remove the spyware with the click of a button.

I squeeze my knees together, just about wetting my pants with relief. The real spyware is safe, the one I installed to spy on him. I emit a false-sounding laugh. "I could have saved you the time."

My phone starts buzzing, and the sound reverberates in the room. *Damn! Too loud.*

Buck moves swiftly to my chair. "Give me that."

"No. It's nothing." I cover my pocket with my hand, daring him to lay a finger on me.

He's not a poker player, and a look of surprise comes over his face. "What happened, Vince? Didn't you give her the, you know, the special drug?"

I glare at Vince, the unsexy man clutching my gun while his clueless little computer thug looks on. I say, "Let me understand the end game tonight, Vince. If I'd been amenable to it, you would have entertained me in your bed, with my mother and her friend in the house, and your henchman over here ... watching? Or was he going to participate? What did you have planned here, a gang rape of a drugged woman?"

"Shut up, Madeline," Buck says, chewing on his lip. He seems unsure of the next move.

As for me, my next moves are well-defined—escape from my deranged stalker and his new henchman, rescue my mother from a locked room, and get us the hell out of this house.

Vince is slumped in his chair, and Buck has relieved him of the gun and is holding it awkwardly at his side. Perhaps they both think I've been cowed into submission. Perhaps they think I'm an easy mark.

I ease myself inch by inch to the edge of my chair.

"Don't move!" Buck says, suddenly alert. He turns to Vince. "Boss man, go get her a good dose of that drug."

"Don't do it, Vince," I say. "Let me go." *Counting on his declaration of love and the potency of his evil drug.*

He looks at me with dead eyes. "Did you forget, Madeline? Tonight is when we get to yes."

The real Phase 6.

A great crack of thunder is followed by a loud splintering of glass that doesn't belong to the storm. Both of my antagonists turn away from me in confusion. In that instant, I somersault myself onto the rug, and with all my strength, I grab Buck's legs in a kind of rugby tackle that takes him down. He cries out as he falls, letting go of the gun, which clatters onto the floor.

Another crash, and the front door slams.

Buck seems dazed as he picks himself up and looks around frantically. In one screaming, adrenaline-fueled lunge, I grab the gun and get a firm hold on it—ready to fire—when two apparitions from Hell burst into the room, soaking wet and dripping rain and mud. One grabs the poker from the fireplace and the other the container of firewood. My mother, shrieking like a banshee, smashes the poker on Vince's head, and Mrs. Auerbach clobbers Buck with the heavy, metal wood holder.

Mom, her face smudged with eyeliner and mascara running down like the ghost of thunder, screams at the bloodied Vince. "We've had enough of you! Leave my daughter alone!" Mrs. Auerbach—not a woman of many words—her eyes like two black sockets, aims a wad of spit on Vince, her tormentor.

We grab our coats and umbrellas and computer and gun and wade through the rivers in the garden out into the rain, which is finally subsiding, and into my Jeep, the three of us screeching out the driveway like the devil's on our tail.

CHAPTER 57

The backstreets of Boston are flooded, but the Jeep soldiers us through to Memorial Drive. Navigating the streams of sloshing water is a bit like my off-road adventures, but it takes concentration, so we drive in silence. I turn the heating to high to warm up the shivering ladies in the back.

Home and dry at last, Mom, having one of her most lucid days in a long while, tells me of her confusion and fury at discovering they were locked into Vince's family room. First, they tried to break the window with a hard-backed chair, but the glass was too strong and the chair bounced off. Then Gretchen got the idea of hurling the small television set at the glass, which must have been the crash I heard.

"How did you get through the front door?" I ask. "You didn't break anything else, did you?"

"I had a key," Mrs. Auerbach says simply. "After you fired me, I stayed in his house." She's matter-of-fact.

"I'm sorry," I say. It comes out before I can think about it.

"He's an evil man," Mom says. "Gretchen has escaped and will stay with us for now."

I nod. She can have the guest room near my mother's room. It's almost midnight, not the right time to discuss Mrs. Auerbach's future.

I text Wanda, who has left worried messages on my phone.

Home safe. It's over. I'll explain later. ♥

Then I text Jessica, my indefatigable lawyer, who has, yet again, warned me to be careful.

Mission accomplished. Will tell all tomorrow.

It is well after midnight, with an eerie silence in the house. Nervously, I slide Vince's flash drive into my computer. The moment of revelation is at hand, giving me a pang of doubt. What if this whole episode has really just been a case of a man who met me online, became obsessed, and when I wouldn't have him, pursued me to distraction? Hard to believe, but possible.

The first file on the drive is entitled *Women.* It has a header: *Manipulation of Mood Compatibility in Animal Pairs Using Frequency Variability of Brain-Implanted Lights.*

This must be it!

Everything is meticulously documented, including an array of women—w1, w2, w3, w4—with names, dates, addresses, tables, progress reports, and precise descriptions of each phase of his experiment. A shiver of recognition passes through me when I see how well I imagined it all.

He recounts how he started out as a young neurologist with a specialty in brain chemistry, who then became interested in mood disorders and switched from medical practice to research. He understood early on how manipulation of light frequencies in rodents improved their moods and sociability. He got the idea of applying this to humans, but couldn't figure out how to get permission to experiment on people. That's when he made the fateful decision to include himself in his experiments and to lure unsuspecting women to participate. With the help of a medical colleague, he implanted a light in himself.

Of *course*! With his obsessiveness it makes perfect sense. But never—not in my wildest imaginings—did I predict he'd go to such lengths. I have an epiphany. This was never about Vince's desire for women or his lack of sex appeal; it was always about his research. Cold and clinical. Could human beings be controlled by computer and electronic signals.

For the first woman, w1, Susan Buffington, he practiced his light-implantation surgery on one of her dogs. Unsuccessfully. The dog died, and Vince moved on. He was relieved when Susan dropped the matter.

Woman number two, w2, was hypnotized before receiving a light at the base of her skull. When Vince set her light frequency to be the same as his, her compliance went off the scale, and she begged him to marry her. This was Kay Fornato, the woman who had the fatal accident. But Vince's surgical technique had been crude, leading to an intolerable buzzing in her head. Not long after surgery, she steered her car into a tree. She was loaded with drugs the day she died. Vince wrote: *Signal frequency too high. And probably too much LSD in the drug mix. For future subjects, lower the ratio of LSD:Oxy:Escitalopram to 40-30-30.*

All science, no remorse.

Vince refined his technique for w3, Gretchen Auerbach, injecting the light through her spinal column. Success. Gretchen became completely compliant, doing Vince's bidding. I feel sick reading about Mrs. Auerbach's abuse at Vince's hands, and here it is, documented down to the last microgram of drugs.

With a feeling of dread, I gird myself to read about my household. Vince refined his spinal technique by practicing on my mother and pets. There are no variable names for them, but they're documented in a sidebar. Thankfully, there were no drugs administered, just the lights controlled by a Squid Link Gateway box. In the file is a table of varying frequencies for Mom and Gretchen, with a subjective description of results reported by Gretchen. Our Mrs. Auerbach— *Vince's faithful foot soldier*—was active in reporting about us.

My poor babies, Torvill and Tosca. They were nothing more than innocent pawns caught up in Vince's cruel experiment, fighting with each other at different light frequencies, their every hiss and growl coldly documented in the notes. If only for this, I hope Vince rots in jail and roasts in hell.

His experiments started to fail when Mom and Gretchen became friends. It was the first indication that people—but not animals—could overcome the effects of the electronic signals. In a footnote, Vince expressed irritation at his inability to exert total control over people. *Humans have free will, an inconvenient new variable that skews the results. Drugs, therefore, will be needed to counteract it.* At some point, he started adding drugs to the experimental mix.

Deep into the night, I come to the write-up about me—w4, the fourth woman. A fresh wave of queasiness courses through me. Vince has documented everything in brutal detail. I discover—to my relief—I'm a difficult subject, smarter than most. He is irritated at my lack of cooperation, documented in detail by the harrowing description of my light-insertion surgery aided and abetted by all-round thug Leo Metzger.

First attempt at spinal entry unsuccessful. Subject was uncooperative even under anesthetic and had to be restrained. Subject was actively resistant and hostile, attempting violence against doctor and assistant.

No wonder I had such awful back pain. Some doctor.

The lights in our heads—Vince's and mine—were set to the same frequency. That's why at times he didn't seem so bad. The different frequencies he tried are documented in a table, from lowest to highest. He reports: *Subject most pliable at a medium-high frequency.* I've long since conquered the egregious effects of the light, but at the time, they were debilitating.

Ice goes down the back of my neck, and I must pause and recompose myself before reading on. Seeing myself written up like a lab rat is terrifying, especially in the dead of night, with the distant echo of rodents in the attic. I force myself to take in the notes about the drug I involuntarily ingested. Initially, it worked all too well, as the pull of Vince operated on my mind.

Last night, before the dinner, Vince wrote: *Subject not susceptible—will need to increase dose to triple strength and tweak hallucinogenic component.* This must be the drug cocktail he himself swallowed.

His final entry about me. *Phase 6: Ongoing.*

It sends more shivers down my poor, violated spine.

I resist the urge to call the police this instant—3:00 a.m. Instead, I open the second file on Vince's flash drive, the one entitled *Men.* I ask myself what's so important about this that it needs to be off the grid and in Vince's safe. The file is a spreadsheet with names, addresses, email addresses, dollar amounts, and *pill quantities.* Pages and pages of them, from all over the country. If the dollar amounts are income, then Vince has an empire that's making him very rich. This must be how he finances his lifestyle and experiments. I don't need to be Einstein to figure it out. He's a drug dealer with a very special product—a drug that makes women sexually compliant. And now I possess his customer list.

I may have the only copy.

When Vince realizes I have this, he won't sit idly by. He'll drop everything and come for me.

Adrenaline has kept me going through the night. Sleep is still out of the question. I jab at the command that brings up my new spyware, *Symbiote*, and to my surprise, detect Vince at his laptop. Like me, he's a night owl. And he hasn't yet discovered his missing flash drive.

He's in an incel chat room on the dark web, where men—aside from Vince—are spewing misogyny. With his most polite voice, Vince is offering relief in the form of his compliance drug for women. He solicits customers right there on the site, and men are signing up in droves.

Some of them have already tested different dosages of the drug on unsuspecting women, and are reporting back about the drug's effectiveness.

Real good, one says. *Date rape, baby.*

I transfer this chat as evidence onto my own little bombshell of a flash drive, snatch it out of my computer, and hotfoot it downstairs.

It's time to go to the police for a third time—*right now!*

CHAPTER 58

Before sunrise, I call Jessica Kim. Unsurprisingly, it goes straight to voicemail.

Hi, Jessica. So sorry to call at this ungodly hour, but I'm heading out to the Cambridge Police Department. I have the goods against V on a flash drive, but need to unload them now because they're radioactive. Will update you later.

When I set out for the Cambridge Police Department, the roads are deserted and the water level is way down. A steel-gray dawn is spreading over Boston.

Inside the CPD, I request to see Officer Larry Corbett, and amazingly, he's there. As I'm being led to the interview room, a miracle happens in the form of a slightly disheveled version of my petite lawyer, wearing snug jeans, stilettos, and carrying a large coffee. I want to hug her, because she must have broken speed limits to get here.

When we're seated at a desk in a small office with Officer Corbett, I update my story. Discretely, I omit details of the gun and smashed window, but I do include the drama of the drugs and flash drives. I'm assertive and confident in the telling, because this time I have the evidence.

Corbett listens intently, as he did before, but when I'm done, he says, "I find it hard to believe, Ms. Geiger, that last night you and your mother went to the house of your stalker. Why not let the police raid the place with a search warrant?"

My lawyer is conspicuously silent. I, however, am ready for this. With my back ramrod straight, I stare him down.

"Because they wouldn't have had the technical know-how to find the smoking guns on Vincent's computer. And because the last two times I was here, you—the cops—didn't believe me."

He sighs deeply and backs off. "Show me what you got. I'm listening."

A kind of euphoria comes over me. Securing the evidence has taken every ounce of my strength and wits. I have outplayed a maniac.

The goods that rest in the palm of my hand have been well and truly backed up on the cloud before reaching this moment.

I place the two flash drives on the desk and invite the officer and Jessica to view their contents. Every last piece of damning evidence—assault, experiments on women, drugs, misogyny—is contained in those small devices.

The viewing takes time, and they do it in silence, each on their own computer.

When they are done, Officer Corbett lets out a long whistle and rubs his chin. "Holy Lord, Ms. Geiger, that's quite a story. You are one spunky lady."

I lean toward him. "It's time, Officer, for you to arrest this man. Right now as we speak, I'm in danger. Vince Cantley knows I have this evidence."

"There are issues with that," Officer Corbett says. "You stole his property from his safe. It may not be admissible."

Jessica places her coffee on the desk, stands, and leans forward with the heels of her palms on the desk. "Excuse me, Officer. That is not illegally obtained evidence. My client was not acting as a representative of the state—she's a private citizen who took the flash-drive evidence as a last resort, in self-defense." My lawyer sits back down, crosses her legs, shuts her eyes, and appears to inhale her coffee through the sippy lid.

I'm tired of dealing with unhelpful cops. "Officer Corbett, I've shown you evidence that Vince Cantley physically harmed me, my mother and pets, and that he poisoned the places I live and work. He's upended my life, and it is high time for you—the police—to arrest him."

Officer Corbett inclines his head, contemplates me and my lawyer, then nods. When I meet his eyes, I finally see a slow capitulation, and more than a hint of admiration.

We've won.

My written complaint is long and detailed. Corbett promises to investigate with due speed. In the meantime, at Jessica's insistence, he will assign protection to me in the form of a bodyguard from the CPD.

Mom comes to the door when the Jeep pulls in. She waves and smiles and is as happy as I've seen her in a while. My heart squeezes. Without her help, I couldn't have done it. I drop my stuff on the porch and envelop her in a bone-crushing hug. My dear, exasperating, big-hearted mother, who smells like sweet peas and bubble bath. I'm so happy she's here, in this house, part of my bedrock. We stand clasped together for so long that Gretchen comes out to look for her. The animals pad outside too, nudging and nuzzling in between us, everyone in the act. Torvill and Tosca seem to have recovered from their ordeals and are friends again.

My mother draws Gretchen into the circle. Mom is luminous. "I'm so proud of you, Madsy," she says. Does she even know why? Does it matter? She's in a happy place.

There's someone missing from this picture, and I'm suddenly fearful about Wanda and whether she'll even see me again. I've disrupted her life every time Vince encroached on mine. What makes me think that, yet again, she'll drop everything and come running? Why do I always act like I'm the most important person in her life?

What is she to me? A poem I was forced to learn at school pops into my mind.

How do I love thee? Let me count the ways.

She's been my lover, roommate, driver, therapist, savior, and best friend.

I love thee with a love I seemed to lose.

No gentle goodbye from me when I stormed out. A pang of sadness envelops me when I press *Favorites* and bring Wanda up on my phone. *Will she pick up?* I shut my eyes and inhale, holding my breath.

"Hey, Madeline." She sounds subdued. "What's up?"

"Wanda ..." And now that she's there, I'm tearing up.

"Is it that time, Mads? Do you need a getaway car?" The familiar husky voice with a smile behind it.

I laugh with relief. Sleep is tugging at me, but so is longing. I hold the phone close. She's still there, breathing.

"Um, Mads, I'm about to leave for the Warhol exhibition with a ... friend."

Why shouldn't she have other "friends"?

The reasonable side of me is about to say, "Enjoy it, we'll talk again some time," but the recently victorious, combative, sleep-deprived, sex-starved version of myself says, "Cancel your plans for tonight and come eat here with me so I can tell you how I nailed him. For real. I mean it, he's gone for good. Bring a toothbrush—and a toy—you know." It's garbled. I'm so tired I don't know what I'm thinking, making it up on the fly. Will we really have noisy, mind-blowing sex in the room above my mother's?

My darling friend doesn't respond immediately, but nor does she tell me to go screw myself.

"Oh, yeah?" she says eventually. "What time?"

When I open the door, Wanda, with her unkempt hair and unselfconscious beauty, is framed in moonlight. "Hiya, Sweetheart," she says. She takes my hands and leans in to kiss my cheek. "What do I see in you?"

Damned if I know.

Much later, in a private moment, Mom says, "Mads, do you really like women?"

"I like *this* woman," I say.

Two weeks later, in early December, Vince is arrested for illegal drug manufacture and trafficking, manslaughter of Kay Fornato, as well as aggravated assault and medical experimentation on women.

Jessica lets me know that Buck is in trouble too, but will get a reduced punishment if he cooperates with law enforcement against Vince. I guess I'll never know what noxious alchemy Vince used to lure Buck to the dark side.

The fall of Vincent Cantley causes a minor splash in the *Boston Herald.* No screaming headlines about injecting bits of hardware into the spines of unsuspecting women, just a small article on page eight mentioning the eradication of a minor drug ring and the incel website that fueled it. The eminence of the perpetrator and the liberation of his rodents get barely one sentence each.

I fear that a good lawyer will mitigate some of the charges against Vince—the death of Kay Fornato, the damaged lives of women he pursued. Will he ever fully pay for the stalking and emotional suffering he inflicted on me and my family? Even now, on a moonless night, I sense shadows on the sidewalk, and glance furtively over my shoulder.

In the matter of my gun, Jessica advises me to turn myself in before Vince vindictively implicates me. After Vince's arrest, on a day the weather cooperates, we make another visit to Officer Corbett.

I place my weapon in the center of his desk.

"My firearm application to the State of Massachusetts was rejected," I say. "So I bought this for my protection after the Cambridge Police Department declined to protect me."

Officer Corbett is a man of a certain age, one who has seen a lot during his colorful career as a cop. And yet he examines my expertly put together ghost gun, with its filed-down edges, in disbelief. It's not clear what bothers him more: the fact of its blatant illegality or my in-your-face expertise.

"You bought this through the mail and put it together yourself?"

I shift in my chair. "Yessir."

"And you've fired it, what, a couple of times?"

"I shot a few at the firing range. Damn good gun, considering."

He's writing in a notebook. Old school. Pauses. "Did you, uh, fire it in any location other than the range?"

I'm ready for this, the part that Vince will report. *Be completely honest with him*, Jessica had advised. I open my laptop on the officer's desk and play him the video from Vince's computer: the image of me in the dark, an ultra-violet villain inside the rodent room; the attack on me by Leo and the accidental firing of the gun. I can't sugarcoat it. It exists. I was there. The gun was mine and it went off.

Officer Corbett puts his gray head in his hands and sighs mightily. "Why was this gunshot not reported?"

I'm on tricky ground, and say matter-of-factly, "I certainly wasn't going to report myself, Officer, and Vince and Leo weren't about to draw attention to their illegal activity, so we all kept our mouths shut." I lean toward the cop, my palms planted flat on my thighs. "This video was used by Vince to blackmail me into seeing him again. That's how he was able to continue stalking me." I pull up on my computer the threatening note written to me by Vince the day after the gun incident in his lab.

Jessica slurps up the last of her coffee through the straw. "My client felt she had no choice and had to take drastic measures to protect herself," she says.

The upshot is my gun gets confiscated, Officer Corbett writes a complaint—signed by me and Jessica—and with mitigating factors, including the fact I turned myself in, I get off with a stiff fine. I'm sorry to lose that gun. It was put together with tender loving care, and had become a friend of sorts.

My mother and Gretchen have developed a symbiotic relationship in my house. Gretchen, who was seriously impaired by Vince's drugs and abuse, has started to heal in the benevolent atmosphere of Mom's friendship. I see it in the renewed sparkle of her eyes as she slowly morphs back into a normal person. As for Mom, Gretchen keeps her grounded in the house, firmly linking arms with her on bad days and keeping her safe.

Even the animals are softening toward Gretchen, slyly sniffing her at the table, nudging her ankles. On a recent day, I came upon them all in the sitting room. Tosca was on Mom's lap, being held firmly but gently, while Gretchen tried to clip the cat's formidable claws. That used to be Mom's job, but she lost the manual dexterity.

By Christmastime, it's clear Gretchen is here to stay. I formally offer her free room and board, plus a salary, for taking care of Mom. All of us are happy and relieved when she accepts. This is a big house we're in. I invite Gretchen to inspect it and decide which room she'd like. She's welcome to have her old suite of rooms at the top of the stairs, but I suspect she's haunted by her unhappiness there. For now, she's content with the lovely big room near Mom's.

I walk into my office one morning in April, and Shawna has a sparkling diamond on her finger. After all that passion and drama, Lonnie has won her over. We squeal and hug and I ask her tearfully if I'll lose her.

"Of course not," she says.

Julie McGuire, my new tech employee, comes into the office to see what the noise is about. Julie is brilliant, edgy, and can program up a storm. She has plugged into Buck's stereo and listens to classical music through her headphones. She loves Shawna and me, and is tickled by our all-female triumvirate in the firm.

Buck the HackMeister is a pale ghost lingering in the walls.

I've become savvier at work since the stalking and ransomware interludes. Sharpened and chastened by bitter experience, I'm a font of good advice for my clients. They kiss my feet, awed by my brilliance, not understanding that an expert is someone who has already made all the mistakes.

I've become the Earth Mother of cybersecurity in Cambridge.

Now that Vince has been expunged from my life, my relationship with Wanda has blossomed with the spring. It's a Saturday night in May following an opera concert at the Boston

Symphony, and I'm staying over at Wanda's condo. It's well after midnight, and I'm wide awake. While Wanda is softly snoring, I prop myself up on my elbow and watch her as she lies close beside me on her pillow. Moonlight filters in through the curtains, illuminating her like a slumbering Madonna. With her thick tumble of hair and warm autumn smell, she seems as lovely to me now as the day I first met her.

She's still able, after all these months, to mesmerize me with her *joie de vivre*, her braininess, her knowing hands, all somehow charged by memories of past danger.

She senses me watching her.

"Cm'ere," she murmurs, putting a soft hand up to my cheek. Then she collapses back and sighs deeply. How I envy her this ability to sleep like a stone.

I love her—how could I not?—but I'm too set in my house and business to change my lifestyle in any significant way. Like me, Wanda is established in her home and professional life. She adores her condo and the charm of her Boston neighborhood. I could no more imagine myself and my furry menagerie frolicking in her pristine living room than I could see Wanda comfortable in my old house with its ghosts and creaking stairs.

For now, we're happy to muddle along and revel in our separate solitudes, sexy sojourns, and feisty independence.

ACKNOWLEDGEMENTS

So many people helped in the creation of *The Fourth Woman*, that I apologize if I inadvertently omitted anyone's name.

First and foremost, thank you, Moh Adam, my irrepressible publicist and production manager, who took care of the nuts and bolts of the novel every step of the way.

Thanks also to American Publishers and the teams who created the magic in so many aspects of the book.

A special thank you to my incredible editor, Elizabeth White, who helped seal the plot-holes and provided an inline edit that polished the manuscript to a sheen. I appreciate her meticulousness and support at a time that extraneous difficulties tried to pull her away. And also many thanks to my dear friend and editor, Lauren Baratz-Logsted, fondly known in my house as "Lauren-Editor," who gave me the benefit of her unique insights and humor.

As always, there's a special place in heaven for my beta readers, who gave me their time and detailed feedback: Lisa David, Dominique Moore, Aryn Youngless, and Tamara Watson.

Thanks also to my many readers and critiquers: Nick Barner, Deb Begley, Steve Browne, Pat Carlson, Curtis Chin, Sara Chisolm, Pat Civale, Julie Dawning, Sharon Durr, Emily Johnson, Janis Kelly, Hiromi Komiya, Edy Krauss, Chris Kowalchuk,

Martha Lasley, Gabi Lorino-Tyner, Jen Mann, Susan Mattern, June Meyer, Axel Milens, Nicky Morris, Linda Myers, BJ Rae, Helen Rivers, Linda Rose, Ellen Ryan, Don Small, Teddy Swanson, and Doris Wright.

A special word for Dominique Moore for her brilliant analysis of the plot and characters, and for going above and beyond. Dear Dominique, the novel is dedicated to you.

Many people have given my writing a boost in so many ways. Thank you Dee Buckingham, Mary Helen Cathles, Kathy Dewart, Karen Dionne, David Flaccus, Trisha Flaccus, Kathy Henion, Lisa King, Aimee Lehmann, Alan Lightman, Paul McEuen, Ellie O'Connor, Barry Passer, Nancy Ridenour, Leslie Schover, and Susan Wiser.

My new life in California has given me the gift of my Vintage Writers group, which has boosted me with love and support beyond description. Thank you Carol Amato, Miranda Chivers, Paulette Scott, Karen Lee Cohen, Denise Cross, Edi Depurna, Ruth Fisher, Colleen Fliedner, Kim Gottlieb-Walker, Deirdre Hennings, Alexis Krasilovsky, and Cynthia Naden,

I will never forget the Bridge Club of Ithaca, whose members supported my writing career for so many years, and thanks also to the players at the Pasadena Bridge Club, who have welcomed me as a writer.

So many thanks go to Kathleen Kaiser, the Queen of Southern California writers: for your many nuggets of marketing advice, the L.A. Times Festival of Books, and Launch Master, which made everything possible. Somehow, caught up in your vision for writers, I got sprinkled with fairy dust.

Yet again, thank you Holly Adams, the wonderful narrator, whose energetic, multi-voice reading of the audiobook continues to bring my characters to vibrant life.

As always, my darling sister, Brenda Cooper, cast her eagle eye over *The Fourth Woman* and gave it the tough-love and shtick treatment it needed.

Love and thank you to the lights of my life, Saul Teukolsky, Rachel Teukolsky, Lauren Teukolsky, Caleb Stapleton, Josh Adams, Noah Adams, and Jacob Adams. My granddog, Gordy Stapleton, the Plott Hound, was a role model for Torvill Eriksson, Madeline's dog. Many thanks to Caleb for some choice Gordy anecdotes. RIP Gordy.

My beloved husband, Saul, as always, gets the last word. How could any of this be possible without you?

ABOUT THE AUTHOR

Former math and computer science teacher, Roselyn Teukolsky, is the author of *A Reluctant Spy*, an unconventional spy thriller, and its sequel, *The Fourth Woman*, a cautionary tale about online dating.

Teukolsky was born in Johannesburg, South Africa, where she graduated from the University of the Witwatersrand with a B.Sc. in Math and Chemistry. She immigrated to the US when she was 23, and graduated from Cornell University with an M.S. in Mathematics Education. She taught Math and Computer Science for many years, mostly at Ithaca High School in Upstate New York.

Roselyn retired from teaching in 2009. After a lifetime of devouring mysteries and thrillers, she decided to have a full-time go at writing her own novels of suspense.

She has long been intrigued by the dilemmas faced by smart women in male-dominated settings. Working as a computer science teacher has given her the familiarity to create an authentic female protagonist, a brilliant computer scientist, who can hack her way into the computers of the wiliest of predators and criminals.

Teukolsky is the author of the Barron's review book for AP Computer Science, which is currently in its 12th edition.

Roselyn's favorite pastime is tournament bridge. She wrote *How to Play Bridge with Your Spouse ... and Survive* (Master Point Press) in 2002.

She lives in Pasadena, California, with her husband, Saul Teukolsky.

917-920-5745

Made in the USA
Las Vegas, NV
01 January 2026